GEORGE FRIDERIC HANDEL

head section of statue by Roubiliac

A
BIOGRAPHICAL
DICTIONARY

OF

ACTORS, ACTRESSES, MUSICIANS, DANCERS,

MANAGERS & OTHER STAGE PERSONNEL

IN LONDON, 1660–1800

Volume 7: Habgood *to* Houbert

by

PHILIP H. HIGHFILL, JR., KALMAN A. BURNIM
and
EDWARD A. LANGHANS

SOUTHERN ILLINOIS UNIVERSITY PRESS

CARBONDALE AND EDWARDSVILLE

Publication of this work was made possible in part through a grant from the National Endowment for the Humanities.

Library of Congress Cataloging in Publication Data   *(Revised)*

Highfill, Philip H.
  A biographical dictionary of actors, actresses, musicians, dancers, managers & other stage personnel in London, 1660–1800.

  Includes bibliographical references.
  CONTENTS: v. 1. Abaco to Belfille.—v. 2. Belfort to Byzand.—[etc.]—v. 7. Habgood to Houbert.
  1. Performing arts—London—Biography. I. Burnim, Kalman A., joint author. II. Langhans, Edward A., joint author. III. Title.
PN2597.H5   790.2'092'2 [B]   71–157068
ISBN 0-8093-0918-1 (v. 7)

List of Illustrations

OFFICIAL DOCUMENTS AND LETTERS

Volume 7

Habgood *to* Houbert

= H =

Habgood, [**Thomas?**] [*fl.* 1758–
*c.*1760?], *clarinetist.*

Between the acts of *Patie and Roger* at the
Haymarket Theatre on 13 March 1758 Mr
Habgood and Mr Pearson played clarinets in a
"grand" concerto. The performance was not
repeated. Perhaps Habgood was Thomas
Habgood, a music seller who had a shop in
King Street, Golden Square. In 1759 Thomas
Habgood published *A Pocket Companion For the
Guittar Containing XL of the newest and most
favourite Minuets Country-Dances Jiggs Airs &c.
All carefully Transposed & properly adapted to that
Instrument, To which is added the Prussian March
in two parts And favourite Hymn for Easter.*
About 1760 Habgood apparently subscribed
to Dupuis's *Six Concertos for the Organ*; the Brit-
ish Library copy has his name added in manu-
script.

Habito, Mrs [*fl.* 1742], *actress.*

Mrs Habito acted Lady Pride in *The Indian
Merchant* at the Phillips-Yeates booth at Bartholomew Fair on 25 August 1742.

Hacket, Mr [*fl.* 1755–1758], *actor.*

Mr Hacket acted Nym in *The Merry Wives of
Windsor* on 5 May 1756 at Covent Garden and
shared in benefit tickets with house servants at
the same theatre on 20 May 1757 and 12 May
1758. He was probably the same Mr Hacket
who had been in the Orchard Street Theatre
Company, Bath, in 1755–56.

Hackett, Mr [*fl.* 1743–1750], *actor.*

A Mr Hackett played Tom in *The Blind
Beggar of Bethnal Green* at the Great Tiled
Booth on the Bowling Green at Southwark
Fair on 8 September 1743. A year later a Mr
Hacket, probably the same person, acted at
the Haymarket Theatre; his roles included Ap-
pletree in *The Recruiting Officer* on 27 Septem-
ber 1744, Harry in *The Mock Doctor* on 29
September, Daniel in *The Conscious Lovers* on 4,

6, and 9 October, Timothy in *The Prodigal* on
11 October, and the Apothecary in *Romeo and
Juliet* on 13 October and 17 December 1744.

Between 10 June and 31 August 1747
Hackett was at the Jacob's Wells Theatre in
Bristol. He seems to have passed most of his
career as an obscure provincial actor, although
from time to time he played at London. On 28
March 1748 he acted the Constable in *The
Author's Farce* at Covent Garden for the benefit
of Theophilus Cibber. Other occasional appearances in 1749–50 at that theatre included
Barnaby in *The Old Bachelor* on 6 October
1749, the Welch Collier in *The Recruiting Officer* on 1 November, Shadow in *2 Henry IV* on
8 November, and the Tooth Drawer in *A Cure
for a Scold* on 26 April 1750. In the autumn he
returned to act Barnaby again on 19 November
and Shadow on 22 November 1750.

Hackett had been at Twickenham and Richmond in the summer of 1750, playing the Earl
of Oxford in *Richard III*, Don Felix in *The
Mistake*, Gardener in *The Drummer*, Corydon
in *Damon and Phillida*, and Snip the Tailor in
Don Quixote. In the bill for the last-named
piece he was also listed for a Country Wench,
with Master Brett playing a second Wench.

Hackett, Mrs [*fl. c.* 1673–1675],
performer?

The Lord Chamberlain's accounts indicate
that a Mrs Hackett was a member of the King's
Company from about 1673 to 1675. She may
have been one of the minor performers. Mrs
Hackett is not otherwise known, and *The London Stage* does not list her.

Hackett, John 1734–1761, *actor, editor.*

John Hackett, born in 1734, entered Westminster School in September 1745, at the age
of 11, and matriculated at Balliol College,
Oxford, on 5 March 1752, at 17. Sometime in
1755, presumably before 1 September, the
Daily Public Advertiser announced that "At the

Little Theatre in the Haymarket this day will be opened a Scheme" for instructing gentlemen to speak from the pulpit, the bar, and the stage, "By Mr. Hackett of Baliol College Oxon." The notice claimed that Hackett would offer, among other pieces, Milton's "L'Allegro" and "Il Penseroso," Gray's "Churchyard Elegy," and Pierre's speech to the Venetian senate (from *Venice Preserv'd*). He also promised to explain "the reason of his not appearing on Covent Garden Stage as was reported." When, or whether or not, Hackett made his solo appearance is not known, but on 21 August 1755 the same paper announced that he was to act Othello for Theophilus Cibber. On 1 September 1755, Hackett, announced as making his first appearance on any stage, did act Othello at the Haymarket, with Cibber making his first attempt at Iago. Hackett repeated Othello on 3 and 6 September, on the latter occasion for his own benefit.

John Hackett seems not to have appeared again on the London stage although there was a "Hacket" who acted Nym in *The Merry Wives of Windsor* at Covent Garden on 5 May 1756 and who shared in benefit tickets with house servants on 20 May 1757 and 12 May 1758.

According to Reed's "Notitia Dramatica" at the British Museum, soon after Hackett had played Othello he went to the West Indies, where he was drowned about the beginning of 1761.

He was, we believe, the John Hackett who in 1757 edited and published *A Collection of Select Epigrams . . . By the Most Eminent Hands. Published by Mr. Hackett* and *Select and Remarkable Epitaphs . . . In Two Volumes, Ed. John Hackett*.

Hacketts, Mr ₁*fl. 1798–1802*₁, *house servant.*

A Mr Hacketts was a minor house servant at Covent Garden Theatre from 1798–99 at least through 1801–2. On 29 May 1799 and 11 June 1800 he shared benefit tickets with numerous other house personnel. His salary in 1800–1801 and 1801–2 was 12*s.* per week.

Hackman, Thomas ₁*fl. 1784?–1794*₁, *violinist.*

A Mr Hackman played second violin in the Handel Memorial Concerts at Westminster Abbey and the Pantheon in May and June

1784. He was probably Thomas Hackman, who was listed in Doane's *Musical Directory* in 1794 as a violist and member of the New Musical Fund from Watford, Hertfordshire.

Hackwood, Francis ₁*fl. 1784–1820*₁, *violinist, violist.*

In 1794, Francis Hackwood, of Half Moon Street, Piccadilly, was listed in Doane's *Musical Directory* as a violist, a member of the Royal Society of Musicians, a performer at the Professional Concerts and the opera, a member of the King's Band, and a player in the Handelian concerts at Westminster Abbey. Hackwood had previously been listed by Dr Burney as a violist in the first Handel Memorial Concerts at Westminster Abbey and the Pantheon in May and June of 1784. In 1791 he was a second violinist for the opera at the Pantheon. Hackwood served the Royal Society of Musicians as a member of the Court of Assistants in 1785, 1795, 1798, 1799, 1807, and 1820.

Haddock, Mr ₁*fl. 1736*₁. *See* HAYDOCK, MR.

Haddock, Mr ₁*fl. c. 1795–1796*₁, *exhibitor.*

Richard Altick in *The Shows of London* cites a playbill of the mid-1790s concerning the exhibitor Haddock. At No 38, Norfolk Street, Haddock displayed an automaton capable of writing and drawing outlines of a bear, lion, elephant, tiger, horse, camel, or stag. Another mechanical device showed a country mansion in which was a fruitress who came out of the door, took orders, and then delivered them. A mechanical dog in front of the house barked until customers returned the fruit they had taken from the woman. Then a chimney sweep came from behind the house, went indoors, and was soon seen coming out of the chimney crying "Sweep!" After finishing his chores he walked out the front door with a bag of soot.

Mr Haddock advertised in the Bristol press on 17 September 1796 for his opening two days later:

MECHANIC THEATRE,
At the TAYLORS'-HALL, *Broad-Street.*
MR. HADDOCK has the honour to announce his
arrival in
Bristol with his *Mechanical Exhibition*,
ANDROIDES,
With which he has had the happiness to entertain a

succession of crowded houses in London these eight months past.

MR. HADDOCK flatters himself the Androides will be found more curious than any thing of the kind ever introduced to the Public, as the principals of action are entirely new. The Theatre (which will be lighted with wax) is neatly fitted up, and every thing calculated to give satisfaction to a polite and discerning audience.

***Doors open at half past Six.—Exhibition begins at Seven, and is over before Nine o'clock.

Boxes 2s.—Gallery 1s.

Hadley, Mr ₍*fl. 1734*₎, *actor.*

Mr Hadley played Sir Trusty in *Fair Rosamond* at the Hippisley-Bullock-Hallam booth at Bartholomew Fair on 24 August 1734.

Hadlow, John *1712–1755, singer.*

John Hadlow, identified as a "singing-man," died on 20 April 1755 and was buried in the North Cloister of Westminster Abbey on 24 April. The Funeral Book records his age as 43. Hadlow's will, describing him as of St John the Evangelist, Westminster, dated 28 March 1754, was proved on 10 May 1755 by his widow, Mary, to whom he left all his estate, including his house in Marsham Street. Mary Hadlow was probably his second wife. A Dorothy Hadlow, probably his first wife, died on 11 May 1749, aged 37, and was buried on 14 May in the North Cloister.

It is likely that John Hadlow sang in the oratorios. He was one of the sacristans of the Abbey, having been appointed on 20 June 1732.

Hadwyn, Thomas *d. c. 1664, trumpeter.*

A warrant in the Lord Chamberlain's accounts dated 6 June 1662 ordered Thomas Hadwyn and three other trumpeters in the King's Musick to attend the Duke of Ormonde in Ireland. On 15 September 1664 Alexander Jackson was appointed trumpeter in the place of Thomas Hadwyn, deceased.

Haessler, Johann Wilhelm *1747–1822, organist, pianist, composer.*

Born at Erfurt, Germany, on 29 March 1747, Johann Wilhelm Haessler was educated in music by his uncle, Kittel, the Erfurt organist. By the time he was 14, Johann was the organist of the Barfüsserkirche at Erfurt, but his father determined to apprentice the lad in his own trade of capmaker. He traveled widely for his father's business, but in 1780 abandoned it and began to give concerts at Erfurt.

From 1790 to 1794, according to Grove, Haessler gave concerts in St Petersburg and London, playing a Mozart concerto in London on 30 May 1792. In 1794, he was listed in Doane's *Musical Directory* as a pianist living at No 29, Clarges Street, Mayfair.

Soon after 1794, Haessler moved to Moscow, where he died on his birthday, 29 March 1822. His compositions for piano and organ were numerous, as were his songs. Many of his sonatas and vocal pieces were published in Germany in the 1770s and 1780s, and after he took up residence in Moscow in the 1790s the works he published there reached opus 49.

Hagan. *See* HAGEN.

Hagemann, John Gotfrid ₍*fl. 1794–1815*₎, *instrumentalist.*

Doane's *Musical Directory* of 1794 listed John Gotfrid Hagemann of Norwich as a performer on the violoncello, violin, and clarinet. Hagemann was a member of the New Musical Fund, the Academy of Ancient Music, and the band of the Second Regiment of the Guards. He was still a subscriber to the New Musical Fund in 1815.

Hagen, V. ₍*fl. 1735*₎, *flutist.*

V. Hagen (or Hagan) played flute in a concert at Hickford's Music Room on 21 February 1735 and was given a benefit there the following 5 May. Perhaps the initial mentioned in the bill was not Hagen's but an abbreviation for "von." If so, Hagen may have been related to the organist, violinist, and composer Peter Albrecht von Hagen (d. 1803) of Rotterdam.

Hagley, Miss, later Mrs Allen ₍*fl. 1789–1794*₎, *singer, actress.*

Miss Hagley, the daughter of a keeper of an alehouse at the top of Sackville Street, near Piccadilly Circus, was apprenticed as a young girl to Thomas Linley, who introduced her to the public at Drury Lane Theatre in the spring oratorios of 1789. She first appeared on 27 February in *The Triumph of Truth*, a collage of instrumental and vocal music in which she sang Arnold's "No more shall Edom" and "On the charmer," Corelli's "On our paternal" (with Reinhold, Dignum, Mrs Crouch, and others), and Jomelli's "Hear a Nation's deep Distress" (also with others). She sang other selections in the oratorios on 18, 20, and 25 March.

Several months later, on 28 May 1789, Miss Hagley was brought forward at Drury Lane for the first time in a speaking role, Narcissa in Colman's comic opera *Inkle and Yarico*, which she repeated on 8 June. Sufficiently successful in this debut to be engaged at Drury Lane at £2 per week for the subsequent season, Miss Hagley played her second character on 15 September 1789, Leonora in *The Padlock*, and was well received. The critic in the *European Magazine* for that month found that she sang with great taste and correctness and possessed a sweet but not powerful voice; her features were regular and her small figure neat and well proportioned. Another reviewer confirmed "a small sweet voice, and the merits of a chaste *clear* articulation," and he thought she might become a "useful actress" in the vocal roles which had been filled by the late Mrs Forster (Ann Field). When she played the Pastoral Nymph in *Comus* on 26 September she sang her air "with great taste." On 12 December 1789 she played Lady Elinor in *The Haunted Tower* in place of the indisposed Mrs Crouch, whose style she imitated; and she was, according to Kemble's notes, "very well approved." Her other roles during that season included Lesbia in *Selima and Azor*, Lauretta in *Richard Coeur de Lion*, Phoebe in *Belphegor*, Philidel in *Arthur and Emmeline*, a Nun in *The Island of St Marguerite*, Gillian in *The Quaker*, Penelope in *The Romp*, Nelly in *No Song No Supper*, Ariel in *The Tempest*, Laura in *The Strangers at Home*, and Columbine in numerous performances of *Harlequin's Frolicks*. On 19 February 1790 she sang in the *Messiah*. When she played Mrs Crouch's role of Nancy in *True Blue* on 11 May 1790, she shared net benefit proceeds of about £115 with Burton and Haymes.

In 1790–91 Miss Hagley's salary was raised to £3 per week, for which she was kept busy in many of the roles already mentioned as well as in a number of performances of Fatima in *The Siege of Belgrade* and Viletta in *Don Juan*. On 27 October 1790 she, Mrs Bland, and Miss DeCamp played the Italian Girls in *The Critic*, and she also sang a song in Act V of *As You Like It*.

Still engaged at £3 per week in 1791–92, she appeared with the Drury Lane company, now playing at the King's Theatre, in her regular roles and also as Ann in *The Doctor and the Apothecary*, Madalon in *The Surrender of Calais*, and Sylvia in *Cymon*. Her playing of Sylvia was "as chaste a performance" as one critic claimed ever to have witnessed. On 31 May 1792 she shared benefit receipts of £516 6s. 6d. (less house charges of £159 1s. 8d.) with four other performers.

Miss Hagley's marriage to a Mr Allen, a sailmaker of property in Liverpool, in late August or early September of 1792 prevented her return to Drury Lane. No doubt she had met him while acting at Liverpool in the summers of 1791 and 1792. It was reported that she, born a Jewess, had converted to Christianity and had retired from the stage to accommodate her husband. The writer of an unidentified press notice lamented her leaving the stage:

If Miss Hagley possessed no other claim to the public patronage, than vocal ability, she still would be entitled to a more than ordinary portion; but if with the science acquired from the able tuition of Mr Linley, we connect the charms of personal beauty receiving additional lustre from the engaging suffusion of modest apprehension, we cannot help regretting that the boards of a theatre can never again be adorned by her presence.

In 1794, Doane's *Musical Directory* listed her mistakenly as "Mrs Hale (late Miss Hagley)," of Liverpool. Doane said she was a soprano, a participant in the Concerts of the Academy of Ancient Music and at Drury Lane Theatre, but she was no longer performing.

Hague, Mr ₁*fl. 1748*₁, *singer*.
A Mr Hague was one of the vocalists in a concert of instrumental and vocal music given at the Haymarket Theatre on 9 December 1748 for the benefit of Mr Waltz.

Hague Mr ₁*fl. 1770–1803?*₁, *actor*.
A Mr Hague acted Oakly in *The Jealous Wife* at the Haymarket Theatre on 2 May 1776. A printing error on the bill for the afterpiece *The Citizen* listed both him and Cresswick for the role of Young Philpot. Perhaps Hague was the

provincial actor of that name who performed at Norwich and Hull in 1770, at Edinburgh in 1771, 1772, and 1773–74 (where he acted many leading roles, including Hotspur in *1 Henry IV*, Horatio in *Hamlet*, Antony in *Julius Caesar*, and Prospero in *The Tempest*), at Glasgow in May 1773, and at Brighton in 1774 and 1779. A Mrs Hague also performed at Edinburgh in 1773–74 and at Brighton in 1779. At the Theatre Royal, Plymouth, on 30 July 1798, a Mr Hague acted Sir George Touchwood, Mrs Hague acted Kitty Willis in *The Belle's Stratagem*, and their two daughters danced a Scotch reel. In May 1803 a Mr and Miss Hague were again performing at Plymouth.

Hague, Charles *1769–1821, violinist, organist, composer, teacher, singer.*

Born at Tadcaster in Yorkshire on 4 May 1769, Charles Hague received his early education from his father and his elder brother, William Hague (fl. c. 1779–c. 1800), a singer and music publisher at Cambridge, who is entered separately in this dictionary. His father may have been the Mr Haigh who was listed in Doane's *Musical Directory* in 1794 as a violinist residing in Yorkshire and a player in the Handelian concerts at Westminster Abbey. It is also possible that the father was a member of the band at the Norwich Theatre as early as 17 August 1770, at which time a Mr Hague was being paid one guinea a week.

In 1779, Charles Hague went to live with his brother William at Cambridge, where he was tutored by Manini in violin and by the elder Hellendaal in thoroughbass and composition. He was probably the "Master Haigh," age nine, who played the piano at the York Theatre Royal on 7 April 1778. On 10 September 1784, Basil Cozens-Hardy was present at a concert in the Assembly Room at Norwich in which Master Hague sang two songs; also performing that night was Manini on the viola.

When Manini died in 1785, Hague went to London to study under Salomon and Dr. Cooke. Returning to Cambridge he took his Mus. B. degree in 1794, composing for the occasion the anthem *By the Waters of Babylon*, which was performed on 29 June 1794 and afterwards published. In the same year he was

By permission of the Trustees of the British Museum

CHARLES HAGUE

engraving by Cardon, after Gilchrist

listed in Doane's *Musical Directory* as a violinist and organist residing at Cambridge, a subscriber to the New Musical Fund, and a player in the Handelian concerts at Westminster Abbey.

Succeeding Dr Randall as Professor of Music in 1799, he became Mus. D. in 1801. For the installation of the Duke of Gloucester as Chancellor of the University on 29 June 1811 in the Senate House, Hague composed music for an ode written by William Smyth, Professor of History; the music was published.

Charles Hague died at Cambridge on 12 June 1821. On 6 February 1822, administration of his estate, valued at £1500, was granted to Philip Knapton, a musician and creditor of the deceased, since his wife, Harriot Hague, and his only surviving child, Sophia Hague, spinster, had renounced the administration. Hague's elder child, Harriot, who had been born in 1793, was a talented pianist and published *Six Songs, with an Accompaniment for the Pianoforte* in 1814, but she died in 1816, at 22.

Charles Hague's other compositions included two collections of glees, rounds, and canons; *Twelve Symphonies by Haydn, arranged as quintets*; and, with Mr Plumptre, a fellow of Clare College, Cambridge, *A Collection of Songs* (1805).

A portrait of Charles Hague painted by G. H. Harlow about 1813 is at the Fitzwilliam Museum, Cambridge; an engraving by H. Meyer, after Harlow, was published by W. D. Jones at Cambridge in 1813. A watercolor portrait of Hague drawn by Thomas Unwins is at the British Museum. A portrait engraved by A. Cardon, after Gilchrist, was published in 1803. An engraving by W. Say of Hague's daughters Harriot and Sophia was published in 1816.

Hague, William ₍*fl. c. 1779–c. 1800*₎, *singer, music publisher and seller.*

The music publisher and seller at Cambridge, William Hague, was the elder brother of the violinist Charles Hague (1769–1821), to whom he taught music; he brought Charles to Cambridge about 1779. William Hague's name appeared as a subscriber to *Six Songs with an accompanyment for the Harpsichord, or two Violins and a Violoncello. Composed by Mr. King*, printed at London by Longman and Broderip about 1786. From his shop in Petty Cury, Cambridge, he published with John Peppercorn *A Collection of Psalm and Hymn Tunes some of which are new & others by permission of the authors with six Chants and Te Deums . . . The whole revis'd & harmonized by Dr. Randall*, 1794. A second edition appeared about 1800. About 1795 he printed and sold *Duett for Two Performers on One Violin composed by Mr. Charles Hague* and, about 1800, *The Gods of the Grape, written by a Gentleman. Compos'd by Is. Nicholls.*

In 1794, William Hague was listed in Doane's *Musical Directory* as a bass singer living in Cambridge and a participant in the Handelian concerts at Westminster Abbey.

Haigh, Mr ₍*fl. 1794*₎, *violinist.*

A Mr Haigh was listed in Doane's *Musical Directory* in 1794 as a violinist residing in Yorkshire who played in the Handelian concerts at Westminster Abbey. The fact that he was from Yorkshire suggests the possibility that Mr Haigh was related to Charles Hague of Yorkshire (1769–1821), a celebrated violin-

ist and Professor of Music. See Charles Hague's entry for additional information on the family.

Haigh, Mr ₍*fl. 1794*₎, *violoncellist.*

A Mr Haigh was listed in Doane's *Musical Directory* in 1794 as a violoncellist living at No 23, Old Cavendish Street, a member of the Amicable Society, and a participant in the oratorios at Drury Lane Theatre.

Haigh, Mr ₍*fl. 1800–1806*₎, *instrumentalist.*

The Minute Books of the Royal Society of Musicians on 30 March 1800 show that a Mr Haigh would be asked to play his trumpet at the commemoration (presumably the Handelian concert in Westminster Abbey) and that on 3 April 1800 he was granted one guinea for doing so. It does not seem likely that this person was the violinist Thomas Haigh (1769–1808), who at that time was living in Manchester. Mr Haigh was also listed as playing the trumpet for the Society's concert at St Paul's in May 1801. He may have been the Haigh who was designated to play the bassoon at the St Paul's concert in May 1800 and the hautbois in 1803 and the Mr Haigh, instrument not designated, who was also on the list for those concerts in 1802, 1804, and 1806.

Haigh, Thomas 1769–1808, *violinist, pianist, composer.*

Although it has been commonly assumed that the musician Thomas Haigh was born in London in 1769, in the records of the Royal Society of Musicians is an extract from the parish register of Wakefield, provided by the parish clerk, which indicates that Haigh was baptized there on 30 January 1769, the son of John Haigh.

Thomas may have been the Mr Haigh, a violinist in the theatre band at Manchester, who composed or selected the music for the production of Ryley's *The Civilian* in that city in May 1789. At the beginning of the 1790s he went to London and studied composition with Haydn in 1791 and 1792. He soon settled in Manchester where he resided from about 1793 to 1801.

In 1794, Thomas Haigh was listed in Doane's *Musical Directory* as a violinist and pianist of Manchester who played in the Handelian concerts at Westminster Abbey. He was probably the Mr Haigh who was one of the instrumentalists in a musical and rhetorical program which was given at the Haymarket Theatre for five nights in March 1795, although that person may have been the violoncellist (fl. 1794).

On 7 April 1799, he was recommended by W. Dance for membership in the Royal Society of Musicians, at which time he was described as a single man, 30 years old, engaged at the Concerts of Ancient Music, and living at No 23, Duke Street, St James. On 7 July 1799 Haigh was unanimously elected and attended and signed the membership book.

Between 1796 and 1807 he was frequently in Ireland, performing in concerts at Dublin, Belfast, Cork, Waterford, Derry, and Youghal. After 1801 he returned to London, where he died in April 1808.

Some 38 published compositions by Thomas Haigh are listed in the *Catalogue of Printed Music in the British Museum*, including numerous arrangements for some of Haydn's symphonies. Haigh wrote at least 12 sonatas for the piano, some with accompaniment for flute or violin, as well as airs, songs, and ballads, often arranged as rondos.

Hailes. *See also* HALES.

Hailes, Henry   ₍*fl.* 1670–1695₎, *scenekeeper, boxkeeper.*

Henry Hailes (or Hales) served the King's Company as a scenekeeper in 1670–71. By the 1674–75 season he was working as a boxkeeper. On 9 December 1675 he was named in the new company rules to guard the door at the sharing table and collect forfeits. One of the few pieces of information we have concerning the company's income during the 1670s concerns Hailes (or, in this instance, "Hayle"): the *Theatrical Inquisitor and Monthly Mirror* (a dubious source) in July 1816 printed the receipts at Drury Lane on 12 and 26 December 1677, and Hailes's boxes brought in £3 and £2 16s. respectively.

Hailes was involved in a lawsuit of some kind in 1679; he and the actor Sheppey were sued by Thomas Johnson, one of the theatre owners, on 9 June of that year. Without knowing the details of the case we cannot tell if it had anything to do with Robert Mather's replacing Hailes on the King's Company roster

on 28 April 1681. Though Hailes may have been employed elsewhere in the years that followed, he kept up his theatrical contacts, for when the prominent actor Charles Hart wrote his will on 10 July 1683 (probate followed on 6 September), he left his "friend" Henry Hailes £10. Hailes seems to have gone back to theatre work in the early 1690s, for his name was listed among the members of the United Company on a warrant dated 22 February 1695. His name was crossed out, however, indicating, probably, that he had just been discharged.

Haim. *See* HAYM.

"Haines, Count." *See* HAINES, JOSEPH.

Haines, Joseph   *d. 1701, actor, singer, dancer, guitar player, fortune teller, author.*

The Life of the Late Famous Comedian, Jo. Hayns (1701), possibly written by the actor's fellow player Tobias Thomas, would have us believe that Joseph Haines (as his name is now most commonly spelled) was "descended of mean Parents, but such as were of known probity," but the forgetful author later had Joe say he was the son of "Sir *Thomas Hayns.*" The *Life* also has it that Joe's mother turned Quaker in her declining years, that young Joseph went to St Martin's School in London, and that he did so well that some gentleman sent him to Oxford. There he attracted the attention of Joseph (later Sir Joseph) Williamson and in time became his Latin secretary. Haines took his M.A. degree at Cambridge, joined a troupe of strolling players there, and eventually wound up in the King's Company in London as a comedian and dancer.

The Duke of Buckingham took Joe into his service, the *Life* says, and, with the Duke, Joe journeyed to France, where he styled himself a Count. Debts forced him to return to England, where he acted again. There followed numerous escapades, another trip to France to investigate opera productions, a brief career as a mountebank named "Signior Salmantius," service with Sir William Soames in Europe, friendship with the Pope, work as a lawyer in London, and a return to his career as an actor.

The *Life* must contain some grains of truth, but it is so riddled with fancy that one can scarcely sift them out. Kenneth Cameron per-

Harvard Theatre Collection

JOSEPH HAINES
artist unknown

Oxonienses has Joe matriculating in 1659, when Williamson was nearing the end of his second stay at Queen's College (he first entered there in 1650, took his B.A. in 1654, and returned as a fellow in 1657).

We know that about 1667 Haines was in Cambridge and joined John Coysh's troupe of strolling players. He journeyed with Coysh to other towns, presumably, and with him joined Edward Bedford's company of young performers at the Hatton Garden "Nursery" in London. The Nursery was sponsored by the two London patent companies, and within a short time Haines was noticed by Thomas Killigrew and became a member of the King's troupe at the Bridges Street Theatre. About the same time Joe was first mentioned in the Lord Chamberlain's accounts in connection with a debt: on 1 February 1668 Thomas Jennings petitioned against Joe, the first of many such citations in the accounts.

By that time Haines was doubtless performing at Bridges Street, though the first sure record we have is dated 7 March 1668, when Pepys saw *The Spanish Gypsies*. It was the second time the play had been performed, the first having been, most likely, on 3 March. "A very silly play," Pepys thought, "only great variety of dances, and those most excellently done, especially one part by one Hanes, only lately come thither from the Nursery, an understanding fellow, but yet, they say, hath spent £1,000 a-year before he come thither."

It is quite possible that Haines participated in the performance of *The Virgin Martyr* at Bridges Street on 7 May 1668, for after the play Pepys went to a gathering at the actress Mrs Knepp's house, and "Here was also Haynes, the incomparable dancer of the King's house, and a seeming civil man, and sings pretty well."

A Lord Chamberlain's warrant dated 5 August 1668 noted that Haines was discharged by Killigrew, but the discharge was canceled. Joe may have been dropped by the company for a short period, but he is known to have done some performing for the King's Company during the 1668–69 season. The prompt notes in a 1635 edition of *The Sisters* show that Haines acted Piperollo sometime during the season (not Stephanio, as *The London Stage* and Cameron report); perhaps he was in the revival

formed a valuable service in *Theatre Notebook* (24) by trying to separate fact from fiction. There is no evidence to prove or disprove the statement that Haines attended St Martin's School. That he may have gone to Oxford and been employed (but not as Latin secretary) by Williamson is possible, and Cameron feels the most likely date would have been 1666, when Williamson was there briefly, editing the *Oxford Gazette*. Anthony à Wood stated that Haines, who was said to have been "a great Actor and Maker of Plays—but I find him not either in Langbain, or Term Cat," matriculated as a servitor of Queen's College, Oxford, on 3 May 1689—a time when theatrical records show Haines to have been busy in London after returning from Rome and a time when Williamson was not at Oxford. Foster in *Alumni* of *Catiline*, which opened on 18 December 1668; on 17 March 1669 he delivered the prologue to *The Coxcomb* (not in March 1668 as Cameron has it); and the *Life* says Joe danced before Cosimo III, who visited the theatre in April 1669.

Most of the factual information we have about Haines in 1668–69 concerns his problems with creditors. On 9 January 1669 Martin Powell (presumably the actor of that name) went to law against Joe, and on the same day Haines and Henry Browne were petitioned against by Will Mathewes. Mathewes's permission to sue was suspended on 3 February, for it appears the matter was settled out of court: a warrant dated 6 March directed Haines to pay Mathewes 5*s.* weekly on his debt. On 30 July John May petitioned against Joe for a debt of £8; on 12 August Haines was ordered to pay Edward Sanger weekly to diminish a debt of £18; and on 14 August similar weekly payments to May were ordered. Joe was again in debt the following October, to John Curll for £5.

Haines was in the King's Company again in 1669–70, for he was granted livery for the period 1668–1670 on 2 October 1669. Perhaps he acted Mr Plot in *Mr Anthony* on December 1669, but the casting comes from the 1690 edition of the play, and the work is listed in *The London Stage* as having been done by the rival Duke's Company at the Lincoln's Inn Fields Theatre. In July 1670 Joe went to France in the train of the Duke of Buckingham, just as the *Life* stated. The Duke returned to England in September, but Joe stayed on to dance before Louis XIV in the first performance of *Le Bourgeois Gentilhomme*, at Chambord, on 14 October. From Paris on 25 October 1670 (new style) William Perwich wrote to Sir Joseph Williamson:

The King will be (here, I mean) at St Germains this day to see the Dolphin, upon whose indisposition the King broke up all his *divertisements* in the very midst to come away. I think I told you some thing of Jo. Haines; now I can add that he has behaved himselfe there [at Chambord] to every body's wonder, & diverted the King by severall English dances, to his great satisfaction & that of all the Court. I believe he will have a present made him. If you should think it convenient, it would doe him a great kindnesse in England to mention

him in the 'Gazette' among the King's *divertisements* at Chambort, where, whilst the Balets were preparing, he hunted the wild bore & pheasants.

By the enclosed you see the severall entries & manner of the Balet; between every one Haines had order to dance by himselfe, & notwithstanding the confronting of the best dancers, carried it off to admiration, & was ordred to dance some things twice over.

With such encouragement, perhaps Haines stayed in France during 1670–71; we have no record of him in England that season, though the *Life* implies that Joe returned to England after his October 1670 success and then soon after made another trip to France, with a scenekeeper (Henry Wright?), to study opera staging techniques.

Joe's next notice in London was on 7 December 1671, when he appeared in *The Rehearsal* at the Bridges Street playhouse. Haines's role is not known, but it seems to have involved some singing and dancing, for a ballad of the time said, "I confess the Dances were very well Writ, / And the Tune and the Time by Haynes as well Hit." The author of *The Rehearsal*, the Duke of Buckingham, wrote into the dialogue at the end of the play a reference to Joe's dancing. Perhaps as early as December 1671 or January 1672 *The Citizen Turn'd Gentleman* (or *Mamamouchi*, an adaptation of *Le Bourgeois Gentilhomme*) was performed at the Duke's Company's new theatre in Dorset Garden; it was certainly acted there the following 4 July. Haines deserted the King's Company to appear as the French Tutor and Singing Master. The prompter Downes stated in 1708 that Haines did not just desert his troupe: "having affronted Mr Hart, he gave him a Discharge and then [Haines] came into our House. . . ."

By November 1672 Joe was back with the King's Company, playing Benito (a role requiring him to sing and play guitar) in *The Assignation* at the troupe's temporary home, the Lincoln's Inn Fields Theatre (Robert Hume and Judith Milhous suggest the play may have been given as early as May 1672). At some point, perhaps during the fall of 1672, Haines performed in a stable in Greenwich; the *Life* suggests that his stint in Greenwich took place sometime after Hart discharged him, but that is not too helpful, since Joe had a history of discharges. After leaving Greenwich Haines wrote a dreadful lampoon on the strolling players there which was printed in 1672 in *The Covent Garden Drollery* and found its way into the *Life* years later.

A Lord Chamberlain's warrant dated 25 March 1672 or 1673—the year is not certain— shows Haines's certificate with the King's Company as renewed but then canceled. Indeed, the next clear theatrical reference to Haines was on 16 May 1674, when, at Drury Lane, he spoke the prologue to *Nero*. The *Life* implies that Joe was responsible for the dances in *The Tempest* at the Dorset Garden Theatre; the Shadwell version of the work was produced there as early as 30 April 1674. Duffett's *The Mock Tempest* was given at the rival Drury Lane playhouse as early as late spring 1674 (and certainly by the following 19 November); the Introduction was spoken by Haines and Betty Mackarel, the prologue was delivered by Haines, and John Harold Wilson suggests that perhaps Joe played Prospero.

The King's Company performed at Oxford in the summer of 1674 and so misbehaved that they were not allowed to return in 1675. The *Life* speaks of Joe's acting at Oxford the summer following his return from France, and though the chronology of his foreign jaunts is not certain, the summer of 1674 seems likely for his Oxford visit. While there, the *Life* tells us, Joe set himself up as a fortune teller, but he was found out and prudently returned to London.

During the 1674–75 season Haines acted Sparkish in the (first?) performance of *The Country Wife* on 12 January 1675 at Drury Lane, Roderigo in *Othello* on 25 January, one of the two Swordsmen in *A King and No King* on 23 April, Visconti in *Love in the Dark* (and the epilogue) on 10 May, the prologue to *Every Man out of His Humour* in July, None-so-fair in *Psyche Debauch'd* on 27 August, and perhaps, as Cameron suggests, the title part in *Trappolin* in July or August. As usual, Joe was frequently named in the Lord Chamberlain's accounts during the season, as on 3 September 1674, when John Tummins petitioned against him; 18 November, when Clement Vincent sued him; 25 January 1675 (the day Joe appeared in *Othello*), when George Tynder went against him for an eight-pound debt; 10 February, when Hannah Barton (his landlady) of Gutter Lane, Cheapside, sued him for food and lodg-

ing; 30 March, when he was ordered apprehended; and 30 June, when his landlady went against him again for £24 and when Hugh Lamb sued him for £10.

Joe began the 1675–76 season in his usual form. On 30 October 1675 permission was granted Sir Edmund Windham to sue Haines for abuse; five days later Joe was suspended from acting because he had "with ill & scandalous language & insolent carriage abused Sir Edmund Windham and his Lady." Hannah Barton and Hugh Lamb were again after Joe on 15 November; Francis East claimed on 22 December that Haines owed him £30; and John Roffey petitioned on 15 January 1676 for a seven-pound debt. On 7 August Joe's creditors were told they would have to suspend their suits against the actor since there was then "noe playing" at the King's playhouse. During the 1675–76 season the only known theatrical activity for Joe was the speaking of the prologue to *Gloriana* on 29 January 1676.

Haines's certificate with the King's Company was renewed on 7 August 1676, and on 11 December he appeared as Plausible in what may have been the first performance of *The Plain Dealer*. During the rest of the season he played Dwindle in *The Country Innocence* in March 1677 or earlier, Harlequin (perhaps Joe was the first English Harlequin) in *Scaramouch* on 5 May 1677, and Sir Simon Credulous in *Wits Led by the Nose* in mid-June. Though the records do not list *Catiline* as having been performed in 1677, the *Life* contains an anecdote concerning it that suggests it may have been acted that year, when Charles Hart was managing the King's Company at Drury Lane (a less likely year for the incident would be 1668, when we know the play was given).

The *Life* tells us:

There happen'd to be one Night, a Play Acted, Call'd *Catilines Conspiracy*, wherein there was wanting a Great Number of Senators.

Now Mr. *Hart* being chief of the House, wou'd oblige *Jo.* to dress for one of these Senators. Altho *Jo's* Sallary being then 50*s. per* Week, freed him from any such obligation.

But Mr. *Hart*, as I said before, being sole Governour of the Play-House, and at a small variance with *Jo.* commands it, and the other must obey. *Jo.* being vex'd at the slight Mr. *Hart* had put on him: He gets a Scaramouch dress, a large full Ruff, makes himself Whiskers, from Ear to Ear, puts on his head, a long Merry Andrews Cap, a short Pipe in his mouth, a little three Leg'd stool in his hand, and in this manner, follows Mr. *Hart* on the Stage, sets himself down behind him, and begins to smoke his Pipe, to Laugh, and Point at him.

Which Comical Figure put all the House in an uproar, some Laughing, some Clapping, and some Hollowing. Now Mr. *Hart*, as those that knew him can aver, was a Man of that Exactness and Grandeur on the Stage, that let what wou'd happen, he'd never discompose himself, or mind any thing but what he then Represented and had a Scene fall'n behind him, he wou'd not at that time look back, to have seen what was the matter, which *Jo.* knowing, remain'd still Smoaking, the Audience continued Laughing, Mr. *Hart* Acting, and Wondering at this unusual occasion of their Mirth, sometimes thinking it some disturbance in the House; again, that it might be something amiss in his dress; at last, turning himself towards the Scenes, he discover'd *Jo.* in the aforesaid Posture, whereupon he immediately goes off the Stage, Swearing he wou'd never set foot on it again, unless *Jo.* was immediately turn'd out of Doors; which was no sooner spoke, but put in Practice.

The *Life* states that after that incident, Haines joined the group of players at Greenwich; Joe's Greenwich experience, we have guessed, may have been about 1672. But 1672, like 1668, seems too early for the *Catiline* incident, because the story, if any of it is to be believed, makes a point of saying the troupe was under Hart's sole command (which was true only in 1677, briefly) and that Joe was one of the leading players in the company (which he was not in 1668, certainly). The weekly salary of 50*s.* sounds absurd for Joe in 1668, highly unlikely in 1672, and perhaps not even possible in 1677 (Mrs Barry, at the height of her career in 1694, earned that amount).

On 18 June 1677 the Lord Chamberlain ordered Haines apprehended "for reciteinge . . . a Scurrilous & obscoene Epilogue"; the reference may have been to the *Wits Led by the Nose* prologue, which the actor playing Sir Simon was supposed to deliver. At Oxford in July Joe served as a member of the Duke of Ormonde's Irish players from Smock Alley Theatre in Dublin and is known to have spoken an epilogue "to the University of Oxford" on 30 July.

His activities in the fall of 1677 are not now known, though he may have been performing with the King's Company at Drury Lane, where he certainly was in the spring of 1678.

In March 1678 Joe acted Whiffler and spoke the Induction to *The Man of Newmarket* and played Launce and spoke the prologue "in a Red Coat like a Common Souldier" when *Trick for Trick* was presented. The sparse records of the time make no mention of Joe again until a year later. In March 1679, if not before, he acted La Marre and spoke the epilogue to *The Ambitious Statesman*. On 14 April he was given a protection warrant and went off to Edinburgh.

Joe was not the only King's Company player to leave for the north; among other deserters were James Gray, Cardell Goodman, Philip Griffin, Thomas Clark, Mrs Corey, and Joe's mistress, Mrs Knepp (Pepys's old friend). Haines was still in Edinburgh as late as 20 January 1682. The second prologue to Ravenscroft's *Titus Andronicus* said "Haynes does head the Rebell-Players there," though it is not certain he was the actual leader of the group. The *Life* said nothing of Joe's Edinburgh adventure. *The London Stage* states that Haines spent part of the 1679–80 season in Paris, but that information derives from a misprint and concerns Joe's 1670 trip. His stay in Edinburgh may have lasted well into 1682.

Two curious documents relate to Joe's visit to Scotland. In the papers of Lord Montagu of Beaulieu as reported by the Historical Manuscript Commission is a letter dated 20 January 1682 (not, as the HMC *Report* has it, 1683) from J. McLachtan in London to the Duke of Albemarle. The writer asked Albemarle to give Haines his protection, for he had been discharged from the King's Company and would get better conditions elsewhere if the Duke offered Haines his good name. "Hae nided goe from this [Edinburgh, presumably, though McLachtan was in London], for hae wanttes nothing, for boath the nobellmen and the gentrye hes a kynese for him," since Joe had been behaving himself civilly and honestly in Scotland and would want for nothing should he stay there. But Joe, after seeing so much of the world, resolved to go back to London and live honestly with his wife.

The other document, a manuscript doggerel poem by Haines which is now at the British Museum, helps clarify some of the statements in McLachtan's letter. It is addressed "To Madam [Nell] Gwin" and is "a Rhymeing Supplication by way of Ballad for Her Intercession to His Matie: in behalf of Heynes." In it Joe reviewed some of his past troubles:

> I have my discharge
> From Cha: Killegrew
> I am none of his Crew
> And betwixt me & you
> I'de have nothing to doe
> With Him whom I knew
> To mee still a Jew
> To his ffriend never true
> Tho' hee has but a few.

Then Joe hinted at an overseas trip (to France?):

> I begg you'd Implore
> The King but once more
> That on some other Score
> I might bee as before
> The seas I went 'ore.

Knowing the sad state of the King's Company in London, Joe hoped for a place with the rival Duke's players.

> Now dear Madam Gwin I think it no Sin,
> Get the King but to speak to my Lord Chamberlin
> That in the Duke's house I may once Act agen,
> And I doe assure you if I have leave to Play
> It shall be twice as much in his Majesties way,
> For I will still make it my endeavour hereafter
> To lengthen His daies with Fattening laughter.

Joe's stay in Scotland had been touched with tragedy:

> And Pray Let His Matie: too understand
> How sad I have been in merry Scotland
> To loose Mrs: Nep that inchanting Dear Lump
> That Fountaine of Love so juicy so Plump
> That delicate Compound of Spiritt & Rump
> . . . .
> In Child birth from mee to 'Lizeum departted
> Since when Spight of Clarret I've bin broken hearted
> . . . .
> I fasted on ffrydayes I drank nought but water
> To signifie griefe for my Unborn Daughter.
> . . . .
> The Babe was carv'd from Her each Limb e're Shee
>   dy'd
> Whilst I in each lovely Morsell tooke Pride
> You'd admire at th'Infant had I brought it hither
> Twas a beautiful Babe when 'twas put together.

Haines also petitioned the King directly and on 10 July 1682 was granted a certificate as one of the King's servants in ordinary.

By that time a working union of the King's and Duke's companies had been formed, so by the time Joe returned from Scotland he would have become a member of the new United Company, which operated both Drury Lane and Dorset Garden theatres. For the 1682–83 season, however, there are no records of Joe's performing. His *Satyr Against Brandy*, a broadside, was published in early 1683 (Luttrell dated his copy 20 February that year). Not until the spring of 1684 was Haines cited as acting in London. Perhaps he did not find the new United Company to his liking and left town for a time. The *Life* tells us that Joe acted briefly at Windsor and that he spent one summer in Hartford as a mountebank named Signior Salmantius, using as his Merry Andrew a chap he called Hayns. There was a "James" (error for Joseph?) Haynes who showed a motion of "The Prince's Ball and Prospect" in Norwich in 1683 and 1684.

In mid-March 1684 *The Northern Lass* was revived at Drury Lane; the 1684 edition indicated that Joe wrote (and perhaps spoke) the prologue and played Bullfinch. About 1 June he delivered the prologue and epilogue to *Sir Hercules Buffoon* at Dorset Garden, and in mid-August he spoke the epilogue to *A Duke and No Duke* at one of the two playhouses. A year later, in the latter half of July, Haines played Bramble in *Cuckolds' Haven*; in mid-August he acted Hazard in *A Commonwealth of Women* and spoke the prologue "Habited like a Whig, Captain of the Scyth-men in the West, a Scythe in his Hand." Later that month, according to Tony Aston, Joe operated a booth at Bartholomew Fair and presented *The Whore of Babylon, the Devil, and the Pope*. Though there is some question whether that production belongs to 1685, or an earlier year (Aston said Joe ran his booth in the first year of the reign of James II), there may be some truth in the anecdote Aston told in his *Supplement* to Cibber's *Apology*. The production won Joe a punishment by the authorities:

Joe was sent for, and roundly admonish'd by Judge *Pollixfen* for it. *Joe* reply'd, *That he did it in Respect to his* Holiness; *for, whereas many ignorant People believed the Pope To be a Beast, he shew'd him to be a fine, comely old Gentleman, as he was; not with Seven Heads, and Ten Horns, as the* Scotch *Parsons describe him*. However, this Affair spoil'd *Joe's* expiring Credit; for next Morning, a Couple of Bailiffs seiz'd him in an Action of 20*l.* as the Bishop of *Ely* was

JOSEPH HAINES

artist unknown

passing by in his Coach.—Quoth *Joe* to the Bailiffs,—*Gentlemen, here's my Cousin, the Bishop of Ely, going into his House; let me but speak to him, and he'll pay the Debt and Charges.* The Bailiffs thought they might venture that, as they were within three or four Yards of him. So, up goes *Joe* to the Coach, pulling off his Hat, and got close to it. The Bishop order'd the Coach to stop, whilst *Joe* (close to his Ear) said softly, *My Lord, here are two poor Men, who have such great Scruples of Conscience, that, I fear, they'll hang themselves.*—Very well, *said the Bishop.* So, calling to the Bailiffs, he said, *You two Men, come to me Tomorrow Morning and I'll satisfy you.* The Men bow'd, and went away. *Joe* (hugging himself with his fallacious Device) went also his Way. In the Morning, the Bailiffs (expecting the Debt and Charges) repair'd to the Bishop's; where being introduced,—*Well,* said the Bishop, *what are your Scruples of Conscience?*—*Scruples!* (said the Bailiffs) *We have no Scruples: We are Bailiffs, my Lord, who, Yesterday, arrested your Cousin,* Joe Haines, *for* 20*l. Your Lordship promised to satisfy us To-day, and hope your Lordship will be as good as your Word.*—The Bishop, reflecting that his Honour and Name would be expos'd, (if he complied not) paid the Debt and Charges.

The *Life* tells us that at some point Haines left London to perform in the provinces, then wound up on the Isle of Wight and joined "Sir W———— S————" on his embassy to Constantinople. (Sir William Soames was named ambassador to Constantinople on 30 September 1685 and died in Malta in 1686 on his way to his post.) The theatrical records of the time contain no mention of Haines in London between the summer of 1685 and April 1689, at which time he was welcomed as just returned from Rome. It is thus very likely that the essential facts concerning Joe's association with Soames as told in the *Life* are correct and that they belong to this period. Yet Theophilus Lucas's *Lives of the Gamesters* (1714) tells a somewhat different story:

In the reign of the late King James [Haines] travelled in my Lord Castlemaine's retinue, when he went Ambassador to Rome, where [Haines] professed himself a member of that church (which was the first time he ever pretended to any religion) and there he made use of his skill in gaming, by which he got considerable sums from the cautious Italians; and being for some misbehavior left behind at my Lord Castlemaine's return, he was obliged to make use of all his wit and sharping to support himself there, and in his passage home to England.

The *Life* has it that Haines, before leaving England, had joined a company of strollers who were on their way to Portsmouth; the troupe ran into debt and disbanded, perhaps even before performing, and Joe took refuge with Sir Robert Holmes on the Isle of Wight. There he met Soames on his way to Constantinople, joined him, and went to Malta, where Soames died. Soames's widow befriended Haines and helped him get to Leghorn, after which he was on his own. Letters in the Medici Collection in Florence, studied by Anna Maria Crinò in *Fatti e figure de seicento Anglo-Toscano*, provide details of Joe's activity late in 1686.

One letter, dated 29 November, was written by a secretary to Cosimo III to an envoy of the Grand Duke in London:

There departed from Florence an Englishman named Joseph Haynes whose profession is to dance with much grace and art in various styles, and it has been said that he is a comic and that he dances on the stage. His Highness Our Lord admitted him to the palace out of curiosity, in order to show his talent to the princesses and princes. But what was best for him is the renunciation he made of heresy, giving himself over entirely to the Catholic religion with signs of great piety and of a true conversion. His Highness would like to know, however, what kind of a person he is and as much as can be discovered about his situation, wherefore, Your Most Illustrious Lordship should do his part in finding him out.

The London envoy, Francesco Terriesi, did, indeed, find out and replied on 17/27 December 1686:

That which I have found out about Joseph Haynes, concerning whom Your Most Illustrious Lordship asked me information, is that he once was in the service of the Duchess of Cleveland [Lady Castlemaine], and that it was he who introduced into her house that comedian [Cardell Goodman] who then, together with herself, made and still makes the world gossip so much, and who took the place of the aforementioned Haynes. Because of

her, and from this occasion, he put himself forth to play the comedian himself. I do not know for precisely what reason—whether for his debts or for the exceeding wickedness I have ascertained him to be composed of—he later took ship for Constantinople with Ambassador Soames, who died on the voyage. Because of [Haines's] iniquity, he could not be suffered to remain on board, and was violently forced to disembark—I do not know whether this was on the voyage going or returning. And whoever hears now of his conversion laughs at it, and believes it neither sincere nor real. (Translation by Kathleen Falvey.)

The *Life* claims that Haines became a favorite of the Pope in Rome, but from what is known of Pope Innocent X, that sounds rather unlikely. That Joe may have met the Pope is possible, for Lucas said that Haines attached himself to the Earl of Castlemaine's entourage, and Castlemaine was Ambassador to the Pope.

After his Italian adventure Haines returned to England and waited on James II—which would mean he came back before the end of 1688. The *Life* implies that upon his return from the Continent Joe practiced as an attorney and preached among the Quakers before returning to the stage. In 1688 theatrical references to Haines reappeared. Mountfort, in his play *The Injur'd Lovers*, performed in February 1688 at Drury Lane, said of himself in the prologue, "*Jo' Hayns's* Fate is now become my share, / For I'm a *Poet, Married,* and a *Player.*" Joe must have been true to his word and returned to his wife.

His first recorded stage appearance after his return to England was in late April 1689 at either Drury Lane or Dorset Garden, when he played Bayes in *The Rehearsal* and gave a "Recantation-Prologue" in "a white Sheet, with a burning Taper in his Hand, upon his Admittance into the House after his Return from the Church of Rome." In *The Reasons of Mr. Joseph Hains the Player's Conversion & Re-conversion* (1691) it was explained that Joe had become a Catholic on Malta on the advice of an Italian friend, to cure a tumor on his left arm, but that he had gone back to being a Protestant, since Protestantism had come back in fashion. Joe's recantation prologue proved so amusing that he offered a second one in 1690.

On 15 October 1689 Joe was in the thick of legal problems again. He was complained against by his colleague Mountfort, perhaps in

Document suspending JOSEPH HAINES, 1676

league with Charles Killigrew, Thomas or Alexander Davenant (whichever one the bailiffs could find, probably), Thomas Betterton, the younger Powell (George, presumably), Bray the dancing master, the United Company bookkeeper and property maker, Mr Ashbury, and Joseph Trefusis. The bone of contention is not known. Later that month, on 29 October 1689, the Lord Mayor's Show inspired a satire attributed to Joe Haines called "The City Regiment," which appeared in *Poems on Affairs of State*.

There is some evidence that *Love in the Dark* was revived in 1691 and that Haines again spoke the epilogue, though it is likely that he did not resume acting until 1691–92. The 1691 edition of George Powell's *Alphonso King of Naples* credited "John" Haines with the authorship of the prologue, which had been presented at Drury Lane in December 1690, and on 31 December 1691 Joe was Robin in *The Merry Wives of Windsor*. In 1692 *A Fatal Mistake* was published, with Haines listed as the author; Gildon, however, claimed that Joe did not write the "abominable Play." The title page informed readers that the play had been lately acted, but no performance dates are known, and the first edition provided no cast. In 1692 Joe's only known role was Depazzi in *The Traytor* in March.

A year later Haines was cited for three assignments: Captain Bluffe in *The Old Bachelor* in March 1693 (Aston said it was one of Joe's best interpretations), Sneaksby in *A Very Good Wife* in late April (and Joe spoke the prologue), and Bully in *The Female Vertuosos* in May. Congreve's prologue to Powell's *A Very Good Wife* had Joe say

Among the few [authors], which are of noted Fame,
I'm safe, for I my self am one of them:
You've seen me smoak at Will's *among the* Wits,
I'm witty too, as they are, that's by Fits.

By 1693 Joe had also set himself up as a fortune teller, as allusions in *The Richmond Heiress* indicate. The next theatrical notice of Haines was in mid-May 1694, when he played Gines de Passamonte in the first part of *Don Quixote* at Dorset Garden, after which he was not named until mid-February 1696, when, at Drury Lane for Christopher Rich's company, he spoke the epilogue "acting the Mad-Man" to *Neglected Virtue*. By then London again had

rival acting troupes, and Joe, oddly, decided to stay with the younger players rather than join Betterton's dissidents. In March 1696 he acted Knowlittle in *The Lost Lover*; in June he spoke the prologue and played Busy in *The Cornish Comedy*; and in July, seated on an ass, he delivered the epilogue to Scott's *The Unhappy Kindness*—and he was so depicted in a crudely drawn print.

The Female Wits, which came out at Drury Lane in the summer or early fall of 1696 (certainly by September), may have been a group effort in which several playwrights, including Haines, had a hand. On 21 November when *The Relapse* opened, Haines played Serringe and in December gave another of his best interpretations (according to Aston) when he acted the bumpkin Roger in the first performance of *Aesop*. He was Roger again in the second part of *Aesop* in March 1697; on 8 May he played Rumour and spoke the prologue to *A Plot and No Plot*; on 31 May he was Spade and spoke the epilogue to *The Sham Lawyer*; and in late June at Dorset Garden he played himself in *The World in the Moon*.

In the 1697–98 season Joe acted Jamy in *Sauny the Scot*, and he wrote the epilogue spoken by Boman to *The Italian Husband*, a work presented at the rival Lincoln's Inn Fields Theatre probably in December 1697. A year later his name appeared in a cast again: he wrote the prologue, wrote and spoke the epilogue, and acted both Rigadoon and Pamphlet in *Love and a Bottle*. The following April 1699 Joe spoke the prologue to *Love Without Interest*. In a letter dated 12 September 1699 in Tom Brown's *Works* is a statement that Joe Haines worked with the Kentish Strong Man, William Joy, at the Dorset Garden playhouse. Joe was "his Master of the Ceremonies, and introduc'd him in a Prologue upon the Stage; and indeed who so fit to do it as this Person, whose Breath is as strong as the Kentish Man's Back?" The earliest notice of Joy in London was on 15 November 1699.

The 1699–1700 season was Joe's last full one. On 28 November 1699 he was the original Tom Errand in *The Constant Couple*, a work that was immensely popular; in March 1700 he acted the Doctor in *The Reform'd Wife*; on 20 March at York Buildings he spoke a prologue at a benefit concert for Mrs "Hudson" (probably Hodgson) and Mr Williams; and on

29 April and subsequent dates he played the Parson in *The Pilgrim*. Haines spoke the epilogue to *The Perjured Husband* in October 1700, after which his name disappeared from cast lists.

Joseph Haines died at his lodgings in Hart Street, Longacre, on 4 April 1701 after a short illness. He was buried at St Paul, Covent Garden, according to *The Era Almanac*—but the registers do not confirm that. A benefit concert for a Mrs Haines was held at York Buildings on 5 May; there is no certainty that she was Joe's widow, but it seems possible.

The facetious Tom Brown in his *Letters from the Dead* fabricated an exchange between Joe and himself. He wrote to Joe under the date 10 January 1701/2: "'Tis well, Mr. *Haines*, you died when you did; for that unhappy place, where you have so often exerted your Talent, I mean Smithfield [where Bartholomew Fair was held], has fallen under the City Magistrate's displeasure. . . ." Brown then said, "since you left this Upper World, your Life has been written by a Brother Player, who pretends he received all his Memoirs from your own Mouth a little before you made a leap into the Dark; and really you are beholding to the fellow, for he makes you a Master of Arts at the University, tho' you never took a Degree there. That, and a thousand stories of other People he has father'd upon you . . ." *The Life of the Late Famous Comedian, Jo. Hayns*, possibly by the actor Tobias Thomas, came out about the time Brown was writing.

Joe Haines was remembered long after his death. Some song lyrics written by him appeared in D'Urfey's *Wit and Mirth* in 1719. The ass-epilogue which Joe popularized was adopted by many later comedians, notably Pinkethman, Cibber, Shuter, and Wilson. Even as late as the nineteenth century Joe's epilogue on an ass was imitated.

Joe was pictured twice delivering an ass-epilogue. One print is an amateurish drawing that served as a frontispiece to *A Fatal Mistake* in 1692, and the other, drawn more professionally, was published in the fifth volume of Tom Brown's *Works*. In the second volume of that collection is a representation of Haines as "the High-German Astrologer and Chymist," which probably dates about 1700. Among Joe's nicknames were "Signior Salmatius" and "Signior Giuseppe Hanesio."

Haines, Mrs [Joseph?] [*fl.* 1700–1701], *singer.*

A Mrs Haines, quite possibly the wife of the comedian Joe, sang at the Lincoln's Inn Fields Theatre on 5 July 1700 in *Don Quixote*. Joe's private life is little known; he mentioned having a wife as early as 1682, though there is no certainty that she was the Mrs Haines who performed 18 years later. *Mercurius Musicus* in March-April 1701 contained a song from *The Mad Lover* as sung by Mrs "Haynes" and Mr Cooper at Lincoln's Inn Fields. The songs from that work were very popular, and it is likely that the play was performed in early 1701, though *The London Stage* does not mention it until April 1703. The same 1701 issue of *Mercurius Musicus* also contained Eccles's *The loud, the loud alarums*, as sung by Mrs Haines and Cooper, and about 1700 was published another Eccles song, *Ye gentle gales that fan the Air*, with Mrs Haines listed as the singer.

Joe Haines died in early April 1701. On 5 May Mrs Haines was given a benefit concert at York Buildings, after which date mention of her in theatrical records ceased.

"Hairy Girl, The" [*fl.* 1793–1805], *freak.*

An engraving of "The Hairy Girl"—"who was exhibited in many parts of Europe"—was published by the engraver J. Holloway at London in 1793. A reverse of the engraving, "from the celebrated Lavater," was published by Hogg in 1805. In the Harvard Theatre Collection are two other engravings, unsigned, of back and side views of the Hairy Girl.

Hale, Mr [*fl.* 1794], *singer.*

Doane's *Musical Directory* of 1794 listed a Mr Hale, of No 18, Little Tower Street, as a bass who participated in the oratorio performances at Westminster Abbey.

Hale, Mr [*fl.* 1794], *singer.*

Doane's *Musical Directory* of 1794 listed a Mr Hale of Cheshire as a tenor who participated in the oratorio performances at Westminster Abbey.

Hale, Mrs [*fl.* 1794]. *See* HAGLEY, MISS.

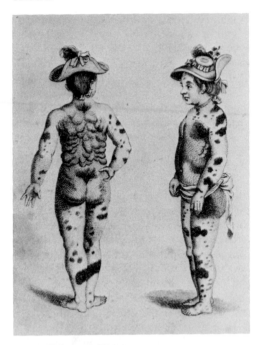

Harvard Theatre Collection

"THE HAIRY GIRL"

artist unknown

Hale, Friend [*fl. 1711*], *musician?*

William Mears and Friend Hale shared a benefit concert at the Town Hall at St Margaret's Hill, Southwark, on 6 February 1711.

Hale, Mary Ann *d. 1805, actress, singer.*

Mary Ann Hale was the daughter of Sacheverel Hale and his wife, the former Ann Hallam. The Hales were married shortly before the opening of the 1739–40 season at Covent Garden, and Hale died in 1746; sometime between those bracketing dates Mary Ann was born. The earliest record of her theatrical activity dates from three years after the end of her mother's career: on 5 August 1776 Mary Ann was named in a playbill for the Richmond Theatre, where *The Runaway* and *Cupid's Holiday* were performed.

The following summer Mary Ann performed at the Haymarket Theatre, which was to become her showplace in summers to the end of her career. On 30 May 1777 she was in *The Nabob*; on 19 June, Damaris in *Polly*; on 15 July, a Lady in *Rule a Wife and Have a Wife*;

on 18 July, Dorcas in *The Sheep-Shearing*; on 9 August, La Bronze in *The Advertisement*; on 12 August, Lucinda in *Love in a Village*; on 19 August, a Kinswoman in *The Chances*; on 25 August, in *The Rehearsal*; on 17 September, Lucy in *The Beggar's Opera*; on 18 September, Belinda in *The Provok'd Wife*; and on 13 October, Peggy in *The Gentle Shepherd*. She returned to the Haymarket on 31 March 1778 to play Ann Lovely in *A Bold Stroke for a Wife*, and she was there again during the summer of 1778 to be Anne Bullen in *Henry VIII*, Lavender in *Tony Lumpkin in Town*, Peggy in *The Suicide*, Violetta in *The Gipsies*, and a member of the singing chorus in *Macbeth*.

Except for the summers of 1786 and 1787, Miss Hale appeared regularly at the Haymarket through 1801–1802, adding such roles to her repertoire as Fidget in *Summer Amusement*, an Actress in *The Manager in Distress*, Dame Furrow in *Harlequin Teague*, Lucy in *George Barnwell*, Judith in *The Young Quaker*, Toilet in *The Jealous Wife*, Zaphira in *A Mogul Tale*, Curtis in *Catherine and Petruchio*, a Villager in *The Battle of Hexham*, a Bacchante in *Comus*, a Peasant in *The Mountaineers*, Kitty in *The Liar*, and Sukey Tawdry in *The Beggar's Opera*.

Perhaps as early as 1778 Mary Ann had been a member of the Drury Lane company in the winters. The accounts there on 3 October of that year show a payment to Miss Hale of 13*s.* 4*d.* "for last week." The fee may have been for her work at the Haymarket during the summer, or perhaps she was a member of the chorus at Drury Lane. She received no citations in the patent house playbills in 1778–79, however, and not until 1780–81 was she advertised there. That season she was Trusty in *The Provok'd Husband* on 26 October 1780, Peg in *The Way of the World* on 22 January 1781, Lucy in *The Recruiting Officer* on 18 April, and Mignionet in *The Way to Keep Him* on 24 April.

She played at Drury Lane again in the seasons that followed, trying such new parts as Florella in *The Orphan*, Mrs Fulmer in *The West Indian*, Jenny Private in *The Fair Quaker*, Jenny Diver in *The Beggar's Opera*, and Cornet in *The Provok'd Wife*. Her last season at Drury Lane seems to have been 1786–87; her only known role there that season was Mignionet on 21 May 1787, just before the close of the season. The following 20 June she turned up at the Royalty Theatre to play Audrey in *As*

You Like It. Ten years later, at the end of the 1796–97 season, Mary Ann returned to Drury Lane briefly to act Susan in *The Spoil'd Child* on 28 April 1797, an Arcadian in *Linco's Travels* on 24 May, and the Nurse in *The Chances* on 15 June (in the early part of the evening, before hurrying over to the Haymarket to act Kitty in *The Liar*, the third piece on that theatre's bill). Mary Ann was styled "Mrs" Hale on most of the playbills; in 1793 she abandoned "Miss," though there is no clue about why.

Little is known of Mary Ann's income. Her benefit tickets were accepted at Drury Lane in the late springs of 1786 and 1787, but there is no record of how much she made. In 1785 she had subscribed £1 1s. to the Drury Lane fund. She was earning £2 weekly at the Haymarket in 1793, but when she appeared briefly at Drury Lane in May and June 1797 her salary was only £1 weekly.

The Haymarket accounts for the summers of 1804 through 1810 list a female Hale as a member of the chorus; possibly Mary Ann was the performer cited in 1804 and 1805, but she died in November 1805, so later citations in the accounts must have concerned another woman, perhaps a relative. Mary Ann Hale's will was written on 31 October 1805 and designated Elizabeth Barbara Sophia Woodeson, spinster, who was then living with Mary Ann, her chief beneficiary. Mary Ann's address when she made her will was in Suffolk Street, Charing Cross. The will was proved on 18 November 1805.

Hale, Sacheverel *d. 1746, actor.*

The first mention of Sacheverel Hale in playbills was on 2 May 1732 when he acted Foodle in *Tragedy of Tragedies* at the Lincoln's Inn Fields Theatre. He may have been playing lesser roles before that for the John Rich company, but the bills took no notice of them. Hale was at Bullock's booth at Bartholomew Fair on 23 August, acting Bellair in *The Perjur'd Prince*. He was back with Rich's troupe in 1732–33 and was more frequently cited in cast lists. He acted Loveworth in *Tunbridge Walks* on 26 December 1732 at Lincoln's Inn Fields; then, at the new Covent Garden Theatre, he played Delio in *The Fatal Secret* on 4 April 1733, Elliot in *Venice Preserv'd* on 12 April, a Gentleman in *Timon of Athens* on 1 May, Pollux in *The Rape of Helen* on 19 May, Courtney in

The Fatal Extravagance and Jupiter in *Momus Turn'd Fabulist* on 26 June, Scipio in *Sophonisba* on 6 July, the first Manager in *The Stage Mutineers* on 27 July, the Governor in *Oroonoko* on 2 August, and Vario in *The Tuscan Treaty* on 20 August.

Though Hale was seen at Covent Garden throughout the rest of his career, he made occasional appearances elsewhere. He was King Henry in *Fair Rosamond* on 24 August 1734 at Bartholomew Fair, Sir George in *The Drummer* on 26 September 1734 at Richmond, the Elder Worthy in *Love's Last Shift* at Lincoln's Inn Fields on 9 April 1735, a Hussar in *The Top of the Tree* at Bartholomew Fair on 23 August 1739.

But until his death in 1746 Hale appeared at Covent Garden. Some of his many roles there over the years were Horatio in *Hamlet*, the Duke in *Venice Preserv'd*, Lenox and Seward in *Macbeth*, the Chaplain in *The Orphan*, Antonio in *The Rover*, Lysippus in *The Maid's Tragedy*, Loveday in *The London Cuckolds*, the Duke and Juan in *Rule a Wife and Have a Wife*, Vizard in *The Constant Couple*, Peregrine and Avocatore in *Volpone*, Axalla, the Prince, and Omar in *Tamerlane*, Bertran in *The Spanish Fryar*, Lodovico and Cassio in *Othello*, Freeman in *The Plain Dealer*, Manuel in *Love Makes a Man*, Poins and Douglas in *1 Henry IV*, Achilles in *Troilus and Cressida*, Juba and Marcus in *Cato*, Trueman in *The Squire of Alsatia*, Tressel and Stanley in *Richard III*, Sir Charles and Aimwell in *The Stratagem*, Raleigh in *The Unhappy Favorite*, Dorilant and Harcourt in *The Country Wife*, Pylades in *The Distrest Mother*, Hemskirk in *The Royal Merchant*, Albany in *King Lear*, Percy in *Richard II*, Lord Bardolph in *2 Henry IV*, Gower in *Henry V*, Foppington in *The Relapse*, Sharper in *The Old Bachelor*, Blandford in *Oroonoko*, Dolabella in *All for Love*, Worthy in *The Recruiting Officer*, Clerimont in *The Tender Husband*, Valentine in *Love for Love*, and Manly in *The Provok'd Husband*.

After 1740 Hale added such new characters to his repertoire as Moneses in *Tamerlane*, Castalio and Polydore in *The Orphan*, Edmund in *King Lear*, Constant in *The Provok'd Wife*, Banquo and Malcolm in *Macbeth*, Torrismond in *The Spanish Fryar*, Carlos in *Love Makes a Man*, Richmond in *Richard III*, Orlando in *As You Like It*, Laertes in *Hamlet* (though he went back to Horatio after a few years), Fenton in *The Drummer*, Townly in *The London Cuckolds*, Florizel in *The Winter's Tale*, Clerimont Senior in *The Tender Husband*, the Mad Scholar in *The Pilgrim*, Young Bevil in *The Conscious Lovers*, Fainall in *The Way of the World*, the title role in *The Gamester*, Hastings in *Jane Shore*, Hotspur in *1 Henry IV*, Prince John in *2 Henry IV*, Bedamar in *Venice Preserv'd*, Antony in *Julius Caesar*, Young Fashion and Worthy in *The Relapse*, Buckingham in *Henry VIII*, Bassanio in *The Merchant of Venice*, the title role in *Henry V* (for his shared benefit with his wife, on 19 April 1744), Hubert in *The Royal Merchant*, Truewit in *The Silent Woman*, the title role in *Timon of Athens* (for his 20 April 1745 benefit; he seldom played leading roles otherwise), Claudio in *Much Ado about Nothing*, and Iachimo in *Cymbeline*. His last appearance at Covent Garden was as Freeman in *A Bold Stroke for a Wife* on 28 April 1746. Hale's salary, during the 1740–41 season at any rate, was 13s. 4d. daily, a good salary; but it is doubtful, considering his continuing string of secondary roles, that he rose much above that in London before he died.

In 1738 a group of London players, including Hale, acted at Canterbury from the end of May to the middle of August. As early as the summer of 1741 Hale became associated during his summer vacations with the company at the Jacob's Wells Theatre in Bristol. He acted there regularly through the summer of 1746—indeed, up to within two days of his death. During all or most of the time Hale was one of the sharers in the troupe. His roles from 2 June to 20 August 1746 have been preserved and indicate how much better his parts were outside London: Captain Plume in *The Recruiting Officer*, Colonel Careless in *The Committee*, Sir Charles Easy in *The Careless Husband*, Farewell in *Sir Courtly Nice*, Brabantio in *Othello*, Heartly in *The Non-Juror*, Lord Hardy in *The Funeral*, the title role in *Timon of Athens*, Benedick in *Much Ado about Nothing*, and Colonel Standard in *The Constant Couple*. Hale's benefits in Bristol compared favorably with other leaders in the troupe. In 1743, for example, he had gross receipts of £57, while Macklin brought in £52, Woodward £55, and Hippisley £55.

Mrs Hale, the former Ann Hallam, was active at Covent Garden and Bristol during those same years. She and Hale were married just before the opening of the 1739–40 season.

Sacheveral Hale died between midnight and 1:00 A.M. on 22 August 1746 at his lodgings near the Hot Wells in Bristol, according to the *Daily Advertiser*. The *Bristol Oracle* called Hale "an Excellent Performer, an indulgent Husband, a tender Parent, an affectionate Brother, and a sincere Friend; Qualities so very rarely united, make him not only an insupportable Loss to the Widow and Fatherless; but, also greatly lamented by all who had the pleasure of his Acquaintance." His widow and their son were given a charity benefit on 27 August, when Mrs Pritchard played in *The Distrest Mother*. Mrs Hale's receipts were £60, less charges of £10 8s. 1d. The Hales also had a daughter, Mary Anne, who acted during the last quarter of the eighteenth century. Mrs Hale married the actor John Barrington in the summer of 1749 and continued performing under her new name until 1773 or longer.

Davies in his *Dramatic Miscellanies* in 1784 remembered Hale as

in person tall and well-proportioned, his voice strong and harmonious, his deportment manly, and his action not displeasing; his ear was so unfaithful, that he was generally monotonous; he wanted that judgment which alone knows how to give dignity to sentiment or warmth and variety to passion. His best performance was Hotspur; he was always to be endured when he restrained himself from doing too much. He was a favourite actor in Bristol, where I think he died in 1746. He was so fond of wearing large full-bottomed wigs, that, to the astonishment of the audience, he acted the part of Charles the First in one which was remarkably long and fair.

Hale, Mrs Sacheverel. *See* BARRINGTON, JOHN.

Hales. *See also* HAILES.

Hales, Mrs [*fl.* 1747–1760], *dresser.*
Mrs Hales, one of the women dressers at the Covent Garden Theatre, was listed in the bills on 22 May 1747 and 7 May 1750 as one of many house servants who shared in benefits; receipts were poor each time, and Mrs Hales realized only half value for her tickets—£1 17s. and £2 10s. On 22 September 1760 she was on the payroll at 1s. 6d. daily.

Haley, Henry $_{[}fl.$ $1786?–1809?_{]}$, *trumpeter.*

Perhaps the Mr "Halley" whose benefit tickets were accepted at Covent Garden Theatre on 2 June 1786 and again on 5 June 1789 was the trumpeter Henry Haley, who served in the royal musical establishment in 1793. Henry may have been the Haley cited on 6 March 1809 in the Minute Books of the Irish Musical Fund as one of the members of the orchestra in the Society's annual commemoration concert.

Halford, Mrs $_{[}fl.$ $1766–1767_{]}$, *singer.*

At Covent Garden Theatre Mrs Halford sang in the choruses of *Romeo and Juliet* on 21 October 1766 and *The Royal Convert* on 21 November. Her last notice was on 20 April 1767, when *Romeo and Juliet* was repeated.

Hall, Mr $_{[}fl.$ $1717_{]}$, *wardrobe keeper.*

Mr Hall, the wardrobe keeper at Lincoln's Inn Fields Theatre, shared a benefit at that house on 3 June 1717.

Hall, Mr $_{[}fl.$ $1743–1749_{]}$, *actor.*

Mr Hall played Sir Harry in *The Constant Couple* on 17 October 1743 at the Aungier Street Theatre in Dublin, and on the following 26 November he acted Hamlet for his benefit. He was Archer in *The Beaux' Stratagem* on 9 January 1744, then moved to the Smock Alley Theatre to play Clodio in *Love Makes a Man* on 2 February. Hall performed at the new theatre in Capel Street in 1744–45, taking the title role in *The Lying Valet* for his benefit on 26 March 1745. Gratiano in *The Merchant of Venice* was another of Hall's roles at Capel Street. In Dublin Hall became associated with "Harlequin" Philips, and on 23 August 1749 at Bartholomew Fair in London Philips produced *The Tempest*, with Hall as Gonzalo.

Hall, Mr $_{[}fl.$ $1770_{]}$, *actor.*

A Mr Hall played Lopez in *The Mistake* and Mungo in *The Padlock* at the Haymarket Theatre on 14 December 1770 for that night only. Possibly Hall was the player of that name who was active in Ireland from 1768 to 1790, but there is not sufficient evidence to make identification possible.

Hall, Mr $_{[}fl.$ $1784–1808?_{]}$, *boxkeeper.*

At Covent Garden from 1784 through the end of the eighteenth century and possibly as late as 1808 was a Mr Hall who worked as a boxkeeper and a John Hall who served the playhouse as a carpenter. Distinguishing them in the bills and accounts is often impossible; one or the other or perhaps both of them earned 12*s*. weekly, but that was a salary earned by many of the employees, including yet another Mr Hall who was a doorkeeper in the 1790s.

The first mention of Hall the boxkeeper seems to have been on 29 May 1784 when his benefit tickets were accepted. He was cited almost every spring thereafter in a similar fashion, though his name was not mentioned in 1785 or 1793, and in 1797 he seems to have been mistakenly cited as Mrs Hall. The accounts in 1807–8 still mentioned a Hall as an employee of the theatre, though they failed to specify his job.

Hall, Mr *d. 1787?, actor.*

A Mr Hall played a principal role in the afterpiece *The Lawyer Non-suited* at the Haymarket Theatre on 6 May 1782, and it was probably he who acted the Lawyer in *'Tis Well It's No Worse* at the same house on 25 April 1785. Charles Beecher Hogan has conjectured that this actor was the Mr Hall whose death at Clonmel was reported in the *Dublin Chronicle* of 26 May 1787.

Hall, Mr $_{[}fl.$ $1792–1795_{]}$, *doorkeeper.*

A Mr Hall had his benefit tickets accepted at Covent Garden on 25 May 1792; he seems not to have been either Hall the boxkeeper or Hall the carpenter, so it is likely that he was the Mr Hall, doorkeeper, who was listed in the account books in 1794–95 at a salary of 12*s*. weekly.

Hall, Mr $_{[}fl.$ $1799_{]}$, *puppeteer.*

A Mr Hall presented a puppet show at Bartholomew Fair in 1799. Possibly he was the Hall who managed a troupe at Potten in 1792, but there is not sufficient evidence to make an identification.

Hall, Mrs $_{[}fl.$ $1728–c.1760_{]}$, *exhibitor.*

After the death of James Salter, his daughter, a Mrs Hall, ran "Don Saltero's," a coffee house and museum of curiosities at what is now No 18, Cheyne Walk.

Hall, Mrs ₁*fl. 1794–1795*₁, *dresser.*
A Mrs Hall was a dresser at the Covent Garden Theatre in 1794–95 earning 12*s.* weekly.

Hall, Mrs ₁*fl. 1797*₁. *See* HALL, MR ₁*fl. 1784–1808?*₁, *boxkeeper*

Hall, Miss ₁*fl. 1783*₁, *dancer.*
Miss Hall danced with the Simonets in a "Mélange Ballet" called *La Noce du château* at the Royal Circus on 18 October 1783.

Hall, Elizabeth ₁*fl. 1664–1683?*₁, *actress.*
Elizabeth H̄all was probably the "Bette" who was cast as Kecka by Thomas Killigrew in his *Thomaso* at the Bridges Street Theatre in November 1664. Sometime during the 1664–65 season *The Siege of Urbin* was performed there, and the servant Clara, according to the manuscript of the play, was acted by Mrs "Bettie." A livery warrant in the Lord Chamberlain's accounts named Elizabeth Hall as a member of the King's Company on 30 June 1666, and from Pepys we learn her nickname: on 23 January 1667 he saw *The Humorous Lieutenant* and backstage "saw Mrs Hall, which is my little Roman-nose black [brunette] girl, that is mighty pretty: she is usually called Betty."

Mrs Hall's name on a warrant dated 22 July 1667 was lined out, suggesting that she had been discharged, though she was named for her livery allowance on 8 February 1668. She did leave the King's Company, probably after the 1667–68 season, for on 19 December 1668 Pepys went to the Bridges Street playhouse and sat "next to Betty Hall, that did belong to this house, and was Sir Philip Howard's mistress, a mighty pretty wench." Pepys implied that she was no longer Howard's mistress, though she was remembered in the *Satyr on Both Whigs and Toryes* in 1683 as "Phil's Player" and was then, presumably, still alive.

Hall, Francis ₁*fl. 1663*₁, *trumpeter.*
On 23 May 1663 Francis Hall was appointed a trumpeter extraordinary in the King's Musick. The term indicated that he had to serve without a salary until a position became vacant, and since the records make no further mention of him, he must have left the royal service.

Hall, Henry *c. 1655–1707, singer, organist, composer.*
Henry Hall, the son of Captain Henry Hall, was born in New Windsor about 1655 and became one of the Children of the Chapel Royal in London under Henry Cooke in the early 1670s. By 17 January 1673 his voice had broken and he was issued clothing, a customary practice with former Chapel boys. Responsible for him then at the Chapel Royal was the musician Pelham Humphrey.

In 1674 the precocious Hall became organist of Exeter Cathedral, succeeding Theodore Coleby, and in 1698 was appointed vicar choral and organist of Hereford Cathedral, where he remained until his death. By 1685 Hall had begun to publish songs; one of them, "A Dialogue betwixt Oliver Cromwell and Charon," was included in the second book of Playford's *Theater of Music* that year. Several other light songs by "Henry Hall, of Hereford" came out in *Mercurius Musicus* in 1699 and 1700, including "Sing, sing, sing, sing," "Shou'd a legion of Cares," "Lucinda has the de'll," and "Why Fair Armida." The *Post Boy* of 5 November 1700 advertised that Hall's *A Comical Song on the Jubilee* had been separately published, and in *Monthly Masks* in 1704 Hall's "Come take of your Liquor" appeared, a piece for which Hall, an accomplished poet, wrote both the words and the music. Another song he wrote and set to music was "To our Arms on Earth and Seas," which the *Diverting Post* advertised on 4 November 1704. His "On the Duke of Marlborough's approaching campaign" was sung at Drury Lane, according to the *Diverting Post* on 31 March 1705.

In addition to his light music he composed a number of anthems and other religious pieces, which have survived in manuscript in the British Library and a *Te Deum* and *Jubilate* which were published.

Henry Hall died at Hereford on 30 March 1707 and was buried in the cloister of the vicar's college there. On the following 28 July was advertised in *Mercurius Musicus* a *Suite of Airs* by the late Henry Hall of Hereford. Henry left a son Henry, also a poet but apparently not a composer; young Henry succeeded to his father's position at Hereford in 1707 and held it until his death on 22 January 1713. *The Dictionary of National Biography* claims that the court musician William Hall (d. 1700) was another son of Henry Hall of Hereford, but Grove does not so identify him.

Hall, Jacob [fl. c. 1662–1681], rope dancer.

Grammont's *Memoirs* tell us that the rope dancer Jacob Hall was fashionable in London as early as about August 1662. On 22 February 1663 Hall, along with Thomas Cosby and William Fuller, was sworn one of the King's "Valters & Dancers on ye Rope and other agillity of Body." Hall became in time a paramour of Lady Castlemaine, who took the King's advice and chose Jacob Hall over Henry Jermyn. The King, said Grammont,

did not think it consistent with his dignity that a mistress whom he had honored . . . should appear chained to the car of the most ridiculous conqueror that ever was [i.e., Jermyn]. His majesty frequently expostulated with the Countess upon the subject, but his expostulations were never attended to. It was in one of these differences that, when he advised her to bestow her favors upon Jacob Hall the rope-dancer, who was able to return them rather than lavish her money upon Jermyn to no purpose . . . she was not proof against his raillery.

Lady Castlemaine provided Hall with a salaried post in return for his favors.

On 26 March 1667 Hall and Fuller were permitted to set up a rope dancing booth near the Maypole in the Strand, and the following year, on 29 August 1668 at Bartholomew Fair, Pepys praised "Jacob Hall's dancing of the ropes; a thing worth seeing, and mightily followed." The following 21 September Pepys saw him again at Southwark Fair:

to Jacob Hall's dancing on the ropes, where I saw such action as I never saw before, and mightily worth seeing; and here took acquaintance with a fellow that carried me to a tavern, whither come the musick of this booth, and by and by Jacob Hall himself, with whom I had a mind to speak, to hear whether he had ever any mischief by falls in his time. He tells me, 'Yes, many; but never to the breaking of a limb:' he seems a mighty strong man.

Harvard Theatre Collection

JACOB HALL

engraving by de Brune, after van Oost

Hall was very popular with the town, much sought after by the ladies, and frequently alluded to by writers. Shadwell called him "a most admirable Rope-Dancer" in *The Sullen Lovers*. Dryden in his epilogue to Lee's *Mithridates* spoke of "Jacob's Cap'ring Tricks," and Dr John King used Hall in one of his riddles.

Hall, Robert Turner, and John Perin were sued on 20 May 1669 by Sir Henry Herbert, the Master of the Revels. Though the reason is not known, it is probable that the trio had performed somewhere illegally. We know Hall participated in the city pageants honoring the Lord Mayor, for he was mentioned in some verses on St Marylebone in Dr Wild's *Rome Rhymed to Death* (1683):

When Jacob Hall on his high rope shews tricks,
The Dragon flatters; the Lord Mayor's horse kicks;
The Cheapside crowds, and pageants scarcely know
Which t'admire, Hall, hobby horse, or Bow.

The occasion may have been 30 October 1671, when Hall is known to have danced in the Lord Mayor's Show. About 1673 Hall performed illegally at Stourbridge Fair, Cambridge; he "shewed and acted unlawfull games two dayes together contrary to the statute," said the charge.

At some point, probably in the 1670s, Hall advertised a performance—but the bill below, undated, was reported by John Payne Collier in 1859 and could be spurious:

These are to give Notice to all Gentlemen and Others, That there is Joyned together Two of the Best Companies in England, viz. Mr. Jacob Hall (Sworn Servant to his Majestie), and Mr. Richard Lancashire, with several Others of their Companies; by Whom will be performed Excellent Dancing and Vaulting on the Ropes; with Variety of Rare Feats of Activity and Agility of Body upon the Stage; as doing of Somersets, and Flip-flaps, Flying over Thirty Rapiers, and over several Men's heads; and also flying through severall Hoops: Together with severall other Rare Feats of Activity, that will be there presented: With the Witty Conceits of Merry Will: In the performing of all which They Challenge all Others whatsoever, whether Englishmen or Strangers, to do the like with them for Twenty Pounds, or what more They please.

The bill was for a performance at Bartholomew Fair, and Hall was, indeed, still appearing there in the late 1670s, one known date being 3 September 1679, when William Blaythwaite saw him.

Manuscript notes in an extra-illustrated copy of *Bartholomew Fair* at the Harvard Theatre Collection state that Hall lived at No 10, Neville Court, Fetter Lane. "There was a symmetry and elegance as well as strength and agility" in his person, the anonymous commentator wrote, and he was regarded by the ladies "as a due composition of Hercules and Adonis. . . . Purcell the musician has made Jacob Hall one of the subjects of his catch beginning 'There's that will challenge all in the fair'."

At some point Hall erected a booth in Charing Cross. Ventris's *Law Reports* in 1771 preserved an account of the problems Hall encountered:

Complaint was made to the Lord Chief Justice by divers of the Inhabitants about Charing-Cross, That Jacob Hall was erecting of a great Boothe in the Street there, intending to shew his feats of Activity, and Dancing upon the Ropes there, to their great Annoyance, by Reason of the Crowd of idle and naughty People that would be drawn thither, and their Apprentices inveigled from their Shops.

Upon this the Chief Justice appointed him to be sent for unto the Court, and that an Indictment should be presented to the Grand Jury of this Matter; and withal the Court warned him, that he should proceed no further.

But he being dismissed, they were presently after informed, That he caused his Workmen to go on. Whereupon they commended the Marshall to fetch him into Court; And being brought in and demanded, how he durst go in Contempt of the Court? He with great impudence affirmed that he had the King's Warrant for it, and Promise to bear him harmless.

Then they required of him a Recognisance of 300 £ that he should cease further Building; which he obstinately refused, and was committed: And the Court caused a Record to be made of this nuisance, as upon their own View (it being in their Way to Westminster) and awarded a Writ thereupon to the Sheriff of Middlesex, commanding him to prostrate the Building.

And the Court said, Things of this Nature ought not to be placed amongst People's Habitations, and that it was a Nuisance to the King's Royal Palace; besides, that it straightened the Way, and was insufferable in that respect.

Apparently Hall's influence at court allowed him to complete his Charing Cross project.

He also set up a stage in Lincoln's Inn Fields but was forced out of business by irate residents who, like their fellow-citizens of Charing Cross, objected to the rowdiness of the crowds Hall attracted. The poem "Bartholomew-Fayre" in *A Choice Compendium*, which was noted in the Term Catalogue in February 1681, said "Here's Jacob Hall that does Jump it, Jump it." But he did not jump much longer. By 1681 Hall had been performing for nearly 20 years, and though he was alluded to after that date, references to his performances ceased.

There is a painting of Hall (supposedly dating about 1650, but that is surely too early) in the collection of F. T. Dent. Possibly that is the painting by van Oost of a finely-dressed gentleman who has been taken for Jacob Hall. In any case, there is a watercolor drawing of the van Oost portrait in the Harvard Theatre Collection, and engravings of the van Oost were made by: an anonymous engraver, published by W. Richardson in 1792; an anonymous engraver, used as a plate to Caulfield's *Remarkable Persons* in 1795; P. de Brune; Scheneker, used as a plate to Hamilton's *Memoirs of Count Grammont*, published by Edwards in 1793; and by E. Scriven, used as a plate to the same, published by W. Miller and J. Carpenter in 1810. S. Freeman made a portrait engraving of Hall. Nell Gwynn owned a statuette of "iacob haale dansing upon ye robbe of Weyer Worck." Oil painting by unknown artist, possibly van Oost. Reported in the collection of F. T. Dent. Oil painting by unknown artist. At Trinity College, Oxford.

Hall, John [*fl.* 1703–1711], *manager?*
On 23 April 1703 a Mr Hall shared a benefit at Drury Lane Theatre with Owen Swiney. They shared similar benefits on 15 October 1703, 6 April 1704, and 21 June 1704; on 19 June 1705 and 14 April 1707 Hall shared benefits with Zachary Baggs, the company treasurer. *The London Stage* lists Hall as an actor at Drury Lane during those years, but no roles are known for him, and the appearance of his name with Swiney and Baggs, both of whom were concerned with theatre administration and finances, suggests that Hall served in a nonacting capacity, perhaps as an assistant manager.

At the Queen's Theatre on 8 March 1708, according to the Coke papers at Harvard, Hall was earning a daily salary of 10*s.*, and though his duties were not specified on the paylist that has survived, he was grouped with nonperforming personnel. His salary was the highest scale listed, equivalent to Mr Porter, who was in charge of the scenemen. On 13 January 1708 Hall had been paid £329 for "stuffs" for the operas.

John Hall also dabbled in real estate, letting the Lincoln's Inn Fields playhouse as a tennis court; the *Daily Courant* of 4 September 1708 advised interested renters to inquire of Hall at the Angel in Little Russell Street.

At Drury Lane on 9 March and the Queen's on 27 April 1710 Hall again shared benefits. Leslie Hotson cites legal documents among the Chancery records dated 10 and 24 February and 15 May 1711 naming Swiney and John Hall in suits over breaches of articles with the Drury Lane managers Cibber, Doggett, and

Wilks. After 1711 Hall's name seems to have disappeared from theatrical records.

Hall, John   *d. 1734, actor, dancer, singer, manager.*
W. R. Chetwood, writing in 1749, claimed that John Hall was a sharer in the Smock Alley company in Dublin "above thirty Years ago" and co-managed the theatre with John Leigh. Hall had a good knowledge of music, Chetwood said, and had once been a dancing master. With Leigh, Hall came to London to join the Lincoln's Inn Fields troupe. Hall's career, we find, began even earlier than Chetwood thought. In the fall of 1714 Joseph Ashbury, the manager of Smock Alley, produced four plays in which Hall appeared: *The Committee*, with Hall as the first Committeeman; *Don Quixote*, with Hall acting Vincent in the first part; *Timon of Athens*, with Hall as Isidore; and *Tamerlane*, with Hall playing Omar. By the end of the year Hall had migrated to London to join John Rich's company at Lincoln's Inn Fields. Of his co-managership at Smock Alley with Leigh we have only Chetwood's word.

In London, Hall acted Bluff in *The Old Bachelor* on 4 January 1715, a Sailor in *The Fair Quaker* on 7 January, Captain Driver in *Oroonoko* and Sir Antony Bounteous in *The Slip* on 3 February, Falstaff in *1 Henry IV* for his benefit on 4 April (and Hall was given a second benefit on 26 May), Justice Hardhead in *The City Ramble* on 2 June, Bounce in *The Doating Lovers* on 23 June, and Francisco in *The False Count* on 11 August. He demonstrated his singing ability on 3 August by offering "'Tis Sultry Weather, Pretty Maid," with Mrs Thurmond. Perhaps he demonstrated his speed, too, if the Mr Hall and his wife who were granted a benefit at the Tennis Court in Edinburgh on 25 June 1715 when *The Beaux' Stratagem* was presented was John Hall. It is worth noting that Hall could have managed a trip to Edinburgh and back: there was no performance at Lincoln's Inn Fields on 24 or 25 June, and *The Doating Lovers* was advertised for 27 June (a Monday) but deferred until the following day. That Hall was married (at least twice) we learn from Chetwood, and he may well have been married by 1715.

John was at Lincoln's Inn Fields again from 1715–16 on, adding to his repertoire such new parts as Kite in *The Recruiting Officer*, Balderdash in *The Twin Rivals*, a Gravedigger in *Hamlet*, Sir Sampson in *Love for Love*, Sir Peter in *The Amorous Widow*, Sackbut in *A Bold Stroke for a Wife*, Day in *The Committee*, Gammer Grime in *The Lucky Chance*, and Madge in *Sir Richard Whittington*. Each spring he received a solo benefit. He was at Angel Court on 24 September 1718 to play Kite at a benefit he shared with Pack and Spiller, and his only appearances at Lincoln's Inn Fields in 1718–19 were as a Gravedigger in March and April 1719. Then Hall's name disappeared from London casts until 5 September 1720, when he and John Leigh presented *Friar Bacon*, a droll, at Southwark Fair. It is possible that when Hall was absent from London he was with Leigh in Dublin.

On 10 October 1720 Hall acted Falstaff in *1 Henry IV* at the Southwark Fair booth he and Leigh operated, and on 28 November at Southwark he ran a booth by himself and produced *The Old Bachelor*. He then rejoined Rich's company at Lincoln's Inn Fields to play Elbow in *Measure for Measure* beginning 8 December. He remained with the troupe for the rest of the 1720–21 season and then joined

Harvard Theatre Collection

JANE GIFFARD as Lucy, JOHN HALL as Lockit, and THOMAS WALKER as Macheath

a detail from scene by Hogarth

Leigh once more to operate a booth at Southwark Fair in September 1721.

Until his death in 1734 Hall was a member of Rich's company, acting at Lincoln's Inn Fields and, from 1732 on, at Covent Garden. Among his roles were Hecate in *Macbeth*, Sir William in *Love's Last Shift*, Bloody Bones in *The Soldier's Fortune*, Sancho Panza in *Don Quixote*, Charino in *Love Makes a Man*, Caius in *The Merry Wives of Windsor*, Hackum in *The Squire of Alsatia*, a Carrier in *1 Henry IV*, Bobadil in *Every Man in His Humour*, Quack in *The Country Wife*, Alphonso in *The Pilgrim*, the original Lockit in *The Beggar's Opera*, Old Hob in *Flora*, Gripe in *The Confederacy*, Poundage in *The Provok'd Husband*, a Cyclops in *Perseus and Andromeda*, Driver in *Oroonoko*, Glumdalca in *The Tragedy of Tragedies*, Cacafogo in *Rule a Wife and Have a Wife*, Peregrine in *Volpone*, Jobson in *The Devil to Pay*, Bajazet in *Tamerlane* (at Bartholomew Fair, though apparently not a droll), and Ajax in *Achilles*. On 16 October 1734 he acted Poundage in *The Provok'd Husband* at his last stage appearance. For a leading player he had a remarkably small repertoire.

Throughout the years John Hall was often active at Richmond and the late summer fairs: in 1722 he appeared at a Southwark Fair booth probably operated by Walker and staffed with performers from Drury Lane; from 1723 to 1726 he skipped the fairs; in 1727 he shared the management of a Bartholomew Fair booth with Miller and Milward; he and Miller ran a booth there in 1728; he joined with Oates to operate a booth in 1729; he did not work the fairs in 1730, though on 16 July that year he and some of his fellow actors from Lincoln's Inn Fields performed at Richmond; in 1731 Hall co-managed booths at both fairs with Hippisley and Fielding after again acting in July at Richmond; he appeared at Richmond in August 1732 but was not at the fairs; in 1733 he joined Griffin, Cibber, and Bullock in a Bartholomew Fair venture; and in the summer of 1734 he worked at Richmond and then joined with Ryan, Laguerre, and Chapman to run booths at both fairs. In his *Londina Illustrata* in 1819 Robert Wilkinson said that Hall at some point "had a dancing school, and, consequently, balls in the [Lincoln's Inn Fields] Theatre: his second wife kept the *Bell and Dragon* tavern and ordinary, opposite, frequented by actors, young lawyers, city youths, &c." W. R. Chetwood identified the keeper of the Bell and Dragon as Hall's second wife's daughter, Grace Moffet.

Hall received regular benefits, both at his home theatre in the spring and at the fairs. In some cases a record of the receipts has survived. On 12 May 1721, for instance, the income at Lincoln's Inn Fields came to £68 4s. 6d., probably before house charges. The highest receipts came in 1728: almost £167; the lowest was in 1723: £30 13s. Hall's first benefit at Covent Garden Theatre in 1733 brought in over £138. His last benefit, shared with Neale, was held on 2 May 1734. Hall's daily salary, as of the 1724–25 season, was 6s. 8d.

John Hall died of consumption on 29 October 1734, less than two weeks after his last stage appearance, at his lodgings in Drury Lane. The following June administration of the estate of a John Hall, probably the actor, was granted to his principal creditor, William Grainger. Hall was described as late of the parish of St Martin-in-the-Fields (which encompassed Drury Lane) and a widower. Sarah Taylor was named as Hall's natural and lawful sister and next of kin.

Hall was called "Fat" Hall, according to a newspaper advertisement for his Bartholomew Fair booth on 18 August 1727. The prompter Chetwood described Jack Hall as "something too corpulent, and [he had] a thickness of Speech that might be mimic'd with Ease."

The name John Hall appears frequently in the parish registers of St Margaret, Westminster, and St Paul, Covent Garden, during the last 30 years of the seventeenth century, but the name was too common to permit conjectures about the actor Hall and his relatives. In view of the reference in the letters of administration of 1735 to a sister of John Hall named Sarah Taylor, however, perhaps the following entry in the registers of St Paul, Covent Garden, concerns our subject: Sarah, daughter of John Hall, from St Giles in the Fields, was buried at St Paul, Covent Garden, on 15 October 1732. The implication in the entry is that Hall was at the time a widower, an implication which matches the reference in the letters of administration. The registers also contain citations in 1733, 1735, 1740, and 1751 to a John Hall who was clearly not the actor,

so we cannot be certain about the 1732 reference.

Hogarth's engraving, "Rich's Glory, or His Triumphal Entry Into Covent Garden" (December 1732, celebrating the opening of the new theatre), pictured John Rich and a procession of his actors in costume. Hall was shown as Kite in *The Recruiting Officer*, though the details of his features are too small to be helpful. A poem accompanied the print, naming the players:

> Then Hall, who tells the bubbled Country men
> That Carolus is Latin for Queen Anne.
> Did ever mortal know so clean a bite!
> Who else, like him can copy Serjeant Kite?

Hall also appeared in Hogarth's several paintings of the Newgate scene in *The Beggar's Opera*. He was shown standing to stage right of Macheath and upstage of the kneeling Lucy. Information on the different versions of the scene, and engravings of it, may be found in the entry for Lavinia Fenton.

Hall, John [*fl.* 1784?–1804?], *carpenter.*

John Hall (for so he was named in the 12 October 1787 issue of the *World*) served the Covent Garden Theatre as a carpenter from perhaps as early as 22 May 1784, when a Hall was listed in a benefit bill, to as late as 1803–4, when a Hall was named in the theatre accounts. But there was also a Mr Hall who worked as a boxkeeper during those same years and another who was a doorkeeper. All three seem to have been paid 12s. weekly. John Hall the carpenter was usually named in benefit bills each spring, along with numerous other house servants, though he appears not to have been cited in 1785 and 1793 (nor was Hall the boxkeeper).

Hall, Thomas [*fl.* 1760], *house servant.*

The Covent Garden Theatre accounts contain an entry dated 28 June 1760 which reads: "By Thos. Thorne & Thos. Hall for a Weeks work in ye womens Wardrobe to 14th instant 1. 13. 0." We know Thomas Thorne (d. 1764) was one of the theatre's carpenters, so we assume Hall was also an employee. The season ended on 28 May, after which the theatre was dark for the summer; Hall and Thorne apparently made some repairs or renovations to the wardrobe during June.

Hall, Thomas [*fl.* *1779–1795*], exhibitor.

Thomas Hall exhibited a collection of stuffed birds and beasts in City Road, Islington, between 1779 and 1782. According to Davis and Waters in *Tickets and Passes of Great Britain and Ireland*, Thomas Hall "was a proprietor of a Travelling Exhibition. The show consisted of Human Monstrosities, Animals, Curiosities, etc. These he exhibited at the fairs in the vicinity of London. He carried on the business of Taxidermist and Curiosity Dealer at No 10, City Road. The tokens served the purpose of small change, and advertised his business." One of the tokens showed Mrs Newsham, the "white negress," on one side and gave Hall's address and the date, 1795, on

the other. Sir Jeffrey Dunstan, the deformed Mayor of Garratt, was also exhibited by Hall, and another token advertised "THE KANGUROO THE ARMADILLO THE RHINOCEROS."

An unknown engraver pictured Hall seated at a table with his hand on a volume of Buffon's *Natural History*.

In the Harvard Theatre Collection is an anonymous engraving of Thomas Hall, seated at a table on which are several stuffed specimens.

Hall, William [*fl.* *1677–1678*], performer?

A warrant in the Lord Chamberlain's accounts dated 7 February 1678 names William Hall as a member of the King's Company at the Drury Lane Theatre. He may have been one of the performers. *The London Stage* lists Hall in the company roster for the 1677–78 season.

Hall, William *d. 1700, violinist, viola da gamba player.*

William Hall was a musician in the Chapel Royal as early as 4 November 1671. On 15 February 1675 he was one of the violinists added to the regular band of 24 at the performance of the court masque *Calisto*. Later that year, from 7 July to 11 September, Hall attended the King at Windsor. He was granted new positions at court on 22 July 1680, a post in the violins replacing John Young and a post as viola da gamba player, with wages of £40 annually plus livery. He accompanied the King to Windsor again in the spring of 1682, for which service he was paid £14 0s. 7 1/2d. When James II came to the throne in 1685 Hall's appointment was renewed, and he went with James to Windsor in the summer of 1686 at 3s. daily, to Windsor and Hampton Court in 1687 for the same fee, and to Windsor in 1688 for 6s. daily. Under the new monarch Hall was earning an annual salary of £50.

When William III became King, Hall's salary dropped to £30, but he was appointed to the King's private music and went with William to Newmarket in the summer of 1689, attended the Queen during William's absence in Holland in January 1691, and by 1697 was back up to an annual income of £40. On 8 March 1699, according to the *Flying Post*, "A Consort of all new Vocal and Instru-

Harvard Theatre Collection

THOMAS HALL

artist unknown

mental Music" was held for the benefit of William Hall, "who formerly had the Consort of Musick at his House in Norfolk-street." The benefit was held, according to *The London Stage*, at York Buildings. The records do not reveal how long Hall had been holding concerts in his own house. He still retained his post at court, however, until his death.

William Hall died in the spring of 1700. He was buried at Richmond, Surrey, on 1 May. The registers there said, "Mr Wm Hall of St Gilses in the fields [buried] over against ye pastry coocks shopp." On 3 June Mr Abrahall replaced William Hall in the King's Musick. A benefit concert for Hall's widow was held at York Buildings on 3 March 1701, and a benefit for his daughters (number and ages not specified) was held there on 2 April 1707. Hall's tombstone at Richmond called him a "superior violinist." He wrote a few airs and harpsichord pieces.

Hallaburton, Mr. *See* HALLIBURTON, MR.

Hallam. *See also* HALLUM.

Hallam, Mr [*fl. 1798–1799*], *actor.*

A Mr Hallam played a Servant in *Douglas* at a benefit performance he shared with Twaits, Ives, Brown, and Mrs Brooks at Wheatley's Riding School in Greenwich on 8 June 1798. Hallam and his companions were evidently country players. Their playbill informed "the Ladies and Gentlemen of Greenwich" that, "being compelled to answer their Engagements in another Town, they jointly solicit their Patronage on this occasion. . . ." Nearly a year later, on 17 May 1799, Hallam and some of the same group of actors rotated back to Wheatley's Riding School, Hallam to play Sir Charles Marlow in *She Stoops to Conquer* and Thomas in *The Agreeable Surprise*. The Hallam concerned in those performances has no known connection with the well-known English and American family of players of that name.

Hallam, Adam *d. 1768, actor, dancer, machinist, pyrotechnist?, booth proprietor?, manager?*

Adam Hallam was born sometime in the second decade of the eighteenth century to the actor Thomas Hallam and his wife. His broth-

ers George, William, and Lewis and his sister Ann (successively Mrs Sacheverel Hale and Mrs John Barrington) were all on the stage. A fourth brother, Thomas, joined the navy and eventually became an admiral. (The baptismal register of St Catherine, Dublin, shows an "Addam Hallum, son of George and Mary" to have been christened on 16 March 1707. We believe that he was not the subject of this entry. He may have been the Adam Hallam said in an eighteenth-century manuscript in the Burney papers to have died in 1738. The George who was that person's father may have been the father also of the elder Thomas. Or they may not have been closely related; the Hallams were numerous and used a few names over and over.)

Adam acted as a juvenile in Dublin from 1723–24 through 1726–27. His only known parts during those seasons were the Boy in *Wife and No Wife* and Howd'ye in *The Northern Lass*. He was evidently in the care of his mother. His father seems to have departed for London in the summer of 1724. Adam was in London as a comic dancer at Drury Lane in 1727–28, 1728–29, and 1729–30, identified variously as "A. Hallam," "Young Hallam," and "Hallam Jr" to distinguish him from his father Thomas, who often appeared on the same bills. For two years Adam's only identifiable named part was Pierrot's Servant in *Harlequin Happy*. Toward the end of 1729–30 he was given two more named parts, Jerry in *The Clown's Stratagem* and Nicodemus in *The Stage Coach Opera*.

In 1730–31 Hallam added the minor roles of Blandford in *Oroonoko*, Cant in *Phebe*, Guyomar in *The Indian Emperor*, Malcolm in *Macbeth*, and a Noble Venetian in *Cephalus and Procris*. But from the beginning of the season of 1731–32 when he helped open Drury Lane's season, playing Laertes in *Hamlet*, he moved steadily into important supporting parts and leads both in comedy and in tragedy, but specializing in youthful leads in comedies of manners and sentimental comedies. In 1731–32, in addition to Laertes, he added to his repertoire the following: both Juba and Marcus in *Cato*, Edgeworth in *Bartholomew Fair*, Leolyn in *Athelwold*, Vernon in *1 Henry IV*, Alonzo in *Rule a Wife and Have a Wife*, Moody in *The Lover's Opera*, Careless in *The Double Gallant*, and (probably) Colonel Courtly in *The Modern Husband*. In 1732–33 he added Pedro in *The*

Spanish Fryar, Lovemore in *The Amorous Widow*, Moneses in *Tamerlane*, Razor in *The Provok'd Wife*, Young Bellair in *The Man of Mode*, Harcourt in *The Country Wife*, both Loveless and Sir John Friendly in *The Relapse*, Carlos in *Love Makes a Man*, Castalio in *The Orphan*, Cassio in *Othello*, Young Loveless in *The Scornful Lady*, Charles in *The Busy Body*, Bellmour in *Jane Shore*, Edgar in *King Lear*, the title role in *Theodosius*, and Lovemore in *The Amorous Widow*.

He was the subject of a critique in *The Auditor* of 6 February 1733 in which his interpretations of Laertes and of Charles in *The Fop's Fortune* were praised.

At the beginning of the 1733–34 season Adam Hallam followed Theophilus Cibber's seceders to the Haymarket, but they had all returned to Drury Lane by early March. He expanded his repertoire during that season, adding Lancaster in *2 Henry IV*, Vainlove in *The Old Bachelor*, Mirabel in *The Way of the World*, Francisco in *Wit Without Money*, Mosca in *Volpone*, Dauphine in *The Silent Woman*, Davison in *The Albion Queens*, Campley in *The Funeral*, Myrtle in *The Conscious Lovers*, and Iago in *Othello*.

In the 1734–35 season Adam joined the company at Covent Garden, leaving his father Thomas behind at Drury Lane. Adam played Laertes on the opening night, 18 September 1734. At Covent Garden he was sometimes at first called "A. Hallam" in the bills, but usually (and finally only) "Hallam," as no other members of his family were then at that theatre. His father was killed in the famous Drury Lane Green Room embroglio with Macklin on 10 May 1735. From 1734–35 to 1736–37, while sustaining many of his former roles, Adam added the following: the title role in *The Mock Doctor*, Felix in *A Woman Keeps a Secret*, Axalla in *Tamerlane*, Mrs Hackum in *The Squire of Alsatia*, Reynard in *Tunbridge Walks*, Horner in *The Country Wife*, Robert in *The Mock Doctor*, the Copper Captain in *Rule a Wife and Have a Wife*, the Irishman in *The Lottery*, Richmond in *Richard III*, Rashly in *The Fond Husband*, Dumont in *Jane Shore*, Hubert in *The Royal Merchant*, Archer in *The Beaux' Stratagem*, Sir Harry Wildair in *The Constant Couple*, Prince Hal in *1 Henry IV*, Gaylife in *The Double Deceit*, Pyrrhus in *Abra Mule*, Frederick in *The Fatal Marriage*, Hephestion in *The Rival*

Queens, Haemon in *Oedipus*, Octavius in *Julius Caesar*, Freeman in *The Plain Dealer*, Alexas in *All for Love*, Altamont in *The Fair Penitent*, Young Mirable in *The Inconstant*, Stanmore in *Oroonoko*, Page in *The Merry Wives of Windsor*, Sir George in *The Busy Body*, Brazen in *The Recruiting Officer*, Bumpkin in *The Funeral*, Freeman in *A Woman's Revenge*, and Arviragus in *Cymbeline*.

In June 1737 Adam was in the Smock Alley company in Dublin. William S. Clark in *The Irish Stage in the County Towns* quotes the *Dublin News-Letter* of 25 June to the effect that the Smock Alley manager, Lewis Duval, was shortly to lead his troupe to Waterford. They were to open there with *The Committee*. Among the London regulars in the Smock Alley company were Adam Hallam, Dennis Delane, and Roger Bridgwater. The extent of the tour is not known, but while at Smock Alley Adam played Townley in *The Provok'd Husband* on 20 June, Iago to Delane's Othello on 23 June, a "principal Part" in *The Orphan* on 24 June, Antony in *Julius Ceasar* on 27 June, on 30 June, and (probably) 12 July, Mosca in *Volpone* and Lorenzo in *The Spanish Fryar* on 14 July.

In September 1737 Hallam returned to Covent Garden and remained all season, adding to his repertoire the following: the Dauphin in *King John*, Garcia in *The Mourning Bride*, Antonio in *The Rover*, Loveday in *The London Cuckolds*, Claudio in *Much Ado about Nothing*, Rovewell in *The Fair Quaker of Deal*, Aumerle in *Richard II*, Cunningham in *The Amorous Widow*, John in *The Chances*, the Mad Scholar in *The Pilgrim*, the title part in *The Gamester*, Fainwell in *A Bold Stroke for a Wife*, and Lysimachus in *Marina*.

Adam Hallam remained at Covent Garden for three more seasons, 1738–39 through 1740–41, and then returned to Drury Lane for two more. During those years he was busy in a selected round of his accumulated roles, and he added: Charmante in *The Emperor of the Moon*, Captain Clerimont in *The Tender Husband*, Emanuel in *The Island Princess*, Grizzle in *The Tragedy of Tragedies*, Elder Wou'dbe in *The Twin Rivals*, Cornwall in *King Lear*, and Careless in *The Double Gallant*. After 11 April 1743, when he played Sharper in *The Old Bachelor*, he does not seem to have acted in a London theatre.

Thomas Davies in his *Dramatic Miscellanies*

(1784) seems unfairly abrupt in his treatment of Hallam:

. . . Mr. Adam Hallam, who, by an imitation of the action of Wilks, especially in a certain peculiar custom of pulling down his ruffles and rolling his stockings, joined to a good degree of diligence, so far gained upon Rich's want of discernment, that he hired him for seven years at a very large Salary. When the term of his engagement was expired, his employer dismissed him, and for the greatest part of his remaining life he was an itinerant actor.

Davies was, very likely, relying on the testimony of the anonymous author of *A Letter to a Certain Patentee* (1747), who had written:

I need go no further back than the Misfortune that befel Mr. [Lacy] R[ya]n, when he was shot in the Mouth: He being, by this Accident, incapable of Playing; the all-wise Manager, Mr. R[ic]h, was so generous, as to engage in his stead, that pretty-friggling Thing Mr. H–ll–m, at six Guineas per Week, who having full as good an Opinion of himself, as Mr. R—h could possibly have, would not condescend to be a stop-gap for this uncertain Interval, and add to the Lustre of that Stage by his Presence, except the Glory of it should be continued for six or seven Years, which was granted.

That was undependable testimony, though. Leaving aside the prejudicial attitude shown toward Rich and Hallam and also the inherent unlikelihood that Rich would have signed so young an actor to a contract of "six or seven Years," the author is plainly wrong on other counts: Adam had played at Covent Garden from the opening night of 1734–35. But the attack on Lacy Ryan did not occur until 16 March 1735, so Hallam was not "engaged in his stead."

But if Davies was correct about the "very large salary," it was a considerable advance over what Hallam had been getting at Drury Lane, for on 4 June 1733 the patentees of that theatre had printed a list of salaries in which had appeared the item: "Hallam, for himself and his father, the latter of little or no service, £3 [per week]."

As to any provincial career of Adam Hallam subsequent to the season of 1742–43, nothing certain can be established on the basis of present evidence. The Hallam family had strolled in both the English and the Irish provinces probably on many occasions, and Sybil Rosenfeld, citing the *Kentish Post* of 13–16 June

1733, located most of the family, including Adam, in Canterbury at the Watling Street Theatre that month. There are scattered references to the Hallams at Bath and Bristol from the later 1740s. One Hallam, possibly Adam, was on the Kentish circuit in the summer of 1741. He is recorded as having played Mark Antony in *All for Love*, one of Adam's parts. On 22 October 1750 a Hallam "of London" spoke a prologue to the Mayor and Corporation at the opening of Simpson's new theatre in Bath. He was a regular member of the company, apparently, and the company played that season at Bristol as well. The only character named for that Hallam was Mark Antony.

Kathleen Barker has cited to us newspaper notices concerning performances at the Jacob's Wells Theatre, Bristol, in 1746 involving Hallams. We believe the following may have concerned Adam: Montano in *Othello* on 19 July, Trim in *The Funeral* (with Mrs Hallam as Lady Brumpton) on 2 August, Beau Mordecai in *The Harlot's Progress* (with Mrs Hallam as a Lady of Pleasure) on 20 August and the Chaplain in *The Double Dealer* (with Mrs Hallam as Lady Pliant) on 30 August. What had been the Hallams' sustenance during the winter months? Perhaps the answer may be found in the advertisement for "Mr and Mrs Hallam's" benefit at Jacob's Wells on 28 August 1747:

After the Performance, the Audience will be Entertained with an *exact Model* of a *Grand Machine* of FIRE-WORKS, That was play'd off at *Vienna*, in Honour of the present Emperor on his Election, and what was shewn in *London* all last Season, to crouded Audiences, with universal Applause. Being two large Fountain Vases, and one Grand Obelisk, that was thirty Feet in height, having four different Revolutions and Changes. Containing, ten Fountains, thirty Pumps, one hundred and forty White Fires, and twelve Moving Fires; with the Form of the Sun in three different colour'd Fires, the Moon, Stars, Crown and Cypher, Prince of *Wales*'s Arms and Motto, Scroll Work, &c. in hollow Fires.

The Whole composed by Mr. HALLAM, (*And done in Miniature, after the Manner of the* Chinese) being the first Work of the Kind that ever was compleated by a *European*; it may be set on a Table, and fired in a Dining Room without Trouble or Nuisance.

N.B. The Whole Machine, as Obelisk, Vases, with their Wheels, Moulds, Rollers, Rammers, &c. and a Parcel of Composition, are to be disposed off [*sic*] (after the Night) for three Guineas, with proper Instructions how to make the Fire and charge it; any Person that have [*sic*] a Mind to purchase, may see it as it stands, now ready charged, at Mr. HALLAM's Lodgings.

The likelihood that the players we have been following in Bristol are Adam Hallam and his wife is increased by Davies's recollection that Adam was an ingenious man with his hands who had "invented the armour and other decorations, preparatory to the single combat between the Dukes of Hereford and Norfolk," in Rich's revival of the original *Richard II* on 6 February 1738, in which Adam played Aumerle. (But the conjecture, like so many tempting ones concerning the Hallams, is blunted by the fact that Lewis Hallam also apparently once exhibited fireworks.)

The Mrs Hallam who acted at Jacob's Wells, if she was Adam's wife, was his first, Elizabeth Carter. They had married in the Chapel Royal, Whitehall, on 22 May 1738. She lived with Adam in London "next door to the Chapel in Great Queen Street." But there is no record of her having performed in London. She died on 9 June 1740, the day following the funeral at Mitcham, Surrey, of her sister-in-law Anne, William Hallam's wife, and was herself buried at Mitcham on 15 June 1740, all according to the *London Daily Post* of 16 June 1740. The administration of her property was granted Adam on 21 April 1741 (in that document she is called "Bethia"). Adam married Isabella Agar, spinster, 25 years old, of the parish of St Stephen, Canterbury, at St Martin, Outwich, on 2 November 1743.

Despite Adam Hallam's obvious importance, we know little about his life aside from the theatre, and even some theatrical episodes are blurred because of confusions with other members of his family. In August of 1731 at the Miller-Mills-Oates booth at Bartholomew Fair, he played Colonel Westford in a droll called *The Banish'd General*. In the late summer of 1732 he was at Hippisley's Booth at the George Inn in West Smithfield during the time of Bartholomew Fair. At the same fair and season in 1733 he was one of a considerable company at the Cibber-Griffin-Bullock-Hallam booth in Hosier Lane. But so was "W. Hallam," his brother William, so it is not possible surely to know which was in management at the booth, though likely it was Wil-

liam. Hallams are ubiquitous at the fair booths for some years, but which ones are concerned either in management or acting is often impossible to tell. Certainly it was Adam who was operating a booth at Bartholomew Fair "Over-against the Hospital Gate," on 22 August 1741, where was presented both *The True and Ancient History of Fair Rosamond, Representing Her Amours with King Henry, and her Being Poisoned by Queen Eleanor in Woodstock Bower* and *The Modern Pimp; or, The Doctor Deceiv'd*. For the proprietor of the booth was identified as "Hallam from the Theatre-Royal in Covent-Garden." (Both drolls had been played by the Hallams at Bartholomew Fair in 1736.)

Adam Hallam was, very likely, the Hallam who appears in scattered Covent Garden notices from the spring of 1764 into the fall of 1768: on 10 February 1764, Charino in *Love Makes a Man*; on 15 May 1764 (his benefit, shared with Davis and Perry), King Henry in *Richard III*; on 10 May 1765 (his benefit, with Mrs Dyer and Davis), Don Charino again; on 31 January 1766, (Popilius) Lena in *Julius Caesar*; on 5 May 1766 (his benefit, with Holtom and Buck), when he evidently did not play; on 22 September 1766, when he doubled as Nym and the English Herald in *Henry V*; on 26 November 1766, when he was Charino again; on 10 March 1768, when he played Oldcastle in *The Intriguing Chambermaid*; and on nine occasions between 20 February 1768 and 1 May 1769, when he played the Old Man in *King Lear*.

After that, the Hallam in question disappeared from theatrical records. In 1767–68 he was earning only £1 per week, according to Arthur Murphy's list of Covent Garden salaries.

We know that Adam Hallam belonged to the Ancient and Honourable Society of Free and Accepted Masons, as did others of the family. When *Jane Shore* was given at Hampstead, "By Desire of several of the Brethren," on 20 August 1734, it was for the benefit of one Hallam, otherwise unidentified. But on 11 April 1741, at Covent Garden, *The Old Bachelor* was performed "With the Songs in Masonry as usual," "For the Entertainment of the Grand Master and the rest of the Brethren. . . ." The play went on "With a proper Prologue by Brother Hallam," and Adam Hallam was the only member of his family then at Covent Garden Theatre.

As far as his appearance and acting ability are concerned, we have to lean on the weak reed of that anonymous writer of *A Letter to a Certain Patentee*. That critic was willing to concede that "Mr H–ll–m [is] a very pretty-fac'd young Man, only, indeed, his Eyes [are] a little too full. But then . . . they [are] a fine Gray, and very fashionable. . . ." However, the "stare and goggle of [his] Eyes, and the Sound of his Voice, in every Character, and in every Sentence, was the exact Resemblance of those of a strangling cat. . . ."

Reed's biographical notation in his "Notitia Dramatica" in the British Library is nearly as unsatisfactory: "Uncle to M^{rs}. Mattocks he died at Kentish Town June ^{2d}3 [*sic*]—1768."

Hallam, Ann. *See* BARRINGTON, JOHN.

Hallam, George ₍*fl.* 1745–1747₎, actor, manager.

George Hallam was probably the eldest child of the actor Thomas Hallam and his wife. George's siblings were William, Lewis, Adam, and Ann (successively Mrs Sacheverel Hale and Mrs John Barrington), all of whom were performers, and Thomas, a naval officer.

Because of crisscrossing careers and the paucity of first names in the playbills, and because some of George's roles were similar to those of his brothers the incidents of his career are sometimes uncertain.

The London Stage lists a G. Hallam in the combined roster of irregular companies playing at the Haymarket in 1732–33. But there are no initials in the bills for the only two performances in which Hallams figure that season, 20 and 26 March 1733. In fact, there seems to be no evidence to place George Hallam on the London boards until 1745–46, though he may have strolled with his family in the provinces before that date. There is complicated but persuasive evidence that George was the oldest of the brothers. While George, William, and Lewis were acting at the New Wells, Goodman's Fields, George was often designated "Hallam Sr," following his first recorded appearance there as Bardolph in *1 Henry IV* on 2 December 1745 (e.g., 9 January 1747 the *General Advertiser* supplied "Hal-

lam Sr" for Bardolph in *The Merry Wives of Windsor*, while the *General Advertiser* gave the part to "G. Hallam." On 3 February 1747 "Hallam Sen" and "W. Hallam" were Recruits in *The Recruiting Officer*.)

George's other known parts, all of them at Goodman's Fields in 1746–47, were: Sycorax in *The Tempest*, Poundage in *The Provok'd Husband*, Comick in *The Twin Rivals*, a Committeeman in *The Committee*, Satin in *The Miser*, Micher in *The Stage Coach*, both Jack and Jemmy Twicher in *The Beggar's Opera*, Tyrrel in *Richard III*, Mirvan in *Tamerlane*, a Recruit in *The Recruiting Officer*, Sir Thomas in *Flora*, an Old Man in *King Lear*, Polonius in *Hamlet*, one of the Boors in *The Royal Merchant*, and Northumberland in *1 Henry IV*.

After the 1746–47 season George's name dropped out of the record. What part, if any, he had in his brothers' endeavors at various fair booths is not known. Evidently he did not accompany his brother Lewis on the American adventure. A George Hallam whom Isabella Hallam Mattocks called her "cousin" in a letter to J. Hill on 19 June 1800 was perhaps his son. Mrs Mattocks declared that the younger George was a colonel in the British Army. He was very likely the George Hallam, "some years before second Lieutenant-Colonel of the 17th regiment of infantry," who in 1831 published *A Narrative Voyage from Montego Bay in the Island of Jamaica*.

Hallam, Isabella. *See* MATTOCKS, MRS GEORGE.

Hallam, Lewis 1714?–1756?, actor, manager, pyrotechnist?

Lewis Hallam was a son of the actor Thomas Hallam and his wife. He seems to have been born about 1714. His brothers Adam, George, and William and his sister Ann (successively Mrs Sacheverel Hale and Mrs John Barrington) were all performers. Another brother, Thomas, joined the navy and in time became an admiral.

Lewis may be that second Hallam who was on the Haymarket bills along with his brother William in the spring of 1730. Perhaps it was he who played Macmorris in *The Half Pay Officers* on 12 March 1730, Heartfree in *Love and Revenge* on 20 March, and First Physician in *Tom Thumb* on 24 April. He seems to have been in the same eccentric line of characters as William, thus no clear distinction can be drawn between William and the other Hallam at the Haymarket except in the case of the cast of *The Author's Farce* on 30 March 1730. The 1730 edition of that piece listed "Hallam" in the role of Murdertext and gave the role of the Poet to "W. Hallam." Those parts cannot be doubled. If Lewis was indeed born in or about 1714 he was very young for at least two or three of the parts listed above. Yet none of the other male Hallams seem to fit.

The *Kentish Post* of 13–16 June 1733 reported that the Hallam family, including a "Young Hallam" who was almost certainly Lewis, was then pausing in Canterbury in what was apparently an acting tour of Kent. And it seems likely that Lewis, like Adam, William, and George, was garnering experience in the provinces and the minor theatres and fair booths of London before the first time any London theatregoer saw "L. Hallam" on a playbill. That occasion, so far as the surviving records show, was on 31 January 1745, when he came to his brother William's theatre, Goodman's Fields, to play Gomez in *The Spanish Fryar*. The bill carried the notation: "being the first time of his performing on that Stage." He repeated the role several times that season and added also to his slender repertoire Marplot in *The Busy Body* (on 9 February 1745, a night when his wife was advertised as Miranda, "being the first time of her performing on that Stage"), "Trincalo" in *The Tempest*, the title role in *The Miser*, Sir Amorous in *A Woman Is a Riddle*, and very likely some parts in other plays among many whose casts were not given that season. He was generously given a benefit night on 1 April, but the receipts are not known.

The 1745–46 season was troubled both by the nervousness engendered by the Jacobite rebellion and by complaints to the Lord Chamberlain about the Hallams' illegal operation. The theatre's management decided to evade the Act of 1737 by advertising "A Concert of Vocal and Instrumental Music," between the halves of which a play would be offered "gratis," and to soothe the government by causing "The Concert to conclude with the Chorus of Long Live the King."

Lewis added to his list of roles the Cardinal in *The Massacre at Paris*, Moody in *The Provok'd Husband*, Teague in *The Twin Rivals*, Lopez in *The Busy Body*, Setter in *The Old Bachelor*, Gardener in *The Drummer*, Daniel in *Oroonoko*, Roderigo in *Othello*, Francis in *1 Henry IV*, an Old Woman in *Rule a Wife and Have a Wife*, Lovegold in *The Miser*, Orator in *The Royal Merchant*, Trappanti in *She Wou'd and She Wou'd Not*, Mizzen *The Fair Quaker of Deal*, Maiden in *Tunbridge Walks*, Amorous in *A Woman Is a Riddle*, Trim in *The Funeral*, Schemewell in *Captain O'Blunder*, Jeremy in *Love for Love*, and Teague in *The Committee*. He noted on his benefit bill, 17 March 1746, that he, "having had the misfortune of dislocating his ancle in a terrible manner," was "render'd incapable of going abroad" to solicit attendance.

In 1746–47 at Goodman's Fields Lewis Hallam added the following parts: Dervise in *Tamerlane*, Sackbut in *A Bold Stroke for a Wife*, Crispin in *The Anatomist*, Macahone in *The Stage Coach*, Sancho in *Love Makes a Man*, Benedict in *The School Boy*, a Gravedigger in *Hamlet*, Razor in *The Provok'd Wife*, Lory in *The Relapse*, the Chaplain in *The Orphan*, Stanley in *Richard III*, Cimberton in *The Conscious Lovers*, Hob in *Flora*, Ben in *The Beggar's Opera*, Francis in *1 Henry IV*, Hecate in *Macbeth*, Evans in *The Merry Wives of Windsor*, Decius in *Cato*, Antonio in *Venice Preserv'd*, Clincher in *The Constant Couple*, the Miller in *The King and the Miller of Mansfield*, the Usher in *King Lear*, and Gibby in *The Wonder*. On 22 April 1747 at the Haymarket Theatre he and Mrs Hallam played unspecified parts in *The Diversions of a Morning; or, A Dish of Chocolate*, and she acted as well in the farce *The Credulous Husband*.

Lewis Hallam and his wife acted once in 1748, on 4 April, at the New Wells (Clerkenwell, according to *The London Stage* but perhaps Lemon Street), he as Kite and she as Sylvia in *The Recruiting Officer*, and he was Hob on 27 February 1749 at the Wells, for his benefit. (The fact that he received a benefit even though he seldom performed argues his concernment in the management.) Lewis was not noticed in a bill again until 26 July 1750 when a casual performance was disguised under the "concert" formula at the Haymarket and he played Slur in *The Wife's Relief; or, The Husband's Cure*, "not acted these Fourteen Years."

On 6 August 1751 Hallam again played

Hob, this time at the slowly expiring New Wells. On 5 September when his wife played Desdemona to Goodfellow's Othello, Lewis was Roderigo. Mrs Hallam took her benefit that night. Those were the last recorded performances of Lewis Hallam and his wife in England.

The Hallams' worsening fortunes goaded them to an expedient which was original and, for those times, daring to the point of recklessness. According to a shaky tradition, the comedian John Moody, who had gone out to Jamaica in 1745 and had succeeded in building up a repertory company there by recruiting actors in England, had excited the Hallams' interest in a theatrical expedition to the New World. There is another tradition, that the actor Robert Upton was given a sum of money and sent to America as an advance agent, to arrange places of performance and permissions to perform, but that once there he forgot his mission and joined the Murray-Kean company.

Whatever the truth of those traditions, the Hallams had by the summer of 1752 organized their expedition. William Dunlap, the early historian of the American Theatre, gave an account of that organization from "memoranda taken from the dictation of Lewis Hallam the second":

The emigrants were . . . assembled at the house of William Hallam; a list of *stock plays* produced by him, with attendant farces, and the *cast* of the whole agreed upon in full assembly of the body politic: which appears to have been a well-organized republic, every member of which had his part assigned to him, both private and public, behind and before the curtain. Lewis Hallam was appointed manager, chief magistrate, or King, and William, who stayed at home, was to be "Viceroy over him," according to Trinculo's division of offices. The brothers were to divide profits equally after deducting the expenses and *shares*. Thus William was entitled to half of such profits as projector and proprietor, and Lewis to the other half as manager and conductor.

The uses Dunlap made of the words "profits" and "shares" seem contradictory, and explanations he undertook later in his narrative were even more confusing. However the scheme worked, whether it provided for proprietorship and salaries, or for outright "sharing," or for something in between, there seems to have been little profit for William. (Dunlap wrote

that William Hallam visited his relatives in America briefly in June 1754. Dunlap thought that during the visit a transfer of "all the property, interest, and good-will" from William to Lewis took place.)

According to Dunlap's account, deriving from the younger Lewis Hallam, Lewis and his wife brought with them a company consisting of Mr and Mrs William Rigby, Mr and Mrs Thomas Clarkson, Mary Palmer, Charles Bell, John Singleton, a Mr Herbert, a Mr Winnell (or Wynel), William Adcock and Mr and Mrs Patrick Malone. They also brought with them 20 plays: *The Merchant of Venice*, *The Fair Penitent*, *The Beaux' Stratagem*, *Jane Shore*, *The Recruiting Officer*, *Richard III*, *The Careless Husband*, *The Constant Couple*, *Hamlet*, *Othello*, *Theodosius*, *The Provok'd Husband*, *Tamerlane*, *The Inconstant*, *A Woman Is a Riddle*, *The Suspicious Husband*, *The Conscious Lovers*, *George Barnwell*, *The Committee*, and *The Twin Rivals*. Dunlap said that "The farces cast and studied for the common stock" were *Lethe*, *The Lying Valet*, *Miss in Her Teens*, *The Mock Doctor*, *The Devil to Pay*, *Hob in the Well*, *Damon and Phillida*, and *The Anatomist*. "Of the pantomimes, the company had but one for many years, which was called Harlequin Collector, or the Miller Deceived."

The Lewis Hallams bid good-bye to their four-year-old daughter, Isabella, who remained behind with her aunt. They collected their sons Lewis and Adam and their daughter Helen and embarked with their company and their playbooks in the *Charming Sally*, Captain William Lee commanding, early in May 1752 and, by way of Barbados, "after a voyage of six weeks, a short passage in those days, arrived safely at Yorktown," on 2 June, having rehearsed their offerings on the quarter-deck "whenever the winds and weather permitted." On 12 June an advertisement in the *Virginia Gazette* (reprinted by Hugh Rankin in *The Theater in Colonial America*) proclaimed:

That Mr. Hallam, from the New Theatre in Goodmansfields, is daily expected here with a select Company of Comedians, the Scenes, Cloaths and Decorations are all entirely new, extremely rich, and finished in the highest Taste, the Scenes being painted by the best Hands in London are excell'd by none in Beauty and Elegance, so that the Ladies and Gentlemen may depend on being entertain'd in as polite a Manner as at the Theatres in London, the Company being perfected in all the best Plays, Opera's, Farces, and Pantomimes, that have been exhibited in any of the Theatres for these ten years past.

The advertisement was an act of faith, for Hallam had several days earlier submitted to the colonial Governor Robert Dinwiddie his application for permission to perform plays, and the recent offstage activities of native players under the management of Murray and Kean had excited opposition to the drama among Williamsburg's inhabitants. The Governor's Council had even sent a bill to the House of Burgesses which would have prevented the performance of any theatrical entertainments within two miles of the capital. The bill had been defeated, but the Council now advised the Governor to turn down Hallam's petition, and he did so. But assiduous courtship and argument finally prevailed, and Hallam received his license. He purchased from Alexander Finnie for £150 10s. the old theatre building used by Murray and Kean, refurbished it, and prepared to play.

On 15 September 1752 Lord Lansdowne's version of *The Merchant of Venice*, "the first play performed in America by a regular company of [British] comedians," took the boards at Williamsburg, introduced by a lengthy prologue penned by John Singleton, one of the company, which began:

> To this New World, from fam'd Brittania's shore,
> Through boist'rous seas where foaming billows roar,
> The Muse, who Britons charm'd for many an age,
> Now sends her servants forth to tread your stage;
> Britain's own race, though far removed to show
> Patterns of every virtue they should know.

Mrs Hallam was Portia in the mainpiece; Hallam doubled as Launcelot Gobbo and Tubal; young Lewis made his debut as "servant to Portia" (and "stood motionless and speechless, until bursting into tears he walked off the stage making a most inglorious exit"); Miss (Helen?) Hallam (also appearing on the stage for the first time) was Jessica. In *Lethe*, the afterpiece, Mrs Hallam was the Fine Lady and the elder Lewis doubled again, as the Drunken Man and Tattoo.

The Hallam company played at Williamsburg three nights a week for 11 months, drawing good houses, with receipts up to £300 per performance. In November they played *Othello* before the "Emperor" of the Cherokee Nation and his Empress and entourage, who had come to the capital to renew a treaty of friendship and to be fêted by the Governor. For their diversion Hallam also exhibited fireworks in Palace Street. According to surviving accounts of tradesmen and court records, several of the actors, despite the success of the season, ended it in the shadow of debtors' jail. To keep his company together, Hallam offered for their bail a deed on his theatre.

Hallam and most of his company (Wynel and Herbert had defected to Murray-Kean) departed for New York, where also the offstage behavior of the Murray-Kean company had stirred up the wrath of the guardians of morality. Again, a public appeal was necessary before a license to play was granted. Hallam razed the old Nassau Street Theatre and built a larger one, opening on 17 September 1753 with *The Conscious Lovers* and *Damon and Phillida*. William Charles Hulett, Charles Love and his wife, Miller, and Mrs Becceley, all English actors, joined Hallam there, and young Lewis, Helen, and Adam began to make regular appearances. The season ended with *The Beggar's Opera* on 18 March 1754, and an advertisement suggested that "Lewis Hallam, Comedian, intending for Philadelphia, begs the favour of those that had any demands upon him, to bring in their accounts, and receive their money."

Once again, at Philadelphia and more stridently than ever before, the cries of religious opposition went up. Quakers and Presbyterians united to combat the menace to morality. Hallam finally received his permission from Governor Hamilton after assurances that he would play nothing indecent and under the stipulation that he would donate to charity the receipts of one performance. Hallam remodeled Plumstead's Warehouse as "The New Theatre in Water Street" and embarked on a season which was apparently profitable but punctuated frequently by the attacks of the censorious devout.

On 30 August 1754 Hallam's company arrived in Charleston, South Carolina, and on 7 October opened with *The Fair Penitent*. Bills and other accounts for the company ceased after 27 January 1755, though Julia Curtis in "The Early Charleston Stage: 1703–1798" disagrees with Rankin's opinion that the company departed because of the arrival of the evangelist George Whitefield.

The next stop for Hallam proved to be his last. Arriving in Jamaica sometime after 1 February 1755, he found David Douglass, whose company had been depleted by disease, on the point of sailing for England to recruit. Hallam and Douglass joined forces. Nothing is known of their repertoire. But the notoriously treacherous climate of Jamaica killed Lewis Hallam within a year. The exact date of his death is unknown. About two years later his widow married David Douglass.

Hallam, Mrs Lewis, née Rich?, later Mrs David Douglass   d. 1774, actress.

Mrs Lewis Hallam's maiden name may have been Rich. Her daughter Isabella Hallam Mattocks, in answering a query for biographical information, told the editor J. Hill in 1800 (in a letter now in the Harvard Theatre Collection) that "Mr Rich the late Patentee of Cov: Garden & his family are my relatives." But neither Mrs Hallam's first name nor her patronym is recorded. Nor is it known when she married.

Lewis Hallam had acted for the first time on the stage at Lemon Street, Goodman's Fields, the family enterprise managed by his brother William, on 31 January 1745. His wife followed, playing Miranda in *The Busy Body*, on 9 February. The bills implied ("first time on that stage") that she had acted elsewhere, and indeed she probably had at least assisted in one or more of the summer fair booths which the Hallams habitually operated. She was named in the Goodman's Fields bills five times during the spring of 1745, playing two additional roles, Hippolito in *The Tempest* on 14, 15, 16, and 18 February and Mariana in *The Miser* on 7 March.

Mrs Hallam made a full and useful contribution in ingenues and pathetic young heroines of tragedy during the following two seasons, 1745–46 and 1746–47, at Goodman's Fields. Her parts, in order of playing, were: Antramont in *The Massacre of Paris*, Constance in *The Twin Rivals*, Angelina in *Love Makes a Man*, Mrs Sullen in *The Stratagem*, Araminta in *The Old Bachelor*, Maria in *George Barnwell*, the title role in *Jane Shore*, Estifania in *Rule a Wife and Have a Wife*, the Countess of Rutland

Harvard Theatre Collection

Said to be MRS LEWIS HALLAM (later Mrs David Douglass)

artist unknown

in *The Earl of Essex*, Monimia in *The Orphan*, Lady Townly in *The Provok'd Husband*, the title role in *The Fair Quaker of Deal*, Hillaria in *Tunbridge Walks*, Angelica in *Love for Love*, Harriet in *The Miser*, Leonora in *The Revenge*, Melinda in *The Recruiting Officer*, Lady Percy in *1 Henry IV*, Arpasia in *Tamerlane*, Beatrice in *The Anatomist*, Millwood in *The London Merchant* (*George Barnwell*), Bertha in *The Royal Merchant*, Elvira in *The Spanish Fryar*, Ruth in *The Committee*, Lappet in *The Miser*, Sylvia in *The Recruiting Officer*, Desdemona in *Othello*, Charlotte in *Oroonoko*, Lady Brute in *The Provok'd Wife*, Amanda in *The Relapse*, Lady Anne in *Richard III*, Indiana in *The Conscious Lovers*, Lady Outside in *A Woman Is a Riddle*, Ann Lovely in *A Bold Stroke for a Wife*, Lavinia in *The Fair Penitent*, Mrs Page in *The Merry Wives of Windsor*, Laura in *Tancred and Sigismunda*,

Charlotte in *The Funeral*, Victoria in *The Fatal Marriage*, and Violante in *The Wonder*.

On 4 April 1748 at the New Wells (Clerkenwell, according to *The London Stage*, but perhaps Lemon Street), *"upon a particular occasion"* Lewis Hallam was Kite and his wife Sylvia in *The Recruiting Officer*. Mrs Hallam acted only twice more in England, so far as is known: Ruth in *The Committee* on 27 February 1749 at the New Wells, Lemon Street, and Desdemona at the same theatre on 5 September 1751, for her own benefit.

Early in May 1752 Mrs Lewis Hallam accompanied her husband and his company to America, by way of Barbados, arriving at Yorktown, Virginia, on 2 June. With the Hallams were their two sons, Lewis, about 12, and Adam, somewhat younger, and a young daughter. A second daughter, Isabella, later Mrs George Mattocks, stayed in England. In the letter to J. Hill quoted at the beginning of this entry, Isabella recalled that "worldly embarrassments compelled" her father, "When I was only 4 years old to quit England & try his fortune in America. My Aunt [Ann, Mrs John Barrington,] with true sisterly affection, prevail'd on my mother to leave me under her Protection—."

On 15 September 1752 Mrs Hallam played Portia in *The Jew of Venice*, the Lansdowne alteration of *The Merchant of Venice*, the first play performed in America by a company of British comedians. For the next two years Mrs Hallam and the rest of the company endured the vicissitudes of playing, usually against stiff "moral" opposition, in crude theatres successively in Williamsburg, New York, Philadelphia, and Charleston. In the late winter or early spring of 1755 the company went to Jamaica and there united with the David Douglass company, which had been decimated by the fevers for which Jamaica was then famous. Sometime during 1756, it is believed, Lewis Hallam succumbed to the island's miasmas.

After about two years, certainly before the amalgamated companies returned northward under David Douglass's leadership in 1758, Mrs Hallam became Mrs Douglass. When Douglass opened his new theatre at Crugar's Wharf in New York she again assumed the female leads and to a large extent retained them, often acting opposite the heroes played by her son Lewis, then 18. She was, in fact, a

Harvard Theatre Collection

MRS LEWIS HALLAM (later Mrs David Douglass) as Daraxa

copy of a print by G. V. Neist.

star of the American Company (as it came to be called) in cities along the eastern seaboard until near her death, only gradually relinquishing younger parts for the statelier, older ones. She played the widest variety of roles ranging from Mary of Scotland in *The Albion Queens* to Mrs Coaxer in *The Beggar's Opera*, from Mrs Heidelberg in *The Clandestine Marriage* to Thermusa in *The Prince of Parthia*. Again and again she introduced new British roles in America.

As Richardson Wright observes in *Revels in Jamaica*, Mrs Douglass was "the Queen Mother of the American Stage." Captain Graydon, in his *Memoirs of a Life Lived Chiefly in Pennsylvania*, called her "a respectable, matronlike dame, stately or querulous as occupation required, a very good Gertrude, a truly appropriate Lady Randolph [in *Douglas*], with her white handkerchief and weeds."

T. Allston Brown believed that "she retired from the stage in declining health in 1769." *Rivington's Gazette* of 23 September 1773 reported that Mrs Douglass had recently died in Philadelphia, but the report was erroneous, as was that of the *Pennsylvania Chronicle* of 27 September, which said she had died in Annapolis. She probably died in Philadelphia in 1774, though there was a Mrs Douglass acting Lady Capulet in Jamaica in David Douglass's company in July 1775. (That actress may have been Mary Peters, whom Douglass married in 1778, acting under his name.) John North, caretaker of the Southwark Theatre in Philadelphia, remembered that our Mrs Douglass had died in a house at Fifth and South Streets, Philadelphia, and had been buried in the grounds of the Second Presbyterian Church at Third and Arch Streets. There is no other record of the burial. North thought, according to Seilhamer, that "Mrs. Douglass was highly respected in Philadelphia," and "all the ladies in the neighborhood of the theatre attended her funeral." David Douglass did not die until 1789. The son and daughter mentioned in his will, David and Mary, appear to have been by his second wife.

Mrs Hallam was pictured as Daraxa in *Edward and Eleanora* in an engraving by G. V. Neist. At the Harvard Theatre Collection is a large drawing in India ink by an unknown artist; it is either the original from which the Neist engraving was made or a drawing based on the Neist engraving.

Hallam, Lewis *1740–1808, actor, dancer, singer, manager, violinist.*

Lewis Hallam "the Younger" was a son of Lewis Hallam and his wife (née Rich?) who headed the first complete company of British actors to perform on the American mainland. The younger Lewis had two sisters, Isabella (who became Mrs George Mattocks) and Helen, and a younger brother, Adam.

When Lewis was 12 years old the company headed by his parents and partially financed by his uncle William went to America by way of Barbados, arriving on the *Charming Sally* in York River on 2 June 1752. On 15 September Lewis (who had been taken from a grammar

Harvard Theatre Collection

LEWIS HALLAM, the younger, as Belville

engraving, artist unknown, after miniature in the Players Club

school in Cambridge to join the expedition) made his dramatic debut as a Page to his mother, who was playing Portia in *The Jew of Venice*, Lansdowne's version of *The Merchant of Venice*. Lewis's debut was ignominious, for according to his own account, later retold by Dunlap, he "stood motionless and speechless, until bursting into tears he walked off the stage making a most inglorious exit."

After 11 months at Williamsburg the little band of expatriate players departed for New York. There, in 1753–54 young Lewis began building his repertoire with Daniel in *The Conscious Lovers*, Dicky in *The Constant Couple*, Prince Edward in *Richard III*, Frisure in *The Twin Rivals*, an Attendant in *King Lear*, Balthazar in *Romeo and Juliet*, and Tester in *The Suspicious Husband*. He also several times sang entr'acte songs.

The Hallam troupe went next to Philadelphia, where they performed from 15 April to 24 June 1754. Master Lewis Hallam was there recorded as a Servant in *The Fair Penitent* and Haly in *Tamerlane.* From Philadelphia they proceeded to Charleston, where presumably young Lewis continued to play. At some time after the last recorded appearance in Charleston, on 27 January 1755, the company embarked for Jamaica, where they remained until 1758, joined with the company of David Douglass. There the elder Lewis died. His widow married Douglass, who took the company, including Lewis the younger and his bride, a girl native to Jamaica, back to the mainland in 1758. Lewis was then 18 years old.

Lewis spent the next 18 years as a principal actor with the "American Company" up and down the eastern seaboard of the mainland—strolling the colonies, playing at Annapolis, Williamsburg, Charleston, Providence, and New York from 1759 until 1762. He was at Philadelphia in 1759, 1766, 1767, 1768, 1769, 1770, 1772, 1773 (see Thomas Clark Pollock, *The Philadelphia Theatre in the Eighteenth Century*); at New York in 1761–62, 1767–68, 1773, and 1775 (see G. C. D. Odell, *Annals of the New York Stage*, I).

The growing troubles in the colonies seem to have forced the Douglass company to suspend performance. (The Hallams were probably Loyalist in sympathy. Two close family connections were officers in the British forces, Admiral Thomas Hallam and Colonel George Hallam.) In 1775 the American Company went again to Jamaica, but Lewis had already left the company and gone to England.

On 3 January 1775, advertised only as "A Gentleman being his first appearance in Europe," Lewis Hallam played Hamlet at Covent Garden. So far as is known it was also his last appearance in Europe. It drew from one "S********" in the next day's *Morning Post* the following spleenful critique:

Last night a young gentleman, whose name we find is Hallam (brother to Mrs. *Mattocks*) made his first appearance at Covent Garden Theatre in the character of *Hamlet.* It seems this theatrical adventurer has put himself to the inconvenience of travelling from a remote quarter of the globe, to make this essay on an English stage; and we are sorry to say, without one necessary qualification for his support in so hazardous an undertaking. His general deportment is unpleasing; his voice naturally not

the most harmonious, is hurt by a glaring lisp, and that insurmountable affectation, which is the never failing consequence of a spouting club education: add to this his conception of some parts of the character seem to be widely erroneous, and his attitudes generally disgusting.

Lewis Hallam had returned to Jamaica by 1779, and his name appeared on playbills at Kingston through at least 21 September 1782. ("Lewis Hallam, Jr" is listed among other actors who subscribed to *The Elements of Free-Masonry Delineated*, printed at Kingston in 1782.) The company was now under the command of John Henry, Hallam's mother having died and her husband David Douglass having retired. The company was at a low point in its fortunes. An undated clipping in the British Library reads:

Extract of a letter from Jamaica, Sept 14, 1783: "Mr. Henry, who formerly belonged to Drury-lane Theatre, and who is the proprietor of the playhouse, in the town of Kingston, upon this Island, arrived here the latter end of June, with some new performers, the want of whom occasioned his voyage to England last Spring. Bad news awaited his return. The wardrobe of the Kingston theatre had . . . been plundered to the amount of 500£ and an account had the day before been received, that a very fine theatre, which belonged to him at Charleston [South Carolina], was entirely burnt to the ground. However, he turned his thoughts towards the entertaining his Jamaica friends with great spirit, had the Play-house new painted, and opened it about a fortnight after his arrival. . . . Since which they have gone very well, tho' they play only once a week. . . . In about a month's time they move off for Philadelphia, where Mr. Henry has a good theatre also.

The account places Hallam in the company, but Lewis had already returned to the mainland by that time.

About 1783, with an actor named Allen, Hallam moved into management while he continued to expand his repertoire, though John Durang in his *Memoir* called him "a sterling actor, but an inactive manager." On 21 January 1784 Hallam, for himself and "The comedians, commonly called the American Company" petitioned the Pennsylvania assembly for repeal of the law against plays. Though the Quakers petitioned to retain the statutes, by 21 February Hallam was thanking his supporters in the Philadelphia *Packet*, and by 1

April in the Old Theatre in South Street he had embarked on a series of "Lectures on Heads." Plays were not mentioned, but were certainly being given, as Durang attests. George Washington "purchased four Play Tickets" for 22 May 1784, and he evidently attended several times in the year or two following. Durang recalls that "When Gen'l Washington visited the theatre, the last stage box was decorated with the United States coat of arms over the box. Mr. Wignell, dress'd in black and powdered, with two silver candlesticks would wait at the box door to receive him and light him to his seat."

In 1785 Lewis Hallam and John Henry formed their much vexed partnership. In 1785–86 they played in New York, returning to Philadelphia in the spring, but "lay idle in the summer," according to Durang. Hallam was, in fact, living in New York during that summer. In the fall of 1786 Hallam and Henry were again at Philadelphia and they alternated between there and New York with excursions to Baltimore and elsewhere until the middle of the 1790s, after which they concentrated on New York, with occasional visits to Boston. In 1794 Henry sold his interest in the John Street Theatre to Hallam for £4,000 (original indenture in the Huntington Library) and John Hodgkinson became Hallam's partner. Hodgkinson's quarrelsome nature and insistence on better and better parts for himself and his wife made life ever worse for Hallam, whose own roles diminished in importance. In 1797 Hallam withdrew from management, but continued on salary as an actor.

In 1796 William Dunlap had joined the enterprise and had attempted fruitlessly to bring peace to the partnership. In 1806 T. A. Cooper obtained the lease of New York's Park Street Theatre and refused to rehire the aging Hallam, who died in Philadelphia on 1 November 1808.

The conditions of Lewis Hallam's professional life in a peripatetic small repertory company, as well as his flexible talent, resulted in the wide variety of his offerings. The fact that his father, mother, and stepfather managed the Old American Company before he himself succeeded to its direction ensured him leading roles before he was mature enough to do them justice, but he developed the quicker because of that circumstance. Often in his earlier years

he played romantic leads (including Romeo) opposite that capable actress his mother. John Durang said of him: "His stile of acting was of the old school. He was celebrated in all the gentlemanly dashing profligateness of young men, in epilogues, correct in Harlequin, and performed them with ease and spirit to a great age. He was particularly admired in Lord Oglebey [in *The Clandestine Marriage*]." Durang recalls that when he was hired by Hallam as a dancer the manager accompanied him on the violin. Hallam also danced as Harlequin and sang.

Until the later 1780s he went on adding parts in comedy, tragedy, and farce. He could alternate King Lear with Aimworth in *The Maid of the Mill*, Ferdinand in *The Tempest* with Bajazet in *Tamerlane*. A partial list of his roles will suggest his range: Balthazar in *Romeo and Juliet*, Lord Townly in *The Provok'd Husband*, Richmond and Richard in *Richard III*, Varanes in *Theodosius*, both Young Norval and Douglas in *Douglas*, Belcour in *The West Indian*, Lovemore in *The Way to Keep Him*, Osmyn in *The Mourning Bride*, the title role in *The Roman Father*, Macheath in *The Beggar's Opera*, Tony Lumpkin in *She Stoops to Conquer*, Pierre in *Venice Preserv'd*, Ranger in *The Suspicious Husband*, Modely in *The Country Lasses*, Benedick in *Much Ado about Nothing*, Cecil in *False Delicacy*, the title role in *Cymon*, Tinsel in *The Drummer*, Oakly in *The Jealous Wife*, Petruchio in *Catherine and Petruchio*, the title role *Don Quixote*, a Drunken Man in *Lethe*; both Shylock and Antonio in *The Jew of Venice*, the title role in *George Barnwell*, Horatio in *The Fair Penitent*, Macbeth, Lovel in *High Life below Stairs*, Sempronius in *Cato*, Block in *The Reprisal*, Zamphineri in *The Orphan of China*, Young Bevil in *The Conscious Lovers*, Marc Antony in *Love for Love*, Beverley in *The Gamester*, the title role in *The Earl of Essex*, Othello, the title role in *Alexander the Great*, Young Belfield in *The Shipwreck*, Lord Aimworth in *The Maid of the Mill*, Mortimer in *The Fashionable Lover*, Posthumus in *Cymbeline*, Modely in *The School for Lovers*, Edgar in *Edgar and Emmeline*, General Wolfe in *The Conquest of Canada*, Hob in *Flora*, Archer in *The Beaux' Stratagem*, Don Felix in *The Wonder*, Captain Le Brush in *The Register Office*, Young Wilding in *The Citizen*, Captain Absolute in *The Rivals*, Touchstone in *As You Like It*, and Marshal Fehrbellin in *Love in a*

Camp. After the arrival of Hodgkinson, Hallam's roles diminished steadily. Toward the last he who had been Benedick was reduced to Dogberry and to such roles as Goldfinch in *The Road to Ruin*, the Fool in *The Battle of Hexham*, Lackland in *Fontainebleau*, and Aircourt in *The Toy*.

During Lewis Hallam's early Jamaican sojourn, 1755–1758, he had married a young Kingston girl whose first name was Sarah, the first of his two wives. Hugh F. Rankin, in *The Theater in Colonial America*, cites a lawsuit of 1769 argued in an Anne Arundel County, Maryland, court in which a Sarah Hallam was plaintiff. Rankin says that she probably was on stage only a few times, perhaps only once, and that she was separated from Hallam by about 1763 and settled in Williamsburg, where she ran a dancing school after 1775. The *Columbian Centinel* for 12 January 1793 reported that she had died lately in Virginia. The Philadelphia *Daily Advertiser* of 17 January 1793 reported the marriage of Lewis Hallam to the beautiful young actress Eliza Tuke, with whom he had lived for some time. She was an excellent actress but, according to Dunlap, drunken and quarrelsome, and her behavior onstage and off complicated the already difficult relations between Hallam and his partners, as Dunlap illustrated copiously in his *Diary*.

Lewis Hallam's first wife, Sarah, brought him two children during the brief time of their association—Mirvan, an inconsiderable actor, and Lewis D. Hallam, who studied medicine and who died at Kingston, Jamaica, in his nineteenth year, on 21 September 1780.

Thomas Clark Pollock, in the "Index to Players" of *The Philadelphia Theatre in the Eighteenth Century*, cites many performances of a "Miss Sarah Hallam" from 1766 through 1773. But inspection of his transcriptions of the playbills, in the body of his text, makes clear that they contain references only to "Miss Hallam." Pollock has confidently supplied the "Sarah." But the references are probably to Nancy Hallam, perhaps William Hallam's daughter, who is regularly confused in earlier accounts both with Sarah, wife of Lewis the younger, and with Lewis's sister, the Miss Hallam whose first name we do not know, but who accompanied the company to America in 1752.

A miniature portrait by an unknown artist of Lewis Hallam the younger as Belville in *The Country Girl* is at the Players Club, New York. A small woodcut copy of the miniature is in the Harvard Theatre Collection.

Hallam, Thomas   *d. 1735, actor, dancer, singer.*

Thomas Hallam was the earliest member of his family of which anything is known and the progenitor of a line of British and American actors and actresses on the stage for at least 120 years.

Thomas is almost certainly the adult Hallam listed among other members of the Smock Alley, Dublin, company for the 1707–8 season in a promptbook of *The Spanish Wives* in the Harvard Theatre Collection. W. S. Clark in *The Early Irish Stage* placed that Hallam (whom he called, incorrectly, "Adam") at Smock Alley from perhaps before 1707 until "past 1720." (We find a T. Hallam on the Smock Alley lists through 1723–24.) At Dublin Hallam played Hidewell in *The Spanish Wives*, the Bookseller in *The Committee*, a Musician in *Timon of Athens*, Nicholas in *The Comical History of Don Quixote*, Sir Jeremy Daudle in *The Hasty Wedding*, Clumsy in *Irish Hospitality*, Tradewell in *The Plotting Lovers*, Mr Seville in *The Sham Prince*, Foresight in *Love for Love* and Commick in *A Wife and No Wife*.

There is hardly any doubt that the Dublin actor of c. 1707–1724 was the Hallam who turned up in London on the Drury Lane stage playing much the same line of parts in 1724–25. On 18 February 1725 he was one of the Witches in *Macbeth* with Benjamin Griffin and Henry Norris. On 30 April he was Statue in *The What D'Ye Call It*. He took his benefit on 19 May 1725, so doubtless he had appeared on other occasions. Many bills for that season are lost.

Hallam served Drury Lane humbly again in 1725–26, adding to his repertoire only (so far as is known) Macahone in *The Stage Coach* at his benefit on 7 May, shared with Miss Tynte and Robert Williams. He returned to the theatre alone in 1726–27, and in 1728–29 his son Adam Hallam joined him there. The elder Hallam remained at Drury Lane dancing and singing, playing small parts, principally in pantomime and farce through the beginning of the season 1733–34, and even after Theo-

Harvard Theatre Collection

THOMAS HALLAM

artist unknown

philus Cibber drew away the seceders, including young Adam, to the Haymarket on 26 September. Thomas himself joined the rebels sometime before 12 February and returned with them to Drury Lane the following March. Other identifiable parts were Sycorax in *The Tempest*, Symon in *Patie and Peggy*, a Shopkeeper in *Harlequin Doctor Faustus*, and one of the Witches in *Macbeth*. He signed on with the company again in the fall of 1734.

Thomas Hallam never finished the 1734–35 season. While dressing for the comedy role of Guzman in *Trick upon Trick* on 10 May 1735 he incurred the ire of the tempestuous Irish tragedian Charles Macklin by putting on a property wig which Macklin had used the previous night and considered ought to be his again. Macklin's memorialist Kirkman reproduced the proceedings of his trial, where various persons gave versions of the tragedy, all agreeing substantially with the recollections of the first witness, Thomas Arne, who testified:

I have the honour to be the numberer of the boxes, of Drury-lane play-house, under *Mr. Fleetwood*. On Saturday night I delivered my accounts in at the property-office; and, then, at eight at night, I came into the scene-room, where the players warm themselves, and sat in a chair at the side of the fire. Fronting the fire there is a long seat, where five or six may sit. The play was almost done, and they were making preparations for the entertainment, when the prisoner came into the scene-room, and sat down next me, and high words arose between him and the deceased about a *stock wig*, for a disguise in the entertainment. The prisoner had played in the *wig* the night before: and now the deceased had got it.— "D——n you for a rogue," says the prisoner, *"what business have you with my wig."*—*"I am not more a rogue than yourself,"* says the deceased; "it's a *stock wig*, and I have as much right to it as you have." Some of the players coming in— they desired the deceased to fetch the wig, and give it to the prisoner, which he did, and then said to him, "Here is *your wig*; I have got one that I like *better*." The prisoner, sitting by me, took the wig, and began to comb it out, and all seemed to be quiet for about half a quarter of an hour: but the prisoner began to grumble again, and said to the deceased "G——d d——n you for a blackguard, scrub, rascal, how durst you have the impudence to take *this wig*?" The deceased answered "I am no more a rascal than yourself." Upon which the prisoner started up out of his chair, and, with a stick in his hand, made a longe at the deceased, and thrust the stick into his left eye; and, pulling it back

again, looked pale, turned on his heel, and, in a passion, threw the stick into the fire— "G—d d——n it," says he; and, turning about again on his heel, he sat down. The deceased clapped his hand to his eye, and said it was gone through his head. He was going to sink; but they set him in a chair. The prisoner came to him, and, leaning upon his left arm, put his hand to his eye. "Lord," cried the deceased, "it is out."—"No," says the prisoner, "I feel the ball roll under my hand." Young *Mr. Cibber* came in, and immediately sent for *Mr. Coldham*, the surgeon.

Macklin's own testimony adds a detail: "[Hallam] sat down, and said to Mr. Arne's son, (who was dressed in woman's cloaths) 'Whip up your clothes, you little b——h, and urine in my eye,' But he could not; so I did." That curious first-aid notwithstanding, Hallam died at six o'clock the next day. When Coldham "opened the scull, [he] found that the stick had passed through the thin bone, that contains the eye, into the brain." Macklin fled, returned and gave himself up, and was indicted for willful murder on 13 May. On 12 December 1735 he came to trial. He was convicted of manslaughter and sentenced to be burned in the hand—a "sentence" which was carried out with a cold iron.

Thomas Hallam's long career was probably not confined to Dublin and the patent theatres of London. Doubtless, like the rest of his family, he strolled in the English and Irish provinces; and he probably worked with his sons in the fair booths. His professional sphere was varied, but humble, singing, dancing, and acting. His known roles, in addition to those named, were: a Beggarman in *The Jovial Crew*, a Senator in *Timon of Athens*, Orbellan in *The Indian Emperor*, a Porter in *The Harlot's Progress*, Pistol in *The Merry Wives of Windsor*, a Toothdrawer in *A Cure for a Scold*, and Sancho in *The Rover*. His good new parts were all too few. He never got to play the last one he prepared. At the time of his death he was already in decline. A salary list published in the *Daily Post* of 4 June 1733 by the Drury Lane management included to "[Adam] Hallam, for himself and his father, the latter of little or no service, £3."

Hallam's wife is not known. Evidently she was never on the London stage. Their children, all but one of whom are noticed separately in this dictionary, were: Adam, Ann (successively

Mrs Sacheverel Hale and Mrs John Barrington), George, Lewis, Thomas, and William. Thomas joined the navy and was said by his niece Mrs Mattocks to have attained the rank of admiral. He is doubtless that "Thomas Hallum" whose career the *Biographia Navalis* (1798) details from the time of his commissioning as lieutenant on 6 January 1742 until 1793 when, "in consequence of the promotion of flag-officers then made . . . he was advanced to the rank of rear-admiral on the superannuated list." He was said to be still alive in 1798.

A letter in the Harvard Theatre Collection from Thomas's granddaughter, the celebrated actress Isabella Hallam Mattocks (daughter of Lewis Hallam) to J. Hill, written in reply to a request for information about the family, asserts that "Mr Rich the late Patentee of Cov: Garden & his family are likewise my relatives." The degree of consanguinity is not known.

An unknown engraver depicted Charles Macklin's fatal assault on Thomas Hallam. In the print a hand holds a stick against Hallam's left eye; Hallam stands with a wig in his left hand, pointing with his right hand to some verses titled "An Infallible Recipe to make a Wicked Manager of a Theatre." The engraving was published by "Mons. Verité" at Chester on 20 August 1750. "A. B." and T. Gilks engraved copies.

Hallam, William   *1712?–1758? actor, dancer, manager.*

William Hallam was one of the children of the performers Mr and Mrs Thomas Hallam. William's sister Ann (successively Mrs Sacheveral Hale and Mrs John Barrington) and his brothers Lewis, Adam, and George were, like William, actors. Another brother, Thomas, joined the navy, eventually becoming an admiral.

It seems probable that William was the Hallam, undistinguished by first name in the playbills, who appeared at Thomas Odell's theatre in Goodman's Fields on 3 November 1729, playing Bonniface in *The Stratagem*. He remained through mid-May of 1730, acting Foresight in *Love for Love*, Woodcock in *Tunbridge Walks*, Thinkwell in *A Woman's Revenge*, Sir Jealous in *The Busy Body*, Deputy Stanmore in *Oroonoko*, Macmorris in *The Half-Pay Officers*, Perriwinkle in *A Bold Stroke for a Wife*,

Antonio in *Love Makes a Man*, Darony in *Hurlothrumbo*, Heartfree in *Love and Revenge*, Petit in *The Inconstant*, one of the Gravediggers in *Hamlet*, Thinkwell in *A Woman's Revenge*, and Galloon in *The Gamester*.

After 30 March 1730 William Hallam seems to have left Goodman's Fields to join the company that had begun to play regularly at the Haymarket. There he was joined by one of his brothers, probably Lewis. The two habitually played roles in much the same line of low comic and eccentric characters, so that their respective parts and performances are hard to separate. Only for 30 March 1730, when *The Author's Farce* was given, does a clear distinction seem probable. The 1730 edition listed "Hallam" for Murdertext and gave the role of the Poet to "W. Hallam." The two parts cannot be doubled. A third "Hallam" appeared opposite Dash in the bill; but that part can be doubled. The only other parts credited to a Hallam at the Haymarket that spring were Darony in *Hurlothrumbo*, Alcimes in *The Rival Father*, Heartfree in *Love and Revenge*, and Dr Churchyard in Fielding's popular new farce *Tom Thumb*. (The edition of 1730 listed a Hallam as First Physician, but in the more than two dozen performances which followed the premiere on 24 April 1730 the playbills listed a Hallam only opposite Churchyard.)

It is not possible to say with assurance whether both William and Lewis were at the Haymarket in the winter season of 1730–31. (Their brothers Adam and George and their father, Thomas, are accounted for elsewhere that season.) But probably there was only one Hallam and that one was William. Certainly one or another Hallam played the following: Francisco in *The False Count*, Woodcock in *Tunbridge Walks*, an unspecified part in *The Merry Masqueraders*, Moody in *The Generous Freemason*, Foigard in *The Stratagem*, Gomez in *The Spanish Fryar*, Patrick O'Thimble in *The Jealous Taylor*, Foresight in *Love for Love*, Snuffle in *The Cobler of Preston*, Softly in *The Letter Writers*, John in *The Welch Opera*, and Berkley in *The Fall of Mortimer*.

That Haymarket company continued to offer performances sporadically past midsummer, but there was opposition from the magistrates and dissension in the company as well. The *Daily Journal* of 22 July noted that "Last Night when the Company . . . was going to perform *The Fall of Mortimer*, the High Constable . . . came with a Warrant from several Justices of the Peace, to seize Mr Mullet [Mullart], who play'd the part of Mortimer, and the rest of the Performers, but they all made their Escapes." The *Daily Courant* of 25 August reported another foray into the Haymarket by "The Constables of Middlesex and Westminster" and another escape by the players on 20 August. Thereafter, the fluctuating group at the Haymarket lost the little cohesion it had possessed. In the winter of 1731–32 the theatre was dark except on the occasions of a few benefits performed by pickup companies in which no Hallam figured.

The Hallam who turned up at Lincoln's Inn Fields Theatre on 7 February 1732 playing Antonio in *Love Makes a Man* was probably also William. The bills gave him one more performance in that part and three as Merlin in *Tom Thumb* (then called *Tragedy of Tragedies*) during the remainder of the season. He played Antonio again at Lincoln's Inn Fields on 7 November 1732 but was credited with no other parts by that theatre's extant bills during the 1732–33 season. Very likely William was the Hallam playing Gregory in *The Mock Doctor* and the "Hallum" who played the Squire in the afterpiece *Love Runs All Dangers* the same evening, 20 March 1733, at the Haymarket, a performance given "at the Desire of several Persons of Quality" (i.e., probably at the desire of the players themselves). The same nonce group gave *The London Merchant*, in which Hallam was Blunt, and repeated *Love Runs All Dangers* on 26 March.

In the early summer of 1733, virtually the whole Hallam clan seems to have gone strolling. The *Kentish Post* of 13–16 June 1733 was quoted by Sybil Rosenfeld: "We are inform'd from London, that during the Vacation of the Theatres there, a Company of Comedians selected from both the Royal Playhouses, design to entertain this City [Canterbury] (for a short Time) with a Sett of the best Plays, Tragedies, Comedies, and Operas. . . ." The group which opened at the Watling Street Theatre consisted in large part of the Hallam family: an elder couple (presumably Thomas and wife), Adam, William, "Young" Hallam (Lewis or George), "Miss Hallam" (no doubt Ann), and a second Mrs Hallam, who attracted great attention as

Lady Macbeth and who was, therefore, William's wife, already famous in the part.

In the late summer of 1733 William Hallam began an activity with which he was to be associated for some years. During the time of Bartholomew Fair in late August and early September he joined the old actors Benjamin Griffin and William Bullock the elder and the 30-year-old comedian Theophilus Cibber in the management of a fair booth in Hosier Lane. He himself acted, as did the other proprietors, his parts being the title role in *Tamerlane* and both Justice Shallow and Mouldy in a droll called *The Comical Humors of Sir John Falstaff, Justice Shallow, Ancient Pistol and Others*. The booth was elaborate, Henry Morley in *Memoirs of Bartholomew Fair* crediting it with rich decorations and "candles in lustres," and the company was large. It included William's brother, Adam, and two dozen others besides the proprietors.

We cannot place William Hallam with certainty anywhere in the winter of 1733–34. It is possible he was again acting in the provinces. He returned to Bartholomew Fair in August 1734, this time in partnership with Bullock and John Hippisley. A slightly different and smaller company included his future brother-in-law Sacheverel Hale and a Master Hallam who was perhaps Lewis or George.

William's wife, Anne, was a starring tragedienne at Covent Garden and both his brother Adam and his in-law to be, Hale, were prospering there. Their combined influence should have procured him a better situation than he apparently obtained at Covent Garden in the winter of 1734–35 when his meagre repertoire consisted of few and infrequent appearances (billed only as "Hallam") in such roles as Robert in *The Mock Doctor*, an Irishman in *The Lottery*, a Gentleman in *The Toy Shop*, and Mrs. Hackum in *The Squire of Alsatia*.

William Hallam then disappeared again from the record for a summer, surfacing in Dublin on 13 November 1735 as a member (W. Hallam) of the company at the Rainsford Street Theatre, playing Higgen in *The Royal Merchant*. He had returned to London, however, by 27 March 1736, when he played the part of a Newswoman in the farce called *The City Ramble* at Covent Garden. Perhaps the management of the theatre gave him a short engagement again to please his friends and relations. But on 16 April 1736 the bill at Lincoln's Inn Fields carried him as Guildenstern in *Hamlet*. Neither theatre took him into the regular company at that time. At Bartholomew Fair time, from 23 to 26 August 1736, a Hallam, very likely William, joined Chapman, presenting in a booth a company playing *Fair Rosamond: Representing her Amours with King Henry, and her being poisoned by Queen Eleanor in Woodstock Bower* and *The Modern Pimp; or, the Doctor Deceiv'd*, with several entertainments of dancing.

The London playbills of 1736–37 are devoid of mention of William Hallam, or of any Hallam who played in his line. At Bartholomew Fair time, for five days from 23 August 1737, at "Hallam's Great Booth, Over against the Hospital Wall," a medley entertainment was presented including dancing and "*The Italian Shadows* by the best Masters from Italy," a kind of show which obtained its effects by throwing silhouettes on a screen.

William joined his wife in the Covent Garden company for the 1737–38 season, and during that and the following season (1738–39) played several rather inconsiderable comic or eccentric parts: a Citizen in *Oedipus*, Jaquez in *The Pilgrim*, Galloon in *The Gamester*, Bumpkin in *The Funeral*, Periwinkle in *A Bold Stroke for a Wife*, Mother Coupler in *Marina*, and Argus in *The Contrivances*. He was also the Duke in *Othello* and, repeatedly, Bardolph (his best characterization) in both parts of *Henry IV* and in *Henry V*.

Hallam's Bartholomew Fair booth opened in August of both 1738 and 1739. It was "in the George-Inn Yard" on 23 August 1738 and five days following presenting a "Lilliputian Company" of youngsters in *The Dragon of Wantley*. During the time the booth was filling Mons Rapinere made surprising postures on the stage. The playbill directed the audience to

Note the extraordinary band of music, Violins, Hautboys, Bassoons, Kettle-Drums, Trumpets, and French Horns. The Passage to the Booth will be commodiously illuminated with several large Moons and Lanthorns, for the Conveniency of the Company, and that Persons of Quality's coaches may drive up the yard.

Some Hallam, possibly William but probably Adam, had a booth "at the bottom of Mermaid-Court" at Southwark Fair on 5 September 1738 and following, presenting the droll *The Man's Bewitch'd*. Again opposite the Hospital Gate at Bartholomew Fair in late August 1739, Hallam's booth gave its audiences *Harlequin Turn'd Philosopher* and *The Sailor's Wedding*.

During the preceding winter season William Hallam had been busily organizing a venture to compete with the patent houses in which he had found so little employment. On 20 April 1739 the *London Daily Post* carried the following announcement:

Mr. W. Hallam, of the Theatre Royal, Covent Garden, having taken the Dwelling-house and Bowling-Green in Hooper's-Square, the lower End of Lemon-street, Goodman's-Fields, has repaired and beautified them both in a very handsome manner, and will open the House on Monday next, and the Bowling-Green on Thursday.

The bowling green opened on schedule, but the Wells, with its entertainments, did not open until 18 June. The *Post*'s notice promised "the Usual Diversions of Rope-Dancing, Posture-Masters . . . and a New Entertainment, call'd Harlequin Hermit; or The Arabian Courtesan . . . to continue every Day 'till the Season is over."

The first season of the Wells was eccentric, cutting across the theatrical offerings of spring, summer, and fall at the other houses, taverns, and fair booths and running for 32 weeks, from 18 June 1739 to 21 January 1740. In June 1740 William Hallam received a crushing blow in the death of his talented wife, Anne, who was earning excellent money as a first-line performer at Covent Garden, and was no doubt also assisting William's management labors.

C. B. Hogan outlines the fortunes of the New Wells in his article in *Theatre Notebook*, (3), to which account we add others. The venture was successful.

After five years Hallam converted the Wells into something like a regular playhouse and on 26 November 1744 began performing "legitimate" dramas, evading the Licensing Act of 1737 (which confined such fare to the winter patent houses) by the expedient of offering the play "gratis" between two halves of a concert. Playing stock pieces from the dramatic repertoire in the winter and giving harlequinades, singing, rope dancing, and tumbling in the summers, Hallam prospered very well until early in 1744, employing his brother Lewis and Lewis's wife, and other minor actors, including some who, like Hannah Haughton, Cushing, and Goodfellow, achieved a mild degree of fame later. If his claims were correct his scenic designers were from the beginning first rate and his effects ambitious, as illustrated by a fugitive bill in the Enthoven collection hand-dated 23 August 1742 describing *Humors of the Jubilee* with "A Grand Representation of Water Works, as in the Doge's Garden in Venice The Scenes, Cloaths, and Musick, all New the Scenes painted by Mons. [John] Devoto. . . ." (DeVoto was still receiving benefits at Goodman's Fields as late as the 1745–46 season.) In that bill "Mr Hallam, the Master of these Wells," noted that "having for several years kept a Booth in Smithfield, during the Time of Bartholomew Fair; this is to inform the Publick, that he is in no Shape concerned in that Fair this Year, but will continue his Performances every Evening at his Wells. . . ."

In May 1744 not only Hallam's booth at May Fair, but also the New Wells—along with two gaming houses in Covent Garden—were presented by the Grand Jury of Middlesex as "places kept apart for the encouragement of luxury, extravagance, idleness, and other wicked illegal purposes," according to Noorthouch's *History of London*. If Hallam was affected by the blast, he did not show it. By Arthur H. Scouten's tabulation there were in 1744–45 over 50 actors and dancers giving more than a hundred performances.

The Goodman's Fields bills for the first half of 1744–45 are sparse and uninformative. Mrs Lewis Hallam was acting throughout the season. Her husband was specifically said to be performing for "the first time . . . on that stage" when he acted Gomez in *The Spanish Fryar* on 31 January 1745. He was always called "L. Hallam" thereafter in the bills. George Hallam (called "Hallam Sen[ior]") joined the venture in 1745–46, when Lewis and his wife continued to act. William, oddly, seems to have confined himself to managing, for when he played Bonniface in *The Stratagem* on 23 December 1745 he was said to be "first time here." In 1746–47 he played only a few

times—Bonniface again, Polonius, Gratiano in *Othello*, Stephano in *The Tempest*, Day in *The Committee*, the Duke in *Venice Preserv'd*, and Lucius in *Cato*.

The theatre in Lemon Street was sparsely attended in 1745–46, giving between 80 and 90 performances by the end of Lent. On Easter Monday it reopened to perform pantomimes only. The theatre revived somewhat in 1746–47, giving some 100 performances and employing about 60 performers, including William, Lewis, George, and Mrs Lewis Hallam. William appeared as Kate Matchlock in *The Funeral*, Lewis in *Love Makes a Man*, Sir Tunbelly Clumsy in *The Relapse*, the Host in *The Merry Wives of Windsor*, Sir Francis in *The Provok'd Husband*, the Captain in *King Lear*, and the Third Witch in *Macbeth*.

From 1747–48 through 1750–51 the New Wells in Lemon Street, Goodman's Fields, again was given over nearly entirely to harlequinades. In the summer of 1751 there were two performances of *Richard III* and one of *Othello*, the latter for Mrs Lewis Hallam's benefit. But complaints about the Wells were already before the Lord Chamberlain. After 18 December 1751 the theatre was closed.

William seems to have turned his attention immediately to organizing the adventure which brought to America the first British theatrical company, under the leadership of William's younger brother, Lewis.

Dunlap, the early historian of the American theatre, gave some erroneous information in his remarks about the Hallams, though he claims to have consulted Lewis the younger for some of it. Thus, his account of the American adventure may not be exact:

The emigrants were . . . assembled at the house of William Hallam; a list of *stock plays* produced by him, with attendant farces, and the *cast* of the whole agreed upon in full assembly of the body politic. . . . Lewis Hallam was appointed manager . . . and William, who stayed home, was to be Viceroy over him. . . . The brothers were to divide profits equally after deducting the expenses and *shares*.

The arrangement evidently did not produce a financial bonanza for William. On 13 November 1752 there was given a "Benefit for Hallam at the New Wells, Lemon St. A Concert . . . by a set of Mr Hallam's Friends." The bill continued: "As the Wells have been shut up all the past Summer, and are now open'd only upon this occasion, Mr Hallam hopes the Town will be so indulgent, as to honour him with their Company, and the Favour will always be gratefully acknowledged." On 16 November Hallam cautiously allowed two of the proscribed "legitimate" dramas, *Othello* and *Lethe*, to be played for his benefit. Grown bolder with success, again for his own benefit, he produced *The London Merchant* and *An Old Man Taught Wisdom* on 20 November 1752, *Venice Preserv'd* and *The Devil to Pay* on 28 November, and the *Recruiting Officer* and *The Devil to Pay* on 30 November. The authorities must have been aroused, for after that there was an abrupt cessation of activity at Lemon Street.

There is no London record of William Hallam from 1752 until 1756. Dunlap testified that William visited his kin in America:

In addition to the pleasure of success, the Thespians were gladdened by a visit from William Hallam, the father of the American stage, the original projector of this prosperous scheme. He landed in June, 1754. There is reason to believe that Lewis purchased all the property, interest, and goodwill, from his brother William the original owner, as he returned to England immediately after a settlement of their accounts, and we hear no more of him.

William had evidently been forced to curb his activity. When on 18 March 1756 Theophilus Cibber delivered "Two Dissertations on Theatrical Subjects: with a Prefatory Address to the Anti-Gallicans, for the Benefit of Mr Hallam," places could "be had of Mr Hallam," who added a pitiful note to the bill: "N.B. As I have been lame for some Time, I hope my friends will excuse my not waiting on them. W. Hallam."

Nevertheless, on 3, 4, and 5 September 1756 at the Swan Inn, West Smithfield, Hallam turned out a company at Bartholomew Fair time. The group acted the droll *Adventures of Half an Hour*. On 9 October Hallam was given a benefit at Sadler's Wells. He noted on the bill: "As I am refused the use of my own House, I hope the Town will indulge me with their Company at this."

William Hallam is thought to have died in 1758.

Hallam's wife, Anne, the brilliant tragedy actress, was commanding good salaries and getting fine roles at Covent Garden during some of the time her husband's activities went unrecorded. She died in June 1740.

Hallam, Mrs William, Anne, formerly Mrs Lewis Parker and Mrs Joseph Berriman *1696–1740, actress.*

The first notice we have of the actress who eventually became Mrs William Hallam is on a Lincoln's Inn Fields Theatre bill of 15 October 1720, when "Mrs Parker" played Regan in *King Lear*. (British Library Additional Manuscript 18,586 states that she went to London from Norwich, and in his *Dramatic Miscellanies* Thomas Davies also remembered that "she had signalized herself so greatly as a member of the company acting at Norwich, when her name was Parker, that she received an invitation from Mr. Rich to join his company at Lincoln's-inn-Fields.") Davies says that at first she was not one of Rich's favorites and did not get good roles, but that she inherited many principal parts from Mrs Boheme. The fragmentary records show that on 18 October 1720 she played Melinda in *The Recruiting Officer*.

By the end of the season of 1723–24 Mrs Parker was playing a list of 16 primary and secondary roles, ranging from the Duchess in *2 Don Quixote* to Charlotte in *Oroonoko* and Isabella in *Measure for Measure*. On 27 April 1724 she and the prompter John Stede shared a benefit (total receipts £102 4s.) at which she played Jocasta in *Oedipus, King of Thebes*. At the beginning of the next season her daily salary was 16s. 8d., according to the entry of 25 September 1724 in the Lincoln's Inn Fields accounts in the British Library. Strangely, however, by 19 December 1724 she was being paid only £2 2s. after every (presumably six-day) week. That payment was continued weekly through 7 October 1726 (at least), after which date there is no evidence. By the time of her benefit on 17 April 1727 (gross receipts £74 4s. 6d.) she was called Mrs Berriman in the accounts. Joseph Berriman was a minor actor at Lincoln's Inn Fields who died in 1730. He is separately noticed.

Anne continued to act at Lincoln's Inn Fields as Mrs Berriman (sometimes Berryman) each season through 1730–31. Her benefit with Chapman on 29 April 1730 totaled £133. She was still in the bill of 20 September 1731 as Mrs Berryman, but by 27 September she had married William Hallam. She continued as Mrs Hallam to the end of her career (though an absent-minded printer called her Mrs Berriman as late as 25 April 1732).

Mrs Hallam played Mrs Marwood in *The Way of the World* at the opening of John Rich's new Covent Garden Theatre on 7 December 1732, and she remained an ornament of that company until her death after the season of 1739–40. Under her successive names she went quickly to the first rank of heroines in tragedy, though she played competently in comedy as well. Her roles, in chronologized order, included Jocasta in *Oedipus, King of Thebes*, Alithea in *The Country Wife*, the Queen in *The Spanish Fryar*, Elizabeth in *Richard III*, Isabella in *The Mistake*, Arpasia in *Tamerlane*, Roxana in *The Rival Queens*, Florinda in *The Rover*, Monimia in *The Orphan*, Maria in *The Fond Husband*, Queen Gertrude in *Hamlet*, Hortessia in *Aesop*, Candare in *The Fall of Saguntum*, Queen Katherine in *Henry VIII*, Lady Macbeth, Belvidera in *Venice Preserv'd*, Portia in *The Jew of Venice*, Lady Touchwood in *The Double Dealer*, Mrs Sullen in *The Stratagem*, Isteria in *Philip of Macedon*, Lady Cockwood in *She Wou'd if She Cou'd*, Cartismandua in *Caradoc the Great*, Mrs Page in *The Merry Wives of Windsor*, Nitocris in *Sisostris*, Cleora in *The Bath Unmask'd*, Elvira in *Love Makes a Man*, the title role in *Mariamne*, Lady Touchwood in *The Double Dealer*, the Duchess in *2 Don Quixote*, Araminta in *The Old Bachelor*, Lady Brute in *The Provok'd Wife*, Dorothea in *Successful Strangers*, the title role in *Sophonisba*, Ann Lovely in *A Bold Stroke for a Wife*, Cynthia in *The Wife's Relief*, Maria in *The Fond Husband*, Artemisia in *Themistocles*, Adelaide in *Frederick, Duke of Brunswick Lunenberg*, Lady Sly in *The Fortune Hunters*, Corinna in *A Woman's Revenge*, Evadne in *The Maid's Tragedy*, Roxana in *The Rival Queens*, Lady Raleigh in *Sir Walter Raleigh*, Antigona in *Philotas*, Circe in *Orestes*, Clarissa in *The Confederacy*, Amanda in *Love's Last Shift*, the title role in *The Prophetess*, Lady Wronglove in *The Lady's Last Stake*, the Duchess in *The Fatal Secret*, Evandra in *Timon of Athens*, Maria in *The Fond Husband*, Lady Traffick in *The Lady's Revenge*, Lady Easy in *The Careless Husband*, Hermione in *The Distrest Mother*, Calpurnia in *Julius Caesar*, Queen Elizabeth in *The Albion Queens*, Alicia in *Jane Shore*, Constance in *King John*, Zara in *The Mourning Bride*, the Queen in *Cymbeline*, Belvidera in *Venice Preserv'd*, Pulcheria in *Theodosius*, the Duchess of York in *Richard II*, and Joan la Pucelle in *1 Henry VI*.

In addition to her frequent and fruitful labors acting at Lincoln's Inn Fields and Covent Garden, Anne Hallam probably assisted her husband in his fair-booth enterprises. She had herself acted at the fairs and the minor theatres. She, with the rest of the Hallams, had trouped through Kent in the summer of 1733. There is a record of a Mrs Hallam, probably William's wife, playing Hoyden in *The Relapse* at York Buildings for a benefit on 17 July 1735. She was one of 22 prominent performers who in 1735 signed an unsuccessful petition to Parliament against the pending bill to regulate the theatres.

Evidently Mrs Hallam ended her career with her performance of her most celebrated role, Lady Macbeth, "in which part she gave greater pleasure than any person who had apper'd before her," said the London *Daily Post*, for her benefit "At the particular desire of several Ladies of Quality," at Covent Garden on 21 April 1740. Tickets could be had "at Hallam's House, Leman Street, Goodman's Fields." (Mrs Hallam's address at the times of her benefits in 1737, 1738, and 1739 had been No 6, Wild Court, Wild Street, Lincoln's Inn Fields. In 1734 and 1735 it had been "at Mrs Hallam's Lodgings, at a Grocer's," Mr Baily's, "Corner of James St. Long-Acre.")

Anne Hallam died on the morning of 5 June 1740, and on Sunday 8 June her corpse was "carried in a very handsome manner" to Mitcham in Surrey "to be buried in the churchyard," according to the London *Daily Post* of 9 June 1740. (One of the mourners, Elizabeth Carter Hallam, wife of her husband's brother, Adam, was taken ill at the funeral, died the next day, and was herself buried in Mitcham Churchyard on 15 June.) Anne's husband wrote a Latin inscription for her tombstone:

Charissimae Tuae uxori Annae Hallam, Histrioni, ultimum hoc amoris munus, moestissimus dedit Gulielmus Hallam.

Intravit		1696	
	Anno		AEt. 44
Exit		1740	

Thomas Davies said that she was "a large un-wieldy person," but so able that she was con-stantly encouraged by her audiences to play roles "which received no advantage from her figure." Davies illustrated with a cruel anec-dote: James Quin ridiculed her one morning at rehearsal by asking the prompter what a large barrel which stood on the stage was doing there. Before the prompter could answer Quin cried: "I see what it is: Mrs Hallam's stays, in which she played Monimia last night."

Hallandall. *See* HELLENDAAL.

Hallet, Benjamin   *b. 1742?, flutist, violoncellist, actor?*

Master Benjamin Hallet, a musical prodigy, was born about 1742, the son of Benjamin Hallet, of the parish of St Mary le Strand, who lived in Exeter Court, near Exeter 'Change. Two of the boy's brothers, both named Joshua, who died in infancy, were buried at St Paul, Covent Garden, on 10 November 1747 and 30 April 1750.

Young Benjamin's name first appeared in the London bills on 27 December 1751, when he played a solo on the violoncello and delivered the epilogue to an entertainment called *The Old Woman's Oratory*, presented by the colorful Christopher Smart under his pseudonym of Mrs Mary Midnight at the Haymarket The-atre. Throughout the rest of the season that entertainment played variously at the Hay-market and the Castle Tavern a total of some 33 times until 12 May 1752. On the an-nouncement for the tenth night, 6 February 1752 at the Castle Tavern, which was for the lad's benefit, Master Hallet was described in the *General Advertiser* as "A Child of Nine Years of Age," and patrons were advised that tickets could be had of Mr Hallet, in Exeter Court. The advertisement also stated that three years previously Master Hallet had played the flute for 50 nights and that in the following year he had played the violoncello at the Castle Tavern, but neither the bills nor other records of that theatre support such a claim. A similar claim, however, is to be found in a marginal inscrip-tion on a copy of a mezzotint of the child, done

Harvard Theatre Collection

BENJAMIN HALLET
engraving by McArdell, after Jenkins

by McArdell after T. Jenkins, which is in the British Museum. That inscription also stated that Master Hallet had been a student of Mr Oswald. The picture itself depicts the boy dressed in a girl's stays and frock.

In 1752–53, Mrs Midnight resumed the performances of *The Old Woman's Oratory* on 7 December, but Master Hallet's name was not on the opening bill. Again the entertainment continued throughout the season, and on 10 April 1753 Master Hallet, advertised for the prologue, shared a benefit with "Sig Gapa-tano," so no doubt the boy had been appearing regularly. Thereafter, he was not heard from.

Hallett, Joseph   *d. 1710, singer.*

The registers of Westminster Abbey reveal that Joseph Hallet, one of the gentlemen of the choir, was buried in the north cloister on 25 November 1710. His will, dated 11 No-vember 1710 and proved hastily on the seventeenth by Hallett's aunt, Joyce Thomas of St Margaret, Westminster, named her as residuary legatee. Hallett left £5 to his aunt Barbara Sweeting of Colwinstone, County Glamorgan, and other bequests to his friends and associates.

Halley. *See also* HALEY.

Halley, Mr [*fl.* 1786–1789], *house servant?*

On 2 June 1786 and 5 June 1789 at Covent Garden the benefit tickets of a Mr Halley were accepted. He was probably one of the house servants.

Halliburton, Mr [*fl.* 1776–1783], *constable.*

Mr. Halliburton, a house constable, shared annual benefits with other house servants at Covent Garden Theatre regularly from 1776–77 through 1782–83.

Halling, Mr [*fl.* 1779], *actor.*

A Mr Halling acted the role of Friar Laurence in *Falstaff's Wedding* at the Haymarket Theatre on 27 December 1779.

Hallum. *See also* HALLAM.

Hallum, M. [*fl.* 1797], *actor, singer?*

One Hallum played unspecified parts in *The Way to Get Married* and *The Maid of the Mill* at the theatre at Richmond, Surrey, on 1 September 1797.

Halpin, John Edmund *b. 1764, painter, actor.*

Born in Dublin in 1764, the son of the engraver Patrick Halpin (fl. 1755–87) and his wife, Eleanor, John Edmund Halpin spent most of his professional life as a painter of miniatures. After early education in art from Robert West and J. J. Barralet in the Dublin Society Schools, he went to study in London. There he was encouraged by Macklin in his ambition to go upon the stage but refrained because of his father's opposition to the idea. After practicing as a miniature painter in Dublin, he finally did give in to his inclination and made his debut at the Crow Street Theatre on 16 December 1789, advertised as "A Young

By permission of the British Library Board

JOHN EDMUND HALPIN as Pierre

artist unknown

Gentleman," in the role of Macbeth. With the same billing he repeated the role on 26 December, and when he played again on 20 January 1790 his name was given in the bills. Although the debut was a fair success, he made little progress as an actor and returned to painting.

On 2 November 1796, again called "A Young Gentleman," he played at Drury Lane Theatre as Norval in *Douglas*. The *European Magazine* (November 1796) incorrectly identified him as "Hamlin." The *Monthly Mirror* (November 1796), recalling that Halpin had acted previously in Dublin, protested the claim in the bills that this performance was his first "on any stage" and also condemned his talents:

His voice is something like the worst part of Mr. Kemble's, but not under the same management, and inadequate to equal exertion. This natural resemblance probably excited him to an artificial imitation of that gentleman's performance of Douglas; but unfortunately, like most other mimics, he trenched too much on the borders of caricature. His figure and countenance are rather in his favour, but for an artist, as he is reported to be, he is extremely ignorant of the picturesque; we never saw action and deportment more disgustingly awkward.

Halpin did not appear on the London stage again. He acted at Bath in 1799, at Birmingham in the summers of 1799 and 1800, and at York in 1801. During a performance at York he was the object of noisy insults from a lady in the audience "*famed* for such conduct." In *A Pasquinade upon the Performers at York* (1801), W. Burton wrote of Halpin:

> *His Kitely discovered his skill as an actor,*
> *Should he follow the trade, must prove a great*
> > *factor;*
> *'Tis not easy to say too much of his merit,*
> *But hard to note down how his calling he'll credit;*
> *I can scarce keep my temper, it adds to my rage,*
> *To hear that performer talk of quitting the stage;*
> *Shall he fly dame Fortune, heap curses upon her,*
> *And throw away that, he could wear with much*
> > *honor;*
> *For shame, let him mend, his good conduct he can't,*
> *I've given my advice—but may he never want:*
> *To a well-studied part conception he fashions,*
> *And no rigid judge can find fault with his passions.*

Eventually Halpin gave up the stage to settle in London as a painter. One of his portraits was of William Macready, engraved by W. Ridley for *Parson's Minor Theatre* (1794). An engraving of Halpin himself as Pierre in *Venice Preserv'd* was published in the *Hibernian Magazine* in March 1790.

Halsted, Mr ₁*fl.* 1710₁, *boxkeeper.*
Mr. Halsted, one of the boxkeepers at Drury Lane, was given a solo benefit there on 18 April 1710.

Haltham. *See* HOLTHAM.

Ham. *See also* HAMM.

₁**Ham?**₁, **Mr** ₁*fl.* 1783₁, *performer?*
An illegible entry, which may read Mr and Miss "Ham," is in the British Library's manu-

script Drury Lane accounts under the date 6 December 1783. The pair were described as not on the regular paylist and were to receive £6 13*s.* 4*d.* for four days. Perhaps they were performers.

₁**Ham?**₁, **Miss** ₁*fl.* 1783₁, *performer?*
See ₁ HAM?₁, MR.

Hambleton, the Misses ₁*fl.* 1731₁, *singers.*
At Goodman's Fields Theatre on 1 June 1731, according to the bills, there was singing "In Scotch and English by the two Misses Hambleton, who never appeared on any Stage before." Two days later at the same theatre they sang "both in Italian and English."

Hamersley, Mr ₁*fl.* 1746–1747₁, *tailor.*
The Covent Garden Theatre accounts for the 1746–47 season indicate that a Mr Hamersley was on the payroll as a tailor. On 17 October 1746 he was placed on the paylist at 4*s.* daily; on 8 November he was paid £8 1*s.* for a black velvet dress for Mrs Cibber; on 28 January 1747 he was apparently paid (though no amount was specified) for an olive waistcoat; on 24 February he was paid for a "Livery Frock & pair of Leather Breeches" for the actor Bencraft; and on 29 May he received 16*s.* for four days' work.

Hamilton, Mr ₁*fl.* 1720₁, *actor?*
A Mr Hamilton, probably an actor, shared benefits with John and Christopher Rich at Lincoln's Inn Fields Theatre on 5 and 10 February 1720. Probably he was the husband of the Mrs Hamilton who had a benefit at the same theatre the previous season, on 6 May 1719, when *Don Sebastian* was given.

Hamilton, Mr ₁*fl.* 1727–1750?₁, *actor.*
The Irish actor Hamilton and his wife, Sarah Hamilton, née Lyddal, were members of the company at the Smock Alley Theatre in Dublin during the season of 1727–28. His known roles at Smock Alley included Blunt in *Richard III* on 22 March 1731, Eumenes in *The Rival Queens* on 29 March 1731, Doran in *Love and Ambition* on 9 December 1731, Aegon in *Damon and Phillida* on 16 December 1731, and the Footman in *The Devil to Pay* on 24 January

1732. Hamilton made his debut on the London stage on 10 October 1732 as Whisper in *The Busy Body* at Goodman's Fields Theatre. A week earlier his wife had first performed there, on 4 October, as Cherry in *The Stratagem*. That little minor house was at the time under the management of Henry Giffard, who was married then to Anna Marcella Giffard (1707–1777), née Lyddal, a sister to Mrs Hamilton. After his appearance as Whisper, Hamilton acted Story in *The Committee* on 8 November; he is recorded for only two more appearances during that season, Whisper again on 25 November and Story on 10 March 1733. He shared a benefit with his wife on 11 April 1733 but did not perform that night.

The following season, 1733–34, Hamilton was more regularly employed at Goodman's Fields, playing Alonzo in *Rule a Wife and Have a Wife*, Jack in *Oroonoko*, Tom in *The Funeral*, Sir Charles in *The Stratagem*, Meleager in *The Rival Queens*, Simon in *A Bold Stroke for a Wife*, Guildenstern in *Hamlet*, and Burgundy in *King Lear*. For two more seasons he was seen in similarly modest roles at Goodman's Fields, and then, in 1736–37, he and his wife accompanied Giffard when he moved his operation to the larger Lincoln's Inn Fields Theatre, where Hamilton first appeared on 28 September 1736 as Guillamar in *King Arthur*. In addition to the roles cited above, at Lincoln's Inn Fields that season Hamilton acted such parts as a Servant in *Harlequin Female Bone-Setter*, Tom Errand in *The Constant Couple*, Blunt in *The London Merchant*, Scale in *The Recruiting Officer*, and Petit in *The Inconstant*. On 1 March 1737 he acted Colonel Tomlinson and the Duke of Gloucester in the first performance of a piece called *An Historical Play*, based on the life of Charles I, by the actor William Havard. At the time the Hamiltons lived at Mr Corey's, in Hemlock Court, Corey Street.

After that season Hamilton had no further London engagements, although his wife did act occasionally at Drury Lane in 1737–38 and regularly there during the second half of 1738–39. Probably Hamilton left his family temporarily in London while he went to play at Smock Alley in 1737–38. He is known to have been at that theatre during 1738–39, and on 12 April 1739 the *Dublin Journal* announced that his wife and children were to join him "next winter." The family was together

playing at Canterbury and probably other places on the Kent circuit in the summer of 1739.

The traces of our Mr Hamilton after 1739 are dim. He may have been that Hamilton who acted tertiary roles at Smock Alley in the 1750s, but we believe that actor to have been one of our Mr Hamilton's sons, either William or Myrton. (In *Thomas Sheridan of Smock-Alley* Esther Sheldon calls the actor at Dublin in the 1750s John Hamilton, husband of Mrs Esther Hamilton; but her husband does not seem to have performed.)

Our subject was no doubt the Mr Hamilton who acted Sir Walter Blunt in *Henry IV* at Edinburgh on 1 March 1749, when Sarah Hamilton was a member of that company. According to Winston in *The Theatric Tourist*, at various periods between 1735 and 1750 "Messrs. Lee, Hamilton, and others, from the Edinburgh Company," performed in a booth erected in the Castle Yard at Newcastle.

For information on Mr Hamilton's children, see the notice of his wife, Sarah Hamilton (fl. 1727–1776).

Hamilton, Mr [fl. 1775–1792], *actor.*

A Mr. Hamilton, or several different persons of that name, acted the female role of Mause in the occasional and traditional Scottish performances of *The Gentle Shepherd* at the Haymarket Theatre on 20 February 1775, 20 November 1775, 7 October 1776, 11 January and 8 March 1779, and 17 January 1780. On 22 October 1792, when Mause was played by Mrs Stichel, Mr Hamilton acted Patie. It is possible, but not likely, that some of these performances were given by William Hamilton (fl. 1735–1805?).

Hamilton, Mrs [fl. 1719], *actress. See* HAMILTON, MR. [fl. 1720].

Hamilton, Miss [fl. 1769], *dancer.*

A Miss Hamilton and Master Blurton, both apprentices to the dancing master Fishar, danced a double hornpipe at Covent Garden Theatre on 12 May 1769.

Hamilton, Miss [fl. 1769–1771], *actress.*

A Miss Hamilton, announced as a "Young Gentlewoman" making her first appearance on any stage, acted Desdemona in *Othello* at the Haymarket Theatre on 30 August 1769. That was her only role there that summer, but she returned a year later to act Serina in *The Orphan* on 22 August 1770 and Lavinia in *The Fair Penitent* on 1 September. No doubt she was the same Miss Hamilton who acted Palmira in *Mahomet* for her benefit at the Haymarket on 6 April 1771 and then played the same role one month later, on 6 May, at Covent Garden Theatre. She may have been the Miss Hamilton who was also a member of the Norwich company at that time; on 17 August 1771 it was recorded in the Minute Books of the Norwich Theatre that "Miss Hamilton be retained in the Company to the End of the Colchester Season ensuing."

Hamilton, Miss ₍*fl.* 1777₎, *actress.*

A Miss Hamilton acted Miss Biddy in *Miss in Her Teens* at Drury Lane Theatre on 13 May and 5 June 1777. Her name was entered in the account books for a salary of £2 per week.

Hamilton, Miss ₍*fl.* 1778–1780₎, *actress.*

A Miss Hamilton acted the role of Harriot in *The Students* at the Haymarket Theatre on 11 January 1779 and 17 January 1780, the same evenings on which a Mr Hamilton (fl. 1775–1792) acted Mause in *The Gentle Shepherd.*

Hamilton, ₍**Catherine?**₎ ₍*fl.* 1785?–1801?₎, *actress.*

A Miss Hamilton, announced as making her first appearance on that stage, acted Patty in *Inkle and Yarico* at the Crown Inn, Islington, on 16 January 1792. Perhaps she was the Miss Catherine Hamilton who had made her debut at the age of four at the Fishamble Street Theatre, Dublin, on 13 January 1785, and who, with her sister Maria Hamilton, had acted at Lincoln in August 1793. Miss Catherine Hamilton, Miss (Sophia?) Lyddal Hamilton, and Miss Maria Hamilton, all sisters, were members of a company headed by a Mr Hamilton at Manchester in the summer of 1789, at Derby in 1794, and at Coleshill in April 1801. They were not, it seems, the children of the actress Sarah Hamilton (née Lyddal) but were related to her through Myrton Hamilton, her brother-in-law, or through John or Marlbor-

ough Hamilton, her grandchildren and the sons of William Hamilton (fl. 1735–1805?).

Hamilton, Mrs Gilbert. *See* CROSS, MRS [JOHN CARTWRIGHT?].

Hamilton, Master J. *See* HAMILTON, JAMES.

Hamilton, James ₍*fl.* 1735–1746₎, *actor.*

As a little boy, James Hamilton made his first appearance when he and his brother William, advertised as the two Masters Hamilton, played Chimney Sweeps in the pantomime *Jupiter and Io* at Goodman's Fields Theatre on 25 January 1735. They were the children of Mrs Sarah Hamilton and her husband, who were also performing at that time at Goodman's Fields, which was managed by Henry Giffard, the brother-in-law of Mrs Hamilton. For information on the Hamiltons' other children and relations see Sarah Hamilton (fl. 1731–1776).

James Hamilton usually appeared with his brother, so their early careers were closely intertwined. Sometimes they were called Master J. and Master W., but often they were identified as Master Hamilton Sr and Master Hamilton Jr; we have arbitrarily designated the senior as James and junior as William. They appeared regularly as the Chimney Sweeps throughout the rest of the season, and on 9 April 1735 they sang the "Waterman's Song" from *Britannia* for their family benefit. The song was repeated on 2 May. In 1735–36 they reappeared several times in the same roles and song.

In 1736–37 the family moved to Lincoln's Inn Fields Theatre, where one of the children played Cupid in *King Arthur* on 28 September. They reappeared as Chimney Sweeps in *The Worm Doctor* on 9 October and were Ballad Singers in *The Beggar's Pantomime* on 31 December. One of them was Cupid again, this time in *Hymen's Triumph* on 1 February 1737, and on 2 April Master James played Squire Sapscull and Master William played Gaylove in a "Lilliputian" performance of *The Honest Yorkshireman.* The evening, which was for the family benefit, also featured "A Dialogue composed by Purcell and sung by the Masters Hamilton." They repeated the dialogue song several times throughout the remainder of the season.

When their mother was engaged at Drury Lane in 1737–38, the boys were found also at that theatre in Lilliputian performances of *The Burgomaster Trick'd* and *The Dragon of Wantley*. In the summer of 1739 the Masters Hamilton sang and acted in Hallam's booth at the Tottenham Court and Bartholomew fairs. Again at Drury Lane in 1738–39 they appeared in *Robin Goodfellow* and *The Burgomaster Trick'd*. With their parents and a sister, the Masters Hamilton were members of a company that played at Canterbury during the summer of 1739.

Presumably the Hamiltons were playing at Smock Alley Theatre, Dublin, in 1739–40, but after that season the activities of the family cannot be followed. As an adult, William acted in Dublin, London, and the provinces for some years. Myrton Hamilton, another brother, who was probably too young during the 1730s to be performing in London, became an actor and manager in Ireland. Little is known of James Hamilton after 1739. As an adult he played at Edinburgh in the summer of 1746, his known roles being Ragoue and the Second Shepherd in *The Amours of Harlequin and Columbine*. We have assumed that the Mr Hamilton who acted in Dublin between 1749 and 1758 was William, but this assumption is made without great confidence, and possibly that person was James. In any event, James was not mentioned along with his brothers in the will of his aunt Anna Giffard in 1776, so he was probably dead by that year.

Hamilton, Mrs John, Esther, earlier Mrs George Bland, later Mrs Sweeny   *d. 1787, actress, singer.*

Esther Hamilton's career on the London stage seems to have begun in 1741–42 at Covent Garden Theatre when, acting under her first-marriage name, Mrs Bland, she was noticed in the bills on 6 March 1742 as Trusty in *The Provok'd Husband*. She was at that time the wife of George Bland (d. 1753), who later acted in London in 1751–52, perhaps after performing for some years in the provinces. Esther, too, probably had provincial experience before coming to Covent Garden in the spring of 1742. She was not, however, born a Lyddal and a member of the Irish theatrical

family of that name, as Clark suggests in *The Irish Stage in the County Towns*. Clark has conflated her career with that of Sarah Hamilton (fl. 1727–1776), who was a Lyddal before her marriage to an actor named Hamilton about 1727. Esther, whose maiden name is unknown, did not become Mrs Hamilton until 1754, and her husband John Hamilton does not seem to have been an actor.

After her debut at Covent Garden as Trusty, Mrs Bland played Belinda in *The Fair Quaker* on 8 March 1742, Mrs Frail in *Love for Love* on 27 March, and Belinda again on 19 April. Continuing to be engaged at Covent Garden for another six seasons through 1747–48, Mrs Bland played numerous minor and supporting roles in a varied repertoire of comedy, farce, and tragedy but seldom enjoyed a part of major consequence. In 1742–43 her roles were Francisca in *Measure for Measure* and Belinda in *The Fair Quaker*; on 4 May 1743 she shared a benefit with Anderson, Miss Ferguson, and Mrs Le Brun, all minor performers. In the summer of 1743 she performed in Chapman and Hippisley's booth at Bartholomew Fair, one of her roles being Jenny in *The French Doctor Outwitted* on 23 August. Her return to Covent Garden in the autumn of 1743 brought no improvement in her fortunes. For in 1743–44 her name was in the bills again for Francisca and for Viletta in *She Wou'd and She Wou'd Not*. In the following season, 1744–45, however, her repertoire expanded greatly to include Juletta in *Measure for Measure*, Dula in *The Maid's Tragedy*, Wheedle in *The Miser*, Betty in *The Old Bachelor*, Mrs Centaure in *The Silent Woman*, Mrs Squeamish in *The Country Wife*, Lady Loverule in *The Devil to Pay*, Thais in *Timon of Athens*, the Queen of France in *Henry V*, Isabella in *The Conscious Lovers*, and Wishwell in *The Double Gallant*. In 1745–46 she added such roles as Camillo in *The Mistake*, Mrs Peachum in *The Beggar's Opera*, Chloris in *The Rehearsal*, Jacqueline in *The Royal Merchant*, Mrs Clearaccount in *The Twin Rivals*, and Helena in *Cymbeline*. Her salary for playing similar roles in 1746–47 was 15s. per week.

Mrs Bland's best moments during those early years came in June 1746, when David Garrick performed a series of his already famous roles in a special engagement at Covent Garden; she acted Regan in *King Lear* on 11 June, Lady Anne in *Richard III* on the sixteenth, Emilia in *Othello* on the twentieth, and Dorinda in *The Stratagem* on the twenty-third. During the remainder of the summer she was a member of the company which played at Richmond and Twickenham (where she returned in the summer of 1747).

After seven years at Covent Garden, Mrs Bland went to Dublin, first playing the summer season of 1748 at the Jacob's Wells Theatre, Bristol. She made her debut at Smock Alley on 7 November 1748 as Clarinda in *The Suspicious Husband*, a role she is not known to have played previously in London, her regular part in that play having been Lucetta. Under Thomas Sheridan's management new opportunities were available, and soon she became Smock Alley's leading actress, playing in her first ambitious season there some 28 roles, most of them of the first rank, including the Queen in *Hamlet* on 21 November 1748, Lady Townly in *The Provok'd Husband* on 27 November, Beatrice in *Much Ado about Nothing* on 5 December, Lady Macbeth on 12 December, Lady Brute in *The Provok'd Wife* on 23 December, Sylvia in *The Recruiting Officer* on 16 March 1749, and Millwood in *The London Merchant* on 12 April. In May of that season she acted Mrs Ford in *The Merry Wives of Windsor*, Dorinda in *The Stratagem*, Calista in *The Fair Penitent*, Sir Harry Wildair in *The Constant Couple*, and Cleopatra in *All for Love*, all for the first time.

In 1749–50 at Smock Alley, Mrs Bland added another 24 roles, which included Rosalind in *As You Like It*, Hermione in *The Distrest Mother*, Queen Elizabeth in *The Earl of Essex*, Alicia in *Jane Shore*, Portia in *Julius Caesar*, Constance in *King John*, Portia in *The Merchant of Venice*, Mrs Sullen in *The Stratagem*, and Epicoene in *The Silent Woman*. When *The Beggar's Opera* was played on 23 April 1750, Mrs Bland spoke a new prologue written especially for the occasion by Dr Clancy. After passing the summer of 1750 in London, she returned to Smock Alley in 1750–51 to play Belvidera in *Venice Preserv'd*, Phaedra in *Phaedra and Hippolitus*, Horatia in *The Roman Father*, Elvira in *The Spanish Fryar*, Monimia in *The Orphan*, and nine other new roles. When Mrs Delany saw her as Lady Macbeth on 9 November 1750, she found her "a very handsome clever woman, acts with spirit, but wants judgment." When Mrs Bland took her benefit on 8 March 1751

she apologized in the press for not being able to "wait on the Ladies in Person, her Time being wholly taken up in the Business of the Theatre." Never again would she enjoy such popularity as was attested by lines which appeared in the *Dublin Journal* of 15–19 January 1751: "But of real Perfection no Mortal e'er tired, / Bland is seen every Night, every Night is admired."

In 1751–52, Mrs Bland's fourth season at Smock Alley, Sheridan was persuaded to engage Peg Woffington at a salary of £400. Although the manager did not believe that she could be superior to Mrs Bland, Peg soon proved otherwise and began to play the leading female roles with enormous success. Mrs Bland soon found herself in secondary roles and allowed to appear in her former capital roles only when Mrs Woffington rested for a night. On 16 October 1751 Mrs Bland was replaced "by Desire" (by Mrs Woffington?) as Hermione in *The Distrest Mother* and was obliged to play Andromache. After being advertised for her usual role of the Queen in *Richard III* for 13 February 1752, she was again replaced "by Desire" by Mrs Woffington. Mrs Bland's other roles became Dol Common in *The Alchemist*, Lady Lurewell in *The Constant Couple*, Victoria in *The Fatal Marriage*, Harriet in *The Man of Mode*, Belinda in *The Old Bachelor*, Hellena in *The Rover*, and Leonora in *Sir Courtly Nice*. On 14 February 1752, however, she acted the leading role of Zara in *The Mourning Bride* for the first time.

Since Mrs Woffington was to be reengaged for a second season, Mrs Bland decided to leave Dublin at the end of the 1751–52 season. During the summer she negotiated with Garrick for an engagement at Drury Lane. On 17 August 1752 the manager wrote to his brother George Garrick that he would not pay her above £7 per week, an offer which Mrs Bland evidently accepted, but then refused. On 14 September 1752 the *General Advertiser* announced that she had arrived in London from Dublin and would soon appear at Covent Garden Theatre, where she had signed on with Rich at favorable terms. Her husband George Bland had played several nights at that theatre the previous season.

After an absence of four years Mrs Bland reappeared at Covent Garden on 25 September 1752 as Clarinda in *The Suspicious Husband*.

Richard Cross, the prompter at Drury Lane, which was dark that night, saw her performance and wrote in his diary: "Mrs Bland, (who first engag'd with us when she came from Ireland, but broke from it) plays this night Clarinda. Indiff[erent]." But it was clear, despite Cross's indifference, that Mrs Bland was now, at the least, a seasoned actress, able to command roles of a stature very much above those she had left in London four years before. She played Leonora in *The Revenge* on 29 September, Lady Brute in *The Provok'd Wife* on 4 October, Portia in *The Merchant of Venice* on 6 October and then followed with Sylvia in *The Recruiting Officer*, Lady Jane in *Lady Jane Gray*, Lady Townly in *The Provok'd Husband*, Jane Shore, Hermione, and Millimant, among others. The author of *The Present State of the Stage* (1753) wrote that "her Performances this Season Shew she had made the best Use of her Time in Ireland." Her figure was reported to be very agreeable. Although she was not without merit in tragedy, she was better and more spirited in comedy.

On 28 October 1753, soon after the new season began at Covent Garden, Mrs Bland's husband died. He had broken his leg when thrown from a horse two days earlier. He had been ill for some time, however, for when he made his will on 6 November 1752, a year before his death, he had described himself as weak in body. He left his estate to his wife. She proved the will at London on 13 December 1753.

The death of her husband did not prevent her from keeping on with a full season of work. She received high praise for her portrayal of Elizabeth in *The Earl of Essex* on 11 December 1753. Arthur Murphy stated in the *Gray's Inn Journal* for 15 December that "it is universally agreed . . . that Mrs Bland performs the queen with great spirit and with more resemblance to a personage of rank, than is commonly seen on the stage."

In the summer of 1754 Mrs Bland acted with the summer company at Jacob's Wells, Bristol. On 15 June 1754 she was married for the second time, at St Martin-in-the-Fields, to John Hamilton, an obscure figure who seems to have relied upon her income and at one time bilked her of £2000. When she returned to Covent Garden in the autumn of 1754 to play Lady Brumpton in *The Funeral* on 2 October,

her name was given in the bills as Mrs Hamilton, late Mrs Bland. When Arthur Murphy appeared as Othello on 18 October 1754, Mrs Hamilton acted Emilia and spoke the prologue he had written for his debut. The author of *A General View of the Stage* was very pleased with the dignity and spirit with which she continued to act Elizabeth and other roles.

Mrs Hamilton remained comfortably engaged at Covent Garden through the 1761–62 season. In 1757 she lived in York Buildings, Buckingham Street. At her benefit on 17 March 1760, when she played Biddy in *The Tender Husband* and Combrush in *The Honest Yorkshireman*, the receipts came to £246 11s. 6d. The following season, after returning from Ireland on 1 October 1761, she was entered on the paylist at £1 10s. per day. At her benefit on 25 March 1761 her proceeds were £211 19s., less £64 5s. in house charges. Her salary in 1761–62 was £272 for the season. A selected list of her regular roles during this second period at Covent Garden includes Bisarre in *The Inconstant*, the Widow in *Wit Without Money*, Angelica in *The Rover*, Millimant in *The Way of the World*, Indiana in *The Conscious Lovers*, Lady Sadlife in *The Double Gallant*, Flora in *The Country Lasses*, Andromache in *The Distrest Mother*, Roxana in *The Rival Queens*, Delphia in *The Prophetess*, Ann Lovely in *A Bold Stroke for a Wife*, "Veturia" in *Coriolanus*, Lady Graveairs in *The Careless Husband*, the Queen in *The Spanish Fryar*, Mrs Ford in *The Merry Wives of Windsor*, Lady Macbeth, the Queen in *Richard III*, and Hypolita in *She Wou'd and She Wou'd Not*.

As Mrs Hamilton felt secure in her long articles with Rich, she grew more quarrelsome and arrogant in personality as well as less attractive in person. Although she had been a handsome woman, somewhat inclined to portliness even in her earlier years, she became quite heavy and often allowed her hair to remain in disorder. In the *Dramatic Mirror* Gilliland related how Mrs Hamilton acquired the nick-name of "tripe." When she appeared on stage the night after she had refused to play for George Anne Bellamy's benefit night, the audience hissed, whereupon Mrs Hamilton, not one to avoid a good argument, challenged the public with "I suppose as how you hiss me because I did not play at Mrs. Bellamy's benefit. I would have performed, but she said as how my audience stunk, and were all *tripe people.*" The audience was won over to her, calling out "Well said, Tripe!"—a title which remained with her thereafter. The *Theatrical Examiner* of 1757 found that by then she was exhibiting a "little roughness" which did her no private advantage. Several years later, in the summer of 1759, when she acted in Edinburgh, a critic observed that she was then "overtaken by Age," but he reminded his readers of her "former Excellencies."

The *Rosciad of C–v—t G–rd–n* in 1762 still mustered praise for her acting, speaking of her "sprightly wit, and unaffected ease" and, in Lee's bombastic scenes, her "noble mein" as the injured queen:

The words thou utter'st 'vibrate in my ear,'
Freeze up my blood, and chill my soul with fear.
Nor less conspicuous does thy merit rise
When Comic-humour decks thy laughing eyes.
In ROSALIND, thy native arts excite,
At once, our admiration and delight.
. . . .
Yet with too great a force her spirits play,
And tear the actress from herself away;
Whilst artificial smiles, and strong grimace,
Contract her eye-brows, and distort her face;
She strips her humour of its native dress.

When John Rich died on 26 November 1761, the new manager, his son-in-law John Beard, found Mrs Hamilton intractable, displaying a vulgar asperity which frustrated Beard, who was led to believe her long-term contract with Rich could not be broken. But Mrs Hamilton overplayed her hand when she refused the role of Lady Wronglove in a projected revival of *The Lady's Last Stake* and remained adamant about her intentions to play Mrs Conquest, a role for which she was by then ill-suited. When threatened with a £20 fine by Beard, she told him that there was a clause in her articles with Rich which did not bind her agreement with future managers. This ploy, which she assumed would cow Beard into acquiesing for fear of losing her, instead gave him an opening to be rid of her, so at the end of 1761–62 she was discharged. Her last role at Covent Garden was Angelica in *Love for Love* on 21 May 1762.

Her arrogant folly in that case set off the misfortunes which followed the remainder of her rapidly declining career. She profited little

by her experience with Beard, for when she engaged with Arthur at the Bath Theatre in 1762–63 she continued in her troublesome ways, refusing parts to the point where she was again discharged. One dispute involved her determination to go on as Lady Townly despite the advertisements that Mrs Lee would play the role. The audience protested, expecting and wanting Mrs Lee, and a disturbance ensued. In order to forestall violence in the pit Mrs Lee persuaded the audience to allow her to decline Lady Townly; they suffered Mrs Hamilton to continue in the role.

Thereafter Mrs Hamilton went to play again at Smock Alley, then under Mossop's management, but audiences in Dublin were not impressed this time. She was ill-paid and ill-received. She found no favor except as Mrs Peachum, a role in which by her person and reputation she seemed comfortable. Her second husband, whom she had left behind in London to open a tearoom, died in the summer of 1763. The following summer she acquired a third husband, a Captain Sweeny whom she married perhaps at Kilkenny, although no record of the ceremony appears in the registers of that parish. At Edinburgh in 1765–66 she acted as Mrs Bland Hamilton but in the following season returned as Mrs Sweeny. By then, according to Dibdin in *The Annals of the Edinburgh Stage* (1888), she had "lost her voice, her looks, her teeth" and was "deformed in her person."

By 1771 she was reduced to acting with a pack of strollers at Malton, Yorkshire, playing the Nurse in *Romeo and Juliet*. There she was found in great distress by Tate Wilkinson. Sweeny, who had pawned her clothes, spoons, and other belongings as they traveled about, had left her. With compassion, Wilkinson engaged her for his York company, and she made her first appearance in that city in January 1772, when she was well received in her established role of Elizabeth in *The Earl of Essex*. But an accident to her false teeth while she was playing Lady Brumpton brought ridicule. Her last appearance at York was probably on 11 April 1772 as Mrs Heidelberg in *The Clandestine Marriage*.

Returning to London, a pitiful spectacle, she was treated kindly with charitable acts by former colleagues. On 4 December 1772 the treasury of Covent Garden Theatre made her a

gift of £21. Her dilemma spurred the establishment of the theatrical funds at both theatres, but it was too late for her to benefit from
them, for she was not at the time a member of
either company. Kitty Clive, comfortably retired at Strawberry Hill, wrote a typically un-
feeling letter on 6 October 1773 about the
poor woman, whose request for assistance she
had rejected:

Mrs Hamilton wrote me a very long melancholy
letter to tell me of her distress, that she was so poor
as to want a dinner and how do you think she
wanted to extricate herself by desiring me to go to
a strolling for her and act for her Benefit at Richmond; I don't believe there ever was an instance of
such a piece of assurance, I answered her letter and
told her she might with more propriety have asked
Mr Garrick to have played for her *there*, as he continued on the *stage and I had left*—notwithstanding
I am really sorry for her, this woman was but a few
years ago in possession of nine pounds a week, had
all the great characters both in comedy and tragedy
and chose to give up an article with five years to
come because she had quarrelled with Mr Beard. . . .

Probably Esther was the Mrs Hamilton who
acted at Birmingham in the summer of 1774
and at Edinburgh in 1775. In the latter city
she had a benefit on 20 May 1775, at which
time she was living on "Ramsay's Land back of
Theatre." In the summers of 1776, 1777, and
1781 she was playing at Richmond, Surrey,
and in 1778–79 she filled the roles of old
women at Bristol. It is most unlikely that she
was the Mrs Hamilton who was a member of
the theatre at Kingston, Jamaica, between
1779 and 1782.

To the credit of the Covent Garden management, Mrs Hamilton was allowed to share in
benefit tickets with minor performers and servants of the house on 19 May 1781, 10 May
1782, 29 May 1783, and 11 and 24 May
1784. Through the influence and generosity of
Mr and Mrs Thomas Hull, performers at Covent Garden, she lived out her last years as
dresser and wardrobe keeper at the Richmond
Theatre until her death there, according to
Fawcett's notebook, now at the Folger Library,
on 27 November 1787. Her death is not recorded in the Richmond parish registers. Despite her unhappy life, according to Wilkinson
she was never "guilty of the smallest dishonest,
or mean action."

Hamilton, Sarah, née Lyddal [fl.
1727–1776], *actress, singer, dancer.*

Sarah Hamilton was the daughter of the
Irish actors Mr and Mrs Lyddal who were performing at Smock Alley Theatre, Dublin, by
1716–17. Two of her sisters, Mary (Molly) and
Anna (Nancy) Marcella Lyddal, were also playing ingenue roles in the company by that time,
but there is no record of Sarah's professional
involvement by that date. Some confusion is
created by the fact that both of her sisters
became the wives of the actor Henry Giffard—
first Mary, who died about 1728, and then
Anna Marcella. Yet a third sister, Christian
name unknown, married the actor James Sterling and made her London debut, as Mrs Sterling, at Lincoln's Inn Fields on 2 October
1723. (Information on the sisters may be
found under their married names.)

It is unlikely that Sarah Lyddal was married
by 1719, so she was probably not the Mrs.
Hamilton who had a benefit at Lincoln's Inn
Fields on 6 May 1719, but that possibility
should be noted. By 1727–28, as Mrs Hamilton, Sarah was a member of the Smock Alley
Company with her husband. Her known roles
as a young actress with that theatre included
Betty in *Flora* on 27 April 1730, Isabella in
The Revenge on 21 May 1730, Prince Edward
in *Richard III* on 22 March 1731, Parisates in
The Rival Queens on 29 May 1731, and Lucy in
The Devil to Pay on 24 January 1732. Announced as from Dublin, she made her first
appearance at Goodman's Fields Theatre, then
under the management of her brother-in-law
Henry Giffard, on 4 October 1732 in the
sprightly role of Cherry in *The Stratagem*. Her
husband, who had been with her at Dublin in
the previous season, also made his debut at the
same theatre a week later, on 10 October
1732, as Whisper in *The Busy Body*. The Hamiltons were to enjoy a regular engagement at
Goodman's Fields for four seasons and in
1734–35 were to introduce their sons William
and James, as the Masters Hamilton, to the
London audience. The identification of Mrs
Hamilton as the former Sarah Lyddal is confirmed by the will of Anna Marcella Giffard,
dated some years later on 9 September 1776,
in which Sarah Hamilton was named as Anna's
sister and William and Morton (Myrton) Hamilton as Sarah's children. James Hamilton, not

named in the will, presumably was dead by 1776. Another child of Sarah Hamilton, named as a niece of Mrs Giffard, was identified as Henrietta Keasberry, the wife of the Bath manager, William Keasberry (1726–1797).

After her debut at Goodman's Fields as Cherry, Sarah acted Sylvia in *The Old Bachelor* on 6 October 1732 and Rose in *The Recruiting Officer* the following night. Her other roles during the 1732–33 season were numerous, suggesting extensive experience in Ireland, and included Elvira in *Love Makes a Man*, Jenny in *The Provok'd Husband*, Angelica in *The Constant Couple*, Ann in *A Bold Stroke for a Wife*, Prue in *Love for Love*, Wishwell in *The Double Gallant*, Hillaret in *The Mad Captain*, Edging in *The Careless Husband*, Zaida in *Scanderbeg*, Hoyden in *The Relapse*, Caelia in *The Mock Mason*, Lucia in *Cato*, and Phyllis in *The Conscious Lovers*. On 11 April 1733 Sarah shared a benefit with her husband and spoke the epilogue to *Richard III*, although neither of them acted that evening.

The Hamiltons remained busily employed at Goodman's Fields through 1735–36, during which period Sarah continued mostly in her line of ingenues, adding several of that type each season. In 1734–35 she began to play columbine, first appearing in the character on 11 October 1734 in *Britannia* and then a week later on 17 October in *Harlequin in the City*; she appeared similarly in *Jupiter and Io* and *The Chymical Counterfeits* in that season. From time to time more serious parts were hers: Lady Percy in *1 Henry IV*, Lady Macduff in *Macbeth*, and Ophelia in *Hamlet* (which she played for the first time on 16 September 1734). In August 1734 she performed at a booth operated by Hippisley, Bullock, and Hallam during Bartholomew Fair.

In 1736–37 the Hamiltons moved with Giffard to the larger theatre in Lincoln's Inn Fields, where she made her first appearance on 28 September 1736 as Philidel in *King Arthur*. That season she offered many of her familiar roles and also appeared regularly as Columbine Polly in *The Beggar's Pantomime*, Columbine in *Hymen's Triumph*, and Emmeline in *King Arthur*. When she and two of her children, the Masters Hamilton, took their benefit on 2 April 1737, they were living at Mrs Corey's, in Hemlock Court, Corey Street. When the Licensing Act forced the closing of the non-

patented theatres in 1737, the Hamiltons lost their regular London employment. Sometime during the year a daughter, Henrietta, was born. Mrs Hamilton secured occasional employment at Drury Lane Theatre during the second half of the 1737–38 season, making her first appearance there on 14 January 1738 as Eliza in *The Plain Dealer*, a role she is not known to have previously played. She repeated Eliza on 16 and 24 January and 6 February. Her only other performances at Drury Lane that season were as Peggy in *The King and the Miller of Mansfield* on 6 February and Belinda in *The Old Bachelor* on 16 May 1738 for her benefit, at which time she was lodging at Mr Strawberry's in Russell Court. Her husband, who had no London engagement that season or the next, had perhaps by now gone to perform in Dublin, temporarily leaving his family behind. During the summer of 1738 Mrs Hamilton acted several times at Covent Garden Theatre: Emilia in *Othello* on 27 June, Lady Wealthy in *The Gamester* on 30 June, and Philoten in *Marina* on 1 and 8 August.

Mrs Hamilton was absent from London during the first half of the 1738–39 season, but on 20 January 1739 she reappeared as Peggy in *The King and the Miller of Mansfield* at Drury Lane, where she made quite regular appearances throughout the balance of the season. Her children were with her at that time, but her husband was engaged at the Smock Alley Theatre. On 12 April 1739 it was announced in the *Dublin Journal* that Mrs Hamilton from Drury Lane and "her two sons" would be at the theatre in Smock Alley the following winter, "Mr Duval having agreed with Mr Hamilton, who is now here, and is to have a benefit 10 May next." In the summer of 1739, however, Mr and Mrs Hamilton were playing in Canterbury and probably in other towns on the Kent circuit. Performing with them were not only their two sons, Masters W. and J. Hamilton, who had appeared with them in London, but also a Miss Hamilton, no doubt their daughter, but certainly not Henrietta, who was then only two years old. Probably she was Catherine Hamilton, mentioned by Anna Giffard in her will of 1776 as her niece.

The Hamilton family presumably took up their engagement at Smock Alley in 1739–40. There is a lacuna in the records of their careers after that. Mr and Mrs Hamilton and their son William acted at the New Concert Hall, Canongate, in Edinburgh in February and March 1749. Sarah's roles there reflected her maturity and included Calista in *The Fair Penitent*, Belvidera in *Venice Preserv'd*, Lady Townly in *The Provok'd Husband*, and Marwood in *The Way of the World*. Though at Edinburgh in 1749–50, she seems to have acted rarely because of an obscure dispute she had with the singer Mrs Salomon. On 17 February 1750 she played Queen Elizabeth in *Richard III*. In 1750–51 she is known to have performed there as Captain Macheath in *The Beggar's Opera* and as Jane Shore. On 22 June 1751, she was given a benefit by some young gentlemen who, as they announced, did so "not so much for their own diversion as to help her in her present unhappy circumstances, having been left some time ago behind by the company, sick, and having part of her family to leave behind her should she follow them." Sarah continued to perform at Edinburgh through 1754–55. On 2 July 1752 she acted Monimia in *The Orphan* and on 24 November 1752 Lucy in *The Beggar's Opera*. With her daughter, Miss Hamilton, probably Catherine, she shared a benefit on 22 March 1754 when *The Rehearsal* was played, and on 10 March 1754 she was a Witch in *Macbeth*.

Sarah was still alive in 1776, when her sister Anna Giffard made her will. The Mrs Hamilton who acted in London between 1754 and 1762 was not she but Esther Hamilton (d. 1787) who earlier had been Mrs George Bland and later was Mrs Sweeney and seems not to have been related to Sarah.

Sarah Hamilton had at least five children, all of whom had stage careers. William Hamilton (fl. 1735–1805?) and James Hamilton (fl. 1735–1746) are entered separately in this dictionary. Catherine Hamilton may have been one of the Misses Hamilton who performed in London between 1769 and 1792. A third son, Myrton Hamilton (called Morton in Anna Giffard's will), evidently not old enough to perform with his brothers in London in the 1730s, had a busy career as an actor and manager in Ireland between 1750 and 1783. In October 1770, Myrton Hamilton married Miss Elizabeth Scott at Waterford. Sarah Hamilton's second known daughter was Henrietta (1737–1812) who also may have been one of the Misses Hamilton who later acted in London. She was married to the Bath manager William Keasberry (1726–1797) by 1776, the year in which her aunt Anna Giffard made her will. William Keasberry, who acted occasionally in London in the 1760s, died on 15 November 1797, and Henrietta died at Berkeley, near Glastonbury, on 15 June 1812, at the age of 75. Sarah Hamilton's known grandchildren included John and Marlborough Hamilton (sons of William Hamilton) and Julia Maria Keasberry (daughter of Henrietta and William Keasberry), who acted at Bath and married Nathaniel Peach at St James's in that city on 19 August 1784.

In the will of her sister Anna Giffard, dated 9 September 1776, Sarah Hamilton, then at least 65 years of age and evidently in ill health, was left among other bequests, clothes, linen, some furniture, silver coffee and tea services, a portrait of her mother (Mrs Lyddal), and a miniature of Mrs Sterling (her sister). After bequests to the members of the Hamilton and Keasberry families, Mrs Giffard left the balance of her personal estate at interest for the benefit of Sarah Hamilton for the rest of her life. The date of her death is not known.

Hamilton, W. *See* HAMILTON, WILLIAM. [fl. 1735–1805?], *actor*.

Hamilton, William [fl. 1735–1805?], *actor*.

Advertised with James as the two Masters Hamilton, William Hamilton made his first appearance, as a Chimney Sweep, in the pantomime *Jupiter and Io* at Goodman's Fields Theatre on 25 January 1735. They were children of the actors Mrs Sarah Hamilton and her husband, who were also performing at that time at Goodman's Fields. For information on the Hamiltons' other children and relations see the entry of Sarah Hamilton (fl. 1727–1776).

The childhood career of William Hamilton is related in the notice of his brother James Hamilton (fl. 1735–1746). After the Hamilton family left London in 1739, it is difficult to follow their traces for some years. William's father perhaps died early. Our subject was probably the grown-up W. Hamilton who acted at Edinburgh in 1748–49, and he was, we believe, the Hamilton who acted at Smock

Alley, Dublin, between 1749 and 1758, although the possibility should be noted that that person could have been his father or one of his brothers, James Hamilton or Myrton Hamilton.

At Smock Alley from 1749–50 through 1757–58, the Mr Hamilton whom we presume to have been William played about 55 roles in the repertory, almost all in a tertiary comic or pantomime line, including, for example: Sapscull in *The Honest Yorkshireman*, Jeremy in *The Amorous Widow*, Supple in *The Double Gallant*, Jeremy in *Love for Love*, Theodore in *Venice Preserv'd*, Gibbet in *The Stratagem*, characters in *Harlequin Ranger*, *The Statue*, and *The Necromancer*, Pantaloon in *The Lovers' Revels*, Sly in *The Cheats of Scapin*, Oxford in *Richard III*, a Witch in *Macbeth*, a Gravedigger in *Hamlet*, Seringe in *The Relapse*, and Squire Richard in *The Provok'd Husband*.

Hamilton returned to the London stage in a company which Spranger Barry brought to the King's Theatre in the summer of 1766; he played Roderigo in *Othello* on 8 August, Gregory in *Romeo and Juliet* on 18 August, the Gentleman Usher in *King Lear* on 25 August, and William in *As You Like It* on 13 September. In the summer of 1767 he returned to London, this time to join Foote's company at the Haymarket, but his only known roles were Coupée in *The Virgin Unmask'd* on 18 September and Roderigo three nights later. At the Haymarket with Foote in the summer of 1768 he acted Coupée, Dick in *Hob in the Well*, Cymon in *Damon and Phillida*, and Drawcansir in *The Rehearsal*.

On 4 November 1768 at Covent Garden, announced as making his first appearance on that stage, Hamilton performed Pistol in *Henry V*. It was his first engagement at a winter patent house since childhood. His other known roles at Covent Garden during 1768–69 were only Cymon in *Damon and Phillida* on 6 November and Hodge in *Love in a Village* on 7 January, but he probably filled some supernumerary roles, for on 12 May 1769 he received £28 17s. as his share of a joint benefit with Holtom, Quick, Fox, and Miss Besford. Within several days he was back with Foote at the Haymarket for the summer of 1769 in such roles as Peter Nettle in *The What D'ye Call It*, Sharp in *The Lying Valet*, Noodle in *Tom Thumb*, and the Poet in *The Author*.

Hamilton remained regularly engaged at Covent Garden in the winters through 1773–74 and at the Haymarket in the summers through 1773. His roles were his usual lot; in addition to many of those mentioned above they included a character in *Harlequin's Jubilee*, Grumio in *Catherine and Petruchio*, Sir Joseph in *The Old Bachelor*, Richard in *The Provok'd Husband*, Eolus in *Dido*, Laird in *A Trip to Portsmouth*, and Cash in *The Man of Business*, among others. According to the *Thespian Dictionary*, Hamilton had been originally cast as Tony Lumpkin in the first production of *She Stoops to Conquer*, which occurred at Covent Garden on 15 March 1773, "but through inattention and volatility lost the part," which was given to Quick. The role brought that actor into prominence. Hamilton was supposedly "shortly after discharged and became a provincial actor." The story about losing Tony Lumpkin may be true, but the fact is that Hamilton was again engaged at Covent Garden for 1773–74. He earned £28 12s. in tickets for a shared benefit on 16 May 1774, and his last performance there seems to have been as Richard in *The Provok'd Husband* two days later, on 18 May. At the end of the summer, on 21 September 1774, he acted an unspecified role in *The Duellist* at the Haymarket.

Between 1775 and 1777 Hamilton was acting at Edinburgh. He is known to have been in Ireland for his debut at the Mill Gate Theatre in Belfast (under the management of his brother Myrton) as Scrub in *The Beaux' Stratagem* on 5 March 1779. By 1779 William Hamilton was only about 50 years old, so it is possible that he lived into the nineteenth century. In 1805 the *Thespian Dictionary* wrote of him as "now superannuated (if still alive)." Perhaps he was the Hamilton who with Brett had a company which began a season at Manchester on 3 October 1788 that lasted several weeks. A Hamilton acted Banquo in *Macbeth* and Sir William Meadows in *Love in a Village* at Leigh on 11 February 1789, and a Hamilton played at Salisbury and Windsor in 1790 and 1791. It is possible, but unlikely, that William Hamilton was the actor who performed the roles of old men at Charleston, South Carolina, between February 1793 and April 1795.

In 1776 William Hamilton had inherited £200 from his aunt Anna Giffard. In her will two of William's children were named: John and Marlborough Hamilton, who each received £50. No mention was made of William's wife, who presumably was dead by now. It is not known whether or not William's sons became performers.

According to the *Thespian Dictionary*, William Hamilton was supported in his old age by a "small stipend" allowed him by his niece, Julia Maria Peach, the wife of the actor Nathaniel Peach. She was the daughter of William's sister Henrietta, who had married the manager of the Bath theatre, William Keasberry.

Hamilton, William *1751–1801, scene painter, portrait and historical painter.*

The painter William Hamilton was born in Chelsea in 1751, the son of William Hamilton, who was a Scotsman and an assistant to the architect Robert Adam. The younger Hamilton was sent by Adam to Rome to study under Antonio Zucchi, but he soon returned to become in 1769 a student at the Royal Academy, where his "King Edgar's First Interview with Elfrida" and three other works were exhibited in 1774. Between 1780 and 1792 he devoted himself primarily to painting portraits, many of theatrical people.

No doubt he was the "Mr Hammilton Painter" who was paid £16 16s. on 11 December 1781 for work done at Drury Lane Theatre. He was a scene painter at Covent Garden Theatre in 1790–91; his contributions included scenes with Richards, Carver, Hodgins, Pugh, Malton, and others for *The Picture of Paris, Taken in the Year 1790* on 20 December 1790. At the King's Theatre he designed scenes, which were painted by Walmsley, for the first performance in London of Bianchi's *Aci e Galatea* on 21 March 1795.

Most of Hamilton's career was spent outside the theatre as a portrait and historical painter of some reputation, working in his studio at No 63, Dean Street, Soho, from as early as 1782 until his death. In 1784 he became an associate of the Royal Academy and, in 1789, an academician. His work, all somewhat theatrical in style, included "The Woman of Samaria" and "The Queen of Sheba entertained at a Banquet by King Solomon" for Arundel Castle (the latter was exhibited at the Royal Academy in 1790 and was engraved by James

Caldwall); "Moses receiving the Law upon Mount Sinai" (1799) and "The Elevation of the Brazen Serpent in the Wilderness" (1801), both for Fonthill Abbey and both exhibited at the Royal Academy; and paintings for Boydell's *Shakespeare Gallery*. Hamilton also did small rural scenes and designs for Macklin's *Bible* and *British Poets*, Bowyer's *History of England*, and Du Roveray's editions of Milton's *Paradise Lost* and the poems of Gray and Goldsmith. Bartolozzi and P. W. Tomkins engraved his drawings for Thomson's *The Seasons* (1797). Hamilton received 500 guineas for decorating the panels of Lord Fitzgibbon's state carriage, which is now in the Victoria and Albert Museum, as are watercolors of his "Gleaners" and "Eve and the Serpent." A portrait of the Rev John Wesley (1789) is in the National Portrait Gallery; it was engraved by James Fittler.

Hamilton's paintings of theatrical persons include a full-length portrait of Mrs Siddons as Isabella, with Sarah's son Henry(?); an engraving by Caldwall was published in 1785, and another engraving by H. R. Cook was published as a plate to Oxberry's *New English Drama*, 1831. Two ink drawings by him of Mrs Siddons are in the British Museum. His watercolor of her as Jane Shore is in the Victoria and Albert Museum; an engraving by Leney was published as a plate to *Bell's British Theatre*, 1791; another engraving, by Houston, appeared in 1792; and a third, by Chapman, was published as a plate to *British Drama*, 1817. Hamilton also painted Mrs Siddons as Cleone, engraved by Thornthwaite for *Bell's British Theatre*, 1792; as Euphrasia in *The Grecian Daughter*, engraved by Caldwall, 1789; and as Matilda in *The Carmelite*, engraved by Thornthwaite for *Bell's British Theatre*, 1791. One of Hamilton's paintings of John Philip Kemble as Richard III is in the Victoria and Albert Museum; an engraving by F. Bartolozzi was published in 1794. Another painting of Kemble as Richard III was sold from the collection of the American Shakespeare Theatre for $400 at Sotheby Parke Bernet, New York, on 15 January 1976. His portrait of Kemble as Edward the Black Prince was engraved by Audinet for *Bell's British Library*, 1791.

Hamilton's 23 paintings of scenes for Boydell's *Shakespeare Gallery* are discussed by W. M. Merchant in *Shakespeare and the Artist* (1959). Among those surviving are:

Folger Shakespeare Library

Twelfth Night, painting by WILLIAM HAMILTON

1. "A Scene from *Love's Labour's Lost*." In Drury Lane Theatre, from the collection of Lord Dudley.

2. "Macbeth and the Witches." Attributed to Hamilton and possibly one of his Boydell works, this painting was sold from the collection of the American Shakespeare Theatre for $90 at Sotheby Parke Bernet, New York, on 15 January 1976.

3. "Isabella and Angelo" in *Measure for Measure*. Signed and dated 1793. In the Folger Shakespeare Library.

4. "Hero Rejected at the Altar" in *Much Ado about Nothing* (possibly after a painting by Francis Wheatley). Sold from the collection of the American Shakespeare Theatre for $175 at Sotheby Parke Bernet, New York, on 15 January 1976. A pen-and-ink with wash drawing of the same was also sold that day for $140.

5. "Hero fainting in Church" in *Much Ado about Nothing*. Signed and dated 1788. Sold at Christie's on 24 July 1953, from the collection of Lt Col W. Bromley Davenport. Another painting by Hamilton (after a painting by M. W. Peters) of "Beatrice, Ursula, and Hero" was sold from the collection of the American Shakespeare Theatre for $125 at Sotheby Parke Bernet, New York, on 15 January 1976.

6. "Richard the Second's Return from Ireland." In the Soane Museum.

7. "Romeo and Juliet: the First Meeting at the Ball." Sold from the collection of the American Shakespeare Theatre for $600 at Sotheby Parke Bernet, New York, on 15 January 1976.

8. "Miranda and Ferdinand" in *The Tempest*. Sold at Christie's on 4 August 1944.

9. "Olivia, Viola, and Maria" in *Twelfth Night*. In the Victoria and Albert Museum.

10. "Sir Toby, Sir Andrew, and Maria" in *Twelfth Night*. In the Folger Shakespeare Library.

11. "The Duke, Viola, Olivia, and the Priest" in *Twelfth Night*. In the National Theatre (from the Maugham bequest). An engraving by Bartolozzi was published in 1797. Hamilton's oil sketch for the painting is at the Yale Center for British Art.

12. "The Shepherd's Cot" in *The Winter's Tale*. In the collection of T. S. R. Boase.

13. "Leontes and Hermione" in *The Winter's Tale*. On loan to the Stone House Mental Hospital, Dartford, from the Guildhall Art Gallery, London.

14. "Leontes looking at the Statue of Hermione" in *The Winter's Tale*. Sold at Christie's on 24 July 1953, from the collection of Lt Col W. Bromley Davenport.

After several days with a fever, Hamilton died at his house in Dean Street, Soho, on 2 December 1801 and was buried in St Anne's Church, Soho. In his will, drawn on 30 November 1801, several days before his death, he left his property, effects, and funds to his wife, Mary, and his three minor children—Charles, Emily, and Henry Hamilton. To his father, William Hamilton, he left a picture of the Adelphi. To his friend Thomas Bell, of Dean Street, he left a gold watch and he named him a co-executor with Thomas Malton (the painter) and Edward Markham. On 7 December 1801 John Woodbridge of Swithin Lane swore to the authenticity of Hamilton's handwriting, and on 11 December the will was proved at London by Bell and Markham.

In his will Hamilton also left to his wife a drawing of himself done in crayons by Lawrence and either the oil painting of him done by Steward (Gilbert Stuart?) or that by Lawrence ("as she may choose"), and the oil painting she did not choose was to be given to Thomas Malton. The drawing by Lawrence, made about 1789, was offered with another drawing, by the artist, of Hamilton's wife (each 13" × 11") at Christie's on 6 May 1910 (lot 76). The location of Lawrence's oil painting is not known to us. Lawrence also painted a portrait of Mrs Hamilton, who in 1805 married John Charles Denham; that portrait is owned by Captain H. M. Denham of London. Hamilton appears in a group portrait of the "Royal Academicians assembled in their Council Chamber . . . in 1793," by H. Singleton, which belongs to the Royal Academy. The painting was engraved and published by C. Bestland, with a key plate, in 1802. A portrait of Hamilton drawn by George Dance, 1793, is at the Royal Academy.

Some of Hamilton's sketchbooks are in the Huntington Library and the Victoria and Albert Museum. A list of his illustrations for books is provided in his notice in *Book Illustrators in the Eighteenth Century*, edited by Hammelman and Boase (1975).

Hamlen, Mr *[fl. 1784]*, *actor.*

Mr Hamlen played Lorenzo in *The Spanish Fryar* at the Haymarket Theatre on 30 April 1784 for Delpini's benefit. Only one performance was given.

Hamlin. *See* HALPIN.

Hamm. *See also* HAM.

Hamm, Leonard *[fl. 1757]*, *actor.*

A Mr "Ham" acted Jaffeir in *Venice Preserv'd* at Drury Lane Theatre on 11 October 1757, when the prompter Cross wrote in his diary, "like a Gent: no voice, upon the whole bad." No other performances are known for this person. He was identified in the *Diary* of John Baker as Leonard Hamm.

Hammond, Mr *[fl. 1786]*, *actor.*

Mr Hammond played the Lord of the Manor in a musical spectacle called *Love from the Heart, A Trial of Skill for a Wife, or Theodore the Heart of a Lion* at Astley's Amphitheatre on 4 September 1786.

Hamoche, Mme *[fl. 1721–1722]*, *actress.*

Mme Hamoche was one of the actresses in the French troupe that performed at the Haymarket Theatre from 4 December 1721 to 10 April 1722. She shared a benefit with three others on 26 February 1722 when *The Unhappy Favorite; ou, Le Comte d'Essex* by Thomas Corneille was performed. No roles are known for her. She may have been related to the French actor Jean-Baptiste Hamoche (fl. 1710–1756).

Hamoir. *See also* HANYOURS.

Hamoir, Miss *[fl. 1765–1790]*, *dancer.*
See HAMOIR, JOHN.

Hamoir, John *d. 1805, dancer.*

A Mr Hamoir (sometimes Hamois, Armois, Amoire, Lamoire, or Armoy) danced with a Miss Hamoir in the London theatres during two periods, 1765 to 1776 and 1783 to 1796. Probably the same two artists were involved in both periods, but the interval of 11 years raises the possibility that there were two pairs. It is

likely that Mr Hamoir was the Hamoire who, as ballet master and dancer at the Variétés Amusantes in Paris, prepared the ballet pantomimes *Le Forgeron, La Place publique*, and *Les Jardiniers protégés par l'Armour* in 1780. At the same theatre he danced with his sister, Mlle Hamoire, in *Les Ruses villageoises* on 23 April 1781. His brother, Louis Hamoire, had been a director at the Variétés Amusantes in 1779.

The Hamoirs were dancing at Sadler's Wells by 1765. On 24 April 1766 he performed there with the elder Grimaldi, Tassoni, and others in the pantomime *Sorceress Dancing*. Miss Hamoir's name appeared in the bills as dancing with Grimaldi, Tassoni, and Duval on 13 May 1767. While continuing to perform at Sadler's Wells until 1776, Mr and Miss Hamoir appeared at the King's Theatre at least on one occasion, 25 November 1766. Their advertised debut at Drury Lane Theatre in a new comic dance, which was scheduled at the end of Act I of *The Merchant of Venice* on 5 November 1768, had to be postponed because Hamoir sprained his ankle at the morning rehearsal. He was sufficiently recovered on 1 December 1768 for them to make their delayed first appearance at Drury Lane in a new dance called *The Hunters*. Although their names did not appear in the bills again that season, perhaps they swelled the ensemble.

In 1769–70 the Hamoirs were performing at the Crow Street Theatre, Dublin. The Committee Books of the Norwich Theatre show on 17 August 1770 the management's interest in engaging them for the ensuing season, but the Hamoirs preferred London. They applied to return to Drury Lane, but on 30 August 1770 Garrick wrote to his brother George: "We can't engage *Armoir*, so pray tell them so: they were dancing Pigmies particularly ye Girl." They were taken on, however, by Covent Garden, making their first appearances on 10 October 1770 in a comic ballet called *The Countryman Metamorphosed*. Throughout that season and the next they appeared together in such pieces as *Mother Shipton, Harlequin Doctor Faustus*, and *The Refusal*. They also danced at Sadler's Wells in the summer through 1776.

After an absence of some seven years, during which time they were performing in Paris and other places on the Continent, Mr and Miss Hamoir returned to Drury Lane (announced as

from Brussels and as making their first appearance on that stage) in a comic dance on 4
December 1783. Their combined careers at
Drury Lane extended through 1786–87, in
which year they were on the paylist for a total
of £1 13s. 4d. per day for dancing in specialty
turns such as *The Sportsmen's Return* and appearing in the dancing choruses of *Harlequin Junior*
and other pantomimes. The *Morning Chronicle*
had reported on 22 September 1785 that Hamoir and his sister had settled as teachers of
dancing in Birmingham. After 1786–87,
Miss Hamoir's engagement at Drury Lane did
terminate, but her brother remained another
seven seasons, through 1793–94. In 1789–90
he was being paid £4 per week. That figure
was reduced to £3 in 1790–91. Both he and
Miss Hamoir appeared at the Royal Circus in
the summer of 1790.

Hamoir's last recorded London performances
occurred in *L'Heureux Naufrage*, a new ballet
"in the Scotch style," at the King's Theatre in
July 1796.

Hamoir had subscribed to the Drury Lane
Fund from 1784 onward. He died, according
to the Fund records (which also give his first
name as John), in November 1805.

Hamois. *See* HAMOIR.

Hamond, Mons [*fl.* 1749–1750], *actor.*

Monsieur Hamond was a member of the
French company led by Monnet which performed to noisy audiences at the Haymarket
Theatre in 1749–50. No parts are known for
Hamond, though he was listed as in the cast
of the troupe's first presentation, *Les Amants
réunis*, on 14 November 1749. He and his
fellow actor Mauly had contracted with Monnet for £301 8s. 9d., but the season was so
disastrous that Monnet wound up in debtors'
prison and the actors had to settle for £175 in
cash and £63 in notes for a total of £238.

Hampstead. *See* HEMSTED.

Hancock, Thomas [*fl.* 1661–1676], *actor.*

Downes the prompter listed Thomas Hancock as one of the early members of the King's
Company at the Vere Street Theatre. A manu-

script cast in a Folger Library copy of *The
Royall King*, dating about 1661–62, has Hancock down for the role of the Princess. The
boy-actor tradition was revived briefly at the
Restoration, and it may be that Hancock
played other female roles. It is also likely that
in 1661 he was still quite young.

Hancock was regularly cited in livery warrants and company lists in the Lord Chamberlain's accounts from as early as 30 May 1662,
though his name did not appear in printed
casts. A manuscript promptbook of *The Change
of Crownes*, which was presented at the Bridges
Street Theatre on 15 April 1667, shows that
Hancock played either Andrugio or Castru-
chio. Another promptbook, for Suckling's
Brennoralt, is at the Bodleian Library; the notes
date about 1673–1675 and suggest that Hancock may have played Stratheman. Hancock
had two small roles in *The Maides Revenge* about
1673–74.

On 8 June 1676 Hancock's name was canceled from the King's Company roster, and his
place was taken by Cardell Goodman.

Hand, [Thomas?] [*fl.* 1735–1738?], *doorkeeper.*

In 1735–36 at Covent Garden a Mr Hand
was paid 1s. 6d. nightly as the gallery office
doorkeeper. Perhaps the house servant in question was Thomas Hand, whose wife Mary was
buried at St Paul, Covent Garden, on 27 January 1738.

Handel, George Frideric 1685–1759, *composer, organist, harpsichordist, impresario.*

George Frideric Handel (for so he signed
himself after settling in England) was born in
Halle-on-Saal, Saxony, probably on 23 February 1685. He was christened Georg Friederich
Händel the following day at the church Zu
unser lieben Frauen. His father was George
Händel, valet to the Elector of Brandenburg
and barber surgeon, aged 63 years; his mother
was Dorothea Händel, née Taust, whose father
was the pastor of the church of St Bartholomew
in Giebichenstein. The pair had married on 23
April 1683. A first son was stillborn in 1684;
after George Friederich in 1685 came Dorothea Sophia on 6 October 1687 and Johanna
Christiana on 10 January 1690. The composer's father had been married once before,
and by his first wife he had had six children.

Handel's father intended a career in civil law for his son, despite the fact that the lad showed an inclination toward music. He was entered in a grammar school at the age of seven and, according to his earliest biographer, Mainwaring, contrived to teach himself music by secreting in a room at the top of the house a clavichord, which could not be heard by his parents when they were sleeping. That story sounds remarkably like the one told about Thomas Augustine Arne in the following century and should perhaps be discounted as a common tale. But the boy did learn music somehow and on a trip with his father to the court at Weissenfels was heard playing the chapel organ by the Duke, who persuaded the elder Handel to give his son some proper musical training. George Frideric was accordingly placed under the organist of the Liebfrauenkirche at Halle, Herr Zachau. From him he learned harmony, counterpoint, composition, organ, harpsichord, violin, and oboe. He was made to compose pieces each week, and from the period before 1696 have survived six sonatas for two oboes and bass.

Harvard Theatre Collection

GEORGE FRIDERIC HANDEL

engraving by J. Faber, Junior, after Hudson

Young Handel went to Berlin in 1696, after having spent three years taking music lessons from Zachau and attending the grammar school at the same time. In Berlin at the Brandenburg court he was briefly in the thick of much musical activity and met, according to Mainwaring, the composers Bononcini and Ariosti. Though the Elector wanted to send young Handel to Italy for further musical study, the elder Handel drew him home to Halle. George Handel died on 11 February 1697 (says Deutsch in his *Handel*, the invaluable chief source of factual information and translations used in this entry; *The Dictionary of National Biography* says the seventeenth). Though that would seem to have left the son free to leave Halle, he stayed on as assistant organist at the Halle Domkirche under Johann Christoph Leporin. A week after his father's death George Frideric wrote a mourning poem, signing himself "George Friedrich Händel, dedicated to the liberal arts." That might be taken as a kind of statement to his dead sire that the arts, not law, were to be his study; on 10 February 1702 Handel entered the University of Halle but not in a special faculty, and he may or may not have continued his study of law.

On 13 March 1702 Handel was appointed organist at the Domkirche in Halle succeeding the disgraced Leporin, who had been dismissed because of misconduct. For 50 thalers annually and lodging Handel was to be on hand to perform at services, look after the organ, "preintone the prescribed Psalms and Spiritual Songs," and, according to *The Dictionary of National Biography*, teach the pupils at the church school. Grove states that about that time Handel came to the attention of the composer Telemann. He also became acquainted with the musician Johann Mattheson, who sang first tenor at the Hamburg opera. Handel went to Hamburg in the spring of 1703 and met Mattheson in the organ loft of the Church of St Mary Madalene on 9 July. The two were introduced to the eminent Dietrich Buxtehude in Lübeck the following 17 August. Buxtehude was looking for someone to succeed him as organist of St Mary's, but a condition of his employment was that the successor should marry his daughter. Neither Handel nor Mattheson was willing, nor, two years later, was Johann Sebastian Bach, though Buxtehude in 1707 was able to snare Johann Christian Schiefferdecker.

At Hamburg Handel was employed first as a second violinist and later as a harpsichordist at the opera under Reinhard Keiser. While there he found an admirer in Prince Gian Gastone de' Medici, later Grand Duke of Tuscany, who visited Hamburg in late December 1703. George Frideric's first oratorio, the *Passion According to St John*, was given its first performance at Hamburg on 17 February 1704. It was not a work of much merit, but Handel was only 19 and just beginning his musical career.

The tuition of Cyril Wyche, the son of the British Resident at Hamburg, was given first to Handel and then to Mattheson, causing a temporary rift between the two musicians. At a performance of Mattheson's opera *Cleopatra* on 5 December 1704 the two quarreled over the playing of the continuo; Handel seems to have been shifted from second violin to harpsichord and refused to give up the keyboard position to Mattheson, who was to conduct the orchestra from that instrument. The squabble led to a duel outside the Theater beim Gänsemarkt in Hamburg, but, according to Mattheson's account, both escaped injury.

The quarrel was quickly made up, for the two dined on 30 December 1704 and then went to a rehearsal of Handel's first opera, *Almira*. The work was given its first performance on 8 January 1705 at Hamburg. *Almira*, which contained 42 German and 15 Italian airs, ran about 20 nights. The librettist of the work, Friedrich Christian Feustking, wrote in a pamphlet in 1705, "To censure Almira, which receives *approbation* from reasonable people as much for its verses as for the artistic music by Herr Hendel, and up to the present is honoured with such approbation, is a sign of *malicious* unreasonableness or unreasonable *malice*." The pair collaborated again on Handel's second opera, *Nero*, which was given its premiere at the Hamburg opera on 25 February 1705 but lasted only three nights. Mattheson made his last stage appearance singing in that work. Handel blamed the failure of the opera on Feustking's uninspiring verses; since the music has not survived, one cannot tell whether or not Handel's contribution was any better.

After *Nero* Handel left the opera house and turned to teaching for a living. Either Prince Gian Gastone de' Medici or his brother, Crown Prince Ferdinand of Tuscany, was responsible for persuading Handel to make a trip to Italy. Before he left Hamburg he completed two more operas, *Florinda* and *Dafne*, two parts of one large work, but they were not performed until later.

Handel was in Rome by the end of 1706 and on his way may have spent some time with his mother and sisters in Halle. He may then have visited Venice and Florence. In Italy, where Handel was referred to as *Il Sassone*, he was well received. The Valesio diary on 14 January 1707 noted that "A German has arrived in this city [Rome] who is an excellent player of the harpsichord and composer. Today he exhibited his prowess by playing the organ in the church of St. John [Lateran] to the admiration of everybody." Handel played regularly with the virtuoso musicians in the employ of Cardinal Ottoboni, and he continued composing, turning out psalm settings, the opera *Rodrigo*, a serenata, a cantata, and the oratorio *La Ressurezione*. The last was given its first performance, in Rome in April 1708. About May 1708 Handel went to Naples, where he remained for a year and then returned to Rome. His opera *Agrippina* was given 27 performances in Venice beginning 26 December 1709.

In the spring of 1710 Handel went to Hanover and on 16 June was appointed Kappelmeister to the Elector at a salary of 1000 thalers annually. He did not stay long in Hanover, for in the fall of 1710 he came to London, by way of Halle and Düsseldorf. On 6 December 1710 at the Queen's Theatre in the Haymarket a Handel aria, partly taken from his oratorio *La Resurrezione*, was introduced into a performance of *Pirro e Demetrio*. Handel's *Rinaldo*, one of his greatest works, was given a sumptuous production by Aaron Hill, manager of the Queen's Theatre, on 24 February 1711, with Handel conducting from the harpsichord. The opera's librettist, Giacomo Rossi, said in his address to the reader in the published libretto that "Mr. *Hendel* [was] the *Orpheus* of our century, and to my great wonder I saw an entire Opera put to music by that surprising genius, with the greatest degree of perfection, in only two weeks." The work was given 15 performances that season. The *Spectator* made much fun of the extravagant scenes and machines in the opera, but the audiences loved the display. The *castrato* Nicolini sang the title role, and in March he went to Dublin to perform in the opera.

In the summer of 1711 Handel returned to Hanover by way of Düsseldorf, where he was detained by the Elector Palatine. But he had found a home in England, was working to learn the language, and was destined to return there. From Hanover in late July 1711 he wrote (in French, which he preferred for correspondence) to Andreas Roner in London, mentioning that he had made some progress learning English. He was quite taken with the poems of John Hughes, he said, and, indeed, Handel's first settings of English words were to works by Hughes. The Elector of Hanover permitted Handel to come back to England in the fall of 1712.

He lived with a Mr Andrews of Barn Elms, Surrey, who also had a house in the City, and at some point Handel moved to Burlington House in Piccadilly, where he remained for three years. On 24 October 1712, according to Handel's own manuscript note, he completed the opera *Il pastor fido*; the work was performed at the Queen's Theatre on 22 November 1712. Among the Coke papers at Harvard is a document attributed to the opera impresario Heidegger which listed payments to several singers and to Handel, possibly in connection with *Il pastor fido*. Handel was to be paid £430. Critical comment on the work is scarce, but the *Opera Register* at the British Library contains a curt note: "ye Habits were old.—ye Opera short."

On 19 December 1712 Handel finished another opera, *Teseo*; it was first performed on 10 January 1713. Four days later the composer completed what came to be called the *Utrecht Te Deum*. That same day, when *Teseo* was given its second performance, the opera manager Owen Swiney, as the *Opera Register* put it, "brakes & runs away & leaves ye Singers unpaid ye Scenes & Habits also unpaid for. The Singers were in Some confusion but at last concluded to go on with ye operas on their own accounts, & divide ye Gain amongst them." When Swiney fled to Italy, Heidegger, who had been largely responsible for introducing Handel to London society and music circles, succeeded to the opera management.

On 6 February 1713 Handel's *Ode for the Birthday of Queen Anne* was performed at court. The following 16 May, when *Teseo* was given for Handel's benefit at the Queen's Theatre, Handel contributed some new songs and played a harpsichord piece; his receipts came to £73 10*s*. 11*d*. In another document among Vice Chamberlain Coke's papers, probably dating about the middle of 1713, Handel was listed as receiving £811, apparently for 1711 and 1712, and £430 for 1713. In addition to his comfortable income from the opera company, Handel was also granted an annual pension of £200 by Queen Anne.

Upon the death of the Queen on 1 August 1714, Handel's master, George, the Elector of Hanover, succeeded to the throne of England. Though Handel had not returned to Hanover as he had promised, George I was reconciled to the composer, perhaps in May 1715, and added another £200 yearly to Handel's pension. By the spring of 1716 Handel was wealthy enough to invest £500 in the South Sea Company. He followed the King to Hanover in July of that year, visited his family at Halle, and renewed his friendship with Johann Christoph Schmidt at Anspach. Schmidt and his four-year-old namesake son (familiar to the English later as John Christopher Smith) followed Handel back to London in late 1716.

On 17 July 1717 Handel's *Water Music* was performed for the entertainment of the King. The *Daily Courant* of 19 July described the occasion:

On Wednesday Evening, at about 8, the King took Water at Whitehall in an open Barge, wherein were also the Dutchess of Bolton, the Dutchess of Newcastle, the Countess of Godolphin, Madam Kilmanseck, and the Earl of Orkney. And went up the River towards Chelsea. Many other Barges with Persons of Quality attended, and so great a Number of Boats, that the whole River in a manner was cover'd; a City Company's Barge was employ'd for the Musick, wherein were 50 Instruments of all sorts, who play'd all the Way from Lambeth (while the Barges drove with the Tide without Rowing, as far as Chelsea) the finest Symphonies compos'd express for this Occasion, by Mr. Hendel; which his Majesty liked so well, that he caus'd it to be plaid over three times in going and returning. At Eleven his Majesty went a-shore at Chelsea, where a Supper was prepar'd, and then there was another very fine Consort of Musick, which lasted till 2; after which, his Majesty came again into his Barge, and return'd the same Way, the Musick continuing to play till he landed.

The entertainment was paid for by Baron Kielmansegg.

Handel left Burlington House in the summer of 1717 and stayed at Cannons as a composer for two years in the service of Lord Bridges, later the Duke of Chandos. By February 1719 Handel and others were laying plans for a new academy for the production of operas. The *Original Weekly Journal* on 21 February reported that "Mr. Hendel, a famous Master of Musick, is gone beyond Sea, by Order of his Majesty, to Collect a Company of the choicest Singers in Europe, for the Opera in the Hay-Market." That news turned out to be premature, for not until 14 May 1719 was Handel given specific orders concerning his recruiting trip for the new Royal Academy of Music:

Whereas His Majesty has been graciously Pleas'd to Grant Letters Patents to the Severall Lords and Gent. mention'd in the Annext List for the Encouragement of Operas for and during the Space of Twenty one Years, and Likewise as a further encouragement has been graciously Pleas'd to Grant a Thousand Pounds p.A. for the Promotion of this design, And also that the Chamberlain of his Ma^ts Household for the time being is to be always Governor of the said Company. I do by his Majestys Command Authorize and direct You forthwith to repair to Italy Germany or such other Place or Places as you shall think proper, there to make Contracts with such Singer or Singers as you shall judge fit to perform on the English Stage. And for so doing this shall be your Warrant Given under my hand and Seal this 14th day of May 1719 in the Fifth Year of his Ma^ts Reign.

To Mr Hendel Master
of Musick   Holles Newcastle.

Instructions to Mr Hendel

That Mr Hendel either by himself or such Correspondenc^s as he shall think fit procure proper Voices to Sing in the Opera.

The said Mr Hendel is impower'd to contract in the Name of the Patentees with those Voices to Sing in the Opera for one Year and no more.

That Mr Hendel engage Senezino as soon as possible to Serve the said Company and for as many Years as may be.

That in case Mr Hendel meet with an excellent Voice of the first rate he is to Acquaint the Govr and Company forthwith of it and upon what Terms he or She may be had.

That Mr Hendel from time to time Acquaint the Governor and Company with his proceedings, Send Copys of the Agreem^ts which he makes with these Singers and obey such further Instructions as the Governor and Company shall from time to time transmit unto him.

Holles Newcastle.

The 63 original subscribers to the Royal Academy of Music included some of the most prominent noblemen in England; the King provided an annuity of £1000. The joint stock was set at £10,000 but may have been oversubscribed by £5600.

In May 1719 Handel went to Düsseldorf and Halle, and in the summer he moved on to Dresden, where he was able to complete his mission. From Dresden in July he wrote—in French—to the Earl of Burlington that he was waiting to settle contractual arrangements with a number of Europe's best singers, among them the *castrato* Senesino and the tenor Berselli. In Dresden Handel also made agreements with the bass Giuseppe Maria Boschi, with Margherita Durastanti, and with Maddalena Salvai. On 30 November 1719 the Academy settled on Handel as Master of the Orchestra at an annual salary that Deutsch suggests may have been more than £800.

The Academy began its first opera season on 2 April 1720 with Porta's *Numitore*. The finances of the new organization, despite the subscriptions, were not stable; Steele in *The Theatre* compared the opera venture to the South Sea Company—both were doubtful investments. Yet Handel's *Radamisto* opened on 27 April 1720 to a huge crowd which included the King and his entourage.

Handel's reputation as a musician and a taskmaster was firmly established. He drove himself as hard as he drove those who worked under him. The Italian poet and librettist Paolo Rolli, who carried on a steady correspondence with the Modenese Representative in London, Abbate Giuseppe Riva, had a whole series of nicknames for Handel: "The Man," "The Alpine Proteus," "The Alpine Faun," but also "the Savage." Yet it was Handel who brought the Academy success, as Mainwaring suggested:

The academy being now firmly established, and Handel appointed Composer to it, all things went on prosperously for a course of . . . years. And this may justly be called the period of musical glory, whether we consider the performances or the performers, most certainly not to be surpassed, if equalled, in any age or country. . . .

The perfect authority which Handel maintained over the singers and the band, or rather the total subjection in which he held them, was of more consequence than can well be imagined. It was the chief means of preserving that order and decorum, that union and tranquillity, which seldom are found to subsist for any long continuance in musical Societies.

Though the Academy had some difficult years, it lasted through the 1727–28 season, and Handel's forceful discipline may well have been essential in giving it so long a life.

By early 1721 there was dissension within the Academy and a jealous rivalry between Handel and Bononcini. The factionalism was increased by the production of *Muzio Scevola*, for which three composers, Filippo Amadei, Bononcini, and Handel, undertook the composition of the first, second, and third acts respectively. When the work was first presented on 15 April 1721 Handel's act won the day, and that victory did not calm the troubled waters.

Francesca Cuzzoni sang Teofane in *Ottone* on 12 January 1723, beginning a fruitful association with Handel and providing Senesino with a prima donna worthy of him. The performances of Handel's new work attracted full houses, with tickets going for two and three guineas instead of the more usual half a guinea. Mons de Fabrice, writing to Count Flemming on 15 January, said, "it is like another Mississippi or South Sea Bubble. Over and above that, there exists two factions, the one supporting Hendell, the other Bononcini, the one for Cenesino and the other for Cussona. They are as much at loggerheads as the Whigs and Tories, and even on occasion sow dissension among the Directors." The Whigs did, in fact, support Bononcini and the Tories Handel. The factions supporting the singers were of a different sort and did not create a problem until Signora Cuzzoni's rival, Signora Faustina, came to London a few years later.

The bad publicity caused by the rivalries did not hurt business. Gay wrote to Swift on 3 February 1723 that

folks, that could not distinguish one tune from another, now daily dispute about the different styles of Handel, Bononcini, and Attilio [Ariosti]. People have now forgot Homer, and Virgil, and Caesar, or at least, they have lost their ranks; for, in London and Westminster, in all polite conversations, Senesino is daily voted to be the greatest man that ever lived.

The combination of Handel, Cuzzoni, and Senesino helped draw full houses to Handel's *Giulio Cesare* on 20 February 1724. It was his most successful opera up to that time.

In the 1720s Handel received attention in several poems. One of the longest and most amusing, *The Session of Musicians* (May 1724), may have concerned Senesino, though the focus is clearly on composers, and Handel must surely have been the hero. The opening sections of the work set the scene:

Folger Shakespeare Library

Title page, HANDEL's *Giulio Cesare*

Apollo (the God both of Musick and Wit)
To summon a Court did lately think fit;
No Poets were call'd, the God found, in vain
He hop'd, that a Bard should the Laurel obtain;
Since what was his Right he could not dispose
To one noted for Sense, in Metre or Prose;
The Laureat's Place to the Court he resign'd,
And the Bays for the best Musician design'd;
As o'er these Twin-Arts he's known to preside,
To Sounds he'd allow, what to Wit was deny'd.

The King's Theatre was used for the judging, and, one by one, the contenders for the crown came before Apollo: "majestick" Pepusch, "soft" Galliard, Ariosti, Corbett, "Merry" Loeillet, "Ill-fated" Roseingrave, Geminiani, Green, Croft, "well powder'd" Dieupart, Amadei, Haym, "grim" Bononcini, and others were all turned down by Apollo. Then

—*Fame's Trumpet, loud and vast,*
Fill'd the large Dome with one amazing Blast;
Straight were they freed from Sleep's lethargick Chains,
And captiv'd Life its Liberty regains;
The Goddess, ent'ring, shook the trembling Ground,
Her breathing Brass from Earth to Heav'n did sound;
One hand her Trumpet held with beauteous Grace,
The other led a Hero to his Place;
Whose art, more sure than Cupid's *bow gives Wounds,*
And makes the World submit to conqu'ring Sounds.
When he appeared,—not one but quits his claim,
And owns the Power of his superior Fame:
Since but one Phoenix *we can boast, he needs no Name.*
The God he view'd with a becoming Pride,
Determin'd not to beg, and easy if deny'd.
Him Phoebus *saw with Joy, and did allow,*
The Laurel only ought t' adorn his Brow;
For who so fit for universal Rule,
As he who best all Passions can controul?
So spoke the God—and all approv'd the Choice,
E'en Ignorance and Envy gave their Voice;
Who wisely judg'd, the Sentence did applaud,
And conscious Shame the poor Pretenders aw'd.

By 1724 Handel was living in a new house in Lower Brook Street, near Hanover Square. His *Tamerlano* began the sixth season of the Academy's opera offerings on 31 October 1724, and on 13 February 1725 came his very successful *Rodelinda*. The continuing rivalry between Handel and Bononcini was satirized

in John Byrom's *Epigram on the Feud between Handel and Bononcini* in May 1725:

Some say, compar'd to Bononcini,
That Mynheer Handel's but a Ninny;
Others aver, that he to Handel
Is scarcely fit to hold a Candle:
Strange all this Difference should be
'Twixt Tweedle-dum and Tweedle-dee!

(In Bononcini's entry, in the second volume of this dictionary, the epigram was said to have been written by Swift, an erroneous attribution by the editor of *The Works of Dr. Jonathan Swift*, 1754. But Swift's modern editor, Harold Williams, does not include the poem in the canon.)

In addition to his operas, Handel was, of course, regularly turning out other compositions: odes, anthems, concertos, arias used in sundry plays and ballad operas, and recitatives for operas by other composers. And his reputation on the Continent was growing with performances of his works in major European musical centers. One way Handel managed to be so prolific was by borrowing from himself and from other composers—his defenders have been hard put to justify his plagiarisms. He frequently revised his earlier works, such as *Ottone*, which he brought out in revised form on 8 February 1726. The *Universal Mercury* said, "Mr Handel had the Satisfaction of seeing an old Opera of his not only fill the House, which had not been done for a considerable time before, but People crowding so fast to it, that above 300 were turn'd away for want of room." On 5 May 1726 his new opera *Alessandro* opened with Signoras Cuzzoni and Faustina as well as Senesino in the cast. Each of these was paid £2000 yearly, and though they attracted crowds, their cost to the Academy and the feud that developed between the two women eventually brought about the Academy's downfall.

On 6 June 1727 the rivalry between Cuzzoni and Faustina—and between the factions supporting them—grew so hot, as the *British Journal* reported, that

a great Disturbance happened at the Opera, occasioned by the Partisans of the Two Celebrated Rival Ladies, Cuzzoni and Faustina. The Contention at first was only carried on by Hissing on one Side, and Clapping on the other; but proceeded at length to Catcalls, and other great Indecencies: And notwithstanding the Princess Caroline was present, no Regards were of Force to restrain the Rudenesses of the Opponents.

The rival ladies seem to have resorted to hair pulling before the fiasco was over. *The Contre Temps; or, Rival Queans* satirized the whole affair.

Despite the turmoil at the King's Theatre, Handel seems not to have broken the even tenor of his ways. On 20 February 1727 he had been granted British citizenship. For the coronation of George II on 11 October of that year Handel composed a coronation anthem, and for the King's birthday on 30 October he wrote some minuets. His *Ricardo Primo* opened at the King's Theatre on 11 November. Mrs Pendarves, writing to her sister Ann Granville on 25 November, said that she did not think the opera venture would survive much longer, which was a fair prophecy, but imminent bankruptcy for the Academy did not slow Handel. On 29 January 1728 Mrs Pendarves wrote again: "Yesterday I was at the rehearsal of the new opera composed by Handel [probably *Siroe*]: I like it extremely, but the taste of the town is so depraved, that nothing will be approved of but the burlesque. The Beggars' Opera entirely triumphs over the Italian one." Handel, despite his occasional interest in writing lighter pieces, was not much interested in the taste of the town. He opened his *Siroe* on 17 February 1728 and his *Tolomeo* on 30 April; in each he used the famous trio of singers, but the Academy went bankrupt at the end of the season, and the three "canary birds" left England.

Though the Academy failed, Handel prospered. On 4 June 1728, just after the Academy ended its final season, the composer bought £700 worth of South Sea annuities; he made similar purchases in July and then sold £1050 of his stock the following December. The December sale may have been to cover expenses of a continental trip. A letter from Rolli to Senesino dated only 21 December and possibly belonging to 1728 said, "The Man returned from his travels very full of Farinello and extremely loud in his praises." (Farinelli was an eminent *castrato*.) Rolli went on to gossip about affairs in London:

The parties of the two prima donnas here are still green-eyed and watchful; and each side wants to have its way, so much so that to put the Opera again on its feet, they have finally decided to have both ladies back. The Man, my good friend, did not want this, but as the ladies have two parties and my friend Senesino has only one, so on that matter there was no other answer but that Senesino must be the first singer. Cuzzona is in his favour, Faustina is for herself and for him besides, Senesino is for everybody. They were wondering about the Impresario but it appears that the Man refuses to undertake the task and I am of the opinion that the Academy will, because that Body is not yet dissolved.

Rolli wondered how Faustina would behave "if the dishonest Barbarian [Handel] turns the tables on her?" Handel did not, in the event, engage Farinelli, nor did he bring back to England Faustina and Cuzzoni.

In early 1729 the defunct Academy agreed to permit Handel and Heidegger to use the scenes and machines, costumes, instruments, and furniture at the King's Theatre for five years. Presumably the pair put up some money for the stock, but no details are known. We do know, however, that Handel and Heidegger each contributed £10,000 to the partnership and lost their entire investment. Under the new arrangement Handel was to receive £1000 for operas, whether they were of his composition or by other composers of his choosing. Handel went off to Venice, then to Hamburg, Hanover, and Halle, and on 29 June 1729 he returned to London, having recruited Bernachi, Riemschneider, Annibale Pio Fabri, and Signoras Merighi, Strada, Pio Fabri, and Bertolli. With that group Handel and Heidegger opened their opera season at the King's Theatre with Handel's *Lotario* on 2 December 1729. Mrs Pendarves was sadly disappointed, not only in the performance but in Handel's opera, which she thought was not up to his standard. Rolli went to the third performance and also found it a "very bad opera." Nevertheless, Henry Carey, one of the few composers in London who admitted Handel's genius, celebrated the maestro with "The Laurel-Grove" in his *Poems on Several Occasions* (1729):

Hail unexhausted Source of Harmony,
Thou glorious Chief of Phoebus' *tuneful Sons!*
In whom the Knowledge of all Magick Number,
Or Sound melodious does concentred dwell.
The Envy and the Wonder of Mankind
Must terminate, but never can thy Lays:

Fitzwilliam Museum, Cambridge

GEORGE FRIDERIC HANDEL, "The Charming Brute"

by Goupy

For when, absorb'd in Elemental Flame,
This World shall vanish, Music will exist:
Then thy sweet Strains, to native Skies returning,
Shall breathe in Songs of Seraphims and Angels,
Commixt and lost in Harmony Eternal,
That fills all Heaven!— — — — —

The new opera venture was not succeeding.
Rolli wrote to Riva on 12 June 1730 of the
"worthless operas" of Handel and Heidegger:

Because in truth they succeed no better than they
deserve. The musicians will be paid, and that is all
that can be done. I perceive besides that either there
will be no operas in the new season or there will be
the same Company, which is most certainly going
from bad to worse. Strada is liked by the very few
who wish to forget Cuzzona—as the rest of the
rhyme goes they are after all most similar: *I ask your*
pardon, Sir. With respect to my ears you were a
thousand times right, but as far as my eyes are
concerned, my dear *Signor Giuseppe*, you were a
thousand times wrong.

The King, according to the *Treasury Minute*
Book on 27 July 1730, allowed his usual £1000
to help discharge the opera managers' debts.

Good news came in August 1730, when it

was reported that Senesino was returning. *Scipione* was revived on 3 November with the *castrato* in the cast (the *Opera Register* said he "charm'd much"). But even if Handel's venture with Heidegger was not succeeding, Handel seems not to have been in serious financial trouble. He regularly helped charities, one of the early occasions being on 25 February 1731 at St Paul's, when his music was played for the benefit of the Sons of the Clergy, and £718 11s. 4d. was collected. He aided such worthy causes throughout his career. The first public performance of Handel's masque *Acis and Galatea*, a work given originally at Cannons privately in 1719, was performed for Rochetti's benefit at the Lincoln's Inn Fields Theatre on 26 March 1731.

In June 1731 Bononcini left England in disgrace. Viscount Percival recorded in his Diary on 31 August:

Bononcini . . . came in the late Queen's time for England, where for a while he reigned supreme over the commonwealth of music, and with justice for he is a very great man in all kinds of composition. At length came the more famous Hendel from Hanover, a man of the vastest genius and skill in music that perhaps has lived since Orpheus. The great variety of manner in his compositions, whether serious or brisk, whether for the Church or the stage or the chamber, and that agreeable mixture of styles that are in his works, that fire and spirit far surpassing his brother musicians, soon gave him the preference over Bononcini with the English. So that after some years' struggle to maintain his throne, Bononcini abdicated.

Bononcini's departure was hurried by a charge of plagiarism.

The year 1732 was a turning point in Handel's career. His *Ezio* was given its premiere at the King's Theatre on 15 January 1732 with Senesino in the title role, but the work did not draw well. *Sosarme* on 15 February met with more success. Then, at the Crown and Anchor Tavern in the Strand on 23 February, Handel's oratorio *Esther* was given a private performance. The following 2 May at the King's Theatre it received a command performance. Originally written at Cannons under the title *Haman and Mordecai*, the 1732 version contained revisions and additions and "no Action on the Stage," according to the *Daily Journal*. Handel's "oratory" did not take London by storm, but the composer had found a form

perfectly suited to his talent which in time became a favorite with the English. On 17 May his *Acis and Galatea* was presented at the new theatre in the Haymarket, "being the first time it ever was performed in a Theatrical Way." After that, though he did not give up composing Italian operas, Handel turned more and more of his energies toward the composition of oratorios in English.

Aaron Hill wrote to Handel on 5 December 1732 pleading for operas written to English texts. "I am of the opinion" he wrote, "that male and female voices may be found in this kingdom, capable of every thing, that is requisite; and I am sure, a species of dramatic Opera might be invented, that, by reconciling reason and dignity, with musick and fine machinery, would charm the *ear*, and hold fast the heart, together." In 1732–33 at the Haymarket Theatre and then at Lincoln's Inn Fields Thomas Augustine Arne began presenting English works in competition with the operas in Italian which Handel, despite Hill's urging, kept producing at the King's. *See and Seem Blind* (1732) commented on the new state of musical affairs:

. . . I left the *Italian* Opera, the House was so thin, and cross'd over the way to the *English* one, which was so full I was forc'd to croud in upon the Stage. . . .

This alarm'd H[ande]l, and out he brings an *Oratorio*, or Religious *Farce*, for the duce take me if I can make any other Construction of the Word, but he has made a very good *Farce* of it, and put near 4000 *l.* in his Pocket, of which I am very glad, for I love the Man for his Musick's sake.

This being a new Thing set the whole World a Madding; Han't you be at the *Oratorio*, says one? Oh! If you don't see the *Oratorio* you see nothing, says t'other; so away goes I to the *Oratorio*, where I saw indeed the finest Assembly of People I ever beheld in my Life, but, to my great Surprize, found this Sacred *Drama* a mere Consort, no Scenary, Dress or Action, so necessary to a *Drama*; but H————l, was plac'd in Pulpit, (I suppose they call that their Oratory), by him sate *Senesino, Strada, Bertolli,* and *Turner Robinson,* in their own Habits; before him stood sundry sweet Singers of this poor *Israel,* and *Strada* gave us a *Halleluiah* of Half an Hour long; *Senesino* and *Bertolli* made rare work with the *English* Tongue you would have sworn it had been *Welch*; I would have wish'd it *Italian,* that they might have sung with more ease to themselves, since, but for the Name of *English,* it might as well have been *Hebrew*.

We have likewise had two Operas, *Etius* [*Ezio*] and *Sosarmes*, the first most Masterly, the last most pleasing, and in my mind exceeding pretty: There are two *Duetto's* which Ravish me, and indeed the whole is vastly Genteel; (I am sorry I am so wicked) but I like one good Opera better than Twenty *Oratorio's*: Were they indeed to make a regular *Drama* of a good Scripture Story, and perform'd it with proper Decorations, which may be done with as much Preverence [*sic*] in proper Habits, as in their own common Apparell; (I am sure with more Grandeur and Solemnity, and at least equal Decency) then should I change my Mind, then would the Stage appear in its full Lustre, and Musick Answer its original Design.

Handel's staging of *Acis and Galatea* may have been an attempt to satisfy those who, like the above writer, wanted their stage spectacle; in time, however, he taught the English to take their oratorios unadorned.

Handel's opera *Orlando* opened at the King's Theatre on 27 January 1733. But the maestro was losing friends among the nobility, and many of his opera singers were turning against him, including Senesino. The Prince of Wales led a group that called itself the "Opera of the Nobility" and set up at Lincoln's Inn Fields in competition with Handel. They lured away from the King's Theatre some of Handel's singers and brought to London the famous *castrato* Farinelli. The Earl of Delawarr wrote to the Duke of Richmond in January 1733 describing the situation:

There is a Spirit got up against the Dominion of Mr. Handel, a subscription carry'd on, and Directors chosen, who have contracted with Senesino, and have sent for Cuzzoni, and Farinelli, it is hoped he will come as soon as the Carneval of Venice is over, if not sooner. The General Court gave power to contract with any Singer Except Strada, so that it is Thought Handel must fling up, which the Poor Count [Heidegger] will not be sorry for. There being no one but what declares as much for him, as against the Other, so that we have a Chance of seeing Operas once more on a good foot. Porpora is also sent for.

Though those plans were afoot to provide Handel with competition, the composer-impresario continued his activities as if there were nothing amiss. His *Utrecht Te Deum and Jubilate* was performed at St Paul's on 1 February 1733

for the Sons of the Clergy; two days later there was a repeat performance of *Orlando* at the King's Theatre ("extraordinary fine & magnificent" according to the *Opera Register*); on 10 February *Hooker's Weekly Miscellany* published an *Ode on Handel's Te Deum*; and on 17 March at the King's was given the first performance of Handel's oratorio *Deborah*, with Senesino as Sisera. Of the last the *Daily Advertiser* reported on 20 March:

An Entertainment, perhaps the most magnificent that has ever been exhibited on the English Theatre. . . . The Composition of the Musick is by no means inferior to the most finish'd of that Gentleman's Works; but the Disposition of the Performers was in a Taste beyond what has been attempted. There was a very great Number of Instruments by the best Hands, and such as would properly accompany three Organs. The Pit and Orchestre were cover'd as at an Assembly [i.e., a masquerade], and the whole House illuminated in a new and most beautiful manner.

Opposition to Handel (and Walpole) was expressed most vehemently in the *Craftsman* on 7 April 1733. Though signed "P———lo R———li" the satirical complaint could hardly have been written by Rolli:

The Rise and Progress of Mr. *H———l's* Power and Fortune are too well known for me now to relate. Let it suffice to say that He was grown so insolent upon the sudden and undeserved Increase of both, that He thought nothing ought to oppose his imperious and extravagant Will. He had, for some Time, govern'd the *Opera's*, and modell'd the *Orchestre*, without the least Controul. No Voices, no *Instruments* were admitted, but such as flatter'd his Ears, though they shock'd those of the Audience. *Wretched Scrapers* were put above the *best Hands* in the *Orchestre*. No Musick but *his own* was to be allowed, though every Body was weary of it; and he had the Impudence to assert, *that there was no Composer in* England *but Himself*. Even *Kings* and *Queens* were to be content with whatever low Characters he was pleased to assign them, as it was evident in the case of Signior *Montagnana*; who, though a King, is always obliged to act (except an angry, rumbling Song, or two) the most insignificant Part of the whole Drama. This Excess and Abuse of Power soon disgusted the Town; his Government grew odious; and his *Opera's* grew empty. However this Degree of Unpopularity and general Hatred, instead of humbling him, only made him more furious and desperate. He resolved to make one last Effort to establish his Power and Fortune by Force, since He found it now impossible to hope for it from the good Will of Mankind. In order to This, he form'd a *Plan*, without consulting any of his *Friends*, (if he has any) and declared that at a proper Season he wou'd communicate it to the Publick; assuring us, at the same Time, that it would be very much for the Advantage of the Publick in general, and his *Opera's* in particular. Some People suspect that he had settled it previously with the Signora *Strada del Po*, who is much in his Favour; but all, that I can advance with certainty, is, that He had concerted it with a *Brother of his own* [Heidegger], in whom he places a most undeserved Confidence. In this Brother of his, *Heat* and *Dullness* are miraculously united. The *former* prompts him to any Thing new and violent; while the *latter* hinders him from seeing any of the Inconveniences of it. As Mr. H——*l*'s Brother, he thought it was necessary he should be a *Musician* too, but all he could arrive at, after a very laborious Application for many Years, was a moderate Performance upon the *Jew's Trump*. He had, for some Time, play'd a *parte buffa abroad*, and had entangled his *Brother* in several troublesome and dangerous Engagements, in the Commissions he had given him to contract with *foreign Performers*; and from which (by the way) Mr. H——*l* did not disengage Himself with much Honour. Notwithstanding all these and many more Objections, Mr. H——*l*, by and with the Advice of *his Brother*, at last produces his *Project*; resolves to cram it down the Throats of the Town; prostitutes *great* and *aweful Names*, as the Patrons of it; and even does not scruple to insinuate that they are to be Sharers of the Profit. His *Scheme* set forth in Substance, that the late Decay of *Opera's* was owing to their *Cheapness*, and to the great *Frauds* committed by the *Doorkeepers*; that the *annual Subscribers* were a Parcel of *Rogues*, and made an ill Use of their Tickets by often *running* two into the Gallery, that to obviate these Abuses he had contrived a Thing, that was better than an *Opera*, call'd an *Oratorio*; to which none should be admitted, but by *printed Permits*, or Tickets of one Guinea each, which should be distributed out of *Warehouses of his own*, and by *Officers of his own naming*; which *Officers* would not so reasonably be supposed to cheat in the Collection of *Guineas*, as the *Doorkeepers* in the collection of *half Guineas*; and lastly, that as the very being of *Opera's* depended upon *Him singly*, it was just that the Profit arising from hence should be for his *own Benefit*. He added, indeed, one Condition, to varnish the whole a little; which was, that if any Person should think himself aggriev'd, and that the *Oratorio* was not worth the Price of the *Permit*, he should be at Liberty to appeal to *three Judges of Musick*, who should be oblig'd, within the Space of

seven Years at farthest, finally to determine the same; provided always that the said *Judges* should be of his Nomination, and known to like no other Musick but his.

The Absurdity, Extravagancy, and Opposition of this *Scheme* disgusted the whole Town. Many of the most constant Attenders of the *Opera's* resolved absolutely to renounce them, rather than go to them under such Exortion [*sic*] and Vexation. They exclaim'd against the *insolent and rapacious Projector of this Plan*. The King's old and sworn Servants of the two Theatres of *Drury-Lane* and *Covent-Garden* reap'd the Benefit of this general Discontent, and were resorted to in Crowds, by way of Opposition to the *Oratorio*. Even the fairest Breasts were fir'd with Indignation against this *new Imposition*. Assemblies, Cards, Tea, Coffee, and all other Female Batteries were vigorously employ'd to defeat the *Project*, and destroy the *Projector*. These joint Endeavours of all Ranks and Sexes succeeded so well, that the *Projector* had the Mortification to see but a very thin Audience in his *Oratorio*; and of about two hundred and sixty odd, that it consisted of, it was notorious that not ten paid for their *Permits*, but, on the contrary, had them given them, and Money into the Bargain, for coming to keep him in Countenance.

This Accident, they say, has thrown Him into a *deep Melancholy*, interrupted sometimes by *raving Fits*; in which he fancies he sees ten thousand *Opera* Devils coming to tear Him to Pieces; then He breaks out into frantick, incoherent Speeches; muttering *sturdy Beggars, Assassination*, &c. In these delirious Moments, he discovers a particular Aversion to the City. He calls them all a Parcel of *Rogues*, and asserts that the *honestest Trader among them deserves to be hang'd*—It is much question'd whether he will recover; at least, if he does, it is not doubted but He will seek for a Retreat in his *own Country* from the general Resentment of the Town.

Though the diatribe was a veiled attack on Walpole, the use of Handel and his musical venture indicates how strong the opposition had grown to him.

Karl Ludwig Freiherr von Pöllnitz wrote from London on 4 May 1733 that London had a splendid Italian opera and that "The Music of these Operas is generally composed by one *Hendel*, who is esteemed by a great many People beyond Expression, but others reckon him no extraordinary Man; and for my own Part, I think his Music not so affecting as 'tis elegant." That independent comment suggests that the *Craftsman*'s satire was not far from the mark. Indeed, by June Senesino had been dis-

Victoria and Albert Museum

GEORGE FRIDERIC HANDEL

statue by Roubiliac

charged by Handel, and when the fourth season of the Handel-Heidegger venture ended, only Signora Strada and a group of English singers remained faithful to Handel. The Italian virtuosi had gone over to the new Opera of the Nobility. The stubborn Handel did not, however, give up his scheme.

Handel was offered an honorary doctorate by Oxford University, but for some reason he turned it down. In July 1733, however, he did go to Oxford with a company of musicians for performances of a number of his works including, on 10 July, his new oratorio *Athalia*. Hearne in his *Diary* said that "'twas computed, that Mr Handel cleared by his Musick at Oxford upwards of 2000 *l*." Much of that sum must have gone toward the payment of expenses, of course. Hearne did not think

much of the Handelian performances at Oxford, though the reports indicate they were
well attended.

Antoine François Prévost was impressed
with Handel and with the idea that Oxford
should encourage the arts through the offering
of honorary degrees to such a person. Handel,
he wrote in *Le Pour et contre*,

has lived in London a long time now; few winters
pass without seeing some admirable work appear
from his pen. Never has perfection in any art been
combined in the same man with such fertility of
production. Every *opera*, every *concerto*, and so on,
is a masterpiece. Recently he has introduced to
London a new kind of composition which goes under the name of *Oratorio*. Although the subject is
taken from Scripture, the audiences are no smaller
than at the Opera. He is master of all the styles:
the sublime, the tender, the gay, the graceful. Some
critics however accuse him of having borrowed the
matter of many beautiful things from Lully, especially from our French Cantatas, which he has the
skill, so they say, to disguise in the Italian style.
But the crime would be venial, were it even certain;
and besides it will be agreed that, [considering] the
multitude of works that Mr. Handel has composed,
it is extremely difficult for there not to be occasionally coincidences with other composers' works.

Prévost attributed to modesty Handel's refusal
of the doctorate.

Handel opened the 1733–34 opera season at
the King's Theatre on 30 October 1733. A
month later the Opera of the Nobility began
their season at the old Lincoln's Inn Fields
playhouse, with Nicola Porpora as the company's composer and conductor. On 26 January
1734 Handel's *Arianna in Creta* came out, in
opposition to Porpora's *Ariadne in Naxus* at the
other house. As might have been expected, the
rivalry inspired satirical comments, including
a pamphlet titled *Harmony in an Uproar*, dated
12 February 1734 and signed "Hurlothrumbo
Johnson"—though probably not written by
Samuel Johnson of Cheshire, the author of
Hurlothrumbo. For a change, the pamphlet accused Handel of bewitching London audiences
with his enchanting music, giving them "good
Musick and sound Harmony, when we wanted
and desir'd bad," and "pleasing us, whether we
would or no."

Handel in the midst of warring factions is
the usual picture. Only occasionally do docu-

ments that have survived from his time show
Handel at ease. One, however, a letter from
Mrs Pendarves to Ann Granville, dated 12
April 1734, gives us a glimpse of the private
man. Mrs Pendarves held a "little entertainment of music" at her house for several friends,
including Handel and Signora Strada. "I never
was so *well* entertained at *an opera*!" she wrote.
"Mr. Handel was in the best humour in the
world, and played lessons and accompanied
Strada and all the ladies that sang from seven
o'the clock till eleven." One would like to
think that Handel enjoyed many such occasions.

On 6 July 1734 Handel's agreement with
Heidegger ended, and on the fifteenth their
opera season at the King's Theatre concluded.
Prévost reported on the failure of the venture:

Mr. Handel, director of one of the two London
operas, had undertaken to keep his theatre going in
face of the opposition of all the English nobility.
He flattered himself—unjustifiably—that his reputation would always bring him a sufficient audience; but deprived of this support, he has incurred
so much ruinous expense and [written] so many
beautiful operas that were a total loss, that he finds
himself obliged to leave London and return to his
native land.

That rumor was not true. Heidegger rented
the King's Theatre to the rival Opera of the
Nobility, and Handel, in a rather unexpected
switch, entered into an agreement with John
Rich, the purveyor of pantomimes at Covent
Garden Theatre, to perform operas there in
1734–35. The King, apparently out of sympathy for Handel's financial distress, directed
that the annual bounty of £1000 for operas
should be paid not to the Lincoln's Inn Fields
company but to Handel. Thereafter, however,
the bounty went to the opera company,
whether Handel was connected with it or not.
For *Il pastor fido* at Covent Garden on 9 November 1734 Handel engaged John Beard, a tenor
who was to become Handel's chief oratorio
singer in the years that followed. (Grove is
incorrect in stating that Handel opened at Lincoln's Inn Fields on 5 October 1734.)

Though Handel was deeply engrossed in
opera and oratorio productions, he regularly
published musical works of all sorts. The
Craftsman of 7 December 1734 carried an ad-

vertisement for a new and larger-than-usual collection that was typically varied

MUSICK,
This Day Published,
Compos'd by Mr. *Handel*,

I. A fourth Volume of Apollo's Feast: Or, the Harmony of the Opera Stage. Being a well chosen Collection of all the favourite and most celebrated Songs out of his late Opera's, with their Symphonies for Voices and Instruments. Engraven in a fair Character.—N.B. In this and the 1st, 2d and 3d Volumes are contain'd the most favourite Songs out of all the Opera's.
Also by the same Author,
II. Six Concerto's for Violins, &c. in seven Parts. Opera terza.
III. Six Sonata's or Trio's for two German Flutes or Violins, and a Bass. Opera seconda.
IV. Twelve Solo's for a Violin, German Flute or Harpsichord. Opera Prima.
V. Thirty Overtures for Violins, &c. in seven Parts.—N.B. The same Overtures are set for the Harpsichord.
VI. The Water Musick and six French Horn Songs. In seven Parts.
VII. The most celebrated Airs out of all the Opera's fitted for a German Flute, Violin and Harpsichord. In 12 Collections.
VIII. Nineteen Operas compleat. Printed in Score.
IX. Esther, an Oratorio, and the Mask of Acis and Galatea.
X. The Te Deum and Jubilate, as performed at St. Paul's.
XI. Two Books of celebrated Lessons for the Harpsichord.
All compos'd by Mr. *Handel*, and
Printed for John Walsh, at the Harp and Hoboy in Catherine-street in the Strand.

Handel's new opera *Ariodante* opened at Covent Garden on 8 January 1735, with special dance music written for the celebrated Mlle Sallé. In March *Esther* was revived "With several New Additional Songs; likewise two new Concerto's on the Organ" played by Handel. The concertos, Mrs Pendarves declared, were the finest things she had ever heard, yet Handel was not drawing a crowd. The *Old Whig* on 20 March gave a glowing report of the success of Farinelli at the King's Theatre but said

Handel, whose excellent Compositions have often pleased our Ears, and touched our Hearts, has this Winter sometimes performed to an almost empty Pitt. He has lately reviv'd his fine *Oratorio* of Esther,

in which he has introduced two Concerto's on the Organ that are inimitable. But so strong is the Disgust taken against him, that even this has been far from bringing him crowded Audiences; tho' there were no other publick Entertainments on those Evenings. His Loss is computed for these two Seasons at a great Sum.

There was precious little sympathy for the man. A letter dated 27 December 1734, probably written to Catherine Collingwood, may well have been typical of the sentiment toward him: "I don't pity Handell in the least, for I hope this mortification will make him a human creature; for I am sure before he was no better than a brute, when he could treat civilized people with so much brutality as I know he has done." Handel's venture at Covent Garden lost £9000 in two seasons (the rival opera at the King's lost £10,000).

Still Handel went on. His *Alcina* was well received in the spring of 1735; his setting of *Alexander's Feast* was given its first performance at Covent Garden on 19 February 1736 (Grove is incorrect in saying that John Beard made his first appearance in it); and Handel's *Atalanta* opened on 12 May 1736. Benjamin Victor wrote to Matthew Dubourg in Dublin that

The two opera houses are, neither of them, in a successful way; and it is the confirmed opinion that this winter will compleat your friend *Handel*'s destruction, as far as the loss of money can destroy him. . . . As to the Operas, they must tumble, for the King's presence could hardly hold them up, and even that prop is denied them, for his majesty will not admit his royal ears to be tickled this season.

The voice of doom had been heard before; Handel remained deaf to it, and the rival opera ventures went on in 1736–37.

Arminio, Giustino, and *Berenice* all came out in the spring of 1737, during which time Handel was struck with rheumatism and a paralytic disorder which affected his right arm and prevented him during part of the season from performing. The *Daily Post* on 30 April reported that he was sufficiently improved that "it is hoped he will be able to accompany the opera of Justin on Wednesday next" before the King and Queen. The rival Opera of the Nobility, unable to outlast the dogged Handel, came to an end on 11 June 1737; the singer Farinelli, who unfortunately never sang for Handel, left England, never to return.

For his health Handel went in September 1737 to take the waters at Aix-la-Chapelle, whence he returned to London in late October or early November. Heidegger reached a new agreement with Handel—the composer was to serve as music director—and opened an opera season at the King's Theatre with *Arsace* on 29 October 1737. Much improved from his continental trip, Handel set to work on a new opera, *Faramondo*, and upon the death of Queen Caroline on 20 November, he composed a funeral anthem. On 26 December he began his opera *Serse*. When *Faramondo* opened on 3 January 1738, according to a London newspaper clipping dated the following day and reported by Deutsch, "It being the first Time of Mr Handel's Appearance this Season, he was honour'd with extraordinary and repeated Signs of Approbation." He doubtless conducted from the harpsichord. London audiences seem to have been willing to accept Handel as long as he was not in competition with someone else. When on 28 March 1738 at the King's Theatre he produced "An Oratorio," the *Evening Post* reckoned "Mr Handel cou'd not get less that Night than 1500*l.*" The Earl of Egmont in his *Diary* estimated the audience at close to 1300 "besides the gallery and upper gallery." Yet the 1737–38 season at the King's was not successful enough to bring a full subscription for the ensuing season, and Heidegger was forced to give up the undertaking and return subscribers' money. Handel was not deterred in the least; he decided to lease the King's Theatre from Heidegger and present the 1738–39 season himself.

Charles Jennens wrote to Lord Guernsey on 19 September 1738, telling him of some of Handel's latest interests (Jennens was one of Handel's librettists):

Mr. Handel's head is more full of maggots than ever. I found yesterday in his room a very queer instrument which he calls carillon (Anglice, a bell) and says some call it a Tubalcain, I suppose because it is both in the make and tone like a set of Hammers striking upon anvils. 'Tis played upon with keys like a Harpsichord and with this Cyclopean instrument he designs to make poor Saul [in the oratorio he was just finishing] stark mad. His second maggot is an organ of £500 price which (because he is overstocked with money) he has bespoke of one Moss of Barnet. This organ, he says, is so constructed that as he sits at it he has a better command of his performers than he used to have, and he is highly delighted to think with what exactness his Oratorio will be performed by the help of this organ; so that for the future instead of beating time at his oratorios, he is to sit at the organ all the time with his back to the Audience. His third maggot is a Hallelujah which he has trump'd up at the end of his oratorio [*Saul*] since I went to the Country, because he thought the conclusion of the oratorio not Grand enough; tho' if that were the case 'twas his own fault, for the words would have bore as Grand Musick as he could have set 'em to: but this Hallelujah, Grand as it is, comes in very nonsensically, having no manner of relation to what goes before. And this is the more extraordinary, because he refused to set a Hallelujah at the end of the first Chorus in the Oratorio, where I had placed one and where it was to be introduced with the utmost propriety, upon a pretence that it would make the entertainment too long. I could tell you more of his maggots: but it grows late and I must defer the rest till I write next, by which time, I doubt not, more new ones will breed in his Brain.

Handel finally followed Jennens's advice on the placement of the Hallelujah in *Saul*.

Handel's 1738–39 season at the King's consisted of only 12 performances, mostly on Tuesdays, beginning with *Saul* on 16 January 1739. *Israel in Egypt* opened on 4 April. To that spring also belong Handel's gorgeous *concerti grossi*. As one would expect, when the Royal Society of Musicians was formed on 28 August 1739, Handel was one of the original subscribers.

In November 1739 Handel hired the Lincoln's Inn Fields Theatre from John Rich for performances of *Alexander's Feast* and his new *Ode for St Cecilia's Day*. *Acis and Galatea* was also revived, and in February 1740 *L'Allegro, il Penseroso, ed il Moderato* was performed, along with some new concertos. *Saul* and *Esther* were revived in March and *Israel in Egypt* in April. Twelve violin concertos, later called Opus 6, were published in April, and seven sonatas for two violins or German flutes also came out about that time. Dr Burney wrote:

Handel's activity and spirit of enterprize at this time, in his fifty-sixth year, were truly wonderful! opposed and oppressed by the most powerful nobles and gentry of the kingdom! suffering with bodily and mental disease! with rivals innumerable; when a Spanish war was just broke out, which occupied the minds, and absorbed the thoughts of the whole nation! Amidst all these accumulated misfortunes and impediments, he composed his twelve grand concertos, and Dryden's second ode; brought out Saul; Israel in Egypt; Jupiter in Argos; published seven sonatas; and revived *Il Trionfo del Tempo*; Acis and Galatea; and Alexander's Feast! And yet this seems to have been one of the most idle years of his public life.

Handel's last opera, *Deidamia*, was given at Lincoln's Inn Fields on 10 January 1741. That season Heidegger, with a superior group of singers at the King's Theatre, worked in opposition to Handel. After the third and last performance of *Deidamia*, on 10 February, Handel left the opera stage. His latest operas had not succeeded, and he had not composed a new oratorio since 1738. Estranged from his London public, Handel may have contemplated leaving England, as an anonymous letter in the *Daily Post* on 4 April 1741 hinted. But in August and September of that year, with his usual speed, he composed the *Messiah*; on 29 October, he completed the oratorio *Samson*. Then, at the invitation of the Lord Lieutenant of Ireland, Handel went to Dublin.

His trip took him first to Chester, where the young Charles Burney saw the great man "smoke a pipe over a dish of coffee at the Exchange Coffee-House. . . ." Handel wanted to try out some of the choruses he planned to offer Dublin audiences, so he applied to Burney's first music master, Mr Baker. Baker introduced Handel to a bass singer named Jansen, but "poor Jansen, after repeated attempts, failed so egregiously that Handel let loose his great bear upon him, and after swearing in four or five different languages, cried out in broken English, 'You scoundrel, did you not tell me that you could sing at sight?' 'Yes sir,' says [Jansen], 'and so I can, but not at first sight.'"

Handel arrived in Dublin on 18 November for a season of his oratorios and other works. He lived in Abbey Street while he was there, and most of his performances took place at the Music Hall in Fishamble Street. The premiere of the *Messiah* was on 13 April 1742, with the celebrated Mrs Cibber singing mezzo-soprano. The event was described in *Faulkner's Dublin Journal* four days later:

On Tuesday last Mr. Handel's Sacred Grand Oratorio, the MESSIAH, was performed at the New Musick-Hall in Fishamble-street; the best Judges allowed it to be the most finished piece of Musick. Words are wanting to express the exquisite Delight it afforded to the admiring crouded Audience. The Sublime, the Grand, and the Tender, adapted to the most elevated, majestick and moving Words, conspired to transport and charm the ravished Heart and Ear. It is but Justice to Mr. Handel, that the World should know, he generously gave the Money arising from this Grand Performance, to be equally shared by the Society for relieving Prisoners, the Charitable Infirmary, and Mercer's Hospital, for which they will ever gratefully remember his Name. . . . There were about 700 People in the Room, and the Sum collected for that Noble and Pious Charity amounted to about 400 *l.* . . .

The normal capacity of the hall was 600. In addition to the Handelian performances in the spring and summer of 1742, Dubliners were treated to a series of presentations by Thomas Augustine Arne, and David Garrick acted at the Smock Alley Theatre.

By the end of August 1742 Handel was back in London. *Samson* was presented at Covent Garden on 18 February 1743, with Beard, Savage, Reinhold, Lowe, and Mesdames Cibber and Clive, and was a good success. Horace Walpole wrote wittily to Horace Mann on 24 February:

Handel has set up an Oratorio against the Operas [at the King's under Gluck], and succeeds. He has hired all the goddesses from farces and the singers of *Roast Beef* from between the acts at both theatres, with a man with one note in his voice, and a girl without ever an one; and so they sing, and make brave hallelujahs; and the good company encore the recitative, if it happens to have any cadence like what they call a tune.

And on 3 March he wrote again that "The Oratorios thrive abundantly—for my part, they give me an idea of heaven, where everybody is to sing whether they have voices or not." But Walpole was more critical than the average London music-lover. A letter dated 8 March 1743 was reported to Irishmen in *Faulkner's Dublin Journal*:

Our Friend Mr. Handell is very well, and Things have taken a quite different Turn here from what they did some Time past; for the Publick will be no longer imposed on by Italian Singers, and some wrong Headed Undertakers of bad Opera's, but find out the Merit of Mr. Handell's Composition and English Performances: That Gentleman is more esteemed now than ever. The new Oratorio (called SAMSON) which he composed since he left Ireland, has been performed four Times to more crouded Audiences than ever were seen; more People being turned away for Want of Room each Night than hath been at the Italian Opera.

Strangely, when the *Messiah* received its first London performance at Covent Garden on 23 March 1743, it was not received as warmly as it had been in Dublin.

Horace Walpole wrote to Mann on 4 May 1743 that Handel was afflicted with a palsy and could not compose, yet the maestro was busy at work on *Semele* in June and July, and during the latter month he almost completed his *Dettingen Te Deum.* Then he turned his attention to the oratorio *Joseph* in August and September. *Semele* was performed on 10 February 1744 at Covent Garden; *Joseph and His Brethren* came out on 2 March. For the 1744–45 season Handel hired the King's Theatre and with a company of mostly English singers attempted an oratorio season. But by 17 January 1745 he announced that he would have to cut the season short and return the subscription money. When some subscribers did not withdraw their money, Handel was able to struggle on and present *Belshazzar* on 27 March. He concluded the season early, on 23 April.

Handel's health became precarious, and, according to a letter dated 24 October 1745 from the Earl of Shaftesbury to James Harris, Handel "has been a good deal disordered in his head." He was well enough the following year to try to make good his promise of the year before to his subscribers. He gave three performances of his *New Occasional Oratorio* in February 1746, but that was all, and he did not try offering subscription performances again. That did not mean that Handelian activity ceased, however. Between the spring of 1747 and the spring of 1749 came performances of *Judas Maccabaeus,* his *pasticcio Lucio Vero, Joshua, Alexander Balus, Solomon,* and *Susanna*—along with revivals of earlier works, constant publications, and numerous concerts and recitals in Great Britain and performances of his works on the Continent.

After much delay, a rehearsal of the Handel music for the Royal Fireworks at Vauxhall took place on 21 April 1749 before an audience estimated at 12,000 people. The event itself took place on 27 April. In May Handel conducted some of his music for the benefit of the Foundling Hospital, another charity he regularly supported. His health improved, and on 13 February 1750 the Earl of Shaftesbury was able to report to James Harris that he had

> seen Handel several times since I came hither [to London], and think I never saw him so cool and well. He is quite easy in his behaviour, and has been pleasing himself in the purchase of several fine pictures, particularly a large Rembrandt, which is indeed excellent. We have scarce talked at all about musical subjects, though enough to find his performances will go off incomparably.

For the 1750 spring oratorio season at Covent Garden Handel's new work was *Theodora,* presented on 16 March, but the audiences were thin. At the end of the season he went to the Continent to visit friends and relatives—for what turned out to be the last time. Between the Hague and Haarlem his carriage was overturned, and it was reported in London in the *General Advertiser* of 21 August that Handel "was terribly hurt" but "now out of Danger." No more is known of the accident.

Handel returned to London soon afterward. On 13 February 1751 he made a personal note in the score of *Jeptha,* on which he was working: "got as far as this on Wednesday 13th February 1751, unable to go on owing to weakening of the sight of my left eye." Though fluent in French, English, and Italian, Handel reverted to German for that brief, distressed note. *The Choice of Hercules* (a new act in *Alexander's Feast*) was presented at Covent Garden on 1 March for the first time; at the performance on the eighth was the Countess of Shaftesbury, who wrote to James Harris a few days later about Handel's plight:

> My constancy to poor Handel got the better of . . . my indolence, and I went last Friday to [the oratorio]; but it was such a melancholy pleasure, as drew tears of sorrow to see the great though unhappy Handel, dejected, wan, and dark, sitting by, not playing on the harpsichord, and to think how his light had been spent by *being overplied in music's cause.* I was sorry to find the audience so insipid and tasteless (I may add unkind) not to give the poor man the comfort of applause; but affectation and conceit cannot discern or attend to merit.

The Triumphal Arches, Mr Handel's Statue &c. in the South Walk of VAUXHALL GARDENS.

Victoria and Albert Museum

Vauxhall Gardens

engraving by Cole

(The year was not given on the letter, but it fits with 1751.)

At some performances Handel did perform, as on 18 April 1751 when the *Messiah* was given at the Chapel of the Foundling Hospital "under the direction of *G. F. Handel*, Esq; who himself played a voluntary on the organ. . . ." But his health continued to fail, and in June he went to Cheltenham Wells to take the waters; upon his return to London he was treated for his failing eyesight by the surgeon Samuel Sharp.

At Covent Garden on 26 February 1752 *Jephtha* was first performed. The following 17 August the *General Advertiser* reported the sad news that "George-Frederick Handel, Esq; the celebrated Composer of Musick was seized a few Days ago with a Paralytick Disorder in his Head, which has deprived him of Sight." Handel was operated on by William Bromfield on 3 November, probably for a cataract, and though the prognosis was at first good, Handel became almost completely blind in nine

months, perhaps because of glaucoma. Contrary to reports, though, he never lost his sight completely, and it was reported on 13 January 1753 that Handel was sufficiently recovered to go out of doors. On 9 March he apparently conducted *Alexander's Feast* and *The Choice of Hercules*—though he did not, as had been his custom, play an organ concerto. He also directed as usual at the Foundling Hospital. But as time went on Handel relinquished his duties to others, chiefly to John Christopher Smith.

Handel had had his will drawn up on 1 June 1750, shortly before his last trip to the Continent. On 6 August 1756 he added a codicil. A second codicil was written on 22 March 1757 and a third on 4 August of the same year. Shortly before he died Handel added a fourth codicil. During his last years he was treated with some success by John Taylor at Tunbridge Wells. The Countess of Huntington wrote, probably in the spring of 1759, of having "a most pleasing interview with Handel—an interview which I shall not soon forget. He is

Harvard Theatre Collection

"Apotheosis of Handel"

engraving by Heath

now old, and at the close of his long career; yet he is not dismayed at the prospect before him." On 7 April 1759 the *Messiah* was to be directed by Handel at the Foundling Hospital, but the performance had to be conducted by Smith. On the same day the *Whitehall Evening-Post* noted that the Handelian oratorio season had just concluded and that Handel was about to make a trip to Bath "to try the Benefit of the Waters, having been for some Time in a bad State of Health." But he was apparently not up to the trip. George Frideric Handel died at the age of 74 on 14 April 1759.

James Smyth, a close friend of Handel's, wrote to Bernard Granville on 17 April:

According to your request to me when you left London, that I would let you know when our good friend departed this life, *on Saturday last at 8 o'clock in the morn died the great and good* Mr. Handel. He

was sensible to the last moment; made a codicil to his will on Tuesday, ordered to be buried privately in Westminster Abbey, and a monument not to exceed £600 for him. I had the pleasure to reconcile him to his old friends; he saw them and forgave them, and let all their legacies stand! In the codicil he left many legacies to his friends, and among the rest he left me £500, and has left to you the two pictures you *formerly gave him*. He took leave of all his friends on Friday morning, and desired to see nobody but the Doctor and Apothecary and myself. At 7 o'clock in the evening he took leave of me, and told me we "should meet again;" as soon as I was gone he told his servant "*not* to let me come to him any more, for that he had *now done with the world.*" He died as he lived—a good *Christian*, with a true sense of his duty to God and man, and in perfect charity with all the world.

In a postscript Smyth noted that Handel "left the Messiah to the Foundling Hospital, and one thousand pounds to the decayed musicians and their children, and the residue of his fortune to his niece and relations in Germany. He has died worth £20,000, and left legacies with his charities to nearly £6000. He has got by his Oratorios this year £1952 12s. 8d." Smyth's figures may have concerned only Handel's real property; Deutsch notes that Handel's credit at the Bank of England was £17,500 and that his legacies came to more than £9000.

Handel was buried with considerable pomp at Westminster Abbey on 20 April 1759. So great a man could hardly have been given the small ceremony he requested; the *Evening Post* estimated that at least 3000 people attended. The following 3 May Handel was remembered with a performance of the *Messiah* at the Foundling Hospital.

Handel's will of 1 June 1750 was a brief document. He left legacies to his servants, £500 to James Hunter, sums to relatives on the Continent, the bulk of his estate to his niece Johanna Friderica Flöerken, and, most important for our interests, £500, his large harpsichord, his little house organ, and all his music books to the elder John Christopher Smith. The first codicil added £1500 to Smith's legacy, adjusted some bequests to Handel's relatives, and added bequests to two men who had helped Handel with librettos, Thomas Morell and Newburgh Hamilton. The second codicil changed some bequests to servants. The third included some interesting additions. Handel left his great organ at Covent Garden

Harvard Theatre Collection

View of the Handel Commemoration at Westminster Abbey, 1784

engraving by Spilsbury, after E. F. Burney

Theatre to the manager John Rich, two pictures to Charles Jennens, "a fair copy of the Score and all Parts of my Oratorio called The Messiah to the Foundling Hospital," and two paintings to Bernard Granville (as indicated in Smyth's letter above). The fourth codicil was more extensive and included bequests of £300 to Thomas Harris (a Master of Chancery), £500 to James Smyth, £100 to the musician Matthew Dubourg, and smaller amounts to a number of others. Handel also included directions about his funeral (as Smyth noted in his letter) and left £1000 to support "decayed" musicians and their families. At some point Handel was apparently ready to disinherit some of his friends, including John Christopher Smith the elder, but, as Smyth mentioned, Handel was reconciled to them on his deathbed.

In August 1759 Handel's household goods

were inventoried and sold to Handel's servant John Duburk for £48; Duburk seems also to have purchased Handel's house in Brook Street, which was not mentioned in the composer's will.

For many years after his death Handel was remembered regularly in London through performances of his music. Most notable among the Handelian memorial concerts were those beginning in 1784 at Westminster Abbey and the Pantheon. Handel is remembered today, of course, as a composer, and an Easter without a performance of the *Messiah* would seem unthinkable. But during most of his life in England Handel was regularly involved in the management and conducting of operas, oratorios, and other musical works, and he was as much respected in his day for his virtuosity at the organ and harpsichord as he was for the enormous outpouring of music of all kinds. He made numerous enemies in his stubborn battle to improve English musical taste, but if London today is one of the great music centers of the world, George Frideric Handel surely deserves much of the credit.

Handel has been treated over the years by many biographers, and musicologists have provided detailed studies of his works. One work must be mentioned here, for it has served as the basis for this biographical entry: Otto Erich Deutsch's *Handel: a Documentary Biography*, a monumental work of scholarship. Lists of Handel's works may be found in *Grove's Dictionary of Music and Musicians*, the *Catalogue of Printed Music in the British Museum*, and the more recent (1969) *Chronological Catalogue of Handel's Works* by A. Craig Bell.

The Dictionary of National Biography described Handel as "somewhat unwieldly" in person; "his features were large, and his general expression (according to Burney) rather heavy and sour. . . . His smile, according to the same authority, was like 'the sun bursting out of a black cloud'." Portraits and busts of Handel partly bear out those descriptions.

The attempt to compile a Handel iconography is frustrated by many problems, not the least of which is the difficulty of distinguishing some originals from copies. Portraits of Handel, authentic or spurious, have changed hands many times over the years, and their provenance is often a tangled skein. Some portraits in the following iconography may be listed more than once, since it has not been possible to follow them all with confidence from sales room to sales room. We make no claim for comprehensiveness. Especially helpful have been J. M. Coopersmith's list of Handel portraits, published in the April 1932 issue of *Music and Letters*, and John Kerslake's *National Portrait Gallery: Early Georgian Portraits* (1978). In the list below those two sources are referred to as Coopersmith and Kerslake.

ORIGINAL PAINTINGS, DRAWINGS, AND MINIATURES.

1. By Christopher Barber. Miniature offered to the British Museum about 1759. Now lost.

2. By Charles Boit. Miniature, oval bust on enamel. In the collection of Lord Beauchamp at Madresfield Court, Worcestershire. Reproduced in Wilhelm Nisser, *Michael Dahl* (1927), pl LV.

3. By Charles Boit. Portrait offered at Christie's on 28 June 1895, from the Henry Doetsch collection. Evidently not the miniature owned by Lord Beauchamp. Present location unknown.

4. By Samuel Bulkeley. Miniature plumbago (on vellum). In the Victoria and Albert Museum.

5. By Michael Dahl. Oil on canvas (29½ × 24); in blue coat and vest with white frills. Sold at Christie's on 17 December 1915 from the collection of Dr W. H. Cummings; bought by Mr Ellis for £5 15s. 6d., then sold to John Lane, of "Bodley Head," London, in whose possession it was in 1917.

6. By Bartholomew Dandridge. Oil on canvas. Three-quarter length, wearing skull cap and holding a roll of music. This portrait has sometimes been attributed to William Hogarth, and as such it was sold at Christie's in July 1909 to Felix Thornley Cobbold, who bequeathed it to the Fitzwilliam Museum, Cambridge, in that year. An engraving by Charles Turner was published in 1821 as "after a painting by Hogarth." A similar portrait, also designated a Hogarth, at the Bibliothek Peters in Leipzig, may be a copy. Coopersmith cautiously attributes the portrait to Dandridge. The attributions of those portraits to Hogarth are not confirmed by Ronald Paulson or other Hogarth scholars.

7. By Balthasar Denner, c. 1726–28. Oil on canvas. Presented to the National Portrait

Gallery in 1923 by A. F. Hill. For reproduction and provenance see Kerslake. Engraving by E. Harding, 1799.

8. By Balthasar Denner, signed and dated 1736, with an inscription on the frame reading: "FREDERICK HANDEL/AETATIS. 52./ OB.ᵀ75." But now commonly considered not to be of Handel. In the possession of Lord Sackville at Knole House, Kent.

9. By Joseph Goupy. Pastel caricature of Handel seated at the organ, with a large wig and enormous tusks on his boarlike head. The drawing once belonged to Horace Walpole; it eventually passed into the hands of Edward F. Rimbault, who wrote an informative article on it in *Notes and Queries*, April 1876. The drawing is now in the Fitzwilliam Museum, Cambridge. Prints of it were published in 1730 and 1754.

10. By Joseph Goupy. In the collection of the Prince of Wales in 1742.

11. By Giuseppe Grisoni, c. 1745. Oil on canvas, in the Fitzwilliam Museum, Cambridge. Similar to the 1756 type Handel portrait by Thomas Hudson and perhaps a copy. A copy of Grisoni's picture is in the Musée de l'Opéra, Paris.

12. By Heins (?), 1738. Handel with a group of friends. In the possession of R. Leitner, Vienna, in 1927.

13. By W. Hoare. Portrait in crayons, owned by the artist's brother, Prince Hoare, in 1809; now lost.

14. By William Hogarth, c. 1724. In the collection of Newman Flower, Sevenoaks, in 1932. Perhaps this is the portrait (13 × 9½) attributed to Hogarth of Handel in brown dress, seated, holding some music, offered at Christie's on 17 June 1929 (No 48). A portrait of similar description was sold as a Hudson at Christie's on 6 February 1931. See No 37.

15. By Hogarth. Oil on canvas, group portrait of "Handel, Farinelli, and Mrs Fox." Owned by Mrs Gough Nichols in 1889.

16. By Hogarth. "The Levée" from "The Rake's Progress" series (No 2), 1734. Showing Handel (or a composite Handel and Porpora) at the harpsichord. In the Sir John Soane Museum. Engraving by Hogarth, 1735.

17. Attributed to Hogarth. Owned by the Earl of Carlisle in 1932. Reproduced in J. J. Foster, *British Miniature Painters* (1898), pl XXX.

18. Attributed to Hogarth, possibly a copy of the Dandridge portrait. In the Bibliothek Peters, Leipzig. See above, No 6.

19. By Hogarth, c. 1731. "A Musical Party" or "The Concert." Sometimes called the Mathias Family Portraits, and wrongly said to be a party at the house of Andrew Millar, the bookseller. Engraving by T. Cook, 1809. Coopersmith places Handel in the painting, but the musicians are probably members of the Popple or Ashley families. In the Fitzwilliam Museum, Cambridge. See R. B. Beckett, *Hogarth* (1949).

Thomas Hudson made at least two portraits of Handel, commonly referred to as the "1747 type" and the "1756 type" (or "Gopsall" portrait). The latter was at Gopsall, Leicestershire, for many years, but in 1968 was purchased by the National Portrait Gallery. A number of pictures of both types are listed below; some may be versions or copies by Hudson himself, and many are probably copies by other artists. We do not know the type of some of the reported Hudsons.

20. By Thomas Hudson, 1747 type. At the Royal Society of Musicians, London, presented by Redmond Simpson in 1780. Reproduced in the *Musical Times*, 14 December 1893. Engravings by Belliard, Bollinger, H. R. Cook, Delpesch, Droehmer, Esslinger, J. Faber, Jr, Heckel, R. Hoffmann, Landon, Miller, Riedel, Weger, and Whessel.

21. By Hudson, 1747 type. At the Royal Society of Musicians.

22. By Hudson, 1747 type. At the Music School, Oxford (Lecture Room A). Engravings by Bromley, Day & Sons, Huncliff, R. Phelps, Rossaux and Grandjean, Sartain, Sichling, and A. Smith.

23. By Hudson, 1747 type. At the Music School, Oxford (Instrument Room), the gift of the elder George Colman, dramatist and manager, c. 1754.

24. By Hudson, 1747 type. Once owned by Dr Samuel Arnold. Engraving by Heath, 1787, after a design by Rebecca.

25. By Hudson, 1747 type. At the Staats and Universitäts-Bibliotek, Hamburg, acquired in 1883. Engravings by C. Becker and by Schuster.

26. By Hudson, 1747 type. Once owned by Dr W. H. Cummings. In the possession of Mrs Robert F. Jeffreys, Philadelphia, in 1932.

Reproduced in the *Musical Times*, 14 December 1893.

27. By Hudson, 1756 type. The "Gopsall" portrait (94 × 57½). Formerly in the possession of Lord Howe at Gopsall, Leicestershire; between 1956 and 1967 on loan to the National Portrait Gallery. Sold at Christie's on 7 July 1967, bought by Leggatt's. Acquired in 1968 by the National Portrait Gallery (No 3970) with the help of a public appeal and a Government grant. Engravings by Harding and an anonymous engraver.

28. By Hudson, 1756, duplicate of the "Gopsall." In the Royal Collection, Buckingham Palace. Engravings by W. Chapman and by J. Thomson. August Selb drew a picture of this painting; it was engraved by M. and N. Hanhart.

29. By Hudson, 1756 type (48⅞ × 39⅞). In the National Portrait Gallery (No 8), purchased in 1857 from Graves, Pall Mall. Engraving by Wintter.

30. By Hudson, 1756 type. At Kensington Palace.

31. By Hudson, 1756 type. In the Royal College of Music, London.

32. By Hudson, 1756 type. In the collection of A. F. Hill, London, in 1932. Reproduced as frontispiece to Flower, *Handel*.

33. By Hudson. Handel in a brown coat and yellow vest, holding a book. Sold at Christie's on 6 March 1914; bought by a Mr Parsons.

34. By Hudson. Drawing in red and white chalk on blue paper, 1743. Sold at the Hotel Drouot, Paris, 12 September 1920. Perhaps the sketch for the portrait presented by Redmond Simpson in 1780 to the Royal Society of Musicians (see No 20).

35. By Hudson. Three-quarter length (54 × 40). Sold at Sotheby's on 19 July 1922; bought by a Mr Field.

36. By Hudson. Three-quarter length, oval (58 × 51), Handel seated in a brownish-green coat. Sold at Sotheby's on 25–26 July 1922; bought by Mr Charles.

37. By Hudson. Handel in a brown coat with embroidered vest, holding some music. Sold at Christie's on 6 February 1931; bought by Mr Glyka.

38. By Hudson. Förstemann, *Handel's Stammbaum* (1844) reported a Hudson portrait at Halle, in the possession of descendants of Johanna Friderica Flörcken, Handel's niece. Authenticity questionable.

39. By Hudson. *Grove's* (fifth edition) reports a copy after Hudson, once in the possession of Lord Mayor Chitty, to be owned by Dr Davan Wetton.

40. By Hudson (?). Handel in a red coat, with white frills, holding the music of the *Messiah*. This portrait, called a Hudson by Coopersmith, was listed as by Richard Wilson when sold at Christie's on 14 June 1929 and bought by Mr Storey. See No 56.

41. By George Knapton (?). Pastel drawing, ownership and provenance unknown. Reproduced without explanation in *The Connoisseur* in September 1920, and again in 1943, CXI, 82.

42. Attributed to Godfrey Kneller. At the Foundling Hospital, London. According to Benedict Nicholson, *The Treasures of the Foundling Hospital* (1972), "Not impossibly a portrait of Handel, but certainly not by Kneller."

43. Attributed to Godfrey Kneller. Owned by D. W. Wise, Ilfracombe, Devonshire, in April 1908. Photographs in the Fitzwilliam Museum. Coopersmith calls it a "very questionable painting."

44. By Francis Kyte, 1742. In the National Portrait Gallery (No 2152). This portrait is after the engraving by Jacob Houbraken, 1738. (See Kerslake.) Other portraits made either from the engraving or as copies of Kyte are noted in this list as Nos 51, 72, and 87. The National Portrait Gallery Kyte probably is the portrait from the Keith Milnes collection, which was acquired by Dr. W. H. Cummings. The canvas came to the National Portrait Gallery in 1927 by the bequest of W. B. Squire, who had bought it in the Cummings sale at Christie's on 17 December 1915. Engravings after the Kyte portrait were done by Angus, Armstrong, Delius, Goldar, Grignois, F. C. Lewis, Riepenhausen, Sohertly, G. F. Schmidt, and an anonymous engraver.

45. By Bernard Lens. Miniature on ivory, c. 1710. Of doubtful authenticity. In the collection of Frances Wellesley in 1921.

46. By Philippe Mercier, with harpsichord, pen, and music. In the collection of Lord Malmesbury at Heron Court. Kerslake suggests a dating in the late 1720s. A copy by a Miss Benson of London, done about 1825, was offered at Christie's in July 1872 and January

1873; it was owned by a Herr Clemen of Bonn, Germany, in 1932.

47. By Christoph Platzer. Miniature on vellum. In the collection of Francis Wellesley in 1921. Reproduced in Flower, *Handel*.

48. Attributed to Joshua Reynolds. Once in the possession of Dr W. H. Cummings, this oil on a panel was purchased at Sotheby's on 21 May 1917 by a Mr Myers of London.

49. Attributed to the elder Jonathan Richardson, c. 1723. Oil painting in the collection of S. Wise, London, in 1932.

50. By John Russell. Pastel, c. 1776, similar to portrait by Van der Myn (No 55). In the collection of Mrs. M. P. H. Simms, 1961. Reproduced by Kerslake.

51. By Susan, Countess of Shaftesbury. Pastel, at St Giles House. Lady Shaftesbury copied either the Kyte painting or, more likely, the Houbraken engraving from which Kyte worked. See Nos 44, 87, and Betty Matthews, "The Handel Portrait at St. Giles," *Music and Letters* (1963), pp. 43–45, 206–7, and 316–17.

52. By James Thornhill, c. 1720. Supposedly of Handel seated at an organ; said to have been painted for the Duke of Chandos. The evidence is scanty and Handel probably is not the sitter. In the Fitzwilliam Museum, Cambridge.

53. By J. A. Tischbein. Oil, life-size, Handel in breastplate. In the possession of Herr Kellner, Hoforganist at Cassel, Germany, in 1790.

54. By Jan Van der Banck. Oil, three-quarter length. In the collection of Felix Cobbold in 1909; owned by Lord Howe in 1932.

55. By Francis Van der Myn (?). Oil on oak. Handel in a brown coat. Sold from the W. H. Cummings collection at Christie's on 17 December 1915; bought by W. B. Squire, who bequeathed it in 1915 to the National Portrait Gallery (No 2151). See Kerslake.

56. Possibly by Richard Wilson. Oil on canvas (49 × 39); in red coat with white frills, holding music of the *Messiah*. Listed as No 103 in the catalogue of pictures by Richard Wilson which were sold at Christie's on 14 June 1929; bought by a Mr Storey.

57. By George Andreas Wolfgang. Sold in the Snoxell sale at Puttick and Simpson, 9 June 1879 (lot 272); bought by W. Clark. Perhaps the portrait reported in 1968 to be in a Swiss private collection.

58. By George Andreas Wolfgang. Holding a book lettered *Alexander's Feast*. Once owned by Dr Harry E. Smith of Streatham; then owned by K. E. Henrici of Berlin (in 1928), it was listed as a Hudson. Now in the collection of Newman Flower, Sevenoaks.

59. By George Andreas Wolfgang, 1737. Pencil and sepia drawing, in the Bibliothek Peters, Leipzig, in 1932. Inscription on back indicating that it was drawn by Wolfgang at London in 1737. This type was the model for the engraving by J. G. Wolfgang, the artist's father, published by 1744, and copied in an engraving by W. Holl published as a plate to *Biographical Magazine*, 1819.

60. By George Andreas Wolfgang. Miniature at Windsor Castle.

61. By Gustav A. Wolfgang, 1710. Recorded in Charles Burney's will of January 1807 as a half-length portrait, "painted by Wolfgang at Hanover in the year 1710, where he stopt at the Elector's Court (afterwards Geo. the first, King of England) on his way from Italy to London." Burney described it the "best picture" of Handel, with "a strong resemblance in his 24th year when it was painted." Evidently never engraved. Present location unknown. See Kerslake.

62. By Christian F. Zincke. Miniature, probably after the "Gopsall" Hudson. Sold at Christie's on 9 May 1922.

63. By Zincke. Miniature in the Barrett Lennard collection in 1896.

64. By Zincke. Miniature enamel, in the Victoria and Albert Museum. Reproduced in the *Musical Times*, 14 December 1893.

65. By Zincke. Miniature enamel. Once owned by Arthur F. Hill of London, then by A. W. Clapham of London; reported to be in the collection of Newman Flower, Sevenoaks.

66. Attributed to Zincke. Miniature enamel, Handel in blue coat. Owned by the Duke of Buccleuch in 1932.

67. Attributed to Zincke. Miniature enamel, Handel in brown coat. Owned by the Duke of Buccleuch in 1932.

68. By unknown artist. Miniature, probably after the Hudson at Gopsall. In the collection of Newman Flower, Sevenoaks, Kent.

69. By unknown artist. Miniature on ring, 1755. Possibly after the Hudson at Buckingham Palace. At the Royal College of Music, London.

70. By unknown artist, school of Kneller. Owned by Mrs. George Madison Millarp, Pasadena, in 1932.

71. By unknown artist. Oil, after the Kyte portrait or the Houbraken engraving. Sold from the Hill collection at Sotheby's on 18 June 1947; then owned by W. C. Smith. Present location unknown.

72. By unknown artist: Oil (?), after the Kyte portrait or the Houbraken engraving. An engraving by Goldar in 1785 was noted as taken from a portrait lately in the possession of John Spencer, late Baron Spencer of Althorp. Lord Spencer owned a Houbraken engraving.

73. By unknown artist. Oil, in the possession of Dr Ernest Foss, Berlin, in 1932; he was a direct descendant of Handel's sister, Dorothea Michaelsen. Reproduced in Newman Flower, *Handel*.

74. By unknown artist. At the Bodleian Library, Oxford.

75. By unknown artist. Handel in a brown dress, with a book of music. Sold at Christie's on 17 December 1915 from the collection of Dr W. H. Cummings; bought by Ellis.

76. By unknown artist. Handel in a green coat. Sold at Christie's on 8 April 1911; bought by a Mr Mallman.

77. By unknown artist. Present location unknown, but according to Coopersmith the National Portrait Gallery has a reproduction presented before 1914 by W. H. Howes, Ipswich.

78. By unknown artist. At Trinity College of Music, London.

79. By unknown artist. Handel with "La Francesina" (Elizabeth Duparc). Red chalk drawing owned in 1935 by Harry Stone of New York. Reproduced in this dictionary, vol v, p. 384.

80. By unknown artist. Miniature, at Windsor Castle (in frame No 3, No 18 in the collection).

81. By unknown artist. In the Städtische Museum, Halle.

82. By unknown artist. Young musician said to be Handel; seated in garden, playing a harp, a pet dog at his feet. In the collection of Newman Flower, Sevenoaks.

83. By unknown artist. In the Foundling Hospital. Called Handel, but "bears little resemblance." See Benedict Nicholson, *The Treasures of the Foundling Hospital* (1972).

ENGRAVED PORTRAITS FOR WHICH NO ORIGINAL PAINTINGS OR DRAWINGS ARE KNOWN.

84. Engraved portrait by H. Adlard.

85. Engraved portrait by F. Bartolozzi, after Cipriani. Seated at a table; pen in hand; a cupid above his head holding a scroll inscribed "Handel," [1784?]. A copy, medallion tablet on a monument, after Cipriani, was published as a plate to *European Magazine*, 1784.

86. Engraved portrait by F. Bartolozzi, after Cipriani. Oval supported by Fame and a cupid. "For Clementi & Co's edition of Handel's Songs."

87. Engraved portrait by Jacob Houbraken. Published 1738. The portrait was published as frontispiece to *Alexander's Feast*, with a scene below designed by Hubert François Gravelot.

88. Engraved portrait by J. Kovatsch, date unknown.

89. Engraved portrait by McRae. Half-length, looking to right, book in left hand.

90. Engraved portrait by D. C. Read, 1830. Supposed after a portrait by Hogarth.

91. Engraving by J. K. Sherwin, after B. Rebecca, 1784. Oval medallion. Admission ticket to the Handel Memorial Concerts, 1784.

92. By unknown engraver. Head, profile. Admission ticket to the Handel Memorial Concerts, 1784.

93. By unknown engraver. Bust; rectangle frame with lions' heads.

94. By unknown engraver. Medallion tablet on a monument. Copy of Cipriani's portrait.

VIEWS AND SCENES CONCERNED WITH HANDEL.

95. Handel directing an oratorio. By unknown engraver. In the British Museum.

96. "Interior View of Westminster Abbey on the Commemoration of Handel's Centenary," 1784. Oil on canvas by Edward Edwards, exhibited at the Royal Academy in 1793. In the Yale Center for British Art.

97. "View of the Gallery prepared for the reception of their Majesties, the Royal Family, Directors, & principal Personages in the Kingdom, at the COMMEMORATION OF HANDEL in Westminster Abbey," 1784. Engraving by J. Spilsbury, after E. F. Burney.

98. "Apotheosis of Handel." Handel seated on a cloud, pen in right hand, music in left.

Fame about to place crown of laurel on his head, an angel with lighted torch at his side. Engraving by J. Heath, after B. Rebecca, published on 21 May 1787 by Richards in connection with the 1787 Handel commemoration. Another impression was published by Cox on 26 May 1787.

99. "View of the Grand Musical Festival Held in September 1823 in the Cathedral Church of York." Engraving by Edward F. Finden, after J. Browne, 1824. In the Yale Center for British Art.

100. Handel's tombstone in Westminster Abbey. Watercolor drawing by Grosden. In the Harvard Theatre Collection.

101. Satirical watercolor, entitled "Amateurs of the Tye Wig Concerts," by E. F. Burney. In the Victoria and Albert Museum.

SCULPTURES, MONUMENTS, IMPRESSIONS, AND MEDALS.

102. Monument, by Heidel, 1857. At Halle. Engraving by A. Alboth, Leipzig.

103. Marble statue, L. F. Roubiliac, 1738. Commissioned Jonathan Tyers for Vauxhall Gardens. Now in the Victoria and Albert Museum. The terracotta model by Roubiliac is in the Fitzwilliam Museum. A view of the statue was engraved by F. Bartolozzi, after B. Rebecca, 1789.

104. Terracotta model, by Roubiliac. In the Fitzwilliam Museum, Cambridge. Model for the Vauxhall Gardens statue (now in the Victoria and Albert Museum).

105. Terracotta modello, by Roubiliac. In the Ashmolean Museum, Oxford. The final model for the monument in Westminster Abbey.

106. Monument, by L. F. Roubiliac, 1761. In Westminster Abbey. The final modello is in the Ashmolean Museum, Cambridge. Another, previously at Bath, is in the collection of Gerald Coke. Engraved views of the monument were done by J. M. Delattre and several unknown engravers.

107. Terracotta modello, by Roubiliac. In the collection of Gerald Coke. A model for the monument in Westminster Abbey.

108. Marble bust, by Roubiliac, 1739. At Windsor Castle.

109. Terracotta bust, by Roubiliac. At the Foundling Hospital, Thomas Coran Foundation for Children. The model for the marble bust, 1739, at Windsor Castle. Engraving by J. Hinton.

110. Plaster bust, by Roubiliac. At the Foundling Hospital, Thomas Coran Foundation for Children. Of the type in marble at Windsor Castle.

111. Bronze bust, by Roubiliac. Owned by B. F. Stevens, London, in 1917. Perhaps the one now in Bremen (see No 112).

112. Bronze bust, attributed to Roubiliac. In a private collection, Bremen.

113. Marble bust, by Roubiliac. Mentioned in the Blackwood sale catalogue in 1778. Perhaps the same mentioned in the Stanley sale catalogue in 1786. Also perhaps one of the other marble busts in this list.

114. Terracotta roundel, by Roubiliac. In the Victoria and Albert Museum.

115. Plaster roundel, attributed to Roubiliac. In the Sir John Soane Museum.

116. Bronze medallion, by Roubiliac (?). In the collection of F. J. B. Watson.

117. Death mask, by Roubiliac. Cast sold in the Cummings sale at Sotheby's, 17–24 May 1917.

118. Marble statue, by Jules Salmson. At l'Opéra, Paris. An engraving was done by J. C. Michelet, after E. Jeanmaire.

119. Bust, white earthenware, painted in enamel colors. Probably by Enoch Wood. In the Victoria and Albert Museum.

120. Bronze bust, by unknown artist. In the Fitzwilliam Museum, Cambridge. Terracotta bust in the National Portrait Gallery (No 878, our No 121), seems to be the model for this bronze.

121. Terracotta bust on a plaster socle. By unknown artist. In the National Portrait Gallery (No 878). Seems to be the model for the bronze bust in the Fitzwilliam Museum.

122. Bronze bust, by unknown French sculptor. In the collection of Mr Cummings (not Dr H. M. Cummings) in 1917.

123. Impression from a gem, by W. Brown. Exhibited at the Royal Academy, 1812.

124. Impression by Thomas Pingo from a bust in steel. Exhibited at the Free Society of Artists, 1771.

125. Bas relief, by Grass, showing Handel and others. Exhibited at the Royal Academy in 1859; possibly the same as the marble medallion exhibited there in 1867.

126. Bronze medal, by F. Wolff, 1823. In the British Museum.

127. Marble medallion, by unknown artist. In the private chapel of Belton House, Lincolnshire.

128. Five medals by anonymous artists, 1769–1859. In the British Museum.

Handler, Miss. *See* ABRAMS, HARRIET.

"Handsome Jack." *See* BANNISTER, JOHN.

"Handsome Leigh." *See* LEIGH, JOHN *1689–1726.*

Handy, Benjamin [*fl. c. 1784–1824*], *equestrian, clown, manager.*

Benjamin Handy served as an ostler in Hughes's equestrian company in London before striking out on his own. The earliest theatrical notice we have found of Handy's activity dates from 26 April 1788, in a yard behind the Angel in Borough Walls, Bristol. The bill claimed that audiences would be entertained by "the unparalleled vaulting horseman MR. HANDY." The troupe was made up of selected performers from Astley's and Hughes's riding schools in London. Also on the bill was "The Child of Promise" (Handy's daughter Mary Ann, who was born about 1784) and Signora Riccardini, Handy's wife.

The three Handys were at Stourbridge Fair near Cambridge in 1788. Also at the Fair was Hughes and his company from the Royal Circus in London. Hughes challenged Handy to ride for £500; if he equalled Robinson or "Ciles" of the Hughes troupe, Handy was to receive a £20 note in the presence of the audience. Giles Sutton, an apprentice to Hughes (and perhaps the "Ciles" mentioned above), challenged Handy to ride at 20 guineas to 10. A third challenge to Handy dared him to produce an equestrienne who could match Miss Huntley or Miss Crofts, riding on one or two horses, for £20. We do not know how the challenges came out, but Handy in his bill claimed he had the best horsemen in England, especially the "Wonderful Child of Promise," only 40 months old. In addition to performing at Cambridge, the Handys appeared at Norwich in 1788.

Astley's troupe appeared in Bristol in Sep-

tember 1789 and the papers there noted that Astley had offered 365 guineas a year to Handy for his little child, but Handy, of course, refused. Mrs Handy died in Bristol on 15 September 1789, but Handy and his daughter carried on. About 1790 or 1791 Handy used the Lyceum in London for "Feats of Horsemanship," and 1790 also found him again at Bristol, advertised in March as from the riding school at Bath. He and Franklin were partners in a venture to erect "a very commodious Amphitheatre, in the Back Field, adjoining the Full Moon, North-street, St. Pauls near Stoke's Croft," Bristol, similar to Astley's Riding School in London. They originally planned to open on 8 March, but delays in construction, the Bristol papers said, forced postponement until 22 March. Meanwhile Handy and Franklin offered riding lessons to ladies and gentlemen. When their new arena opened, Handy served as a clown to the horsemanship.

On 10 May 1790 at Bristol, Handy and Franklin advertised a subscription for 1000 guineas to enable them to build a new riding school. They continued at Bristol until November, then on 6 March 1792 they were there again, at a new amphitheatre in Limekiln Lane. But at the end of May they dissolved their partnership and headed individual equestrian troupes. Handy's group was at Limekiln Lane again in March 1793, but in mid-April he left the field to Franklin's company. Handy then spent the summer performing in Manchester, offering in addition to horsemanship, the typical fare of equestrian troupes: acrobatics, rope dancing, and pantomimes.

After Astley's Amphitheatre in London burned, Astley and Handy formed a partnership and converted the Lyceum into a circus, according to Frost's *Circus Life*, but most of the contemporary records concerning the Lyceum link Handy not with Astley but with Mr Lingham, a breeches-maker in the Strand who had been involved in performances at the Lyceum since 1790. In February and March 1795 in the Drury Lane Theatre accounts Handy and Lingham were named as receiving money for horses (which they doubtless had rented to the patent house for a spectacle production). On 10 February at Handy's New Circus at the Lyceum the manager presented an equilibrist, slack wire dancers, horsemanship (with Handy as one of the equestrians), unnamed feats of activity by "THE FAMOUS AFRICAN," tightrope dancers (including the ever-popular Child of Promise, who had developed a new specialty), tumblers (including "The Little Devil"), "HANDY'S LITTLE PONEY" that could "do more than any horse in the kingdom ever did," and *The Taylor Riding to Brentford* (a pantomime, one supposes) with Mr Sanderson leading the band. As usual, Handy was offering riding lessons on the side.

At Astley's on 27 July 1795 Handy served as a clown horseman; then he and his company appeared at the New Circus in Manchester from August to October. After that he took his group to Ireland, whence Handy was hailed when he set up again at Limekiln Lane, Bristol, in February 1796. By then he had added to his company some "Catauba" Indians, who displayed their native abilities. Handy remained in Bristol through March, went again to Manchester for the summer of 1796, and was again at Bristol in early 1797. His benefit bill of 25 March noted that he was living at No 2, Lower College Street, Bristol. He and his troupe were engaged in June 1797 by the elder Astley for performances in London.

Handy and William Davis took over the Dublin Amphitheatre Royal, but at the end of 1797 Davis's wife and child, Handy's daughter Mary Ann, and 20 horses were among the losses suffered when the packet *Viceroy* went down on a trip from Liverpool to Dublin. In 1804 Handy and Davis joined with Crossman, Smith, and Parker to form a new company in London. They bought a half share of the management of Astley's Amphitheatre, with John Astley holding the other half. At some point after that Benjamin Handy retired. De Castro in his *Memoirs* in 1824 said Handy "lives as an independent gentleman, and a magistrate for the county of Somerset, very near the famed city of Bath. . . ."

Perhaps the following entry in the registers of St Paul, Covent Garden, concerned our subject: Benjamin Handy of that parish, widower, married Mary Grant, widow, on 7 June 1818.

Handy, Mrs Benjamin, stage name Signora Riccardini *d. 1789, equestrienne.*

The equestrienne Signora Riccardini was the wife of Benjamin Handy and performed with him on 26 April 1788 in a yard behind the Angel in Borough Walls, Bristol, and at Stourbridge Fair and Norwich the same year. Perhaps Mrs Handy's stage name was her maiden name, for a rope dancer named Miss Riccardini performed in London and Bristol a few years later and could have been a sister. No record of the marriage of the Handys has been found, but their daughter, Mary Ann, was born about 1784 and began performing in 1788. Little is known about Signora Riccardini's performances, though the bill for 3 May 1788 in Bristol said she would "perform on One and Two Horses in a capital Manner." The *Bath Chronicle* on 17 September 1789 reported that Mrs Handy had died two days before in Bristol. Though we have found no records of specific performances by Mrs Handy in London, when Handy's troupe arrived in Bristol in the spring of 1788 they were hailed as from London. She probably performed at Astley's Amphitheatre or at the Royal Circus, where her husband had worked.

Handy, Mary Ann, stage name "The Child of Promise" *c. 1784–1797, equestrienne, rope dancer.*

Born about 1784, Mary Ann Handy was the daughter of the equestrians Mr and Mrs Benjamin Handy (Mrs Handy was called Signora Riccardini, which may have been her maiden name). Little Miss Handy, advertised as "The Child of Promise," was an equestrienne in a troupe of performers from the Astley and Hughes companies in London on 26 April 1788 in Bristol. The group performed "In a large commodious yard at the back of the Angel, in the Borough Walls, leading from Redcliff-street to Thomas-street" in Bristol, with Miss Handy, "only forty months old," exhibiting her horsemanship. In the company were her father and mother and Franklin, who soon became Benjamin Handy's partner.

The bill at Bristol for 3 May boasted that "THE CHILD OF PROMISE, will, for this Evening, ride on Mr. *Franklin's* Shoulders, Without the Assistance of Hand or Rein, having nothing to keep her up but her perpendicular Balance, and which is allowed to be the greatest balance ever attempted." Philip Astley was so impressed by Miss Handy that, according to the Bristol papers in September 1789, he offered to pay Handy 365 guineas a year for her services, but Handy refused. She was with the Handy-Franklin company at Bristol in March 1790, performing in a new, covered riding school behind the Full Moon, Stoke's Croft, hailed as "the *never to be equalled* LITTLE CHILD OF PROMISE." At the new amphitheatre and riding school in Limekiln Lane, Bristol, on 6 March 1792 she was again performing with the Handy and Franklin troupe. Frost's *Circus Life* places her at the Royal Circus in London in 1793, performing with Franklin, and the Bristol bills (examined by Kathleen Barker and communicated to us) show that Mary Ann was again with the circus there on 11 March 1794. The following October "the Child of Promise" was advertised as performing dances on the tightrope with an Italian company at a booth in St James's churchyard, Bristol, and though Benjamin Handy was not connected with that venture, the child in question was evidently Mary Ann Handy. She performed with her father at the Lyceum in London in 1795, offering tightrope dancing and equestrienne feats.

By 1796 Miss Handy was advertised sometimes as Miss Mary Ann or Miss Marianne, as when she rope-danced in Bristol in February and March. Indeed, her benefit bill in March called her "Miss Mary Ann, the original Child of Promise." The bills no longer mentioned her as an equestrienne, and she seems to have developed instead her rope-dancing ability. She was at Limekiln Lane on 6 February 1797 and subsequent dates, taking a benefit on 14 March. She was one of the company lost in December 1797 when the packet *Viceroy*, bound for Ireland out of Liverpool, went down to St George's Channel. She and others were on their way to Dublin.

"**Hanesio, Signior Giuseppe.**" *See* HAINES, JOSEPH.

Hangler. *See also* HENGLER.

Hangler, ₁Mrs?₁ ₁*fl.* 1786₁, *actress.*
An actress named Hangler played the second Columbine in a pantomime called *At the Village Sports* on 4 September 1786 at Astley's Amphitheatre. A Miss "Hengler" was a rope dancer at the Royal Circus in 1803, but there

is not sufficient evidence to prove that the two women were identical.

Hankins. *See* HAWKINS.

Hanmer or **Hanmeuze** *See* HANMORE.

Hanmore, Mr ₁*fl.* 1740–1750₁, *porter.*
The Covent Garden Theatre accounts first mentioned Mr Hanmore in the 1740–41 season, when he was earning 10s. weekly as one of the porters. From time to time during the season Hanmore received an extra shilling for "laying the matt last night"—probably the carpet for tragedy. He was cited again in 1746–47, and on 7 May 1750 he received half value for his benefit tickets—a pitiful £1 18s.

Hanmore, Mrs ₁*fl.* 1726?–1760₁, *house servant.*
The Lincoln's Inn Fields accounts mention a Mrs "Hanmer" on 17 October 1726 as the recipient of 2s. for flowers for *Camilla*, which opened a month later, and 13s. 6d. for unspecified properties. On the previous 25 February she had been paid £4 for properties for "Proserpina" *The Rape of Proserpine*, which did not open until 13 February 1727. During the 1726–27 season her name was cited on the theatre free list, and the ticket accounts occasionally mentioned "Ch. Rich by Mrs. Hanmer." It is not clear just what the woman's post was in the company, but she seems not at that period to have been serving as a charwoman, the job she (cited as Mrs Hanmore) held in later years.

The accounts for Rich's troupe in 1735–36, when Covent Garden Theatre was in operation, show Mrs "Hanmer" to have been receiving 12d. daily as a charwoman. She worked 179 days that season. On 22 May 1747 Mrs "Hanmore" received £1 15s. as her half-value share of benefit tickets. She was cited again as a beneficiary on 3 May 1749. Mrs "Hanmeuze" had her benefit tickets accepted on 14 May 1751, and since the names of the other beneficiaries match those usually cited along with Mrs Hanmore on such occasions, we take that woman to be our subject. Mrs Hanmore's name was listed among the charwomen at Covent Garden on a pay list dated 22 September 1760.

Her relationship to Mr Hanmore, who worked at Covent Garden in the 1740s, is not known.

Hanning, Mr ₁*fl. 1767*₁, *pit office keeper.*
As of 14 September 1767 a Mr Hanning was earning 2*s* 6*d*. daily at Covent Garden as the pit office keeper.

Hanson, Mr ₁*fl. 1722–1724*₁, *house servant?*
Mr Hanson was apparently one of the house servants at Lincoln's Inn Fields. He shared a benefit with two others on 29 May 1722 which brought in a total of £128 18*s*., probably before house charges. The following year he shared £111 19*s*. with two others. The theatre accounts show him to have been paid £2 6*s*. for six days on 7 December 1724, a salary that suggests a post of some importance in the company.

Hanson, Mrs ₁*fl. 1719–1725*₁, *dresser.*
Mrs Hanson was a dresser at the Lincoln's Inn Fields playhouse. On 28 May 1719 she shared a benefit, as she did again on 3 June 1724, when the receipts came to £156 17*s*., probably before house charges. On 24 May 1725 she shared £123 8*s*. 6*d*. with two others. *The London Stage* season roster for 1724–25 lists her as a dresser. Her relationship to Mr Hanson, who worked at the theatre from 1722 to 1724, is not known.

Hanyours. *See also* HAMOIR.

Hanyours, Master ₁*fl. 1756*₁, *actor.*
Master Hanyours was one of the children in the Drury Lane company who performed in *Lethe* on 5 May 1756. One might suspect that the name should have been spelled Hamoir and that the boy was the performer of that name who danced at Sadler's Wells in 1766 and at Drury Lane two years later, for that dancer's name was variously spelled Armoir, Armoy, and Hamois. Hanyours is also a close approximation. Yet the parish registers of St Paul, Covent Garden, contain four entries concerning what would appear to have been a Hanyours family, all from the parish of St Martin-in-the-Fields: Robert was buried on 2 February 1758; James Henry, on 14 May 1761;

John, on 15 January 1764; and Mary, on 14 January 1768. Further, a James Heymours was buried at St Paul, Covent Garden, on 24 October 1767. Without more information about Master Hanyours, however, it is impossible to establish a relationship between him and the information in the registers or to identify him as Hamoir.

Haplin. *See* HALPIN.

Harbin, ₁ **Thomas?** ₁ ₁*d.* 1765?₁, *actor.*
Charles Beecher Hogan in his *Shakespeare in the Theatre* takes the actor Harbin who performed in the mid-1730s at Goodman's Fields to have been Thomas Harbin, who was granted a benefit at Covent Garden in 1748, but we question that identification. Harbin's first notice came on 25 September 1733, when he played Vernon in *1 Henry IV* at Goodman's Fields. During the rest of the 1733–34 season and in 1734–35 Harbin also acted Clerimont in *The Double Gallant*, Thessalus in *The Rival Queens*, Rosencrantz in *Hamlet*, Manuel in *Don Quixote*, an Earthly Spirit in *The Indian Emperor*, the Soothsayer in *Julius Caesar*, Seyward in *Macbeth*, a Waterman, Citizen and a Gentleman in *Britannia*, Rossano in *The Fair Penitent*, Nicodemus in *The Stage Coach*, Douglas in *1 Henry IV*, Norfolk in *Richard III*, Pyracmon in *Oedipus*, Raleigh in *The Unhappy Favorite*, Decius in *Cato*, the Duke in *Rule a Wife and Have a Wife*, and Manuel in *Love Makes a Man*. He shared benefits on 7 May 1734 and 22 April 1735.

Thomas Harbin's 1748 benefit, at which he apparently did not perform, was preceded with an inordinate amount of hullabaloo. On 7 November 1748 "Jack Friendly" wrote to the *General Advertiser* from Grigsby's Coffee House:

I beg leave by means of your paper, to acquaint the friends of Tom Harbin, that he intends shortly to have a Benefit at the Theatre Royal in Covent Garden: Having in consequence of the advice of many of them, apply'd himself to Mr Rich, on that account who very generously and readily said he would contribute anything in his power to serve him; and as one night of the week might be better than another, (as his Interest lay) he gave him his choice, whereupon he chose Wednesday, as being a night of most leisure amongst people eminent in trade, on whom the city depends. He persuades himself that those who have laughed with him, will not laugh at him for requesting a favour (which his circumstances could never be supposed to put him above accepting) from persons of affluent fortunes, which the generality of his friends are; and whose Experienc'd good nature, he doubts not, will serve him on this occasion. In a few days Publick notice will be given of the time, the Play, &c.

A response to that was written on 14 November by "T. Meanwell" at Lloyd's Coffee House, and how much of what he said was facetious is difficult to tell:

When I read the letter in your paper concerning Tom Harbin's intention of having a Benefit at Covent Garden, I own I was much pleas'd, as it would give me the opportunity of making him merry, who has often made me so: But I have since been in some concern to hear he was to perform himself— I would not have him appear in an Ill-Light; and as it is easy to conceive what confusion a Man unus'd to the stage must be in, to appear on it, I would in Friendship advise him to desist from that design.— If he does it from an opinion of his Capacity, I am sorry for him: but if it is only to draw people together, I think he need not have any Apprehensions on that Account:—For there ever was and ever will be in London, a number of Persons of Fortune and Generosity, sufficient to do what he wants, whenever they have an Inclination to serve a man they like.—And as he is Generally allow'd to be what is call'd a Fiddle in Company, and plays as often as anybody, it would be but right to keep him in tune. . . .

The benefit was held on 14 December. *The Provok'd Husband* and *Damon and Phillida* made up the bill, but Harbin was not mentioned in either cast. On 15 December 1748 he wrote a letter of thanks to the *General Advertiser*. According to the *Public Advertiser* of 30 July 1765, Thomas Harbin died on the twenty-seventh of that month.

Harbour, Jacob [*fl.* 1784–1815], *violinist, instrument maker, music seller and publisher.*
Jacob Harbour, musical-instrument maker and music seller, issued three books of country dances. The second book, in 1784, was published from No 25, Duke Street, Lincoln's Inn Fields, and the third, about 1797, from No 15, Lamb's Conduit Street. In 1794, when he lived at No 34, Red Lion Street, Holborn, he was listed in Doane's *Musical Directory* as a violinist and a member of the New Musical Fund; in the subscription list of that fund in 1794 he was named as on the Court of Assistants and in 1815 he was still a subscriber.

The James Harbour who was recommended by Robert Shaw on 6 March 1791 for membership in the Royal Society of Musicians was probably the same person. By a vote of five yeas and ten nays on 7 August 1791, he was rejected.

Harbour, James. *See* HARBOUR, JACOB.

Harbour, Thomas [*fl.* 1794–1815], *musician.*
Thomas Harbour was listed in 1794, 1805, and 1815 as a subscriber to the New Musical Fund.

Harcourt, Mrs. *See* HOOK, MARY.

Harden. *See* HORDEN.

Harder, Mr [*fl.* 1744], *actor.*
Mr Harder played Furnish in *The Miser* at the Haymarket Theatre on 10 May 1744.

Hardham, John 1712–1772, *numberer, treasurer, teacher, tradesman.*
John Hardham was born in 1712 in Chichester, the son of a wholesale provision merchant. According to *The Dictionary of National Biography* he was trained to be a diamond cutter and may have worked for a while as a servant, but after settling in London he was attracted to the theatre and became David Garrick's principal numberer and undertreasurer at Drury Lane. His work at the theatre, at least in 1765, brought him only 15s. weekly, but he was also in business (perhaps as early as 1744) as a tobacconist and snuff merchant, and that made him a wealthy man. He attracted a very elegant clientele to his shop, aided by Garrick's occasional ad libs on stage; Colton's *Hypocrisy* (1812) quotes a quatrain:

A name is all—from Garrick's breath a puff
Of praise gave immortality to snuff;
Since which each connoisseur a transient heaven
Finds in each pinch of Hardham's Thirty-seven.

No 37 was one of Hardham's most popular mixtures.

Gray's Inn Journal on 19 January 1754 contained an amusing note:

From Mr. Hardham's *Snuff-shop in* Fleet street. Besides the Right *Dramatic Strasburgh*, mentioned in our last, Mr. *Hardham* has lately laid in a Store of various Kinds of Snuff, which are acknowledged to possess several excellent Qualities, and are a sovereign Remedy for all Disorders in the Head, as can be attested by many eminent Critics who have experienced the same. His *Right Orthodox Snuff* expels the noxious Vapours arising from Theatrical Parties, and instantly enables the Taker to distinguish genuine Merit in an Actor from false Fire, and mechanic Imitation. He has Snuff very proper to be taken at a new Play, as it totally obstructs the petulant Sensations of Pleasure arising from a malevolent Hiss: he also enlivens the Spirits for Comedy, and composes them for Tragedy; prevents the ill Effects of a dull Writer, or a soporific Actor. In short, he sharpens the Discernment of a Critic, opens his Intellects, gives him some Degree of Taste, and renders him fit for his Profession, or, as *Horace* expresses it, *emunotae naris*, and raises agreeable Images in the Fancy of every one who chuses to take his *pungent Grain of titillating Dust.*

Given that kind of advertising and the easy contact with fashionable people which house servants at the theatres had, it is little wonder that Hardham built a fortune of some £20,000.

According to W. J. Lawrence in *Old Theatre Days and Ways*, Hardham's box at Drury Lane was next to the stage on prompt side, in the upper boxes, where actresses used to sit with him in veils—possibly true, though he was supposed to have been at work as a numberer and undertreasurer, not watching the show. Hardham is also said to have taught acting in the back room at his shop, at the sign of the Red Lyon in Fleet Street. Hardham loaned money (Garrick was security for £100 which Mr. Leach borrowed from Hardham in 1764) and was very generous. He paid stipends, said the *Biographia Dramatica* of 1812, to "unfortunate women" whose patrons had died or lost interest, not letting the ladies know that he had become the source of their annuities.

John Hardham died on 25 September 1772 at the age of 60 and was buried four days later at St Bride, Fleet Street. He had begun drawing up his will the previous 20 January. He wanted a no-nonsense funeral costing no more than £10, "for none but vain fools spend more." When he wrote his will (which he did in his own hand) he had £15,500 invested in reduced three percent government securities, and he wished to have whatever goods he or his chief beneficiary, Mary Binmore, did not dispose of otherwise, similarly invested. Mary Binmore, known in Hardham's house as "Nanny," was the wife of William Dewick Binmore, and, Hardham said, he wished his estate to be invested for her benefit during her lifetime and not subject to her husband's control. He requested that after Mrs Binmore's death £30 annuities should go to the jeweller John Elliot and Mrs Dorothy Rion, but the bulk of the dividends and interest on the £15,500 Hardham wished to go to John Condell, the boxkeeper at Covent Garden Theatre. The residuary legatee was the Poor House of Chichester, "to ease the inhabitants of the said City in their poor Rate forever." Hardham left a number of small bequests to friends, including 10 guineas to Garrick. The will was finally signed on 6 February 1772 and proved on 3 October. Hardham's bequest to Chichester, which went to the city in 1786, did not, as it turned out, help the citizens; for some reason it caused the rents to be higher within the city walls than without.

John Hardham was married, and *The Dictionary of National Biography* states that his wife died before he did. He evidently had a daughter, for Garrick, in a letter to Colman on 23 August 1764, asked, "What is become of Hardham's Girl? & of Jack himself?" Garrick was still concerned about the girl's whereabouts the following February.

Hardham wrote a farce, *The Fortune Tellers: or, The World Unmask'd*, which was published about 1750 but was never produced.

Harding, John   *d. 1684, violinist, violist, singer.*

John Harding was sworn a Gentleman of the Chapel Royal on 25 March 1638, replacing the deceased Thomas Holmes. In the Chapel Royal as early as 1625 had been John, Edward, and James Harding, one of whom may have been our subject's father and all of whom were probably related to him. During the Commonwealth our John Harding taught music; Playford's *Musical Banquet* in 1651 listed him as one of the London teachers of "Voyce or Viole." At Rutland House in 1656 when Davenant's *The Siege of Rhodes* received its first performance, Harding and Alphonso Marsh were double cast as Pirrhus.

At the Restoration Harding was reappointed to the King's Musick; an order granting him livery on 17 July 1662 was noted as retroactive to 24 June 1660. Harding's position under Charles II was in the private music for lutes, viols, and voices, replacing Edward Wormwell, who had been a violist and a singer. Harding was also a violinist, according to other entries in the Lord Chamberlain's accounts. His livery allowance, which the accounts show was rarely paid on schedule, was £16 2*s.* 6*d.* yearly; his annual salary was £40. Most of the information we have concerning Harding comes from the court accounts, but Samuel Pepys mentioned him once, on 7 January 1660, when the diarist heard Harding and others performing at Dr "Whores."

Harding augmented his income on occasion by performing extra services at court. On 30 March 1661, for instance, he was paid 7*s.* 4*d.* for attending at the funeral of Princess Mary; in the summers of 1671, 1675, and 1678 he attended the King at Windsor for an extra few pence daily. Harding seems to have remained solvent through the years, which was a rarity among court musicians. The accounts occasionally cited payments to him by other musicians, to whom, one supposes, Harding had loaned money. One instance was on 24 December 1662 when Mr Young paid John £15 14*s.* 6*d.*, and another was on 6 July 1672 when Henry Cooke's will mentioned a debt of £10 to Harding. John managed to remain a creditor even though his own livery payments seldom arrived on time; in 1683, for example, he was still owed for 1677 through 1682. He may have had a private source of income, but the only post we know of for Harding outside court was his position as a warden in the Corporation of Music, and that probably brought him no fee.

On 7 November 1684 John Harding died. He was buried on 10 November in the cloisters of Westminster Abbey, and on 26 November he was replaced in the King's private music by John Boman. Harding left a will, dated 23 September 1684 and proved on 27 November. He described himself as of the parish of St Margaret, Westminster. To the poor of his parish he left 40*s.*, to be distributed by Mr Tinker (Tynchare) alias Littleton, and to Tinker he

also left a ten-shilling ring. He left to Lord Viscount Newport his own picture (then at Mr Morgan's house, now lost), plus a gold ring worth 20*s.* To Mrs Morgan he left another such ring plus his blue stone ring, all his glasses, silver, and his watch. Rings worth 20*s.* also went to Dr (John) Blow, Mr (Edward) Braddock, and Benjamin Colinge. Rings worth 10*s.* each were left to Willaim Colinge, Mrs Healmes, and Margery Bomer. Mrs Morgan's maid received an eight-shilling ring. Harding's executors, Thomas Fordham and Thomas Morgan, received the rest of his estate. On 23 March 1697 John Gostling was appointed to Harding's place in the private music, Boman having left the royal service.

Hardy, Mr. [*fl. 1726*], *performer?*
A Mr Hardy received a benefit at the Lincoln's Inn Fields playhouse on 19 May 1726 that brought in a total of £151 1*s.* 6*d.* (probably before house charges). Hardy's function in the company—if, in fact, he was a member—is not known.

Hardy, D. J. [*fl. 1799–1802*], *actor.*
D. J. Hardy, of No 32, High Holborn, was a member of the company at the Richmond Theatre in the summer of 1799, according to some Winston papers now in the Richmond Reference Library. At the theatre in Gloucester on 6 October 1802 Hardy played Lord Duberly in *The Heir at Law* and Deputy Bull in *The Review*.

Hardy, Henry [*fl. 1781–1804*], *violinist.*
Henry Hardy of Oxford was, according to Mee's *Oldest Music Room in Europe*, a student of Pinto on the violin. An advertisement in the Oxford *Journal* of 24 February 1781 announced that Hardy had been appointed resident violinist by the Oxford Musical Society and wished to acquaint "the Gentlemen of the University that he teaches on that Instrument." Hardy published *The Violoncello Preceptor* about 1785, and by about 1790 he had set up shop in High Street, Oxford, as a music seller and publisher, succeeding William Mathews, whose publications Hardy reissued.

Doane's *Musical Directory* of 1794 listed Hardy as a participant in the Handel performances at Westminster Abbey in London, though the violinist did not take up a London residence. Mee says that Hardy became a member of the Oxford Loyal Volunteers but was expelled in 1800 for insulting the adjutant. By 1804 he had left Oxford to live near Carfax, where he sold musical instruments belonging to gentlemen of the University who had gone down.

Harford. *See* HOLLAND, CHARLES *1768–1849*

Hargrave, Mr. [*fl. 1784*], *singer.*
Mr Hargrave sang bass in the Handel Memorial Concerts at Westminster Abbey and the Pantheon in May and June 1784.

Hargrave, Mr, stage name of Robert Snow [*fl. 1791–1847*], *actor.*
An anonymous "Young Gentleman" made his debut at Covent Garden Theatre on 7 October 1791 as Osman in *Zara*. The *European Magazine* that month was blunt in its comments on the novice, who was identified as Robert Snow:

Of an attempt which was not heard by anyone in the theatre we shall say but little. To a voice inaudible, the gentleman added a redundancy of action which could not but have a ludicrous effect. He seemed to have a proper conception of the character, but from a want of power is not likely to be again seen as a candidate for stage patronage.

Hiding under the name of Hargrave, Snow tried to gain experience outside London. John Bernard said Hargrave acted at Dover in 1791; the *Thespian Magazine* in June 1792 reported him at the theatre in Plymouth. On 18 March 1793, according to the *Hibernian Journal*, he made his Irish debut at the Crow Street Theatre in Dublin, disguised again under the description "A Young Gentleman" and claiming his Dublin debut was his first appearance on any stage. On the following 30 April, at his third appearance, Hargrave's name was cited on the Crow Street bill. He performed at that playhouse through the 1795–96 season and also appeared at Cork in 1794 and 1796.

Having thus seasoned himself, Hargrave tried London again. The *Monthly Mirror* in 1796 reported that "Mr. Hargrave, from Dub-

lin, is . . . engaged for the next season" (1796–97) at Covent Garden. The periodical noted that Hargrave had been unsuccessful in his attempt in London six years before, "but he is wonderfully improved since that period." For his return Hargrave chose Octavian in *The Mountaineers*, which was performed on 6 October 1796. The first reaction from *How Do You Do?* on 8 October was lukewarm: Mr Hargrave, the critic said,

possesses an uncommon powerful voice, but is by no means happy in the modulation of it. We do not approve his speaking nearly the half of Octavian's speech behind the scenes before he appears. It is not what we have been used to, and reminded us of PUFF, who says, *it is necessary to prepare you for who is coming.*

The critic hoped to see Hargrave succeed better in subsequent performances.

The same periodical on 22 October was kinder:

So in Mr. HARGRAVE, though there is no even tenor of acting—no Siddonian maintenance of the impression once made, yet he at times harrows the heart, and proves that he has requisites for the stage that are invaluable. His lowest note fills the theatre. He requires no straining of his voice, no scream, no bellowing to reach the ear of the highest god or goddess in the house; it is as musical as it is clear, and therefore with the modulation which proceeds from judgment, there is nothing in the histrionic art which he may not achieve. Thus, in a fortunate moment, he proved his powers; his description of the murder was truly impressive, and this alone compensated for all the faults which he committed. We think that those faults are rather of the ear than of the judgment; and we know that a defective ear, however pride and ignorance may question the doctrine, is to be corrected, and melody of speech to be acquired, even by the man who cannot distinguish the gradations of a tune.

The *Monthly Mirror* also devoted a lengthy criticism to Hargrave, beginning by saying that "while we condemn his performance of Octavian as a whole—while we affirm that it was ill-conceived, and ill-executed throughout, we hesitate not to affirm, that he will become a very FINE ACTOR, and a great favourite with the public." The critic cautioned the performer not to change earlier interpretations (the critic was thinking of those of Kemble and Elliston, both of whom had been successful in the role) unless the changes were to be improvements. Then:

The grand fault of Mr. Hargrave consisted in his being too *uniform*; he seemed to have contemplated the madman in his *lucid intervals* only, for except so far as the *dress* promoted the idea, there was nothing that indicated any symptom of derangement. His dialogue and all simple recitation—one speech gave the clue to the other—regulated the measurement and the key in which it should be uttered; and the whole maintained a consistency and equality which run exactly counter to the import of the character;—there were no bursts of passion—no transitions—none of the *maniacal* properties of CERVANTES' CARDENIO: which, by the by, we recommend every performer of *Octavian* to look to, for a lesson how to play it.

Mr. Hargrave has the advantage of a very elegant figure, and a voice of uncommon strength and extensiveness; but the former requires management, and the latter *modulation*; he was unfortunate enough to excite the audience to laughter in some of the speeches of Zaphna, his *second character*; but, as we are confident his intonation is more the effect of habit, or probably choice, (for we are often captivated ourselves by certain peculiarities which are disgusting to others) than of any defect in the nasal organ; a little attention and practice will soon remove the source of such unseasonable merriment.

The countenance of Mr. Hargrave wants significance, and his action grace; and since his *genius* cannot be disputed, we may safely recommend him to apply very sedulously to the decorations of *art*. Some actors start at the term art, as if it were foreign to their profession, and they disdained to associate their fine natural talents with so mechanical a principle; but through art can raise no superstructure but on the *basis* of genius, it will do wonders when once the foundation is laid; for the adjustment of attitude and of action, the study of the *Greek statues* is admirably adapted.

We have no doubt but this gentleman, with due care and observation, will make a very delightful tragedian; he is at present too *laborious* an actor, and would probably raise more powerful effects if his efforts bore less the appearance of toil and difficulty.

The *Monthly Mirror*'s reference to Zaphna was to Hargrave's second part, in *Mahomet*, which he acted on 13 and 18 October 1796. On 26 October he played Glenalvon in *Douglas*. The *Monthly Mirror* found his character full of originality, but Hargrave only "subdued in some measure the disagreeable peculiarities of his utterance" which the critic had previously noted. On 19 December he acted Osman in *Zara* and then once again left the London stage.

John Williams in *A Pin Basket to the Children of Thespis* (1797) put it all in verse:

> Half-fledg'd and half-finish'd, lo! HAR-
>   GRAVE *appears*,
> For my plaudits too callow—too bright for my
>   sneers;
> When he burst in Octavian some laugh'd and some
>   wept,
> And many applauded, yet many more slept;
> . . . .
> Some prais'd him, and loudly, till Zaphna ap-
>   pear'd,
> And then his escutcheon was blotted and smear'd;
> All the critical saw the same o'erheated rage,
> And that Lunacy govern'd his aims on the Stage!

But Williams, too, admitted that "Some occasional flashes illumin'd his deed. . . ."

Hargrave played in York and Newbury in early 1797 and at Liverpool in 1798; then he left the stage to serve as a Captain in the Staffordshire militia, going by his own name, Robert Snow. According to the *Monthly Mirror* in 1802, he was acting again by that time, in Manchester. He returned to Dublin that year, is known to have acted Iachimo in *Cymbeline* on 7 May 1803, and remained until August 1804. Then he tried London once more.

He was engaged at Covent Garden for the 1804–5 season at £7 weekly and is known to have acted King Henry in *Richard III* on 15 October 1804. In the O. Smith collection at the British Museum is a contemporary commentary on Hargrave's reappearance: "He has very just conceptions, keen sensibility and strong powers. . . . [T]he lower division of his voice, for roundness, solemnity, and equality of tone, is superior to that of any other performer on the stage; but when it ascends above its level" it sounds nasal and strained. Hargrave also appeared as Glenalvon in *Douglas* with Master Betty.

A Mr Hargrave appeared at the Theatre Royal, Edinburgh, from January to August 1805 as Ataliba in *Pizarro*, Captain Beldare in *Love Laughs at Locksmiths*, Captain Belville in *Rosina*, Captain Vain in *Lock and Key*, Mr Collooney in *The Irishman in London*, Sir Rowland in *The Children of the Wood*, and Silvius in *As You Like It*. The roles do not appear to have been the sort our subject would have been assigned, but we know of too few of his parts to be certain, and the Edinburgh performer may have been our man. Our Hargrave was at Covent Garden again for at least the first months of the 1805–6 season. But on 23 December 1805, according to John Philip Kemble's notes, when Hargrave was performing the title role in *Barbarossa*, "(hurt at some disapprobation from the audience) at the end of the second act [he] left the theatre & withdrew himself entirely from the stage—I believe he will take a Commission in the Army."

Years later, on 10 August 1847, Robert Snow wrote to the scholar-scoundrel John Payne Collier from his lodgings at No 9, Savile Row:

Sir

In your Edition of Shakespeare Vol. II. page 338 is the line "With men, like men of strange inconstancy." and in the Note at the foot, you have given various readings.

In reading the above line . . . I have always endeavoured to give the sense—"With *men*-like men, of strange inconstancy," that is, with men, *men*-like, and consequently fickle and inconstant.

Or the same meaning, nearly, would be conveyed by writing the line thus "With men, like men, of strange inconstancy." But a vast deal of the point of Biron's wit throughout the Play is lost without great care in the enunciation.

Pray excuse this trouble from one who has not the pleasure of knowing you, excepting through your edition of Shakespeare, which I esteem one of the best ornaments of my shelves.

Collier noted in pencil on the letter (now at the Folger Shakespeare Library) that Snow's stage name had been Hargrave; "I saw him act Pierre in 1805."

Hargrave, Miss. *See* HEMET, MISS.

Haris, T. *See* HARRIS, JOSEPH.

Harland, Mr [*fl. 1694–1698*], *actor.*

Mr Harland was one of the members of the United Company under Christopher Rich in 1694–95 who stayed with Rich instead of joining Thomas Betterton and the older players in their rebellion. Consequently, Harland found himself frequently mentioned in the bills from 1695 through 1698, whereas before he had been unnoticed. For Rich, usually at Drury Lane though occasionally at the troupe's

other house in Dorset Garden, Harland acted Acacis in *The Indian Queen* in mid-April 1695, Petilius in *Bonduca* in September, Blanford in *Oroonoko* in November, Lycastes in *Neglected Virtue* in mid-February 1696, Solyman in *Ibrahim* (by Pix) in late May, Manley in *The Cornish Comedy* in June, Frederick in *The Unhappy Kindness* in July, Oronces in *Aesop* in December, Lord Lovemore in *Woman's Wit* in January 1697, Perollo in *The Triumphs of Virtue* in February, Oronces in *2 Aesop* in March, Belvil in *A Plot and No Plot* on 8 May, Friendly in *The Sham Lawyer* on 31 May, King Antigonus in *The Humorous Lieutenant* in late July, Tranio in *Sauny the Scot* sometime during the 1797–98 season, probably Alonza in *Imposture Defeated* in September 1697 (Horden was listed, but he died in 1696, so Harland may have been intended), and Gabinius in *The Fatal Discovery* in February 1698.

"Harlequin." *See* MILES, FRANCIS, and MOYLIN, FRANCISQUE.

Harley, Mr [*fl. 1790*], *actor.*

A manuscript in the British Library notes a payment of £10 10s. as "A Donation to Harley & Lewis Supernumerary Men, who fell from the Scaffold" during a performance of *The Crusade* which opened at Covent Garden Theatre on 6 May 1790 and was performed a total of 13 times before the end of the season. This notation would not seem to be a reference to George Davies Harley who was playing major roles at Covent Garden that season.

Harley, Mrs [*fl. 1768?–1781*], *actress.*

A Mrs Harley acted Mrs Graspall in *A Wife to be Lett* on 22 January 1781 and Bullfinch in *Love and a Bottle* on 26 March 1781 at the Haymarket Theatre. Perhaps she was the Mrs Harley who had acted at York in 1768. A Miss Harley, perhaps her daughter, acted at Bath in 1787–88 and at Bristol in 1787–88 and 1788–89.

Harley, "Fat" [*fl. 1797–1806*], *actor.*

A manuscript in the British Library names a "Fat" Harley as an actor of servants' roles at Covent Garden Theatre in 1797 and 1800, but we found no such name in the bills. He was probably the Mr Harley who was paid £1

10s. per week at that theatre between 1801–2 and 1805–6.

Harley, George Davies   d. 1811, actor, author.

George Davies Harley, whose real surname was Davies, was probably born in London, where as a young man he served first as a banker's clerk (or as a tailor, according to one account) at No 28, Cornhill, then as a lottery clerk, and finally as an employee in an insurance office, until he was lured to the stage by a friendship with the fine actor John Henderson (1747–1785). Having been given lessons by Henderson, he obtained an engagement at the Theatre Royal, Norwich, making his debut under the name Harley on 20 April 1785 as Richard III. There he proved successful enough to be called the "Norwich Roscius." Extant Norwich press notices indicate that he acted Benedick in *Much Ado about Nothing* for his benefit on 5 May 1787, the title role in *Tamerlane* for Quin's benefit on 23 May 1786, and King Lear for his own benefit on 30 April 1788. When Mrs Siddons made her first and only professional visit to Norwich in late sum-

Folger Shakespeare Library

GEORGE DAVIES HARLEY as Richard III
by Loftis

mer of 1788, Harley acted Dumont to her Jane Shore (on 1 September).

After performing in Norwich for four years he was engaged at £2 per week for 1789–90 by Harris at Covent Garden Theatre, where he made his debut as Richard III on 25 September 1789. One news account, noting he was a student of Henderson's, stated that, while he had the action, deportment, and utterance of his teacher, he was wanting in "the mind—the passion—and the truth" but conceded that at a period when there was a dearth of good tragedians Harley, who possessed some power, "may be useful." The *Biographical and Imperial Magazine* for October 1789 described his first London effort:

> His voice is powerful; his person well suited to the character; his action free and various, and his manner totally unembarrassed; with these advantages he went through the character with some success, and much applause; he was by far the best in the third and fourth acts, and in which he appeared to have exerted himself too much to give the requisite force to the fifth. In several of the soliloquies, he discovered nice discrimination, gave them in a very judicious manner, and often reminded us of our late favourite Henderson.

After two more performances of Richard, Harley acted Iago on 16 October. He played the role again on 26 October and later in the season, on 15 May 1790, at which time he was reviewed again by the *Biographical and Imperial Magazine*, whose critic judged that performance the best specimen of Harley's acting he had seen all season:

> In his soliloquies in particular, he *painted* the villain which Shakespeare drew. Still, however, he has not forgot that strut, and swell of the chest, which presents no faint idea of a bantum cock, strutting before his partlets at the barn door. In some places also, his mistaken emphasis evidently discovered that he had not correctly the sense of his author: particularly "Thus do I ever make my *fool* MY purse." Instead of which, he should have pronounced "Thus do I ever make my *fool* my PURSE;" the connection plainly shewing that he alludes particularly to *the use he makes of his fool*, not the manner in which his purse is supplied. Perhaps also, if he had discovered *less fear* and *more confusion*, when Othello seized him by the throat, he would have better characterized the *villainous*, but certainly not *dastardly* Iago.

On 6 November 1789 he played Shylock, followed by Hernandez in *Marcella* on 10 November, Jaques in *As You Like It* on 20 November, and King Lear on 23 November. When Henry Crabb Robinson saw his Lear again on 4 January 1790, he wrote in his *Diary* that "Harley's youth and vigour so repeatedly got the better of his endeavors to conceal them under the veil of assumed debility that it was rather the grandson of Lear . . . than the good old King himself." Harley acted Lear again on 18 January, 1 and 15 February, and 19 April. The last performance was seen by the critic of the *Biographical and Imperial Magazine* (May 1790), who thought it cold and uninteresting and wanting in dignity and power, as well as imitative of Henderson; and the writer found "disgusting" the actor's sudden and unnatural transitions of voice. Several years later John Williams (as "Anthony Pasquin") wrote of Harley's Lear in *The Children of Thespis* (1792):

> By HENDERSON tutor'd, whom GARRICK had made,
> He is but the shadow at best of a shade
> . . . .
> Had your Lear, servile HARLEY, but less of that whine,
> Competition should shake and my plaudits be thine.

Harley's other roles during his first London season included Montfort in *The Force of Passion* on 5 December 1789, Horatio in *The Fair Penitent* on 14 December, Verino in *Eudora* on 29 January 1790, Austin in *The Count of Narbonne* on 22 March, a character in *Arden of Faversham* on 14 April, Macbeth on 3 May (when he took £360 12s., less house charges of about £108; tickets had been available from him at No 252, Holborn), Chief Bramin in *The Widow of Malabar* on 5 May, and Ventidius in *All for Love* on 24 May. The familiar critic of the *Biographical and Imperial Magazine* took him to task severely for his overplaying of Chief Bramin, but proclaimed him, in balance, to be a fine player:

He did, it is true, all that convulsive twinges of the eyelids, distortions of countenance, and abundance of black lead pencilling could do to remedy the want of expression, so evident in his features; but these cannot give the eye which speaks the meaning of the soul, or the flexible muscles which sympathise with the internal passions; neither can his affected and sudden transitions of tone supply the absence of that powerful and copious harmony of voice which so nicely discriminates the feelings of the real player. Mr. Harley is not, however, without merit; he conceives his character justly; and so far as his powers extend, does justice to his author: and considering the present state of the theatres, we know not how his characters could be so ably filled.

In 1790–91 Harley's salary was raised to £5 per week. He again played Lear, Richard, Iago, and Chief Bramin, and took on Tamerlane, Pierre in *Venice Preserv'd*, Glenalvon in *Douglas*, Burleigh in *The Earl of Essex*, Carlos in *Isabella*, Don Fabio in *Lorenzo*, Duke Angelo in *The Double Falsehood*, and Don John in *The Chances* (for his benefit on 1 June at which he received £242 1s. 6d., less house charges; tickets had been available from him at No 22, Great Queen Street, Lincoln's Inn Fields). He also appeared regularly to deliver the prologue to *Wild Oats*. Harley acted in Yorkshire in August 1791. In 1791–92, his third year at Covent Garden, he again played some of his major roles, such as Chief Bramin, Lear, Richard, and Polydore, and added Creon in *Medea*

Harvard Theatre Collection

GEORGE DAVIES HARLEY

engraving by Ridley, after Edridge

and Leontes in *The Winter's Tale*, but he also appeared in the less substantial parts of Laertes, Comus, Milford in *The Road to Ruin*, Antipholis in *The Comedy of Errors*, and Guiderius in *The Winter's Tale*. On 18 May 1792, now living at No 51, Great Queen Street, he received at his benefit £308 14s. 6d., less £105 house charges.

After playing at Birmingham in the summer of 1792, Harley returned once more to Covent Garden, and although he acted again as Iago and also played Petruchio, never again in London was he to enjoy a business in so capital a line, for he was now relegated to the likes of Captain Seymour in *The Irishman in London*, Sealand in *The Conscious Lovers*, Edwin in *Elfrida*, Solasco in *Columbus*, Jaques in *As You Like It*, the Ghost in *Hamlet*, and the Duke of Norfolk in *Henry VIII*. For his benefit on 23 May 1793 he chose Stricland in *The Suspicious Husband* and collected gross receipts of £341 5s. 6d. He was now living at No 1, Castle Street, Bloomsbury. On 23 April 1793, he substituted for Kemble with the Drury Lane company at the Haymarket as Horatio in *The Fair Penitent*.

Harley continued at Covent Garden for three more seasons, through 1795–96, at a steady salary of £6 per week, in a repertoire of modest roles, most now in a more mature line which included Clytus in *Alexander the Great*, Pisanio in *Cymbeline*, Kent in *King Lear*, Gloster in *Jane Shore*, Count Montoni in *The Mysteries of the Castle*, Banquo in *Macbeth*, King Henry in *Richard III*, and the Earl of Devonshire in *The Days of Yore*. For his benefit on 27 May 1795, when he played Southampton in *The Earl of Essex*, his gross proceeds were £287 3s., and on 12 May 1796, his last benefit at Covent Garden, at which he acted Shylock (for the first time since he had played the role in the autumn of 1789), the gross receipts were £219 12s. 6d. His address was still in Castle Street. On 22 February 1796 he acted Perez in *The Mourning Bride* for a benefit given to Miller at the Haymarket. In his *Candid and Impartial Strictures on the Performers*, F. G. Waldron summarized Harley's attributes and defects as an actor in 1795:

A performer of great assiduity and no inconsiderable degree of merit. His person too short, but well proportioned. His action wants variety; and

there is a hardness in it that resembles much the same defect in the late Mr. Henderson, a gentleman he always appears to have in his mind's eye. His voice is . . . good, but wanting in sweetness and harmony . . . and possesses not one strain of the tender and pathetic. There is an inflexible something in his features that he cannot throw off, and which suits well the flinty countenance of a *Richard*, or a *Shylock*, but is little adapted to the grief worn . . . *Lear*. We think this gentleman's abilities ought to be better directed than they have been of late. His comedy, into which he had been occasionally thrust, is in our opinion insufferable. . . .

In the summer of 1796 Harley returned to Birmingham, where he had also played the previous summer, to prove a great favorite. The *Monthly Mirror* in July 1796 reported that his poems, which he had been writing since his days at Norwich, made him accepted at the tasteful literary parties of Birmingham. Evidently stories circulated that he had quarreled

Harvard Theatre Collection

GEORGE DAVIES HARLEY as Caleb engraving by Wilson, after De Wilde with William Macready the Birmingham manager, so Harley inserted the following letter "To the Public" in the press on 22 August 1796:

Injurious reports, tending to depreciate the character of Mr. M'Cready, being in circulation, falsely asserting and insinuating, that a mis-understanding or quarrel existed between him and myself,—I take this public opportunity of avowing, that no such circumstances has ever taken place; and in the most sacred and solemn manner assert, that directly or indirectly, through myself or friends, I have neither said, suggested, written or circulated any thing whatever, that could in the slightest degree militate against the character of Mr. M'Cready, either as a man or manager; whose behaviour, on every occasion, has been that of a Gentleman and sincere Friend towards me.

Dissatisfied with his salary, and no doubt unhappy with his roles, Harley left Covent Garden—one report stated that he was dismissed—and joined the company at Bath and Bristol for 1796–97, making his debut at both theatres as Richard III toward the end of August 1796. He subsequently enjoyed success in old men of comedy; it was said that he resembled a popular clergyman of Bath. He acted regularly in the winter seasons at Bristol until 1799 and during the summers at Birmingham from 1797 through 1802; he was also at Sheffield in 1799 and at Liverpool and Worcester in 1801. At Manchester in 1800 he acted Richard III, Shylock, and Iago during Whitsun Week. He was at Dublin in 1799–1800 and 1802, in the latter year supporting Mrs Siddons's farewell visit to that city.

Probably he was the Mr Harley who acted a role in *The Battle of Edmonton* and Colonel Ormsby in *The Romance of an Hour* at the Haymarket on 10 May 1797 and Roger in *The Mayor of Garratt*, Harry Halliard in *A Naval Interlude*, and Sir Stephen Bertram in *The Jew*, all at the Haymarket on 26 March 1798.

Harley died at Leicester on 28 October 1811. His obituary notice in the *Gentleman's Magazine* in November 1811 described him as "a poet of some eminence, and a comedian of much provincial celebrity; much esteemed as an independent, upright, and honourable man." Another news report of his death stated that he had been much respected for his suavity of manners and his integrity.

On 4 March 1788 at Chelmsford Harley had married his first wife, Elizabeth Griffith, the daughter of "the late" John Griffith. She seems not to have been on the stage. The Ann Davies, daughter of George and Elizabeth Davies, who was baptized at St Paul, Covent Garden, on 14 July 1799, may have been their child.

Earlier, before 1792, two sons had been born to them. One named George, had died in infancy. The other, also named George, was the subject of a very long poem by Harley, "To His *only* Child; His dear Boy George;—the Second; A Legacy of Love," which was published at London in his *Poems*, 1796, when the boy was four years of age.

By the time Harley drew his will at Sheffield in his last year of life, on 21 January 1811, he had a second wife, Susanna, to whom he left his estate. In the will he mentioned two children (but not by name) who he claimed were well provided for and charged them not to disturb their mother's unquestionable possession. The will was proved at London on 30 May 1812 by his widow.

Harley's writing included the volumes of poems mentioned above; *A Monody on the Death of Mr. John Henderson, late of Covent Garden Theatre* (Norwich 1787); *Ballad Stories, Sonnets &c.* (Bath 1799); *Holyhead Sonnets* (Bath 1800); *An authentic biographical sketch of the Life . . . of W.H.W. Betty, the Celebrated Young Roscius* (London 1804); and *The Fight off Trafalgar. A descriptive poem* (London and Sheffield 1806). In reviewing the publication of the *Ballad Stories, Sonnets &c.*, the *Monthly Mirror* in August 1799 wrote that "The metre is as various as the subjects, and, if the general merit of these pieces be not equal to the former volume, they are nevertheless the production of a man of extensive reading and good taste."

Portraits of Harley include:

1. An engraving by W. Ridley, after Edridge. Published as a plate to *Parson's Minor Theatre*, 1793.

2. As Caleb in *The Siege of Damascus*. By De Wilde. In the Garrick Club. Engraved by Winslow for *Bell's British Theatre*, 1793.

3. As Kent in *King Lear*. Pencil and watercolor by De Wilde. In the Victoria and Albert Museum. Engraved by W. Ridley for the *Monthly Mirror*, 1803.

4. As Lusignan in *Zara*. By De Wilde. In the Garrick Club. Engraved by W. Bromley for *Bell's British Theatre*, 1791. Another en-

graving, by an anonymous engraver, was published in *British Drama*, 1807.

5. As Maskwell in *The Double Dealer*. Engraving by Audinet, after De Wilde, for *Bell's British Theatre*, 1795.

6. As Mosby in *Arden of Faversham*. Watercolor by W. Loftis. In the Folger Shakespeare Library.

7. As Richard III. Watercolor by W. Loftis. In the Folger Shakespeare Library.

Harlowe, Master [*fl.* *1792–1794*], actor.

A Master Harlowe acted the role of a Child in performances of *Isabella* with the Drury Lane company at the King's Theatre on 21 January, 24 March, and 17 December 1792, and on 4 May 1793. He also played a Bloody Child in the production of *Macbeth*, which was the first dramatic presentation to be given at the new Drury Lane Theatre on 21 April 1794.

Perhaps Master Harlowe was the child of the actress Sarah Harlowe by an alliance prior to her relationship with Francis Godolphin Waldron.

Harlowe, Sarah, stage name [of Miss Wilson? and later] of "Mrs" Francis Godolphin Waldron the second *1765–1852, actress, singer, dancer.*

The actress who performed under the stage name of Sarah Harlowe was born in 1765, probably in London, and perhaps with the maiden name of Wilson. The specification by *The Dictionary of National Biography* of her stage debut at Colnbrook, near Slough, in 1787, is manifestly wrong, for according to all accounts of her life (including that in the *DNB*), she had had some theatrical experience before she became a member of Francis Godolphin Waldron's summer company which was based at Richmond but sometimes played at Windsor. Waldron's management of the Richmond Theatre occurred in 1779 and 1780, some eight years before the reputed debut at Colnbrook.

According to *The Secret History of the Green Room* (1792) Sarah had assumed the name of Harlowe because she thought it would look good on a playbill. Although her theatrical career remained closely allied to that of Waldron in the 1780s, it is not possible to state with certainty when their personal relationship began, for Waldron had a wife who was with

Harvard Theatre Collection

SARAH HARLOWE as Dorothy

engraving by E. Harding, Junior, after S. Harding

him at least until 1788. In fact Mrs Waldron was a member of the company headed by her husband that played at the Windsor Castle Inn in King Street, Hammersmith, in the summer of 1786, when Mrs Harlowe made her first London appearance of notice on 19 July as Kitty Sprightly in *All the World's a Stage*. On 24 July Mrs Harlowe acted Trusty in *The Provok'd Husband* and two nights later played Lady Frances Touchwood in *The Belle's Stratagem* and Laura in *The Fool*.

During the ensuing winter season Mrs Harlowe made two appearances in specially licensed performances at the Haymarket: as Anna in *Douglas* and Melissa in *The Lying Valet* on 18 December 1786 and as Harriet in *The Devil upon Two Sticks* on 8 January 1787 for the benefit of Harwood, formerly prompter at Drury Lane. She was with the Richmond company in the summer of 1788. Through the influence of Waldron she was soon engaged at Sadler's Wells, where, according to Winston, she was much noticed as a "sprightly actress of chambermaids" and enjoyed special success in *The Guardian Frigate*. The song *Jack the Guinea Pig*, as sung by her in *The Guardian Frigate* at the Wells, was published in 1790. She cut a good "breeches" figure and exhibited a "good flow of spirits and some humour."

Probably about that time she began living with Waldron, whom she never seems to have married, seeking—as one memoir put it— "the comforts of a matrimonial life without the ceremonies." She was now 25 years old, he 50. Mrs Waldron had left him or died sometime after she gave her last performance on record at the Haymarket as Tag in *Miss in Her Teens* and Damaris in *Barnaby Brittle* on 30 September 1788.

Mrs Harlowe's growing reputation in a mixture of roles as singer, dancer, and actress secured her an engagement at Covent Garden, where she made her first appearance on 4 November 1790 as one of the unspecified principal characters in O'Keeffe's new comic opera *The Fugitive*. After three more performances of that piece she appeared as Sophia in a new musical interlude called *A Divertissement* on 23 November and repeated that role numerous times that season. Her other roles included Patch in *The Busy Body*, Colombine in *The Picture of Paris, Taken in the Year 1790*, Miss Jenny in *The Provok'd Husband*, Donna Clara in *Two Strings to your Bow*, Nancy in *Three Weeks after Marriage*, Belinda in *Modern Antiques*, Emma Tudor in *National Prejudice*, Wishwell in *The Double Gallant*, and a principal character in *Primrose Green*.

After spending the summer of 1791 under Fox's management at Brighton (where she played "splendidly" Roxalana in *The Sultan* and Peggy in *The Country Girl*), Mrs Harlowe returned to Covent Garden, in the next two seasons sustaining pert chambermaids, romps, and shrews such as Lucy in *The Beggar's Opera*, Marianne in *The Dramatist*, Jenny in *The Road to Ruin*, Rachel in *The Prisoner at Large*, Wowski in *Inkle and Yarico*, Grace in *The Fashionable Levities*, and principal characters in *The Woodman, Hartford Bridge*, and *Harlequin's Museum*. At her benefits on 19 May 1792 and 10 June 1793 she shared with Marshall net receipts of £151 7s. and £273 13s. 6d., respec-

tively, and in each instance her address was given as No 54, Drury Lane, the same address as Waldron's. In the summer of 1792 she acted again at Brighton and also at Margate.

In 1793–94 Mrs Harlowe joined Colman's company for a winter season at the Haymarket (where Waldron was prompter), a season made possible by Colman's renting the patent from the Drury Lane proprietors, who were awaiting the completion of their new theatre. There she acted Dorothy in *Heigho for a Husband* (written by Waldron), Diana Grampus in *The Box-Lobby Challenge*, and the male role of William in *Rosina*, which she played for the first time on 11 February 1794. Her neat figure suited her for male roles, or breeches' parts, which she often assumed. In *The London Theatres* (1795) Thomas Bellamy wrote of her in dreadful verse:

> *When well form'd* HARLOW's *seen in breeches*
> *Her dainty leg the eye bewitches,*
> *Sure none has seen and none will see*
> *Her* Dolly *give a dish of tea [in Heigh Ho]*
> *Without a free approving smile*
> *Join'd with just share of praise the while.*

In the same year her *cher ami* Waldron characterized her in his *Candid and Impartial Strictures on the Performers* with a playful tweak: "Serious, comic, or operatic parts, are all the same to her, in the whole of which she uniformly displays a most happy self-possession, which sometimes approaches *a little* too much to the *impudent*."

For six consecutive years, 1794 through 1799, Mrs Harlowe was regularly engaged at the summer Haymarket in her usual line, to which she added in 1794 Betsy Blossom (with a song) in *The Deaf Lover*, Floranthe in *The Mountaineers*, Queen Philippa in *The Surrender of Calais*, Flora in *She Wou'd and She Wou'd Not*, Mrs Sneak in *The Mayor of Garratt*, Tag in *Miss in Her Teens*, and Comfit in *The Dead Alive*; in 1795 Mrs Scout in *The Village Lawyer*, Adeline in *The Battle of Hexham*, Lucy in *The Recruiting Officer*, and Dorcas in *The Mock Doctor*; and in 1796, Mrs Cadwallader in *The Author*, Juba (breeches role) and Caroline in *The Prize*, and Cecilia in *The Son in Law*. She also made rare excursions into more serious drama: Elizabeth in *Richard III* on 27 August 1794, Gertrude in *Hamlet* on 18 August 1795, Nerissa in *The Merchant of Venice* on 28 August 1797, and

Emilia in *Othello* on 4 September 1797 (in the last two Elliston acted Shylock and Othello), but she was sensible enough to limit herself to characters of the second or third walk.

During those years at the Haymarket she did not have an engagement at either winter house, a circumstance that bothered a writer in *How Do You Do?* on 13 August 1796: "She is an improving little performer, and we think it would be to the interest of all parties if she had a situation in Town the whole Year. We have seen many *Adelines* [in *The Battle of Hexham*], but . . . never saw the character so well played as when by the Lady in question, which is rather astonishing, sentimental declamation being out of her general line of acting."

For a brief time she joined William Macready's undertaking at the Royalty Theatre, in the East End, which he reopened on 27 November 1797 for a desperate season; there she appeared in a musical sketch called *Amurath the Fourth, or the Turkish Harem* and in the pantomime *The Festival of Hope, or Harlequin in a Bottle*. But otherwise she was obliged to take winter work in the provinces, playing at Exeter in December 1795 and in March 1797 (when she was "a particular favorite"), at the Theatre Royal, Birmingham, in 1797, in June and September 1798, and at Wolverhampton in February 1799. In the last place she had been engaged for only 12 nights but then was retained for the whole season. The reporter to the *Monthly Mirror* in February 1799 called her "a pleasant actress" who performed "many characters with great spirit." She acted at Sheffield in October 1799 and in the summer of 1800 was at the Theatre Royal, Weymouth, performing Letitia Hardy in *The Belle's Stratagem* and Kitty Sprightly in *All the World's a Stage* on 6 August and Moggy in *The Highland Reel* and Lady Racket in *Three Weeks after Marriage* on 13 August. She was again at Weymouth in 1801.

At the turn of the century Mrs Harlowe received an engagement at Drury Lane Theatre at 10*s.* per night (£3 per week). She made her first appearance on that stage on 2 Feburary 1801 in the role of Cora in *Pizarro* and continued there for 26 years, including three seasons with the Drury Lane company at the Lyceum from 1809 to 1812. She was also a member of the "English Opera" at the Lyceum in the summer of 1816. Her salary from 1804–5 through

Courtesy of the Garrick Club

SARAH HARLOWE as Adeline
by Wellings

1808–9 was £6 per week, and during that period Waldron nearly always signed for its receipt. By 1811–12 she was earning £8 per week, an amount she still received in 1819–20. She also acted summers at the Haymarket from 1802 to 1810. A Drury Lane casting book dating about 1815 (now in the Folger Library) lists 39 roles for Mrs Harlowe, including Lady Loverule in *The Devil to Pay*, Lucy in *The Rivals*, Lady Freelove in *The Jealous Wife*, Mrs Frail in *Love for Love*, Lady Sneerwell in *The School for Scandal*, Judith in *The Iron Chest*, and a Witch in *Macbeth*—parts which reflected her advancing years.

On 29 January 1818 a substitute had to be found for her part at Drury Lane, she "being absent on account of the very dangerous state of Mr. Waldron's health." He died in March of that year at his home in Orange Street, Red Lion Square. In his will, made 13 years earlier on 12 December 1805, Waldron described himself as of Duke Street, Lincoln's Inn Fields, and of the parish of St Giles in the Fields and left all his property to Mrs Sarah Harlowe of the Theatre Royal, Drury Lane, in trust for his four younger children Sarah Elizabeth, Frances Anne, Francis, and William Waldron. To his eldest son, George Waldron, and to his foster son, George Rusdon, he left £5 each. On 28 July 1818 Sarah Harlowe, widow, of Seymour Crescent, Eustace Square, appeared to swear to Waldron's handwriting and on the following day she was granted administration.

According to the *Authentic Memoirs of the Green Room* (1799), in the earlier time of their "matrimonial" life, Sarah and Waldron suffered temporary separations brought on by quarrels, but their "tender pledges" of love (presumably children) kept their union firm, although Sarah never changed her name. The 1806 edition of the *Authentic Memoirs* stated that they then had "four fine and promising children," evidently the four younger children mentioned in his will of 1805. (On 17 May 1814 Mrs Harlowe was absent from rehearsal having "gone to the Bishop to get her children confirmed.")

Waldron's oldest son, George, was the issue of his marriage with Mrs Waldron. Advertised as Waldron Junior, George played at the Haymarket Theatre as early as 11 June 1793.

The elder son of Sarah Harlowe and Waldron, probably Francis, was 16 in 1809; on 26 June of that year his father wrote to Field at Brighton to recommend the lad, unnamed, for the position of messenger or other minor service; he said the boy was 16, that he was his eldest son, and that he had performed Douglas with "much approbation, for my last Benefit, at the Haymarket Theatre." The Mrs Hale who acted with her husband at Lynn, Norfolk, in 1815 was identified by John Brunton in a letter to Winston in March 1815 as "a Daughter [probably Sarah Elizabeth] of Mrs Harlowes & clever both of them if you want such persons you will find it difficult to get better in the country. . . ." The Hales were acting at the Surrey Theatre, London, in 1827. The Master Harlowe who acted on occasion the role of a child in the Drury Lane company at the King's

Theatre in 1792 may have been Sarah's son by a previous alliance.

After a career of some 37 years, Mrs Harlowe retired from the stage in 1826, her last role being Mrs Foresight in *John Bull* at Drury Lane on 21 February 1826. Having been a long-time subscriber to the Drury Lane Fund, beginning in 1827 she received an annuity of £140, which was in 1837 reduced to £112. She died of heart failure in her lodgings at No 5, Albert Place, Gravesend, Kent, on 2 January 1852, at the age of 86. According to her obituary notice in the *Gentleman's Magazine* in March 1852, "she enjoyed her faculties to the end." Her death was registered at Somerset House as that of "Sarah Waldron, annuitant."

Portraits of Sarah Harlowe include:

1. As Adeline in *The Battle of Hexham*. Watercolor by W. Wellings, 1795. Presented to the Garrick Club by Mrs Harlowe in 1839.

2. As Beatrice in *The Anatomist*. Pencil and watercolor by Samuel De Wilde, 1805. In the collection of Her Majesty, Queen Elizabeth II. Engraving by R. Cooper. Published as a plate to Cawthorn's *Minor British Theatre*, 1807.

3. As Dorothy in *Heigho for a Husband*. Watercolor by S. Harding. Presented to the Garrick Club by Mrs Harlowe in 1836. Engraving by E. Harding, Jr, published by T. Arrowsmith, 1794.

4. As Jenny, with Harriet Grist as Sophia, in *The Road to Ruin*. Engraving by Barlow. Published by J. Roach, 1793. Reproduced with the entry of Harriet Grist in this dictionary.

5. As Lady Lambert, with William Dowton as Dr Cantwell and John Liston as Maw-Worm, in *The Hypocrite*. Drawn and engraved from life by W. Gear. Published by J. W. Gear, July 1824.

6. As Miss Pickle, with Claire Fisher as Little Pickle and John Tayleure as Tag, in *The Spoiled Child*. Painting by George Clint. Exhibited at the Royal Academy in 1823. Now in the Garrick Club, presented by F. J. Nettlefold in 1924.

7. As Mrs Sneak, with William Dowton as Major Sturgeon and S. T. Russell as Jerry Sneak, in *The Mayor of Garratt*. Painting by Samuel De Wilde. In the Garrick Club. Reproduced with the entry of William Dowton in this dictionary.

8. As Widow Warren. Engraving by J. Rog-

ers. Published as a plate to Oxberry's *Dramatic Biography*, 1825.

Harm. *See* HAYM.

Harman, Mr *d. c. 1759, actor, singer.*

About 1750 at Lymington Mr Harman married Catharine Maria Charke, the daughter of the eccentric Charlotte Cibber Charke. He apparently was an actor before they met. The couple performed in and around Bath and on the Isle of Wight. On 3 September 1756 they were with Hallam's company at the Swan Inn at Bartholomew Fair, playing Sir Politick and Lady Tagg in *Adventures of Half an Hour*.

The Harmans went to America and by 1758 were with David Douglass's company. Between 25 June and 14 December 1759 at the new theatre on Society Hill in Philadelphia Harman is known to have acted the title role in *Tamerlane*, Richard III, Sir Francis Wronghead in *The Provok'd Husband*, Old Norval in *Douglas*, Brazen and a Recruit in *The Recruiting Officer*, Polonius and the Gravedigger in *Hamlet*, Vellum in *The Drummer*, Atticus in *Theodosius*, Blunt in *George Barnwell*, Macheath in *The Beggar's Opera*, Lothario in *The Fair Penitent*, King Lear, Duncan and a Witch in *Macbeth*, Mercutio in *Romeo and Juliet*, the Conjurer in *Harlequin Collector*, and Lewson in *The Gamester*. He was performing at the new theatre on Society Hill in Philadelphia.

Harman's death is usually given as about 1759; since he is known to have acted on 14 December of that year, his death must have been in the last two weeks of December or early the following year. Mrs Harman retired from the stage temporarily after his death, but she returned to act with Douglass in Charleston in 1763. She died in New York in 1773. A Mr Harman acted in Philadelphia in 1799; he may have been a son of Catharine Charke Harman and her husband.

Harman, Mr ₁*fl. 1800₁, doorkeeper.*

Mr Harman, a doorkeeper at Drury Lane according to the theatre accounts, had his benefit tickets accepted on 14 June 1800.

Harman, Mrs. *See* **Charke, Catherine Maria.**

Harman, George ₁*fl. 1670₁, manager.*

A warrant in the Lord Chamberlain's accounts dated 29 August 1670 ordered the apprehension of George Harman, who had been putting on dumb shows and rope-dancing exhibitions, apparently without authority.

Harman, John *d. 1663, trumpeter.*

John Harman of the parish of St Olave, Southwark, Surrey, wrote his will on 22 July 1663, describing himself as a trumpeter "sicke in body." To his friend John Jolleff he left £8 and to Jolleff's wife 40*s*. for a pair of gloves. To a Mr Sornder of Whitechapel he left £5 to be paid within six months of Harman's death. A similar bequest was made to Susanna and Mary Swinford. Harman asked that £10 be distributed to the poor of St Olave's parish. The rest of his estate he left to Elizabeth Swinford, the wife of Peter Swinford, trumpeter, and he named Mrs Swinford his executrix. She proved the will on 28 July 1663.

Harman, Thomas ₁*fl. 1709₁, actor.*

Thomas Harman, an otherwise unknown actor, was listed in 1709 among the members of the Drury Lane troupe who protested the silencing of their company in June of that year.

Harmozin. *See* KARMAZIN.

Harnege, Thomas ₁*fl. 1668–1670₁, scenekeeper.*

The London Stage lists Thomas Harnege as a scenekeeper in the King's Company at the Bridges Street Theatre in 1668–69 and 1669–70. A Lord Chamberlain's warrant dated 13 July 1669 cites Harnege as a company member.

Harnell, Mrs ₁*fl. 1790₁, performer.*

Mrs Harnell was named in the Sadler's Wells advertisements as making her first appearance in an unspecified role or function in *The Incas of Peru* on 12 April 1790.

Harold, ₁ Henrietta?₁ ₁*d. 1738?₁, actress.*

Mrs Harold (or Herold) played Manila in *The Female Fop* at the Haymarket Theatre on 12 December 1723 as one of a group of "Persons who never yet appear'd in Public." The inexperience of the amateur performers made for an unsuccessful presentation, though the play was repeated on 13 and 31 December. On 5 February 1724 Mrs Harold acted Leonora in *Sir Courtly Nice*, and on 9 March she shared a benefit with three others when *Venice Preserv'd* was presented.

Mrs. Harold acted at Lincoln's Inn Fields in 1725–26, playing Calpurnia in *Julius Caesar* on 15 December 1725, Maria in *The Fond Husband* on 24 June 1726, and Isabella in *The Man's the Master* on 15 July.

Possibly the following entries in the registers of St Paul, Covent Garden, concern Mrs Harold and her family: Thomas Henry Herrold, son of Henry Herrold, was buried on 14 November 1736; Henrietta Maria Herold, widow, was buried on 14 March 1738.

Haron. *See* HERON.

Harper, Mr [*fl.* 1755–1770], *actor, pantomime deviser.*

Mr Harper played Jarvis in *The Gamester* and Pierrot in *The Spell, or Harlequin Salamander* with Simpson's company at the Jacob's Wells playhouse in Bristol on 31 March 1755. He was probably the Harper who acted Sir Anthony Laycock in *The Happy Gallant* on 6 September of the same year at Bence's Room in Swan Tavern at Bartholomew Fair. Mrs Harper, presumably his wife, acted Mrs Brittle. Harper played at the Orchard Street Theatre in Bath from 1756 to 1770, though he was not there in 1761–62, and in 1764–65 he was at the Smock Alley Theatre in Dublin. A letter has survived concerning Harper's Dublin engagement. On 23 July 1763 Dr Thomas Wilson wrote from Dublin to Samuel Derrick at Bath:

Harper is a very valuable acquisition. I must request of you to conclude a positive agreement with him, reduc'd to writing (His performances as Inventor or Conductor of Pantomimes to be included). . . . If he can't stay for the Money till M. arrives, I must request of you to advance him the 3 Guineas.

Evidently the agreement was not made until a year later.

Harper, Mr [*fl.* 1787–1790], *actor.*

Mr Harper played Sadi in *Barbarossa* on 28 March 1787 at the Red Lion Inn, Lordship

Road, Stoke Newington; and at the Haymarket Theatre on 29 September 1790 he acted Diggory in *She Stoops to Conquer* and offered Hippisley's Drunken Man monologue. Perhaps he was the Mr Harper who acted at Brighton in 1789 and who, with his wife, acted at Dover the same year. Thomas Dibdin in his *Reminiscences* spoke of that Harper as "a tall, gaunt, meagre-looking gentleman, who from some nasal defect, snuffled out dramatic quotations with an irresistibly ludicrous effect." Dibdin said Harper "was blest with a form and face, the component parts of which were still more discordant than his voice." In 1789, Dibdin recalled, Harper was in Richland's troupe at the end of the Eastbourne season and came to blows with Russell and Richland over a quarrel between the manager and Mrs Harper. Harper was expelled from the company. Mrs Harper, described as a handsome woman, seems not to have performed in London.

Harper, Mrs [*fl.* 1755], *actress. See* HARPER, MR [1755–1770].

Harper, Master [*fl.* 1737–1738], *dancer.*

As one of the "Lilliputian" dancing scholars of Leviez, Master Harper appeared as a Country Lad in *The Burgomaster Trick'd* at Drury Lane on 19 November 1737 and subsequent dates and again the following season beginning on 4 December 1738. He may have been the son of the Drury Lane actor John Harper, though when Harper died in 1742 his widow was referred to as "in years," and no mention was made of a son. Harper's will named no son.

Harper, Elizabeth. *See* BANNISTER, MRS JOHN.

Harper, John *d. 1742, actor, dancer, singer, manager.*

Little is known of John Harper's early stage career, but he was probably the Mr Harper who wrote and spoke the epilogue and acted Theophilus at a performance of *Injured Virtue* at the King's Arms in Southwark on 1 November 1714. The troupe was called the Duke of Southampton and Cleaveland's Servants; they are known to have presented the same play at

Richmond the previous summer, but the cast was not then advertised. The next mention of Harper in the records was on 5 September 1719, when he appeared at the Bullock-Leigh booth (apparently at Southwark Fair) dancing a comical scene "mimicking a Drunken Man." The players on that occasion were hailed as from Lincoln's Inn Fields Theatre, though Harper's name was not cited in any playbills there the previous season. John repeated his drunken man dance for his own benefit at Bullock's booth in Southwark on 24 September.

In 1719–20 Harper acted a full schedule at Lincoln's Inn Fields, and the size of some of his roles suggests that he would not have been unnoticed in the bills the previous season had he been in the company. Indeed, the evidence points to a considerable amount of stage experience somewhere prior to 1719–20. Harper acted the Murderer in *Macbeth* on 13 October 1719, Balderdash in *The Twin Rivals* on 15 October, the second Boor in *The Royal Merchant* on 5 November, Montmorency in *King*

Harvard Theatre Collection

JOHN HARPER as Jobson
engraving by Miller, after White

Henry IV of France on 7 November, the Mad Tailor in *The Pilgrim* on 17 November, Kite in *The Recruiting Officer* on 18 November, Casca in *Julius Caesar* on 19 November, Teague in *The Committee* on 23 November, Grogram in *The Pretenders* on 26 November, Loadham in *The Half Pay Officers* and Old Hob in *Hob's Wedding* on 11 January 1720, Sir Rowland Heartfree in *Whig and Tory* on 26 January, Driver in *Oroonoko* on 13 February, Hackum in *The Squire of Alsatia* on 15 March, and Sancho Panza in *Don Quixote* on 5 May. During the season his drunken man dance was often presented, and for his benefit with Miss Stone on 3 May 1720 he embellished it with the song, "Four and Twenty Stock-Jobbers," which thereafter became as popular as Harper's dance. John's line was almost identical with that of John Hall, who was beginning his career with the Lincoln's Inn Fields troupe about the same time. As will be seen, Harper soon changed to Drury Lane, where he spent the bulk of his career, giving Hall stiff competition.

In 1720–21, however, Harper was still at Lincoln's Inn Fields. Before the regular season commenced he appeared in Southwark playing Kite in *The Recruiting Officer* and Bardolph in *1 Henry IV*. Then he worked at Lincoln's Inn Fields, adding such new parts as Dr Caius in *The Merry Wives of Windsor*, Ajax in *Troilus and Cressida*, Flip in *The Fair Quaker*, Mopus in *The Cheats*, and Fondle in *The Quaker's Wedding*. At benefit time he again offered his song and dance; he and Miss Stone shared receipts of £92 9s. 6d. on 4 May 1721. In the summer Harper showed his dance at the Haymarket Theatre, played Booby in *The Country Wit* and Tom in *The Lancashire Witches* at Drury Lane, and acted Roderigo in *The Siege of Bethulia* at Bartholomew Fair and Fearful in *The Noble Englishman* at Southwark Fair.

Harper became a permanent member of the Drury Lane troupe in 1721–22, his first role in the regular season being Sir Epicure Mammon in *The Alchemist* on 25 October 1721. He played at that house regularly until his death in 1742, though his activity the last few years of his life was curtailed because of illness. Over the years he tried such new parts as Sir Jealous in *The Busy Body*, Puzzle in *The Funeral*, Surly in *Sir Courtly Nice*, Ventoso, Trinculo, and a Waterman in *The Tempest*, Heartwell in *The Old Bachelor*, Falstaff in *1 Henry IV* (for the first time on 11 May 1723 for his benefit; the role became one of his best), Cacafogo in *Rule a Wife and Have a Wife*, Sosia in *Amphitryon*, Bonniface and Sullen in *The Stratagem*, Trapolin in *A Duke and No Duke*, the title part in *The Spanish Fryar*, Sir Harry in *The Tender Husband*, Kate Matchlock in *The Funeral* (one of several skirts parts he played), Old Bellair in *The Man of Mode*, Sir Wilful in *The Way of the World*, Lory in *The Relapse*, Mrs Midnight in *The Twin Rivals*, Falstaff in *2 Henry IV*, Henry VIII, Pinchwife in *The Country Wife*, Ben and Sir Sampson in *Love for Love*, Jobson in *The Devil to Pay* (which won Harper a raise in 1731), Ursula in *Bartholomew Fair*, Huncamunca in *The Tragedy of Tragedies*, Lady Termagant in *The Boarding School* (which elicited a commentary in *The Auditor* in February 1733), the Mayor in *Richard III*, Lolpoop in *The Squire of Alsatia*, Lockit in *The Beggar's Opera*, the Host in *The Merry Wives of Windsor*, Gripe in *The Confederacy*, Antonio in *Love Makes a Man*, the Alderman in *The Plain Dealer*, and Sir Tunbelly in *The Relapse*.

Over the years Harper continued his interest in the late summer fairs and made occasional appearances at other playhouses. He was at Richmond in the summer of 1722 and then shared with Lee and Spiller the management of a Bartholomew Fair booth; in 1723 he was not at the fairs but appeared in some late summer performances at Drury Lane; and in the summer of 1724 Harper acted several of his standard roles, such as Boniface, Trapolin, Sir Jealous, and the Spanish Fryar, at Richmond, acted and danced at Lee's Bartholomew Fair booth, and then ran a booth with Lee at Southwark Fair. John was inactive—in London and vicinity at any rate—in the summer of 1725; he shared the operation of booths at both fairs in 1726; in 1727 he and Lee were in charge of a Bartholomew Fair venture; he shared booth management at both fairs in 1728 (he even helped run two different booths that summer at Southwark Fair); Lee and Harper worked at both fairs in 1729, 1730, and 1731 (their team effort was pictured: "Lee and Harper is here" said their sign); and the same pair ran two booths at Southwark Fair in 1732.

In 1733 Harper teamed with Lee and Petit to run a booth theatre at Tottenham Court; Harper and Lee worked at both fairs in 1733 and had their Southwark booth shown in a

Hogarth engraving that year; and Harper acted with Theophilus Cibber and his dissenting Drury Lane players at the Haymarket during the first half of the 1733–34 season and then turned up on 29 May 1734 at Lincoln's Inn Fields to play Stocks in *The Lottery* and on 2 September at Richmond to act in *The Stagecoach* and *The Fair Penitent*. He engaged in no activity at the fairs after 1733, and after an appearance at Lincoln's Inn Fields on 14 April 1736 as Falstaff in *1 Henry IV* for Macklin's benefit, he acted only at Drury Lane.

Of Harper's income we know very little. He had yearly benefits, usually solo, but records of the receipts have not been found for Drury Lane during the years Harper acted there. Occasionally the benefit bills and other records reveal where he lived. From 1732 to 1735 he gave Catherine Street, Covent Garden, as his address, and from 1737 to 1741 he lived there still; but in the spring of 1736 he was living in Bridges Street, and he lived there, too, in 1739, 1740, and 1741.

John made a trip to France in the early summer of 1735, but the theatrical records show that he barely had time to get there and back. On 26 June the *Daily News* reported:

The facetious John Harper, Comedian—alias Plump Jack, is hourly expected from France to join the Summer Company [at Drury Lane]. 'Tis not to be doubted but that Country will greatly improve him in his dancing by which performance he has already acquir'd no small reputation. We hear he brings over with him a new bag wig & solitaire in which he is to perform the character of Mr. Basinghall in a new comedy . . . called The Citizen turn'd Gentleman—taken from 'Le Bourgeois Gentilhomme' of Moliere.

Harper had been acting at Drury Lane through 11 June.

Harper's life had taken an interesting turn in 1733 when Theophilus Cibber's group defected from Drury Lane. Some of the actors there, led by Cibber and including Harper, engaged in a dispute with the patentees Mary Wilks, John Ellis, Hester Booth, and, most particularly, John Highmore. On 4 June 1733 in a letter to the *Daily Post* the patentees stated their case, arguing that the actors, contrary to their complaint, were well paid. Harper's weekly salary was cited as £4, which was about average in the troupe for performers of the first

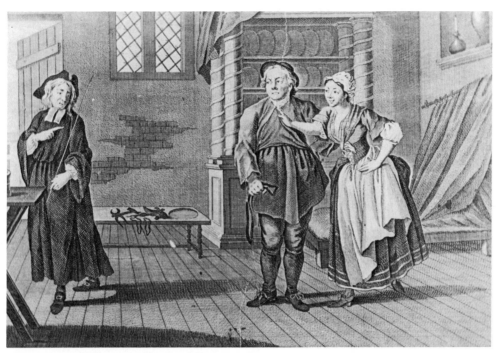

Possibly a scene from *The Devil to Pay*, depicting RICHARD CHARKE as Ananias, JOHN HARPER as Jobson, and CATHERINE CLIVE as Nell

engraving by B. Cole, of an original painting in Vauxhall Gardens

rank. The patentees also noted that they had given Harper a present as well, though they did not state what it was. In September Cibber and his followers, Harper among them, set up at the Haymarket Theatre. Highmore, having lost most of his best performers, brought the seceders to court for infringement of the patent, but when the case came to trial on 5 November 1733 it was dismissed on a technical plea. Highmore pleaded unsuccessfully with the Lord Chamberlain to close the Haymarket; then he invoked the Vagrant Act against the seceders, and John Harper was used as an example.

On 12 November Harper was taken from the Haymarket stage and committed to Bridewell; Cibber had to read the part of Falstaff. The *London Evening Post* reported on 17 November that "Yesterday the Court of King's Bench granted Habeas Corpus, directing the Keeper of Tothill-Fields Bridewell, to bring up the Body of John Harper, one of the Hay-

market Comedians; and he is accordingly to be brought up on Monday Next . . . that he may be admitted to Bail." The *Daily Advertiser* on 21 November reported that "Yesterday Mr Harper was brought up . . . and it was agreed, that Mr Harper should be discharg'd out of Bridewell, on his own Recognizance, to appear the last Day of this Term; and an Action on a feign'd Issue is to be tried, whether he is a Vagrant within the Statute of the 12th of Queen Anne, next Term."

Highmore had apparently thought that picking Harper and thus ruining a performance of *1 Henry IV* at the Haymarket would effectively hurt Cibber's troupe, and he knew Harper to be a man of timid character. But on the last day of the term it was shown that Harper was a freeholder in Surrey and a householder and voter in Westminster and consequently anything but a vagrant. He was carried in triumph from the hall by his friends. On 12 February 1734 Harper was officially discharged, for Highmore was unwilling to go to trial. Highmore lost out and sold his shares to Charles Fleetwood. On 12 March the seceders returned to Drury Lane.

At the beginning of the 1738–39 season Harper was in poor health. On 14 September 1738 he was to play the Carrier in *1 Henry IV* (Quin was cast as Falstaff), but Macklin had to take the role; two days later Griffin acted Silence for Harper in *2 Henry IV*. On 21 September Harper was well enough to play one of the Citizens in *Julius Caesar*; on 28 September he acted Bonniface in *The Stratagem*; on the thirtieth he played the Lord Mayor in *Richard III*; on 10 October he was Sir Tunbelly in *The Relapse*; on the eighteenth he acted (Mrs) Midnight in *The Twin Rivals*; two days later he played the Murderer in *Macbeth*; and on 21 October 1738 he acted Cacafogo in *Rule a Wife and Have a Wife*—his final stage appearance. Harper was granted a benefit on 5 April 1739,

another on 28 April 1740 (when the bill stated he was indisposed), and another on 24 April 1741 (when the *Daily Advertiser* noted that Harper was incapacitated with "a Paralytick Disorder, which has taken away the Use of his Limbs"). John Harper died on 1 January 1742 and was buried at St Paul, Covent Garden, on 29 January.

On 30 April 1742 the *Daily Advertiser* carried a note concerning a benefit for John's widow:

The Case of the Widow of the late John Harper, Comedian: Mr Harper, having been siez'd about four years ago since with a Paralitic Disorder, which not only rendered him incapable of acting, but depriv'd him of the use of his limbs, and in some degree affected his senses so as to make him an object of great compassion; during which long and dreadful Indisposition of near four years all possible means were tried (tho' in vain) to recover him,

By gracious permission of Her Majesty Queen Elizabeth II

"Falstaff examining his Recruits," possibly depicting JOHN HARPER as Falstaff

sketch by Hogarth

Private Collection

"Falstaff examining his Recruits," possibly depicting JOHN HARPER as Falstaff
painting by Hogarth

which impair'd and hurt his Circumstances, so greatly, as not to permit him to leave a sufficient support for his Widow, who is in Years and unprovided for.

Mr. Harper dying in January last, according to a custom in the Theatre, his Widow is entitled to a Benefit and the Comedy of the MISER is to be Acted To-morrow Night for her Benefit, at the Theatre-Royal in Drury Lane; but as she is incapable of making a proper Interest for it, without applying to the Compassion and Generosity of the Publick, she hopes to be excused in giving them the Trouble of this her Case.

The receipts came to a mere £50, the warm weather having discouraged many playgoers from attending. Consequently, Garrick played Chamont in *The Orphan* for Mrs Harper's benefit on 11 May, and the receipts totalled £240.

John Harper had written his will in August 1737, a little over a year before he became so incapacitated that he could no longer perform. There were no witnesses to the document,

which may account for the fact that his widow, Ann, was not able to prove the will until 23 June 1742, six months after his death. Harper left to his brother William his best suit and all his periwigs and to his nephew Harper Perkins all his other clothes. To his wife he bequeathed the rest of his estate, which may, in 1737, still have included his holdings in Surrey and the house worth £50 which Harper owned in Westminster.

Benjamin Victor praised Harper as a low comedian, but *The Auditor* on 6 February 1733 found the actor's grotesque playing of Lady Termagant "the vilest and lowest Degree of Buffoonery." Davies, in his *Life of David Garrick*, said:

Harper was a lusty fat man, with a countenance expressive of much mirth and jollity; his voice was strong and musical, well adapted to many parts in ballad operas, and farces. This actor had the honour to be a competitor with Quin in Falstaff; and the critics agreed, that though the latter was more judicious, Harper caused more laughter. He was a just representative of our country gentlemen, of booby 'squires, and fox-hunters. The brutal and jolly ignorance of his Sir Harry Gubbins in the Tender Husband afforded much sport, and the absurd humour, aukward bashfulness, and good-natured obstinacy of Sir Wilful Witwood in the Way of the World, were, in Harper, as diverting as any groupe of spectators could wish. In the Wives Metamorphosed, his Jobson the Cobler was an admirable second to Mrs. Clive's inimitable Nell.

John Harper was pictured as Falstaff in "The Stage Mutiny" print by John Laguerre in 1733. Hogarth reproduced that scene as part of his "Southwark Fair" in 1733. The Hogarth engraving was issued in a number of copies during the eighteenth century. Harper was probably the model for the central figure of Falstaff in Hogarth's "Falstaff Examining His Recruits." That painting, once owned by David Garrick, is now in a private collection. An engraving by Thomas Ryder was published in 1779. Hogarth made a preparatory black-and-white chalk sketch, which is in the collection of Her Majesty Queen Elizabeth II, at Windsor. Harper was also pictured as Jobson, with Mrs Clive as Nell, in The Devil to Pay, in an engraving by A. Miller, from an original drawing by G. White at Vauxhall. The engraving was published by A. Miller and W. H. Thomas.

Harricks, William ₁fl. 1778–1783₁, actor.

On 26 January 1778 at the Haymarket Theatre William Harricks from the Theatre Royal in York played Torrismond in The Spanish Fryar. The performance was for the benefit of "Brother Harricks and Mrs. Robinson" and was given "At the desire of the Jerusalem Lodge." The following year Harricks applied for and received a license to perform A Mirror for the Ladies at the Haymarket; the work was probably written by him. It was presented on 15 March 1779 as the second piece, with Harricks playing Lieutenant Generous. In the mainpiece, The Humours of Oxford, Harricks acted Gainlove. On 15 December 1783 at the Haymarket Harricks shared a benefit with Williams at which he played the title role in Richard III and Sir Patrick O'Neale in The Irish Widow.

Harrington, Mr ₁fl. 1780₁, actor.

On 3 January 1780 at the Haymarket Theatre a Mr Harrington acted Charles Prudent in The Modish Wife.

Harrington, Mr ₁fl. 1787₁. See HERIOT, JOHN.

Harrington, Miss. See HORSINGTON, MARGARETTA.

Harrington, Hurloe. See HARRINGTON, JOHN d. 1749.

Harrington, J. ₁fl. 1734₁, actor. See HARRINGTON, R.

Harrington, John d. 1749, actor, prompter.

John Harrington was first noticed in London playbills on 1 May 1733, when he acted the Jeweller in Timon of Athens at Covent Garden. On the sixteenth he appeared as a Planter in Oroonoko. He joined Theophilus Cibber's group of Drury Lane seceders at the Haymarket Theatre in the fall of 1733 and was seen as Alonzo in Rule a Wife and Have a Wife, Poins in 1 Henry IV, Ralph in Wit Without Money, one of the Avocatori in Volpone, a Neighbor in The Alchemist, and Gifford in The Albion Queens. When Cibber's troupe returned to Drury Lane in March, Harrington went to Covent Garden to finish out the 1733–34 season, playing the Jeweller in Timon of Athens and the Attorney in The Squire of Alsatia.

He was not mentioned in London bills again until 9 October 1736, when he was a Drawer in The Worm Doctor at Lincoln's Inn Fields. Then, after another absence, he returned to Covent Garden for the 1739–40 season. There he remained through 1746–47, with occasional appearances elsewhere. At Covent Garden Harrington tried such new parts as Pembroke in King John, Burgundy in Henry V, Robert in The Mock Doctor, Diego in She Wou'd and She Wou'd Not, Doodle in The Tragedy of Tragedies, the Priest, Marcellus, and the Player King in Hamlet, Alphonso in The Spanish Fryar, Ratcliff in Richard III, Arcas in Damon and Phillida, the Duke in Othello, Scruple in The Recruiting Officer, Belford in The Fatal Marriage, Duncan and Seyton in Macbeth, Hastings in *2 Henry IV*, Old Atall in *The Double Gallant*, Spinoza in *Venice Preserv'd*, Bardolph in *The Merry Wives of Windsor*, Stratocles in *Tamerlane*, and Jack Stanmore in *Oroonoko*. He was also seen at Bartholomew Fair in August 1741 and spent the summers of 1742, 1743, and 1744 at the Jacob's Wells Theatre in Bristol.

In the 1743–44 season Harrington's name appeared rarely in the bills, and it is probable that during that season he began serving Covent Garden as a prompter, supporting John Stede. On 6 May 1745 Harrington received a shared benefit and was called the prompter. The accounts show that as an actor playing minor roles in 1740–41 Harrington was paid 3*s*. 4*d*. daily; as a prompter in 1746–47 he received 16*s*. 6*d*. weekly. He shared a benefit on 12 May 1747 and received only half value for his tickets: £4 3*s*. His last benefit, shared with three others, was on 26 April 1748, after which he left London.

Harrington joined the Smock Alley company in Dublin as prompter for the 1748–49 season and shared a benefit on 21 April 1749 with the theatre's printer. Victor in his *Original Letters* noted that sometime in 1748 Harrington had gone to London to recruit actors for the Smock Alley troupe. The *Dublin Journal* reported that on "September the 14th Mr Harrington, prompter to the Theatre Royal [Smock Alley], being delerious and in a high fever, in the absence of his nurse-keeper, threw himself out of his lodging-window, and was killed by the fall." Administration of John Harrington's will was granted the following 6 October.

Harrington's tragic death inspired a satirical pamphlet called *A Full and True Account of the Woefull and Wonderfull Apparition of Hurloe Harrington*, which was an attack on the enemies of the politician Charles Lucas. In this twisted story the Smock Alley manager Thomas Sheridan hired Harrington, a sane and well-behaved prompter, but Harrington began usurping the manager's powers, was threatened by the actors, and fell into the fever that led to his suicide. Then, the pamphlet tells us, Harrington's ghost returned to Smock Alley, disrupting things by prompting everyone to do the wrong things. Coming so hard upon Harrington's death and containing as it does some unflattering comments on the prompter ("He was buried, not greatly lamented by many,"

for example), the pamphlet may contain some grains of truth about Harrington.

Harrington, John [*fl.* 1792–1805], *oboist, violoncellist?*

In his *First London Notebook* Haydn listed among the musical folk in London in 1792 one Harrington, a violoncellist, who had played at Haydn's concerts. John Harrington seems to be the only likely candidate for that reference, though he was celebrated as an oboist. He had been born in Sicily and studied under Lebrun. On 29 May 1792 he played oboe in a concert at the Crown and Anchor tavern in the Strand, and during 1793 and 1794 he performed in Salomon's concerts. In 1794 he also began playing regularly at the King's Theatre at opera performances, an activity which continued at least through the 1804–5 season. Doane's *Musical Directory* of 1794 noted that Harrington was a member of the Academy of Ancient Music and lived at No 24, Cumberland Street, Middlesex Hospital. In addition to his work at the opera house, Harrington is known to have performed in the *Messiah* when it was presented at the Haymarket Theatre on 15 January 1798. Smith in *The Italian Opera in London* notes that the oboist "Harrison" mentioned in King's Theatre bills in 1796–97 was Harrington.

Harrington, R. [*fl.* 1734], *actor.*

At a performance of *Tamerlane* on 4 November 1734 at the Great Room in the Ship Tavern, by a group claiming to be from the theatres, J. Harrington played Moneses and R. Harrington played the title role.

Harris, Mr [*fl.* 1726–1727], *musician.*

Mr Harris was a member of the band at the Lincoln's Inn Fields playhouse in 1726–27, according to citations in the theatre's free list for that year.

Harris, Mr [*fl.* 1729–1735], *actor.*

A Mr Harris played Temo in *Hurlothrumbo* on 18 December 1729 at the Haymarket Theatre. The following 30 March 1730, when Fielding's *The Author's Farce* was performed at the same house, Harris probably played Robgrave, as the 1730 edition of the work has it, though the playbill put him down as Somebody. The printed play listed Harris Junior for Somebody—the only notice of him in theatrical records. On 6 April 1730 the elder Harris shared a benefit with Jones and played Leander in *The Cheats of Scapin*. On 20 April *The Pleasures of the Town*, which was part of *The Actor's Farce*, was performed; Harris was listed as Somebody. The same Harris, we believe, acted Butler in *The Drummer* at Lee's booth at Tottenham Court on 28 May 1735.

Harris, Mr ₍*fl. 1730*₎, *actor.*
The 1730 edition of *The Author's Farce* listed a Harris Junior in the role of Somebody; another Harris, his senior and possibly father, was down for Robgrave. The playbill for the Haymarket Theatre on 30 March 1730, when the play was performed, gave the role of Somebody to the elder Harris and made no mention of the younger man.

Harris, Mr ₍*fl. 1746–1749*₎, *actor, manager.*
Mr Harris played the first Witch in *The Imprisonment of Harlequin* at Warner's Southwark Fair booth on 8 September 1746. On 23 August 1749 a Harris, presumably the same performer, joined with Godwin to operate a booth at Bartholomew Fair. They offered *The Intriguing Footman* and *Trick Upon Trick*, "With the Escapes of Harlequin into a Quart Bottle." Harris spoke a prologue to the mainpiece "in the Character of a Seaman."

Harris, Mr ₍*fl. 1782?–1789*₎, *actor.*
A Mr Harris played Snuffle in *The Mayor of Garratt* at the Haymarket on 8 March 1784. Perhaps he was the same Harris who played a Planter in *Inkle and Yarico* and the Cook in *Chrononhotonthologos* at the White Horse, Fulham, on 9 November 1789. A Mr Harris had acted at the Capel Street Theatre, Dublin, in 1782–83.

Harris, Mr ₍*fl. 1789–1791*₎, *dancer.*
A Mr Harris was a dancer at Drury Lane Theatre in 1789–90 and 1790–91, sharing in benefit tickets on 2 June 1790. Earning £1 per week in 1790–91, Harris began to perform Scaramouch on 27 December 1790 and then was switched to Pantaloon on 7 February

1791 in the pantomime *The Fairy Favour*, which received 24 performances that season.

Harris, Mr ₍*fl. 1791*₎, *See* HARRIS, MRS ₍*fl. 1785–1792*₎.

Harris, Mr ₍*fl. 1794*₎, *singer.*
In 1794, a Mr Harris of No 83, Longacre, was listed in Doane's *Musical Directory* as a tenor, a member of the Handelian Society, and a participant in the Handelian concerts in Westminster Abbey.

Harris, Mr ₍*fl. 1794–1803*₎, *watchman.*
A Mr Harris was a watchman at Drury Lane Theatre from as early as 1794–95 through at least 1802–3, at a salary which seems for some reason to have varied from 12s. 6d. to £2 2s. per week. As late as 1815–16 a Mr Harris was on the paylist as a messenger.

Harris, Mrs ₍*fl. 1695–1715?*₎, *singer.*
Mrs Harris was a member of Christopher Rich's company at Drury Lane in 1695–96, the only known role for her that season being Lady Youthly in *The Younger Brother* in February 1696. *The London Stage* lists her in the troupe again in 1698–99, during which season she sang *'Twas in the month of May* in *Sauny the Scot*, a song which was separately printed in 1699. At Drury Lane in December 1701 Mrs Harris sang "Let not love on me bestow" in *The Funeral*. In 1715 or thereabouts was reprinted *'Twas in the month of May*, but though Mrs Harris was cited as the singer, she may not have been performing at the time.

Harris, Mrs ₍*fl. 1708*₎, *house servant.*
Mrs Harris was listed among the house servants at the Queen's Theatre on 8 March 1708 in a paylist preserved in the Coke papers at Harvard. Her daily salary was 2s. 8d. but her duties were not specified.

Harris, Mrs ₍*fl. 1736*₎, *actress.*
Mrs Harris acted Lamorce in *The Inconstant* at the Haymarket Theatre on 19 February 1736.

Harris, Mrs ₍*fl. 1775*₎, *actress.*
A Mrs Harris acted Nell "by particular desire" in *The Devil to Pay* at the Haymarket

Theatre on 2 February 1775. She was announced as a fruitress from Tunbridge Wells who had performed the role at that place three times with applause.

Harris, Mrs ₍fl. 1785–1792₎, *house servant?*

A Mrs Harris, evidently an obscure house servant, shared benefit tickets with other minor personnel at Covent Garden Theatre annually from 1785–86 through 1791–92. (The reference in *The London Stage* to a "Mr" Harris receiving benefit tickets at Covent Garden on 14 June 1791 we believe to be an error for Mrs Harris.) Perhaps Mrs Harris was related to the Covent Garden ballet master Peter Harris, who died in 1789.

Harris, Mrs ₍fl. 1789–1795₎, *dancer.*

A Mrs Harris was a member of the Drury Lane corps de ballet from 1789–90 through 1794–95 at a salary of £1 5s. per week. She danced regularly in the choruses of such extravaganzas as *Don Juan*, *The Pirates*, *The Cherokee*, and *Alexander the Great; or, the Conquest of Persia.*

Harris, Master. *See* HARRIS, PETER.

Harris, Miss ₍fl. 1779–1781₎, *singer.*

A Miss Harris sang the role of Miss Diamond in the interlude *A Mirror for the Ladies* at the Haymarket Theatre on 15 March 1779. Later in the season, on 10 May, at the same theatre she sang "He's aye kissing me" and a "Hunting Song." Her only known subsequent appearance was as Leonora in *The Padlock* at the Haymarket on 26 March 1781.

Harris, "Cat" ₍fl. 1749₎, *imitator.*

In his *Dramatic Miscellanies*, Thomas Davies related that once Samuel Foote engaged a man named "Cat" Harris, famous for mimicking the mewing of cats, to give a concert of cat music at the Haymarket. One day, requiring "Cat" Harris for rehearsal, Foote sent Shuter to seek him in a court in the Minories where the fellow lived. Not knowing the house, Shuter began a "cat-solo" in the street, whereupon Harris looked out a window and answered with "a cantata of the same sort."

Cat Harris sang a cat duet with Shuter

which spoofed the Italian opera, on the opening night of Foote's comedy *The Knights* on 3 April 1749 and in the next two performances. Foote advertised: "The Company to be waited on by two Knights, from the Land's End, and a Brace of Cats from Italy. The Ladies and Gentlemen are desired to leave their Lapdogs and Spaniels at home because of the Cats."

Harris, George ₍fl. 1784₎, *singer.*

George Harris, a countertenor, was listed by Dr Burney as one of the vocal performers in the Handel Memorial Concerts at Westminster Abbey and the Pantheon in May and June 1784.

Harris, Henry *c.* 1634–1704, *actor, singer, dancer, manager, scene painter?*

According to a Chancery warrant dated 12 November 1691, Henry Harris was then about 57. He was, therefore, born about 1634. Nothing is known of his early years.

On 5 November 1660 Harris became the third party to an elaborate agreement concerning the establishment of the Duke's Company of players under Sir William Davenant. Davenant himself was the party of the first part, and the second part was made up of the actors Betterton, Sheppey, Robert and James Nokes, Lovell, Mosely, Underhill, Turner, and Lilleston. Harris was described as "of the Citty of London, painter." The players agreed to act at the old Salisbury Court theatre until Davenant could provide a new playhouse fitted with scenes and machines and staffed with a company including women. Until the new theatre was ready, there were to be 14 shares, four of which were to be assigned to Davenant; after the new playhouse was finished, there were to be 15 shares, ten going to Davenant to cover rent, management, costumes, properties, scenery, and maintenance of the actresses. The remaining five shares were to be divided among the players and "the said Henry Harris is to haue an equall share with the greatest proporcions in the said fiue shares or proporcions." Each actor in the group posted a £500 bond; Harris was bonded for £5000.

Harris's exact position in the troupe is not clear from the agreement, but the fact that he was specified a painter and treated separately from the actors suggests that his responsibilities may at first have concerned the scenes and

Harvard Theatre Collection

HENRY HARRIS as Cardinal Wolsey
engraving by Dawe, after Greenhill

machines with which Davenant hoped to dazzle Londoners. Though Pepys later mentioned Harris's interest in painting, no other theatrical documents indicate that he served as a scene painter; indeed, all they tell us of him concerns his considerable career as an actor.

Harris may have performed at Salisbury Court in late 1660, but the first role recorded for him was Alphonso in both parts of *The Siege of Rhodes* at the Lincoln's Inn Fields playhouse beginning 28 June 1661. On 15 August and subsequent dates he was Young Palatine in *The Wits*, and on 24 August he played Horatio to Betterton's Hamlet. From the beginning of his association with the Duke's Company, then, he was apparently the second man in the troupe. The following season he acted Sir Andrew Aguecheek in *Twelfth Night* on 11 September, Prince Prospero in *Love and Honour* on 21 October (the work was later performed at the Middle Temple), Young Trueman in *Cutter of Coleman Street* on 16 December 1661, and Romeo to the Juliet of Mary Saunderson, later Mrs Betterton, on 1 March 1662. He doubtless acted many other parts for which there is no documentation.

During that 1661–62 season the only other reference to Henry is not to his credit: he was one of several actors in the company, all described as from the parish of St Clement Danes, who assaulted and held prisoner for two hours a messenger from the Office of the Revels who attempted to deliver a warrant to stop the troupe from acting. The event took place on 4 July 1662; the actors were brought to trial on the eighteenth and fined 3*s*. 4*d*. each.

By 1662 Harris had sufficient experience to begin training others. The prompter Downes later claimed that Harris had brought Joseph Williams into the Duke's Company as a boy and had given him his early theatrical education. In 1662–63 Harris acted Duke Ferdinand in *The Duchess of Malfi* ("exceeding Excellently *Acted* in all Parts," said Downes), Beaupre in *The Villain*, Antonio in *The Adventure of Five Hours*, and Salerno in *The Slighted Maid*. All of those plays had extremely good runs.

The Lord Chamberlain ordered Harris arrested on 21 June 1663, and perhaps the apprehension had to do with Harris's brief flirtation with the rival King's Company (actors were not allowed to change company affiliations). Pepys got the story on 22 July from his shoemaker, Mr Wotton,

who tells me the reason of Haris's going from Sir W. Davenant's house—that he grew very proud and demanded 20 *l* for himself extraordinary there, [more] then Batterton or anybody else, upon every new play, and 10 *l* upon every Revive—which, with other things, Sir W Davenant would not give him; and so he swore he would never act there more—in expectation of being received in the other House; but the King will not suffer it, upon Sir W. Davenants desire that he would not; for then he might shut up house, and that is true. He tells me that his going is at present a great loss to the house. And that he fears that he hath a stipend from the other House privately.

He tells me that the fellow grew very proud of late, the King and everybody else crying him up so high, and that above Baterton, he being a more ayery man, as he is endeed. But yet Baterton, he says, they all say doth act some parts that none but himself can do.

Harris did not, in the end, change companies.

According to a Lord Chamberlain's warrant dated several months later (20 February 1664), Henry Harris—the actor, as later information assures us—received pay as a Yeoman of the Revels beginning 24 June 1663, three days after the apprehension order. On 6 August Henry was officially sworn to his Revels post, which he apparently held until at least 1704. His salary consisted of 6*d*. daily, £15 annual house rent, and £13 6*s*. 8*d*. (annually, we suppose) for board wages and attendance. The duties of the Office of the Revels included keeping the royal apparel for masques, disguisings, and similar court events.

Henry's new post may have been a sinecure, for it did not prevent him from busying himself at the public theatre in the years that followed. Pepys found out from his shoemaker on 24 October 1663 that "by the Duke of Yorkes persuasion, Harris is come again to Sir W Davenant upon his terms that he demanded, which will make him very high and proud." At Lincoln's Inn Fields Theatre on 22 December Harris played Wolsey in a highly successful production of *Henry VIII*. Downes said that Betterton was excellent and Harris "was little Inferior to that, he doing it with such just State, Port and Mein, that I dare affirm, none hitherto has Equall'd him. . . ."

It was as Wolsey that Greenhill later painted Henry Harris.

On 3 February 1664 Pepys wrote in his diary:

In Covent-garden tonight, going to fetch home my wife, I stopped at the great Coffee-house there, where I never was before—where Draydon the poet (I knew at Cambrige) and all the wits of the town, and Harris the player and Mr. Hoole of our college; and had I had time then, or could at other times, it will be good coming thither, for there I perceive is very witty and pleasant discourse.

It was to be a while yet before Pepys would make the acquaintance of Harris and report to his diary more of Henry's social life, but it is obvious that by 1664 Harris was moving in important circles. He was also, for a while at least, occupying quarters at court. An order dated 26 May stated that George Johnson, the court theatre-keeper, should take over the lodgings in the Cockpit at court which Harris "now possesseth."

In March 1664 Harris was Sir Frederick Frolick in *The Comical Revenge*; on 20 July he had a part in *Worse and Worse* (Pepys saw it and said, "I begin to admire Harris more than ever"); and on 13 August and ensuing dates Henry played the title role in Boyle's *Henry V*, in which production he wore the Duke of York's coronation suit.

On 10 September 1664 Pepys saw *The Rivals*, with Harris as Theocles and Pepys's former maid, Winifred Gosnell, as Celania. Mrs Gosnell went off key in a duet she sang with Harris, "so that the Musique could not play to her afterward; and so did Harris, also, go out of the tune to agree with her"—which would have taken some skill. Harris acted Macduff in *Macbeth* on 5 November 1664 and the title role in *Mustapha* on 3 April 1665—and surely other parts we know not of. During that season he was cited on 16 March 1665 in an order directed to him as Yeoman of the Revels, and his position was again cited on 15 June. After the conclusion of the 1664–65 season Harris and all the other players in London found themselves without theatrical employment because of the plague.

Harris, with his court connections, was in a good position to seek other offices. In the latter half of 1665 he petitioned for the post of chief engraver of seals, which had become vacant owing to the death of Thomas Simon. He stated that he had previously engraved seals for the King, but his petition was not successful; five years later, when he tried again, he was granted the post.

After the plague and fire the players resumed their activity, and Harris was again a member of the Duke's Company at Lincoln's Inn Fields in 1666–67. By then Pepys had met him, and on 24 January 1667 Harris was one of several guests at the diarist's home. "Harris I first took to my closet," confided Pepys to his diary, "and I find him a very curious and understanding person in all pictures and other things, and a man of fine conversation. . . . [Later] Harris sung his Irish song—the strangest in itself, and the prettiest sung by him, that ever I heard." Pepys had planned for Harris to spend the night, but the actor walked home. The following month Henry acted the title role in *The Cardinal*, but on the twentieth of February Pepys "heard discourse how Harris of the play-house is sick, and everybody commends him, and above all things, for acting the Cardinall." A week later the actress Mrs Knepp told Pepys that Harris was well again, "having been very ill." By 7 March Henry was busy acting the Duke of Richmond in *The English Princess*.

Four days before that stage appearance Henry's post as Yeoman of the Revels had been reconfirmed, though that order was, for some reason, stopped the following 4 April. Finally, on 1 June 1667, letters patent passed the great seal, granting Harris the office for life. His duties were described as follows: "yeoman or keeper of our vestures or Apparrell of All and singuler our masks Revells and Disguiseings And also of the Apparrell or Trappers of all and singuler our horses ordeyned and appoynted for our Iusts and Tournies." As before, he was to receive 6*d*. daily, but his pay was in arrears, and the order of 1 June directed that Harris be paid his arrears since 1660. That suggests that Henry had held a post at court since the Restoration, though most information concerning it dates from 1663. Harris was still waiting for his arrears on 17 December 1667.

The only part in addition to the Cardinal and Richmond known for Harris during 1666–67 is Warner in *Sir Martin Marall*, which he acted on 15 August 1667, and the only other reference to the actor that has been found for that period is an unexplained petition against him in April 1667 by a William Watkins. Perhaps that petition concerned a debt. Henry was frequently petitioned against in 1667–68—by Mathew Capell on 8 October 1667, by Thomas Halfepenny on 26 November, by Robert Bird on 8 January 1668, by Richard Snow on 3 February, by Sir Henry Herbert (the Master of the Revels) on 21 March, and by one Levett on 27 March.

Though regularly harassed with law suits in 1667–68, Harris kept up a full schedule of acting and socializing, both of which are fairly well documented. On 4 September 1667 Pepys saw Henry play the title role in *Mustapha*, but "both Betterton and Harris could not contain from laughing in the midst of a most serious part, from the ridiculous mistake of one of the men upon the stage; which I did not like." On 7 November Harris played Ferdinand in *The Tempest*; on 19 November he probably acted Theocles in a revival of *The Rivals*; on 28 December he may have come on as Sir Frederick in a revival of *The Comical Revenge*; and he was in *The Tempest* again on 6 January 1668. On 6 February Harris was Sir Joslin in the first performance of *She Wou'd If She Cou'd*; Etherege, according to the eavesdropping Pepys, did "mightily find fault with the actors, that they were out of humour, and had not their parts perfect, and that Haris did do nothing, nor could so much as sing a ketch in it. . . ." On 26 March Henry played the Master in *The Man's the Master* and delivered the epilogue with Sandford "in the form of a ballet," said Pepys; on 2 May he was Sir Positive At-All in *The Sullen Lovers*; on 6 July he revived his title role in *Henry V*; and on 29 August he may have repeated his role in *The Sullen Lovers* (Pepys thought the attendance was so small that the play might be canceled). *The Session of the Poets* (1668) had Apollo "The laurel on Lacy and Haris put on, / Because they alone made the plays go off."

During 1668 Harris and Pepys became good friends, and the *Diary* is full of references to the actor. On 6 January 1668 Henry arrived unexpectedly at Pepys's house at noon:

However, we did get a pretty dinner ready for him; and there he and I to discourse of many things, and I do find him a very excellent person, such as in my whole [acquaintance] I do not know another better qualified for converse, whether in things of his own

trade, or of other kinds, a man of great understanding and observation, and very agreeable in the manner of his discourse, and civil as far as is possible. I was mightily pleased with his company; and after dinner did take coach with him, and my wife and girl, to go to a play. . . .

Then, "after the play, stayed till Harris was undressed, there being acted 'The Tempest,' and so he withall, all by coach home." In the party Pepys held at his house after the play was also Mrs Knepp, and the group spent the evening singing and dancing, much to the host's delight, though he was concerned about the expense.

On 23 March Pepys was at Mrs Pierce's, singing and dancing with Harris, Mrs Knepp, and others, and on 26 March he entertained Henry and others at the Blue Balls, near the Lincoln's Inn Fields playhouse, where the gathering made merry with singing and dancing until midnight. Three days later Pepys invited Harris and the composer John Banister to his home for dinner. They were "most extraordinary company both, the latter for musique of all sorts, the former for everything. . . ." Harris "do so commend my wife's picture of Mr. Hale's, that I shall have him draw Harris's head; and he hath also persuaded me to have [Samuel] Cooper draw my wife's. . . ." On the thirtieth Harris and Pepys went to see Cooper's work and arranged to have the artist paint Mrs Pepys; then they went to a coffee house where Pepys and Hales agreed that Hales would paint Harris's portrait. By 26 April the painting of the actor was well along, and after seeing it Pepys wrote, "I think [it] will be pretty like, and he promises a very good picture."

On 29 April 1668 Pepys saw *The Comical Revenge* at Lincoln's Inn Fields, and "after the play done, I stepped up to Harris's dressing-room, where I never was, and there I observe much company come to him, and the Witts, to talk, after the play is done." The diarist became enamoured of Banister's echo song in *The Tempest* and on 7 May persuaded the composer to "prick me down the notes." On the eleventh he went to see the play, hoping to jot down the lyrics, but he botched the job. So, "between two acts, I went out to Mr Harris, and got him to repeat to me the words of the Echo, while I writ them down, having tried in the play to have wrote them; but, when I had done it, having done it, without looking upon my paper, I find I could not read the black-lead."

Poor Pepys was fascinated by the theatrical world his friends opened to him, but he was in anguish over the cost. On 26 April, for instance, he had written in his diary that he "did begin to think that the pleasure of these people was not worth so often charge and cost to me, as it hath occasioned me." But that thought did not stop him. On 30 May he met Harris and some other wild fellows and went with them to

Fox Hall, and there fell into the company of Harry Killigrew, a rogue newly come back out of France, but still in disgrace at our Court, and young Newport and others, as very rogues as any in the town, who were ready to take hold of every woman that come by them. And so to supper in an arbour: but Lord! their mad bawdy talk did make my heart ake! And here I first understood by their talk the meaning of the company that lately were called Ballers; Harris telling how it was by a meeting of some young blades, where he was among them, and my Lady Bennet and her ladies [the procuress and her whores]; and their dancing naked, and all the roguish things in the world. But Lord! what loose cursed company was this, that I was in to-night, though full of wit; and worth a man's being in for once, to know the nature of it, and their manner of talk, and lives.

After that initiation into low life among the upper orders, Pepys may have found, on 29 August, that inspecting Holbein's painting of Henry VIII (at "Chyrurgeon's-hall") with Harris was rather tame. Following their viewing, Pepys took Harris to the playhouse to act in *The Sullen Lovers*.

Hales's portrait of Harris as Henry V was completed in September 1668. On the fifth Pepys called it "mighty like a player," yet he was dissatisfied with it. The painting has not been traced.

After the death of Sir William Davenant the artistic direction of the Duke's Company passed into the hands of Betterton and Harris, beginning about April 1668. They were each paid 20*s.* weekly out of the gross receipts, which was not a sensible arrangement; their fees should have been taken from shares held as payment for managerial duties. Harris's acting is not well documented in the late 1660s and early 1670s, though his new duties may

have kept him from making many stage appearances. He is known to have danced in *The Royal Shepherdess* on 25 February 1669 and subsequent dates (Pepys: "a good martial dance of pikemen, where Haris and another do handle their pikes in a dance to admiration") and played Appius in *The Roman Virgin* on 12 May, Peregrine Woodland in *Sir Salomon* in April 1670, Tysamnes in *The Women's Conquest* in November, Prexaspes in *Cambyses* on 10 January 1671 (and possibly the following 12 July in Oxford), Mr Franckman in *The Six Days' Adventure* on 6 March, and the Cardinal in *Juliana* in late June—his last known role at the little Lincoln's Inn Fields playhouse.

Henry was less frequently mentioned in the Lord Chamberlain's accounts in suits for debts: Mary Inglesby sued him on 15 December 1668 and William Keene on 9 January 1669. But his new managerial post at the theatre involved him in occasional litigation. He and Betterton had to appear for a hearing soon after 8 January 1670 in a case brought against them by the actor Matthew Medbourne. Perhaps it was in connection with that case that two bailiffs were ordered arrested on 6 April that year for seizing Harris's goods without the Lord Chamberlain's permission.

It is surprising that Harris did not get into more legal trouble than he did as one of the company managers, for, according to Pepys, he was high-handed with playwrights. A script was offered Harris by Captain Silas Taylor, wrote Pepys on 7 May 1669:

. . . Harris told him that he would judge by one Act whether it were good or no, which is indeed a foolish saying, and we see them out themselves in the choice of a play after they have read the whole, it being sometimes found not fit to act above three times; nay, and some that have been refused at one house is found a good one at the other. This made Taylor say he would not shew it him, but is angry, and hath carried it to the other house, and he thinks it will be acted there, though he tells me they are not yet agreed upon it.

The work seems not to have been acted.

Henry petitioned again in 1670 for the office of chief engraver of seals, and on 11 November it was granted him. The post paid him £50 annually plus a profit on every seal cut by the chief engraver. Harris was frequently mentioned in the Treasury books in connection with his new position as well as his old one of Yeoman of the Revels. And in the Lord Chamberlain's papers he was also regularly cited, as on 15 December 1674, when he received costumes for the court masque *Calisto*, or on 9 February 1675, when he was to be given braziers for warming the actors at court performances. *The Dictionary of National Biography* was unaware that Harris the engraver of seals and Yeoman in the Revels office was Harris the actor, and it confused Henry with other Harrises who acted during the Restoration period. It may seem unlikely that the actor should also have been the royal employee, but the evidence is clear: on 11 August 1675, for example, the Committee of Trade and Plantations wrote a letter to "Mr. Harris at the Duke's Play House to hasten the seal for St. Christopher's" and on 21 October 1678 "Mr. Harris of the Play House" was ordered to cut two seals for the Leeward Islands for £100. References to Harris in the State Papers and Treasury Books have been found from 1671 to 1679 and then again from 1691 to 1703 connecting him with his government positions.

It is not likely that Henry did much actual work in his Yeoman and engraver posts; he was busy most of the time at the theatre. In late 1669 or early 1670 the Duke's Company began considering a site for a new theatre. On 11 August 1670 Harris and John Roffey (who held a share in the Lincoln's Inn Fields playhouse) leased a site at the south end of Dorset Garden, fronting the Thames near Dorset Stairs. They were acting in trust for Lady Davenant, Betterton, and the rest of the sharers. On 12 August it was agreed by the troupe that Harris and Roffey would reassign the lease to Nicholas Davenant and Thomas Cross in trust for Lady Davenant. Whether or not they actually did so is not clear, for several years later, on 21 July 1674, Harris and Roffey assigned the lease to two trustees, John Baker and Thomas Franklin, who in turn leased the theatre and the site to Nicholas Davenant and John Atkinson. Why the company went through such elaborate leasing and releasing arrangements is mystifying, but the example is fairly typical for the period.

Since Harris was a leading member of the Duke's Company it is not surprising that by 1670 he had bought two and three-quarter building shares at a cost of about £1237. After

the new playhouse in Dorset Garden was completed in 1671 Harris moved into one of the apartments at the front of the building; he was living at the playhouse by 1677, when a survey of St Bride's was taken.

The Dorset Garden Theatre opened on 9 November 1671 with *Sir Martin Marall*, a play in which Harris earlier had acted Warner. Later in November he played Ferdinand in *Charles VIII*. Before his retirement in 1681 he is known to have acted the following new parts: Trickmore in *The Citizen Turn'd Gentleman*, Merry in *The Morning Ramble*, Rains in *Epsom Wells*, Antonio in *The Reformation*, Muly Labas in *The Empress of Morocco*, Zungteus in *The Conquest of China*, Theramnes in *Alcibiades* (and he spoke the prologue), Merry in *The Country Wit*, Ulama in *Ibrahim*, Medly in *The Man of Mode*, Don John in *Don Carlos*, Ferdinand in *Abdelazer*, Don Gusmun in *The Wrangling Lovers*, Mecaenas in Sedley's *Antony and Cleopatra*, Thoas in *Circe*, Ranger in *The Fond Husband*, Cassander in *The Siege of Babylon*, Apemantus in Shadwell's *Timon of Athens*, Valentine in *Friendship in Fashion*, Antonio in *The Counterfeits*, Tiresias in *Oedipus*, Hector in *The Destruction of Troy*, Ulysses in Dryden's *Troilus and Cressida*, Beverly in *The Virtuous Wife*, the King in *The Loyal General*, the Cardinal in Crowne's *1 Henry VI*, and he spoke the epilogue to *Fatal Jealousy*.

In 1673 Harris inadvertently wounded his fellow actor Philip Cademan. On 9 August in a stage duel with Cademan, Harris pierced Cademan under his right eye; according to Cademan's testimony in later years, the stroke "touch'd his Brain by means whereof he lost his memory his speech and the use of his right side . . . " The play was *The Man's the Master* (not, as was reported, *Macbeth*); Cademan was apparently replacing Sandford as Don Lewis, and Harris must have been substituting for Underhill as Jodelet. Those two characters have a sword fight in Act V, and if both players were acting roles they were not accustomed to, the accident is understandable.

Of Henry's personal life during the 1670s we know little. By 1672 he had married, for on 7 November of that year "Petter Dod" petitioned against Harris for rent due him from Harris's wife. A few years later, on 25 January 1676, Harris was sued by his wife for maintenance, and on 19 May 1677 Emma Worcester petitioned against Henry for a debt his wife had not paid. Mrs Harris sued her husband for maintenance again on 2 November 1677, and on 24 November 1679 Joseph Dodd sued Henry for a debt. The identity of Harris's wife is not known for certain, though the St Marylebone registers show that a Henry Harris married an Anne Sears on 6 January 1672. At that time, however, Henry Harris the actor seems to have been of the parish of St Bride, Fleet Street.

A map of the Covent Garden area made by John Lacy in 1673 shows plots owned by a Mr Harris. (Again we cannot be sure that the actor was the Harris in question, but in later years Henry's will mentioned property owned in London.) Three parcels were owned by Mr Harris. They fronted on Rose Street between New Street and Longacre. The largest measured about 125′ × 50′ and the others 40′ × 100′ and 40′ × 80′. A Mr Harris (the same man or possibly a different one) owned a slim 100′ × 15′ strip running north and south, fronting on the north side of Hart Street. And a Mr Harris owned a 12′ × 100′ plot fronting on Bow Street, north of Russell Street. The possibility that Harris the land-owner may have been Harris the actor is increased by the fact that among the other owners' names on the map are several who may have been performers: Bartholomew Baker (the actor?), Mr Humphreys (Pelham, the musician?), Mr and Mrs Long (Jane the actress?), Mr Outin (Outom the musician?), Mr Reeves (Thomas the actor?), Mrs Bampfield (the actor's relative?), Mr Watson (Marmaduke the actor?), Mr Kinnaston (Edward the actor?), Mrs Meggs (Mary the orange woman at the theatre?), and Mr Smeedon (Smeaton the actor?). If Henry Harris the actor was dabbling in real estate, perhaps that is what ran him into debt.

But Harris also dabbled in high society, and his debts may have come from his hedonism. Nell Gwyn wrote to Laurence Hyde about August 1678 saying that "My lord of Dorseit apiers wonse in thre munths, for he drinkes aile with Shadwell & Mr. Haris at the Dukes House all day long." We know that Harris spent less and less time at the theatre as the 1670s wore on. About 1677 he may have relinquished some of his managerial duties to William Smith, an actor who had gradually taken over some of Henry's roles, but Henry was still living at the playhouse in 1678 and may not have given up all his duties until 1681, when he is last known to have performed.

Before the union of London's two acting troupes in 1682 Harris retired. In April 1681, or perhaps a month or two earlier, he acted the Cardinal in 1 Henry VI; after that the sparse records of the time show no stage activity for him. Perhaps he was the Henry Harris who went abroad on a pass issued on 23 August 1681, and he was probably the "Harris, the player" described in a letter from Roger L'Estrange to Secretary of State Jenkins on 30 June 1683 as "a venomous fellow." No other actor named Harris was prominent enough to have been talked about in high political circles.

Henry had lost his position as chief engraver of seals about 1680, but he was appointed an assistant engraver at the Mint—a post which he may well have deputized to someone else, as he doubtless had his Revels position. During the brief reign of James II Harris held no office except that of Yeoman of the Revels. Typically, he was in debt in the 1680s. He owed £5 on his poll tax in March 1686, and on 14 July 1687 his Yeoman's salary was paid to a William Richards in trust for Harris (a debt? or was Harris abroad?). When William and Mary came to the throne Harris was reconfirmed as engraver of seals. On 19 March 1690 he applied for the position of chief engraver to the Mint, agreeing to use James and Norbert Roettier as assistants. He was granted the post at an annual salary of £325, from which he paid the Roettiers £175. Harris may not have been the skilled cutter of dies and medals he claimed to be, but he was clever at using talented assistants who did the actual work; that practice continued, despite some complaints from the Roettiers, until Harris died in 1704.

In addition to his income from the government, Harris continued as a shareholder in the Dorset Garden Theatre. That investment did not turn out to be a good one after the rival companies joined in 1682, for Drury Lane became the United Company's chief playhouse, and Dorset Garden was often dark and eventually fell into disuse. On 9 May 1693 Harris brought a complaint against the proprietors of the old playhouse. He said that on 18 July

1674 it had been agreed that as an investor in the Dorset Garden Theatre he was to have received 19*s*. 3*d*. every acting day, a sum which was to have been reduced to 15*s*. 9*d*. after he sold part of his interest. Until March 1687, Harris said, he received his money regularly, but then Alexander and Ralph Davenant stopped his payments and put him off with excuses. Harris then became involved in lengthy litigation which led to the complaint of 1693. The Davenants responded in July and October, saying that the reason they had not paid Harris was that he had not paid his yearly ground rent of £130. The outcome of the case is not known, but it is not likely that Henry won. Alexander Davenant fled to the Canary Islands in late October 1693 to avoid arrest as a swindler, leaving behind a number of people who had lost money because of him.

When Philip Cademan brought his sad case to the Lord Chamberlain about 1696 he spoke of Henry as "the late Mr Harris ye player." But that only meant that Harris had formerly been a performer, for Henry was as busy as ever in the 1690s and early 1700s wangling money from the government. He had been, for reasons now obscure, recommended for military employment by the Lords of the Treasury on 15 May 1694 when he was about 63, and he was thereafter called in some government documents Captain Harris. On 15 May 1697 he added to his sinecure posts that of one of the commissioners of stamps at £300 yearly. When Gildon wrote of Harris in his *Lives and Characters* in 1699 he seemed unaware of Henry's government posts; he called Harris "A Player yet living, and Brother to the Famous Organist [Renatus Harris?] of the City of London . . ."

Harris sued for his share in the Dorset Garden rent again in July 1700. By that time London once more had rival companies, but the crafty lawyer Christopher Rich was in charge of both Drury Lane and Dorset Garden. Rich claimed he was poor and could not pay Harris. A second suit brought by Harris was still pending at Harris's death.

When Queen Anne ascended the throne in 1702, Harris lost his post as commissioner of stamps, though he kept his other positions. On 10 June 1704 he was paid £1002 for seals completed in 1702 and 1703 (probably made by John Croker, an assistant, who succeeded to

Harris's post as engraver to the Mint after Henry died). On 26 July 1704 Harris was still getting his salary as Yeoman of the Reveis. But he did not have long to live and may have been ill. On 2 August 1704 Henry Harris made his will.

Serving as witnesses were John Colbatch, Robert Manning, and William Boen (the actor William Bowen?). Harris specified that his debts were to be paid by selling as much of his property as necessary and establishing a trust. To Joseph Johnson and Drue Deane, who were to set up a trust, Harris left all his houses in London and Middlesex and their rents, and all his plate, ready money, and debts owed him. Half of the income from the trust was to go to Harris's daughter Elizabeth Furness, wife of the merchant George Furness; the other half was to provide for her children Henry, George, and Elizabeth until they should become of age. Harris specified that Elizabeth's husband was not to meddle with the estate.

On 3 August 1704, the day after he wrote his will, Henry Harris died. On the sixth he was buried at St Paul, Covent Garden, his parish church since at least 1693. Luttrell called him "Captain Harris, her majesties engraver of money and medalls" when he reported Henry's death. He made no mention of Harris's having once been a player, but perhaps by 1704 most people had forgotten that Henry Harris had been, in the 1660s and 1670s, one of London's foremost actors.

The late William Van Lennep contributed to *Studies in English Theatre History* in 1952 a very helpful article on Harris that for the first time identified the player as the government employee.

Harris was pictured by John Greenhill as Cardinal Wolsey in *Henry VIII*. There are three versions of the portrait. One in colored chalks and wash on buff paper is in the Ashmolean Museum; another, a pastel, is at Magdalen College, Oxford; the third, an oil on canvas, was at Strawberry Hill until 1842, when it was purchased by Ralph Willett, who presented it to the Garrick Club, where it now hangs. Engravings were made by H. Dawe, published by W. J. White in 1820; by E. Harding, Jr, after S. Harding's copy of the Greenhill, published in 1793 and also as a plate to Waldron's *Shakespeare Miscellany* in 1802; and by an anonymous engraver, undated. The Greenhill work is presumably the first portrait of an actor in a Shakespearean role. The Harvard Theatre Collection and the British Museum catalogues of engraved portraits incorrectly call the subject Joseph Harris.

Harris, James ₁*fl. 1689*₁, *actor.*

James Harris was ordered arrested on 9 September 1689 for playing drolls, presumably without authority.

Harris, John ₁*fl. 1690–1723*₁, *puppeteer.*

One of the earliest playbills extant (reproduced here) is for a puppet show at Bartholomew Fair presented by John Harris about 1700. Harris had performed earlier, in the 1690s, but the exact date of his first presentations is not known.

In 1721 he presented his puppets at Tower Hill, and in 1723 he was in Oxford. There he ran into trouble with the authorities, as

Harvard Theatre Collection

Advertisement by JOHN HARRIS

George Speaight relates in his *History of the English Puppet Theatre*. Harris was hauled before the Chancellor's Court and his goods confiscated when he failed to pay a bill to a carrier. The inventory was as follows:

10 Boxes with Figures and Pieces of Figures Show Boards Sceens Machines Sconces Show Cloaths and other Lumber . . .

Box No.	
1 . . .	13 Figures
2	12 Figures
3	15 Figures
4	8 Figures undress and Lumber
5	Pieces of Old Figures
6	Scenes and machines
7	Scenes and machines
8	Scenes and machines
9	Scenes and machines
10	Show Cloaths and Lumber
	12 Pannells of Painted Boards.

Perhaps one of the figures at the top of the Bartholomew Fair playbill is supposed to represent John Harris, but we have no way of knowing.

Harris, John ₁*fl. 1714–1739*₁, *trumpeter.*

In the Lord Chamberlain's accounts John Harris was listed as one of the trumpeters in the royal musical establishment as early as 1714. He was replaced by Thomas Harris (probably a relative, perhaps his son) on 8 May 1731. We believe he was the John Harris who was one of the original subscribers to the Royal Society of Musicians when it was formed on 28 August 1739.

Harris, John ₁*fl. 1795–1815*₁, *musician.*

A John Harris was listed among the subscribers to the New Musical Fund in 1795, 1805, and 1815.

Harris, Joseph *c. 1650?–c. 1715*, *actor, singer.*

The Mr Harris who acted Duprete and the Yeoman of the "Seller" in *The Bloody Brother* on 20 January 1685 at Drury Lane or Dorset Garden (the United Company operated both playhouses) was probably Joseph Harris. Citations for a Mr Harris from 1667 to 1677 would appear to concern an earlier and lesser actor, William Harris, though one should be aware that the important player Henry Harris was also active in the 1660s and 1670s with the Duke's Company. The *New Cambridge Bibliography of English Literature* gives Joseph Harris's dates as c. 1650–c. 1715, though on what grounds we know not; 1650 seems early for his birth date, though 1715 for an approximate death date is possible.

For the United Company from 1685 until the troupe split in 1694–95 Harris is known to have acted (at Drury Lane unless otherwise noted) Bourcher in *A Commonwealth of Women* in mid-August 1685, Corigidore in *The Banditti* in January 1686, Noysey in *The Luckey Chance* probably in April 1686, Syana in Tate's version of *The Island Princess* at court in April 1687, Alberto Gondi in *The Massacre of Paris* on 7 November 1689, Colonel Downright in *The Widow Ranter* on 20 November 1689, Bassanes in *The Treacherous Brothers* about January 1690, Dorrel in *Madam Fickle* in the spring or summer of 1691, Lanoo in *Bussy D'Ambois* in March 1691, Guillamar in *King Arthur* in early June 1691 at Dorset Garden, the Music Master in *The Wives' Excuse* in December 1691, Almeric in *The Rape* in February 1692, and Cosmo in *The Traytor* in March 1692. On 2 March 1692 a Lord Chamberlain's warrant listed Joseph Harris a member of the United Company (that was certainly not his initial appointment, as has sometimes been thought), after which there is a gap in the records until 1694.

Harris acted Bellford in *The Fatal Marriage* in February 1694 and Nicholas in the first part and Diego in the second part of *Don Quixote* in mid and late May (at Dorset Garden). The United Company divided in 1694–95.

Like several other players of the time, Joseph Harris tried his hand at playwriting—with the help of friends, according to Gildon's *Lives and Characters* (1699). In 1691 he published *The Mistakes, or, The False Report*, a tragicomedy, one scene of which was written by William Mountfort. The work was performed at Drury Lane in mid-December 1690. Langbaine in 1691 said:

This Young Author is beholding to the Poets to rig him out; Mr. *Dryden* having bestowed a Prologue on his Play, and Mr. Tate an *Epilogue*; and the ever Obliging and Compassionate Mr. *Montford*, (as the Author with Gratitude acknowledges) 'Not only corrected the Tediousness of the Fifth Act, by cut-

ting out a whole Scene; but to make the Plot more clear, has put in one of his own, which heightens his own Character [Ricardo], and was very pleasing to the Audience.'

Langbaine concluded that actors "had better confine themselves within their own Sphere of Action" and leave playwriting alone. For a while, Harris did.

When the United Company broke up, Harris moved with Betterton and his seceders to Lincoln's Inn Fields. There, before the end of the century, he played Major Buff in *Love's a Jest* in June 1696, possibly Martin in *The Anatomist* on 14 November (the printed cast has "T. Haris" down for the role—a typographical error, probably, unless the troupe had another Harris in it), Pedanty in *The City Lady* in December 1696, Gentil in *The Innocent Mistress* in late June 1697, Roderigo in *The False Friend* in May 1699, and Sir Richard Vernon in *Henry IV* on 9 January 1700.

For Betterton's company during those years Harris wrote two more plays. *The City Bride, or, The Merry Cuckold*, an adaptation of Webster's *A Cure for a Cuckold*, was performed at Lincoln's Inn Fields in March 1696, and was, according to *A Comparison Between the Two Stages* (1702), "Damn'd." It was printed in 1696. *Love's a Lottery, and Woman the Prize*, with a masque, *Love and Riches Reconcil'd*, was published in 1699 and performed by Betterton's players in March of that year (*The London Stage* gives the play to Rich's company in error).

In his *Lives and Characters* in 1699 Gildon spoke of one Harris as "A Player yet living, and Brother to the Famous Organist of the City of London," a reference, perhaps, to the eminent organ-builder Renatus Harris. Gildon made the actor Harris sound like an older, possibly retired player; but Gildon is more likely to have been writing about Henry Harris than about Joseph.

Joseph Harris is recorded as acting the Duke of Venice in *The Jew of Venice* about January 1701, Fedor in *The Czar of Muscovy* about March 1701, and the Duke of Venice in *The Jew of Venice* about May 1701 (according to Christopher Spencer) at Lincoln's Inn Fields, a Boor in *The Royal Merchant* on 12 June 1705 at Drury Lane, the Coachman in *The Man's Bewitch'd* on 12 December 1709 at the Queen's

Warrant concerning JOSEPH HARRIS, 1692

Theatre, and a Servant in *The Contrivances* on 9 August 1715 at Drury Lane. Perhaps one should question the citations from 1705 onward, for the Harris mentioned may have been another, younger actor and not Joseph.

It is worth noting that references to a Harris on stage stop for some time after 1715, as do publications listed in the *New Cambridge Bibliography of English Literature* for Joseph Harris—though the works listed for him in the eighteenth century are all nondramatic and perhaps are incorrectly attributed. Cited are *Luzara, a Pindaric ode on Prince Eugenius of Savoy* (1703), *An Ode Inscribed to the Queen's Most Excellent Majesty* (1714), *Great Britain's Glory* (1714), *A Funeral Ode to the Memory of Queen Anne* (1714), and a *Congratulatory Ode [to the] Prince of Wales* (1714). Worth mentioning also is the fact that a Mrs Harris, who may have been related to Joseph, acted and sang in London beginning in 1696 and was last mentioned in 1715.

Harris, Joseph *1743–1814, composer, organist, singer.*

Joseph Harris was born on 8 September 1743 and was baptized soon after at St Nicholas, Bristol, the son of John Harris (b. 18 March 1715), "a writing master and accomptant at Bristol," and his wife Mary. He was the grandson of Thomas Harris (b. 22 February 1686?) and Jane (née Goodman, of Byford, Herefordshire).

Perhaps he was the Harris who with Linley gave a concert in the Long Room at Bristol Hotwells on 20 August 1764. Some of his earlier compositions were sung at the Oxford Music Room: "Menalcas" on 1 July 1766, a "Te Deum" and "Jubilate" on 6 July 1768 and 3 July 1770, and "Milton's Hymn" on 16 November 1772.

Harris matriculated at Magdalen College, Oxford, on 16 March 1773 and proceeded B. Mus. on 24 March 1779. After having been organist at Ludlow Parish Church he succeeded to the same position at St Martin's, Birmingham, in 1787. Possibly he was the Mr Harris of Birmingham listed by Dr Burney as a bass singer in the Handel Memorial Concerts at Westminster Abbey and the Pantheon in May and June 1784 as well as J. Harris (of Henley), the bass listed in Doane's *Musical Directory* (1794) as a participant in the Han-

delian concerts at the Abbey. Although Harris's papers are not in the archives of the Royal Society of Musicians, he was probably the Joseph Harris who was appointed to play in the Society's annual benefit concert at St Paul's in 1813 but requested that a deputy be appointed in his place.

At Ludlow in 1767, Harris had married Ann, his first wife, who was buried on 2 November the same year. In 1771 at Birmingham he married Ann Silvester (1748–1812). He died at Liverpool in 1814.

Harris published six pianoforte quartets in 1774 and two collections of songs. His work was strongly influenced by Handel.

Harris, Morgan *c. 1649–1697, violinist, singer.*

On 4 July 1674 Morgan Harris and other members of the King's Musick were directed to practice under Robert Cambert at the theatre in Whitehall, to prepare for playing before the King at Windsor a few days later. Harris and his colleagues were at Windsor from 11 July to the beginning of September. A Mr Harris, probably Morgan, was one of the regular band of 24 violinists who participated in the production of the court masque *Calisto* on 15 February 1675. Two months later, on 26 April, Morgan married Ursula Fawcet, the daughter of the widow Elizabeth Fawcet of St Martin-in-the-Fields. That marriage was consented to by Mrs Fawcet, which fact suggests but does not necessarily prove that Ursula was still a minor. Morgan was described in the register as a bachelor 26 years old (hence he was born about 1649) from the city of Westminster.

The Lord Chamberlain's accounts, after mentioning Harris in 1674 and 1675, did not cite him again until 20 February 1680, when he was sworn a Gentleman of the Chapel Royal, replacing the deceased Richard Gadbury. The rest of Harris's career was spent, it would appear from the accounts, as a singer, but he kept up his interest in stringed instruments, for John Hingeston's will of 12 December 1683 directed that Morgan should be given Hingeston's "Base Viall in a leather case."

Harris was reappointed to the King's Musick upon the succession of James II in 1685 and marched in the coronation procession among the tenors. Similarly, he participated in the coronation of William and Mary in 1689 and was appointed to the King's private music. In January 1691 Harris went with the King to the Hague for a stay of 103 days, for which he received extra pay. The musician John Goodwin's will was proved on 20 July 1693, and Morgan Harris was named to receive one of Goodwin's silver-headed canes (he was cited simply as Mr Harris, but it seems certain Morgan was intended). Morgan was called by his nickname (or possibly his middle name) "Pelagio" in some Lord Chamberlain's warrants. At the end of his life Harris was earning £40 annually plus livery.

On 2 November 1697 Morgan Harris died. He was buried in the South Cloister of Westminster Abbey on the fifth, and the following day William Williams replaced him in the King's Musick. Thomas Jennings succeeded to Harris's position as Gospeller of the Chapel Royal on 8 November. Harris had drawn up a will on 3 January 1691 leaving all his arrears in salary and all his worldly goods to his wife and executrix Ursula. She proved the will on 12 November 1697. Ursula was still alive on 7 July 1708, when Elizabeth Bentham, the widow of the elder Samuel Bentham, a court singer, made her will. Mrs Bentham left a bequest of £10 and her bed to Mrs Harris and named her one of her three executrices.

Harris, Peter   *d. 1789, dancer, ballet master, actor.*

Cited as Master Harris and a scholar of Miles, Peter Harris made his first appearance at Covent Garden Theatre on 1 May 1767 dancing a hornpipe, which he repeated on 6 and 13 May. He may have been the "young gentleman" announced as making his first appearance on any stage who acted Prince Edward in *Richard III* on 29 December 1767, for "Master" Harris was named in the role when the play was next performed at Covent Garden, on 11 April 1768. On 17 March 1768 he had appeared as a Child in *Medea*.

As Master Harris, he remained at Covent Garden through 1772–73, making regular appearances in specialty dances and playing Prince Edward, Robin in *The Merry Wives of Windsor*, a Page in *The Inconstant*, and the Brother in *Comus*. Early the next season, on 16 October 1773, when he played the last-men-

tioned role, he was called "Mr" Harris, and so he continued to be listed for the rest of the season, except in two instances. On 8 December 1773, with Miss Twist and Aldridge (whose student he had become), Master Harris danced in *The Old Ground Young*, and on 16 April 1774, for Aldridge's benefit, he danced with Miss Matthews in *The Pilgrims*.

Harris served as a dancer at Covent Garden for another 15 years; in 1782–83 he also became a ballet master and his salary rose from £1 10*s.* to £3 per week. In 1783–84 it was £4. Harris shared annual benefits with other Covent Garden dancers, usually Dumai and Holloway. His address in May 1777 was No 12, Duke's Court, Bow Street; by May 1779 he lived at No 42, Wells Street, Cavendish Square, where he was still to be found in May 1784. Harris also danced at Richmond, Surrey, in the summers of 1775 and 1776.

Between 1773–74 and 1784–85 Harris served as a principal dancer in such pieces as *The Fair*, *The Sylphs*, *Daphne and Amintor*, and *The Weathercock* and appeared in numerous specialty dances. He was still acting Prince Edward in June 1775 and earlier, on 15 March 1774, had played Prince John in *1 Henry IV*. He danced at Sadler's Wells in the summer of 1786.

While at Eling, near Southampton, on 23 March 1789, Harris died of injuries he had suffered when he was thrown from his horse on Wednesday 13 March. On 19 March he had made his will orally to the Rev Robert Ashe at Southampton, parish of Twyford, in the presence of Richard Maut and Susan Holloway. Harris left everything to his wife, Sarah Harris. On 6 February 1790 Richard Maut testified that the deceased having been "most violently bruised" it had been decided not to trouble him to sign the will which he had dictated but to have him make a mark. Administration was granted to Sarah Harris on 19 February 1790.

Harris's widow and seven children were given a benefit at Covent Garden on 4 June 1789 at which their receipts were £311 1*s.*, less house charges.

Harris, Richard   *1766–1799, violinist, violist.*

The musician Richard Harris was born at Towyn, in the county of Merioneth, Wales, on

1 April 1766 and was baptized in the parish church of Towyn on the fifth of the same month, the son of Richard Harrys, a tanner, and his wife, Mary. Nothing is known about his education or early career. Dr Cooke proposed him for membership in the Royal Society of Musicians on 5 June 1785. But he was rejected on 3 July by a vote of 17 nays to three yeas.

In 1794, Harris was listed in Doane's *Musical Directory* as employed at Drury Lane Theatre and in the oratorios and a participant in the Handelian concerts in Westminster Abbey; he lived in Paradise Buildings. On 6 November 1796, he was again proposed for membership in the Royal Society of Musicians by Lesarre Purney, at which time he was described as a single man, a violinist and violist, with engagements at Covent Garden Theatre and Vauxhall Gardens. He also taught at a boarding school. His mother, a widow, then residing with Richard at No 3, Paradise Buildings, Lambeth, in a deposition to the Society on 5 November 1796 confirmed the dates and place of her son's birth and baptism.

Harris was finally elected to the Royal Society of Musicians on 5 February 1797 by a unanimous vote; he signed the membership book and paid his subscription the following 7 May. In May 1797, 1798, and 1799 he played the violin for the Society's annual benefit concerts at St Paul's.

Harris was dead, however, by 1 December 1799, for on that date his mother advised the Society that he had been "deprived of all emolument from the Covent Garden Theatre," where he had been engaged for that season in the band at 5*s*. per night, and that she had been required to dispose of much of her property to supply him with medical care during his last illness. The Governors awarded her ten guineas for the medical costs and £8 for his funeral expenses.

Harris, Richard [*fl.* 1784–1786], *singer.*

Richard Harris, a bass singer, was listed by Dr Burney as one of the vocal performers in the Handel Memorial Concerts at Westminster Abbey and the Pantheon in May and June 1784. Perhaps he was the Mr Harris who sang in 1785 and 1786 at Bermondsey Spa Gardens.

Harris, Thomas [*fl.* 1731–1759], *trumpeter.*

The Lord Chamberlain's accounts show that Thomas Harris replaced John Harris as a trumpeter in the royal musical establishment on 8 May 1731. Thomas was probably a relative of John Harris, perhaps his son. On 28 August 1739 Thomas became one of the original subscribers to the Royal Society of Musicians. Perhaps he was the Thomas Harris, bookseller and music publisher at the Looking Glass and Bible on London Bridge between 1741 and 1745. His name appeared in the imprint of *A Collection of Tunes, Set to Music, As they are commonly sung at the Foundery* (1742). Thomas Harris was still a member of the King's Musick in 1759.

Harris, Thomas *d.* 1820, *patentee, manager.*

Thomas Harris was the son of a prosperous merchant. Entering the soap-manufacturing business, Thomas acquired a small fortune. According to the *Thespian Dictionary* (1802) "He [had] received a liberal education, which he improved by a constant application to literature. . . ." His devotion to literature notwithstanding, his plan to purchase, with the wine merchant John Rutherford, Covent Garden Theatre, looked principally toward financial gain.

Harris and Rutherford sought to compensate for their theatrical inexperience by drawing into the partnership the brilliant actor William Powell and the aristocratic playwright George Colman, who had gained extensive managerial experience at Drury Lane during Garrick's absence on the Continent. The four men acquired Covent Garden's property and patent for £60,000 in the summer of 1767.

Colman naturally assumed that he was expected to manage the affairs of the stage and did so. But the contractual agreements among the partners had been vaguely and ambiguously drawn. Harris and Rutherford were incensed over imagined slights to their authority in the hiring of theatrical personnel. The personalities of Harris and Colman clashed. Colman said that "Mr Harris must be humoured, and has in his nature, among many worse qualities, the tyranny of a school-boy, who will have every-thing his own way." Harris fulminated over Colman's supposed extravagance "lavished away . . . upon superfluous servants, greedy favorites, and a numerous standing army of undisciplined and useless performers." Harris thought Colman unfairly discriminatory in his assignment of parts to Jane Lessingham, Harris's new mistress. Harris and Rutherford fired Joseph Younger, the veteran prompter, without Colman's knowledge, demanded the account books from Jonathan Garton the treasurer, and insisted on the return of the wardrobe from Powell's house, adjoining the theatre, where Mrs Powell presided as wardrobe mistress. They demanded also that Mrs Lessingham and George Ann Bellamy, Rutherford's mistress, be accommodated with private dressing rooms.

By the end of the first season, 1767–68, violence had broken out, with Colman ordering Covent Garden's doors and windows barricaded against Harris and Rutherford, and Harris bringing an armed band to break into the theatre. Throughout 1768 and into 1769 newspaper and pamphlet warfare raged. In July 1770 the affair came to litigation. (A lengthy series of depositions taken preparatory to the trial, involving theatrical persons of many specialities giving various testimony on the operation of Covent Garden Theatre, is in the British Library.) The principal ostensible allegation of Harris and Rutherford against Colman had been the wastefulness of his theatrical expenditures. But, since he was able to show a considerable profit for the partnership through the first three seasons of his management, a verdict was returned in his favor, and he was continued, for the time, in the management. Meanwhile, William Powell had died (on 3 July 1769) and John Rutherford had sold his share to the solicitor Henry Dagge and the bookseller James Leake. In 1771 Harris and Colman had patched up their difficulties, but after the 1773–74 season ended Colman retired from the enterprise and turned over his shares in Covent Garden Theatre to the actor Thomas Hull for £20,000, leaving Harris as the only survivor of the original partnership.

He had learned much about both the artistic and the practical aspects of theatre in the previous seven years, and he took over the management and prosecuted the affairs of Covent Garden with vigor until his death. His partners, after the departure of Colman, seem to have been content to be silent and leave major policy decisions in his hands. (By 1799–1800, other exchanges of property had occurred, and the proprietors were William Thomas Lewis—who assisted in the management—John Martindale, and George White.) From 1776–77 through 1787–88, when the record falls silent, Harris paid himself a salary of £500 in addition to his share of profits from the theatre. And substantial profits there certainly were, all during the years when (especially under Sheridan) Drury Lane was sinking into debt.

Modern judgments on the causes and consequences of Harris's success as manager-proprietor of Covent Garden vary from that of Cecil Price (that "his businesslike methods verged on the grasping") to that of C. B. Hogan (that his relationships with authors and his catering for their needs was excellent). Both points of view can be sustained with evidence. Harris did encourage writers like Sheridan, Morton, Reynolds, and Mrs Inchbald by furnishing them excellent production facilities and paying them well. On the other hand, in 1800 he was embroiled in a squabble with his actors over an increase in benefit charges, salaries, and forfeitures for refusing parts. Certainly he accelerated the drift toward musical pieces, pantomime, and spectacle and away from serious drama.

Harris was concerned in two other theatrical ventures, one of them unprofitable and the other abortive. In 1778 he and R. B. Sheridan purchased the King's Theatre and its opera enterprise for £22,000, mortgaging the property for £12,000. The opera dancer and impresario Giovanni ("Sir John") Gallini purchased the mortgage, expecting shortly to swallow up the shares of the debt-ridden Sheridan. But Sheridan sold out to William Taylor. Taylor remodeled the theatre in 1782, over-extending his resources, and while he was in jail for debt his portion was auctioned off to Harris. Harris sold to Gallini but apparently gained nothing by the transaction. In 1782, a plan by Harris and Sheridan to erect a third theatre, to be called the Prince of Wales, on some land owned by Henry Holland the architect "behind Grosvenor Place," failed for want of subscribers. An undated clipping in the Burney Collection in the British Library states that Harris had taken a company of players, including John Philip Kemble, Lewis, Johnston, and others, to play in Paris in the summer of 1784. During the perturbations of 1768 Harris penned two pamphlets and published them anonymously: *The Ring. An Epistle, Addressed to Mrs. L————m* and *A Narrative of the Rise and Progress of the Disputes Subsisting between the Patentees of Covent-Garden Theatre.* The first pamphlet defended Mrs Lessingham against her detractors in the Covent Garden Company.

Harris maintained a house close to the theatre, in Bow Street, from 1808 or earlier until his death. But he died on 1 October 1820 at his cottage near Wimbledon and was buried in his family vault at Hillingdon, near Uxbridge. He had a daughter, who died at age 15 in 1802, and at least four sons. One son, Henry, was himself manager of Covent Garden Theatre for some years. Another, Captain George Harris, was, according to T. J. Dibdin's *Reminiscences*, "eminently distinguished, as a captain in the navy," commanding the *Sir Francis Drake* "at the conquest of Java. . . ." A letter (now in the National Library of Scotland) dated 6 January 1815 from Thomas Harris to the Prince Regent solicited his son George's inclusion "in the second Class of the Most honb.^le Military Order of the Bath." When Jane Lessingham died in 1783 she left her entire estate to Thomas Harris, in trust for three of her sons, Thomas, Charles, and Edwin, who were probably children by Thomas Harris.

Thomas Harris left a large collection of theatrical portraits which was dispersed in a sale by Robins in the Covent Garden Piazza in 1819. His own portrait was painted by Opie and in 1885 was in the possession of the family of Longmans, the publishers, one of whose members had married a sister of Thomas Harris. The family also inherited a large number of documents relating to Harris's management of Covent Garden Theatre.

Harris, William   [*fl.* 1663?–1677], actor.

The prompter Downes stated that William Harris was one of four who "were Bred up from Boys, under the Master ACTORS" in the King's Company, and he listed the four among those who joined the troupe after it left the Vere Street Theatre in 1663. We may guess, then, that Harris may have been playing small parts earlier than 1667, when he was first named for a role. *The Change of Crownes* was acted at the Bridges Street playhouse on 15 April 1667, and the manuscript promptbook for that unpublished play indicates that William Harris had a role, apparently that of a Gentleman. On 6 November 1668 he acted Pedro in *The Island Princess*. Another promptbook, for *The Sisters*, shows that Harris played Contarini in that play, probably between January and August 1669, and that on 24 June of that year he acted Charinus in *Tyrannick Love*. A Lord Chamberlain's warrant dated August 1669 listed Harris as discharged from the King's Company, but the discharge was canceled, and on the following 2 October he was granted livery for the period 1668–1670.

He was Servilius in *The Roman Empress* in August 1670 and Zulema in both parts of *The Conquest of Granada* in December 1670 and January 1671. On 28 February 1671 he and three other players were ordered apprehended for some unspecified misdemeanor. His name did not appear in any cast lists again until March 1673, when he was noted as playing Don Fenise in *The Spanish Rogue* at the King's Company's temporary home in the Lincoln's Inn Fields Theatre—but records for the period are scanty, and he may have been performing regularly. Probably in the summer of 1673 he was in the prologue and acted Morena in *The Empress of Morocco* burlesque by Duffett, and he played the first Witch in the *Macbeth* burlesque that served as an epilogue to Duffett's piece. Harris acted Diego in *The Maides Revenge* about 1673–74. He or Haines spoke the epilogue and Harris played Flavius in *Nero* on 16 May 1674 at the new Drury Lane playhouse, Lodovico in *Othello* on 25 January 1675, Bomilcar in *Sophonisba* on 30 April (though Downes and the 1681 edition of the play give Wintershall the role), Satana in *Love in the Dark* on 10 May, and Bruine the white bear in *Psyche Debauch'd* on 27 August. A promptbook of *Brennoralt* at the Bodleian Library, dated 1673–1675, has Harris playing Marinell.

On 29 January 1676 Harris acted Araspes in *Gloriana*, and a Lord Chamberlain's warrant of about 7 February 1677 listed a Mr "Haris"

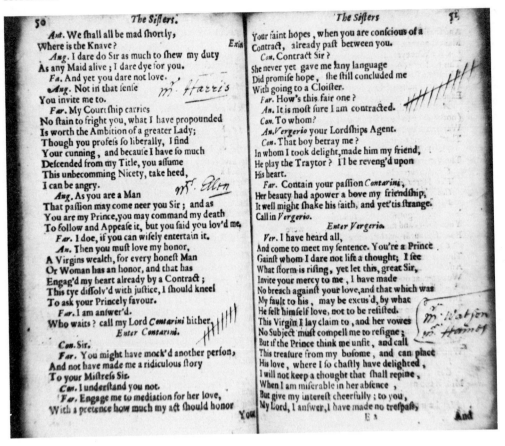

Folger Shakespeare Library

Promptbook opening, *The Sisters*,

with the name of WILLIAM HARRIS

as a member of the King's Company. After that the name Harris disappeared from that troupe's records. The Harris of 1685 and later we take to have been Joseph, not William. The Harris in the rival Duke's Company in the 1660s and 1670s was Henry. The William Harris who was buried at St Paul, Covent Garden, on 21 December 1690 may have been our subject, but there is not enough evidence to make a positive identification.

In *The Restoration Theatre* Montague Summers printed the frontispiece to Duffett's *The Empress of Morocco* and identified the pictured actor as William Harris in the role of the Empress. John Harold Wilson in his biography of Cardell Goodman reproduced the picture as possibly of Goodman as Mariamne the cinderwench, a more likely identification, which is discussed in Goodman's entry.

Harris, William *d. c. 1749, trumpeter.*

In October 1725, according to the Lord Chamberlain's accounts, William Harris replaced Thomas Weir as a trumpeter in the royal musical establishment. Harris became one of the original subscribers to the Royal Society of Musicians on 28 August 1739 and died about 1749, in which year Jonathan Snow replaced him in the King's Musick.

Harrison, Mr [*fl. 1721–1728*], *house servant.*

Mr Harrison, listed as a boxkeeper at the Lincoln's Inn Fields Theatre, shared a benefit with Mines on 23 May 1721; they split almost £150 in receipts before house charges. Thereafter Harrison was cited in benefit bills through at least 1725, and his name appeared in the account books as pit office keeper through 1728. The accounts also noted Harrison's wife and son on the free list.

Harrison, Mr [fl. 1724–1730], singer?, dancer?, actor.

Mr Harrison played Ostorius in *Merlin* at the Norris-Chetwood-Orfeur-Oates booth at Southwark Fair on 2 September 1724. On 21 January 1725 at Lincoln's Inn Fields Theatre (where another Harrison was a house servant) Mr Harrison was a (dancing and singing?) Witch in *Harlequin a Sorcerer*. He repeated that role a number of times through October 1730. Harrison shared benefits in the spring of some years, though it is difficult to determine whether a benefit for a Harrison in the late 1720s was for our man or the house servant. Harrison was cited on the theatre's free list in 1726–27 and 1727–28 as "Mr Harrison Musick," so he probably sang in the chorus. He was an Ethiopian in *Perseus and Andromeda* in January 1730 and again in October and December, after which he seems not to have been named in the bills.

Harrison, Mr [fl. 1726], performer?

A Mr Harrison shared a benefit with three others at Drury Lane on 10 May 1726. Possibly he was a performer, though the bill gave no indication of his participation in the performance, which was of *Oroonoko*.

Harrison, Mr [fl. 1733], actor.

Plume in *The Recruiting Officer* at the Haymarket Theatre on 18 April 1733 was played by a Mr Harrison. The "Miss Harrison" listed in the 1732–33 season roster in *The London Stage* as a Haymarket performer seems clearly to be an error for Mr Harrison.

Harrison, Mr [fl. 1784?–1803], actor, singer.

A person, or persons, named Harrison performed in London between 1785 and 1795. Perhaps he was the Mr Harrison who had acted at Exeter in 1784–85 and then played at Tun-

bridge Wells in 1795. With a company at the Windsor Castle Inn, King Street, Hammersmith, in the summer of 1785, a Mr Harrison played Jupiter in *Midas* on 15 July, Fairfield in *The Maid of the Mill* on 22 July, and Sir Penurious Muckworm in *The Honest Yorkshireman* on 26 July.

In the summer of 1788 a Mr Harrison played the title role in *The Mock Doctor* and Pantaloon in *Harlequin's Frolic*, in performances given at Wayer's booth in Greyhound Yard at the time of Bartholomew Fair. He also sang "The Golden Days of Good Queen Bess," the song which, according to Wayer's advertisement, Harrison had sung at the Royalty Theatre, presumably at its opening night on 20 June 1787.

Between 1793 and 1803 Harrison was a member of the Sadler's Wells company, appearing in *The Honours of War*, *Pandora's Box*, and *Sans Culottes* in 1793; *William Tell* in 1794; a ballet character in *The Lord of the Manor* and the Earl of Northumberland in *Chevy Chase* (in which a Miss Harrison played a Fairy) in 1795; a vocal character in *The Talisman* in 1796; Bolabar in *Sadak and Kalassade*, Chief Sealdi in *Alfred the Great*, and Heraclitus in *The Mountain of Miseries* in 1797; an Officer in *Peter Wilkins* in 1800; and an Officer in *The Old Man of the Mountains*, Friar Bacon in *Wizard's Wake*, and a Sailor in *British Amazons* in 1803.

Harrison, Mr [fl. 1796–1797], oboist.
See HARRINGTON, JOHN [fl. 1792–1805].

Harrison, Mrs [fl. 1733], house servant?

Mrs Harrison shared a benefit with two others at Covent Garden on 16 May 1733. She may have been a house servant, possibly the wife (or widow) of one of the Harrisons who were active in the troupe at the Lincoln's Inn Fields playhouse in the 1720s.

Harrison, Mrs [fl. 1774?–1776], actress.

A Mrs Harrison played Molly in a performance of *The Beggar's Opera* at the Haymarket Theatre on 20 September 1776. Perhaps she was the Mrs Harrison who had acted at Brighton in 1774.

Harrison, Master [fl. 1748–1749], dancer.

A Master Harrison performed with Mme Dominique in the dance *Foote's Vagaries* at Hussey's Great Booth from 24 to 27 August 1748, at Bartholomew Fair. In the following winter season he was employed at Drury Lane Theatre, dancing as a Follower of Pan in the ballet *Vertumnus and Pomona* (with Cooke, Anne Auretti, Matthews, and others) for some 11 performances between 27 October 1748 and 11 January 1749. Probably he was the son of J. Harrison, a dancer at Drury Lane during that period.

Harrison, Miss [fl. 1732–1733]. See HARRISON, MR [fl. 1733].

Harrison, Miss [fl. 1745–1746], actress.

At Goodman's Fields Theatre on 24 February 1746 a Miss Harrison, announced as making her third appearance on the stage, acted Mrs Sullen in *The Stratagem* and delivered the epilogue in the character of a Volunteer, for her own benefit night. Probably she was the gentlewoman, new to the stage, who had played Cherry in the same play at the same theatre on 13 November 1745 and had acted Prue in *Love for Love* a week later on 21 November.

Harrison, Miss [fl. 1763], actress.

A Miss Harrison was named for one of the principal parts in Foote's *The Diversions of the Morning* at the Haymarket Theatre on 6 and 7 July 1763.

Harrison, Miss [fl. 1767], dancer?

On 10 March 1767, a Miss Harrison was paid £2 2s. along with ten other young persons for performing ten nights, probably as a dancer, in *The Fairy Favour*, a masque afterpiece by Thomas Hull which had its first performance at Covent Garden on 31 January 1767.

Harrison, Miss [fl. 1781], actress.

A Miss Harrison acted Celemena in a specially-licensed performance of *A Wife to be Lett* played by actors from the north at the Haymarket Theatre on 22 January 1781.

Harrison, Miss [fl. 1791–1795], dancer.

A Miss Harrison danced with others in a new comic dance called *The Irish Fair* at Astley's Amphitheatre on 6 May 1791. Perhaps this was the same Miss Harrison who danced a Fairy in *Chevy Chase* at Sadler's Wells on 4 August 1795. In the latter performance a Mr Harrison acted the Earl of Northumberland.

Harrison, J. [fl. 1748–1760], dancer.

J. Harrison was very likely the person who performed a *Punch Dance* in Act III of *Volpone* at Covent Garden Theatre on 18 April 1748. The following summer he played the Coachman in *The Unnatural Parents* at Lee and Yeates's Bartholomew Fair booth from 24 to 27 August and also appeared in *The Fair Maid of the West* at Southwark Fair several weeks later, on 7 September.

In 1748–49 he began an engagement at Drury Lane Theatre that lasted for 12 seasons through 1759–60. In a letter to the *Public Advertiser* on 8 May 1749 regaring his first benefit (to be shared with three other performers) on the following evening, he signed as J. Harrison. Except for some specialty numbers, such as a *Drunken Peasant* or hornpipes offered for his annual shared benefits, Harrison was obscurely placed in the choruses of such ballets and pantomimes as *The Triumph of Peace* and *Harlequin Ranger*. He performed one of the Furies in *Macbeth* in 1750–51.

The Master Harrison who danced at Drury Lane in 1748–49 was probably his son. On 21 May 1759 Harrison and a young gentleman named as his scholar danced a hornpipe. On that night, as well as a year later, on 8 May 1760, two of his scholars performed a minuet.

Harrison, James [fl. 1779–1803], singer, music seller and publisher.

The Mr J. Harrison, of Derbyshire, who was a bass singer in the Handel Memorial Concerts at Westminster Abbey and the Pantheon in May and June 1784 was the older brother of the singer Samuel Harrison (1760?–1812).

His first name was given as James in "The Manager's Notebook" in an account of a litigation between him and Madame Gertrud Mara. She accused Harrison of sending a letter over the *nom de plume* "Common Sense" to the editor of *The World* in March 1793 which re-

counted a number of abuses and insults that
the difficult soprano had heaped upon the British public, especially in the recent oratories at
Covent Garden. Harrison gave evasive replies
to her accusations in his letters to her, but she
obtained the original manuscript, which proved
to be in his handwriting, whereupon she sued.
She won the verdict but obtained a judgment
of only one shilling. When Mme Mara refused
to sing at the benefit of John Ashley, the manager of the oratorios, he brought an action
against Harrison for the losses he claimed to
have sustained by her absence provoked by
Harrison's publication. But the court "was of
the opinion that the plaintiff had not proved
any injury done him, and he was nonsuited."
If there is truth to this account—for "The
Manager's Notebook" must be approached
with caution—one wonders at Harrison's
provocation. In the previous two years his
brother Samuel had been co-promoter of the
Covent Garden oratorios with Ashley, but in
1793, the year of the trouble with Mme Mara,
Samuel was in the Drury Lane oratorios.

In 1794, Harrison was listed in Doane's *Musical Directory* as a bass singer at the Derby
Meeting of 1793 and as living at No 19, Percy
Street, Rathbone Place, which was the same
address as that of his brother Samuel. His surname, however, was given incorrectly by
Doane as John.

Also listed by Doane was a firm, Harrison
& Co, music sellers of No 18, Paternoster
Row. The establishment, founded by James
Harrison, had been at that address from 1779
to 1798, with a second address at Dr Arne's
Head, No 141, Cheapside, in 1788. The firm's
principal publications were *The New Musical
Magazine* (1783), *The Songs of Handel* (1786–
87), and *The Pianoforte Magazine* (1797–1802).
The establishment became Harrison, Cluse,
& Co in 1798, when it moved to No 78, Fleet
Street; in 1802, it moved again to No 108,
Newgate Street, where it was to be found in
1803.

Harrison, Samuel   *1760?–1812, singer,
conductor, promotor.*

According to his notices in both *Grove's Dictionary* and *The Dictionary of National Biography*, Samuel Harrison was born at Belper,
Derbyshire, on 8 September 1760. A notation
on a manuscript in the Burney papers at the

Harvard Theatre Collection

SAMUEL HARRISON
engraving by Daniell, after G. Dance

British Museum, while agreeing with the day
and the month, states the year as 1766. When,
however, Harrison was recommended for
membership in the Royal Society of Musicians
on 4 November 1781, he was described as 23
years of age; thus his year of birth was supposedly 1758. He was from his earliest years,
according to Sainsbury's *Dictionary of Music*
(1827), "among the choristers of the chapel
royal of England." One of his first teachers,
about 1773, was George Burton (d. 1784) a
bass singer at Marylebone Gardens at that
time. Harrison was trained as a soprano for the
Concerts of Ancient Music and at the Society
of Sacred Music in 1776.

As Master Harrison he sang as one of the
principal characters in *The Sirens*, a new
masque, at Covent Garden Theatre on 26 February 1776. A month later, on 27 March and
again the next night, he sang at the same
theatre in Dr. Arnold's new oratorio *The Prodi-*

gal Son. On 11 May of that year, at a benefit which he shared with numerous other performers at Covent Garden, he sang the song "The Soldier Tir'd of War's Alarms." In the summer of 1777, still billed as Master Harrison, he performed at the Haymarket as one of the Lilliputians in *Lilliput* and as a Fairy in *The Fairy Tale*, Colman's adaptation of *A Midsummer Night's Dream*. He also sang again in *The Prodigal Son* at Covent Garden on 1 April 1778.

Harrison was engaged to sing in the Gloucester festival in 1778, but his voice then began to change. Over the next six years he cultivated his tenor and busied himself with teaching the harpsichord. On 4 November 1781 he was recommended by Parke for membership in the Royal Society of Musicians, at which time he was described as a person who "has practised Music for a livelihood seven years, as a vocal performer and teacher of the harpsichord. He sings one of the principal parts at the old concert, is a single man (23 years of age)."

The story was told that upon hearing the young Harrison sing at one of the Queen's musical parties, so impressed was George III that he recommended his engagement as a vocalist in the Handel Memorial Concerts at Westminster Abbey and the Pantheon in May and June 1784, at which the tenor sang "Rend' il sereno al ciglio" from *Sosarme* and the opening recitative and air in the *Messiah*. Whether or not the King's influence was involved remains conjectural. Samuel's brother James also sang in the great commemoration.

Harrison soon distinguished himself as one of the leading singers in the various concert meetings throughout the country. He had first sung at the Three Choirs meeting in 1781 at Gloucester. From 1786 until 1806 he sang at the Hereford meetings and from 1801 to 1808 was the principal tenor at Gloucester and Worcester. During three mornings in the second summer assize week at York in mid-August 1791, Harrison, Kelly, Mrs Crouch, and Mme Mara gave Handelian concerts at the Minster. Harrison managed the Three Choirs meeting of 1811. At London he was a member of the Catch Club, and he sang at the Professional Concerts from about 1783, at Salomon's from 1786, and at the Society of Sacred Music from 1785 until 1790. He was also principal tenor at the Ancient Concerts from 1785 until 1791. "No Divine from the pulpit," wrote Michael Kelly in his *Reminiscences*, "could have inspired his auditors with a more perfect sense of duty to their Maker than Harrison did by his melodious tones and chaste style." Kelly thought him deficient, however, in "the animated songs of Handel" and once heard him sing "the laughing song, without moving a muscle," a technique that Kelly later rejected.

Harrison and Charles Knyvett then initiated the Vocal Concerts, the first of which was offered on 11 February 1792 at Willis's Rooms. Although the performances were of a high calibre, they did not succeed and after a few years Harrison returned to the Ancient Concerts. He and Knyvett revived the Vocal Concerts, now with Greatorex, in 1801 through 1803. Each spring between 1807 and 1812, Harrison, Bartleman, and Greatorex were granted licenses to present nine subscription concerts at the Hanover Square Rooms.

For a number of years Harrison was a leading figure in the oratorios at the several London theatres. He was the director and principal singer at the Covent Garden oratorios in the springs of 1789 and 1790. In reviewing the performances of the *Messiah* in 1789 the critic in the *Biographical and Imperial Magazine* (May 1789) wrote: "Among the singers, it is almost unnecessary to remark the rich mellow notes of Harrison; whose charming execution and profound judgment in music are so universally known." With Ashley he directed and sang in the Covent Garden oratorios in 1791 and 1792; and in the oratorios at the Haymarket in 1793, at the King's Theatre in 1793, 1794, and 1795 and at Drury Lane in 1793 and 1794. For his services in the Drury Lane oratorios in 1794 he was paid £210, in full on May 5. In June of that year he sang for a "Choral Night" of the Oxford Musical Society, in their Music Room, where he also appeared occasionally early in the nineteenth century.

In 1786 Harrison became one of the successive lovers of the celebrated and high-spirited singer Mme Gertrud Mara. In that summer they ran off to enjoy the sea at Margate and then set off for a brief visit to Paris. The affair seems not to have survived long. Seven years later, in 1793, James Harrison, a bass singer and Samuel's brother, engaged in a public altercation with Mme Mara when she accused him of leading a cabal against her.

On 6 December 1790 at St James, Clerkenwell, Samuel had married the soprano Ann Cantelo, who was the daughter of the instrumentalist Hezekiah Cantelo (d. 1811) and his wife, Sarah, and the sister of the musicians Master H. Cantelo (d. 1797) and Thomas Cantelo (1774–1807). As Mrs Harrison her career closely paralleled her husband's in concerts and oratorios.

In the last year of his life, Harrison sang some of his favorite numbers at a benefit concert given for him on 8 May 1812. He died suddenly of "internal inflammation" seven weeks later, on 25 June, at his home, No 12, Percy Street, Rathbone Place, where he and his wife had lived since 1794 or earlier, and was buried at the old church of St Pancras. The following lengthy inscription was placed on his monument in the churchyard:

Sacred
to the Memory of
Mr. SAMUEL HARRISON
who to a most pleasing and melodious Voice,
added
a very extensive knowledge and correct Judgment
in the SCIENCE of MUSIC.
The chaster Style, refined Taste, and impressive
manner
with which he delivered
The beautiful Composition of
HANDEL,
will cause his loss to be severely felt
and lamented by
The Admirers of SACRED MUSIC:
And the many amiable qualities which adorned
his Character in private life, will long endear
his Memory to
His affectionate Relatives and numerous Friends.
He was born the 8th of September 1760, and died
the 25th of June, 1812

Then followed eight lines of verse alluding to the song "Gentle Airs," which included a portion from an elegiac ode on Harrison written by the Rev Thomas Beaumont and set to music by William Horsley.

Administration of Harrison's estate, valued at £3500, was granted to his widow by the Consistory Court sometime in July 1812. Mrs Harrison died on 25 July 1831 at the age of 65 and was buried with her husband at old St Pancras.

Samuel and Ann Harrison had at least one child, named Charles Thomas Harrison, who by 1821 lived with his wife Emma Haden in Sloane Street. According to an inscription on the reverse of Samuel Harrison's tombstone, their daughter Jane died on 6 January 1821 at the age of four and was buried with her grandfather. The Miss Harrison who sang at the Royal Circus in 1804 and 1808 and in the "English Opera" company at the Lyceum in 1816 may have been related to our subject.

A number of songs published as sung by Samuel Harrison are listed in the *Catalogue of Printed Music in the British Museum*. According to Sainsbury, Harrison's favorites were Pepusch's *Alexis*; Handel's *Lord, remember David* and *Pleasure, my former ways resigning*; Boyce's *Softly Rise*; Zingarelli's *Ombra adorata*; Webbe's *A Rose from her bosom had strayed*; Attwood's *Soldier's Dream*; and Horsley's *Gentle Lyre*.

Harrison possessed a range of two octaves (A to a'), of limited power "but of a tone enchantingly rich and sweet," in the judgment of Sainsbury. His distinction lay in his taste, judgment, and control. In a letter to Sainsbury on 22 December 1823, Mrs Harrison wrote that "It has been allowed by the Whole Musical World that the late Mr Harrison from the Transcendency of his Vocal Talents stood alone!" Sainsbury somewhat extravagantly judged Harrison "the most finished singer of his age or country, or perhaps of Europe."

An engraved portrait of Harrison done by W. Daniell, from a drawing by George Dance, was published by the engraver in 1814. Dance's original drawing was sold at Christie's on 1 July 1898 (lot 61), but its present location is unknown to us.

Harrison, Mrs Samuel, Ann, née Cantelo *1766–1831, singer.*

According to the inscription on her tombstone, Ann Harrison died in 1831 at the age of 65 and therefore was born in 1766. Probably she had been born at Bath, the eldest of six children of the Bath musician Hezekiah Cantelo (d. 1811) and his wife, Sarah. One of Ann's brothers, Thomas Cantelo (1774–1807), became an instrumentalist and teacher at Bath and London; one of her sisters, Bathsheba or Barbary, married the musician John Loder.

Ann was only a child when she first sang as a soloist at the Oxford Music Room in the middle of March 1783. In May and June 1784 she sang with the sopranos in the Handel Memorial Concerts at Westminster Abbey and the Pantheon; her future husband, Samuel Harrison, was a featured singer in those famous events. Sylas Neville attended the Pantheon concert and wrote in his *Diary* that "Miss Cantelo has a sweet voice & a very pretty person."

She sang again at the Oxford Music Room in March 1786, at Bath in April 1786, and probably on numerous other occasions, and in the Covent Garden oratorios in 1789 and 1790. On 6 December 1790 at St James, Clerkenwell, she married Harrison and as Mrs Harrison became a favorite at the various concerts of the Academy of Ancient Music and the Three Choirs. In 1793 she was a soloist in the Drury Lane oratorios presented at the King's Theatre and the Haymarket. At Oxford in June 1794 she appeared in a "Choral Night" and returned to the Music Room there on 23 November 1801. She was, by Burney's account, a "pleasing and well-toned soprano singer, free from English brogue and vulgarity."

Her husband died on 25 June 1812 at their home, No 12, Percy Street, Rathbone Place, where they had lived since 1794 or earlier. His estate, valued at £3500, was bequeathed to her.

On 19 December 1823, when she wrote to Sainsbury about his dictionary, Mrs Harrison was living at No 3, George Street, Portman Square: "Mrs Harrison . . . feels much obliged and highly flattered by his wish of inserting her name in the 'Biographical Dictionary;' but as she has taken leave of the Public, many years ago, it would be painful to her feelings, to bring herself again into notice." Several days later, on 23 December, she wrote again, requesting that Sainsbury "entirely omit *her* name in the forthcoming publication, but offered very high praise of her late husband's talents.

She died on 25 July 1831 and was buried with her husband's remains in old St Pancras churchyard. The inscription to her memory found on the reverse of her husband's tombstone stated she was "aged 65 Years" at the time of her death and was "Beloved and regretted by all who know her." Ann Harrison had at least one child, Charles Thomas Harrison, who married Emma Haden. His daughter Jane, who died on 6 January 1821 at the age of four, was buried with her grandparents.

Harrolt, Mr [*fl.* 1740], *actor.*
At Bartholomew Fair on 23 August 1740 at the Lee-Phillips booth *Harlequin Restored* was presented with "Comedy" played by "Sunderland, Harrolt, Jones, &c."

Harrop, Mr [*fl.* 1794], *singer?*
A Mr Harrop from Lancashire was a bass (singer, one would guess) who participated in the Handel performances at Westminster Abbey, according to Doane's *Musical Directory* of 1794. He was very likely related to Sarah Harrop Bates, the singer and actress who was married to Joah Bates. Sarah was also from Lancashire.

Harrop, Sarah. *See* BATES, MRS JOAH.

"Harry, Old." *See* "OLD HARRY."

Hart, Mr [*fl.* 1744–1747], *actor.*
Mr Hart acted Worthy in *The Relapse* at the Haymarket Theatre on 6 April 1744 (Mrs Hart played the Nurse) and Seyward in *Macbeth* on 5 January 1747 at the Goodman's Fields playhouse. At the latter theatre Mrs Hart had played Sukey Tawdry in *The Beggar's Opera* on 29 December 1746.

Hart, Mr [*fl.* 1776–1777], *numberer.*
A Mr Hart worked at Drury Lane Theatre in 1776–77 as a numberer at 15s. weekly. *The London Stage* quotes an entry in the accounts dated 20 March 1775: "Mr G. Garrick on acct. per Mr Hart £100." That Mr Hart was probably not the numberer but David Garrick's personal servant Charles Hart.

Hart, Mr [*fl.* 1790], *manager.*
According to the Pie Powder Court Book at the Guildhall the managers Jobson and Hart

paid 8*s.* on 4 September 1790 for a license to perform drolls at Bartholomew Fair.

Hart, Mrs [*fl.* 1744–1746], actress. See HART, MR [*fl.* 1744–1747].

Hart, Mrs [*fl.* 1789–1801?], dresser?

The Drury Lane account books cited a Mrs Hart as an employee of the theatre in 1789–90 at 9*s.* weekly. That lowly wage suggests that she may have been the Hart (no sex mentioned) who was cited in the accounts as a dresser at that same salary in 1801.

Hart, Miss [*fl.* 1760–1761], actress.

On 22 October 1760 at Drury Lane Theatre Miss Hart, cited only as a gentlewoman making her stage debut, played Lady Townly in *The Provok'd Husband.* The prompter Hopkins identified her in his notes and said, "Some Applause." Miss Hart made her second appearance on 11 May 1761, playing the Queen in *The Spanish Fryar.*

Hart, Charles c. 1630–1683, actor, manager.

Charles Hart must have been born about 1630 or earlier (John Payne Collier suggested about 1625) if he acted as a boy before the theatres closed in 1642. The story that he was the eldest son of William Hart, who was the eldest son of Shakespeare's sister Joan, has been largely discredited, chiefly on the basis of Charles Hart's detailed will of 1683 (and the fact that William Hart died a bachelor). The usually reliable Wright in his *Historia Histrionica* of 1699 said that ". . . *Hart* and *Clun,* were bred up Boys at the *Blackfriars* and Acted Womens Parts, *Hart* was [Richard] *Robinson's* Boy or Apprentice: He Acted the Dutchess in the Tragedy of *the Cardinal,* which was the first Part that gave him Reputation." *The Cardinal* was licensed in 1641, and if Hart acted so important a role as the Duchess, he must have been apprenticed some years before. David George discovered a manuscript cast for *Philaster* at the Folger Shakespeare Library which dates between 1638 and 1642 and lists "Charles" as Euphrasia, disguised as the page Bellario. It is very likely that the reference was to Hart.

After the closing of the theatres, Hart, again according to Wright, became "a Lieutenant of Horse under Sir *Thomas Dallison,* in *Prince Rupert's,* Regiment. . . ." Then:

When the Wars were over, and the Royalists totally Subdued; most of [the actors] who were left alive gather'd to *London,* and for a Subsistence endeavour'd to revive their Old Trade, privately. They made up one Company out of all the Scatter'd Members of Several; and in the Winter before the King's Murder, 1648 [i.e., 1648/49], They ventured to Act some Plays with as much caution and privacy as cou'd be, at the *Cockpit.* They continu'd undisturbed for three or four Days; but at last as they were presenting the Tragedy of the *Bloudy Brother,* (in which *Lowin* Acted Aubrey, *Tayler* Rollo, *Pollard* the Cook, *Burt* Latorch, and I think *Hart* Otto) a Party of Foot Souldiers beset the House, surprized 'em about the middle of the Play, and carried 'em away in their habits, not admitting them to Shift, to *Hatton-house* then a Prison, where having detain'd them sometime, they Plunder'd them of their Cloths and let 'em loose again.

Just before 1660 acting resumed on a somewhat larger scale and without such harassment. Hart performed with a troupe at the Red Bull in 1659–60, but the only role conjectured for him (on the basis of a manuscript cast) is Florez in *The Beggar's Bush.* An actor list in the Lord Chamberlain's accounts dated 6 October 1660 indicates that Hart was with a group at the Cockpit for a time. On the thirteenth he and some of his fellow actors signed a petition complaining that Thomas Killigrew had been suppressing them and that Sir Henry Herbert, the Master of the Revels, wanted a weekly payment from the actors as a fee for protecting them. Herbert, it appears, was "a continual disturbance" to the players rather than a protector.

By 5 November 1660 the two official Restoration acting companies, the King's and the Duke's, had been formed under Thomas Killigrew and Sir William Davenant, respectively. The King's players, among whom was Charles Hart, began acting at the Red Bull. There they performed *Wit Without Money, The Traitor,* and *The Beggar's Bush* in quick succession; the casts are not known, though one may guess that Hart probably acted Florez in the last play and doubtless participated in some way in the other two. On 8 November the company opened their Vere Street Theatre, a converted tennis court, where they performed for three years. Their first offering was *1 Henry IV*, but Hart's role, if he had one, is not known. A manuscript cast at the Folger Library, discovered by David George, shows Hart as Amintor in *The Maid's Tragedy* about 1659.

In 1660–61, in addition to the role of Florez, Hart played Dorant in *The Liar*, possibly the Prince in *Erminia* (the playwright, Flecknoe, asked for that casting, at any rate), Amintor in *The Maid's Tragedy*, Arbaces in *A King and No King*, Rollo in *The Bloody Brother*, and probably many other roles, records of which have not been found. As a member of the King's Company, Hart was granted a livery allowance for the period 1660–1662 on 29 July 1661.

The following season he is known to have acted the Prince of England in *The Royall King* and Michael Perez in *Rule a Wife and Have a Wife*. *The London Stage* suggests that when *The Cardinal* was performed on 23 July 1662 Hart may have played the Duchess, the role he took years before, but that assignment seems highly unlikely for a man who was probably in his thirties and at a time when the all-male acting tradition had passed. The only other role known for Hart before the troupe left the Vere Street Theatre in 1663 was Jolly in *The Cheats*, which was acted about 16 March of that year.

During the 1661–62 season the King's Company had been busy planning a new theatre in Bridges Street, the first Restoration playhouse to be built. Hart joined in the signing of an indenture for the ground on 20 December 1661, and on 28 January 1662 he became one of the building investors by buying two shares. On the previous 10 January he had invested in one and a quarter acting shares in the company. We do not know how much Hart paid for his building and acting shares, and it is not clear how much he realized from them. The building sharers as a group (there were 36 shares) were to be paid £3 10*s*. per share for each acting day, and Leslie Hotson conjectured that a single share may have brought in £280 annually at the most.

Hart was not only one of the troupe's leading players and shareholders; sometime after 1663 he joined with Michael Mohun and John Lacy as a co-manager of the company. Thomas Killigrew gave the trio a power of attorney to superintend the company; to pay themselves, the managers divided three-fourths of one acting share. Where they got the share is not clear, but apparently they took portions of shares from some of the minor actors and turned the bit-part players into hirelings. That created dissension in the ranks, and the delegated powers were withdrawn. That was not, however, the end of Hart's managerial career, as will be seen.

On 7 May 1663 the King's Company opened their new theatre in Bridges Street with *The Humorous Lieutenant*; Hart played Demetrius. Between then and the closing of the playhouses because of the plague, Hart's known new parts were Fernando and Ferentes in *Love's Sacrifice* (not in the same performance), The Duke in *The Siege of Urbin*, Mosca in *Volpone*, and Cortez in *The Indian Emperor*. Smith and MacMillan, the editors of Dryden's *The Rival Ladies* and *The Indian Queen*, suggest that Hart may have acted Gonsalvo in the former and Montezuma in the latter.

Of Hart's private life in the early 1660s we know little. He was living in Henrietta Street, Covent Garden, in 1665, according to *The Survey of London*. Charles was a lover of Nell Gwyn. She apparently began working as an orange girl at the Bridges Street Theatre shortly after it opened in 1663, when she was about 13. Perhaps within a year and a half she was onstage. Colley Cibber, years later, said Charles Hart was her patron, lover, and tutor in acting, just as John Lacy was, perhaps before Hart, Nell's lover and dancing teacher. Mary Knight and a merchant named Robert Duncan may also have had a hand in helping Nell to a stage career, so perhaps Hart's influence was not all that strong. A satire, "The Lady of Pleasure," attributed to Etherege in Buckingham's *Works* in 1715 but probably not by Sir George, said

> *Then Entred* Nelly *on the publick Stage,*
> *Harlot of Harlots,* Lais *of the Age;*
> *But where what Lacy's fumbling Age abus'd,*
> *Hart's sprightly Vigor more robustly us'd.*
> *Yet* Hart *more manners had than not to tender,*
> *When noble* B[uckhurst] *begg'd him to Surrender:*
> *He saw her roll the Stage from side to side,—*
> *And thro' her Draw'rs the powerful Charm De-*
>   *cry'd,*
> Take her my Lord, *quoth* Hart *since you're so*
>   *mean,*

To take a Player's leavings for your Q[ueen].
For tho I love her well, yet as she's poor,
I'm well contented to prefer the Whore.

Buckhurst (Charles Sackville, later the sixth
Earl of Dorset), according to Pepys, lured Nell
from the playhouse in the summer of 1667,
and when she returned in the early fall Hart's
love for her had turned to hate. Between the
middle of 1663, then, and mid-1667 Hart
became Nell's chief lover, and the most likely
time would seem to have been after the plague
and fire, when the pair acted opposite one
another in important parts.

Tracing the activities of the players during
the period when the theatres were closed is
virtually impossible. Not until 25 February
1666, when Hart's name appeared on a livery
warrant, do we hear of him again. From then
until the burning of the Bridges Street playhouse in early 1672 Hart was Valerio in *Da-
moiselles à la Mode* (Flecknoe's intended casting), Amintor in *The Maid's Tragedy*, Welford
in *The Scornful Lady*, Don John in *The Chances*,
Celadon in *Secret Love* (with Nell as Florimel),
Rollo in *The Bloody Brother*, possibly Forecast
in *The Mulberry Garden* (Pinto's conjecture),
Philidor in *All Mistaken*, Lord Delaware in *The
Black Prince*, Hotspur in *1 Henry IV*, the title
character in *Philaster*, Wildblood in *An Evening's Love*, Armusia in *The Island Princess*, Catiline, Cassio in *Othello*, Arbaces in *A King and
No King*, Porphyrius in *Tyrannick Love*, Brutus
in *Julius Caesar*, Almanzor in both parts of *The
Conquest of Granada* (and he may have spoken
the epilogue to Part One and, according to a
Harvard manuscript, the prologue to Part
Two), Ranger in *Love in a Wood*, and Palamede
in *Marriage à la Mode*. His last role before the
theatre burned in January 1672, so far as is
known, was Brutus.

Comments on Hart's acting, so rare in the
early 1660s, are more easily come by later.
Pepys, after seeing *All Mistaken* on 28 December 1667, wrote in his diary that " . . . Nell's
and Hart's mad parts are most .excellently
done, but especially her's. . . ." Settle in 1695
remembered in his prologue to the revised *Philaster* how fine Hart and Nell had been in the
1667 production:

*The good old Play Philaster ne're can fail
But we Young Actors, how shall we prevail?
Philaster and Bellario, let me tell ye,*

*For these Bold Parts we have no Hart, no Nelly;
Those Darlings of the Stage, that charm'd you
there.*

But when Pepys saw *Othello* on 6 February
1669 he was disappointed in Hart's Cassio as
well as Mohun's Iago and Burt's Moor; the
parts, he wrote, were "ill-acted."

The production of *Catiline* caused more
comment than any other play in which Hart
acted. Pepys observed on 7 December 1667
that the play was planned for the King's Company but that the Bridges Street Theatre had
been closed for several days because of "some
difference" between Hart and his fellow actor
Mohun. The cause of the postponement was,
apparently, the King; some clothes he promised for the production were not forthcoming.
Finally, a year later, on 18 December 1668,
the play was performed. There was a flurry of
criticism because Mrs Corey, in the role of
Sempronia, imitated Lady Harvey. When
Pepys saw the play the following day he found
that it did not play nearly as well as it had
read.

The most notorious story connected with
Catiline may concern the 1668 production but
more likely dates from 1677, when Hart was
sole manager of the King's Company. The tale,
possibly a fiction, was told in *The Life of . . .
Jo. Hayns* in 1701. The *Life* dated the incident
as happening when Hart was "sole Governour
of the Play-House, and at a small variance with
Jo. . . ." Hart needed some extra Senators in
the play and insisted that Haines appear as one
even though Joe was not a mere hireling in the
troupe. To get even, Haines dressed up as a
scaramouch and clowned behind the unsus-
pecting Hart during one of the scenes.

Which Comical Figure put all the House in an
uproar, some Laughing, some Clapping, and some
Hollowing. Now Mr. *Hart*, as those that knew him
can aver, was a Man of that Exactness and Grandeur
on the Stage, that let what wou'd happen, he'd
never discompose himself, or mind any thing but
what he then Represented, and had a Scene fall'n
behind him, he wou'd not at that time look back,
to have seen what was the matter, which *Jo.* knowing, remain'd still Smoking, the Audience continued Laughing, Mr. *Hart* Acting, and Wondering at
this unusual occasion of their Mirth, sometimes
thinking it some disturbance in the House; again,
that it might be something amiss in his dress; at
last, turning himself towards the Scenes, he dis-

cover'd Jo. in the aforesaid Posture, whereupon he immediately goes off the Stage, Swearing he wou'd never set foot on it again, unless Jo. was immediately turn'd out of Doors; which was no sooner spoke, but put in Practice.

Hart's break-up with Nell Gwyn in 1667 did not deter the actor from again playing musical beds, and he chose this time a strumpet from higher social circles, Barbara Palmer, Lady Castlemaine, sometime mistress of Charles II. Pepys learned on 7 April 1668 the

mighty news, that my Lady Castlemayne is mightily in love with Hart of their house; and he is much with her in private, and she goes to him, and do give him many presents; and that the thing is most certain, and Becke Marshall [the actress] only privy to it, and the means of bringing them together, which is a very odd thing; and by this means she is even with the King's love to Mrs Davis [the actress].

In time Lady Castlemaine threw over Hart for another actor, Cardell Goodman.

Another anecdote in the Joe Haines biography cannot be easily dated but is worth repeating because it gives us a clue about where Hart had his lodgings. Haines persuaded a parson to go to Hart's house, which was described as in or near the theatre and perhaps was in the passageway leading from Bow Street to the front of the playhouse. Haines instructed the parson to go to "the 3d Door of your left hand." When the parson came "down the Passage Ringing his Bell, and bauling out, Players come to Prayers, Players come to Prayers; coming to Mr. Hart's door he finds it open, and up he goes one pair of stairs, where Mr. Hart was then busie at his Study. . . ." As instructed by Haines, the parson increased his clanging as Hart's aggravation grew.

Hart's income during the 1660s and 1670s is not certainly known, though he must have been one of the highest-paid actors in his troupe. The *Historia Histrionica* stated later that for several years after 1660 Hart and other leading players in the King's Company cleared £1000 a season—an impossibly high figure and perhaps a misprint for £100. Malone put Hart's salary at £3 weekly, plus 6s. 3d. for each acting day, which amount would add up to about £50 to £60 annually, a reasonable figure for the time.

Hart and his fellow players, after the Bridges Street fire, moved to the Lincoln's Inn Fields Theatre, which had recently been vacated by the rival Duke's Company when their new playhouse in Dorset Garden had been completed. In the tiny tennis court theatre Hart is recorded as reciting the prologue to *Henry III* in March 1672 and then speaking the prologue to *Arviragus and Philicia* and playing Aurelian in *The Assignation* and Captain Towerson in *Amboyna*. In July 1673 at Oxford he spoke a special prologue and epilogue written by Dryden. Sometime between about 1673 and 1675 Hart played Almerin in *Brennoralt*, according to the prompt notes in a Bodleian copy of the work.

We cannot be sure how deeply involved Hart may have been in the management of the King's Company, but even after he, Mohun, and Lacy were demoted, Hart may have continued influential in the troupe's affairs. Warrants in the Lord Chamberlain's accounts sometimes cited Hart and Mohun as the company representatives in legal tangles, as in 1669 in a controversy between the scene painter Isaac Fuller and the King's Company.

The troupe, after the Bridges Street fire, began laying plans for a new playhouse to be built on the site of their old one. On 17 December 1673 Hart and other sharing actors agreed to perform in the new Drury Lane Theatre and to pay the building investors (chiefly business men) a daily rent of £3 10s. if the cost of the building should come to £2400. The figure ultimately soared to £3908 11s. 5d., so the rent was £5 14s. daily. Hart still held a share and a quarter. For the first few years at the new playhouse, then, Hart and his colleagues may not have fared well financially.

Drury Lane opened on 26 March 1674 with *The Beggar's Bush*; the cast is not known, but surely Hart must have been in it. His first recorded role at the new house was the title part in *Nero* on 16 May 1674. At Drury Lane from that date until his retirement in 1682 Hart is known to have played Bussy D'Ambois, Horner in *The Country Wife* (and he spoke the prologue), Othello, Arbaces in *A King and No King*, Massanissa in *Sophonisba*, probably Valentinian in *Lucina's Rape*, the title part in *Aureng-Zebe*, Caesario in *Gloriana*, Manly in *The Plain Dealer*, Phraartes in *The Destruction of Jerusalem*, Alexander in *The Rival Queens*, Marc Antony in *All for Love*, Ziphanes in *Mithri-*

dates, and Monsieur Thomas in *Trick for Trick*. Hart and Mohun acted rarely after 1679. The prologue to Crowne's *The Ambitious Statesman* (performed before March 1679) lamented: "The Time's Neglect, and Maladies have thrown / The two great Pillars of our Playhouse down." In September 1680 or perhaps a few months earlier, when *Fatal Love* was performed, the author Settle in his dedication, referring to Hart, said the "sweetest Pipes" in the troupe "were stopt." By that time Hart may well have ceased acting entirely and settled for a pension.

During the last half of the 1670s Hart had not only served as the company's leading man but had been, either again or still, active in company affairs, and he remained so to the end of his stage career. In 1675 Thomas Killigrew's son Charles took over the company and entered into new articles with the players. Hart was granted £100 annual salary, the highest sum any of the players received. On 1 May 1676 the actors signed new articles with Charles Killigrew. Each sharer was to receive after three months notice, 5*s*. each acting day for life, and after his death his executors were to be paid £100. Holders of a share and a quarter (Hart was one) were to receive 6*s*. 3*d*. each acting day and the same benefit to executors.

But Thomas Killigrew failed to turn over the company patent and governorship as he had promised, and a quarrel ensued. The upshot was that Hart, Mohun, and Kynaston were made a committee of control by the Lord Chamberlain on 9 September 1676 to serve until the Killigrews settled their differences. Even that failed to work satisfactorily, and Hart later became sole manager. On 22 February 1677 the law forced Thomas Killigrew to resign his power and authority to his son; on that date, presumably, Hart had to relinquish his managership to Charles Killigrew, though the records suggest that he still remained active in company business matters. On 8 August 1677, for instance, Hart, Mohun, Kynaston, and Cartwright were ordered, as King's Company representatives, to pay the scene painters Aggas and Towers. In 1678 Hart, Charles Killigrew, Burt, Goodman, and Mohun complained about Dryden's giving *Oedipus* to the rival troupe, in violation of his agreement with the King's Company.

The troupe did not prosper. On 30 July 1680 the troubles in the company came to a head. The Duke's Company had better actors and playwrights, and the King's players found the competition too strong. Their income kept dropping, the younger actors grumbled that the older players, chiefly Mohun and Hart, were sitting on the best parts and yet not acting as frequently as they once had done. On 30 July 1680, then, Charles Killigrew and some of the players in the troupe drew up a new agreement. Several younger actors were to become sharers, and Hart and Mohun were to be dropped.

Though Hart was acting very little, if at all, by 1681, on 14 October of that year he and Kynaston signed an agreement with the rival Duke's Company, promising not to act for or aid the King's troupe; the pair made over their King's Company stock to the Duke's Company managers and agreed to do what they could to promote a union of the two groups. Kynaston, but not Hart, made arrangements to perform for the Duke's players as soon as he could. The agreement was a sensible one for Hart, for the days of the King's Company were numbered, and if the rival troupe wanted to pay him for not acting at Drury Lane at a time when he seems not to have been acting anyway, why should he not accept? He stood to gain by signing over his stock in his own company to the rival actors, for they agreed to pay him 5*s*. daily whenever they acted, for life—as long as he did not act for or aid the King's Company. In June 1682 a draft agreement was signed leasing Drury Lane to the leaders of the Duke's Company at £3 daily; in this arrangement Hart held two shares. But the agreement was canceled in November and a new one made up leasing Drury Lane to Charles Davenant. As of June 1683 Hart still held two building shares in the United Company.

According to the prompter Downes, Charles Hart retired completely at the union of the troupes:

Upon this Union, Mr. Hart being the Heart of the Company under Mr. Killigrew's Patent never Acted more, by reason of his Malady; being Afflicted with the Stone and Gravel, of which he Dy'd some time after: Having a Sallary of 40 shillings a Week to the Day of his Death.

Settle had indicated in 1680 in *Fatal Love* that Hart had then left the stage:

'Tis true, the Theatre Royal was once all Harmony, where the Heroick Muses sung so sweetly, and with Voices so perfectly Musical, as few Ears could escape Enchantment. . . . But, *Oh, that their Oracle should be quite silent! Ah, that their* Golden Head *would speak agen, and* bring once more the scatter'd Quire around him! *Then* Tragedy *might re-assume its Majesty.* . . . This I may modestly say of him . . . that the best *Tragedies on the* English *stage* have receiv'd that Lustre from *Mr.* Hart's *Performance*, that he has left such an Impression behind him, that no less than the Interval of an Age can make them appear agen with half their Majesty from any second Hand.

Hart retired to Stanmore Magna. On 10 July 1683 he wrote his will, a lengthy and detailed document which was witnessed by, among others, Nicholas Strawbridge, one of the nonacting sharers in the old King's Company. Hart described himself "sick and weake in body," and, indeed, he did not have long to live. Luttrell recorded in his diary that "that Worthy and Famous Actor, Mr. Charles Hart . . . departed this Life Thursday August the 18th. 1683." He was buried two days later in Stanmore Magna.

Charles Hart left 40s. to the minister (not named) who preached at his funeral. To his servant Alice Girdler, Hart left 20 guineas, all his plate (which he itemized in his will), the furniture in the room in his house which he described as hung with purple and white, the furniture in the bedroom where Alice slept as well as that in the room next to that of his servant James Allen, all the brass and pewter in the kitchen, all the linen, and all of his clothes. To a Mrs Carpender Hart left a looking glass; to his friend Thomas Napper the furniture in the room called the bed chamber and some pictures; to Barbara (Flenno?) the furnishings of his own bedchamber; and to his friends Mr Fenne, Mr Carpender, and Mr Norwood, all his books.

Hart directed his executors to sell the movables in his little parlor, the hall, and the withdrawing room, and to give the profits as follows: two-thirds to the poor of Stanmore Magna and one-third for repairing the highways of the town.

To the daughter of Mathew Hart, late clerk of the parish of St Botolph, Bishopsgate, Charles Hart left £20 plus £5 for her to distribute to any of Hart's relatives whom she knew; if she knew none, she was to keep the money herself. To his fellow actor Edward Kynaston, of St Giles in the Fields, Hart left his one building share in Drury Lane Theatre (presumably Hart had disposed of his other share before he wrote his will). He indicated that the building share was to be held by Kynaston for the remainder of the 41 years "which I have therein yet to round out." Out of the revenue from the share Kynaston was to pay the Earl of Bedford and his heirs (who had leased the land to the players) £50 ground rent yearly. If Kynaston should default on the payment, the share was to go to Hart's executor. Kynaston was also left £5 for mourning.

Hart's friends Gilbert Soper and Henry Hales, both theatre folk, were left £10 each. To Thomas Betterton, William Smith, and Thomas Costyn (Coffyn?) Hart left £5 each for mourning; Betterton and Smith were leading actors in the rival Duke's Company. Hart left gold rings worth 20s. each to his friends Lady Dray, Lady Digby, Mrs Rogers Lake, Thomas Napper, Mr and Mrs Carpender, Mr and Mrs Fenne, Mr and Mrs Norwood, Captain and Mrs Lloyd, Mr and Mrs (Field?), Mr and Mrs (Fenche?), Mr and Mrs Hooke, Mr and Mrs Nicholls, Mr and Mrs Ashborne, Mr Jordan, the widow Hooke, Mrs Mary Norwood, Mrs Anne Carpender, Mrs Ellen Lloyd, Mrs Bircher, Mr Powell (the actor?), Mrs Powell (the will separated the two, as though they were not man and wife), Mrs Betterton (the actress), and Mrs Corey (the actress). Hart left his servant James Allen £5, to be paid to his father, James, and given to the lad when he should reach 21. To Thomas Napper, who was named Hart's executor, Hart bequeathed £5 for mourning and the rest of his estate, the size of which it is impossible to determine.

Both during his life and for many years after, Charles Hart was admired for his talent, especially in tragic roles, and it is clear that he was for a time Thomas Betterton's chief rival. In the King's troupe only Michael Mohun came close to matching Hart in importance. Rymer in *The Tragedies of the Last Age* (1678) wrote:

These [critics] say, for instance, a *King* and no *King pleases.* I say the *Comical* part *pleases.*
I say that Mr. *Hart pleases*; most of the business falls to his share, and what he *delivers* every one takes upon *content*; their *eyes* are prepossest and charm'd by his *action* before ought of the *Poets* can

approach their *ears*, and to the most wretched of *Characters* he gives a lustre and *brillant* [sic] which dazles the *sight*, that the *deformities* in the Poetry cannot be perceiv'd.

As for *The Maid's Tragedy*:

We may remember (how-ever we find this Scene of *Melanthius* and *Amintor* written in the Book) that at the *Theater* we have a good Scene Acted; there is work cut out, and both our *Aesopus* and *Roscius* are on the Stage together. Whatever defect may be in *Amintor* and *Melanthius*, Mr. *Hart* and Mr. *Mohun* are wanting in nothing. To these we owe for what is pleasing in the Scene; and to this Scene we may impute the success of the *Maids Tragedy*.

John Downes the prompter was also struck by Hart's ability. In commenting on Griffin's playing of Manly in *The Plain Dealer*, he said no one had ever equalled him "except his Predecessor Mr. Hart." And " . . . Mr. Hart, in the Part of Arbaces, in King and no King; Amintor, in the Maids Tragedy; Othello; Rollo; Brutus in Julius Caesar; Alexander, towards the latter End of his Acting; if he Acted in any one of these but once in a Fortnight, the House was fill'd as at a New Play. . . ." Downes called Robert Wilks "the finisht Copy of his Famous Predecessor, Mr. Charles Hart." Like his rival, Betterton, Hart had a wide range. Downes said he "was no less Inferior in Comedy; as Mosca in the Fox; Don John in the Chances, Wildblood in the Mock Astrologer; with sundry other Parts. In all the Comedies and Tragedies, he was concern'd he Perform'd with that Exactness and Perfection, that not any of his Successors have Equall'd him."

Thomas D'Urfey, in the dedication to his version of *Bussy D'Ambois* in 1691 said:

About Sixteen Years since, when first my good or ill Stars ordained me a Knight Errant in this Fairy Land of Poetry, I saw the *Bussy D' Ambois* of Mr. *Chapman* Acted by Mr. *Hart*, which in spight of the obsolete Phrases and intolerable Fustian, with which a great Part of it was cramm'd, and which I have altered in these new Sheets) [*sic*] had some extraordinary Beauties, which sensibly charmed me; which being improved by the graceful Action of that eternally Renowned, and Best of Actors, so attracted not only me, but the Town in general, that they were obliged to pass by and excuse the gross Errors in the Writing. . . . For a long time after it lay buried in Mr. *Harts* Grave, who indeed only could do that noble Character Justice. . . .

An *Elegy* that appeared after Hart's death also praised the actor:

> *Such Pow'r He had o'r the Spectators gain'd,*
> *As forc'd a Real passion from a Feign'd.*
> *For when they saw Amintor bleed, straight all*
> *The House, for every Drop, a Tear let fall;*
> *And when Arbaces wept by sympathy,*
> *A glowing Tide of Wo gush'd from each Eye.*

In 1702 *A Comparison Between the Two Stages* praised the quality of the plays in earlier years and said "Hart and Mohun acted 'em so well." Steele honored the pair, too. In the *Tatler* on 25 November 1709 he lauded "My old friends, Hart and Mohun, the one by his natural and proper force, the other by his great skill and art, never failed to send me home full of such ideas as affected my behaviour, and made me insensibly more courteous and humane to my friends and acquaintances." On 24 February 1710 Hart was again mentioned in the *Tatler*: "I have heard my old friend Mr. Hart speak it as an observation among the players, 'that it is impossible to act with grace, except the actor has forgot that he is before an audience.'" But certainly one of the most flattering anecdotes about Hart was one told years later by Davies; if true, it was a high compliment indeed. At a rehearsal of *The Rival Queens*, in which Hart had played Alexander in earlier years, Thomas Betterton, displeased with one of his own line readings in the part, asked if anyone in the cast could remember how Hart had spoken the line. "At last, one of the lowest of the company repeated the line exactly in Hart's key. Betterton thanked him heartily, and put a piece of money in his hand as a reward for so acceptable a service."

Unfortunately, no portrait of Charles Hart survives.

Hart, George *d. 1699, singer, composer.*

Though George Hart was not recorded in the *Old Cheque Book of the Chapel Royal* until 1694, Sanford's description of the coronation of James II on 23 April 1685 listed Hart as marching in the procession among the tenors from the Chapel, substituting for Henry Smith. Hart composed some songs which Playford published in his *Theater of Music* in 1686 and 1687, among them "While Orpheus in a heavy strain," "Th'ambitious Eye," and "In th'Evening's Dawn." Hart was apparently supposed to sing in the St Cecilia's Day festivities on 22 November 1692, but a Bodleian manuscript of Purcell's music shows that he was replaced by Woodson.

On 10 September 1694, according to the *Cheque Book*, George Hart was sworn a Gentleman of the Chapel Royal extraordinary—unsalaried until a position should become vacant. On 1 June 1696, upon the death of John Frost, George was sworn a Gentleman in the pay of Epistler, and on 9 November 1697 he was granted a salaried post. Jeremy Noble in his *Purcell and the Chapel Royal* states that George Hart died on 29 February 1699.

Hart, James   *1647–1718, singer, composer.*

James Hart was born in York in 1647 and served as a bass singer in York Minster until he joined the Chapel Royal in London in 1670. He was appointed a lay vicar of Westminster Abbey and a Gentleman of the Chapel Royal, replacing Edmund Slater, on 10 September 1670. In May, June, and July 1671 he attended the King at Windsor for 8s. daily, and he waited on the King there again in 1674. On 30 April 1674 the opera version of *The Tempest* was produced at the Dorset Garden Theatre with some of the vocal music by Hart and Pietro Reggio. Hart contributed a "lament" in Act IV, and either James or Richard Hart sang in the production. On 15 February 1675 James sang the roles of Europe and Strephon in the court masque *Calisto*, and then he spent the summer again in Windsor.

In 1676 Hart and Jeffrey Banister ran a boarding school for young ladies in Chelsea, where they produced Duffett's masque *Beauties Triumph*. At the Chapel Royal, too, Hart served as an instructor: on 15 April 1678 he was paid £30 (a yearly sum) for maintaining Edward Butler, a former Chapel boy who had probably been trained by Hart.

James was reappointed to the Chapel Royal under James II and marched in the coronation procession on 23 April 1685. That year a number of his songs were published in Playford's *Theater of Music*, among them "When absent from my fair Corinna," "Say my Heart, what shall I do," and "Happy as Man in his first Innocence." Subsequent editions of Playford's work included more of Hart's songs. In 1689 Hart was once more reappointed to the Chapel under William and Mary. By 1694 his salary was £73 annually, though the Lord Chamberlain's accounts in the 1690s made no mention of Hart's activities. He continued serving in the royal musical establishment until his death in 1718.

Of Hart's personal life little is known. Hawkins in his *General History* guessed that Philip Hart, the organist and composer, was the son of James Hart, and one suspects that Richard Hart, a bass singer and lutenist in the Chapel Royal and contemporary with James, may have been our subject's brother. The parish registers of St Bride, Fleet Street, contain three entries which could concern James: James and Anne "Harte" christened a son Fredericke on 20 February 1675, a son John on 19 August 1677, and a son Robert on 9 February 1679.

James Hart died in York on 8 May 1718 at the age of 71 and was buried on 15 May in the West Cloister of Westminster Abbey. Administration of his estate was granted to his widow Anne on 23 May 1718, at which time Hart was described as late of the parish of St Andrew, Holborn. No will has been found. Mrs Hart was buried in the West Cloister of the Abbey on 10 April 1722.

A number of Hart's songs remained popular enough after his death to be included in D'Urfey's collection *Wit and Mirth* in 1719. Among them were "Phillis lay aside your Thinking" (for which Etherege wrote the words), "When Wit and Beauty meet," "Now ev'ry Place fresh Pleasure yields," "Happy is the Country Life," and "Honest Shepher'd." Several of his pieces are in the British Library either in printed or manuscript form.

Hart, Nathan   *d. 1765, dancer, proprietor.*

Nathan (or Naphthali) Hart, according to Wroth's *London Pleasure Gardens*, was the proprietor of Marble Hall, Vauxhall, from about 1752 to 1756. He was a dancer and a teacher of music and dancing and held assemblies at Marble Hall in the summers and at his Academy in Essex House, Essex Street, Strand, in the winters. At Marble Hall he advertised that he would rent boats, teach fencing and dancing, and provide breakfasts. At his Academy, he assured the public, "grown gentlemen are taught to dance a minuet and country dances in the modern taste, and in a short time." He claimed he could teach gentlemen to play on any instrument, to use the small sword and spadroon, to master navigation and mathematics, and to speak French, Italian, Spanish, Portuguese, High German, and Low Dutch.

Nathan Hart died on 22 June 1765, according to the *Public Advertiser*.

Hart, Polly. *See* REDDISH, MRS SAMUEL THE FIRST.

Hart, Richard *d. 1690, singer, lutenist, actor.*

Richard Hart was one of the Children of the Chapel Royal under Henry Cooke sometime before 7 April 1668, when Cooke received two suits of clothes to be given young Richard—a standard grant to former Chapel boys whose voices had broken. As late as 20 July 1670 Hart was still receiving clothing.

A Richard Hart was a member of the King's Company of players in the 1670s, and it seems probable that he was the former Chapel boy. On 19 January 1671 Zonch Herbert sued Hart and his fellow actor John Littlewood for unpaid rent. The only known role for Hart is Abbibar in *Generous Enemies*, which was acted in June 1671 at the Bridges Street Theatre. By that time James had rejoined the Chapel Royal; he was sworn a Gentleman on 26 April 1671, replacing Gregory Thorndell, deceased. The Lord Chamberlain's accounts note Hart occasionally thereafter: at Windsor attending the King in the summer of 1671 for 8s. daily and at Windsor again in the spring of 1674. His attendance at Windsor in 1674 was only on Saturdays and Sundays and only when occasion demanded, for Hart and other members of the Chapel Royal, both men and boys, were allowed to remain in London or return there if they were involved in *The Tempest* at the Dorset Garden Theatre. Either Richard or James Hart, both Chapel members, sang in the production. A royal order dated 16 May 1674 granted Chapel members that privilege, one of the proofs we have of occasional if not regular participation by court musicians in public theatre productions.

Hart attended the King at Windsor again in the summer of 1675, was granted Robert Smyth's position as a lutenist on 22 November of that year at £40 annually plus livery, journeyed to Windsor again in the late summer of 1678, and marched in the coronation procession of James II on 23 April 1685 as one of the basses.

On 18 November 1683 Richard Hart had married Elizabeth Hopwood at Westminster Abbey; she was the widow of the court musician William Hopwood. Hart died on 8 February 1690 and was buried on 11 February in the cloisters of the Abbey. His will, dated 26 December 1689, when he described himself as of the parish of St Margaret, Westminster, and "sick of body," was proved on 25 February 1690, presumably by his widow and designated executrix Elizabeth Hart. Richard left his entire estate to his wife. On 26 November 1690 she appointed Jonas Watson her attorney, probably because she found herself in debt. On 20 August 1691 she had to assign £28 in arrears due her late husband to William Bushell of Tothill Fields.

Hart, Richard [*fl. 1792–1815*], *singer.*

Richard Hart sang in the chorus when Gluck's *Orpheus and Eurydice* (with additions) was presented at Covent Garden Theatre on 28 February 1792. Doane's *Musical Directory* of 1794 indicated that Hart was a tenor and also participated in oratorio performances at Covent Garden, in the Handel concerts at Westminster Abbey, and in concerts presented by the New Musical Fund and the Choral Fund. In 1793 Hart was a member of the Oxford Meeting. In London he lived at No 6, Little New Street, Shoe Lane. He was a subscriber to the New Musical Fund and a member of that society's Court of Assistants in 1805 and 1815.

Hartford. *See* HOLLAND, CHARLES *1768–1849.*

Hartland. *See* HARLAND.

Hartle. *See also* HARTLEY.

Hartle, Mrs M. [*fl. 1768–1775*], *dancer.*

Mrs M. Hartle was an obscure chorus dancer at Covent Garden Theatre between 1768–69 and 1773–74. She signed her name as Mrs M. Hartle to an open letter from Covent Garden performers to the manager George Colman which was printed in the *Theatrical Monitor* on 5 November 1768. Annually she shared benefit tickets with other minor dancers, taking a net of £15 7s. 6d. on 19 May 1769, £5 12s. on 18 May 1770, and £5 2s. on 29 May 1772. Her known performances included appearances in a comic dance on 22 May 1771, the chorus of *The Recruits*, a new pantomime dance on 1 May 1772, and various minuets and cotillions.

At the beginning of 1774–75, Mrs Hartle transferred to Drury Lane Theatre, where on 29 October 1774 she was paid £2 for 12 days' work. She shared in benefit tickets on 8 May 1775 and was paid £1 10s. on 25 May, after which date her name dropped from the records.

The William Hartle who was buried at St Paul, Covent Garden, on 6 September 1773 may have been her relative.

Hartley, Mrs [*fl.* 1735–1736], *dresser.*
A Mrs Hartley was paid a total of £12 18s. (1s. 6d. per day for 172 days) as a dresser at Covent Garden Theatre in 1735–36.

Hartley, Edward [*fl.* 1663–1670], *scenekeeper.*
The London Stage lists Edward Hartley as a member of the King's Company in 1663–64 and again in 1669–70. A Lord Chamberlain's warrant of 20 February 1665 cited him as a scenekeeper in the troupe, which then performed at the Bridges Street Theatre.

Hartley, Elizabeth, née White 1750?–1824, *actress.*
Elizabeth Hartley was the daughter of James and Eleanor White of Berrow, Somerset, who were, according to her earliest memoir in the *London Magazine* for October 1773, persons who "occupied a position of great obscurity." Since she was described in her burial register in January 1824 as aged 73, Elizabeth must have been born in 1750 or early in 1751. She was probably baptized in the parish church of Berrow, although entries for the years between 1745 and 1753 are absent from those records. The *London Magazine* memoir claimed that while she was a chambermaid in a gentleman's family she became the mistress of a Mr Hartley, who upon becoming poverty-stricken persuaded Elizabeth to take up acting.

The identity of Mr Hartley, whose name she took but whom she never married, remains a mystery. Possibly he was the "Heartly" who was in Roger Kemble's touring company for part of 1768 but who on 3 June left the troupe at Bath "clandestinely." A Mr and Mrs Hartley (hardly Elizabeth) performed with Durravan's company at Derby in 1763–64. A child named Hartley performed at Bristol in 1766 and later, as an adult, played in a company at Glasgow in 1770. Perhaps he was James Hartley, an actor formerly of Scarborough, who died at Durham in December 1790.

It has been said that Mrs Hartley made her theatrical debut under Foote's management at the Haymarket about 1769 in the role of Imoinda in *Oroonoko*, but we find no record of such a performance, either under its main title or under its alternate title, *The Royal Slave*, which would confirm that assumption.

Nothing is known, in fact, of her theatrical experience prior to her first appearance on the Edinburgh stage as Monimia in *The Orphan* on 4 December 1771. In that season under Digges's management she also acted Desdemona in *Othello*, Cordelia in *King Lear*, and a substantial line of other tragic figures including Almeria in *The Mourning Bride*, Angelica in *The Constant Wife*, Belvidera in *Venice Preserv'd*, Calista in *The Fair Penitent*, Constance in *The Twin Rivals*, Lady Percy in *1 Henry IV*, Mary Queen of Scots in *The Albion Queens*, and Anne Bullen in *Henry VIII*. Soon after, she joined Dodd's company at Bristol for the summer of 1772 where she made her debut as Jane Shore. The prologue spoken by Dodd upon that occasion is preserved in a manuscript in the Folger Shakespeare Library:

To night before this awful Court, appears
With Diffidence quite sunk—half dead with Fears
A Female, who requests me to intreat
Her Inexperience may Your Candour meet.
Untaught by Garrick's or by Colman's Rule
She brings no Lessons, but from Nature's School
By these instructed, 'tho devoid of Art,
Her Aim to please, is levell'd at the Heart.
E'en Scotland's hardy Natives will confess,
She taught them first to feel for Shore's Distress.
To Them Her endless Gratitude is due
For Favors, which She dares not hope from You;
Who Younge's Accomplishments will call to mind,
Where Art and Nature's highest Pow'rs are join'd.

ELIZABETH HARTLEY, as a Nymph with a Young Bacchus
by Reynolds

Yet if from Sensibility's pure Source
Quick Feelings She displays, & Passion's Force,
Your Favor will enliven, like the Spring,
Those Seeds which Time may to Perfection bring.

*   For me,—who seldom serious am you know,*
Smit with Her Form—my Gallantry to show,

I told Her on Her Beauty to depend,
Each Manly Heart is Female Beauty's Friend.
The Generous Englishman, whose Haughty Soul
Stands forth for Liberty, and scorns Controul,
To Beauty's Tyranny a Slave will prove,
And as in Arms He conquers, yields in Love.
Hence to this Point my word I'll boldly stake
You'll spare the Actress, *for the* Woman's *sake.*

At Bristol she also acted Indiana in *The Conscious Lovers* on 17 July, Louisa Dudley in *The West Indian* on 27 July, and Euphrasia in *The Grecian Daughter* on 3 August. On 19 September 1772, two days after the Bristol season closed, she wrote an indignant letter to *Felix Farley's Bristol Journal* to deny the accusation that she had refused to take on new parts. On the contrary, she argued, although on one occasion (9 July) she had refused a role with good reason, Dodd had from that day "*never offer'd her a single Part* (excepting that of one of the Women in the *Beggar's Opera* by way of Insult)." She accused the manager of deliberately holding her back "lest *she* should be

mistaken for the *principal* Actress," Mrs Bulkley. On 26 September a correspondent to the same paper replied that Dodd "might very safely have ventured her playing *every* Night in the Season without the least Danger of her having been ever taken—or (as she herself expresses it) *mistaken* for the *principal* Actress."

While Mrs Hartley was still in Edinburgh in the spring of 1772, Garrick had become interested in her as a potential acquisition for the Drury Lane company. In a letter on 2 March 1772 he asked James Boswell to advise in confidence "What You & ye Wisest folks in Edinburgh think of Mrs *Heartley* y^e *Actress?*— has she the Merit which she is said to have?" Boswell's reply is not extant, but Garrick's interest persisted. On his behalf the actor John Moody scouted her performances at Bristol and wrote to George Garrick, David's brother and right-hand man, on 26 July 1772:

. . . Mrs Hartley is a good figure, with a handsome small face, and very much freckled; her hair red, and her neck and shoulders well-turned. There is not the least harmony in her voice; but when forced (which she never fails to do on every occasion) is loud and strong, but such an inarticulate gabble, that you must be acquainted with her part to understand her. She is ignorant and stubborn: the latter might be got the better of at Drury Lane, and the former mended; but I despair of either at Covent Garden, where she is engaged. . . .

Had she not already been signed with the other house, it is doubtful that Garrick would have offered her a position on the strength of Moddy's recommendation, for, he continued, although "there is a superficial glare about her that may carry her through a few nights" she would not last long on the London stage. "She has a husband, a precious fool, that she heartily despises," concluded Moody, and "She talks lusciously, and has a slovenly good-nature about her that renders her prodigiously vulgar."

Within a week after finishing the Bristol summer season of 1772, Mrs Hartley was in London preparing for her debut at Covent Garden and apparently trying to earn a few extra pounds by giving acting lessons. Almost surely she was the "E. H." who advertised on 29 September 1772 to teach and coach ladies for the profession or for their private amusement—"Enquire for E. H. No 2 Queen St. near

Harvard Theatre Collection

ELIZABETH HARTLEY as Elfrida, ISABELLA MATTOCKS as one of the chorus, and THOMAS HULL as Edwin

artist unknown

Windmill Street, Haymarket." She described herself as a gentlewoman "who had played Capital Characters . . . in the three King-doms" (thus indicating she had played in Ire-land as well).

On 5 October 1772 she made her debut at Covent Garden as Jane Shore. The critic in the *Town and Country Magazine* for that month judged her deserving "of much praise" and described her figure as elegant, her face pleas-ing and expressive, her action just, and her voice—contrary to Moody's report—"in gen-eral melodious." After another four perform-ances as Jane Shore, she appeared on 6 Novem-ber as Queen Catherine in *Henry VIII*. But now the critic of *Town and Country Magazine* (No-vember 1772), noting his preference for her acting in *Jane Shore*, remarked that she had as Catherine "frequently sunk into a whining monotony which from the length of some of the speeches became very disagreeable."

During that 1772–73 season she frequently acted Catherine and Jane Shore as well as the title role in *Elfrida* (first time on 21 November 1772). When she played Orellana in the pre-miere of Murphy's *Alzuma* on 23 February 1773 the critic in the *Covent Garden Journal* for that month wrote that Mrs Hartley, "from her beautiful figure and sweet face, made every auditor wish that nature had given her a voice less dissonant, and monotonous." She also per-formed Alcmena in *Amphitryon* on 20 March, Statira in *The Rival Queens* on 30 March, Is-mena in *Timanthes* on 3 April, Cleopatra in *All for Love* on 28 April, Portia in *Julius Caesar* on 4 May, and Juliet on 17 May. For her benefit on 22 March 1773, when she acted Lady Mac-beth for the first time, she took a substantial profit of £180 2s. 6d.

If by the end of her first London season Mrs Hartley had not charmed the critics and the public by her histrionic talents, that deficiency was more than compensated for by her acclaim as a very beautiful woman. After Garrick vis-ited Covent Garden in May 1774 to see her play Rosamond in Thomas Hull's *King Henry II*, in a letter to Peter Fountain he proclaimed that he had never seen "a finer creature than

Courtesy of the Garrick Club

ELIZABETH HARTLEY
by Angelica Kauffmann, detail of full-length painting

Mʳˢ Hartly," describing her "make" as "perfect." In October 1773 the critic in the *London Magazine* swooned:

This lady's figure seems to have been moulded by the hand of Harmony itself. It presents to us all those fine inclinations which compose the essence of real grace; and the whole form is so admirably put together, that the parts seem to be lost into each other, and to defy the eye with their beauties. The features of her face are marked with the same regularity. Her eye is lively, though not brilliant; her skin is singularly fair; and her hair is dark red. In a word, taking her altogether, she gives us the idea of a Greek beauty."

A similar tribute to her stunning physical attributes was paid by William Hawkins in *Miscellanies in Prose and Verse* (1775), who summed her up as "the finest figure on the London stage." Such appreciation was echoed in the *Macaroni & Savoir Vivre Magazine* (October 1773): "she is tall and elegant, her face is remarkably handsome, her carriage easy." It was therefore no wonder that a lady endowed with such requisites for the stage would gain great applause "had she little or no merit in her profession." The effect was marred only, it seems, by her voice: "it is somewhat harsh, though not discordant, but she is apt to wind it sometimes beyond the keys of harmony."

Her beauty also wound up her admirers at times beyond the bounds of propriety. On 23 July 1773, a summer night at Vauxhall Gardens, the impolite attentions paid to her by Thomas Lyttelton (commonly known as the wicked Lord Lyttelton), George Robert Fitzgerald (commonly called Fighting Fitzgerald, who was executed for murder in Ireland in 1786), and Captain Crofts resulted in what came to be known as "The Vauxhall Affray." A quarrel began when her companion, the Rev Henry Bate, editor of the *Morning Post* (later Sir Henry Bate Dudley, who married Mary White, Elizabeth's sister, in 1780), became incensed by the insults of these "gentlemen" and in a boxing match thrashed a professional "bruiser"—Captain Miles, one of Fitzgerald's servants. Mrs Hartley's champion thus earned for himself the nick-name of the Fighting Parson. According to the *Thespian Dictionary* (1805), that incident spawned another duel between the author John Scawen and Fitzgerald, which ended without injury to either party. The dispute over Mrs Hartley's honor continued in the press during August 1773 and in occasional pamphlets, including *The Vauxhall Affray, An Appendix to the Vauxhall Affray* (with an engraved frontispiece), and *The Rape of Pomona*, all published in 1773. Satirical prints also appeared in the *Macaroni and Theatrical Magazine* (November 1773).

Mrs. Hartley's theatrical reputation was, no doubt, considerably enhanced by the time she began her second season at Covent Garden on 22 September 1773 as Queen Catherine. In 1773–74 she was seen again as Rosamond, Elfrida, Jane Shore, Cleopatra, Juliet, Lady Macbeth, Statira, and Ismene. She also added to her repertoire Hermione in *The Winter's Tale*, Mariamne in *Herod and Mariamne*, Lady Percy in *1 Henry IV*, Almeyda in *Don Sebastian*, and the title role in *Lady Jane Gray*. On 13 April 1774, when she played Lady Macbeth and also appeared in *Henry and Emma*, a "New Poetical Interlude" adapted by Henry Bate, she made

Harvard Theatre Collection

ELIZABETH HARTLEY as Andromache
engraving by Sherwin

a modest profit of £116 13s. in benefit receipts.

After giving her last performance of the season as Rosamond on 23 May 1774, Mrs Hartley set the tongues of the town wagging again by running off to France with the actor William "Gentleman" Smith, who also played her stage lover in the title role of *Henry II*. The French leave was brief, but the *affaire* was not. Smith accompanied Mrs Hartley to Dublin, where both he and she acted in the Smock Alley company. On 10 July 1774 the pair arrived at Cork "with a large party for the Lake[s] of Killarney," reported the *Hibernian Chronicle*. But they tarried at Cork for two weeks to play *Richard III*, *Hamlet*, *Macbeth*, *The Recruiting Officer*, *All for Love*, *Jane Shore*, and *The Conscious Lovers*. When they returned to London in the autumn, Mrs Hartley resumed her engagement at Covent Garden, but Smith transferred to Drury Lane. The duration of their affair is not known, but when Garrick wrote to Smith about contract renewal on 15 March 1775 it was still warm: "You may depend upon my not mentioning a certain person indiscreetly . . . but a Gentleman told me yesterday, Unconnected with any theatre, that M^r S's reason for quitting me & offering himself Elsewhere, was that ye Person in question wanted a protector: M^r S: sh^d desire his *present* friends not to be indiscreet." Smith remained at Drury Lane.

Mrs Hartley continued to be engaged at Covent Garden through 1779–80, raising no special stir but acquitting herself with competence in roles that were not beyond her powers, especially in creatures of tenderness. Among the characters she "created" in premiere productions were the title role in *Cleonice* on 2 March 1775, Evelina in *Caractacus* on 6 December 1776, Isabella in *Sir Thomas Overbury* on 1 February 1777, Miss Neville in *Know Your Own Mind* on 22 February 1777, Rena in *Buthred* on 8 December 1778, Julia in *The Fatal Falsehood* on 6 May 1779, and Lady Frances in *The Belle's Stratagem* on 22 February 1780. Her other roles included Rutland in *The Earl of Essex*, Andromache in *The Distrest Mother*, Marcia in *Cato*, Indiana in *The Conscious Lovers*, the title role in *Ethelinda*, Almeria in *The Mourning Bride*, Olivia in *Twelfth Night*, Miss Willoughby in *A Word to the Wise*, Sigismunda in *Tancred and Sigismunda*, Cordelia in

King Lear, Leonora in *The Revenge*, the Abbess in *The Comedy of Errors*, Mary Queen of Scots in *The Albion Queens*, Monimia in *The Orphan*, the Queen in *Richard III*, Eudocia in *The Siege of Damascus*, and Agapea in *The Widow of Delphi*.

On 20 November 1779 she acted Hermione in *The Winter's Tale* at Drury Lane, a role she repeated at that theatre on 23 and 26 November and 3 and 11 December (it was played by Elizabeth Farren on 29 November and 1 December). She also acted in the summer seasons at Liverpool in 1776 and 1777 at a salary of £2 10s. per week and at Stroud in the early 1770s. The Mrs Hartley who acted at Manchester evidently was another actress.

During her last several seasons at Covent Garden she occasionally was prevented from playing by illness. In 1778–79 her bad health delayed her first appearance until 8 December, when she acted Rena in the premiere of *Buthred*, she having passed the autumn recuperating at Bath. After acting Lady Frances in *The Belle's Stratagem* on 29 May 1780, she retired from the stage, when she was only about 30 years old.

By permission of the City Art Gallery, Manchester, the Thomas Greg Collection

ELIZABETH HARTLEY as Lady Jane Gray

on a Delftware tile, from the engraving by Thornthwaite, after Roberts

In June 1782 the *Gentleman's Magazine* reported that Mrs Hartley, "the celebrated actress," had died "Lately, in the South of France." But the following month the journal retracted the story: "The report of Mrs. Hartley's death is not true; that lady now resides at Orleans in good health, and passes by the name of White." How she passed the remaining 42 years of her life is undocumented. At Leeds in April 1786, G. S. Carey imitated her in the character of Jane Shore as part of his "Lecture on Mimicry." She died in "easy circumstances" on 26 January 1824 at her house in King Street, Woolwich, at the age of 73 (according to the burial register for the Union Independent Chapel in Woolwich, and not on 2 February 1824 as given in manuscripts at the British Museum and the Folger Library). She was buried in the graveyard of the Union Chapel (Section 11, No 102) on 6 February.

In her will dated 25 January 1824, the day before her death, and proved on 25 February 1824 (calling herself White, her maiden name), she left the interest on her money "in the funds for life," to her sister, Lady Bate Dudley, in the event that her husband Sir Henry should not leave her a full £500 per year. To Elizabeth Mesuard, Elizabeth's niece, the wife of Stephen Mesuard of Woolwich, she left her investment in the French funds. To a Mrs White, her deceased brother's widow, she gave £50, and to her nephews John Davis White and Joseph White she bequeathed £600 and £500 in stocks, respectively. An Elizabeth Hyde of Garlick Hill also received £50. To the trustees of the Covent Garden Theatrical Fund she gave £100 in eight per cent consolidated bank annuities. There was no mention in the will of Mr Hartley or of any issue by him or by any other alliances. When Hartley disappeared from her life is not known to us. According to Boaden's *Life of Mrs Inchbald*, Mr and Mrs Hartley were numbered among Mrs Inchbald's acquaintances and Mr Inchbald was particularly fond of them, although his wife disapproved of their conduct. In the account books of the Liverpool Theatre on 20 June 1777, when Mrs Hartley was playing there, is a record of orders having been given out to "Mrs Hartley's son," but that person was probably her "boy" or "servant" to whom references are made in other notations. A child, Miss Hart-

ley, and a young woman, Miss L. Hartley, were acting in the Theatre Royal, York, in 1799 and 1780 respectively, but we can establish no relationship to Elizabeth Hartley.

Both Northcote and Mrs Thrale declared Elizabeth Hartley to have been among the most truly beautiful women they had ever seen. Hull regarded her as the only woman fit to personate the character of the fair Rosamond—a name by which she became known—in his *Henry II*. Thomas Davies, who himself had a most beautiful wife, claimed that "The most serious satirist who bestows one look on Mrs. Hartley must be instantly charmed." It is said that when Joshua Reynolds complimented her looks while painting her as Jane Shore, Mrs Hartley replied, "Nay, my face may be well enough for shape, but sure 'tis freckled as a toad's belly."

Portraits of this eighteenth-century beauty with the Titian-red hair that made men rave include:

1. By Robert Cosway. Mrs Hartley is said by *Macaroni Magazine* to have been the original for Cosway's "Venus Victrix."

2. By Angelica Kauffman. Painting in the Garrick Club.

3. By Joshua Reynolds. "Mrs. Hartley as a Nymph with a young Bacchus." In the Tate Gallery, given by Sir W. Agnew in 1903; exhibited at the Royal Academy in 1773. Another version by Reynolds was owned successively by Captain Walsh, the Marchioness of Thomond in 1821, and Mrs. Howard in 1871; sold in the Morton sale at Christie's, 8 June 1928 (lot 125); perhaps this is the painting reported to be in the collection of Lord Northbrook. A third version, copied after Reynolds, is in the Walker Art Gallery, Liverpool. Engravings were done by Lacour; by R. W. Macbeth; by G. Marchi, 1773; by W. Nutter, published by R. Cribb, 1801; and by S. W. Reynolds. Engravings, omitting the child on Mrs Hartley's shoulders, were done by J. Hopwood, as a plate to *The Cabinet*, published by Mathews & Leigh, 1807; by Kennerley, published as a plate to Oxberry's *Dramatic Biography*, 1826; and by Page, undated. These last three engravings are incorrectly identified in the Hall catalogue of portraits in the Harvard Theatre Collection as Mrs Hartley in the role of Calista.

4. By George Romney. In 1780, a Mrs Hartley, probably the actress, sat a number of times for Romney and paid him 100 guineas for the painting. Present location unknown. She also sat for him in 1783 and 1795. Mrs Hartley also paid Romney £52 10s. for half the fee, and gave a promissory note for the remainder, for a portrait of Master Hartley in 1795. A Miss and Master Hartley sat for Romney in 1781, 1782, and 1783. A Mr Hartley, perhaps the actress's elusive husband, sat for Romney in 1780, 1782, and 1783 and in January 1785 paid the artist £18 18s. for his portrait.

5. Engraving by R. Houston, after H. D. Hamilton. Published by R. Sayer & J. Bennett, 1774.

6. Engraving by J. Sharples. Published by the engraver, 1779.

7. By unknown engraver. Published as plate to *London Magazine*, October 1773.

8. As Almeyda in *Don Sebastian*. Colored drawing on vellum by J. Roberts. In the British Museum. Engraving by B. Reading as a plate to *Bell's British Theatre*, 1777.

9. As Andromache in *The Distrest Mother*. By J. K. Sherwin. Originally in the Mathews Collection Catalogue (No 71), but not found in the Garrick Club. Engraving by the artist published 1782.

10. As Andromache. Engraving by G. Sherwin. Published by Lowndes as a plate to *New English Theatre*, 1776.

11. As Andromache. By unknown engraver. Published by J. Wenman, 1777.

12. Called "Calista" in *The Fair Penitent*, but incorrectly identified. See item 3, above.

13. As Cleopatra in *All for Love*. Engraving by Page, after J. Roberts. Published as a plate to *Bell's British Theatre*, 1776.

14. As Cleopatra. Engraving by Thornthwaite, after J. Roberts. Published as a plate to *Bell's British Theatre*, 1776.

15. As Cleopatra. By unknown engraver. Published as a plate to an edition of the play, by J. Wenman, 1778.

16. As Elfrida in *Elfrida*. Engraving by W. Dickinson, after J. Nixon. Published by Dickinson and Watson, 1780.

17. As Elfrida. Engraving by J. Leney, after J. Roberts. Published as a plate to *Bell's British Theatre*, 1796.

18. As Elfrida, with a portrait of William Smith as Kitely. By unknown engraver. Published as a plate to *Town and Country Magazine*, 1776. A reverse engraving was published by T. Walker.

19. As Elfrida, with Mr Hull as Edwin and Mrs Mattocks as one of the chorus. Engraving, without artist or engraver named, undated, in Harvard Theatre Collection but not in catalogue of portraits.

20. As Elvira in *Elvira*. Colored drawing on vellum by J. Roberts. In the British Museum. Engraving by Thornthwaite published as a plate to *Bell's British Theatre*, 1778.

21. As Evelina in *Caractacus*. Study by John Downman. Present location unknown. In Downman's sketch books from Butleigh Court, he noted doing studies in 1777 of six performers in *Caractacus*, which opened at Covent Garden on 6 December 1776. The performers were Mrs Hartley, Hull, Leone, Wroughton, Lewis, and Reinhold. Dowman wrote that "I had not time to make a picture of it as I intended."

22. As Hermione in *The Winter's Tale*. Engraving by C. Grignion. Published as a plate to *Bell's Shakespeare*, 1775.

23. As Hermione. By unknown engraver. Published by Fielding and Walker, 1780.

24. As Imoinda in *Oroonoko*. Colored drawing on vellum by J. Roberts. In the British Museum. Engraving by Thornthwaite published as a plate to *Bell's British Theatre*, 1777. A likeness, after Thornthwaite, is on a Delftware tile in the City of Manchester Art Gallery.

25. As Jane Shore in *Jane Shore*. By Joshua Reynolds. In the Garrick Club. A study for the painting was once in the possession of the Marchioness of Thurmond.

26. As Jane Shore. Colored drawing on vellum by J. Roberts. In the British Museum. Engraving by Thornthwaite for *Bell's British Theatre*, 1777. Different from No 26.

27. As Jane Shore. Colored drawing on vellum by J. Roberts. In the British Museum. Engraving by unknown artist for *Bell's British Theatre*, 1777.

28. As Lady Jane Gray in *Lady Jane Gray*. Engraving by Thornthwaite, after J. Roberts. Published as a plate to *Bell's British Theatre*, 1776. A reverse copy, engraved by Page, was published in the same work. A likeness, after

Thornthwaite, appears on a Delftware tile in the City of Manchester Art Gallery.

29. As Lady Jane Gray. Engraving by G. Sherwin. Published by Lowndes as a plate to *New English Theatre*, 1777.

30. As Lady Jane Gray. By unknown engraver. Published as a plate with an edition of the play, by J. Wenman, 1778.

31. As Marcia in *Cato*. Engraving by Walker, after D. Dodd. Published as a plate to *New English Theatre*, 1777.

32. As Mariamne in *Mariamne*. By unknown engraver. Published by Harrison & Co, 1781.

33. As Mary Queen of Scots in *The Albion Queens*. Colored drawing on vellum by J. Roberts. In the British Museum. Engraving by Thornthwaite published as plate to *Bell's British Theatre*, 1777.

34. As Rosamond in *Henry II*. Engraving by Pegg, after J. Roberts. Published as a plate to *Bell's British Theatre*, 1795.

35. In the "Immortality of Garrick." A large canvas by G. Carter. In the Art Gallery of the Royal Shakespeare Theatre, Stratford-upon-Avon. This group, depicting some 17 actors watching Garrick being lifted from his tomb to Mount Parnassus by winged females, was engraved by J. Caldwall & Smith, and published by the artist, with a key-plate, in 1783.

Hartley, Joseph ₁*fl. 1794*₁, *singer, violist.*
Joseph Hartley, of No 9, Bride's Passage, Fleet Street, was listed in Doane's *Musical Directory* in 1794 as a violist, a tenor, and a performer in the Handelian concerts in Westminster Abbey. Joseph Hartley, Junior, was his son, and Theophilus Hartley, another musician, was no doubt related.

Hartley, Joseph ₁*fl. 1794*₁, *singer.*
Joseph Hartley, Junior, of No 19, Air Street, Piccadilly, was listed in Doane's *Musical Directory* in 1794 as a tenor who was a member of the Choral Fund and the Handelian Society.

Hartley, Theophilus ₁*fl. 1794*₁, *singer, violoncellist.*
Theophilus Hartley was listed in Doane's *Musical Directory* in 1794 as a bass singer and violoncellist, a member of the Choral Fund and the Handelian Society, and a participant in the Handelian concerts in Westminster Ab-

bey and the oratorios at Drury Lane Theatre. His address was given as "St Catherine," perhaps meaning St Katherine by the Tower. No doubt he was related to the Joseph Hartleys (fl. 1794).

Hartly, Mr ₁*fl. 1784*₁, *singer.*
Mr Hartly of Windsor sang countertenor in the Handel Memorial Concerts at Westminster Abbey and the Pantheon in London in May and June 1784.

Hartman, Mr ₁*fl. 1792–1796*₁, *clarinetist, flutist.*
Mr Hartman was mentioned in Haydn's *The First London Notebook* in 1792 as a flutist in London. On 29 January 1796 the *Morning Herald* described him as a clarinetist. H. C. Robbins Landon, editor of the *Notebook* says that at some unknown date Hartman left England poverty-stricken, soon lost his wife by death, and became a derelict.

Hartog, Mme ₁*fl. 1794*₁, *violinist.*
Doane's *Musical Directory* of 1794 listed Madame Hartog of No 12, Leadenhall Street, as a violinist.

Hartry. *See also* HAWTRY.

Hartry, John *d. 1774, actor.*
John Hartry first appeared on the London stage on 9 September 1760, when at the Haymarket Theatre he presented an evening of *Comic Lectures*, "Calculated for the use and entertainment of the town in general, but particularly the admirers of *The Minor*, and more especially those who have been present at the humorous representations of that piece." Although his program was advertised for a second night, 11 September, it was not given because Hartry obviously on the first night had offended certain members of the audience and had been interrupted. Hartry published a lengthy apology in the press:

Mr. Hartry is oblig'd to postpone his Comic Lecture . . . being engaged in making many alterations therein. The serious part will be considered shortened, some other pieces expunged, and many scenes of humour added, which he hopes will be entertaining. He is extremely troubled that anything in his Lecture on Tuesday should have given offence to any one person present, and is no less concerned that those Ladies and Gentlemen who were desirous to hear him perform (that part which appeared exceptionable to others) were disappointed. . . . It was his first appearance in public, and in such a situation it is no wonder he was robb'd of his comic powers; but he hopes when his Lecture is alter'd there will be found in it nothing which can give offense, or deprive him of that generous indulgence to a young performer which characterizes a British audience.

The promised revised program seems never to have been given. He was probably the Hartry who acted at the Orchard Street Theatre, Bath, in 1760–61, taking a benefit on 22 January 1761. The following spring, however, on 5 May 1761, he made his first appearance as an actor at Covent Garden Theatre as the title character in a "Lady Pentweazle Scene," and on 23 June he acted Feeble in *The Upholsterer*. But he seems not to have performed again in London until he was engaged by Drury Lane in 1766–67 at a salary of 6s. 8d. per day, or £2 per week. His first role there was as Tribulation in *The Alchemist* on 31 October 1766, followed by Stockwell in *Neck or Nothing* on 18 November. No doubt he also filled supernumerary roles, but his only other known roles during this first season at Drury Lane were an unspecified one in *The Young Couple* on 21 April 1767, and Moody in *The Provok'd Husband* and Clackit in *The Guardian* on 19 May for a benefit which he shared with Weston and Fawcett, resulting in a deficit of £18 18s.

Over the next six seasons through 1773–74, Hartry remained regularly engaged at Drury Lane, serving in the most modest of supporting roles, usually in the line of old men. The following is an incomplete selection from his repertoire: Old Hob in *Flora*, Justice Shallow in *The Merry Wives of Windsor*, Snuffle in *The Mayor of Garratt*, Quillit in *The Plain Dealer*, a Countryman in *The Lottery*, Lucianus in *Hamlet*, Corin in *As You Like It*, the Old Man in *King Lear*, Justice Silence in *2 Henry IV*, Sir Harry in *The Double Gallant*, a Shepherd in *A Peep Behind the Curtain*, Verges in *Much Ado about Nothing*, a Justice in *Harlequin's Invasion*, Sir Samuel Mortgage in *The Humours of the Turf*, and Sir Harry Sycamore in *The Maid of the Mill*. On 28 April 1769 he played once

more at Covent Garden, acting Justice Woodcock in *Love in a Village* for the benefit of Barrington and Mrs Pitt. He shared each year in a benefit with other actors, usually Fawcett; he split a net of £116 9s. on 22 May 1772 (when he acted Old Philpot in *The Citizen* for the first time), a net of £149 14s. 6d. on 15 May 1773, and a net of £134 6d. on 12 May 1774 (his last benefit), each time with Fawcett.

On 14 May 1774, Hartry was named as one of the 13 actors to be on the committee "to make such rules and orders as should . . . seem most conducive" to setting up the Actors Fund at Drury Lane Theatre. Within a year three of the committee, Ellis Ackman, Edward Rooker, and John Hartry himself were dead. Hartry evidently became ill soon after the end of 1773–74. He acted only once at Drury Lane in the next season, as Corin in *As You Like It* on 1 October 1774. Three days later, on 4 October, he died.

In his will, made on the day of his death, Hartry left his unspecified estate to his wife Harriet. There seems to have been no evident connection between John Hartry and the Mr and Mrs Hartry (Hawtry) of Edinburgh and Dublin who performed in London in 1775.

Hartwell, John   *d. 1779, musician.*
John Hartwell, a musician from Cripplegate, became a freeman in the Worshipfull Company of Musicians on 7 February 1764. He died in 1779.

Harvay, Mlle   [*fl. 1725*],   *dancer.*
On 18 March 1725 at Drury Lane Theatre, Mlle Harvay, "lately arriv'd from France," danced "Harlequin" and "Peasant" dances. She continued to dance at Drury Lane until mid-May, and on 19 May, now billed as Mlle Harve, she performed "Saraband" and "Pierot" dances at Lincoln's Inn Fields Theatre.

Harve. See HARVAY.

Harvelt, Mr   [*fl. 1740*],   *actor.*
A Mr Harvelt played one of the Furies in the pantomime *Harlequin Doctor Faustus* at Lee and Phillips's booth on 9 September 1740 during the Southwark Fair.

Harvey. See also HERVEY.

Harvey, Mr [*fl. 1701–1704*], *ladder dancer.*

Tom Brown in his *Letters from the Dead* on 10 January 1701 spoke of Mr Harvey exceeding Jevon "in the Ladder-dance." Harvey performed in London under the auspices of Clinch of Barnet in late 1704. The *Daily Courant* ran advertisements on 28, 29, and 30 November calling attention to "Dancing on the Ladder by Mr. Harvey, the only Artist in the World, and Vaulting on the Horse" at Clinch's show at the Leg Tavern.

Harvey, Mr [*fl. 1741?–1765?*], *dancer, actor.*

The dancer named Harvey who made his first noticed appearance at Drury Lane Theatre on 27 October 1748 as a Follower of Vertumnus in the ballet *Vertumnus and Pomona* perhaps was the Mr Harvey who had been a member of the Aungier Street Theatre, Dublin, between 1741 and 1744. In his first season at Drury Lane, Harvey was also assigned as a Follower of Mars in the ballet *The Triumph of Peace* and danced a hornpipe in *The Beggar's Opera*. His name did not appear in the bills in 1749–50, although he probably danced in various choruses. He remained at Drury Lane through 1752–53, dancing such roles as a Bird Catcher in the comic entertainment *The Bird Catchers* and a Peasant in *The Savoyard Travellers*. Frequently he appeared in specialty numbers such as a Scots' dance or a rural dance with Miss Shawford, Mrs Preston, Mlle Camargo, and Mrs Addison. On 2 January 1751 he replaced McNeil in a dance with Mlle Camargo in Act IV of *The Way of the World* and thereafter continued in that assignment. On 27 April 1752 Harvey shared gross benefit receipts of £140 with G. Burton and Harrison.

In 1753–54, Harvey left Drury Lane to join the company at Smock Alley, Dublin, where he was engaged through 1758–59. In the middle of the last season he went over to the Crow Street Theatre until at least through 1759–60. At Smock Alley he appeared in such roles as a Dancing Witch in *Macbeth* on 24 November 1753 and again in 1757–58 and as a Lilliputian in *The Tempest* and Theseus in *The Formation of Harlequin*, also in 1757–58. On 17 April 1758 he acted Rigadoon in Farquhar's *Love and a Bottle*. Perhaps he was the Harvey who performed with Parsons's company at Derby in September 1756.

Harvey, Mrs [*fl. 1753–1758*], *actress.*

A Mrs Harvey, announced as from the Theatre Royal, Dublin, was a member of the summer company at Richmond, Surrey, in 1753. Her known roles there were Lady Dainty in *The Double Gallant* on 11 August 1753 and the Countess of Rutland in *The Earl of Essex* on 25 August. In 1753–54 and 1754–55 she acted at Bath. Perhaps she was the Mrs Harvey who as a member of Theophilus Cibber's pickup company acted at the Haymarket in January 1758. On 12 January, announced as a gentlewoman making her first appearance on any stage, Mrs Harvey played Flora in *She Wou'd and She Wou'd Not*; on 16 January she was again named in the bills for the role. She also acted Miranda in *The Busy Body* on 25 January.

Harvey, Mrs [*fl. 1794–1798*], *actress, singer.*

As a member of the younger George Colman's company at the Haymarket in the summer of 1794, a Mrs Harvey sang in the choruses for *The Surrender of Calais*, *The Battle of Hexham*, and *The Mountaineers* and as the Third Bacchant in *Comus*. On 29 August she acted Charlotte in *My Grandmother*, announced as her first appearance in that character.

Evidently making little progress in London, Mrs Harvey went to play in America the following year. Announced as from the Haymarket, she made her debut in Philadelphia on 22 May 1795 as Lady Contest in *The Wedding Day*. On 25 May she acted Phyllis in *The Conscious Lovers*. Her other roles at Philadelphia that spring included Angelica in *The Constant Couple*, Theresa in *The Prisoner*, and Lady Sarah Savage in *Rage*. She made her debut at Baltimore on 31 July 1795 as Louise in *The Irishman in London* but failed to please. In the 1795–96 season at Philadelphia she was very busy in numerous roles, such as Lucy in *The Rivals*, Marmalet in *All in the Wrong*, Jenny in *The Contrast*, Ethelinda in *Henry II*, Lucy in *The Married Man*, and Donna Isabella in *The Widow's Vow*.

Mrs Harvey remained in Philadelphia through July 1797. By spring 1798 she may have returned to London, for on 23 April 1798 a Mrs Harvey acted Anna in *Douglas* at the Haymarket.

Harvey, Miss *[fl. 1783–1788]*, *dancer.*

In a list of persons in the opera company at the King's Theatre, dated 1783, a "Mrs Hervey" was named as a figure-dancer. This person was probably the Miss Harvey (sometimes Hervey) whose name appeared in the King's Theatre bills as a dancer between 1784–85 and 1787–88. On 18 June 1785 she danced with others in a new divertissement added to Act I of *I viaggiatori felice* and also danced on 25 June. Her known assignments included dancing in *Acis and Galatea*, *Les Deux Solitaires*, *Les Amans surpris*, and *L'Amour jardinier* in 1785–86, in a pas de deux with Henry on 15 May 1788, and in *La Bonté du seigneur* on 31 May 1788.

Harvey, J. *[fl. 1795–1820?]*, *oboist.*

In 1794 J. Harvey was listed in Doane's *Musical Directory* as an oboist who played at the Apollo Gardens and lived at No 7, Green Street, Blackfriars. Harvey played for the oratorios at Covent Garden Theatre in 1795 and 1796, and he may have been a regularly engaged musician there during the 1790s. From 1812–13 through 1819–20 a Harvey was engaged as a member of the Covent Garden band at £4 per week. A Harvey, Junior, no doubt his son, was also a band member at Covent Garden during the same period, 1812–1820, at £1 16s. per week.

Harvey, John *d. 1735, scene painter.*

John Harvey, about whose life little is known, was a scene painter at Lincoln's Inn Fields Theatre from 1724 to 1732 and then at Covent Garden until his death. He may have been the Mr Harvey who was paid £3 for painting the scenery called the Pastry Cook Shop at Drury Lane Theatre at some time between 1713 and 1716. The accounts of the Lincoln's Inn Fields Theatre show the following payments to him: £50 on account on 4 December 1724; £54 on 30 December 1724 "for work in the fall of Siam" (the revival of Hill's *Fatal Vision; or, the Fall of Siam*); £10 10s. on account on 29 January 1725; £200 "in part of a Bond" on 8 February 1725; £60 "in full of his Bond" on 15 February 1725; £30 "in part of Interest on a Bond for 400 *l*" on 13 January 1727;

and £50 "upon Bond" on 9 March 1727. On 5 July 1728 "Mr. Harvey Painter and wife and 2" were put on the Lincoln's Inn Fields free list.

On 18 September 1732 the *Daily Advertiser* reported that Harvey and Lambert had been engaged for some time in painting the scenes for the new Covent Garden Theatre which was to open on 3 December. Harvey also was supposed to have assisted Amiconi in the decoration of the proscenium and the allegory of Shakespeare, Apollo, and the Muses on the ceiling of the new playhouse.

In 1726 Harvey became a steward of the Society of St Luke. He died on 20 June 1735 and was buried three days later at St Paul, Covent Garden. The previous month, on 1 May 1735, he had been given a benefit at Covent Garden. Rich's inventory of his Covent Garden Theatre effects in 1743 listed "Harvey's palace," "the arch of Harvey's palace," 12 wings for a palace, and a figure in palace as scenes still in use.

Harvey, Mary Ann. *See* DAVENPORT, MRS GEORGE GOSLING.

Harvey, Philip *[fl. before 1787]*, *actor?*

In his *Life and Times* Frederic Reynolds related dining in a Swiss restaurant in 1787 and being attended by an English waiter, about 18, who told Reynolds that "he was related to an old retired comic actor on the London stages, named Phil. Harvey." Melancholy and lachrymose after his retirement, Harvey was reminded by a friend that the Duke of Devonshire still allowed him 2s. 6d. per day, to which, "in a paroxysm of grief," Harvey replied, "His Grace might as well make it *three shillings*. Oh, oh, oh!"

We find in the records, however, no performer by the name of Harvey who would seem to be the person described.

Harwood, Mr *[fl. 1726]*, *dancer, musician.*

Mr Harwood was paid 10s. 6d. "pip[e]. & tabor for his attendance this nt." at Lincoln's Inn Fields Theatre on 17 October 1726 when the pantomime *Jupiter and Europa* was played. A month later, on 17 November, he received 15s. 6d. for "pipe & tabor & trav[el?]" on the night *Apollo and Daphne; or, the Burgomaster*

Trick'd was given. Perhaps the Miss Harwood who danced in a pipe and tabor in the latter pantomime at Drury Lane in 1738 was his daughter. The Gertrude Harwood, "a Dancing Master's Wife," who was buried years earlier at St Clement Danes on 22 February 1712, may have been related.

Harwood, Mr *[fl. 1784–1785]*, *singer, musician.*

A Mr Harwood of Lancashire was listed by Dr. Burney as one of the countertenors who sang in the Handel Memorial Concerts at Westminster Abbey and the Pantheon in May and June 1784. Perhaps he was the Mr Harwood who was on the Court of Assistants in the Royal Society of Musicians in 1785. Some 42 years later, on 4 February 1827, a Mrs Harwood sent a letter of thanks to the Society for their donation, but there can be no certainty that she was the widow of our subject.

Harwood, Mr *[fl. 1789–1801]*, *dresser.*

A Mr Harwood received 10*s.* per week at Drury Lane Theatre in 1789–90 for services unknown. Perhaps he was the same Mr Harwood who was paid 9*s.* per week as a dresser in 1801. Probably he was related to Ralph Harwood, the Drury Lane prompter.

Harwood, Miss *[fl. 1738–1739]*, *dancer.*

Miss Harwood performed in the chorus of Country Lads and Lasses, with pipe and tabor, in *The Burgomaster Trick'd*, a pantomime acted by a cast of children at Lincoln's Inn Fields Theatre on 6 January 1738. In May of that year she danced a minuet with Master Ferg several times on the same stage. The following season at Drury Lane Theatre she appeared in *The Burgomaster Trick'd* on 4 and 5 December 1738.

Perhaps Miss Harwood was the daughter of the Mr Harwood who was at Lincoln's Inn Fields Theatre in 1726.

Harwood, Miss *[fl. 1784–1794]*, *singer.*

A Miss Harwood was listed by Dr Burney as a soprano in the Handel Memorial Concerts at Westminster Abbey and the Pantheon in May and June 1784. On 8 April 1786 she sang in a concert of the Academy of Ancient Music in Tottenham Street. About 1790, several songs were published at Liverpool as sung by Miss Harwood: *Dear is my little native vale*, *The Death of Edwin and Emma*, and *Yes Henry, yes, with thee I'll go*. A Miss Harwood, a vocalist of Bath, was listed in Doane's *Musical Directory* in 1794.

Harwood, Ralph *d. 1792, prompter, actor.*

Ralph Harwood was a house servant at Drury Lane Theatre by 1773–74 and shared in benefit tickets on 19 May 1774. The theatre treasury paid him gratuities of £5 5*s.* on 28 May 1775 and 24 June 1776, on which dates his full name was given in the account books; he was a regular sharer in benefit tickets through 1779–80.

Upon the death of William Hopkins in 1780, Harwood succeeded as prompter, receiving a benefit in that capacity on 17 May 1781. He continued as prompter at Drury Lane through 1785–86. On 16 October 1786, he paid up the balance of his benefit charge (£19 5*s.* 6*d.*) from the previous season and was dismissed on the same day, with a gratuity of £25. Several months later, on 8 January 1787, he was given a benefit at the Haymarket Theatre. Harwood also served as prompter at the summer theatre at Richmond in 1775, 1777, 1781, 1785, and 1788, and perhaps other years. At Richmond on 1 September 1788 he played the role of Cryer in *Barataria* and no doubt from time to time acted other parts.

Harwood had lived at Mrs Powel's in New Nelson Street in 1779; by 1786 he was in Little Russell Street, Covent Garden.

Having been an original subscriber to the Drury Lane Fund in 1775, he claimed a benefaction in December 1789. He busied himself as prompter to the private theatricals given by the Earl of Wargrave from 1790 to 1792. According to a notation in a British Library manuscript, Ralph Harwood died in November 1792.

The Mr Harwood who was paid 10*s.* per week at Drury Lane in 1789–90 for services unknown to us was probably related to Ralph Harwood, and was, very likely, the person who was paid 9*s.* per week in 1801 as a dresser at that theatre.

The actor Joseph Edmund Harwood who performed in America (but not in London evidently) between 1794 until his death at Germantown, Pennsylvania, on 21 September 1809 was probably Ralph Harwood's son. In America he married Eliza Franklin Bache, grand-daughter of Benjamin Franklin.

Another son of Ralph Harwood acted in the provinces and at the Surrey and Coburg theatres in the nineteenth century; he was the father of the actor and equestrian James Harwood (1816–1900), who by his marriage to Lucia Eliza Podmore (1836–1898) produced five actors of the twentieth century: Robb Harwood (1869–1910), John Harwood (1868–1944), and Lucy, Florence and Isabella Harwood.

In his *Reminiscences*, T. J. Dibdin mentioned a Mr Harwood's Circulating Library at No 21, Great Russell Street, Bloomsbury, operating in the early part of the nineteenth century.

Haseler, Mr [*fl. 1793–1817*], *boxkeeper.*
A Mr Haseler (sometimes Haseley, Hasley, Hasler) was a boxkeeper at Covent Garden Theatre from 1793–94, when his salary was 12*s.* per week, until at least 1817. Each season he shared benefit tickets with other house servants. By 1802–3 his salary was 15*s.* per week.

Haseley. *See* HASELER.

Haskey, Mr [*fl. 1787*], *house servant? performer?*
A Mr Haskey shared benefit tickets with 11 minor performers and house servants at Covent Garden Theatre on 5 June 1787.

Haskey, Mrs [*fl. 1784–1803*], *dancer, actress, singer.*
Mrs Haskey's name was first noticed in the bills as a dancer in the chorus of the new pantomime *Hurly-Burly* at the Drury Lane Theatre on 26 December 1785. She had, however, shared in benefit tickets on the previous 20 March and had probably been a member of the company in 1784–85. In the summer of 1785 she had performed at Richmond.

She continued as a hardworking but obscure member of the ensemble for at least 19 years, sharing annually in benefit tickets with other minor personnel and earning a constant £1 5*s.* per week through 1800–1801; she was raised to £1 10*s.* in 1801–2, a salary she had in

1802–3, the last season in in which we find her name in the Drury Lane accounts. Mrs Haskey danced and sang regularly in such pantomimes and spectacles as *Don Juan* (1791–92), *The Pirates* (1792–93), *The Cherokee* (1794–95), *Alexander the Great* (1794–95), and *Harlequin Captive* (1795–96) and played Colombine in *Robinson Crusoe* (1796–97) and a Female Slave in *Blue-Beard* (1797–98).

Mrs Haskey also performed at the Haymarket in the summers from 1793 to 1801, usually in a similar capacity, such as the Bridesmaid in *Royal Clemency* in 1793, a Maid in *Harlequin Peasant* in 1794, and an Attendant in *Love and Madness* in 1795. At the Haymarket on occasion she also had the opportunity to fill more substantial parts: Lucy in *The Devil to Pay* (1796), Molly Brazen in *The Beggar's Opera* (1798 and 1799), Cloe in *High Life below Stairs* (1798 and 1799), a Maid in *Cross Purposes* (1797 and 1798), and Margery in *The Spoil'd Child* (1799).

The Miss Haskey who was an occasional dancer and singer in London at this time no doubt was her daughter.

Haskey, Miss [*fl. 1792–1802*], *dancer, singer.*
A Miss Haskey performed in the dances of *The Enchanted Wood* at the Haymarket Theatre on 25 July 1792 and five additional times that summer. In the Drury Lane company at the King's Theatre Miss Haskey was in the dances of *Harlequin's Invasion* six times between 27 December 1792 and 14 January 1793. In the choruses of both pieces was Mrs Haskey, no doubt her mother.

Probably this person was the same Miss Haskey who was at Drury Lane in 1800–1801 and 1801–2 as a chorus singer.

Haslehurst, John [*fl. 1714*], *trumpeter.*
John Haslehurst was a trumpeter in the royal musical establishment in 1714, according to the Lord Chamberlain's accounts.

Hasler or **Hasley.** *See* HASELER.

Hasse, Johann Adolph *1699–1783, director, singer, harpsichordist, composer.*
Johann Adolph Hasse was born, according to Grove, on 25 March 1699 at Bergedorf,

near Hamburg, the son of a schoolmaster and organist. He went to Hamburg when he was 18 and on the recommendation of the poet Ulrich König was hired by Keiser to sing tenor at the Hamburg Opera. Four years later König was able to get Hasse a similar position at Brunswick, and there in 1721 Hasse's first opera, *Antioco*, was performed. It was an apprentice work in the currently popular Italian fashion. Hasse then went to Naples where he studied briefly with Porpora and then with Alessandro Scarlatti and became proficient on the harpsichord. *Tigrane*, Hasse's second opera, was produced there in 1723; *Sesostrate* was presented there in 1726, by which time Hasse's reputation was fully established.

He was attracted to Venice in 1727 by a professorship at the Scuola degli' Incurabili, for which he composed a *Miserere*. Though not a Saxon, he became known in Italy as *il caro Sassone* and continued turning out operas and intermezzi. In 1729 "Giovanni Adolfo," as the Italians styled him, met the singer Faustina

Harvard Theatre Collection

JOHANN ADOLPH HASSE
engraving by Riedel, after Rotari

Bordoni and for her composed his first versions of *Artaserse* and *Dalisa*. They were produced in Venice in 1730, and in that year Hasse married Faustina. With her in 1731 he went to Dresden to take a post as Kappelmeister and director of the opera at the court of Augustus II, Hasse's first opera there being *Cleofide*.

The couple traveled in the 1730s to Venice, Milan, and Naples; and Hasse (evidently without his wife) went to London, where Faustina had sung in the 1720s. According to Grove, Hasse was to take over the direction of the Opera of the Nobility in competition with Handel. His *Arteserse* was performed with great success in 1734–35, but Hasse did not care for England and soon returned to the Continent. Mainwaring in his biography of Handel (1760) said of the 1734–35 season:

HASSE AND PORPORA were the Composers at the Hay-market. When the former was invited over, it is remarkable, that the first question he asked, was, whether Handel was dead. Being answered in the negative, he refused to come, from a persuasion, that where his countryman was (for they were both Saxons by birth) no other person of the same profession was likely to make any figure. He could not believe that in a nation which had always been famous for sense and discernment, the credit of such an artist as Handel could ever be impaired. However, this mystery was explained to him in such a manner, and this explanation accompanied by such offers, that at length he got the better of his scruples, and consented to be engaged. He is remarkable for his fine elevated air, with hardly so much as the shew of harmony to support it. And this may serve not only for a character of HASSE in particular, but of the Italians in general, at the time we are speaking of.

Hasse was back in Dresden by 1739. His second version of *Arminio* was performed on 7 October 1745 at the command of Frederick the Great. During the siege of Dresden in 1760 much of Hasse's property, including many of his musical manuscripts, was destroyed. Hasse and Faustina left Dresden for Vienna, where Hasse with Metastasio was in competition with Gluck. Hasse kept writing operas (Dr Burney claimed that he wrote over 100), his last one being *Ruggiero* in 1771. Hasse died in Venice on 16 December 1783.

Grove provides a very detailed list of Hasse's many works. Hasse's portrait by C. P. Rotari was engraved by S. Kauche, C. F. Riedel, and

L. Zucchi (Dresden 1783). An engraved portrait by Bonatti, after Bosio, was published at Milan, 1818, and an engraved portrait by Haster was published in 1825. Hasse was included in an engraving, after L. Scotti, of a group of composers, published at Florence between 1801 and 1807.

Hasse, Signora Johann Adolph. *See* "Faustina, Signora."

Hassler. *See* Haseler.

Hastings, Mr ₁*fl. 1717–1722*₁, *house servant.*

Mr Hastings, a servant at the Lincoln's Inn Fields Theatre, shared benefits on 28 May 1717, 13 May 1719, and 19 May 1722. In the last instance, he and Randall shared £102 19*s.*, presumably before house charges were deducted.

Haswell, Mr ₁*fl. 1744–1745?*₁, *actor, singer.*

Mr Haswell played Peachum in *The Beggar's Opera* at the Haymarket Theatre on 26 December 1744. The performing troupe was called the "Queen of Hungary's Company of Comedians," and Charlotte Charke led the cast as Macheath. The work was played again on 25 January 1745, but no cast was listed.

"Hatchet, The Marquis of." *See* Mc George, Horatio Thomas.

Hatchet, Mr ₁*fl. 1748–1749*₁, *house servant?*

A Mr Hatchet, presumably a house servant, shared a benefit with Stede, Page, and Miss Morrison at Covent Garden Theatre on 22 April 1749.

Hatfield, Elizabeth ₁*fl. 1727*₁, *dresser.*

The Lincoln's Inn Fields Theatre accounts show a payment of 16*s.* on 2 March 1727 to Mrs Elizabeth Hatfield, dresser to Mrs Pelling.

Hatfield, F. ₁*fl. 1784*₁, *singer.*

Mr F. Hatfield sang bass in the Handel Memorial Concerts at Westminster Abbey and the Pantheon in May and June 1784.

Hathorne, Mr ₁*fl. 1745*₁, *treasurer.*

Mr Hathorne, the Covent Garden treasurer, was granted a benefit on 1 May 1745.

Hatley, Mr ₁*fl. 1788*₁, *house servant.*

A Mr Hatley was announced to share benefit tickets with eight other house servants at Covent Garden on 24 May 1788.

Hatten, Mr ₁*fl. 1734*₁, *actor.*

Mr Hatten played Bajazet in a performance of *Tamerlane* presented at York Buildings on 8 July 1734.

Hatton, Mrs ₁*fl. 1725*₁, *dancer.*

Mrs Hatton was a Shepherdess and a Follower of Daphne in *Apollo and Daphne* at Drury Lane on 20 February 1725, but she was replaced two days later by Mrs Walter.

Hatton, Mrs William, Ann Julia, née Kemble, formerly Mrs C. Curtis *1764–1838, actress, lecturer, author.*

Ann Julia Kemble, the seventh child of Roger Kemble and his wife Sarah (née Ward), was born at Worcester on 29 April 1764. The lack of affection and attention which she alleged that she suffered in her childhood accounted for the bitterness she felt about her family in later life. In letters to J. P. Collier written from Swansea in August 1832 (now in the Folger Shakespeare Library), Ann revealed the psychic scars she still carried at the age of 68. She was precocious, like all the Kembles, but eccentric like none, a distinction which caused her to become an embarrassment and the family blacksheep. She claimed that because she was afflicted with a lameness from infancy and a squint, her parents assumed that "education and mental improvment" for her would be useless. She taught herself to write "three years before it was discovered by the family that I could make a letter." Then she spent six months at "a writing school" but never had a grammar put into her hands.

At the age of 11 she wrote a play which was performed at her father's theatre in Brecon. At the age of 14 she composed a number of childish poems, which she published in 1783 as a collection entitled *Poems on Miscellaneous Subjects: By Ann Curtis, sister of Mrs Siddons;* dedicated to the Duchess of Devonshire, the volume had an impressive list of subscribers. Her family ridiculed her by referring to her ironically as "The Genius," and "every thing was done to extinguish every spark if I possessed any."

Ann was apprenticed to a mantua maker, but like all the Kembles she soon turned actress, "in spite of my bodily infirmity." She also became an authoress, "sans education."

In his manuscript notes William Smith Clark suggests that the Miss Kemble who acted at the Smock Alley Theatre, Dublin, in the summer of 1783 was Ann. About that time, however, Ann married C. Curtis, a provincial actor. Soon she suffered hard times. Curtis was proved a bigamist and the couple separated. (When he died at Lymington, Hampshire, in November 1817, the *Gentleman's Magazine* identified him as "a comedian of considerable provincial fame, and a relative of the Kemble family.")

In October 1783 an advertisement in the London papers solicited donations for Mrs Curtis, identifying her as the youngest sister of the Messers Kemble and of Mrs Siddons, to all of whom she had applied in vain, for relief. The notice stated that her lameness had rendered her unfit for the stage and that she had been unable to get her bread by needlework and making artificial flowers.

Next she was employed by the quack doctor James Graham to give lectures at his establishment located in Schomberg House, Pall Mall. On 19 November 1783 a notice was published in the press that:

Mrs Siddons's youngest Sister, Mrs Curtis, desires most respectfully to inform the Public, that This and every Evening This Week, She will read a Lecture at the Temple of Health, in Pall-Mall, on the present State and Influence of Women, on Society, in England, in France, in Spain, and in the Eastern Countries; and on the relative and reciprocal duties, which are incumbent on BOTH Sexes, to advance their particular, as well as mutual happiness. In the course of the Lecture will be introduced a few words reprehending the present indecent and unnatural phrenzy of the British Stage of turning Men into Women, and Women into Men.

The advertisement was incorrect in styling her as Mrs Siddons's youngest sister (for that was Jane Kemble, born 1777, who later became Mrs Henry Mason), but perhaps it was correct in promising that the lecture would be "per-

fectly chaste and delicate." It is doubtful that she was, as Winston claims in his notes at the Garrick Club, "the Goddess of Health" who performed nude in Graham's "Celestial Bed." According to the dramatist Frederic Reynolds, who knew Graham well, that goddess, whoever she was, died in the doctor's service. Ann had better luck, at least, when an attempt she made at suicide in Westminster Abbey failed.

Six years after Ann Curtis had lectured in Pall Mall, she suffered a dreadful accident which, according to one press clipping in the British Library, nearly killed her. One night in December 1789 at a bagnio in the Covent Garden Piazza "the celebrated Mrs. Curtis" was handling a pistol which belonged to her gentleman companion. The pistol was thought to be unloaded but actually was charged with shot. Her companion, thinking he would frighten her, "presented it at her, pulled the trigger, and lodged the contents in her face! . . . Her right eye was driven from the socket, and her face exhibited an indescribably shocking spectacle!" It was further reported that she "at present barely exists, and Mr. Cruikshank, who attends her, has no hopes of her recovery." The account continued in that dolorous tone, signifying that Mrs Curtis was capitalizing on the opportunity to embarrass her prominent family once more.

What makes this accident truly to be lamented is, that the wretched victim, is a woman of *uncommon intellect*, and a *proud and strong mind*. If her avocation has been *immoral*, it has been excited by poignant distress, for she was obliged even by the sacrifice of her person, to provide 'for the calls of the morrow'—for her vices were not so much founded in the errors of her *own nature*, as they were excited by the *avarice* of her *nearest relatives*!

With abilities more splendid for the stage than any of her family, she was deprived of procuring a livelihood, by a decent and honorable profession, in consequence of a trifling imperfection in her person.

The story of her having taken poison in Westminster Abbey, is fresh in most persons minds; and those who have seen the effusions of her muse in print, must sigh for her foibles, while they shed a tear in reflecting on her sufferings—her persecutions—and her misfortunes!!

That press report was greatly exaggerated. Winston's account of the event and the extent of the injury is somewhat different and certainly more correct. He states that she had been accosted at the bagnio and shot in the face but that the next day she had inserted a letter in the papers, signed Ann Curtis, claiming that she was not seriously hurt and her family was caring for her wants. Yet Winston must have seen the more colorful newspaper story cited above, for he continues his account with a precise verbal echo: "she was eccentric, of uncommon intellect, & a proud and strong mind." As we learn from a letter to be cited below, Ann had not suffered the loss of an eye.

On 30 January 1792 Ann married William Hatton at St Marylebone, London. He seems not to have been an actor, though sometimes he has been mistaken for the actor William Thomas P. Hatton. That confusion is compounded by the facts that about the same year W. T. P. Hatton married Ann Hinds, who acted as Mrs Hatton in the provinces and London over the next two decades, and he left for America, without his wife, at about the same time that our subject crossed the Atlantic.

Late in 1793 Ann Hatton went to New York, accompanied by her husband, whom William Dunlap in his *History of the American Theatre* called "a vulgar man." Quickly she became involved in theatrical and literary circles. On 26 December 1793, *Needs Must, or, The Ballad Singers*, a musical trifle based on her libretto, was produced at the John Street Theatre. Its plot was so arranged that Mrs Pownall, who performed in it on crutches because she was recovering from a broken leg, would be able to sing the ballads without moving about the stage.

Mrs Hatton became, as George Seilhamer observed in his *History of the American Theatre*, "at once the bard of the American Democracy" by writing an ode for the Democratic Society of New York which celebrated the recapture of Toulon. At the urging of the Tammany Society the Old American Company produced her *Tammany; or, The Indian Chief* at the John Street Theatre on 3 March 1794. Composed by James Hewitt, *Tammany* is regarded as the first American opera on an Indian subject. Dunlap called it "a melange of bombast" and the *New-York Magazine* dismissed it as a "wretched thing"; however, it enjoyed modest success and was performed also in Philadelphia and Boston. Book and music are lost, but Mrs Hatton published *The Songs of Tammany* at New York

in 1794. Dunlap found *Tammany* too pro-French to suit his Federalist sympathies and referred to it as being "seasoned high with spices hot from Paris."

While in America Mrs Hatton gave some lectures. On 20 September 1794 at "Tammanial Hall," she offered select readings from Dryden, Milton, Sterne, Smollet, Cooper, and Garrick, in addition to a lecture on hearts, compiled and written by herself. According to Winston, she also acted with an amateur company. Her husband is reported by Julian Mates in *The American Musical Stage before 1800* to have "become a celebrated musical-instrument maker in New York," but we find no other evidence that Hatton pursued that occupation. Tickets for Mrs Hatton's program of readings on 20 September 1794, however, could be obtained "at Hatton's Tavern, upper end of Broadway."

About 1800 the Hattons returned to England. According to Winston, Sarah Siddons settled an allowance of £100 a year upon Ann provided she should remain at least 100 miles away from London. But there is no evidence to corroborate that statement. After William Hatton's death, Mrs Siddons did, indeed, allow Ann £30 a year. Brother John also gave her £40 a year, an allowance he raised to £60 in his will. In 1802 her father, Roger Kemble, made the following bequest in his will (which was proved on 6 April 1803):

I give to my Daughter Ann Hatton twenty pounds a year during her life to be paid by my son John out of Money that will be put into his hands for that purpose and in part of the fforty pounds a year my son John allows Ann Hatton[.] I will that my son John does not pay the said twenty pounds a year without a Receipt under the said Ann Hattons own hand. . . .

The Hattons settled at Swansea, where for a while they kept a hotel. William Hatton died there in 1806. From about 1810 until 1831, using the pen name Ann of Swansea, Mrs Hatton wrote a series of novels and romantic tales which were published by A. K. Newman and Company at London. They included:

1. *Cambrian Pictures; or, Every One Has Errors*, 3 vols (1810?).

2. *Sicilian Mysteries; or, the Fortress Del Vecchi*, a romance (1812).

3. *Conviction; or, She is innocent!*, a novel in 5 vols (1814).

4. *Secret Avengers; or, the Rock of Glotzden*, a romance in 4 vols (1815).

5. *Chronicles of an Illustrious House; or the Peer, the Lawyer, and the Hunchback*, a novel in 5 vols (1816).

6. *Gonzalo de Baldiva; or, a Widow's Vow*, a romantic legend in 4 vols (1817).

7. *Secrets in Every Mansion; or, the Surgeon's Memorandum Book*, 5 vols (1818).

8. *Cesario Rosalba; or, the Oath of Vengeance*, a romance in 5 vols (1819).

9. *Lovers and Friends; or Modern Attachments*, a novel in 5 vols (1821).

10. *Guilty or not Guilty; or, a Lesson for Husbands*, a tale in 5 vols (1822).

11. *Woman's a Riddle*, a romantic tale in 4 vols (1824).

12. *Deeds of the Olden Times*, a romance in 5 vols (1826).

13. *Uncle Peregrine's Heiress*, a novel in 5 vols (1828).

14. *Gerald Fitzgerald; an Irish tale*, 5 vols (1831).

In 1811 Anne Hatton published a volume entitled *Poetic Trifles* at Waterford.

On 7 July 1832, from her home in Park Street, Swansea, Mrs Hatton wrote to J. P. Collier to solicit a subscription for a proposed volume to be entitled *Fifty-Two Poetic Cumaean Leaves, Predicting the Destiny of Ladies and Gentlemen*—"which I think I may without vanity assert is Superior to any thing of the sort that has yet appeared, because it conveys lessons of morality and is a fit present for young people of either Sex." Describing herself as "Sick and Poor," she hoped to raise £30 in order to liquidate her "trifling debts." Through Collier she offered to provide information to Thomas Campbell, who was embarking on his *Life of Mrs Siddons* (which was published in 1834):

I certainly can supply a more correct and extended biography than Mʳ Boaden has given the world [*Memoirs of Mrs Siddons*, 1827] being in possession of anecdotes, letters, &c. from which much relative matter may be collected, on the terms I have stipulated [through James Winston]. I shall be ready to give you or Mʳ Campbell all the information in my power, nor can it be thought I ask unreasonably for my communications, when it is remembered I, a member of the family, am still capable of writing

a History of the House of Kemble.— —perhaps Sir, you will think I speak without much observance of ceremony but I believe you will pardon me, when you reflect that poverty agravated by mental suffering and great bodily infirmity urges me to speak my meaning plainly.

She wrote again to Collier on 11 August 1832, acknowledging receipt of his sovereign for the subscription but advising him that since some gentleman—"whom I assisted by writing love sonnets for him"—had helped clear her debts down to £6, she would not be printing her Cumaean Leaves. She did not, however, intend to return Collier's money because she had "only Ninety pounds a year to pay Rent, Taxes, and maintain myself and Servant—and having as I said before paid the best part of my debts, I am driven so short of money that your Sovereign is just now of consequence to me." In recompence, she promised to send Collier, in about a fortnight, a set of fortune-telling cards which she had designed in her own hand and an account of the early days of Mrs Siddons.

It was in that letter that Ann told in bitter terms some aspects of her own youth with which this notice begins. She complained that at her death Sarah had left her sister Jane Mason not one shilling and "from me who have been nine years owing to a fall unable to walk across my room without assistance, she took off by her Will *ten pounds a year*, from the thirty she had for the last twenty years allowed me," though Sarah had left her companion Patty Wilkinson £5500. John Philip Kemble had left Ann £60 per year, to be paid quarterly, in his will proved on 26 April 1823. At her death in 1836, her sister Elizabeth Whitlock bequeathed Ann an annuity of 3½ per cent on the principal of £700. Though she had suffered the neglect and oppression of both Sarah and John, she promised to let their ashes rest and not expose their faults to public view. Ann closed her letter with a touching plea:

I entreat of yourself, and of Mʳ Campbell as you are gentlemen, let my indiscretions rest. Draw not forth my frailties in your intended work, I am now in my Sixty eighth year,—my unfortunate Story has been long forgotten—I have lived in Swansea thirty two years respected, do not deprive my last days of the soluce [sic] I derive from the kindness of those who believe my every way worthy of their regard. my faults were those of compulsion and necessity, and I have deeply and bitterly repented them—Remember I am on the verge of the grave, a creature whose whole life has been a series of persecutions and misfortunes, do not you increase the weight. . . .

True to her promise, on 27 August 1832 Mrs Hatton sent to Collier a manuscript of 11 pages concerning mainly her maternal grandfather John Ward and her father Roger Kemble, information which we include in their respective notices. She added little to what was already known about Mrs Siddons and she had the years of Sarah's and John's births wrong. Yet again she railed against Sarah's stinginess and hard-heartedness—"I did not see Mrs Siddons for more than fifty years." Campbell, no doubt, felt he did not need Mrs Hatton's help, because Mrs Siddons had supplied him with her own autobiographical notes. Those were revised in Campbell's book, but in 1942 the original manuscript in the Harvard Theatre Collection was published by William van Lennep as *The Reminiscences of Sarah Kemble Siddons*.

In 1834 Ann tried to raise another subscription. On 20 April she wrote to R. Bentley in London hoping to publish her latest poetic effort, "The Raconteur," for which she claimed the patronage of the Duchess of Kent. The only payment she requested from the publisher was 100 copies, eight of which were to be "handsomely bound." She was still trying to peddle her life of Mrs Siddons, and though it had been two years since her original offer to Collier and Campbell, she told Bentley: "I have lately been written to by two gentlemen who not satisfied with Mr Boadens life of Mrs Siddons, wish me to supply the material for an authentic memoir.—as yet I have not complied with their request—but if you think a brief account of my sister, and the Kemble family generally, would assist the sale of the Book (which I presume to think it would) I would give it in the way preface." "The Raconteur" seems not to have been printed.

In a letter of 17 August 1734 by "A Resident of Swansea" (not in Ann Hatton's hand but with those by her now in the Folger Library), we are given a description of her at the age of 70:

I beg to inform you that she has not lost an eye. She has still the perfect use of a pair of dark, brilliant, and impressive ones her skin remains smooth and unwrinkled—her teeth of which she has not lost one, are regular and white, and her particularly handsome mouth retains the crimson glow and freshness of youth—She is still a splendid woman in her youth she must have been extremely beautiful. . . .

In her own hand, still neat and clear, Mrs Hatton wrote in October 1838 to her "dearest friend," Douglas Cohen, of No 21, Great George Street, Liverpool, to relate her physical suffering and of the anguish caused by his absence and the neglect of her acquaintances. In Mrs Hatton's papers at the Folger Library are verses, dated 28 September 1838, written as "Farewell Lines" to Cohen, in which she calls him

The only friend to whom I could reveal,
Each cherish'd thought, each secret wish unfold,
Whose mind could understand, whose kindness feel,
When my sad destiny in life I've told.

In Mrs Hatton's last letter to Cohen on 21 December 1838, signed by her but written by her servant, she assured him that, having settled her worldly affairs, she had hopes of meeting him "in a happier world." She died on 26 December and was buried in St Mary's New Cemetery, behind St John's Church, Swansea. Ann, like the other Kemble daughters, probably had been christened a Protestant, her mother's faith, to conform to the practice then prevailing in such mixed marriages. She died, however, a Catholic, like her father.

In her will drawn on 21 December 1838 she left some of her personal effects and books and a portrait of herself by Walker, to Douglas Cohen, with the prayer that he would convert to Christianity. Other effects she gave to her step-daughter Mary Hatton ("now Mary Lawrence") at that time soon to be married to William Lucas. A small ring was bequeathed to the Rev William Bond, Catholic priest of Swansea. The remainder of her estate, including wardrobe, furniture, plate, and linens, Mrs Hatton left to her devoted servant, Mary Johns, who was also named executrix. The will was proved on February 1839 by Mary Johns, to whom administration was granted.

No issue by either of Mrs Hatton's marriages was mentioned in the will, nor is any known. The location of her portrait by Walker is unknown to us.

Hatton, William Thomas P. *d. 1807, actor.*

William T. P. Hatton (as he signed his name in a letter to the *Morning Post* on 20 July 1805) passed most of his career acting in the several provincial theatres managed by Henry F. Thornton. A Mr Hatton was with Roger Kemble's company at Worcester in 1722 and at Edinburgh in 1773–74. A mimic named Hatton performed in James Whitley's booth at Stourbridge Fair, Cambridge, in 1776.

Our subject was most likely the Hatton who acted the Doctor in a performance of *Chrononhotonthologos* given by a troupe of itinerants at the White Hart, Fulham, on 9 November 1789. He was at the Duke Street Theatre, Brighton, in July 1790. With Thornton's company he acted at Chelmsford, Newbury, and Salisbury in 1792 and at Manchester in 1794; he probably appeared regularly at those and other places on the circuit throughout the 1790s.

Hatton made an appearance at Drury Lane Theatre as Will Steady in *The Purse* on 25 November 1801. In 1803 he obtained a summer engagement at the Haymarket. Winston expressed surprise in the *Theatric Tourist* that "with his abilities" Hatton should have stayed so long with Thornton's company at Andover, for he was certainly "beyond mediocrity." The comic line, particularly country characters and sailors, formed Hatton's usual repertoire, with his chief characters at the Haymarket being Jack Junk in *The Birthday* and Crazy in *Peeping Tom*. He also acted Hotspur, Glenalvon, and Pizarro. He paid "great regard to character and dress," reported the *Thespian Dictionary* (1805), and was "a serviceable and meritorious actor, but colour[ed] rather too coarsely."

Hatton remained at the Haymarket for 1804 and 1805 but then went to act at Charleston, South Carolina. His death in that city, probably of yellow fever in October or early November 1807, was reported in the Boston *Columbian Centinel* on 11 November 1807. Other dates given for his death, such as 31 December 1807 on a Folger Library manuscript and 1813–14 on a British Museum manuscript, would seem incorrect. The announcement in the *Morning Post*, 11 November 1811, of the death "lately in America" of Mr Hatton must refer to another actor of that name.

According to Henry Lee's *Memoirs of a Man-ager*, Hatton was married to one of Thornton's daughters. If so, she was his first wife, the Mrs Hatton who was in Kemble's company at Worcestershire with Hatton in 1772. By 1792 he was married to Miss Ann Hinds, a provincial actress, who later acted at London. Ann Hatton (not to be confused with Ann Julia Hatton, a member of the Kemble family) acted under her married name for some years into the nineteenth century; but when she died in 1841 her name was Mrs Brooks. She had at least one child, a son named John, by Hatton before he left her for America.

Hatton, Mrs William Thomas P. the second, Ann, née Hinds, later Mrs Brooks *1775–1841, actress, singer.*

By 1792, at the age of 17 and about the time she became the second wife of the actor William Thomas P. Hatton at Lyme, Ann Hinds was a member of Henry Thornton's provincial company. Hatton's previous wife, according to Henry Lee in *Memoirs of a Manager*, had been one of Thornton's daughters.

With her husband, Ann acted with Thornton's company at Newbury, Chelmsford, and Salisbury in 1792. In the summer of 1793 she was engaged for a salary of £3 per week by the younger George Colman at the Haymarket Theatre, where she made her first appearance on 14 June 1793 as Kitty in *Seeing is Believing*. Next she sang in *The Surrender of Calais* on 17 June and then acted Nancy in *The Pad* on 21 June. During July she appeared as the Fishwoman in *The London Hermit* on the ninth, Trippit in *The Lying Valet* on the eighteenth, the Maid in *The Deaf Lover* on the nineteenth, and Dorothy in *All in Good Humour* on the twenty-ninth. In August she sang in *The Mountaineers* and *Caernarvon Castle* and played Nelly in *No Song No Supper*. On 2 September she was one of the Bacchantes in *Comus* and during the rest of the month appeared frequently in *The Mountaineers*, singing for the last time in that piece—and in London—on 14 September 1793.

At Chester in 1794 Mrs Hatton, reported the *Thespian Magazine*, played "Mrs Jordan's line of characters very successfully." She was at Manchester by 23 March of that year when she acted—"very pleasing"—the role of Agnes in *The Mountaineers* and shared a benefit with Miss Daniels. Announced as from Manchester and

Edinburgh, she acted at Crow Street, Dublin, in 1796–97 and then returned to Manchester to become a regular in that company for some nine years. She was probably the Mrs Hatton who played at Brighton in September 1801 and at Chester in 1805.

Mrs Hatton would have been "a most engaging actress," judged the critic of the Manchester *Townsman* of 13 December 1803, if only she had contrived to "allay her skipping spirit with a few cold drops of *modesty*." Though she was in her characters equal to the rest of the company,

she is certainly too bulky, even when at her least size, for many of the girlish parts she is required to undertake. Her performance, however, is frequently very good, and would make her a great favorite here if she could remember not to outstep the *modesty* of nature.

Perhaps when she performed Ninetta in *The Wife of Two Husbands* in February 1804 she was pregnant, for the *Townsman* critic thought that "in her present situation she would be much more respectable *off* the stage." If she was not pregnant, she evidently was misbehaving: "if she plays the pert parts on the stage, that's no reason she should play them off," complained the *Townsman* and advised her to heed Hamlet's advice to his mother to "assume a virtue if you have it not."

Probably these insinuations about her off-stage character had something to do with the fact that at about that time her husband left her for America. After acting in Charleston, South Carolina, for several years, he died in 1807. Remaining in Manchester, Mrs Hatton acted on that stage until at least 1806. In her playing of Shelah in *The School of Reform* in March 1805 she proved herself to be "the best *Irishman* in the house," and as Flora in *A Wonder! A Woman Keeps a Secret!* on 21 February 1806, she was "a proper waiting maid."

No doubt she was the Mrs Hatton who played at the Royal Circus in 1809 and 1810 and at the Surrey in 1812. She died at Brighton on 31 March 1841 at the age of 66 and was buried at St Nicholas's in that city. Her obituary notice in the *Gentleman's Magazine* of May 1841 advised that at the time of her death her name was Mrs Brooks and she had been an actress of considerable popularity at Brighton and at the Surrey, though a performer of the old school "of which Mrs Glover is still the living model." She had at least one child, a son named John, by William Hatton.

Haughton. *See also* HOUGHTON.

Haughton, Mr [*fl.* 1710], *pit doorkeeper.*
Mr Haughton, a pit doorkeeper at Drury Lane, was given a benefit on 10 May 1710.

Haughton, Mr [*fl.* 1757], *actor.*
A Mr Haughton acted the Fine Gentleman in *Lethe* at Covent Garden on 16 May 1757, advertised as never having appeared on that stage before. What stage he *had* appeared on previously is not known. He cannot certainly be identified as one of the Haughtons of earlier years, nor as James Haughton, the Bristol actor of the 1770s.

Haughton, G. [*fl.* 1724–1741], *dancer, singer.*
G. Haughton (or Houghton) danced in a piece called *The Union of the Two Nations* at the Richmond Theatre on 27 June 1724. With him in that work were Bridgwater, Mrs Willis, and a Mrs Haughton who was probably his sister-in-law, Mrs James Haughton. Two days later Haughton and Mrs Willis performed an untitled dance, and on 4 July he offered the *Running Footman* and joined Mrs Willis in a *Union Dance*. At the Bullock-Spiller booth at Southwark on 24 September, Haughton and Mrs Ogden gave the *Swedish Dal Karle*, and Mrs Haughton and Mrs Ogden danced *Tollet's Ground*. Not until a year later were Haughton and Mrs Haughton mentioned again, so far as existing bills show: on 23 August 1725 at the Pinkethman-Norris booth at Bartholomew Fair "Houghton and Mrs Houghton" danced (Mrs Haughton, who was also an actress, played Ulamia in *Semiramis*). The careers of the Haughtons apparently separated the following season.

In 1725–26 Haughton was a dancer with the Drury Lane troupe, first appearing on 19 November 1725 with several others in a dance called *Le Badinage champêtre*. The piece was repeated several times. On 11 February 1726 Haughton was a Shepherd and Scaramouch Singing Master in *Apollo and Daphne*, a work which was performed many times in the following months. Haughton also appeared in entr'acte dances and, on 3 June, was Scaramouch in *Harlequin Doctor Faustus*. Haughton did not appear at the late summer fairs in 1726.

Haughton danced regularly at Drury Lane through the 1732–33 season, appearing in such specialty dances as a *Grand Devil's Dance* (he was the Chief Fury), *The Fawns*, *The Cobler's Jealous Wife*, a *Dance of Ethiopians*, a *Village Dance*, a *Grand Dance of Infernal Spirits*, a *Tambour Dance of Moors*, *The Masques*, and *Les Bergeries*. He also continued to perform small and medium-sized parts in plays and pantomimes, such as a Countryman in *Harlequin's Triumph*, a Bridesman in *Acis and Galatea*, a Gorgon, a Follower, and a Triton in *Perseus and Andromeda*, a Triton in *Cephalus and Procris*, a Waterman and a Grand Spirit in *The Tempest*, a Yeoman in *Country Revels*, and a Hungarian and a Companion of Paris in *The Harlot's Progress*.

Once, on 23 April 1731, Haughton danced at Goodman's Fields Theatre, for the benefit of R. Williams and Mrs (James) Haughton. The appearance was advertised as "positively the only Time of his performing on this Stage."

G. Haughton ventured to France in 1731 with Renton and performed at the St Laurent fair on 28 July with the French dancer Roger in *La Guinguette anglaise*. Haughton and other English dancers performed before the Queen at Versailles in September. By 16 October Haughton was back at Drury Lane, dancing as a Triton and a Mandarin Gormogon in *Cephalis and Procris*. He returned to France in the summer of 1732, for at Drury Lane on 23 September he, Essex, and Miss Robinson were welcomed as just having returned from Paris. Appropriately, they appeared in a ballet titled *Les Bergeries*.

In the fall of 1733 Haughton joined Theophilus Cibber's group of dissenting players and left Drury Lane for the Haymarket. There, as at Drury Lane, he served in entr'acte pieces and pantomimes, though he was less frequently cited in the bills. Haughton was in the ballet *Les Amants constants* on 25 October, his first notice in the Haymarket bills, and played a Swain in a *Grand Dance* in *Momus* within an *Impromptu Revel Masque* on 24 November. When Cibber's troupe returned to Drury Lane, Haughton did not go with them. His name disappeared from London bills until

26 February 1734, when he made his first appearance at Covent Garden Theatre as Theseus in a new ballet called *Bacchus and Ariadne*, which was introduced in *The Necromancer*. The work did not enjoy many performances. Haughton also danced *English Maggot* with Mrs Laguerre at her benefit, but he seems clearly to have made little impression on the Covent Garden management, and he moved to Giffard's company at Goodman's Fields the following fall. His first notice there was on 7 October 1734, when he offered an untitled solo dance and was incorrectly advertised as one "who never appeared on this stage before."

Haughton stayed with Giffard in 1734–35 and 1735–36 and moved with him to Lincoln's Inn Fields for the 1736–37 season. He appeared frequently, as the First Fury in *The Necromancer*, in a new *Scots' Dance*, as Nereus in *Jupiter and Io*, in a solo "After the Italian Manner," in a *Moor's Dance* and an *English Maggot*, as Damon and Myrtillo in *Harlequin Shipwrecked*, as Mars in *Britannia*, and as Sylvania in *Hymen's Triumph*. At Goodman's Fields Haughton enjoyed solo benefits, whereas previously he had shared them with others. On the bill for his benefit on 24 March 1737 at Lincoln's Inn Fields he said that his tickets were available at the Wheatsheaf in Little Russell Street, Covent Garden—possibly Haughton's lodgings.

On 22 October 1737 Haughton returned to Drury Lane, Giffard's venture having failed. Haughton was kept very busy throughout the season in specialty dances and pantomimes, and he received an individual benefit on 6 May 1738.

In the fall of 1738 Haughton returned to Covent Garden, where he remained for the rest of his career. His first notice was on 4 October, when he was one of the Furies in *The Necromancer*. Between then and the conclusion of the 1740–41 season he danced such characters as Mars (Leander) in *The Royal Chace*, Fire in *The Rape of Proserpine*, an Infernal in *Perseus and Andromeda*, a Swain in *Orpheus and Eurydice*, and other small parts and was seen in such specialty turns as *The Yorkshire Maggot* and *Satyrs and Nymph*. On 21 April 1741 he shared a benefit with Mrs Bellamy and probably danced in *The Sham Conjuror*. His salary during his final season was 10s. daily.

Though almost nothing is known about

Haughton beyond what appeared in the play-bills, an accident in early 1739 brought some comment in the papers and preserved for us Haughton's initial. On 20 January that year Haughton was an Infernal in *Perseus and Andromeda* and participated in a dance in the mainpiece, *Macbeth*. On 22 January the *Daily Post and General Advertiser* reported that, with the King and some members of the court present "In the Fury Dance of Macbeth, Mr Haughton had the misfortune to dislocate his Ankle-Bone, and fell down upon the Stage, and was obliged to be carried off; upon which his Majesty was graciously pleased to send him Ten Guineas instantly, and to order him to be taken Care of." A few days later the *Daily Post* of 24 January stated that the princesses inquired after Haughton's health and sent him an additional present of ten guineas. The same paper on 29 March ran a letter signed "G Haughton": "As I continue so lame that I am unable to make a personal application [for my benefit], I humbly hope this misfortune (which befell me in my performance this Season on the Stage)" will be excused by patrons. The benefit was held on 3 May 1739.

Haughton, Hannah *d. 1771, actress, dancer.*

Hannah Haughton made her first stage appearance on 6 December 1734 at Goodman's Fields playing the Duke of York in *Richard III*. She was advertised simply as Miss Haughton. As early as 1742–43 she began occasionally styling herself Mrs Haughton, though she seems to have been a spinster all her life. No other parts were recorded for her at Goodman's Fields her first season, and she was not mentioned again until 26 November 1742, when she was in a *New Peasant Dance* at Lincoln's Inn Fields. Then she was not noticed until the following 14 February 1743, on which date she acted Mrs Vixen and Molly in *The Beggar's Opera*. For her shared benefit with three others on 4 April she played Kitty in *The Lying Valet*, and on 11 April she was the Nurse in *Love for Love*.

Again Hannah's name dropped from London's playbills. She turned up on 20 October 1744 playing Cleone in *The Distrest Mother* with Theophilus Cibber's short-lived troupe at the Haymarket. She then moved to Hallam's company at Goodman's Fields and was seen first as Lucy in *The Virgin Unmask'd* on 4 December 1744 and then Lappet in *The Miser*, Imoinda in *Oroonoko*, Angelica in *Love Makes a Man*, Prue in *Love for Love*, Rose in *The Recruiting Officer*, Jane Shore, Kitty in *The Lying Valet*, and Miranda in *The Tempest*. Her benefit bill on 25 March 1745 stated that her lodgings were at Mrs Simpson's in Church Lane. Hannah played Jenny in *The Provok'd Husband* for Morgan's benefit at Drury Lane on 5 June.

The London Stage lists Miss Haughton as a member of the Covent Garden company in 1745–46, but she played there only in June 1746 and was at Goodman's Fields during the regular season. She began the season late, making her first appearance, so advertised, on 13 February 1746. The only new parts she tried were Cherry in *The Stratagem* and, for her benefit on 6 March, Hoyden in *The Relapse*. At Covent Garden after the regular season she played Goneril in *King Lear* on 11 June and Lady Macduff in *Macbeth* on 27 June. Hannah's chief affiliation during the summer of 1746 was with the players at Richmond and Twickenham. She acted Phillis in *The Conscious Lovers* on 4 June at Twickenham and then, at Richmond in August and September, Tib Tatter in *Sir Courtly Nice*, Rose in *The Recruiting Officer*, Lucy in *The Resolute Husband*, and Teresia in *The Squire of Alsatia*. She may have appeared in other works, for she shared two benefits at Twickenham and one at Richmond in August. That fall she returned to Covent Garden at 10s. weekly, but during the 1746–47 season she was mentioned in the bills for only two roles: Hoyden in *The Relapse* and Milliner in *The Suspicious Husband*.

At Richmond in the summer of 1747 she attempted two new roles, Miss Biddy in *Miss in Her Teens* and Lady Betty Frisk in *Diversions of the Morning*. Through November 1752 Hannah acted regularly in the winters at Covent Garden, adding to her repertoire such new parts as Betty in *Woman is a Riddle*, Anne Page in *The Merry Wives of Windsor*, Wishwell in *The Double Gallant*, Lady Loverule in *The Devil to Pay*, Colombine in *Apollo and Daphne*, Juliet in *Measure for Measure*, Lucy in *The Recruiting Officer*, Parisatis in *The Rival Queens*, Busy in *The Man of Mode*, Honoria in *Love Makes a Man*, Trusty in *The Provok'd Husband*, Colombine in *Perseus and Andromeda* (an oft-repeated role), Sentry in *She Wou'd If She Cou'd*, Catherine in *Henry V*, Lucinda in *The Conscious Lovers*, Lucy in *Oroonoko*, Mincing in *The Way of the World*, and Colombine in *Merlin's Cave*. She usually shared benefits or had her benefit tickets accepted, and by 1749–50 she was earning 5*s*. daily.

During the summers Miss Haughton played with the Richmond-Twickenham company through 1750, trying such new parts as Millwood in *George Barnwell*, Lady Lurewell in *The Constant Couple*, Hillaria in *Tunbridge Walks*, Mary Queen of Scots in *The Albion Queens*, Juliet (on 22 August 1749 at Twickenham, when she also acted Beatrice in *The Anatomist*), Arethusa in *Philaster*, Lady Anne in *Richard III*, Jacinta in *The Mistake*, Calista in *The Fair Penitent*, Abigail in *The Drummer*, Moll the Buxom in *Don Quixote*, Mrs Clerimont in *The Tender Husband*, Colombine in *The Inconstant*, and Gertrude in *Hamlet*. On 26 July 1750 she was at the Haymarket to act Arabella in *The Wife's Relief*—a single performance in the middle of her summer at Richmond and Twickenham. Perhaps Miss Haughton acted at Richmond in the 1750s as well, though we know of no roles for her; on 19 June 1760 she played Lady Grace in *The Provok'd Husband* at Drury Lane in a troupe advertised as the Richmond Company.

Hannah began the 1752–53 season at Covent Garden, but after playing Mincing in *The Way of the World* on 16 November 1752, she moved to Drury Lane, where she began her engagement on 18 December as Amanda in *Love's Last Shift*. During the rest of the season she acted Belinda in *The Provok'd Wife*, Monimia in *The Orphan*, Juliet, Charlotte in *The Gamester*, Cherry in *The Stratagem*, and Lavinia in *The Fair Penitent*. On 12 April 1753 she shared a benefit with Shuter. *The Present State of the Stage* in 1753 observed that Miss Haughton had finally risen from obscurity after several seasons at Covent Garden, where her talents had been overlooked. She had managed, apparently, to get the better of a lisp and a Newcastle manner of pronouncing "r" and she "struck all who heard her with amazement," giving "vast satisfaction." She had, the critic said, a very agreeable appearance, good understanding, but a rather weak voice.

Wilkes in *A General View of the Stage* (1759) said that Miss Haughton had "strong feeling; but the weakness of her voice prevents her from making so good an impression as her judgment enforces. She has life and spirit in comedy; and we never see her without satisfaction." *The Battle of the Players* in 1762 said "The prudent *Hughtonia*, whose Abilities in the Art of War, though far from indifferent, must yield to her amiable Qualifications in private Life."

Miss (or, by the 1760s, Mrs) Haughton remained at Drury Lane until her retirement at the end of the 1763–64 season. Among her many new roles there were Belinda and Laetitia in *The Old Bachelor*, Harriet in *The Man of Mode*, Angelica in *Love for Love*, Mrs Ford in *The Merry Wives of Windsor*, Mrs Sullen in *The Stratagem*, Clarinda in *The Suspicious Husband*, Laura in *Tancred and Sigismunda*, Elvira in *Love Makes a Man*, Regan in *King Lear*, Beatrice in *Much Ado about Nothing*, Alicia in *Jane Shore*, Miss Kitely and Bridget in *Every Man in His Humour*, a principal character in *Mercury Harlequin*, Lady Graveairs in *The Careless Husband*, Mrs Strictland in *The Suspicious Husband*, Anne Lovely in *A Bold Stroke for a Wife*, Anne Bullen in *Henry VIII*, Olivia in *Twelfth Night*, and Elvira in *The Spanish Fryar*. Her last performance seems to have been on 17 January 1764, when she acted Angelica in *Love for Love*.

Only a few scraps of information have been found concerning Hannah Haughton's private life and finances during the 1750s and 1760s. On 12 April 1755 her benefit tickets were available from her in "Chandois" Street (presumably at her lodgings); the receipts came to a poor £100. On 27 April 1756, her benefit, the prompter Cross confided to his diary: "She play'd and was brought to Bed 4 hours after." Her role that day was the Second Constantia in *The Chances*; the receipts came to £180. Nothing is known of Hannah's child. Hannah was acting again two and a half weeks after the baby was born.

The *Gentleman's Magazine* in December 1771 reported that Hannah Haughton, formerly of Drury Lane Theatre, died on the sixth of that month. She was buried at St Paul, Covent Garden, on 10 December. The will of a Hannah Haughton of the parish of St Marylebone, dated 24 February 1770 and proved on 16 January 1772 is certainly that of the performer, though it contains no mention of any theatrical connections. The burial registers at St Paul Covent Garden, stated that Hannah

Haughton was from the parish of St Marylebone; apparently she had preferred burial at
the "actors'" church instead of her own church.

The will is a lengthy and involved document
and not always easy to interpret. It would
appear that by the time she wrote her will
Hannah, because of the death of her uncle
William Horsley, had come into rental profits
from two parcels of land in Queen Anne Street
in St Marylebone parish. The income from the
properties had been granted first to Horsley
and then to Hannah by the trustees of the
Duke of Portland. The Duke in question was
William, second Duke of Portland, who had
died in 1762. His connection with Hannah's
uncle is not clear; the Duke's will, dated 27
December 1759 and proved on 12 May 1762,
did not mention Hannah or Horsley.

The income from the properties in Queen
Anne Street had, by 1777, devolved upon
Hannah Haughton, and in her will she arranged for the disposal of it and for the future
of her children. Major General William Keppel was in possession of the two parcels of land,
one of which was occupied by General Irwin
and the other by Lady Downing. Hannah bequeathed the rights to the income from the
property occupied by Lady Downing to Keppel, with the understanding that he should
permit Hannah's daughter, Emelia East, to
have those rights; after Emelia's death the
rights were to go to Hannah's son Lt John
Wood of the 56th Foot. After both he and
Emelia died, the income was to be put in trust
for Hannah's sons William, George, and John
Christopher Frederick Keppel.

The income from the property occupied by
General Irwin was to be disposed of in a similar
fashion, except that John Wood was to receive
the income first, followed by Emelia East.
Then Major General (later Lieutenant General
and M.P.) William Keppel was the fourth of
eight sons of William Anne Keppel (1702–
1754), second earl of Albemarle, and his wife
Lady Anne Lennox. His more famous brothers
were George, the third earl of Albemarle
(1724–1772); Augustus, Viscount Keppel,
the Admiral (1725–1786); and Frederick,
Bishop of Exeter (1729–1777). There were
also seven sisters.

Emelia East was also to have Hannah
Haughton's jeweled watch and the money
Hannah had invested in the public funds

(amount unspecified) when Emelia should
reach 21 or if she should marry. (Emelia was
thus a minor in 1770 and may have been the
child born to Hannah in 1756.) Those bequests were to go to John Wood should Emelia
die before marrying or reaching her majority.

On 24 May 1770 Hannah added to her will
a codicil granting William Keppel permission,
should he deem it necessary, to sell the property occupied by General Irwin in order to
bring John Wood a better commission. Hannah also authorized the sale of her jewelry,
including a number of diamond rings, bracelets, earrings, and other valuables, the proceeds to go into public funds for the interest
and benefit of Hannah's sons William, George,
and Christopher. Each son was to receive a
third of the principal upon reaching 21 (all
three were minors in 1770). Hannah Haughton was described in the codicil as a spinster.
A gloss on the margin of the will shows that
on 16 July 1795 administration of the estate
was granted to the younger William Keppel,
the elder having died.

Haughton, James   d. c. 1739, actor.

James Haughton (or Houghton) was probably the "Horton" who was listed in the
promptbook of *Money the Mistress* as playing
the part of Nathan; the work was presented at
Lincoln's Inn Fields on 19 February 1726. On
the following 17 May Haughton shared a
benefit with two others and acted Vernon in
1 Henry IV; the total receipts came to £86 3s.
He remained at the same playhouse through
the summer, playing Lewis in *The Man's the
Master*, Kick in *Epsom Wells*, Peregrine in *The
Spanish Wives*, and Meager in *The Wits*.

Like most of the lesser members of the
troupe, in 1726–27 Haughton's name did not
begin appearing in the bills until near the end
of the season, though the account books show
he was on salary at 10s. weekly on 16 September 1726 and doubtless played small parts all
season. He was probably the "Horton" who
was scheduled to play an Old Counselor in
Philip of Macedon on 29 April 1727, but the
performance was dismissed. The following 2
May he played Onomastus when the play was
finally given; the bill still spelled his name
Horton. James acted the Mad Priest in *The
Pilgrim* on 8 May and Bernardo in *Hamlet* for
his shared benefit on 15 May. He and two

others took in £152 2s. 6d. before house charges; the attendance was estimated at 1076.

Haughton stayed with the manager John Rich at Lincoln's Inn Fields and, beginning in 1732, at Covent Garden, playing such parts as Seward in *Macbeth*, Crookfingered Jack in *The Beggar's Opera*, a Page in *Don Quixote*, Octavio in *The Successful Strangers*, Menander in *Sophonisba*, Horatio in *The Wife's Relief*, Loveday in *The London Cuckolds*, Fenton in *The Merry Wives of Windsor*, Lorenzo in *The Jew of Venice*, Indent in *The Fair Quaker of Deal*, Phalantus in *Merope*, Sealand in *The Conscious Lovers*, Alcander in *Oedipus*, Spinosa in *Venice Preserv'd*, Noodle in *The Tragedy of Tragedies*, Diphilus in *Timon of Athens*, Stanmore Junior in *Oroonoko*, Basset in *The Provok'd Husband*, the Governor in *Love Makes a Man*, Aeneas in *Troilus and Cressida*, Mortimer in *1 Henry IV*, Termagant in *The Squire of Alsatia*, Cinna in *Julius Caesar*, and Surrey in *Richard II*. Haughton's last appearance at Covent Garden may have been on 2 May 1738 when he acted Surrey, though on 5 May he shared a benefit with Ford at a performance for which he was not listed as a participant. The company accounts show that in 1735–36 Haughton was paid 3s. 4d. daily and worked 172 days; the statistics for other seasons were probably similar.

Occasionally Haughton augmented his income by performing elsewhere. On 25 August 1729, for instance, he acted Dorastus in *Dorastus and Faunia* at Bullock's booth at Bartholomew Fair, and he played Whisper in *The Busy Body* on 24 June 1730 at Richmond. In 1731 James returned to Richmond to be Tom in *The Constant Couple*, Young Worthy in *Love's Last Shift*, and Sealand in *The Conscious Lovers*. He played Memnon in *The Perjur'd Prince* at Bartholomew Fair in 1732, Hephestion in *Love and Jealousy* in 1733, and John in *Don Carlos* in 1734.

James Haughton's name disappeared from playbills after the 1737–38 season, and on 16 May 1739 a benefit was given at Covent Garden at which Widow Haughton's tickets were accepted. James died, therefore, about 1739.

In *Shakespeare in the Theatre* Charles Beecher Hogan identifies our subject as James "Houghton," which spelling could certainly be correct; the name was variously spelled in the bills. If Hogan is correct in giving the actor's Christian name as James, perhaps some of the entries in the parish registers of St Paul, Covent Garden, refer to him. The name James Houghton appears in the registers between 1715 and 1737. On 23 December 1715 Mary, the wife of James Houghton, was buried; on 30 April 1716 Anne, the daughter of James Houghton of Hammersmith, was buried; on 30 May 1737 James, the son of James and Frances Houghton, was christened, and on 17 June he was buried. Two different James Houghtons may have been cited in the registers. The Haughton-Houghton name was remarkably common in the eighteenth century.

Our subject's wife would seem to have been the Mrs Haughton (d. 1755?) who first appeared at Richmond in 1724 and performed at Drury Lane, Goodman's Fields, Lincoln's Inn Fields, and Covent Garden through about 1750. The G. Haughton who danced in London from 1724 through 1741 may have been James Haughton's brother.

Haughton, Mrs James *d. 1755?, actress, dancer.*

A Mrs Haughton (or Houghton) danced in an entr'acte called *The Union of the Two Nations* at the Richmond Theatre on 27 June 1724. In the dance also was a Mr "Houghton," but we take him to have been the dancer G. Haughton, possibly Mrs Haughton's brother-in-law, for whenever the two danced together they were cited as Haughton and Mrs Haughton rather than as Mr and Mrs Haughton. Mrs Haughton was probably the wife of the Lincoln's Inn Fields and Covent Garden actor James Haughton, though she often performed at a different playhouse.

During the rest of the summer of 1724 at Richmond, Mrs Haughton acted Mrs Sullen in *The Stratagem* on 29 June, Prudentia in *A Duke and No Duke* on 4 July, Miranda in *The Busy Body* on 11 July, Flora in *The Country Lasses* on 13 July, and Elvira in *The Spanish Fryar* on 18 July. She was clearly one of the leading members of the troupe. On 24 September she acted Jocasta in *Oedipus* and danced *Tollet's Ground* with Mrs Ogden at the Bullock-Spiller booth at Southwark. In the company, again, was the dancer G. Haughton. The Southwark performance was a benefit for Ward and Mrs Haughton.

At the Pinkethman-Norris Bartholomew Fair booth on 23 August 1725 she played

Ulamia in *Semiramis*. The performance also included dancing by "Houghton and Mrs Houghton." Then Mrs Haughton's name again dropped from the bills until 24 February 1726, when she attempted Monimia in *The Orphan* and spoke a new epilogue at the Haymarket Theatre. No male Haughton was named in the bill, nor was one cited when Mrs Haughton's name turned up again on 8 September 1726; at the Spiller-Egleton booth at Southwark Fair she played the Fair Maid in *The Unnatural Parents*.

A year later Mrs Haughton joined the Drury Lane company, making her first appearance (as far as one can tell from the bills) on 6 October 1727 as the Shopkeeper's Wife in *Harlequin Doctor Faustus*. Then she was seen as Flora in *The Adventures of Five Hours*, Lady Dupe in *The Feign'd Innocence (Sir Martin Marall)*, and a Bridesmaid in *Acis and Galatea*. Her second season was even less distinguished: she was the First Attendant on Andromeda and the First Hour of Sleep in *Perseus and Andromeda* and participated in a *Village Dance*. She doubtless took other assignments that were too small to deserve mention in the bills. Having made little progress at a patent house (she had been competing with Mrs Heron), Mrs Haughton wisely changed companies.

On 31 October 1729 she acted Lucy in *The Recruiting Officer* at Goodman's Fields as a member of Odell's troupe. In November and December, in quick succession, Odell presented her as Mrs Sullen, Mrs Frail in *Love for Love*, Hillaria in *Tunbridge Walks*, Alicia in *Jane Shore*, Patch in *The Busy Body*, Elvira in *The Spanish Fryar*, the Queen in *The Unhappy Favorite*, Anne in *A Bold Stroke for a Wife*, Elvira in *Love Makes a Man*, Lavinia in *The Fair Penitent*, Lucy in *The Recruiting Officer* again, and Angelica in *The Constant Couple*. She also appeared in an unnamed dance and *The Shepherd's Holiday*. During the remainder of the season she was seen in such new parts as Corinna in *A Woman's Revenge*, Colombine in *Jealousy Deceived*, Gertrude in *Hamlet*, Lady Wealthy in *The Gamester*, Lady Trueman in *The Drummer*, Lady Gravely in *The Temple Beau*, Lady Wronghead and Lady Grace in *The Provok'd Husband*, Lady Betty in *The Careless Husband*, Mrs Page in *The Merry Wives of Windsor*, Widow Lackit in *Oroonoko*, Margarita in *Rule a Wife and Have a Wife*, Flareit in *Love's Last Shift*, Arabella in *The Committee*, Melinda in *The Recruiting Officer*. Laetitia in *The Old Bachelor*, Emilia in *Othello*, and Young Lady Languish in *The Widow Bewitch'd* (and she spoke the epilogue). Throughout the season she also appeared in entr'acte dances. The summer found her at Tottenham Court on 1 August 1730 playing Esabella in *Mad Tom of Bedlam* with other members of the Goodman's Fields troupe and then at Bartholomew Fair later in the month acting Aurelia in *Wat Tyler and Jack Straw*.

Mrs Haughton stayed at Goodman's Fields through 1735–36, adding to her extensive repertoire such roles as Nell in *The Devil of a Wife*, Gertrude in *The Royal Merchant*, Selima in *Tamerlane*, Lucia in *Cato*, Oriana in *The Inconstant*, Alinda in *The Pilgrim*, Lady Easy in *The Careless Husband*, Andromache and Cephisa in *The Distrest Mother*, Violante in *Sir Courtly Nice*, Florinda in *The Rover*, Sylvia in *The Double Gallant*, Kitty in *The What D'Ye Call It*, Belinda in *The Fair Quaker of Deal*, Sophonisba, Mrs Foresight in *Love and Love*, Araminta in *The Old Bachelor*, Parly and Lady Darling *The Constant Couple*, the Duchess of Suffolk in *Lady Jane Gray*, Maria in *The London Merchant*, the Duchess of York in *Richard III*, Tattle in *The Busy Body*, Mrs Motherly in *The Provok'd Husband*, Isabella in *The Conscious Lovers*, Dolly in *The Beggar's Opera*, Lady Loverule in *The Devil to Pay*, Goneril in *King Lear*, Calphurnia in *Julius Ceasar*, Leonora in *The Mourning Bride*, Sysigambis in *The Rival Queens*, an Attendant on Britannia in *Britannia*, Nottingham in *The Unhappy Favourite*, Lady Bountiful in *The Stratagem*, and Louisa in *Love Makes a Man*.

During that period Mrs Haughton also spoke prologues and epilogues on occasion and danced, and in the late summer of 1733 she appeared at Bartholomew Fair. She shared benefits at Goodman's Fields, usually with one other person. In 1736–37 she moved with Henry Giffard's company to the Lincoln's Inn Fields playhouse, but the season was not successful, and Mrs Haughton dropped from sight at the end of it.

On 16 May 1739 at Covent Garden the benefit tickets of a "Widow Houghton" were accepted; she was probably our subject, the widow of the Covent Garden actor James Haughton. The Mrs Haughton who played Medlar in *Harlequin Scapin* at Bartholomew

Fair on 23 August 1740 was also our subject in all probability. Wewitzer's *Dramatic Chronology* in 1817 listed a "Miss Haughton" as dying in 1755, but it seems more likely that the woman who died was Mrs James Haughton.

Hauksbe or **Hauksby.** *See* HAWKSBY.

Hautott, John [*fl.* 1794], *singer.*
Doane's *Musical Directory* of 1794 listed John Hautott of No 6, Brick Street, Spitalfields, as a tenor who sang for the Choral Fund, the Handelian Society, and in the oratorios at Westminster Abbey and Drury Lane.

Hautrey. *See* HAWTRY.

Havard, Mr [*fl.* 1791], *actor.*
A Mr Havard acted Harley in *The Double Amour* at the Haymarket Theatre on 26 September 1791. Perhaps he was related to the well-known Drury Lane actor William Havard.

Havard, William *1710–1778, actor, playwright.*
William Havard, whose career on the London stage as a serviceable actor lasted 39 years, was born on 12 July 1710 in Dublin, the son of a vintner. Having been given a liberal education (evidenced by the sophistication of his various writings), Havard was originally apprenticed to a surgeon but soon turned to the stage. Arriving in London in 1730 he made his first appearance of record on 20 August as Young Walworth in *Wat Taylor and Jack Straw* in a booth operated by Pinkethman and William Giffard at Bartholomew Fair. The piece was repeated twice that month and four times in early September.

After appearances at the Haymarket Theatre as Whitemore in *The Author's Farce* on 21 October 1730, Manuel in *Love Makes a Man* on 9 November (when his name was given as "Haverd"), Dugard in *The Inconstant* on 13 November, and Worthy in *The Coffee-House Politicians* and Dangle in *The Battle of the Poets* on 30 November, Havard joined Giffard's company at Goodman's Fields Theatre, where he made his first appearance on 10 December as Fenton in *The Merry Wives of Windsor.*

Harvard Theatre Collection

WILLIAM HAVARD
engraving by Fisher, after Worlidge

In his first season at Goodman's Fields, earning a salary described as "modest," Havard acted about 20 supporting roles, a repertoire which suggests he had enjoyed some practical experience before arriving in London. His second role at Giffard's theatre was Sir Charles in *The Stratagem* on 12 December; that was followed by Freeman in *A Bold Stroke for a Wife* on 17 December and then by Seberto in *The Pilgrim*, the Doctor in *The Devil of a Wife*, Alphonso in *The Spanish Fryar*, Rossano in *The Fair Penitent*, a Conspirator in *Venice Preserv'd*, Clerimont in *The Cobler of Preston*, Stratocles in *Tamerlane*, Belguard in *Sir Courtly Nice*, Hephestion in *The Cynick*, Montano in *Othello*, King Arthur in *Tom Thumb*, Jack in *Oroonoko*, a Player in *The Cobler's Opera*, Purser in *The Fair Quaker of Deal*, and Trebellius in *Sophonisba*. He closed the season by acting two major roles, Prospero in *The Tempest* for a benefit he shared with the prompter Boucher on 2 June 1731 and Polydore in *The Orphan* the following night.

Havard remained at Goodman's Fields through the season of 1735–36, playing dozens of roles, the more notable perhaps being Blunt in *1 Henry IV*, Bellmour in *Jane Shore*, Frederick in *The Rover*, Catesby in *Richard III*, Worthy in *The Recruiting Officer*, Vizard in *The Constant Couple*, Careless in *The Double Gallant*, Mortimer in *1 Henry IV*, Horatio in *Hamlet*, Myrtle in *The Conscious Lovers*, and Aimwell in *The Stratagem*. His performance of Heli in *The Mourning Bride*, a role he played for the first time on 16 December 1731, was supported by his "comely and genteel Person, a clear and distinct Voice, and commonly knowing very well the true Meaning of what he has to say," according to Chetwood in *A General History of the Stage* (1749).

Perhaps Havard's earliest effort at writing was his epilogue to *The Provok'd Husband*, which was spoken by Mrs Giffard on 29 October 1732 and was printed in the *Grub Street Journal* the following 7 December. His polite manner and good sense sufficiently impressed Giffard to produce Havard's tragedy *Scanderbeg* on 15 March 1733. Havard did not play a role in the piece but he spoke his own prologue. Several days before the premiere he placed an advertisement in the *Daily Post* on 12 March to deny the accusation that he had stolen the plot incidents from a play of the same title "which Mr. Giffard had in his custody some time." In a note appended to the advertisement Giffard attested to the truth of Havard's statement. Yet *Scanderbeg* is founded on the same story as Thomas Whincop's tragedy of the same name (published posthumously in 1747) and George Lillo's *The Christian Hero* (1735). Havard's play was based on the life of George Castriot, King of Epirus.

Havard's *Scanderbeg* was played only one more time, on 26 March 1733, and was published the same year. In the judgment of Thomas Davies (*Life of Garrick*), the play was a juvenile effort with unnaturally swelling language but with many vigorous and pathetic passages. Havard also wrote a prologue on the royal marriage, which was spoken by Mrs Giffard before the afterpiece *The Happy Nuptials* on 12 November 1733 and was printed with the edition of the "Pastoral Epithalium" that year.

When Giffard took over Lincoln's Inn Fields Theatre in the summer of 1736, Havard joined

him as actor and author. He made his first appearance at that theatre on 8 June 1736 as Townly in *The Provok'd Husband*. Before the passage of the Licensing Act closed down Giffard's operation at Lincoln's Inn Fields in June 1737 Havard was seen there in his many familiar parts which by then included, among others, Egmont in *Alzira*, Horatio in *The Wife's Relief*, Standard in *The Constant Couple*, Vernon in *1 Henry IV*, Vasquez in *The Indian Emperor*, Hardy in *The Funeral*, and Plume in *The Recruiting Officer*. On 9 November 1736 he acted the leading role of George Barnwell in *The London Merchant*.

At Lincoln's Inn Fields on 1 March 1737 he brought out his *King Charles I* (given in the bills as *An Historical Play*), written "In Imitation of Shakespear." Havard had undertaken to write the play, according to Davies, in order to relieve his manager's financial distress. Legend has it that in order to get the script finished and needing to restrict Havard's lust for drink and pleasure, Giffard locked up Havard in a room, letting him out at his pleasure only, until the author completed the work. With Giffard in the title role and Havard as Bishop Juxon, the tragedy was a fine success, playing to large crowds for 20 nights (13 in March, five in April, and two in May). Lord Egmont saw it on 8 March and wrote in his *Diary* that "the Characters are as the historians represent them, the language good and the sentiments, but the players are bad, he who represented General Fairfax [Johnson] and Cromwell [Wright] excepted."

Chesterfield evidently was referring to Havard's play when he said in the House of Lords that "a most tragical story was brought upon the stage, a catastrophe too recent, too melancholy, and of too solemn a nature to be heard of anywhere but from the pulpit," A revival of the play at Hull in 1777 or 1778, reported Tate Wilkinson, so grieved a young lady named Terrot that at its conclusion she "dropped down dead" in a stage box.

Havard's name was not given on the title page of the first edition of *King Charles I*, published on the day of the premiere. Evidently the publisher, John Watts, was so staggered that an actor had written the play that he refused to pay the usual £100 for it. Havard and Watts contested for some time over the fee, according to Davies, with Watts offering only £80 if the author insisted on having his name on the title page. But although the intention was to keep the author's name secret, when the play proved to be a success, Havard could not resist the fame: "The moment Havard put on the sword and tie-wig, the genteel dress of the times, and professed himself to be the writer," claimed Davies, ". . . the audiences were thinned, and the play was supposed to be inferior to what its real merit had a right to claim." The play had four editions in 1737 and also was published in editions dated 1765, 1770, 1779, 1787, 1793 (*recte* 1797), and about 1810.

With Lincoln's Inn Fields now closed, in 1737–38 Havard engaged with Drury Lane, where he made his debut on 3 September 1737 as the Duke in *Rule a Wife and Have a Wife*. He acted Lucius in *Cato* on 8 September and Story in *The Committee* on 10 September. His other roles in his first season at Drury Lane included a number he had filled at Goodman's Fields and Lincoln's Inn Fields as well as, among others, Lancaster in *2 Henry IV*, Pylades in *The Distrest Mother*, the original Hartly in Miller's *The Coffee House* on 26 January 1738, and Talthybius Herald in the premier of Thornton's *Agamemnon* on 6 April.

Acting similar roles of the second and third rank, Havard's first period at Drury Lane lasted nine seasons through 1745–46. On occasion he was permitted to venture into a major role. In a revival of his *King Charles* for his benefit on 9 May 1740 he played Fairfax. He acted Castalio in *The Orphan* on 28 April 1742, Hamlet (for his benefit) on 3 May 1742, Edgar in *King Lear* (with young Garrick as Lear) on 28 May 1742, Horatio in *The Fair Penitent* (for his benefit) on 8 April 1743, and Richmond in *Richard III* (with Garrick) on 17 December 1744. Other roles during this period included Albany in *King Lear*, Octavius in *Julius Caesar*, Frederick in *The Miser*, Norfolk in *Henry VIII*, Salisbury in *Sir Walter Raleigh*, Trueman in *The Twin Rivals*, Malcolm and Banquo in *Macbeth*, Dauphine in *The Silent Woman*, Oliver in *As You Like It*, Voltore in *Volpone*, Loveless in *The Relapse*, Priuli in *Venice Preserv'd*, Lovewell in *The Gamester*, the King in *1 Henry IV*, and Angelo in *Measure for Measure*.

Havard's third play, a tragedy called *Regulus*, was produced under Fleetwood's management at Drury Lane on 21 February 1744, with

Garrick in the title role, Delane as Corvus, and Havard as Decius. The author spoke his own prologue, and the epilogue contributed by Garrick was given by Mrs Woffington. The next morning the *London Daily Post* reported that *Regulus* had been performed to "a numerous and polite Audience, and met with Applause." A somewhat stilted piece, *Regulus* was turned into a minor success by Garrick's acting and ran a total of seven performances during the rest of the season (not 11 as has sometimes been stated). Havard received his benefits as author on 25 February and 1 March, when tickets could be had at his lodgings at the corner of the Great Piazza, James Street, Covent Garden, incidentally the same address given by Garrick for his benefit that season. On 18 April 1744 Havard had his benefit as actor, which he shared with Mrs Ridout. *Regulus* was published on 1 March, printed by H. Woodfall, Junior, for Paul Vaillant in the Strand. Two other editions appeared in London in 1744 and one in Dublin in 1745. "But if you are for a good sober piece, that has a great deal of good sense in it, but few absurdities, pray read the play of *Regulus*," wrote Mrs Elizabeth Carter to Miss Catherine Talbot at the time of the first printing. "The run of the Town is against it, but whether it is the dulness of the poetry, or the nobleness of the sentiments that makes fine folks dislike it, I am unwilling to determine."

On 30 March 1743 Havard played Plume in *The Recruiting Officer* with other actors from Drury Lane in the Great Theatrical Booth on the Bowling Green, Southwark, for the benefit of a "Family in Distress." In the summer of 1741 he had acted with the company at Jacob's Wells Theatre, Bristol, and in the summer of 1743 he toured with Whitley's company in the north of England but left them in time to play Hamlet at the Aungier Street Theatre in Dublin on 11 July 1743. In the summer of 1746 he was with the company at Richmond and Twickenham playing Young Bevil in *The Conscious Lovers*, Vizard in *The Constant Couple*, Farewell in *Sir Courtly Nice*, Cassio in *Othello*, Tancred in *Tancred and Sigismunda*, Worthy in *The Recruiting Officer*, Trueman in *The Squire of Alsatia*, and Mat o' the Mint in *The Beggar's Opera*.

Havard did not return to Drury Lane in 1746–47 but engaged, at £2 per week, at

Covent Garden, where he made his first appearance on 29 September 1746 as Horatio in *Hamlet*. On 6 October he acted Worthy in *The Recruiting Officer*, on 8 October Charles in *The Busy Body*, and 10 October Octavio in *She Wou'd and She Wou'd Not*. This was the season when Garrick had also defected to Covent Garden to join a company which included as well Quin and Ryan. When Quin acted Richard III on 20 October and Cato on 24 October, Havard played Richmond and Juba, respectively. On 27 October he was Gloucester to Garrick's Lear. That season, the only one he would ever spend at Covent Garden, he also played, among other roles, Moneses in *Tamerlane*, Polydore in *The Orphan*, Orlando in *As You Like It*, Captain Loveit in *Miss in Her Teens*, Hastings in *Jane Shore*, Hubert in *The Royal Merchant*, the original Bellamy in Hoadly's *The Suspicious Husband* on 12 February 1747, and Hotspur in *1 Henry IV*—in all a somewhat more substantial lot of assignments. On 27 April 1747, when he acted in *Jane Shore* and *Miss in Her Teens*, he shared his first benefit with Mrs Havard, a widow who as Mrs Elizabeth Kilby had been performing in London since 1727. They had married on 22 May 1745 at St Benet, Paul's Wharf. At the time of their benefit, at which they brought in a total of £150 (probably less house charges of £60), the Havards lived in Hanover Street, Longacre.

After finishing the Covent Garden season, Mr and Mrs Havard went to act for the summer of 1747 at Jacob's Wells Theatre in Bristol, where she had a benefit on 10 August and he on 14 August. When Garrick was forming his company for the first year of management at Drury Lane he wrote to Havard with an offer of an engagement, and since Havard's articles at Covent Garden were running out, he accepted on what Davies called "very liberal terms." It is unclear whether or not Mrs Havard was also engaged by Garrick. She did not act at Covent Garden in 1747–48, nor did her name appear in the Drury Lane bills that season, but she shared a benefit there with her husband on 31 March 1748. She did join the Drury Lane company, however, in 1748–49.

Havard reappeared at Drury Lane on the first night the theatre opened under Garrick's management, 15 September 1747, as Bassanio in *The Merchant of Venice*, with Macklin as Shylock. He acted Horatio to Barry's Hamlet on

22 September and Dick in *The Confederacy* on 1 October. His other roles that season (during which he acted almost every night), included his usual characters as well as Lelio in the premiere of *Albumazar* on 3 October 1747, Frankly in *The Suspicious Husband*, Sebastian in *Twelfth Night*, Altamont in *The Fair Penitent*, Valentine in *Love for Love*, and the original Colonel Raymond in *The Foundling* on 13 February 1748.

In a great variety of characters, chiefly secondary but occasionally of primary cast, Havard was a work horse for Garrick for the next 20 years. His salary by 1764–65 was £5 per week. It was at the same figure in 1766–67 and probably did not rise much by his last season, 1768–69.

Havard was the original actor of Abdalla in Samuel Johnson's *Mahomet and Irene* on 6 February 1749, Arnold in Shirley's *Edward the Black Prince* on 6 January 1750, Poliphontes in Hill's *Merope* on 31 January 1750, Othman in Brown's *Barbarossa* on 17 December 1754, Amphares in Hume's *Agis* on 21 February 1758, Timurkan in Murphy's *The Orphan of China* on 21 April 1759, Aeson in Glover's *Medea* on 24 March 1767, and Megistus in Murphy's *Zenobia* on 27 February 1768.

No doubt Harvard acted as many different roles as did any actor in the century. In addition to those cited above, a list of the roles he acted in 1761–62, in the maturity of his career, will be illustrative: Friar Lawrence in *Romeo and Juliet*, Sealand in *The Conscious Lovers*, Horatio, Sir Charles Easy, Shore in *Jane Shore*, Gonzales in *The Mourning Bride*, Constant in *The Provok'd Wife*, Osmond in *Tancred and Sigismunda*, Fainall in *The Way of the World*, King Henry in *Richard III*, Adam in *As You Like It*, Wolsey in *Henry VIII*, Mellefont in *The Double Dealer*, Iago in *Othello*, Old Knowell in *Every Man in His Humour*, Norvall in *Douglas*, Careless in *The Double Gallant*, Macduff in *Macbeth*, Tamerlane, the Duke in *Rule a Wife and Have a Wife*, Othman in *Barbarossa*, Belarius in *Cymbeline*, Melanthus in *Hecuba*, Edgar, Valentine in *Love for Love*, Frederick in *The Miser*, Polixines in *Florizel and Perdita*, Sir George Truman in *The Drummer*, the title role in *Amphitryon*, Priuli in *Venice Preserv'd*, Prospero in *The Tempest*, and Ford in *The Merry Wives of Windsor*.

In July 1765 the *Gentleman's Magazine* had

reported Havard's death at Dublin, but the *Public Advertiser* on 31 July 1765 correctly advised that the report had been "without foundation." Illness prevented Havard from playing most of the season of 1768–69, which he began on 23 September 1768 with Thorowgood in *The London Merchant*. He acted Gonzales in *The Mourning Bride* on 26 September and King Henry in *Richard III* on the twenty-ninth, but on 20 October it was announced that he was ill, and he was replaced as Leonato in *Much Ado about Nothing* by Aickin. Havard did not reappear until his benefit on 8 May 1769, the bill for which announced that his "bad State of Health obliges him to retire from the Stage." He did not perform that night (therefore his last performance was as King Henry on 29 September 1768) but after *Zara*, the mainpiece, he came out to deliver *A New Epilogue Upon his Leaving the Stage*, written by himself. It was printed soon after in the *General Evening Post*. In the Folger Library is the manuscript of the epilogue in Havard's hand:

> The Epilogue As spoken by Me upon leaving the
> Stage.
> Batter'd with War in many an hard Campaign
> Tho' the maim'd Soldier quits the martial Plain;
> Yet Fancy whirls him to the Battle's Rage,
> And temporary Youth inflames his Age:
> Again he fights the Foe—counts o'er his Scars—
> Tho' Chelsea's now the Seat of all his Wars—

Harvard Theatre Collection

WILLIAM HAVARD as Edgar, DAVID GARRICK as King Lear, and ASTLEY BRANSBY as Kent

engraving by Spooner, after Wilson

> And, fondly hanging on the lengthen'd Tale,
> Re-slays his Thousands—o'er a Pot of Ale.
>
> So I, long since accustom'd to engage
> In all the noisy Bustle of the Stage;
> Have been employ'd in ev'ry Post of State,
> And seen the Revolutions of the Great
> Seen Patriot Quin with falling Rome expire—
> And Alexander set the World on fire:
>
> Heard plaintive Cibber dignify distress,
> And well-earn'd Plaudits Pritchard's pow'rs confess;
> Have heard the Theatre's incessant Roar
> When Comic Clive Thalia's standard bore.
>
> Myself unworthy, made a little stand
> Where Gen'ral Garrick holds the first Command:—
> My humble Merits did his Choice approve—
> I was his Friend in War—his Friend in Love;
> And now, as in the various Scenes we've past—
> He proves his Friendship to the very last:
> For now Alas! Infirmity denies
> A longer stay, & sage Discretion cries
> "Retire,—Retire!—unable now to please—
> "Enjoy your Chelsea Pittance & your Ease."
> But oh! my Heart!—how warmly dost thou beat
> To those who give this Pittance—this Retreat!
> No study'd Phrase of Gratitude can pay—
> 'Tis extasy of Thanks—'tis more than I can
> say!—
> The Want of Words the full fraught Mind reveals;
> And the Tongue faulters—when the Heart most
> feels."

In the bills for his final benefit, the receipts of which are unknown (his previous benefit on 24 April 1767 had brought him £131 13*s*.), Havard's lodgings were given as at Mr Chaloner's, the linen-draper, in Tavistock Street, Covent Garden. His last-known address prior to that had been a house in Broad Court on the upper end of Bow Street, where he had resided from 1749 through 1761.

Several weeks after his retirement, on 30 May 1769 Havard wrote a pleasant note of gratitude to Garrick in which he asked to be allowed to walk in the procession that Garrick was planning in connection with the Shakespeare Jubilee at Stratford for the coming September:

> I give you Joy S! of your approaching Shakespearean Jubilee. The people of Stratford could not err in their choice of a President—They had properly no other. Might I not be permitted Sir to be a

Walker in ye Cavalcade, & to hold up the Train of Part of the Ceremony.

Garrick's reply has not survived, but Henry Angelo recorded Havard's presence at Stratford, so perhaps he did participate in some way, although a pouring and unremitting rain cancelled the procession. Havard had, however, made a certain contribution by reminding Garrick of one of his compositions: "I have already written an Ode in Honour of our Great Master wch you have formerly thought well of, Doct^r Boyce has set it excellently to Music & Voices, I should think will not be wanting on this Occasion." Havard was referring to his *Anniversary Ode in Commemoration of Shakespeare*, set to music by Boyce and sung by Beard, Champness, and others for the first time at Havard's Drury Lane benefit on 1 April 1756, on a night that Garrick had acted Romeo and the ode's author played Friar Lawrence. It had been printed in the *London Magazine* that year (p. 214), and indeed the *St James's Chronicle* reprinted it in its issue of 3–5 August 1769. Havard's *Ode* was shorter than Garrick's proved to be but the manager did lift a line or two and took from it the idea of using familiar lines from Shakespeare upon which to play his own variations. He especially echoed Havard's lines:

O for a muse of fire
Such as did Homer's soul inspire!
Or such an inspiration as did swell
The bosom of the Delphick Oracle!

According to James Boaden's note in the *Correspondence of David Garrick*, Havard had intended to pass his retirement in Islington, but finding he could not stay away from old friends he settled into his old lodgings in Tavistock Street. From that address on 4 June 1772 Havard wrote to the *Public Advertiser* to deny a report that he had a pension of £50 per year from the Drury Lane Theatrical Fund (to which he had contributed from 1766, according to a notation in the Winston fund book). He died at his lodgings of "a gentle decay" (in the words of Davies) on 20 February 1778 at the age of 68 and was buried in the nearby churchyard of St Paul, Covent Garden, on 26 February.

The satirist Paul Whitehead, Havard's close friend, wrote the following verses for the actor's tombstone:

Views of ambition ne'er his hopes employ'd,
Yet honest fame he courted and enjoy'd;
Fair peace he cherish'd, as he hated strife,
And lov'd and liv'd an inoffensive life.
Not unaccomplish'd in the scenic art,
He grac'd the stage, and often reach'd the heart;
From his own scenes he taught distress to flow,
And manly virtue wept for civil woe.
Malevolence and envy he ne'er knew;
He never felt their darts and never threw.
With his best care he form'd into his plan
The moral duties of the social man.

He honour'd virtue, and he lov'd his friend;
Oft from his little to the poor would lend;
And prais'd his great Creator at his end.

According to Thomas Davies in his biography of Garrick, the last three lines were not written by Whitehead, who died about three years before Havard. Garrick also provided an epitaph for Havard, which as printed in the *Gentleman's Magazine* of May 1779 reveals that he used the same lines he had written for William Gibson's epitaph in 1771, substituting only Havard's name for Gibson's and changing the word "deficient" to "defective":

Havard from sorrow rests beneath this stone:
An honest man,—belov'd as soon as known;
Howev'er defective in the mimic art,
In real life he justly play'd his part!
The noblest character he acted well,
And heaven applauded—when the curtain fell.

In his will with two codicils dated 25 February 1778, Havard requested to be buried in the parish in which he should die and that "it is likewise my pleasure that a Brickwork be raised around my grave of about two ffoot high on which a fflat stone will be laid with an Inscription." He made a number of modest bequests to friends including £20 to the widow of his old friend the actor Michael Stoppelaer and his "seal of Milton's head set in gold and a Mourning ring as a token of Old respect and ffriendship" to David Garrick. The largest bequest was to Mrs Ann Berkham who was to receive "twenty Guineas and five Shillings to be paid to her every week during the term of her natural Life to Commence the Monday after my interment." Mrs Berkham was not identified by Havard but perhaps she was his companion, his wife Elizabeth having died on 27 April 1764, or a daughter, although no issue are known. (A Mr Havard, however, acted Harley in *The Double Amour* at the Haymarket Theatre on 26 September 1791.)

To his barrister, Edmond "Swyny" (Swiny) were left £20 and "a Manuscript Book and papers tied together with a letter addressed to him." These papers, discussed below, are now in the Folger Library. The remainder of his unspecified estate Havard left to Griffith Howell, farrier, of Swallow Street, and his wife Elizabeth Howell. Havard failed to name an executor, but administration was originally granted to Griffith Howell, after whose death it was granted on 29 January 1799 to Elizabeth Howell. Property still remained after her death in 1834, when administration was granted on 5 August 1834 to Daniel Davies.

In the 39 years Havard toiled on the London stage he became a great favorite of the public and was most successful in the roles of kings or ministers. Davies claimed that Garrick encouraged Havard to try roles to which neither his voice nor manner were best adapted, but the critic in the *Theatrical Review* (1757–58) found that Havard was "rather apt to mould his part to his disposition, than his disposition to his part." His reliability, steadiness, good sense, and taste were qualities frequently attested by his contemporaries; his philosophic nature, however, hindered his passion and tended to make his acting predictable and monotonous. In *The Rosciad* Churchill assailed him for being always the same when he "loves, hates, and rages, triumphs, and complains." *The Rational Rosciad* agreed that "Judgement and taste, raise Havard to the sky," but "Mention performance, and applause must dye." In *Thespis*, Kelly affirmed that plain sense and memory were his great merits but exaggerated cruelly by claiming that he had no voice, figure, or face. Of him, the author of *The Anti-Rosciad* wrote:

Havard, 'tis true does seldom play with fire,
Which Havard's parts but rarely do require.
But who can say his strain unvary'd floes,
That sees him counterfeit brave Edgar's woes?

His Edgar in *King Lear* was, indeed, accounted among his very best portrayals. Even the critic in the *Theatrical Review* (1757–58), who found Havard's success in tragedy to be "mediocre," praised his Edgar: "that man must

indeed look the gentleman, who will preserve as he does, the appearance of it, under the blanket and rags of poor Tom." The jealous and disgruntled actor, Charles Adams (fl. c. 1745–1751), however, wrote to his friend John Gilbert Cooper after seeing a performance of *King Lear* on 31 December 1748 that Havard "who is esteem'd the third Man in the Theatre did Edgar last Saturday so execrebly Spiritless, I would whip a Boy of ten Years old who, with a Month's Study, did not perform it better: So void of nature! so very insipid— Some Masterly Strokes indeed he had, but they were so uncouth in him. . . ."

Havard was most comfortable in characters of "a genteel grave cast" and thus did well with Sir Charles Easy in *The Careless Husband*, Manly in *The Provok'd Husband*, and the Friar in *Romeo and Juliet*. Numerous testimonies to his private character were summed up by Davies: "This player deserved to be remembered, not so much for his stage abilities, which were indeed far from contemptible, as for his probity, the gentleness of his manners, and the benevolence of his disposition."

In addition to *Scanderbeg*, *King Charles I*, and *Regulus*, Havard wrote *The Elopement*, a farce which was played for his benefit at Drury Lane on 6 April 1763. It was never printed, but a review of the piece appeared in the *Theatrical Review* of 1 May 1763, and the play's authorship was attributed to Havard in the *London Magazine* for April 1763. An *Occasional Prologue* written by him for the benefit of the Marine Society was spoken by Havard on 5 December 1759; it was printed in the *British Magazine* in January 1760 and survives also in Larpent MS 163 at the Huntington Library. "An occasional prologue to *Miss in Her Teens* . . . Spoken by Master and Miss Simpson," written by Havard, was published in *The Theatrical Bouquet* in 1778. In the Folger Library, in his own hand, is the text of an extempore verse "Made at the Monument of Shakespeare, / in Stratford upon Avon," on 29 May 1752:

These Lines I dedicate to Shakespeare's Name;
Not to add Lustre to his deathless Fame;
But that I think all Mankind who admire,
Who honour, or who feel the Muse's Fire
Shou'd to this Darling Son of Nature bow,
And pay that Revremce [sic] w^b. I offer Now.
W^m. Havard

Also in the Folger Library are the "Manuscript Book and papers" that Havard left to Edmond Swiny. They consist of some 212 pages in his hand, containing many original pieces of prose and poetry. In the letter to Swiny, dated from "Islington [illegible] ber 26th 1775," Havard called these papers his "Jeu d'Esprit"—"The most of them never publish'd, nor intended."

> . . . Yet, tho' I decline sending them into Ye world I wou'd not have them quite Buried.

> I know not under whose Wing so properly to shelter them, as under that of a Friend, a Kinsman, & a Man of Letters, and hope you will gratify this Posthumous Vanity, and suffer them to occupy a Place in your Library, where, if in a vacant Hour they can contribute to y^r Amusement my End will be fully answer'd. . . .

The papers show Havard to have been an indifferent-to-competent rhymster, sometimes touched with Miltonic inspiration, indulging in Latin, and studious of learned effects. His subjects vary from odes on royal birthdays to lines on the loss by his friend John Trevanion of his seat in Parliament. He writes "Lines Upon the Death of my friend Bentham's Dog" and "On the Duke of Cumberland's Return after the Battle of Culloden." It is evident from the papers that Havard had many friends and acquaintances in middle-class London society and some among the nobility. He belonged to the Bedford Coffee House and Beefsteak clubs. He dealt with subjects religious, political, theatrical, musical, and literary. He seems to have intended at one time to publish a new periodical paper "to be called The Friend." With these papers are also a "character" of his friend, George Lambert, the landscape painter, "A Song in One of Mr. Rich's Pantomimes," and his "Coronation Ode," which here he states was "Set to Music by Mr. Bates." Taken together, these documents reveal a man without a serious enemy, warm, intelligent, gregarious, a bit eccentric, cautiously deistic, and fond of comfort. Indicative is his verse "Written in Dick Grindall's Dining Room waiting for the Company to come to Dinner 1773":

> Oft at this Board in Plenty did I dine,
> And season'd luscious Viands with Good Wine;
> A little longer, & impartial Death
> Shall this poor Body to a grave bequeath;

> The Worms will make a just Reprisal there
> On this cold Carcass that so feasted here:—
> But, as I first have feasted, understand,—
> The Worms can have me but at second Hand.

A portrait of Havard was engraved in 1773 by E. Fisher, after T. Worlidge. He also was pictured as Edgar, with Garrick as Lear and Bransby as Kent, in a painting by Benjamin Wilson, now lost. Engravings of this painting are enumerated in this dictionary in the illustration list for David Garrick (item No 173). Possibly he is pictured as Horatio in a painting by Zoffany which supposedly depicts Garrick meeting the Ghost in *Hamlet*, though the figure of Hamlet does not much resemble Garrick. The painting is now in the Folger Shakespeare Library. Havard played Horatio at Drury Lane until September 1767, when the role was assumed by Packer. The other figures in the painting may be Bransby as the Ghost and Ackman as Marcellus. Despite his long career and his numerous roles, these remain the only portraits of William Havard known to us.

Havard, Mrs William, Elizabeth, formerly Mrs Elizabeth Kilby *d. 1764, actress, dancer, singer.*

Prior to her marriage to William Havard (1710–1788) at St Benet, Paul's Wharf, London, on 22 May 1745, when she was identified as a widow, Elizabeth Havard had acted on the London stage under the name of Mrs Kilby, presumably the surname of her earlier husband. She had begun a long but inconsequential career on 1 July 1728 when she acted Selima in *Tamerlane*, for one night only, at the Haymarket Theatre. At that same theatre on 5 August 1728 she had a benefit as Lucy Lockit in *The Beggar's Opera*, and on 9 August she spoke the prologue to *The Spanish Fryar* but seems not to have played a role. She did, however, act the Queen in *The Spanish Fryar* and spoke the epilogue on 6 September 1728, at which time she gave out benefit tickets at her lodgings in the West Indian Coffee House, Portugal Street.

During the following season Mrs Kilby was engaged at Lincoln's Inn Fields Theatre where she made her first appearance of record as a Peasant, probably dancing, in *Apollo and*

Daphne on 23 November 1728. She acted Betty, this time probably singing, in *Hob's Opera* on 17 and 23 April 1729, then Lucy in *The Country Wife* on 7 May (for her benefit shared with Newhouse at which a total of £84 17s. 6d. was taken) and Mrs Snare in *The Fond Husband* on 15 May.

On 25 August 1729 Mrs Kilby played an unspecified role in *The Beggar's Wedding* at Reynold's booth at Bartholomew Fair; and probably she was in performances of the same piece at Southwark Fair on 8, 12, and 15 September. At Lincoln's Inn Fields again in 1729–30 she played her previous role of the Peasant in *Apollo and Daphne* as well as Betty in *Flora*. At the Haymarket on 5 March 1730 she acted Dorinda in *The Stratagem*, and in the summer she was performing in Oates and Fielding's booth at both Bartholomew and Southwark fairs.

During the next two seasons at Lincoln's Inn Fields she continued in her cast of pert and pretty lasses, playing a Country Lass in *The Rape of Proserpine*, Dorothy Stitch in *Sylvia*, Mrs Staff in *The Coffee House Politician*, Jane in *The London Cuckolds*, Mariana in *Measure for Measure*, Mrs Slammekin in *The Beggar's Opera*, Betty in *The Sequel to Flora*, and Parly in *The Constant Couple*. In 1732–33 she acted at both Lincoln's Inn Fields and the new Covent Garden Theatre, at the latter house appearing for the first time on 16 December 1732 as Mrs Slammekin, and then as Betty, Margery in *The Wedding*, Cariola in *The Fatal Secret*, Lady Loverule in *The Devil to Pay*, and Artimona in *Achilles*.

From 1733–34 through 1746–47 Mrs Kilby was regularly engaged with Rich at Covent Garden. A selection of her numerous roles in comedies and pantomimes includes Termagant in *The Squire of Alsatia* (her first appearance in boy's clothes, on 6 April 1734), a columbine in *The Rape of Proserpine*, *Perseus and Andromeda*, *The Royal Chace*, and *Orpheus and Eurydice*, Foible in *The Way of the World*, Flareit in *Love's Last Shift*, a Haymaker in *The Necromancer*, Lady Wronghead in *The Provok'd Husband*, Situp in *The Double Gallant*, and Lucy in *The Recruiting Officer*. In 1735–36 she was paid 5s. per night for 172 nights and was "charged with moiety of her tickets that came in 26 April at £15. 16." She also had played at Richmond, Surrey, in the summer of 1735.

In 1745–46 she began to be billed as Mrs Havard, the first time being on 2 October 1745, when she acted Lady Loverule in *The Devil to Pay*. In the summer of 1746 she acted at Richmond with her husband and at Jacob's Wells Theatre, Bristol. During her last season at Covent Garden, 1746–47, her salary was £1 per week, but she seldom performed.

When Garrick began his management at Drury Lane Theatre in the autumn of 1747, William Havard, who had been with his wife at Covent Garden the previous season, was a member of the company, but it is unclear whether or not Mrs Havard had also been engaged by Garrick. (She had acted at Bristol again in the previous summer.) Her name appeared in no bills for either patent house in 1747–48, but at Drury Lane on 31 March 1748 she shared a benefit with her husband. Mrs Havard was, however, a member of the Drury Lane company in 1748–49, making her debut on 15 October 1748 as Diana Trapes in *The Beggar's Opera*. She then acted Jane in *The London Cuckolds* and Margaret in *Much Ado about Nothing*, her only other roles of the season.

Probably Mrs Havard's engagement at Drury Lane had been offered in order to mollify her husband, for although she continued to be seen there for another 13 years, her roles were few and her appearances spasmodic. In 1749–50 she acted Diana Trapes, Margaret, and Jane, roles she usually filled again when these pieces were revived over the next decade. Her only other role seems to have been Lady Woodvil in *The Man of Mode* on 22 January 1755. Her name did not appear on the bills in 1763–64, so evidently she was ill all season. She died on the morning of 27 April 1764, and Havard sent word to the prompter Hopkins that he would be unable to play Belarius in *Cymbeline* that night. The place of her burial is unknown to us.

Critical notices of Elizabeth Havard's acting are indeed sparse. In the mock-heroic *Battle of the Players* (1762), she was referred to, probably ironically, as: "The blue-eyed Havardia; famed for her mellifluous Voice, and for softening the most rugged Disposition." According to William Cooke, the biographer of Samuel Foote, Mrs Havard was a notorious shrew and drunkard. If that characterization was accurate, then she must have been a burden to William Havard, who by all reports was a man of gentility and taste.

Haward. *See also* HOWARD.

Haward, Esther ₁*fl. 1779–1780*₁, *dresser.*

Mrs Esther Haward was noted in the Drury Lane accounts on 17 October 1780 as having received £13 8s. 6d. for dressing Mrs Abington the previous season.

Hawes. *See also* HOWES.

Hawes, Henry *d. 1680, string instrumentalist.*

Henry Hawes was appointed to Robert Tomkins's position among the violists in the King's Musick on 9 November 1660 at a daily salary of 1s. 8d. and an annual livery allowance of £16 2s. 6d. On 12 November 1663 he was listed in the Lord Chamberlain's accounts among the lutes and voices, and though he may not actually have been a singer, it is likely that he played the lute. The bass viol was another of his instruments, for on 17 June 1664 he was paid £10 to buy one (plus £5 for strings). Hawes was serving in the King's private music on 9 January 1669 for £46 10s. 10d. yearly. On 17 February 1680 Joseph Fashion was appointed a replacement for Henry Hawes, deceased—such appointments usually took place within days of a court musician's death.

Hawes, Samuel ₁*fl. 1794*₁, *singer.*

Doane's *Musical Directory* of 1794 listed Samuel Hawes of No 5, Castle Court, Fulwoods Rents, Holborn, as a tenor who sang for the Cecilian Society.

Hawes, Thomas ₁*fl. 1794*₁, *singer.*

Doane's *Musical Directory* of 1794 listed Thomas Hawes of No 24, James Street, Westminster, as a singer at the Chapel Royal and a member of the Academy of Ancient Music and the Concert of Ancient Music.

Hawes, William *1785–1846, instrumentalist, singer, composer.*

Grove states that William Hawes was born in London on 21 June 1785 and that he was a chorister in the Chapel Royal from 1793 to 1801. In 1802 he joined the band at Covent Garden Theatre as a violinist and about the same time began a teaching career. Hawes was made a Gentleman of the Chapel Royal on 15 July 1805, and in 1812 he was appointed a vicar choral and master of the choristers at St Paul's Cathedral. The following year he became an associate of the Philharmonic Society when it was founded. In 1817 he was given the post of lutenist and master of the children of the Chapel Royal, and in the same year he became a lay vicar of Westminster Abbey. During his musical career Hawes was a member of the Harmonic Institution, conductor of the Madrigal Society, and organist of the German Lutheran Church in the Savoy.

Hawes also had a career as a music seller, printer, and publisher. He was in partnership with Thomas Welsh from about 1825 to 1828. Then he had a shop at No 7, Adelphi Terrace from about 1828 to 1830, according to Humphries and Smith's *Music Publishing in the British Isles.* From about 1830 to 1846 he had premises at No 355, the Strand.

William Hawes was closely connected with London opera productions in the 1820s, and from 1824 he was the musical director at the English Opera House in the Strand (the Lyceum Theatre). He had worked with Kelly on an adaptation of Grétry's *Les Événements imprévus* in 1804; it was presented at the Haymarket Theatre as *The Gay Deceivers.* But it was his adaptation of von Weber's *Der Freischütz* in 1824 that began Hawes on an extensive career as an adapter of foreign operas to the English stage. The von Weber work was produced on 22 July 1824 and was an immediate success. Between then and 1833 he adapted von Weber's *Preciosa,* Salieri's *Tartare,* Winter's *Opferfest,* Paer's *I fuorusciti,* Maurer's *Der neue Paris,* Mozart's *Così fan tutte,* Marschner's *Vampyr,* Ries's *Die Räuberbraut,* Mozart's *Don Giovanni,* and Hérold's *Le Pré aux clercs.* Hawes also composed some operettas: *Broken Promises, The Quartette, The Sister of Charity,* and others, as well as a *Requiem* and some glees. He edited *The Triumphes of Oriana* (1818) and some collections of glees and chants.

On 30 January 1841 William Hawes drew up his will, calling himself a Professor of Music and giving his address as No 7, Adelphi Terrace, the Strand. He left all his property to his wife Elizabeth and asked her to provide for their children Thomas Hawes, William Henry Bartleman Hawes, Elizabeth Hawes, Emma Hawes, Maria Billington Dowding Hawes (1816–1886; she was a singer and composer of some note in the nineteenth century), and John Hawes. Hawes specified that his publishing and music-selling business should be continued for the benefit of his wife, that his insurance with Equitable and Westminster Life should be paid to her, that the mortgage on his premises at No 355, the Strand, should be paid, and that his wife should have all his household furnishings, books, and musical instruments. His children were to share all else—except the contents of his shop—and Hawes's business was to be carried on by his children and his wife.

On 17 February 1846, shortly before his death, Hawes added a codicil making William Rogers of Southern Lodge, Brixton Road, Surrey, co-executor with Mrs Hawes and William Henry Bartleman Hawes. Rogers, as it turned out, did not share in the execution of the will on 10 March 1846. The twentieth-century English composer Malcolm Arnold is a great-great-grandson of William Hawes.

Hawker, Essex ₁*fl. 1723–1729*₁, *actor, playwright.*

Essex Hawker played Manworth in *The Female Fop* on 12 December 1723 at the Haymarket Theatre with a group of amateur performers. The following 27 February 1724 at the same house he shared a benefit with Thomas. He seems to have turned professional when he acted Sir Novelty in *Love's Last Shift* on 10 April 1729 and Maiden in *Tunbridge Walks* the following 19 April—both at the Lincoln's Inn Fields Theatre. On 6 May at that playhouse he played Rako in his own ballad opera *The Wedding*; that was the first performance of the work, and it was given for the benefit of Hawker and Neale. The gross income for the evening was £175 10s. 6d. *The Wedding* was published in 1729, as was an alteration of it called *The Country Wedding and Skimmington.*

Hawkes, Samuel Tanfield ₁*fl. 1739–1763*₁, *organist.*
On 28 August 1739 Samuel Tanfield Hawkes became one of the original subscribers to the

Royal Society of Musicians. *Mortimer's London Directory* of 1763 listed Hawkes as organist at Dulwich College that year.

Hawkins, Mr ₁*fl. 1741*₁, *actor.*
A Mr Hawkins (or Hankins) played the title role in *The Spanish Fryar* at the James Street Theatre on 9 November 1741.

Hawkins, Mr ₁*fl. 1793–1810*₁, *actor, singer, manager?*
Mr Hawkins was first noticed in playbills on 26 December 1793, when he played the Constable in *Harlequin Peasant* at the Haymarket Theatre. Drury Lane hired him for one performance of *The Mountaineers* on 31 October 1794; he was used as a member of the chorus of singing Guards. Hawkins was at Drury Lane again in the same capacity in the same production on 11 January 1796. He was probably the Hawkins who performed at the theatre in St Mary's Hall, Coventry, from February to May 1797. Back in London at the Haymarket on 2 July 1800 Hawkins was an Officer of Government in *Obi*, and he continued appearing in small parts at the Haymarket through 1801. From September 1800 he was on the Covent Garden payroll at 15s. weekly, having earlier that month performed at Richmond. Perhaps he was the Mr Hawkins who was granted a license to perform plays and entertainments at the Haymarket in 1800; if so, it may be that he was mostly concerned with theatre management and occasionally filled out casts when needed. He may have been the Hawkins who performed at Manchester in May and June 1803.

Hawkins played Conrad in *The Hero of Hungary* at the Royalty Theatre in London on 27 November 1809 and Hardacre and the Oracle in *The Mystic Cup* on 25 January 1810.

Hawkins, John ₁*fl. 1794*₁, *organist, singer.*
Doane's *Musical Directory* of 1794 listed John Hawkins, of No 35, Goswell Street, as a paper ruler by profession who played the organ and sang bass for the Choral Fund and the Handelian Society.

Hawksby, Mr ₁*fl. 1757–1768*₁, *actor.*
Mr Hawksby (or Hauksby, Hawksly) shared benefits at Drury Lane on 13 May 1757, 9 May

1758, and 22 May 1765. Though he was not cited for any roles over the years, on 14 January 1768 the playbill for Drury Lane indicated that Hawksby was to replace Watkins in the cast of *The Elopement*.

Hawley, Rouse ₁*fl.* *1718–1719*₁, *violinist*.

It seems very likely that the following three citations concern the same person, Rouse Hawley the violinist. At York Buildings on 10 December 1718 "the famous Mr Reuse" played a solo violin piece by Geminiani; at Hickford's Music Room on 6 March 1719 a benefit was held for Rouse Hawley at which he played some concertos; and at Coignand's Great Room on 18 March "Rousesini" played the violin.

Hawthorn, Robert ₁*fl.* *1739*₁, *musician*.

Robert Hawthorn was one of the original subscribers to the Royal Society of Musicians when it was founded on 28 August 1739.

Hawtin, Mr ₁*fl. 1792–1802*₁, *actor*.

Mr Hawtin worked at the Covent Garden Theatre from 1792 through 1802, playing a number of pantomime roles. His wages were £1 10s., and his benefit tickets were usually accepted each spring. He was first mentioned in the bills as playing a principal character (Sir Gregory Whimsey, evidently) in *Harlequin's Museum* on 20 December 1792. Thereafter, over the years, Covent Garden audiences saw him as Gardner in *The Invasion*, the Miller in *Harlequin and Faustus*, Columbine's Father in *Mago and Dago*, Tythe Parson in *The Tythe Pig*, Pantaloon in *Harlequin's Treasure*, the Father in *Harlequin and Oberon*, an Irish Peasant in *Bantry Bay*, a Bailiff in *Wives as They Were, and Maids as They Are*, a Bailiff in *The Honest Thieves*, a Grandee in *Harlequin and Quixote*, Columbine's Father in *Harlequin's Return*, the Landlord in *The Magic Oak*, Don Felix in *Raymond and Agnes*, the Boatswain in *The Death of Captain Cook*, an Old Beau in *The Volcano*, a Jailer in *The Deserter of Naples*, a Fisherman in *Don Juan*, and other small parts. Once, on 12 October 1793, he took over the role of Harlequin in *Harlequin's Chaplet*.

Hawtin appeared as Jonkanoo in *Obi* at the Haymarket Theatre in the summer of 1800

and was at that house again in the summer of 1801.

Hawton, John ₁*fl. 1794*₁, *trumpeter*.

John Hawton, of No 4, Whitcomb Street, Haymarket, was a trumpeter in the Third Regiment of the Guards, according to Doane's *Musical Directory* of 1794. Hawton was a member of the New Musical Fund and performed in the oratorios at Drury Lane and Westminster Abbey.

Hawtry, Mr ₁*fl. 1761–1775*₁, *actor, singer, dancer*.

Mr Hawtry was a member of the Smock Alley company in Dublin in 1761–62, and he performed also at Cork in 1762. During the following decade he perhaps had been itinerant. We believe him to have been the "Mr Hartry" who acted Sir William in *The Gentle Shepherd* at the Haymarket Theatre on 20 February 1775 with performers from Scotland. On that evening, when he was advertised as from Edinburgh, he also offered a song and danced a hornpipe burlesque of *Tinker's Travels*.

About 1762–63 Hawtry married the singer Miss McNeil. As Mrs Hawtry, her occasional performances in London included Peggy in *The Gentle Shepherd* at the Haymarket on the night that her husband made his only appearance in the metropolis. There seems to have been no connection between this Mr Hawtry and the Drury Lane actor John Hartry, who died in 1774.

Hawtry, Mrs, née McNeil ₁*fl. 1761–1777*₁, *singer, actress*.

Miss McNeil, the daughter of the Irish dancer Gordon McNeil, performed at Crow Street, Dublin, by 1761–62. At that theatre on 22 January 1762 Miss McNeil played Mysis in the first performance of Kane O'Hara's burletta *Midas*. Soon afterward she became Mrs Hawtry and acted under that name at Smock Alley in 1764–65, at Crow Street from 1766–67 through 1769–70, at Cork in July and August 1769, and at Smock Alley again in 1771–72. She sang at Ranelagh Gardens, Dublin, in 1772–73.

The "Mrs Hartry" who acted Peggy in *The Gentle Shepherd* at the Haymarket Theatre on 20 February 1775 with performers from Scotland was no doubt the person known to the provincial theatres as Mrs Hawtry. Her husband also appeared that evening.

After the single Haymarket appearance, she and her husband seem never again to have acted in a London theatre. A press clipping from the *Morning Chronicle* in 1777 reports her singing at the Patagonian Theatre in Dublin. About 1780, a rondeau *By my Sighs* as sung by "Mrs Hautrey" at the New Gardens was published in Dublin. There seems to have been no connection between Mrs Hawtry and the Drury Lane actor John Hartry, who died in 1774.

Hay. *See also* HAYES and HAYS.

Hay, de la. *See* DE LA HAY.

Hay, Mr ₁*fl.* 1794–1800₁, *house servant?* *See* HAY, MRS ₁*fl.* 1794–1800₁.

Hay, Mrs ₁*fl.* 1794–1800₁, *dresser.* A Mrs Hay was paid 16*s.* per week as a dresser at Drury Lane during 1794–95. Presumably this was the person named Hay who shared in benefit tickets at that theatre each subsequent year through at least 1799–1800, although a Mr Hay may have been referred to in these instances. On 8 May 1797, Mrs Hay took the "Ready Money" in the amount of £42 14*s.* from her impending shared benefit on 7 June.

Hay, Harriett Sylvester. *See* LITCHFIELD, MRS JOHN.

Hay, Richard *d.* 1785, *violinist, band leader.* The musician Richard Hay appeared as a violin virtuoso in London as early as 1758. On 3 March of that year he played a concerto on the violin at Drury Lane Theatre. Although he probably enjoyed an active career in his earlier years, his public notices were few. They included solos at the Long Room, Hampstead, on 13 August 1759, at Covent Garden Theatre on 30 November 1759, and at the King's Theatre on 24 April 1760 in a performance of the *Messiah* given for the benefit of the Musicians' Fund.

By 1763, according to *Mortimer's London Directory*, Hay was living in Vine Street, Picca-

dilly. On 13 November 1764 he played a solo on the violin and led the music for a performance of *Acis and Galatea* at the Haymarket Theatre. In the oratorio season of 1765 at Covent Garden he played a solo every night, but in the following season, according to the *Gazetteer* (25 February 1766), such solo performances were severely curtailed, although Hay seems to have been a member of the oratorio band. He served as first violin during the summer of 1765 at Ranelagh Gardens, where he returned in 1766. During the latter summer he occasionally played the violin at the Haymarket.

By 1767 Hay was appointed the Master of the State Musick in Ireland, in which capacity he served until his death. Although residing in Dublin, he made occasional visits to London, playing in a performance of the *Messiah* at Haberdasher's Hall, Maiden Lane, on 10 December 1768, at the King's Theatre on 5 February 1773, and at the Chapel of the Foundling Hospital for another performance of the *Messiah* on 23 November 1775.

From an unknown date Hay was the leader of the Concerts of Ancient Music until he was succeeded in 1780 by Wilhelm Cramer. Hay and Cramer served as the two alternate leaders of the enormous band of 525 vocal and instrumental performers, under the conducting of Bates, at the Handel Memorial Concerts given at Westminster Abbey and the Pantheon in May and June, 1784. Sylas Neville was present and thought that Hay's manner was "graceful & easy to be observed by the band."

At Paris, on the way to the south of France, Richard Hay died on 29 January 1785. His obituary in the *Gentleman's Magazine* for that month described him as "leader of the king and queen's band of musicians, master of his majesty's band of musicians in Ireland, &c."

In his will made on 14 December 1784 with a codicil added on 16 December, prior to his departure for France, Hay described himself as of the parish of Marylebone. To Sarah Bretton of Bath, spinster and cousin of his late wife, he left £10 for mourning and an annuity of £20 during her life. Hay had remarried, for his wife Jane Hay was bequeathed the bulk of his substantial estate, with trust provisions for his four minor children: Richard John, Lionel, Elizabeth Meliora, and Mary Ann. The will was proved in London on 16 February 1785.

Hayden, Mr ₍fl. 1797?–1799₎, actor.

A Mr Hayden acted Old Norval in *Douglas* and Father Luke in *The Poor Soldier* at the Old Crown Inn, Highgate, on 15 May 1799. The bill announced that the company would play on Monday, Wednesday, and Friday, but the number of performances they gave is not known. Perhaps this person was the Mr Haydon who had acted at Cork in 1797.

Hayden, Miss. *See* HEYDON, MISS.

Hayden, George ₍fl. c. 1710–c. 1732₎, organist, composer.

George Hayden began publishing songs about 1710, one of his earliest and most popular being *As I saw fair Clora*, which was sung by Cook and Newberry at the Lincoln's Inn Fields playhouse. Hayden composed a number of songs during the two or three decades that followed, some of which were still being reprinted late in the century. He also tried his hand at cantatas, three of which were published in 1723 and some of which were popular at the Goodman's Fields Theatre in 1730, 1731, and 1732.

Hayden was an organist, and sometime before 1717 he, as organist of St Mary Magdalen, Bermondsey, signed a notice in the newspapers supporting the candidacy of John Jones for the post of organist to the United Parishes of Allhallows, Bread Street, and St John the Evangelist. Other signers included Edward Henry Purcell and Daniel Purcell.

Haydn, Franz Joseph 1732–1809, composer, instrumentalist, singer, teacher.

Franz Joseph Haydn was born in a small house near the marketplace in Rohrau, Lower Austria, on 31 March or 1 April 1732. He was the second child of the master wheelwright Matthias Haydn and his wife Maria, née Koller, daughter of the Markrichter of Rohrau and cook in the household of Count von Harrach. Matthias and Maria Haydn had eleven other children, two of whom became musicians: Johann Michael, a notable composer, and Johann Evangelist, a tenor singer of some ability.

(A lengthy genealogy of Haydn's paternal line and a discussion of the various hotly-disputed theories of his family's ethnic origins— Teutonic, Croation, Slavic, or Czech—is given

in the entry in *Grove's Dictionary* by Carl Ferdinand Pohl and William H. Husk, revised in the fifth edition by Marion M. Scott. That admirable biography, based on the still-definitive three-volume life by Carl Friedrich Pohl and Hugo Botstiber but employing also an exhaustive bibliography of more recent studies, has been drawn on heavily for this entry. It should be consulted for a full treatment of Haydn's continental career, for a catalogue of his works, and for criticism of his music. We provide here some additional details of Haydn's London visits from recent discoveries and have broadened the treatment of his character. For that we have had the valuable assistance of *Haydn, Two Contemporary Portraits*, Vernon Gotwals's excellent 1963 translation of two memoirs, by G. A. Griesinger and by A. C. Dies, both rich in anecdote.)

Both of Haydn's parents sang, and his father played the harp. Franz Joseph early disclosed an aptitude for singing and, over the objections of his mother (who would have preferred to see him a schoolmaster or a priest), he was taken at six years of age to Hainburg and placed under the tutelage of a distant relation, the music teacher Johann Mathias Franck. His relative was a stern but thorough taskmaster and Franz Joseph (or "Sepperl" as he was called) was an apt learner of singing and of several instruments. He later said, "I shall be grateful to that man as long as I live for keeping me so hard at work, though I used to get more flogging than food."

When Haydn was eight years old, George Reutter, *Hofcompositor* and *Kapellmeister* at St Stephen's in Vienna, heard him sing and offered him a place in the choir school of that church where, from 1740 onward, he studied Latin, writing, and arithmetic and where he also learned to play the clavier and the violin. His singing masters were Gegenbauer and Finsterbusch. Though he apparently was not then (or ever) given much formal instruction in composition or harmony, his own inner compulsions drove him to fill every piece of paper he could find with musical notation.

In 1745 Haydn's younger brother Michael was brought to the choir school. Franz Joseph assisted Michael in his studies, only to be supplanted by him when his own voice broke. He was now useless as a choirboy, and Reutter, instead of finding a way to employ his instru-

Courtesy of the Royal College of Music

FRANZ JOSEF HAYDN
by T. Hardy

mental ability, sought a pretext for his dismissal. The young musician left St Stephens in 1748 after being upbraided harshly for playing some practical joke.

Resisting his parents' renewed insistence that he study for the priesthood, Haydn borrowed some money, rented a garret room in the old Michaelerhaus of the College of St Barnabas in the Kohlmarkt, and made ends meet by taking a few pupils while he applied himself earnestly to the study of the music of his early model, Carl Philipp Emanuel Bach. He also practiced the violin and the clavier. By 1751 he was composing his first Mass, in F major. In the spring of 1752 the comic opera *Der krumme Teufel*, by his friend the comedian Felix Kurz, was produced with Haydn's music at the Kartnertor Theatre.

Haydn and the librettist Pietro Metastasio were living in the same house. Metastasio was responsible for the education of the children of an eminent Spanish family and obtained for Haydn the post of music master to the elder daughter. That situation led to an acquaintance with Nicola Porpora, who engaged him as accompanist. Haydn went with Porpora to the baths at Mannersdorf, where for several months Porpora instructed him in composition with strict and even harsh discipline and where he met influential musicians, including Christoph Willibald Gluck (later von Gluck) and Karl Ditters (later von Dittersdorf) at the soirées of Prince von Hildburghausen. He also continued to collect works on theory. His small Latin training proved sufficient to allow him to probe Fux's *Gradus ad Parnassum*, which he always afterward used in his teaching.

During a long visit in 1755 to the country house of Karl Joseph, Edler von Furnberg, at Weinzerl near Melk, Haydn composed his first string quartets. Returning to Vienna in 1756 he attracted more pupils and raised his fees from two to five florins a month. In 1759 he was appointed *Musikdirecktor* and *Kammercompositor* to Count Ferdinand Maximilian Morzin and proceeded to the Count's seat at Lucaveč near Plzeň to direct the private band, for an annual salary, according to Pohl, of 200 florins. (Dies, probably exaggerating, said 600 florins.)

On 26 November 1760, at St Stephen's in Vienna, he married (impulsively, according to Dies) Maria Anna Keller, daughter of a wigmaker. She was a shrew who was to be an agonizing trial to Haydn's spirit and a clog on his work until she died on 20 March 1800. (Haydn once described her as a "bestia infernale.") No children were born of the union.

Count Morzin's dissolution of his band soon after the marriage left Haydn without employment, which situation appeared at the moment disastrous but proved to be the most fortunate single occurrence of his career. He was immediately engaged by the reigning Prince Paul Anton Esterházy of Galantha as *Vicekapellmeister* under the aging Gregor Joseph Werner. He was to enjoy the patronage of the Esterházy family for the rest of his life.

At Eisenstadt Haydn was paid 400 florins a year for conducting an accomplished band of 16 pieces. After the death, in 1762, of Prince Paul Anton and the succession of his humane and generous brother Nicolaus, a fine musical amateur, Haydn's responsibilities multiplied. He received successive salary increases to 782 florins, hired new musicians, and rehearsed them every day. He continued to compose music of every variety—symphonies, cassations, divertimentos, minuets for orchestra, songs, operettas, sonatas, trios, and concertos. In 1766, Werner died and Haydn became sole *Kapellmeister*.

In the mid-1760s the magnificent palace of Esterház, with its elaborate facilities for concerts, musical comedy, opera, and even puppetry, was built near Suttor in an isolated spot on Neusiedler Lake. Here Prince Nicolaus entertained lavishly for eight months of the year, receiving crowds of nobility and gentry. Haydn remained at Esterház during the season every year from 1766 through 1790, conducting his musicians in his fatherly fashion, rehearsing and producing over 100 operas, 88 of them premieres, many of them his own compositions. His works during that period were commanding steadily greater attention throughout Europe. Occasionally the entire suite of musicians under his direction sallied forth to Vienna to perform concerts or, with the Prince himself, to the sitting of the Hungarian diet. The reciprocal devotion between Haydn and his Prince continued to grow. Haydn twice had small houses burned, in general conflagrations, in 1768 and in 1776. Each time Prince Nicolaus rebuilt them.

Of Haydn's personal life during this time much anecdote is recorded but little hard fact is known. In 1779 Antonio Polzelli, a violinist, and his wife Luigia (née Moreschi), a singer, came into the musical establishment at Esterház, and Haydn suffered a painful infatuation for her. She extracted large amounts of money from him and treated him unkindly. It has sometimes been supposed that the younger of her two sons, who was Haydn's pupil, was also his son. But though Haydn showed much regard for the boy, he did not leave him anything in his will.

In 1779 Haydn composed music for *L'isola disabitata*, a libretto by Metastasio, and sent the score to the King of Spain, who returned a gold snuffbox set with precious stones. Haydn was then nominated a member of the Accademia Filarmonica at Modena. Also in 1779 the theatre at Esterház burned, but a fine new one opened on 15 October 1780 with Haydn's *La fedelta premiata*. During the visits of the Grand Duke Paul of Russia and his grand duchess to the Emperor Joseph in 1781 and 1782, Haydn was given another snuffbox (this one studded with diamonds) because of the effect of his quartets on the grand duchess. In the winter of 1781–82 at Vienna Haydn met Mozart for the first time, inaugurating mutual respect and esteem which was to continue until Mozart's death in 1791.

In the 1780s Haydn began to be pulled toward Europe's new musical lodestone, London. In August 1781 he began publishing in England with William Forster the elder, a violin maker. It has been suggested that Johann Christian Bach and Friedrich Abel invited Haydn to come to London in 1781 or earlier. In 1782, after the death of "English" Bach, the Earl of Abingdon tried unsuccessfully to induce Haydn to come to London to take over the direction of the subscription concerts. Haydn's music was played more and more frequently in England. When Robert Jephson's comic opera *The Campaign; or, Love in the East Indies* came from Smock Alley Theatre, Dublin, to Covent Garden Theatre on 12 May 1785, there was "A new Overture by the celebrated Haydn."

Periodically, from 1781 to 1791, London newspapers published rumors of Haydn's imminent advent only to retract and replace them with fanciful reasons why he could *not* come: his religion ("he will never honor this land of *heresy* with his presence"), dislike of his music by King George III and by Joah Bates the organist and influential concert organizer, and his advancing age. Not only was Haydn called a religious bigot (though "the Shakespeare of music") but also his master, Esterházy, was portrayed as a tyrant, keeping his slave "immured in a place little better than a dungeon" (or, from another pen, in "a miserable apartment in the barracks, in which are his bed and an old spinet. . . .") It was suggested at one point that Haydn should be kidnapped and brought forcibly to "Great Britain, the country for which his music seems to be made."

In 1787 both Wilhelm Cramer, leader of London's Professional Concerts, and Giovanni Gallini at the Italian opera urgently pressed Haydn to come to London. Johann Peter Salomon, who in 1786 had already produced a symphony by Haydn at his subscription concerts at the Hanover Square Rooms, even sent John Bland, a Holborn music-seller, scurrying to Esterház in November of 1787 to persuade Haydn to desert. But Haydn was too well situated, and for three years none of those overtures bore fruit.

Late in 1787 and early in 1788 occurred one of those incidents which several times late in Haydn's career slightly sullied his general reputation for probity. He seems to have been paid by the proprietors of the Hanover Square concerts to send them several pieces of original music. But when the scores arrived it was discovered that they had already been published in London. Excuses were made by Haydn and the money was returned, but the affair sparked a month-long skirmish in the newspapers, and it seems also to have blunted momentarily the desire of London's entrepreneurs to bring the composer to England. But only momentarily.

In 1790 Dr Charles Burney published his *General History of Music*, near the end of which he exclaimed:

I am now happily arrived at that part of my narrative where it is necessary to speak of HAYDN! the admirable and matchless HAYDN! from whose productions I have received more pleasure late in my life, when tired of most other Music, than I ever received in the most ignorant and rapturous part of my youth, when every thing was new, and the disposition to be pleased undiminished by criticism or satiety.

On 28 September 1790 Haydn's beloved patron Prince Nicolaus died, leaving the composer an annual pension of 1000 florins, contingent on his retaining his title as *Kapellmeister*. Salomon at once renewed his importunities, and though the King of Naples, Ferdinand IV, then visiting Vienna, also insisted on obtaining Haydn's services, the composer braved his indignation. With the permission of his new master, Prince Anton, he embraced Salomon's offer.

Haydn bade farewell to his friend Mozart

and left Vienna on 15 December 1790. The journey was broken at Munich and Bonn, where, said Dies, he was flattered by the Elector Maximilian by a dinner engagement and almost adored by the local musicians. Haydn and Salomon shipped from Calais on New Year's Day 1791, landed at Dover, and took coach for London, where Haydn was received into the house of John Bland the music seller at No 45, Holborn. He subsequently removed to Salomon's house, No 18, Great Pulteney Street, Golden Square, where he was welcomed by the flattering attention of throngs of noblemen and musicians and by Charles Burney's poem "Verses on the Arrival of the Great Musician Haydn in England."

Haydn had been engaged to compose six new symphonies and, from his pianoforte, to conduct the performance of those works by Salomon's forty musicians. A letter from Burney to Christian Latrobe, dated 3 March 1791 (recently discovered in the Osborn Collection at Yale), expresses distress that Salomon and Haydn have been obliged to put off their opening concert repeatedly because the celebrated tenor Giacomo Davide, whose services they sought, had been contractually prevented from singing in any public place until he had been heard in the new King's Theatre, recently completed. Burney deplored the fact that these excellent musicians should have suffered the consequences of British "fidling quarrels & *feudal Sins.*" But the difficulty disappeared when on 23 February, despite the refusal of the Lord Chamberlain to license the King's for opera, Gallini put on a semi-private rehearsal at the new house, with Davide in the character role in *Pirro.* On 11 March the first concert of the season was given at the Hanover Square Rooms, and the first of Haydn's new series of symphonies (No 93, Salomon No 2) was presented in a highly successful performance. Haydn realised £350 at his first benefit on 16 May.

Gallini persisted in his campaign for a patent at the King's Theatre and was at length granted instead a temporary license. He had repeated his "rehearsal" on 10 March, and although no money was taken, the *Oracle* of 11 March reported that "the Proprietors of this undertaking saw company to the number we imagine of Four Thousand Persons. . . ." Apparently Haydn had no part in this campaign

to secure legitimacy until, perhaps, 26 March, when Gallini dared one step further by staging *Entertainments of Music and Dancing.* Gallini announced in his bills that it had been "found that, without offence to law, the entertainments advertised for the Hanover-Square Rooms may be given at this place." The proprietors of the King's would ("until the hardship and justice of their case [should] produce the proper influence upon his Majesty's benevolent mind") employ the musical and choreographical talents "engaged at an expense of £18,000" in running through the airs of various operas and dancing before theatrical scenery but not in costume.

Very likely Haydn was assisting with that performance and five others that spring of what Walpole called "opera in déshabille." Haydn was named house composer for the first time in the bill of 31 March, for which he wrote "a new Overture," and on 9 April there were "Chorusses in both Parts, composed by Haydn, who will preside at the Harpsichord." The *Entertainments* continued into July. During that period several works of Haydn's had been placed in the program, including the chorus "The Storm" with the words by "Peter Pindar." Haydn had also composed his opera *Orfeo ed Euridice* and Gallini had paid him for it, though it could not then be produced.

Haydn, who at that time was living at Lisson Grove, had been honored on 30 May with his second benefit at the insistence of some influential music lovers. On that occasion he offered two of his symphonies and introduced his *Seven Words.* Invited to the annual dinner of the Royal Society of Musicians, he composed a march and presented it. He attended the final Handel Commemoration and was so moved by the "Hallelujah" chorus that he wept and exclaimed, "He is the master of us all." In July 1791 he received the degree of Doctor of Music at Oxford, where his G Major "Oxford" Symphony (No 92) was performed, with Haydn giving the tempos from the organ.

When he returned from Oxford he sojourned five weeks at the country house of the Brassys, attended two Lord Mayor's dinners, and was fascinated by the Fantoccini Theatre in Savile Row. He gave lessons to several pupils of later renown, among them the glee composer John Wall Callcott and the instrumentalist and composer Thomas Haigh. Mature musicians absorbed his counsel, too. (The seasoned violist and composer William Shield was wont to say that in a journey of four days, in which he accompanied Haydn to Taplow and back, he absorbed more musical knowledge than in any four years of his life.) He visited the newly-married Duke of York at Oatlands for three days and was captivated by the friendly little seventeen-year-old bride, the Princess of Prussia. The Prince of Wales played Haydn's works on the cello, Haydn sang his songs, and, by command of the Prince, Hoppner painted his portrait. Haydn then visited Cambridge University and the music patron Sir Patrick Blake at Langham.

He signed a new contract with Salomon, displeasing Prince Esterházy, who wished him to return to help prepare a fête for the Emperor. Salomon's concerts began on 17 February 1792, this year in competition with those of Ignaz Pleyel, Haydn's favorite pupil, with whom, however, Haydn remained friendly. He was present when Pleyel conducted his first Professional Concert, on 13 February 1792, and heard among other selections one of his own symphonies. The good-tempered Haydn wrote in his diary, "Since his arrival Pleyel has been so modest to me that my old affection has revived; we are often together, and it does him honour to find that he knows the worth of his old father. We shall each take our share of success, and go home satisfied."

During the concert season which ended on 6 June 1792 he produced a steady stream of new trios, airs, symphonies, cantatas, and other works. He contracted friendships with the astronomer Sir William Herschel, the violinist François Barthélemon, the surgeon John Hunter, and the engraver Bartolozzi. Haydn also inspired a deep affection in Rebecca Schröter, widow of the Queen's music master Johann Samuel Shröter. She was then over 60, and Haydn was 50. He later testified that he would have married her had he been free. Though short, dark, stout, and decidedly unhandsome, Haydn was attractive to women, and Mrs Schröter was not the only one whose attention he caught in London. Two others—a Mrs Shaw and a Mrs Hodges—he at various times called the most beautiful women he had ever seen, and he kept mementoes of both. His difficult wife kept herself in his memory by writing him for money to buy a house (Windmühle, 73 Kleine Steingasse, in the suburbs of Vienna), saying that it would be a suitable place for her when she was widowed. Later he did buy it and alter it, and they lived in it together from 1797 until her death in 1800.

In June 1792 Haydn left London and went back to Vienna by way of Bonn—where he saw Beethoven—and Frankfort on the Main, where he was present at the coronation of the Emperor Francis II. In December he began to give instruction to Beethoven. Haydn remained in Vienna, teaching and writing, for a year and a half, enjoying the plaudits of his countrymen. But on 19 January 1794 he turned again toward London, accompanied by Johann Elssler, his music copyist and servant, who would remain devotedly in his service for the rest of Haydn's life. His patron Prince Anton Esterházy died three days after Haydn's departure.

Back in London, Haydn settled in at No 1, Bury Street, St James's. His second visit was even more successful than the first. He had agreed with Salomon to compose and conduct six new symphonies, and he did so in a series of concerts from 10 February through 12 May 1794. At the King's Theatre on 20 February 1795, at the end of a performance of Guglielmi's oratorio *Debora and Sisara*, Haydn conducted a "Grand Overture of his composition." From 2 February through 1 June (his last performance in England) he was concerned, with Salomon, Dussek, Dragonetti, J. B. Cramer, Viotti, and others, in a new series, called Opera Concerts, at the King's Theatre. Haydn was given flattering attention by the royal family, several of whose members were accomplished musical amateurs. He was invited often to the Queen's concerts at Buckingham House, and he attended 26 Times at Carlton House, the residence of the Prince of Wales. The King and Queen pressed him to spend the summer of 1795 at Windsor, but he demurred, citing his loyalty to the Esterházy family. He left London on 15 August 1795 and made his way back to Vienna by way of Hamburg, Berlin, and Dresden.

Haydn collected many friends and admirers besides the royal family on his second London visit. He stayed with Sir Charles Rich near Waverly Abbey in Surrey, visited Taplow again with Shield, and accompanied Lord Abingdon

Harvard Theatre Collection

FRANZ JOSEF HAYDN

engraving by Daniell, after G. Dance

to Lord Aston's house at Preston near Hitchin. He visited Rauzzini at Bath with Asher and Cimadoro and wrote a canon or round for four voices as a setting for part of an inscription on the tombstone of Rauzzini's lamented dog "Turk": "Turk was a faithful dog and not a man." He was of course thrown into close contact with all the notables of the London musical scene—the Ashleys, Brigitta Banti, J. B. Cramer and F. Cramer, Clementi, Incledon, Reeve, Mrs Mountain, Bartleman and Parke, Lindley, Giornovichi, and the ballet dancers Noverre, Mlle Del Caro, D'Auberval, and the D'Egvilles. His amiable and whimsical deportment seems to have been attractive to all except the aged and choleric violinist Felice de Giardini, who conceived a violent antipathy and refused to meet him, saying, "I don't want to see the German dog."

On his return to Vienna Haydn was graciously received. Count Harrach escorted him to view a monument which had been erected to him in a Park near Rohrau. Haydn gave a concert, performing three of his London symphonies, at which Beethoven played one of his piano concertos. He resumed his service to the Esterházys but now resided at Esterház only in the summers and autumns. In January 1797 he set Hauschka's poem "Gott erhalte Franz den Kaiser," producing therewith a national anthem. On 12 February, the Emperor's birthday, it was sung in theatres throughout the country. It was Haydn's most popular song and his own favorite work. In 1798 he finished his great oratorio *The Creation*, another result of his London sojourn, based on a compilation of verses from *Paradise Lost* translated by Baron Gottfried Van Swieten. Its popularity was immediate, immense, and lasting, after the publication of the score in 1800.

Haydn was no longer present in London to adjudicate the dispute which broke out between Salomon and John Ashley over its English premiere, which occurred under Ashley's direction at Covent Garden Theatre on 28 March 1800. On 29 March Salomon sent the following notice to the newspapers:

Mr. Salomon having received from Dr. Haydn an early Copy of his New Oratorio called THE CREATION OF THE WORLD, and having been favoured by him exclusively with particular directions on the style and manner in which it must be executed, in order to produce effects required by the Author, begs to acquaint the Nobility and Gentry, that he means to perform it on Monday, the 21st of April next, at the King's Theatre.

On 2 April Ashley published his riposte:

Mr. Salomon having insinuated that he alone is in possession of a correct Score of this celebrated Oratorio, I feel compelled, in justice to myself, to state that the Oratorio was published by subscription at Vienna, and that the printed Copy, from which I had the Parts transcribed, was delivered by Dr. Haydn to a subscriber in Vienna, and brought from thence expressly for me, and on which is the Doctor's initials. The accuracy with which it was performed, and the enthusiasm with which it was received, are, I hope, convincing proofs that no other directions are necessary to 'produce the effect required by the Author.'

Ashley hoped to escape the "imputation of having attempted to impose a spurious production" on the public. Though out-maneuvered, Salomon went ahead to produce his version.

Van Swieten persuaded a reluctant Haydn to go to work on a musical setting of an adaptation of James Thomson's *The Seasons*. It was first performed on 24 April 1801 at Schwarzenberg Palace. But the strain of the composition of this second oratorio weakened Haydn, and his appearance as conductor of *The Seven Words* at the Vienna Assembly Hall on 26 December 1803 was his last in public. The rate of his compositions finally began to decline, though he did revive his memories of Britain by arranging for publication by George Thomson of Edinburgh numbers of Scottish, Welsh, and Irish airs.

The last half dozen years of Haydn's life were spent in infirmity and honor, receiving visits of homage from musicians and music lovers, great and obscure. He lived through the French occupation of Vienna in 1805 and died in the midst of a second occupation, on 31 May 1809. His body reposed in state at the Schottenkirche under a guard of French soldiers on 15 June while Mozart's "Requiem" was performed, and he was buried in Hundsturm churchyard. In 1820 his remains were re-interred at Eisenstadt by order of Prince Esterházy. When the coffin was opened the skull was missing. It had been stolen but was afterwards recovered and given to the Gesellschaft der Musikfreunde in Vienna. In 1954 it was returned to Eisenstadt.

The salient points of Haydn's personality were his humor, his benevolence, his generosity, and a self-discipline which was lightened by a mischievous streak which, he said, was sometimes perfectly beyond control. He was industrious, neat in his dress and habits, fond of children, and helpful to young musicians under his direction. As all his biographers agree, his importance to the development of western music was crucial. The Grove entry finely summarizes his special qualities:

All his works are characterized by lucidity, perfect finish, studied moderation, avoidance of meaningless phrases, firmness of design and richness of development. The subjects principal and secondary, down to the smallest episodes, are thoroughly connected, and the whole conveys the impression of being cast in one mould. We admire his inexhaustible invention as shown in the originality of his themes and melodies; the life and spontaneity of the ideas; the clearness which makes his compositions as interesting to the amateur as to the artist; the childlike cheerfulness and drollery which charm away trouble and care.

Lists of engraved portraits of Haydn will be found in *Katalog der Portrait-Sammlung der k.u.k. General Intendanz der k. k. Hoftheater* (Vienna) and *Ritratti di musicisti ed artisti di teatro conservati nella Raccolta delle Stampe e dei Disegni* (Milan). The following is a list of portraits painted or engraved in England or in English collections.

1. By George Dance, 1794. Pencil drawing. Sold at Christie's on 1 July 1898 in the property of the Rev George Dance, grandson of the artist. Now in the Royal College of Music, the bequest of Barclay Squire. Engraving by William Daniell, 1809.

2. By Thomas Hardy, canvas exhibited at the Royal Academy, 1791. Owned by Arthur Hill in 1932. Now in the Royal College of Music. Engraving by the artist published by J. Bland, 1792. Published as frontispiece to edition of *The Creation*, 1800.

3. By John Hoppner, painted by command of the Prince of Wales, 1791. The canvas is at Buckingham Palace. An engraving by G. S. Facius was published in 1807. An engraving by N. Hanhart (copying Facius's) was published as a plate to *Complete Set of Haydn's Celebrated Eighty-three Quartets*.

4. By Rösler, depicting Haydn as an old man. The canvas once belonged to J. F. Rochlitz, who bequeathed it to Mendelssohn, at whose death it passed to his daughter, and then to her son P. V. M. Benecke. In 1932 the portrait was in the possession of Benecke in England. An engraving by Sichling was published at Leipzig.

5. After Wingfield. Haydn in a red coat, holding a quill pen. Owned by the Royal Society of Musicians.

6. By unknown artist. Canvas with the Faculty of Music, Oxford.

7. Engraved portrait by F. Bartolozzi, after A. M. Ott. Published by H. Humphrey, 1791.

8. Engraved portrait by Landseer, in a group of medallions picturing 25 other musicians and singers of the time; designed by De Loutherbourg, from miniature cameos by J. de Janvry. Published by de Janvry; sold by Colnaghi & Co, 1801.

9. Engraved portrait by Newton, after T. E. Mansfeld. Published by Sewell, 1784. The same portrait was issued in an engraving by Adlard.

10. Engraved portrait by J. Thomson, from a bust taken from life.

11. Engraved portrait by L. Schiavonetti, after Guttenbrun.

12. By unknown engraver, titled "Haydn the Celebrated Musician," no date; in oval, pedestal suspended, bearing sheets of music and instruments. In the Harvard Theatre Collection, but not listed in Hall catalogue.

Haydock, Mr ₍*fl. 1721–1736*₎, *dancer, dancing master.*

John Weaver in his *Anatomical and Mechanical Lectures upon Dancing* in 1721 listed a Mr Haydock as one of London's dancing masters. Weaver's lectures were presented at the Academy in Chancery Lane. For the 16 May 1734 performance of *The Island Princess* at the Lincoln's Inn Fields playhouse tickets were to be had at Haydock's Great Room at that Academy. The work was presented for his benefit, and it is likely that he had a hand in coaching the dancers in the production. He was a beneficiary at Drury Lane on 22 May 1735, and the Mr "Haddock" who received a benefit at Covent Garden Theatre on 10 May 1736 was doubtless he.

Hayes. *See also* HAY *and* HAYS.

Hayes, Mr ₍*fl. 1752–1777*₎, *pit office keeper.*

A person, or persons, by the name of Hayes, served as pit office keeper at Drury Lane Theatre from 1752–53 through 1776–77 and perhaps beyond. On 5 May 1753, Hayes shared gross benefit receipts of £160 with Scrase and Mozeen. He also shared tickets on 2 May 1757, 27 April 1758, 15 May 1759, 21 April 1760, and 21 April 1762. In 1764–65, Hayes was earning 15*s.* per week; he was still being paid at that rate in 1776–77.

Hayes, Mr ₍*fl. 1757*₎, *violinist.*

According to van der Straeten (*History of the Violin*), a Mr Hayes appeared in 1757 as a violin virtuoso in London.

Hayes, Miss ₍*fl. 1739–1740*₎, *dancer.*
See HAYS, MR ₍*fl. 1736–1740*₎.

Hayes, ₍F.?₎ ₍*fl. 1758–1800?*₎, *actor.*

An actor named Hayes was a member of the Smock Alley Theatre company, Dublin, in 1758–59. When he made his debut there on 19 December 1758, he was announced as acting for the first time in Ireland, so perhaps he was the Mr F. Hayes who had performed at Edinburgh earlier that year. Hayes had a benefit at Smock Alley on 14 May 1759. In 1759–60 he moved to the Crow Street Theatre, where he remained through 1761–62.

On 18 October 1762, Hayes made his first appearance at Covent Garden Theatre, as Mr Honeycomb in *Polly Honeycomb*. Since it was a "part of little consequence," the critic in the *Theatrical Review* (1763) declined to offer his opinion of Hayes at that time. A week later, on 25 October, Hayes played Master Matthew in *Every Man in his Humour*, a role he repeated regularly throughout the season. His other roles included the Welsh Collier in *The Recruiting Officer*, Coupler in *The Relapse*, and the Mad Welshman in *The Pilgrim*.

In the summer of 1763, Hayes was engaged by Foote at the Haymarket Theatre and in his first appearance there "created" the role of Sir Jacob Jollup in the manager's comedy *The Mayor of Garratt* at its premiere on 20 June. He also acted the King of Brentford in *The Rehearsal* on 1 and 11 August.

In 1763–64 Hayes returned to Covent Garden and his line of very modest roles which now included the Third Bravo in *The Inconstant*, Feeble in *The Upholsterer*, Sir Hugh in *The Merry Wives of Windsor*, Charino in *Love Makes a Man* (for a benefit he shared with Tindal on 16 May 1764), and unspecified roles in *The Apprentice* and *The Absent Man*. Back with Foote at the Haymarket in the summer of 1764 he acted again in *The Mayor of Garratt*, Puff in *The Patron*, and a role in *The Orators*. At Covent Garden in 1764–65, his last season there, he added Mordecai in *Love à-la-Mode* to his repertoire.

After leaving Covent Garden in May 1765, Hayes became an itinerant actor. A Mr Hayes was in London ten years later for a performance as a Servant in *Love in a Village* at the Haymarket on 2 February 1775, for the benefit of the widowed Covent Garden actress Mrs Wood-

man and her five children. Perhaps this Mr
Hayes was the earlier actor. A Mr Hayes also
played Young Apeall in *The Humours of Oxford*
and Lord Duke in *High Life below Stairs* at the
Haymarket on 28 March 1780 and Roebuck
in *Love in a Bottle* at the same theatre on 26
March 1781. In 1781–82, Mr and Mrs Hayes,
identified as from the Haymarket Theatre,
acted with Gosli's company at Derby. A Mr
Hayes, perhaps not our subject, played at the
Town Hall in Abergavenny in July 1793 and
at Bury in 1800.

It was believed that the Mr Hayes who was
the original Sir Jacob Jollup at the Haymarket
in June 1763 was the person shown with
Samuel Foote (as Major Sturgeon) in Zoffany's
painting of a scene from *The Mayor of Garratt*.
But in the catalogue of the "Georgian Playhouse" exhibition at the Hayward Gallery in
1975 the painting is said to depict performances at Drury Lane Theatre between 30 November and 7 December 1763, when Robert
Baddeley played Sir Jacob Jollup.

Hayes, Mrs [F?] [fl. 1758–1789?], actress.

A Mrs Hayes acted Madge in *The Gentle
Shepherd* at the New Concert Hall in Edinburgh in April and May 1758. No doubt she
was the wife of F. Hayes, also an actor in
Edinburgh at that time. Although there is no
record of her having acted at London, when
she and her husband were playing with Gosli's
company at Derby in 1781–82, they were
identified as from the Haymarket Theatre. A
Mrs Hayes acted in *The Triumph of Liberty* at
Gloucester on 21 October 1789; she may have
been our subject.

Hayes, Philip 1738–1797, organist, composer, singer.

Born at Oxford in April 1738 the son of the
musician William Hayes (1706–1777) by his
wife Ann (d. 1786), Philip Hayes was educated in music by his father. After serving as
a chorister in the Chapel Royal under Bernard
Gates, Philip matriculated on 3 May 1763 at
Magdalen College, Oxford, where he took his
Bachelor of Music degree on 18 May of that
year. Until 1765 he was organist to Christ
Church Cathedral. He became a Gentleman of
the Chapel Royal on 30 November 1767 and
a member of the Royal Society of Musicians on

Faculty of Music, Oxford

PHILIP HAYES
by Cooper

1 January 1769. In 1776 he was appointed
organist of New College, Oxford, and upon
his father's death in 1777 Hayes succeeded him
as organist of Magdalen College and Professor
of Music. On 6 November 1777 he was created
Doctor of Music. He succeeded Thomas Norris
as organist of St John's College in 1790.

Hayes was a member of the Catch Club
founded in London in 1761 "for the encouragement of the composition and performance
of canons, catches and glees." Many of his
songs and catches, sung by leading London
performers, are listed in the *Catalogue of Printed
Music in the British Museum*. He wrote the music for George Graham's *Telemachus*, a masque
advertised for performance at Hickford's Room
for 14 February 1765, but it seems never to
have been given. Editions were published at
London in 1763 and 1765, Dublin 1763, and
Glasgow 1767. The manuscript of the full
score, lacking the last several pages, is at Oxford. His song "The Highland Laddie" was
sung by Johnstone at the end of Act I of *Robin
Hood* at Covent Garden Theatre on 28 April
1786. He also wrote accompaniments to "Fairest Isle" from Purcell's *King Arthur* and a setting of Shakespeare's "What shall he have that
killed the deer" (1780).

During his 20 years as Professor of Music, Hayes, it was said, never gave a professional lecture and treated his posts as organist of three colleges with neglect. He did, however, raise funds to renovate the academic rooms of the Music School, which had deteriorated in the middle of the century, making the premises sufficiently convenient and elegant for concerts to be revived there. Hayes also was responsible for increasing the collection of portraits, at least 13 of which he contributed to the school.

Hayes received £500 for conducting the "Actus Publicus" concerts at Oxford in July 1791. He was a conductor of the annual performances by the New Musical Fund, the first of which was held on 12 April 1787. Having gone to London in March 1797 to preside at such a festival, he was stricken on the morning of the nineteenth of that month and died within several hours. He was buried in St Paul's Cathedral on 21 March, attended by the choirs of St Paul's and Westminster Abbey singing Dr Green's funeral anthem "Lord, let me know my end."

On 26 May 1797 administration of his estate, valued at £1000, was granted to his "natural brother," the Rev Thomas Hayes, and his sister Sarah Viner, wife of the Rev Samuel Viner. Philip Hayes had died a bachelor. His brother William Hayes had died in 1790.

In addition to many songs, Hayes composed *Six Concertos, with Accompaniments for Organ, Harpsichord, or Pianoforte, to which is added a Harpsichord Sonata* (London, 1769); *Eight Anthems* (Oxford, 1780); *Prophecy, an Oratorio*, performed at the Oxford Commemoration in 1781; *An Ode performed in the Music School, Michaelmas Term, Cambridge, 1785*; and an *Ode for St Cecilia's Day*. He was the editor of *Harmonia Wiccamica*, a collection of music sung at meetings of Wykehamists (alumni of Winchester School), published in London, 1780; of the manuscript *Memoirs of Prince William Henry, Duke of Gloucester, from his birth July 24th, 1689, to October 1697, from an original Tract, written by Jenkin Le Lewis . . .* ; and of his father William Hayes's *Cathedral Music in Score* (1795).

Philip Hayes was reputed to have been the largest man in England, equal in weight to Bright, the celebrated miller of Malden, Essex. According to Rees's *Cyclopaedia*, Hayes had a "very limited genius for composition"

but an "unlimited vanity, envy, and spleen," with a power "to render all other musicians uncomfortable."

A portrait by John Cooper of Philip Hayes as a young man hangs in the common room of the Faculty of Music, Oxford. A portrait by Joshua Reynolds (29½" × 24½"), earlier in the collection of J. C. Robinson, was bought by Leggatt's in the Princess Royal's sale at Christie's on 18 July 1924 (Lot 72). Presumably that portrait was the same Reynolds which was sold at Parke-Bernet on 21 May 1952; its present location is unknown to us, but in the British Museum is a photograph of it, showing Hayes full face, in doctor's robes. A portrait by an unknown artist of Hayes in gown and bands, with his back to an organ, about to conduct, is mentioned by J. H. Mee in *The Oldest Music Room in Europe*. A portrait by James Roberts drawn in pastel is at St. John's College, Oxford.

Hayes, Richard [*fl.* 1687–1717], painter.

Richard Hayes helped paint the pageants for the Lord Mayors' Shows from 1687 to 1708, in collaboration with George Holmes at first and then by himself. Hayes became Master of the Painter-Stainers in 1709 and Beadle in 1717.

Hayes, William 1706–1777, composer, organist, conductor, singer.

William Hayes, progenitor of a family of English musical scholars and composers, was baptized at St John's Church, Gloucester, on 27 January 1706 (and thus he was not born at Hanbury in Worcestershire late in 1706 as stated in *The Dictionary of National Biography*). While a chorister at Gloucester Cathedral he was taken under the patronage of Mrs Viney, who taught him the harpsichord and subsequently placed him under articles to William Hine, the cathedral's organist. On the expiration of his apprenticeship in 1729 Hayes was appointed organist of St Mary's Church, Shrewsbury. In 1731 he became organist of the Worcester Cathedral, a position he resigned in 1734 to assume the posts of organist and master of the children choristers at Magdalen College, Oxford. Also in 1734 he conducted the Worcester Festival. On 8 July 1735 he received

Faculty of Music, Oxford

WILLIAM HAYES
by Cornish

the degree of Bachelor of Music, *pro forma*, at Oxford.

Hayes was one of the original members of the Royal Society of Music upon its establishment in 1739. He succeeded Richard Goodson as Professor of Music at Oxford on 14 January 1742. On the occasion of the opening of the Radcliffe Library on 14 April 1749 Hayes directed the performance and was made Doctor of Music. In 1754 he was the deputy steward and in 1763 the conductor of the Three Choirs meeting at Gloucester. A member of the Catch Club, he won three prizes in their first competition in 1763 with his canons "Alleluja!" and "Misere Nobis" and a glee "Melting airs soft joys inspire."

In *English Theatre Music in the Eighteenth Century* (1973), Roger Fiske lists a full-score manuscript dating about 1747 (now at Oxford) by Hayes for Lord Lansdowne's *Peleus and Thetis*. That opera was sung at the Swan Tavern in London on 29 April 1747, but according to the *General Advertiser* of that date it had been set to music by William Boyce (1710–1779). On 8 May 1760 Hayes's "Ode to Echo" was sung by Miss Young at Drury Lane Theatre.

Hayes was eminent in part-writing for the voice, and many of his glees were great favorites. His canon "Let's drink and sing together" was praised by Dr Burney as the "most pleasant" composition in that form. His published compositions included a set of *English Ballads* (printed at Shrewsbury), *Twelve Arietts or Ballads and Two Cantatas* (Oxford, 1735); *Six Cantatas* (London, 1740?); *Vocal and Instrumental Music, containing* (1) *The Overture and Songs in the Masque of Circe*; (2) *a Sonata or Trio, and Ballads, Airs, and Cantatas*; (3) *An Ode, being part of an Exercise performed for a Batchelor's Degree in Music* (London, 1742); *Catches, Glees, and Canons* (London, 1757, with a second set in 1765); *Instrumental Accompaniments to the Old Hundreth Psalm for the Sons of the Clergy* (London, 1770); *Sixteen Psalms from Merrick's Version* (London, 1775); *Collins's Ode on the Passions* (1775?); and *Cathedral Music in Score* (published by his son Philip Hayes in 1795). He was also the author of *Remarks on Mr. Avison's Essay on Musical Expression* (1753), a defense of Handel against Avison's attack. Many of his ecclesiastical compositions for the different colleges were never printed.

William Hayes died at Oxford on 27 July 1777, at the age of 69, and was buried in the churchyard of St Peter in the East in that city. In his will drawn on 17 February 1776 William Hayes left two-thirds share of his house to his widow Ann Hayes (the other third being entitled to a Mr Smith of Carfax) and all his plate, china, linen, and furniture in trust to his son Philip Hayes and son-in-law Daniel Prince for the use of his wife until her death, whereupon all the effects and property were to be sold and the proceeds to be divided equally among his two daughters, Ann Prince and Sarah Viner, and his grandson Thomas Corne. To his son Philip he gave all his music books. The will was proved at Oxford by his widow on 6 August 1777.

Ann Hayes, his widow, died on 14 January 1786, aged 83. Their eldest son, Thomas Hayes, a cleric who was not mentioned in his father's will, and the daughter Sarah (who married the Rev Samuel Viner) were alive in 1797 when administration of their brother Philip's estate was granted to them. The second son, Philip Hayes (1738–1797), is noticed separately on these pages. The third son, William Hayes (1741–1790), a minor canon, is noticed in *The Dictionary of National Biography*. Another daughter Ann, mentioned in the will, married Daniel Prince. Yet another daughter, Christian name unknown and probably deceased by the time William Hayes drew his will, married the Rev Mr Corne, Rector of Tixal in Staffordshire: their daughter, Hayes's granddaughter, died in January 1779 at the age of 13.

The inscription on William Hayes's family tombstone informs us that his father, W. Hayes, died in November 1758 at the age of 73 and that five of William's children who died in infancy and two grandchildren were also buried there.

A painting of William Hayes by J. Cornish hangs in the rooms of the Faculty of Music, Oxford. An engraving by T. Park of Cornish's portrait was published in 1787; an engraving by J. K. Sherwin, after Cornish, was published in the title to Hayes's setting of Collins's *The Passions, an Ode*. In the British Museum is a silhouette profile of Hayes's head, done by an unknown engraver. A small copy of the Cornish portrait made by Smith is at Magdalen College. A bust of Hayes, done at the request of Edward, Lord Leigh, High Steward of the University from 1767 to 1786, is also with the Faculty of Music.

Hayle. *See* HAILES.

Hayles. *See* HAILES and HALES.

Haym, Nicola Francesco   *c.* *1679–1729, violoncellist, bass violist, librettist, composer, impresario.*

Nicola Francesco Haym was born in Rome about 1679, but he was of German extraction and spent most of his musical career in England. He began composing before he left Rome about the turn of the century, his earliest known works being a cantata and an oratorio written in 1699. He was in England in the service of the second Duke of Bedford by 1701 or 1702, serving as a violoncellist and composer and, probably, living in Southampton House along with his fellow musician Nicola Cosimi. Haym's annual salary from the Duke was £100, but his expenses were also paid. Haym sometimes accompanied Bedford on trips out of London, and on at least one occasion, in 1704–5, Haym was sent to Rome to purchase music for the Duke's library.

Though Haym continued in the service of Bedford until the Duke died in 1711, he was permitted to engage in activities outside the Duke's household. In September 1705, for instance, his edition of Corelli's *Works* was advertised in the *Post Man*; each of the master's compositions was "carefully corrected by the Ingenious Signior Nicolini Haiam, who is very well acquainted with the Author and his Works." In the 25–27 September issue of the same periodical Haym advised all "Lovers of Musick" that

Whereas in the last Post-Man there was an Advertisement publish'd by Mr. John Walsh, that I Nicolini Haym, have corrected his Edition of Corelli's Works: I do hereby give notice for my own credit, that I did not correct the same directly nor indirectly. I do acknowledge to have revised and corrected the Amsterdam Edition by Stephen Roger, which will be speedily published, and will excel in Beauty and Exactnes any Edition of Corelli's Works hitherto printed. . . .

Walsh offered a rebuttal immediately, saying that his edition was "3 months under the said Nicolini Haym's Correction." The reason for the quibbling is not clear, but the implication seems to be that Haym had had a hand in correcting two different editions of Corelli's *Works* and preferred to puff the one from which he would receive the most income.

In addition to his editorial work Haym busied himself as an impresario. He and the violinist Charles Dieupart joined to promote Thomas Clayton's opera *Arsinoe*, which was first performed on 16 January 1705 at Drury Lane. It was London's introduction to opera in the Italian manner and the beginning of a long association for Haym with opera productions.

Haym set to work on an Italian opera of his own, *Camilla*. In connection with it he signed articles (preserved in the Public Record Office) with the Drury Lane manager Christopher Rich on 14 January 1706:

Articles of Agreement Indented made & agreed upon the ffoutheenth [*sic*] day of January Anno-Dñi 1705 [i.e. 1705/6] By & Between Nicolas Hyam gent on the one part and Christopher Rich Esqr one of the Patentees of the Theatres in Covent Garden & Dorset Garden London on the other part as followeth ffirst Whereas the said Nicolas Hyam hath a fair score of the Vocall and Instrumentall Musick with yᵉ words in Italian written under the Notes being the Opera called Camilla which words Mͬ Hyam hath att his' owne charge procured a

Gentleman to Translate into English prose and M.ʳ Rich hath att his owne charge procured one M.ʳ Northman to putt the said prose into English Verse as suitable to the Notes of the Score of yᵉ Italian Musick as he can, and M.ʳ Haym is writing out a new Score & incerting M.ʳ Northmans words under the Same with some necessary additions alterations and abbreviations as he in his Iudgement thinks best which he promises to finish with all possible Speed & to advise M.ʳ Rich in casting the parts to yᵉ Singers and to teach up the same parts and Musick and to give his best dilligence and assistance therein as a Master Composer in the practices of the Vocall and Instrumentall musick & to make proper Tunes for the Dances in Such Opera and att his owne Charge to provide two fair Scores of such Opera with yᵉ English words and Notes . . . Now the said Nicolas Hyam in Consideration of one hundred pounds . . . doth bargaine and Sell unto yᵉ Said Christopher Rich [the Italian and two English scores] and M.ʳ Hyam is not publickly to Performe any parts of the Musick of the said Opera of Camilla as Sett in Italian or as now new alter'd by him or as yᵉ same shall be Alter'd by M.ʳ Motteux or any other person [without Rich's permission].

Haym also agreed to play the bass viol at performances of *Camilla*. At the time, Haym was the singing teacher to Joanna Maria Lindelheim, called "The Baroness," and Rich agreed to allow Haym to accompany his student in performances at the rival Queen's Theatre.

On 1 March 1706 Haym made an oral agreement with the Queen's Theatre management that the Baroness should be paid 100 guineas for 10 performances there, so Haym served his pupil not only as an accompanist and teacher but as her agent. He also played cello in the band at the Queen's, but during the early months of 1706, as the bills indicate, he was performing at Drury Lane as well. At the latter house on 3 April, in fact, a new "solo composed by Haym" was played "by him and Gasperini" the violinist.

On 30 March 1706 *Camilla* was presented at Drury Lane, the libretto having been translated by the impresario Owen Swiney (and then put into verse by Northman, presumably) and the music having been adapted by Haym from Bononcini. Mrs Tofts sang the title role, but she was replaced in April, as the following letter of 21 April from Haym (at his lodgings in Bow Street) to Vice Chamberlain Coke proves:

Sir this is to let you know that Signora Margherita [de l'Épine? Gallia?] desires the favour you would pardon her for tomorrow morning she cannot come to you because she is obliged to learn the part of Camilla by heart for Tuesday next [23 April]— I desire further directions from you to know whether I shall bring Mr Pepuch along with me, & if it is necessary for me to find any violins, or any voice, & I assure you I shall ever be ready to obey your commands. . . .

Haym, it appears, was the Signora's agent, and perhaps he also served as an agent for the composer Pepusch. *The London Stage* does not list the cast change in *Camilla* that is indicated in Haym's letter.

A similar letter from Haym to Coke dated 18 April (1706?) informed the Vice Chamberlain that the singer Ramondon and his boy could not meet with Coke until after the play performance (*The Island Princess* was given that date at Drury Lane, and though *The London Stage* lists no performers, Ramondon and his boy must have appeared). Haym went on to suggest to Coke that if that was too late, the Baroness should begin (rehearsing before Coke?) and Haym would arrive at nine in the evening. Another note from Haym dating about May 1706 indicated that Haym spent much of his time helping to locate and recommend performers to Coke. On 6 May Haym told Coke he had completed setting the *Ode of Discord* to music and had taught it to the singer Leveridge; Haym also mentioned that the violin parts were especially difficult and that Gasparini and Corbett should be chosen to play them.

Records of Haym's busyness between the summer of 1706 and the beginning of 1708 have not been found, and perhaps he was out of London for a time. In 1708 he was again performing at the Queen's Theatre, at a daily fee of £1 5s.—the highest scale for the musicians and more than many of the singers and dancers received. Haym entered into an agreement with Christopher Rich in connection with the opera *Pirro e Demetrio* in 1708. The work was out of Scarlatti, but Haym wrote an overture, adapted the original, and added 18 numbers of his own. For that opera plus a projected alteration of *Thomyris* Rich was to pay Haym £300. Haym also struck a bargain for his students. Rich agreed to pay the Baroness £300 for singing 30 times (and Haym was to receive a percentage of her salary); Rich was to pay the travel expenses from and back to Italy plus an unspecified salary for Signor Cassanino; and Rich was to pay Haym two guineas every time the musician played at the Queen's Theatre (after 10 January 1708 Drury Lane and the Queen's were under joint control). Haym also declared to Rich that he wished to be the sole authority over the musicians. At the time he was also master of the Duke of Bedford's chamber music, received his pay from Bedford, and earned £70 annually at the opera house. By 1710 Haym's opera daily salary was up to £1 15*s*.

Pirro e Demetrio was first presented on 14 December 1708 at the Queen's Theatre; Haym wrote the preface to the printed edition of *Etearco*, which was performed on 10 January 1711; *Dorinda*, for which he arranged the music, was given on 10 December 1712; and *Creso*, according to the *Opera Register* at the British Library, was "sett on ye Stage by Mr. Haym" on 27 January 1714. The *Register* also tells us that for the production of *Lucio Vero* at the King's (previously the Queen's) on 26 February 1715 "ye Musick [was] managed by Nic° Haym."

By that time Haym was no longer in the Bedford service and had become involved in concert promotion. With his colleagues Clayton and Dieupart, Haym sponsored a series of concerts at York Buildings which featured English poems with musical accompaniments. The first one took place on 24 May 1711, before the opera season was quite over and when one would think Haym should have been busy enough already. The quality of the music at the concerts left much to be desired, but the sponsors persisted. On 26 December 1711 they wrote to the *Spectator* (or perhaps Steele, one of their supporters, wrote for them):

Musick . . . must always have some Passion or Sentiment to express, or else Violins, Voices, or any other Organs of Sound, afford an Entertainment very little above the Rattles of Children. It was from this Opinion of the Matter, that when Mr. *Clayton* had finished his studies in Italy, and brought over the Opera of *Arsinoe*, that Mr. *Haym* and Mr. *Dieupart*, who had the Honour to be well known and received among the Nobility and Gentry, were zealously inclined to assist, by their So-

licitations, in introducing so elegant an Entertainment as the *Italian* Musick grafted upon *English* Poetry. For this End Mr. *Dieupart* and Mr. *Haym*, according to their several Opportunities, promoted the Introduction of *Arsinoe*, and did it to the best Advantage so great a Novelty would allow. It is not proper to trouble you with Particulars of the just Complaints we all of us have to make; but so it is, that without Regard to our obliging Pains, we are all equally set aside in the present Opera. Our Application therefore to you is only to insert this Letter in your Papers that the Town may know we have all Three joined together to make Entertainments of Musick for the future at Mr. *Clayton*'s House in *York-Buildings*. . . . We aim at establishing some settled Notion of what is Musick, at recovering from Neglect and Want very many Families who depend upon it, at making all Foreigners who pretend to succeed in *England* to learn the Language of it as we ourselves have done, and not to be so insolent as to expect a whole Nation, a refined and learned Nation, should submit to learn them.

Apparently the extracurricular activity of the three musicians had brought about their discharge from the Queen's Theatre, at least temporarily.

The venture encountered opposition, for just as Italian opera was catching on in England, Haym and his cohorts seemed bent on stopping it. On 18 January 1712 the three wrote a letter (or, again, Steele may have written) to the *Spectator*, trying to explain their position:

It is industriously insinuated that Our Intention is to destroy Operas in General; but we beg you to insert this plain Explanation of our selves in your Paper. Our Purpose is only to improve our Circumstances, by improving the Art which we profess. We see it utterly destroyed at present; and as we were the Persons who introduced Operas, we think it a groundless Imputation that we should set up against the Opera it self. What we pretend to assert is, That the Songs of different Authors injudiciously put together and a foreign Tone and Manner which are expected in every Thing now performed amongst us, has put Musick it self to a stand; insomuch that the Ears of the People cannot now be entertained with any Thing but what has an impertinent Gayety, without any just Spirit; or a Languishment of Notes, without any Passion, or common Sense. We hope those Persons of Sense and Quality who have done us the Honour to subscribe will not be ashamed of their Patronage towards us, and not receive Impressions that patronising us is being for or against the Opera, but truly promoting their own Diversions in a more just and elegant Manner than has been hitherto performed.

Then the trio added a postscript: *"There will be no Performances in* York-Buildings, *until after that of the Subscription* [i.e., after the opera season]." Haym, Clayton, and Dieupart sounded like losers, and they were; the venture failed. But Haym ran his own series of four concerts at Hickford's Music Room in April and May of 1713, showing off the talents of the Baroness and another, unnamed, scholar of his. And he was not dropped completely by the opera house; in 1716–17 he seems to have worked as a copyist and translator, and it is likely he continued playing 'cello in the band. (The Nicolini Haym who was a second violinist and waiting page at Cannons about 1717–1720, earning £7 10*s.* per quarter, was surely not our subject but was perhaps his son.)

From 1713 to 1728 Haym worked with Handel as a librettist. He seems not to have written much that was original, but his alterations and adaptations evidently pleased Handel. Their first collaboration was apparently on *Teseo*, which was given its premiere on 10 January 1713. Then, after a gap of several years, they renewed their partnership and brought out a steady stream of works: *Radamisto* (1720), *Ottone* and *Flavio* (1723), *Giulio Cesare* and *Tamerlano* (1724), *Rodelinda* (1725), *Admeto* (1727), and *Siroe* and *Tolomeo* (1728). Haym also served other composers in a similar capacity, providing texts for such works as *Cajo Marzio Coriolano* (1723), *Vespasiano* (1724), *Elisa* (1726), and *Astianatte* (1727).

In 1722 Haym succeeded Rolli as the Italian Secretary and librettist of the Royal Academy of Music, which for many years provided London with Italian operas. Reference was made to his post in the *Session of Musicians* in May 1724. In the poem, Apollo holds a trial to see who is the best musician in England (Handel wins, of course).

> *The God turn'd round and found, just seated by him,*
> *His old Acquaintance, Nicolino H[a]yam;*
> *With a kind Smile he whisper'd in his Ear,*
> *But what—no living Creature then could hear;*
> *Since that we're told, the God of's special Grace*
> *Confirm'd him in his Secretary's Place.*

Giuseppe Riva, writing from Hanover on 7 September 1725 to Ludovico Muratori, was not so complimentary to Haym:

The operas performed in England, fine though they are as regards the music and the voices, are so much hackwork as regards the verses. Our friend Rolli, who was commissioned to compose them when the Royal Academy was first formed [in 1720], wrote really good operas, but having become embroiled with the Directors, the latter took into their service one Haym, a Roman and a violoncellist, who is a complete idiot as far as Letters are concerned. Boldly passing from the orchestra to the heights of Parnassus, he has, for the last three years, been adapting—or rather making worse—the old librettos which are already bad enough in their original form.

After 1727 Haym's activities decreased, and he was rarely mentioned in advertisements. On 11 August 1729 Nicola Haym died in London, and on 9 March 1730 his considerable library was sold at J. Cook's auction room in Poland Street. He was not forgotten in London, however; on 21 March 1735, for example, the *Daily Advertiser*, puffing a benefit for a musician named Davis, noted that Davis had been trained by Haym. Perhaps it was as a teacher that Haym made his most important contribution.

Haym turned out some oboe and flute sonatas, an anthem, and some songs. He also left behind his opera "librettos," two books on medals, two tragedies, and editions of Tasso and Maffei. He planned a history of music, to be written in Italian, but he did not publish it. Haym was also an amateur artist and drew pictures of Tallis and Byrd, copied from unknown originals.

Haym, Nicolino [*fl.* 1717–1720], *violinist.*

"Nicolino Hayme" was a second violinist and waiting page at Cannons under the Duke of Chandos. He was probably there from 1717 to 1720. He earned £7 10*s.* per quarter. The musician was surely not Nicola Haym, who by that period could have commanded a much higher fee and who was, in any case, a violoncellist in his thirties. This younger musician may well have been his son.

Hayman, Mr [*fl.* 1743–1757?], *actor.*

Announced as a gentleman making his first appearance on any stage, a Mr Hayman acted

Macheath in *The Beggar's Opera* at Lincoln's Inn Fields Theatre on 14 February 1743. His surname had been given in an advertisement in the *London Daily Post* on 11 February. Five weeks later, on 21 March, now announced as the gentleman who had performed Macheath, he played Sir John Loverule in *The Devil to Pay* at the same theatre. The bills identified him as Hayman when he acted Basset in *The Provok'd Husband* and Sir John again, for his benefit on 5 April.

Hayman was found in supporting roles during the following four seasons at Covent Garden Theatre, where he made his debut as Sir John on 5 October 1743. There in 1743–44 he acted Leander in *The Mock Doctor*, Westmoreland in *1 Henry IV*, a Priest in *Hamlet*, Poins in *2 Henry IV*, Wormwood in *The Virgin Unmask'd*, and Shamwell in *The Squire of Alsatia*, the last-mentioned on 2 May 1744 for a benefit he shared with Stede and Neale. In 1744–45 he supplemented his repertoire with Orchan in *Don Sebastian*, Sylvius in *As You Like It*, Mirvan in *Tamerlane*, Bagshot in *The Stratagem*, Verdugo in *The Pilgrim*, Hazereth in *Miriamne*, a number of parts in *The What D'Ye Call It*, Diphilus in *Timon of Athens*, Lorenzo in *The Merchant of Venice*, Friendly in *Flora*, and the Second Gentleman in *The Maid's Tragedy*. In 1745–46 he added Ramilie in *The Miser*, Scrip in *Phebe*, Balthazar in *The Merchant of Venice*, Balthazar in *Much Ado about Nothing*, Trippet in *The Lying Valet*, a French Gentleman in *Cymbeline*, and the Dauphin in *Henry V*. On 5 February 1746 he appeared for the first time on the Goodman's Fields stage, as Macheath for the benefit of Mrs Hooper, who played Polly.

In 1746–47 Hayman was paid 10s. per week, but his name was removed from the Covent Garden pay list on 25 April 1747 for the remainder of the season. The Mrs Hayman who shared in benefit tickets at Covent Garden on 22 May 1747 was probably his wife.

Hayman seems to have made no other appearances in London, but probably he was the "Mr Heyman" who acted as a member of Digges's company at the New Concert Hall in Edinburgh between 1755 and 1757. There he played Norval in the premiere of Home's *Douglas* on 14 December 1756 and enjoyed more substantial roles than had been his lot at London, including among numerous others Bel-

lamy in *The Suspicious Husband*, Horatio in *The Fair Penitent*, Horatio in *Hamlet*, Prospero in *The Tempest*, Truman in *The London Merchant*, Aimwell in *The Beaux' Stratagem*, Tattle in *Love for Love*, and Sealand in *The Conscious Lovers*.

We find no relationship between our subject and the landscape artist and scene painter Francis Hayman (1708–1776), who by the 1740s had a good acquaintance with the theatrical world and had in earlier years painted scenery for Henry Giffard at Lincoln's Inn Fields Theatre.

Hayman, Mr [*fl. 1754*]. *See* PACKER, JOHN HAYMAN.

Hayman, Mrs [*fl. 1747*], *actress? house servant?*

A Mrs Hayman received £3 18s. as her share of benefit tickets at Covent Garden Theatre on 22 May 1747. Her function at the theatre is unknown, but she was probably the wife of the Covent Garden actor Mr Hayman (fl. 1743–1757?).

Hayman, Francis 1708–1776, *scene painter, painter.*

Born at Exeter in 1708 of "a respectable family," Francis Hayman was apprenticed by 1718 to Robert Browne, the Exeter portrait painter. After his training, Hayman was employed by Henry Giffard on the decorations of the new Goodman's Fields Theatre which was opened on 2 October 1732. Hayman's work on the ceiling over the pit was described in the *Daily Advertiser* on 4 October: "On a large Oval over the Pit is represented the Figure of his Majesty, attended by Peace, Liberty, and Justice, trampling Tyranny and Oppression under his Feet; round it are the Heads of Shakespear, Dryden, Congreve, and Betterton. . . ." On the sounding board over the stage was a "handsome Piece of Painting of Apollo and the Nine Muses" done by Hayman and William Oram. For a production of *Britannia, or the Royal Lovers* at Goodman's Fields on 11 February 1734, in celebration of the wedding of Princess Anne and the Prince of Orange, Hayman again adorned the house with portraits of the Royal Family and the Prince of Orange; the advertisement also credited him with a new ceiling piece of Apollo and the Muses, but that painting is believed to have been done by Oram.

By permission of the Trustees of the British Museum

FRANCIS HAYMAN

engraving by Every, after Reynolds

Probably Hayman also painted scenery at Goodman's Fields. The first notice of his work in that line, however, was at Drury Lane, where he was employed by Fleetwood to provide new scenes for *The Fall of Phaeton*, a masque invented by Pritchard, with music by Thomas Arne, which had its first performance on 28 February 1736. The details of Hayman's scene painting activities at Drury Lane during the late 1730s and early 1740s are unknown, but they were extensive enough to have him characterized in a footnote to *An Essay on the theatres; or, the art of acting* (1745) as "a young Gentleman, a Painter, very excellent in his Art, whose Scenes at Drury-lane Theatre have always met with greatest approbation." The main text of the *Essay* offered an appreciation of his art:

> *Hayman by Scenes our Senses can controul,*
> *And with creative* Power *charm the Soul;*
> *His easy Pencil flows with just Command,*
> *And Nature starts obedient to his Hand:*
> *We hear the Tinkling Rill, we view the Trees*
> *Cast dusky Shades, and wave the gentle Breeze:*

> *Here shoots through leafy Bow'rs a sunny Ray,*
> *That gilds the Grove, and emulates the Day:*
> *There Mountain Tops look glad; there Vallies sing,*
> *And through the Landscape blooms eternal Spring.*

Sometime in 1741 Lord Radnor, for whom Hayman had done decorative painting at Twickenham, wrote to Dr Macro about Hayman: "I really think him a genius, and if he had not fooled away many years at the beginning of life in painting Harlequins, trapdoors, etc. he would certainly by this time be the greatest man of his age, as he is now of his country." By the mid 1740s Hayman abandoned scene painting to concentrate on the numerous commissions which were coming his way.

Among these were decorations for the boxes at Bermondsey Spa and for Jonathan Tyers' house at Denbies in Essex. He also did portraits of the Tyers family. The association with Tyers, who became proprietor of Vauxhall Gardens, led to Hayman's perhaps best known works, the series of pictures which ornamented the alcoves of the Prince's Pavilion at Vauxhall. Hayman's paintings for Vauxhall often have been attributed to Hogarth, with whom he shared the project. The paintings were sold at low prices when the pleasure garden was closed in 1841. Several were placed in Lowther Castle and then were sold in 1947, two finding their way to the Victoria and Albert Museum. Three of the Vauxhall paintings by Hayman and two by Hogarth are in the possession of Major A. S. C. Browne at Alnick, Northumberland. Four of Hayman's Vauxhall paintings were of Shakespearean subjects, depicting scenes from *King Lear*, *Hamlet*, *Henry V*, and *The Tempest*. Apparently only the Hamlet painting, of the play scene, survives, but its location is unknown to us; it was offered at an anonymous sale at Robinson & Fisher's on 29 May 1924 (lot 66); a photograph appeared in the sales catalogue and is reproduced in William Merchant's *Shakespeare and the Artist* (plate 8a). A smaller painting by Hayman of the same scene—but one which includes more characters and was probably a study for the Vauxhall one—is in the Folger Shakespeare Library. Hayman also designed illustrations for Thomas Hanmer's edition of Shakespeare's plays (1744–1746), which were engraved by Gravelot. The drawings for the plates to the Hanmer edition and the manuscript agreement between Hayman and the editor are in the Folger Shakespeare Library. Hayman also designed illustrations for the Jennens edition of *Shakespeare* (1771–1774), engraved by Ravenet; from Garrick, Hayman received advice about the composition of the scenes for *King Lear* and *Othello*. A painting by Hayman of the wrestling scene in *As You Like It* is in the Tate Gallery.

Hayman also designed illustrations for Tonson's edition of *The Works of William Congreve* (1753); Smollett's edition of *Don Quixote* (1755), the original drawings of which are in the British Museum print room; Newton's edition of Milton's *Paradise Lost* (1749–1752); Moore's *Fables for the Female Sex* (1744); and *The Spectator* (1747). His scenes—"Caractacus," "The Conversion of the Britons to Christianity," and "The Battle of Hastings"—were engraved by Grignion and Ravenet for a series of historical prints published by Knapton and Dodsley; in a set of smaller engravings they

appeared in Smollett's *History of England* (1757).

In 1745 Hayman presented his painting of "Moses Striking the Rock" to the Foundling Hospital, where it still hangs. On 31 December 1746 he and the other artists (including Hogarth, Highmore, Gainsborough, and Richard Wilson) who had contributed to the hospital's art collection were made governors of that institution and soon began the custom of an annual dinner on the anniversary of the landing of William II. These dinners drew attention to the emergence of native painting and consequently led to a design by a committee under Hayman's chairmanship for a public exhibition of the works of British artists. The first exhibition in the great room of the Society of Art, in the Strand, was offered in 1760; in it Hayman showed his painting of Garrick as Richard III (which is now in the possession of the National Theatre).

The artists split into two groups in 1761,

Courtesy of the National Gallery of Ireland

"Sir John Falstaff raising Recruits" (1761)

by HAYMAN

with Hayman joining those who established the Incorporated Society of Artists of Great Britain, and held an exhibition that year in Spring Gardens, to which Hayman sent his painting of "Sir John Falstaff raising Recruits," a subject also treated by Hogarth. Hayman's 1761 Falstaff scene is in the National Gallery of Ireland. Another version by him of the same scene, exhibited at the Society of Artists in 1765, is in the Birmingham City Art Gallery. A small canvas (14 × 12) depicting Falstaff and his companions in 2 *Henry IV* (act II, scene iv), attributed to Hayman, was sold for $225 in the sale of paintings (lot 119) from the American Shakespeare Theatre held on 15 January 1976 at Sotheby Parke Bernet, New York. A black and white chalk drawing by Hayman, probably a preparatory sketch for one of his pictures on the subject of Falstaff and his Recruits, is in the Yale Center for British Art. These pictures are discussed by Geoffrey Ashton in *Shakespeare and British Art* (New Haven, 1981).

In 1766 Hayman succeeded Lambert as president of the new society and contributed work to its exhibitions nearly every year through 1768. Another secession resulted in the establishment of the Royal Academy of Arts of London by royal charter on 10 December 1768. Hayman, one of the 40 original academicians, contributed scenes to their exhibitions from 1769 (the first) until 1772; from 1771 until his death he served as librarian.

By 1763 Hayman lived at No 104, St Martin's Lane, opposite May's Buildings, in a house which previously had been occupied by the painter Sir James Thornhill and the sculptor Van Nost; the Duke of York's Theatre now stands on the site. Later Hayman moved to a house in Dean Street, Soho, where he died on 2 February 1776, probably of complications of the gout from which he had greatly suffered. He was buried in St Anne's Church, Soho.

On 23 April 1753 at Petersham, Hayman had married Susanna, the daughter of Thomas and Grace Williams of the parish of St James, Westminster. Susanna was the widow of Hayman's old friend, Charles Fleetwood, the Drury Lane patentee, who had died in 1747. The marriage was evidently unhappy. She died before him, and the story is told that when his friend, the architect James Paine, found him

settling some bills for his wife's funeral, Hayman told him "she would have paid such a bill for me with pleasure." By her the artist had one child, Susannah Hayman ("spinster, daughter & only child"), to whom administration of his unspecified estate was granted on 16 February 1776.

A bon vivant, with rough manners and a convivial disposition, Hayman spent much of his time in taverns and clubs. He was a member of the Old Slaughter's, the Beefsteak, and other clubs and enjoyed the fellowship of Quin, Woodward, Garrick, and Johnson. Presumably Hogarth, his boon companion, used him as a model for the husband in the "Marriage-à-la-Mode" series and for the Falstaffian sign-painter in his "Beer Street" print.

Though his reputation was as one of the foremost historical painters of his day, Hayman succeeded at portraits of individuals and conversation groups and also at landscapes. Two excellent pictures of a cricket game were in the possession of the Marylebone Cricket Club. Several of his landscapes are in the Yale Center for British Art, as is his painting of the Tyers family. Among his portraits are those of George Dance, the elder, now at the Fitzwilliam Museum, and George Dance, the younger, with his sister Hester Dance Smith.

Hayman's portraits of theatrical people include:

1. Spranger Barry as Hamlet and Mrs Elmy(?) as the Queen, c. 1748. In the Garrick Club.

2. Samuel Foote. Pen and ink wash in the British Museum.

3. David Garrick with William Wyndham. Formerly at Lowther Castle. Sold at Sotheby's on 17 March 1971.

4. Garrick as Richard III. In the National Theatre. See the list of portraits for David Garrick in this dictionary, No 211.

5. Garrick as Ranger and Mrs Pritchard as Clarinda in *The Suspicious Husband*. Paintings in the Museum of London and the Yale Center for British Art; the latter version was until 1970 in the Garrick Club. See the list of portraits for David Garrick in this dictionary, No. 202.

6. Garrick as King Lear. Engraved by Ravenet for Jennens's edition of *Shakespeare*, 1771–74.

7. Mrs Pritchard. Two portraits in the Garrick Club. Engravings by McArdell and others.

8. Edward Shuter as Falstaff (formerly thought to be James Quin). In the Garrick Club.

9. Margaret Woffington. Attributed to Hayman. In the National Portrait Gallery.

10. Henry Woodward as the Fine Gentleman in *Lethe*. Pencil drawing in the Fitzwilliam Museum. Probably for McArdell's engraving, 1748 (?).

A list of Hayman's illustrations for books will be found in Hammelman and Boase, *English Book Illustrators of the Eighteenth Century* (1975). Information on his Vauxhall paintings is given by L. Gowing, "Hogarth, Hayman and the Vauxhall Decorations," *Burlington Magazine*, XCV (1953) and by W. M. Merchant, *Shakespeare and the Artist* (1959). Garrick's advice for Hayman's scenes of *King Lear* and *Othello* for the Jennens edition is discussed by K. A. Burnim, "The Significance of Garrick's Letters to Hayman," *Shakespeare Quarterly* IX (Spring 1958). An exhibition of Hayman's paintings was held at Kenwood in 1960. A catalogue was published.

Portraits of Hayman include:

1. By Pierre Falconet, 1769. In a series of drawings of 12 of the most important artists in London. Engravings by D. P. Pariset and B. Reading (published by E. Jeffery, 1792).

2. Self-portrait. Hayman in his studio painting a gentleman seated, about 1740–1745. Hayman's sitter was identified as Robert Walpole when the painting was first offered (but not sold) at Christie's on 1 March 1861 (lot 28). At Christie's on 15 June 1866 (lot 93) it was bought by the National Portrait Gallery (No 217). Recent scholarship suggests the sitter is Grosvenor Bedford. See John Kerslake, *Early Georgian Portraits in the National Portrait Gallery* (1978).

3. Self-portrait, in a "Conversation Piece with a Portrait of the Artist," sometimes called "Lord Chesterfield and his Friends." c. 1740–45. Acquired by Paul Mellon in 1960; now in the Yale Center for British Art. Hayman is seated on the floor at the left of the scene. His pose and appearance resemble those of another self-portrait in the Royal Albert Memorial Museum, Exeter (No 4, below).

4. Self-portrait. Whole length, seated before easel. Sold at Christie's on 6 November 1953. In the Royal Albert Memorial Museum, Exeter.

5. Self-portrait. Three-quarter-length, seated, with brush in hand. Sold at Christie's on 6 November 1953. In the Royal Albert Memorial Museum, Exeter.

6. Self-portrait. In a black hat. Given by Percy Moore Turner to the Exeter City Art Gallery, 1935. Sitter doubtful.

7. Self-portrait, a drawing. Acquired by the Exeter City Art Gallery, 1944. Sitter doubtful.

8. By Joshua Reynolds, 1756. In the collection of the Royal Academy of Arts, Burlington House. Engraving by G. H. Every, published by H. Graves & Co.

9. In Johann Zoffany's painting of the Royal Academicians in 1772. In the possession of Her Majesty Queen Elizabeth II, at Windsor Castle. Engraving by Earlom, published by Sayer, 1773.

10. By unknown artist. Drawing in India ink. Half-length, seated by table; a picture on chair at right. In the British Museum.

11. Terra-cotta bust by Louis François Roubiliac. Called Francis Hayman, wearing artist's turban. In the Yale Center for British Art.

Reproductions of portraits above, Nos 1, 2, 3, 4, 5, and 8, are provided in John Kerslake, *Early Georgian Portraits in the National Portrait Gallery*.

Hayman, Mrs. Francis. *See* WILLIAMS, [SUSANNA?].

Hayman, Michael [*fl.* 1791], *scene painter?*

On 19 December 1791 Michael Hayman "of the Parish of Saint Clement Danes, Gentleman" and Henry Hodgins of St Paul, Covent Garden, attested to the handwriting in the will of Robert Carver (d. 1791), the Covent Garden scene painter. Hodgins was also a scene painter, and although there exists no record of scene painting by a Michael Hayman, it seems possible that he followed the profession.

Hayme. *See* HAYM.

Haymes, Joseph [*fl.* 1736–1737], cashier.

Joseph Haymes, who evidently served as cashier at the King's Theatre in 1736–37 for the "Opera of the Nobility" in opposition to Handel's company at Covent Garden, on 5 July 1737 received £250 from the Prince of Wales.

Haymes, Thomas [*fl.* ante 1789–1810], actor, manager, singer.

A native of Devonshire, Thomas Haymes left his intended craft of coachmaker to go upon the stage at Exeter and Margate, where he became a favorite in the 1780s. He made his debut upon the London stage at Drury Lane as Belcour in *The West Indian* on 19 September 1789. His performance exhibited few marks of skill, according to the *European Magazine* of September 1789; his accent seemed provincial and his manner far from agreeable—"His mode of speaking is the reverse of propriety." The critic in the *Biographical and Imperial Magazine* for that month judged that although he was miscast Haymes had a "very accurate" conception of the part and possessed a manner and figure which were in his favor and predicted that his many good requisites would "in a little time, with proper application, render him a very respectable performer." In his notebook (now in the Folger Library) John Kemble recorded that Haymes was "indulgently received, but is not fit for leading Characters— He is a good person."

Kemble's assessment was confirmed by the modest roles assigned to Haymes for the remainder of the season, during which he was paid £2 per week. His second appearance, on 24 September 1789, was as Robin Bagshot in *The Beggar's Opera* and his third Mountjoy in *Henry V* on 1 October, roles in which he continued to be seen. He also acted Captain Bygrove in *Know Your Own Mind*, Dugard in *The Inconstant*, Sir Charles Freeman in *The Beaux' Stratagem*, Harry Bevil in *Cross Purposes*, Beaufort in *The Citizen*, Sir Julius Caesar in *The Life and Death of Sir Walter Raleigh*, a Spouter in *The Apprentice*, unspecified characters in *Trick Upon Trick*, *Harlequin's Frolicks*, and *Harlequin Junior*, Panthino in *Two Gentlemen of Verona*, Young Wrongward in *The Deaf Lover*, the Nephew in *The Irish Widow*, a Gentleman in *The Belle's Stratagem*, Aurelius in *Arthur and Emmeline*, Conrade in *Much Ado about Nothing*,

a Noble Buck in *The Buck's Lodge*, a Spirit in *Comus*, and Jack Stanmore in *Oroonoko*—in all some 22 roles which suggest useful experience in the provinces. At his benefit on 25 May 1790, when tickets could be had of him at No 2, Broadway, Blackfriars, Haymes shared net receipts of about £116 with Burton and Miss Hagley.

In the summer of 1790 Haymes acted at Richmond and then returned for his second season, 1790–91, at Drury Lane, where his lot did not alter. He was seen as Bouquet in *The Son-in-Law*, Don Antonio in *Love in Many Masks*, Sir James Blount in *Richard III*, Carlos in *Don Juan*, a Chairman in *The Fairy Favour*, Lord Ruff in *The Intriguing Chambermaid*, and the Sea Captain in *Twelfth Night*, among similar assignments. At the end of the season he was paid £16 3s. 8d. for 1789–90 and £10 on account "for this Season."

After those two seasons of playing characters of inferior note, Haymes was relegated to the provinces once more, acting at Bristol and Bath in the spring of 1792, in 1792–93, and in 1793–94. He also played at Windsor in the winter of 1793, the King and Queen attending his benefit there on 13 February.

In the middle of 1794–95, Haymes was taken on at Covent Garden at a salary of £4 per week. Announced as from the Bath theatre, he made his first appearance on 2 January 1795 as Farmer Giles in *The Maid of the Mill*, a character that evidently better suited his talents. The *European Magazine* of January 1795 testified that his performance manifested "considerable improvement." During the remainder of the season at Covent Garden he acted Major O'Donnelly in *The Telegraph*, Bob in *The Woodman*, a Robber in *The Battle of Hexham*, and Bob Spanker in *The Frolics of an Hour*.

The statement in the *Thespian Dictionary* (1805) that Haymes's success was only temporary (for he was suddenly discharged because of the jealousy of the acting manager) would appear incorrect, as Haymes remained engaged at Covent Garden for the following two seasons. In 1795–96, still earning his £4 per week, he acted among other parts Tibalt in *Romeo and Juliet* a Lieutenant in *Richard III*, Captain Dash in *The Highland Reel*, the Sheriff in *1 Henry IV*, a principal vocal character in 32 performances of *Merry Sherwood*, and a Sailor in the highly successful *Harlequin's Treasure*, the pantomime which ran for 17 performances between March 1796 and the end of the season. At his benefit on 28 May 1796 Haymes played the Sultan in *Such Things Are* and received £236 2*s*. 6*d*., less house charges of £106.

In 1796–97, his salary now raised to £5 per week, Haymes continued in his cast of supporting roles, which now also included among others Rosencrantz in *Hamlet*, Father Paul in *The Duenna*, Salanio in *The Merchant of Venice*, Rapino in *The Castle of Andalusia*, Bruin in *The Mayor of Garratt*, Captain Broadside in *Bantry Bay*, and Ben in *Love for Love*. When he played the last-mentioned role for his benefit on 13 June 1797, tickets could be had from him at No 8, Duke Street, St James's; he received £228 18*s*. 6*d*., less house charges of £106.

Haymes had become a co-manager of the summer theatre at Richmond with Follet, Cross, and Rees in 1796. The season was, according to the *Monthly Mirror*, "tolerably successful." On 12 September 1796, the night he had announced for his benefit at Richmond, Haymes also found himself obliged by his winter contract to play in the opening bill at Covent Garden. He began the evening by acting Rosencrantz at Covent Garden, then posted down to Richmond, where the boxes were all let, to play Ben in *Love for Love*, and dashed back to London in time to be seen as Captain Slash in the afterpiece, *The Doldrum*.

Haymes left his position at Covent Garden after 1796–97 to devote his energies to the Richmond venture, where he became the sole manager. On 12 April 1797 he leased the Richmond Theatre from James Hubbard, Colonel of the East Middlesex Militia, from 9 June to 31 October 1797 at a fee of £105. Haymes was entitled to the use of all the scenery, wardrobe, and effects. The manuscript lease, now in the Richmond Library, obliged him to retain the incumbent housekeeper, John Rogerson, at a salary of 15*s*. per week.

The summer of 1797 at Richmond was not a success, despite the fact that Haymes kept the theatre open longer than usual in September to present Mrs Jordan for six nights. Her fee was so large that Haymes, according to the *Thespian Dictionary*, had little left to reemburse the caterer. The company, which played at Hampton Wick once a week, was respectable enough: it included Holland, Bland, Blurton, Swendall, Bowden, Mrs Martyr, and Miss

Poole; but the management arrangement at Richmond had always been, in the words of the *Monthly Mirror* of July 1797, "a bad scheme." That season it was "worse than ever, on account of the unpopularity of the manager Haymes, who from some domestic connection or other, is perpetually bringing out women of *loose character*, who are enabled to pay him for their own theatrical diversion."

After passing the winter in the provinces (he is known to have made his first appearance at Tunbridge Wells on 26 October 1797) Haymes renewed his lease at Richmond for the period 29 June to 15 October 1798 but after that summer gave up his management there to join the Brighton company as an actor. The Richmond enterprise had cost him dearly, for on 1 November 1800 he was declared a bankrupt.

Soon Haymes again ventured into management, taking over the direction of the theatre at Brighton on 2 July 1802. After two summer seasons there he deferred to John Brunton in 1804 but on 13 November of that year resumed the reins to become Brighton's first winter-season manager. He was still acting at Brighton in 1810. In 1808 he had been granted an annual license to give theatrical performances at Windsor during Eton vacation while the king was resident there.

Haymes's wife, whom he had married at Bath in the early 1790s, formerly kept a small day school and then was a milliner while they resided in London. She also had shops in Richmond and Brighton—on 1 September 1797 benefit tickets could be had of "Mrs Haymes, Milliner and fancy dress maker, at the Dwelling-house ajoining the theatre." Her trade brought from the press the contemptuous epithet "haberdasher" upon her husband when he was declared a bankrupt.

Thomas Haymes's brother had also gone on the provincial stage as a young man, but a "derangement of mind," according to the *Thespian Dictionary*, prevented him from obtaining a permanent situation. He was no doubt the G. Haymes, reported as brother to Haymes of Drury Lane, who had married Miss Eliza Traffry at St Martin-in-the-Fields on 26 December 1789.

Haymours. *See* **HANYOURS.**

Hayne, Mr ₍*fl.* 1797₎, *performer.*
A Mr Hayne played Henry in Thomas Dib-din's *The Magician* at Sadler's Wells in 1797.

Haynes. *See also* HAINES.

Haynes, Mr ₍*fl.* 1764₎. *See* HAYES, MR ₍F?₎.

Haynes, Mr ₍*fl.* 1779₎, *actor.*
A Mr Haynes spoke the prologue on 18 October 1779 at the Haymarket Theatre.

Hayns. *See also* HAINES.

Hayns, Mrs ₍*fl.* 1730₎, *actress.*
Mrs Hayns played Ben Budge in a perform-ance of *The Metamorphosis of the Beggar's Opera* at the Haymarket Theatre on 11 March 1730.

Hay. *See also* HAYES and HAYS.

Hays, Mr ₍*fl.* 1736–1740₎, *dancer, ac-tor.*
A Mr Hays was a member of Henry Giffard's company at Lincoln's Inn Fields Theatre in 1736–37, where he made his first appearance on 21 October 1736 as one of the Haymakers in *Harlequin Shipwrecked*, a pantomime which was repeated numerous times throughout the season. In the autumn of 1737 he played Har-lequin in *The Necromancer* several times at Cov-ent Garden Theatre, making his debut there on 17 October. In the summer of 1738 he was Harlequin in *The Man's Bewitch'd* in Pinketh-man's booth at Bartholomew Fair. Hays was with Covent Garden during 1738–39, playing Harlequin in *The Necromancer* regularly, and on 21 May 1739 he shared a benefit with several other dancers. Advertised as Mr Hayes, he performed the role of Harlequin in *Harlequin Turn'd Philosopher* on 23 August 1739 and in *The Rambling Lovers* on 23 August 1740, both times at Hallam's booth during Bartholomew Fair. Probably he was related to the Miss Hayes who appeared as a Sea Nymph in *Neptune's Palace* on the same bills.

Hays, Mr ₍*fl.* 1760–1761₎, *dresser.*
A Mr Hays was listed in the Covent Garden Theatre accounts in 1760–61 as a men's dresser at a salary of 1*s.* per day.

Hays, Mrs ₍*fl.* 1717₎, *actress.*
Mrs Hays played Mrs Fancy in *The Fair Example* at Lincoln's Inn Fields on 7 December 1717. She may have been in the play when it was repeated in January and February 1718, but the casts were not announced for those performances.

Hayward. *See also* HAYWOOD and HEY-WARD.

Hayward, Clara ₍*fl.* 1770–1772₎, *ac-tress.*
The 1772 edition of *Theatrical Biography* re-ported that Miss Clara Hayward came from an obscure and humble background (her mother dealt in oysters, said the *Town and Country Magazine* in February 1776). She attracted the attention of a young guards officer who ini-tially wished only "temporary gratification," but, charmed with her mind as well as her person, he taught her to read. When he left her, she "fled to her books as an asylum, which she occasionally relieved with a lover." Her reading attracted her to tragedy and to the

Harvard Theatre Collection

CLARA HAYWARD

artist unknown

stage, and through a friend who knew Samuel Foote, she was introduced to theatrical circles. Sheridan "voluntarily became her instructor in the histrionic mysteries," and on 9 July 1770 she made her first appearance on any stage at the Haymarket Theatre playing Calista in *The Fair Penitent*. The bill cited her only as a gentlewoman.

Clara then played Monimia in *The Orphan* and Rutland in *The Earl of Essex*. The *Town and Country Magazine* in August 1770 was generally pleased with her in both roles. "The tender and pathetic seem to be her particular forte," the critic said, "and were she more attentive to express the passions upon every occasion, with the assistance of those minutiae of acting which she has not yet attained, her fine figure and descriptive countenance would soon class her at least a second-rate tragedian."

Though Clara claimed to be making her first stage appearance in that summer of 1770, it is probable she had had some theatre experience at Drury Lane earlier in the year. On 28 May 1770 a "Mrs Haywood" had been mentioned in a Drury Lane bill as one of a number of employees whose benefit tickets were acceptable that night. We cannot certainly identify that woman as anyone but Clara. Yet the Drury Lane prompter Hopkins, on 27 October 1770, when Miss Hayward appeared as Calista on the Drury Lane boards, noted in his diary, "Miss Hayward made her first appearance upon this stage—a pretty figure,—some requisites and very wild—Time must discover what she will be. Well receiv'd." She went on that season, sometimes advertised in error as *Mrs* Hayward, to play Emmeline in *King Arthur* (Hopkins: "Miss Hayward play'd Emmeline very bad."), Lady Sharlot in *The Funeral*, and, for her spring benefit, Athanais in *Theodosius*. In 1771–72 she added Selima in *Tamerlane* (Hopkins: "Miss Hayward shamefully imperfect . . ."), a Spirit in *The Institution of the Garter*, Hero in *Much Ado about Nothing*, and Cleone in *Timoleon* (on 28 March 1772—her last mention in the bills).

The *Theatrical Biography* said:

The establishment of her theatrical reputation drew fresh groupes of admirers. The favours of a pretty woman are doubled when she appears on the stage to any advantage, and Clara had now this stand to make her conquest from. Many *pig-tailed puppies of quality* dangled in her train;—but in vain,

their solicitations were severally rejected. . . . After looking round her . . . for some time, she accepted the heart of a *young gentleman in the guards*, as remarkable for the *oddity* of his taste in dress, as the delicacy of his person; which last is so remarkable that he has often gone into *keeping* himself, when his *finances* have run short. Such is her present connexion.

The *Town and Country Magazine* in February 1776 reported that Clara went "into the keeping of P—— M——" and left the stage. He was Philip Medows, deputy ranger of Richmond Park.

An engraved portrait of Clara Hayward, bust in oval, with a companion portrait of Medows, was published in *Town and Country Magazine* in March 1776, with an account of their relationship.

Hayward, Clementina. *See* COLLINS, CLEMENTINA.

Hayward, Thomas [*fl.* 1791–1794], *bassoonist.*

Thomas Hayward of Oxford scheduled a benefit concert there for himself on 18 May 1791 and advertised that Haydn had promised to come to Oxford for the occasion and play the harpsichord. Haydn did not appear, and Hayward published a protest on 21 May. A letter of apology from Haydn appeared on 28 May in *Jackson's Oxford Journal*.

On 26 January 1792 Hayward played in the band for the subscription series of concerts of the Oxford Musical Society when the Oxford Music Room was reopened. He also played at the Oxford Meeting in 1793. Hayward performed in London, for Doane's *Musical Directory* of 1794 mentions his participation in concerts there by the New Musical Fund and in the Handel concerts at Westminster Abbey.

Haywood. *See also* HAYWARD AND HEYWARD.

Haywood, Mrs Valentine, Elizabeth, née Fowler *c.* 1693–1756, *actress, playwright, novelist.*

Eliza Fowler was born about 1693, the daughter of a London tradesman. When young, she married the Reverend Valentine Haywood. Haywood in 1711 held a post in Norfolk and had recently been appointed lecturer of St Matthew, Friday Street, London, according to Eliza's biographer G. F. Whicher. Her enemies said that Eliza had had two illegitimate children, one by a peer and one by a bookseller, while her supporters claimed that Haywood had been the father of both children. Half of each story could be true; Eliza and Valentine Haywood are known to have had a son, Charles, who was christened on 3 December 1711 at St Mary Aldermary, where Valentine held a post. Of the other child we have no certain knowledge. In any case, Eliza left her husband, but whether she did so only once, when Haywood made a public complaint of it in the *Post Boy* in 1721, or twice—in 1714 when she began a three-year stay at the Smock Alley Theatre in Dublin, and again in 1721— we cannot tell.

Her first notice as an actress seems to have been in Ireland. Clark in *The Early Irish Stage* places Eliza in Dublin from 1714 to 1717 with

By permission of the Trustees of the British Museum

ELIZA HAYWOOD

engraving by Vertue, after Parmentier

Joseph Ashbury's company at Smock Alley. About 1715, Chetwood tells us, she acted Chloe in *Timon of Athens*. Perhaps she was the gentlewoman advertised as lately arrived from Ireland who played Louisa in *Love Makes a Man* at the Lincoln's Inn Fields playhouse on 4 February 1717. She certainly played Nottingham in *The Unhappy Favourite* there on 23 April, under her own name and hailed as lately arrived from Ireland.

She then acted in the provinces. Richard Savage in the preface to *An Author to Be Lett* in 1725 said: "When Mrs. H—yw——d grew too homely for a *Strolling Actress*, why might not the lady (tho' once a Theatrical Queen) have substituted by turning Washer-woman?"

In the *Post Boy* on 7 January 1721 Rev Haywood advised the public that

Whereas Elizabeth Haywood, Wife of the Reverend Mr. Valentine Haywood, eloped from her Husband on Saturday the 26th of November last past and went away without his knowledge and Consent: This is to give Notice to all Persons in general, That if any one shall trust her either with Money or Goods, or if she shall contract Debts of any kind whatsoever, the said Mr. Haywood will not pay the same.

Valentine Haywood dropped out of Elizabeth's life after 1721. He served as the rector of St Helen, Bishopsgate, from at least 12 July 1731 to his death in 1744, as the parish registers there show. He was buried at his church on 17 February 1744.

In 1721 John Rich, the manager of the Lincoln's Inn Fields Theatre, engaged Mrs Haywood to revise *The Fair Captive*, a play by a Captain Hurst. The work opened on 4 March but was not successful. Mrs Haywood's benefit on 7 March brought in only £46 16s. 6d.

Eliza's *A Wife to Be Lett* was performed on 12 August 1723 with her as Mrs Graspall. The *Daily Post* on 10 August had informed the public:

From the Theatre Royal in Drury-Lane, we are inform'd that on Monday next will be acted a new Comedy, call'd *A Wife to be Lett*, Written by Mrs. Eliza Haywood, author of *Love in Excess* [a novel of 1719], And on the Occasion of the Indisposition of one of the Actresses, she intends to perform the Principal Women's Character herself. If we may judge by her writings we may reasonably expect she will bid fair to entertain the Town very agreeable. . . .

Eliza also spoke the epilogue. The play lasted only three performances, a fate that was to dog most of her stage pieces.

By 1725 Mrs Haywood had quite a reputation in London as a writer of scandalous literary works. Her *Love in Excess*, for example, had gone through five editions. Her literary career, traced and critically examined in Whicher's work, was one of almost compulsive writing, mostly of novels but also of poems, translations from the French, and periodical articles, from 1719 to her death in 1756. Ironically, one of her last works, *Betsy Thoughtless*, was probably her best. Whicher provides a detailed bibliography of her writings, as does the *New Cambridge Bibliography of English Literature*. Most of Mrs Haywood's works were designed for popular consumption and caused the literati to sneer. Alan McKillop in the September 1954 *Notes and Queries* quotes a letter written about 1725, probably by David Mallet, in which "Mrs. H." is referred to: "if I may judge by that Fury's writings, one that thoroughly knows her is acquainted with all the vicious part of the sex."

In *Notes and Queries* in December 1955 John Elwood argues convincingly that Swift's "Corinna" probably dates about 1726 and refers not to Mrs Manley but to Mrs Haywood. Her acting seems to be described at one point:

> *Her Talent she display'd betimes;*
> *For in twice twelve revolving Moons,*
> *She seem'd to laugh and squall in Rhimes,*
> *And all her Gestures were Lampoons.*

And the penultimate stanza gives a fairly accurate description of Eliza's behavior over the years:

> *At twelve, a Wit and a Coquette;*
> *Marries for Love, half Whore, half Wife:*
> *Cuckolds, elopes, and runs in Debt;*
> *Turns Auth'ress, and is Curll's for life.*

The allusion to Curll could concern Eliza's association with Curll as a publisher or Pope's satirical remarks in *The Dunciad*, where Eliza is the prize for which Curll raced; Pope made Eliza Curll's own.

In *The Dunciad* (1728) Pope called Eliza one of those "shameless scribblers" who "in libellous memoirs and novels, reveal the faults or misfortunes of both sexes, to the ruin of public fame or disturbance of private happiness." In response, Eliza contributed in 1729 to *The Female Dunciad*, which contained attacks on Pope by Curll. In a letter to the Countess of Suffolk on 26 October 1731 Swift called Eliza a "stupid, infamous, scribbling woman."

Mrs Haywood's next play, produced at the Lincoln's Inn Fields Theatre by John Rich on 4 March 1729, was *Frederick, Duke of Brunswick-Lunenberg*. Like her earlier attempts, it closed after three performances. She continued a popular novelist, however. In the last half of the 1720s she turned out more works of a scandalous nature, having discovered with her *Utopia* (1725) what appealed to the public. For example, in 1727 she brought out *The Secret History of the Present Intrigues of the Court of Caramania*, providing, as she had in her *Utopia*, a key to the actual people represented by her characters.

On 8 April 1730 at the Haymarket Theatre Eliza played Briseis in William Hatchett's *The Rival Father* and spoke the epilogue (according to *The London Stage*) or the prologue (according to Elwood's article on her stage career in *Theatre Survey* in 1964). Hatchett, who was Eliza's paramour, played Achilles. The play lasted two nights. On 2 March 1732 at the same house Eliza appeared as Lady Flame in *The Blazing Comet*, by the eccentric Samuel Johnson of Cheshire. She called herself in the playbill Madame de Gomez (Eliza had translated Mme Gomez's *La Belle assemblée*, which was evidently published about the time of her appearance in *The Blazing Comet*). When Lady Flame received a benefit at a performance of the play on 19 April, the audience was presented an additional scene: "the Ceremony of Lady Flame's being made a Free Mason, wherein the Grand Mystery is discover'd."

With Hatchett, Eliza wrote *The Opera of Operas*, a ballad opera based on Fielding's *Tom Thumb*, with music by Thomas Augustine Arne; it was performed at the Haymarket on 31 May 1733 with great success. A slightly different version, with music by Lampe, was published in 1733. Eliza was Mrs Arden in *Arden of Feversham* at the Haymarket on 21 January 1736; the bill said the role would be played "by Mrs. Eliza Haywood, the Author"— which seems to imply that she adapted the work, but it is more likely that she was simply being identified as a writer. The play was given only one performance.

Then Eliza joined Henry Fielding's "Great Mogul's Company of Comedians" at the Haymarket to play the First Queen Incog in *A Rehearsal of Kings* on 14 March 1737 and on two subsequent dates. On 21 March *The Historical Register* was presented, with Eliza playing a Lady and Mrs. Screen. On 13 April *Eurydice Hiss'd* opened, serving as an afterpiece to the popular *Historical Register*; Mrs Haywood was seen as the Muse. On 23 May the two works were presented for Eliza's benefit. The following day Walpole introduced a measure in Parliament which led to the Licensing Act that closed such nonpatent theatres as the Haymarket. That ended Eliza's stage career, but she continued in the 1730s, and until her death in 1756, to grind out literary works, though she wrote no more plays.

Marcia Heinemann in the January 1973 issue of *Notes and Queries* wrote a study of Eliza's stage career and transcribed a British Museum manuscript dated 15 March 1734 which shows that Eliza had contracted with the publishers Cogan and Nourse to write a collection of summaries of popular British plays; the collection came out in 1735 as *The Dramatic Historiographer*, was reissued as *The Companion to the Theatre* in 1740, and was printed again, with a second volume, in 1747. The work had not been listed among her writings.

Eliza Haywood, according to the Winston manuscripts, died on 10 December 1743. That report was clearly erroneous. Eliza died after three months of illness on 25 February 1756.

There is an engraved portrait of her by G. Vertue, after J. Parmentier. She was also depicted with the eccentric Samuel Johnson of Cheshire in a scene from his *The Blazing Comet*, published as a satirical print by an unknown engraver in 1732, reproduced with Johnson's notice in volume VIII of this dictionary.

Hazard, Mr ₍*fl. 1748*₎, *actor.*
For Bridges, Cross, Burton, and Vaughan at Bartholomew Fair on 24 August and at Southwark Fair on 7 September 1748, a Mr Hazard played Gillensternia in *The Northern Heros*.

Hazard, Thomas *d. 1667, singer.*
Thomas Hazard (or Hassard, Hazzard) was a singer in the King's Musick in 1625 under Charles I and was reappointed under Charles

II. On 16 January 1660 Pepys heard him sing "alone after the old fashion, which was very much cried up, but I did not like it." Hazard marched in the procession at the coronation of Charles II on 23 April 1661 and sang in the Chapel Royal at least through 10 December 1663, the last mention of him in the Lord Chamberlain's accounts. He died on 23 January 1667 and was buried two days later in the East Cloister of Westminster Abbey. Administration of his estate was granted on 1 May 1667 to Magdalen Williams, his principal creditor, for Hazard had died a pauper. Nothing is known of Hazard's wife, but the Westminster Abbey Registers reveal that Thomas had a son Richard, who was baptized on 21 February 1643, and a daughter (whose name is not known) who was buried there on 15 May 1645.

Hazeler. *See* HASELER.

Head, Mr ₍*fl. 1744*₎, *actor.*
Mr Head played Coupler in *The Relapse* on 6 April 1744 at the Haymarket Theatre.

Heale, Edward ₍*fl. 1686*₎, *musician.*
Edward Heale, a musician in the King's Musick, attended James I at Windsor from 14 May to 1 October 1686. He was paid 3s. daily over and above his regular salary. Edward was doubtless related to the violinist Henry Heale, who was a member of the King's Musick from 1683 to the end of the century.

Heale, Henry ₍*fl. 1683–1702*₎, *violinist.*
The violinist Henry Heale replaced the deceased John Myers in the King's Musick on 26 February 1683. The Lord Chamberlain's accounts cited him frequently from then to the end of the century: practicing for a ball at the court theatre on 26 January 1685, attending the King and Queen at Windsor in 1685 and 1687 and Newmarket in 1689, and journeying with the King to the Hague from 1 January to 13 April 1691. For his regular duties, under William and Mary at any rate, he received a yearly salary of £30 and livery, and for his extra services on trips he earned a few shillings extra each day. Only one warrant mentioned Heale's personal life: on 20 April 1691

he appointed his wife Mary his executrix. It is probable that the warrant was a copy of an earlier one, made before Henry's trip to Holland and its attendant risks. Henry Heale was still in the royal musical service in 1702.

Heaphy, Mary. See O'KEEFFE, MRS JOHN.

Heaphy, Mrs Tottenham, Alice, née Mason *b. c. 1736, actress.*

In *The Irish Stage in the County Towns* Clark gives Alice Mason's birth as about 1736. As early as the 1746–47 season she was acting at the Capel Street Theatre in Dublin. The following season she played at Smock Alley; then she returned to Capel Street in 1749–50. From 1752–53 through 1758–59 she was at Smock Alley. She appeared at the Crow Street playhouse in 1759–60 and then again at Smock Alley in 1760–61 and 1761–62. By 1757 she had begun acting during the summers at Cork; she was there again in 1758, 1760, 1761, and 1762. During those years she was cited, as she was in Dublin as well, as Miss Mason. One of her known roles was Amanda in *The Relapse.*

Sometime between 1762 and 1770 Alice Mason married the Dublin actor and provincial manager Tottenham Heaphy. As Mrs Heaphy she appeared fairly regularly in Dublin, usually at Smock Alley but during some seasons at Crow Street, from 1774 through 1792. From 1771 through 1788 she was also seen at the theatres in Limerick and Cork, which her husband managed. The scanty Irish records reveal only one role for her: Lady Dove in *The Brothers*, for Tate Wilkinson's benefit at Crow Street in 1772. In 1780 and 1781 Mr and Mrs Heaphy ventured to Edinburgh.

Some of Mrs Heaphy's parts at the Theatre Royal, Edinburgh, during the 1780–81 season were: Audrey in *As You Like It*, Dorcas in *The Mock Doctor*, Dorcas in *Thomas and Sally*, Flora in *The Wonder*, the Hostess in *1 Henry IV*, Lady Freelove in *The Jealous Wife*, Lady Mary Oldboy in *Lionel and Clarissa*, Mrs Hardcastle in *She Stoops to Conquer*, Mrs. Lovemore in *The Way to Keep Him*, Mrs Malaprop in *The Rivals*, and Mrs Peachum in *The Beggar's Opera.*

Alice Heaphy made only one appearance at a London theatre, at the end of her career: she acted Mrs Warner in *The Chapter of Accidents* at the Haymarket Theatre on 2 June 1794—the last mention of her that has been found. Tottenham and Alice Heaphy had at least two daughters, the elder of whom, Mary, married the playwright John O'Keeffe on 1 October 1774 and acted in London in 1778.

Heard, Mr [*fl. 1776–1779*], *box inspector.*

Mr Heard (or Hird, Hurd) served Drury Lane Theatre as a box inspector and was first mentioned in the accounts on 3 June 1776, when he was paid 7s. 6d. Two days later he was given £3 as an extra allowance and £5 5s. on a note. His weekly salary during the 1776–77 season was 15s. The Mr "Hind" who shared benefits in May 1778 and May 1779 was, we believe, Mr Heard. He may have been related to Ann Heard, the actress and dancer, but he was not her husband William.

Heard, Elizabeth *b. c. 1775, actress, singer.*

Elizabeth Heard was born about 1775, probably in London, the daughter of William Heard, a physician and playwright, and his wife Ann, née Madden. Sometime after the production of his musical play *Valentine's Day* at Drury Lane on 23 March 1776, William Heard died in Africa at the age of 34, and his wife resumed her stage career, presumably to support herself and her infant Elizabeth.

On 26 December 1782, "before she was seven years old," according to the *Authentic Memoirs of the Green Room* (1801), Elizabeth made her debut at Drury Lane as the Page in *The Orphan*. On 10 March 1783 she was the Duke of York in *Richard III* at Drury Lane; a few weeks later, on 29 March, she played Prince Arthur in *King John* at Covent Garden. On 10 April 1783 she returned to Drury Lane to appear as Cupid in *A Trip to Scotland*, a role she repeated on 1 and 24 May. That season, when Mrs Siddons sent her son Henry off to school, Miss Heard may have replaced him as the Child in *Isabella*, as *The Secret History of the Green Room* (1792) claimed, but the bills do not so indicate.

From time to time over the ensuing six seasons, Miss Heard was seen in children's roles at Drury Lane, where her mother had a regular engagement. In 1783–84 she appeared there several times as the Duke of York and also acted Lord William in *The Countess of Salisbury*

Harvard Theatre Collection

ELIZABETH HEARD as Aurelia

engraving by Wilson, after Roberts

gay manner well suited her for the roles of giddy and sentimental girls. She made her debut at the Haymarket on 25 May 1789 as Miss Elizabeth in *Half an Hour after Supper*, a role she repeated frequently that summer. She also appeared there as an Actress in *The Manager in Distress*, La Blonde in *The Romp*, Celia in *As It Should Be*, Sheba in *A Mogul Tale*, Diana in *Seeing is Believing* Lucy in *The Minor*, and Laura in *The Family Party*. On 9 June 1789, she acted, for the first time, Perdita in *The Winter's Tale*, at Drury Lane for her mother's shared benefit.

Over the next ten years, in which she regularly played winters at Drury Lane and summers at the Haymarket, Miss Heard developed into a "solid and useful" actress, as the *Authentic Memoirs of the Green Room* (1801) described her. In addition to her reliable service to her profession, she maintained "a reputation free from spot, impeachment, and reproach." Her salary at Drury Lane between 1789–90 and 1792–93 was £1 per week; in 1793–94 it was raised to £1 5s. and in 1797–98 to £2 10s. At the Haymarket in 1792–93 she earned £4 per week and probably more as the decade progressed. In June 1793 she lived at No 13, Penton Street, the Haymarket, and in June 1797 at Mrs Fletcher's, No 239, Piccadilly.

Among Miss Heard's many roles at Drury Lane during the 1790s were Kitty in *The Adventurers*, Maria in *The Spoil'd Child*, Isabella in *Don Juan*, a Niece in *The Critic*, Myrtilla in *The Provok'd Husband*, Angelica in *The Constant Couple*, Dorinda in *The Beaux' Stratagem*, Lucia in *The Cheats of Scapin*, Phebe in *As You Like It*, Hannah in *The Wedding Day*, Lucy in *The Country Girl*, Miss Ogle in *The Belle's Stratagem*, and Lydia in *The Wandering Jew*. She acted Maria in *The School for Scandal* on 3 June 1796 and Maria in *The London Merchant* on 26 December 1799. Her roles at the Haymarket were similar. In 1799, her last summer there, she acted Adelaide in *The Prisoner at Large*, Zorayda in *The Mountaineers*, Juliana in *False and Good*, Sophia in *All in Good Humour*, Olivia in *The Italian Monk*, Mrs Die in *Seeing is Believing*, Rosolia in *Zorinski*, Maria in *The Spoil'd Child*, Diana in *The London Hermit*, Helen in *The Children in the Wood*, a Maid in *High Life below Stairs*, Caroline in *The Irishman in London*, and Zapphira in *A Mogul Tale*.

In his reviews of the season 1799–1800 in

on 6 March 1784 and a Page in *Love Makes a Man* on 10 May. On 15 May 1784, when she again played Cupid, she shared in benefit tickets. That season she also appeared again at Covent Garden as Prince Arthur on 16 January and Charles in *The Shipwreck* on 10 February 1784. Her subsequent appearances at Drury Lane as a child included Cupid on 16 September 1784, the Duke of York on 5 November 1784 and 7 November 1785, a Country Boy in *The Plain Dealer* on 1 June 1787 and 6 June 1788, and Prince Edward in *Richard III* on 10 December 1787, 18 February 1788, 14 October 1788, and 29 December 1788.

In the summer of 1789, then about 14, Elizabeth became a member of the younger George Colman's company at the Haymarket, where she was permitted to come on in more important characters. Her pleasant voice and

ELIZABETH HEARD as Celia

engraving by Audinet, after De Wilde

his *Dramatic Censor*, Thomas Dutton consistently praised and encouraged Miss Heard. He particularly commended her for laboring "very assiduously and almost constantly, in the dramatic vineyard" and for her "steadiness, willingness, and punctuality." In Dutton's opinion she was an "amiable actress who possesses from nature a refined sensibility of soul, strictly congenial with the character she represented":

We have only to regret the constitutional delicacy of her frame, which seems inadequate to the vocal exertion, which the theatrical professional so frequently demands. Some of her occasional tones, however, convince us, that judicious attention, and skilful management of her voice, under the auspices of an intelligent friend, would enable her, in great measure to overcome the obstacles, which diffidence, and a degree of native modesty, rarely to be met with in the profession, throw in her way.

An ambitious actress and a quick study who needed the prompter less than anyone in the company, Miss Heard could always be relied upon to fill in with little notice for indisposed colleagues. She appeared to special advantage in breeches, in parts like Melissa in *The Lying Valet*. Among the roles she played in 1799–1800, her next-to-last season at Drury Lane, were Cora in *Pizarro*, Maria in *The School for Scandal*, Fanny in *The Clandestine Marriage*, Oriana in *The Inconstant*, Angelica in *Love for Love*, and Jessica in *The Merchant of Venice*.

Despite Dutton's opinion that "in point of *real utility*," the proprietors of Drury Lane had "not a more deserving performer in their employ," Miss Heard was discharged after the 1800–1801 season. Among her last roles there was Miranda in *The Tempest* on 3 June 1801. She joined the company at Newcastle in the winter of 1802, where, according to the *Monthly Mirror* of January 1802, she proved to be "an acquisition of the highest importance," whose "perfect knowledge of the business of the stage" fitted her admirably for the higher walks of comedy.

An engraving by Wilson, after J. Roberts, of Miss Heard as Aurelia in *The Twin Rivals* was printed by Cawthorn in 1796. An engraving of her as Celia in *The School for Lovers* was made by Audinet, after De Wilde, as a plate to *Bell's British Theatre* in 1793. In the *Catalogue of Dramatic Portraits* in the Harvard Theatre Collection, Elizabeth is confused with her mother Ann Heard, who died in 1797. The roles of Aurelia and Celia, however, were not played in London by either mother or daughter.

Heard, Mrs. William, Ann, née Madden 1750–1797, actress, dancer.

Born in 1750, Ann Madden made her first appearance on the London stage as Aranti in *King Lear*, performed by Spranger Barry's summer company at the King's Theatre on 25 August 1766. Two nights later she acted Myrtilla in *The Provok'd Husband*. She played Aranti again on 29 August, Myrtilla on 1 September, Lucinda in *The Conscious Lovers* on 9 September, Myrtilla on the eleventh, and Lucinda on the twelfth. Her last performance that summer was as Phebe in *As You Like It* on 13 September.

Described as a scholar of Duquesney, Miss Madden performed in a new dance called *The Gallant Shepherd*, devised by her master for his benefit at Drury Lane on 18 May 1767. Her appearance was announced as her first at that theatre. In 1767–68 she was a member of the dancing chorus at Covent Garden, where on 27 May 1768 she danced a minuet with Hussey and received £5 19*s*. as her half-value share of benefit tickets. As a dancer at Covent Garden for the next three seasons her share of benefit tickets was £7 2*s*. on 6 May 1769 and £7 17*s*. on 18 May 1770. Incorrectly named in the bills as Miss "Madan," she danced in *The Rape of Proserpine* on 4 November 1769 and at other times that season. She also appeared occasionally with Hussey in minuets, as at her shared benefit on 22 May 1771. On 5 November 1768 she signed her full name, with other Covent Garden performers, to a letter sent to Colman, the manager.

On 25 May 1771 Ann Madden married William Heard at St Martin-in-the-Fields. On 28 May the press, identifying her as the Covent Garden performer, announced the marriage. As Mrs Heard, she continued to dance at Covent Garden through May 1777. On 23 May 1772 she performed a minuet with Dumai and received £4 18*s*. 6*d*. in half value for her benefit tickets. She danced on occasion at Bristol in 1776.

Her husband, William Heard, the son of a bookseller in Piccadilly, was a physician who had two plays produced without success: *The Snuff Box; or, A Trip to Bath*, a comedy, at the Haymarket on 23 March 1775, and *Valentine's Day*, a musical entertainment, at Drury Lane on 23 March 1776. He was reported to have died in Africa at the age of 34, at a date unknown but probably sometime between mid-1776 and early 1778. The Mr Heard who was a box inspector at Covent Garden between 1776 and 1779 may have been related to William Heard.

Mrs Heard returned to acting parts with a company at the China Hall, Rotherhithe, in the early summer of 1778. She played Mrs Trippet in *The Lying Valet* on 25 May and Bianca in *Catherine and Petruchio* on 29 May. During June she was seen as Corinna in *The Citizen*, Scentwell in *The Busy Body*, Lettice in *The Devil to Pay*, a Masked Lady in *A Bold Stroke for a Wife*, and Mrs Wisely in *The Miser*. After China Hall was consumed by fire on 26 June 1778, Mrs Heard probably continued to perform with the struggling company in the

temporary booth they erected, but no further records of their performances have survived.

Nothing is known of Mrs Heard's activities over the ensuing five years until she shared in benefit tickets at Drury Lane Theatre on 23 May 1783. Perhaps she had served in a supernumerary capacity that season. Her daughter, Elizabeth Heard, not yet seven years of age, had been brought on at Drury Lane on 26 December 1782 as a Page in *The Orphan* and also appeared as Prince Arthur in *King John* at Covent Garden on 29 March 1783.

In 1783–84 Mrs Heard's name was found regularly in the Drury Lane bills as Lucy in *The Gamester*, a role she first played on 22 November 1783; on 15 May 1784 she appeared as Sukey Tawdry in *The Beggar's Opera*. In 1784–85 she played Colombine in 13 performances of *The Caldron* and Trusty in *The Provok'd Husband* on 20 May 1785, when she shared in benefit tickets. After performing at Richmond, Surrey, in the summer of 1785, she returned to Drury Lane where she continued to be engaged the rest of her life.

Over the next ten years at Drury Lane, Mrs Heard remained youthful enough to play a variety of soubrettes and confidantes, such as Furnish in *The Way to Keep Him*, Lettice in *The Plain Dealer*, Kitty in *The Lyar*, Callis in *Love in Many Masks*, a Maid in *The School for Scandal*, a Maid in *The Jealous Wife*, Margery in *The Spoil'd Child*, and Cook in *High Life Below Stairs*. She also acted, among other roles, Madame Le Rouge in *Know Your Own Mind* and the Justice's Lady in *The Critic*. Toward the end of her career, she was relegated to the characters of old women, appearing as a Waiting Woman in *First Love* in 1794–95, a Country Woman in *Harlequin Captive*, and Agnes in *The Follies of the Day* in 1795–96. At Drury Lane her salary was £1 5*s*. from 1789–90 through 1794–95, after which it was raised to £2. In 1786 she had subscribed 10*s*. 6*d*. to the Drury Lane Fund.

In the summer of 1793 Mrs Heard joined the Haymarket company at a salary of £1 per week. She made her first appearance there on 21 June 1793 as one of the Ladies in *The Pad*. The following summer at the Haymarket she acted Mrs Sturdy in *Half an Hour after Supper*, a Fishwoman in *The London Hermit*, and Lucy in *The Gamester*. At the Haymarket in 1795 her roles were Mrs Sturdy and the Landlady in

The Prisoner at Large, and in 1796 again Mrs Sturdy, the Landlady, and a Sweeper in *A Peep Behind the Curtain*. When the Drury Lane company disbanded in the winter of 1793–94 while it awaited the completion of its new theatre, Mrs Heard appeared as Pantaloon's Wife in many performances of *Harlequin Peasant* at the Haymarket.

Probably Mrs Heard's last performance was as Lucy in *The Gamester* at Drury Lane on 23 December 1796. She died on 5 February 1797, according to the *Gentleman's Magazine* that month, at the age of 47. On 11 February her name was removed from the Drury Lane paylist. She had been, reported the *Authentic Memoirs of the Green Room* (1801), if not a great, at least "a very meritorious actress."

Mrs Heard's daughter, Elizabeth, performed at Drury Lane through 1800–1801 and then was a member of the Newcastle company. We find no relationship between Ann Heard and the Mr and Mrs (Margaret) Heard who acted in America in the 1780s. She was, however, the aunt of the Miss Townsend who made her debut at Covent Garden on 5 October 1796 in the title role of *Rosina*.

Heartless, Mrs ₁*fl. 1746*₁, *actress*.

A Mrs Heartless performed the role of Leonora in *The Fate of Villainy* at Warner's booth on the Bowling Green, Southwark, on 8 September 1746, at the time of the fair.

Heartly. *See* HARTLEY.

Heath, Mr ₁*fl. 1799?–1814*₁, *doorkeeper*.

The doorkeeper Heath cited at a salary of 18*s.* weekly in the Drury Lane accounts in 1812–13 and 1813–14 was probably the Heath named in the accounts on 17 June 1799.

Heath, Ann. *See* PHILLIMORE, MRS JOHN.

Heath, Francis *d. 1782, wardrobe master, actor?*

Francis Heath's first notice in the bills was on 31 May 1739 at Drury Lane, when he shared a benefit with two others. Heath may already have been married by that time; his daughter Ann acted as a child at Drury Lane from 1755 to 1767 and later married the Drury Lane actor John Phillimore. Mrs Heath was the wardrobe mistress at the theatre, and the accounts show that she and her husband were usually paid a joint salary. During the 1740s, however, the only mention of Heath was of his irregular, shared benefits. Mrs Heath was not mentioned in theatre documents until 1765, though she may have been laboring at Drury Lane along with her husband throughout the 1740s and 1750s.

The prompter Richard Cross jotted down in his diary an unhappy occurrence that took place on 19 May 1753 when *Merope* was being performed: "The lamp at yᵉ Alter boil'd over & Frank Heath was burnt in ye loins getting it out."

A pay list dated 9 February 1765 has Mr and Mrs Heath down for a joint salary of 6*s.* 8*d.* daily, or £2 weekly. They were at the same scale on 24 January 1767. Occasionally the Drury Lane accounts from the mid-1760s on cite payments of rent from the Heaths (£10 annually), and it would seem that they lived either in the theatre or in nearby lodgings belonging to Drury Lane.

The accounts cite Heath from time to time during the 1770s. On 14 November 1771, for example, he was paid 9*s.* for point lace; on 30 September 1775 he and his wife were paid the same £2 weekly they had received a decade before, for a season income of £76; by 26 October 1776, on the other hand, they had been raised to £3 weekly. Mr Heath (Frank?) acted a Chairman in *The Committee* at Drury Lane on 15 October 1776. After the 1776–77 season London theatre documents cease mentioning Heath and his wife.

Francis Heath made his will on 28 July 1780. He gave his address as Russell Street, Covent Garden, and styled himself "yeoman." To his daughter Ann Phillimore, wife of the Drury Lane actor John, he left his entire estate, and he asked that no more than £10 should be spent on his funeral. He made no mention of his wife, so it seems probable that she had died before he wrote his will. On 10 August 1782 Heath died. His will was proved on 15 March 1783.

Unless Frank Heath led a double life, there were other Heaths working in the eighteenth-century theatre. During the summers of 1754,

1762, and 1764, and perhaps other summers as well, there was a Mr Heath with the company at the Jacob's Wells Theatre in Bristol. He is known to have acted Nat Matchlock in *The Funeral* there on 30 July 1762. Interestingly, between 1753 and 1765 the Drury Lane bills and accounts do not mention Frank Heath the wardrobe master. From 1775 to 1778 the ledger kept by the scene painter Michael Edkins at the Bristol Theatre Royal mention "Frank Heaths Office." That Heath, according to Kathleen Barker, was a box bookkeeper. The Drury Lane accounts contain a number of references to a Mr Heath, doorkeeper, from June 1799 through the 1813–14 season. And at Covent Garden from 1805 to 1808 a Thomas Heath served as a pit doorkeeper.

Heath, Mrs Francis [fl. 1765–1777], wardrobe mistress.

Mrs Francis Heath, the wife of the wardrobe master at Drury Lane, served in a parallel capacity as wardrobe mistress from at least as early as 9 February 1765, when she and her husband were noted on a pay list as receiving 6s. 8d. daily, or £2 weekly. By 26 October 1776, at the beginning of the last season in which the Heaths were mentioned in the bills and accounts, their joint salary was up to £3 weekly. They may have lived at the playhouse or in lodgings owned by the company. Mrs Heath probably died before 28 July 1780, when Francis Heath drew up his will, for he made no mention of her.

Heath, Richard [fl. 1739], treasurer.

On 3 February 1739 the *London Daily Post* published an affidavit signed by Richard Heath, assistant treasurer of the Drury Lane Theatre.

Heathcot, Mr [fl. 1790–1795], doorkeeper.

Mr Heathcot (or Heathcote) was a doorkeeper earning 12s. weekly at Covent Garden Theatre from 1790 to 1795 (and perhaps earlier and later). His benefit tickets were accepted each spring.

Heather, Stephen [fl. 1784–1794], singer.

Stephen Heather sang tenor in the Handel Memorial Concerts at Westminster Abbey and the Pantheon in May and June 1784. Doane's *Musical Directory* of 1794 listed Heather, of Windsor, as a member of the Chapel Royal and Windsor choirs as well as a participant in the Handel performances at the Abbey.

Heather, William Edward b. 1784, actor, singer, organist, composer.

The Master Heather who appeared at Drury Lane at the end of the eighteenth century was William Edward Heather, who was born in 1784. His parents, according to Heather's own account of his life furnished for Sainsbury's dictionary, ran an upholstery business for 25 years in Rutland House, Charterhouse Square— where Sir William Davenant over a century before had produced *The Siege of Rhodes*. Young William "first tried his skill in generating a [musical] scale, by suspending irons, called holdfasts, used by cabinet-makers and joiners, proportioning them according to their acuteness or gravity, and then striking them with a wooden mallet so as to produce, what he then termed, music." To the exasperation of his father he experimented further with "Saws, chisels, mortises, scrapers, and other tools." At the age of four he experimented with a harpsichord, "hammering this away until it had lost all vitality," and then a virginal.

Heather was placed under Hudson, the master of the boys at St Paul's Cathedral. He continued there under Bellamy, receiving vocal and educational training, then sang at various chapels at the west end of town (Heather did not name them), in choirs, and with glee clubs. He sang at Rev Perry's chapel near Bedford Square and there became apprenticed to the musician Costellow, who also played piano in the Drury Lane band. Sometimes Heather substituted for his master in rehearsals at the theatre.

On 15 October 1798, advertised as Master Heather, William made his first appearance on any stage playing Edward in *The Smugglers* at Drury Lane. The *Authentic Memoirs of the Green Room* the following year commented that Heather "is very young, has a charming voice and much taste. He is an admirable substitute for Welsh, who has not only outgrown those characters, but whose voice, on account of the approach of manhood, is at present defective." The *Monthly Mirror* in October 1798 said that William "bid fair to become a singer of merit." Heather remained at Drury Lane, so far as one can tell from the account books, through the 1803–4 season. Thomas Costellow sometimes received young Heather's payments for him, which seem to have been £1 and then £1 5*s.* weekly. William's repertoire did not expand much, but, in addition to Edward in *The Smugglers*, he played Dick in *The Shipwreck*, Juba in *The Prize*, a Page in *Lodoiska*, and a Boy in *The Adopted Child*. But, wrote Heather years later to Sainsbury, "this occupation, combined with provincial and minor engagements, terminated his theatrical career."

His voice matured into a "pleasing countertenor," which enabled him to find endless engagements in London and provincial towns, but when his health began to fail him, he determined to give up that pleasant life and travel—on foot. He took the post of organist of the parish of Walthamstow and settled down there as a teacher. Later (he did not say when) he returned to London, established himself as a teacher, conducted the musical proceedings of "the Caledonian institution," and produced *The Nondescript* (1813), a musical work, at Covent Garden. It was not successful. He composed symphonies for the Duke of Kent's orchestra, helped young composers prepare their works for publication, and continued teaching.

Then (said he) he decided to change careers and take up medicine, but in time he returned to his first love. He visited Devonshire and found it pleasant enough that he stayed for a time, but he finally returned to London. When he wrote to Sainsbury on 19 December 1823, he was living at West Lodge, Tottenham. Heather supplied Sainsbury with a sizable list of his compositions—a number of songs and glees, piano pieces, harp works, duets and trios, and a few orchestral pieces.

Heatley, Matthew [*fl. c.* 1701], puppeteer.
About 1701 Matthew Heatley presented at his booth at Bartholomew Fair "a Little Opera, called the Old Creation of the World, newly

reviv'd, with the addition of the glorious Battle obtained over the French and Spaniards, by the Duke of Marlborough."

Heatly, Mr [*fl.* 1770], actor.
On 19 December 1770 at the Haymarket Theatre Mr Heatly played Selim in *The Mourning Bride*, and Mrs Heatly was seen as Doodle in *Tom Thumb the Great*.

Heatly, Mrs [*fl.* 1770], actress. See HEATLY, MR.

Hebden, John 1701–1765, bassoonist, violoncellist, viola da gamba player.
John Hebden of York was born in 1701. He was one of the original subscribers to the Royal Society of Musicians when it was founded on 28 August 1739, and at that time he was still living in York. At a benefit concert on 10 March 1743 at the Haymarket Theatre (not recorded in *The London Stage* but reported by Latrielle) Hebden played the bassoon, and he was a bassoonist under Richard Collet at Vauxhall in 1745. On 14 March 1745 at the Devil Tavern, John played a concerto on the bassoon. Dr Burney said in his "Memoirs" collected by his daughter that Hebden played in the band at Drury Lane, apparently about 1748. Grove says that at a concert he gave in 1749 Hebden produced a piece for five 'cellos.

In May 1754 Hebden was paid 10*s.* 6*d.* for playing the violoncello at a performance of the *Messiah* at the Foundling Hospital, and he was similarly engaged at the same fee in the spring of 1758. With his fellow musician John Perkins, John Hebden was sworn one of the King's musicians at a fee of £16 2*s.* 8*d.* on 20 February 1759. Grove states that Hebden, in addition to his skill on the bassoon and violoncello, was accomplished on the viola de gamba. The *Public Advertiser* of 28 February 1765 reported that John Hebden had died recently. Another John Hebden, also a musician, died in 1741; he may have been our subject's father. Our Hebden, playing a violoncello, was painted by P. Mercier; an engraving of the painting was made in 1741 by J. Faber, Jr, with a verse by Lockman below. The Mercier painting we have not been able to locate.

"Hecate." *See* DE L'ÉPINE.

Harvard Theatre Collection

JOHN HEBDEN

engraving by J. Faber, Jr, after Mercier

Hedgeley, John [*fl.* 1794–1859?], singer.

Doane's *Musical Directory* of 1794 listed John Hedgeley of No 24, James Street, Westminster, as a singer in the Chapel Royal and a member of the Academy of Ancient Music and the Concert of Ancient Music. The singer Thomas Hawes lived at the same address and was a member of the same groups. John "Hedgely" was left £50 by the musician General Christopher Ashley in a codicil dated 21 August 1817 to his will of a few months before. The will was proved on 4 September 1818. Hedgeley was a cousin to General Ashley and his brother Charles Jane Ashley. When Charles Jane's will was administered on 4 June 1844 by one of his creditors, John "Hedgley" was named Ashley's lawful cousin and next of kin. But Ashley died in debt and Hedgeley inherited nothing.

Our subject was probably the John "Hedgley" who was a music seller and publisher with premises at No 12, Ebury Street, Pimlico, from about 1830 to 1859. His stock-in-trade was up for auction in January 1863, which might indicate that Hedgley had died.

Hedges, Mr [*fl.* 1780–1782], actor.

A Mr Hedges acted Putty in *The Detection* at the Haymarket Theatre on 13 November 1780. The performance was given by the desire of friends of the author, who remains unknown. At the same theatre on 21 January 1782, Hedges acted Valentine in *An Adventure in St James's Park*.

Hedges, Mrs, later Mrs Horton? *d.* 1811, actress, singer.

Announced as "A Lady" making her first appearance on any stage, Mrs Hedges acted Mrs Sullen in *The Stratagem* at the Haymarket Theatre on 9 June 1780. The *Morning Chronicle* identified her incorrectly as "Miss Hodges" and stated that she was "a candidate for public fame under the immediate protection of the Duchess of Devonshire." Her performance was "no bad compliment to the judgement of her noble patroness," wrote the critic; "few actresses are capable of speaking the part with more sense, with greater ease, or more like a Gentlewoman." Although she wanted "pointedness & nerve" in her delivery, her action and deportment, "though not supereminently graceful, were natural & unembarrassed." At Stourbridge Fair on 5 October Mrs Hedges was in *The Constant Couple*, and on 8 December 1780 at Drury Lane Theatre she acted Mrs Sullen again, still billed as "A Lady." Her name, however, was given in the *Morning Chronicle* the next day and was noted by J. P. Kemble on his playbill. Probably she was the Mrs Hedges who in 1780–81 acted at the Orchard Street Theatre, Bath, where she received a benefit on 26 May 1781, playing Mrs Sullen.

Mrs Hedges's name did not reappear in the Drury Lane bills until near the end of the following season, when on 8 May 1782 she acted Isabella in *The Conscious Lovers* at the benefit of Burton, Williams, and Harwood; but evidently she had been employed all the season of 1781–82 in supernumerary roles, for on 10 November 1781 her salary was raised five shillings. After playing Isabella, she acted Bridget in *The Chapter of Accidents* for a benefit she shared with Lamash on 11 May 1782, at which a total of £201 5s. 6d. was received (less house charges of £105). On 31 May she acted Mrs Sullen again.

Over the next four seasons, her career showed little promise. From time to time she was brought on in a major role: on 20 May 1784, for example, she acted Mrs Strickland in *The Suspicious Husband*. But generally she appeared in a variety of tertiary roles, such as Mrs Bentley in *The Fair American*, the Duchess of York in *Richard III*, the Player Queen in *Hamlet*, Lady Faulconbridge in *King John*, Sisigambis in *Alexander the Great*, and Mrs Lovemore in *The Way to Keep Him*. In the summer of 1785 she acted at Richmond.

The Drury Lane account books at the British Library reveal that Mrs Hedges fared badly in her annual benefits, encountering regular deficits: £53 9s. 6d. shared with Miss Wright on 9 May 1783; £69 16s. 5d. shared with Staunton on 20 May 1784 (when her address was opposite Old Bond Street, Piccadilly); £77 10s. 10d. shared with Spencer on 11 May 1785. In May 1786 her address was No 168, opposite New Bond Street, Piccadilly.

Mrs Hedges was absent from Drury Lane in 1786–87 and 1787–88, perhaps touring the provinces, but she returned in 1788–89, her only role given in the bills being Viletta in *She Wou'd and She Wou'd Not* on 5 June 1789, for a benefit she shared with Fawcett; the account books show a deficit of £65, with £178 taken in tickets. In 1789–90, when her salary was £3 per week, she acted Moretta in *Love in Many Masks*, a Lady in *The Belle's Stratagem*, and Widow Lackit in *Oroonoko*. On 16 June 1790 she acted Lucy in a performance of *The Country Girl* given at Covent Garden for the benefit of Fearon's widow and eight children.

After the season 1790–91, Mrs Hedges was again absent from Drury Lane for three years. She returned in 1794–95 to act Sukey Tawdry in *The Beggar's Opera* and Parisatis in numerous performances of *Alexander the Great*. In 1795–96, having been put on the pay list on 2 December 1795 for 10s. per day (£3 per week), she sang in the chorus of Knights and Ladies in *Harlequin Captive* for 37 nights. In 1797–98 she was still on the list for £3 per week. On 11 June 1798 tickets were admitted at the door for the benefit of Mrs Horton, alias Hedges, suggesting that Mrs Hedges may

have married again. After that date she disappeared from the bills.

According to Winston's notations in the Drury Lane Fund Book at the Folger Library, Mrs Hedges had subscribed 10s. 6d. in 1781 and died in 1811.

Heemskirk. *See* HEMSKIRK.

Heidegger, John James *1666–1749, impresario, librettist.*

Grove tells us that John James Heidegger was born on 13 June 1666 in Zurich, the son of a professor of theology and philosophy from Nuremberg. John James (or, originally, Johann Jakob) married and had four children but left his family. Caulfield's *Remarkable Persons* has it that Heidegger traveled around Europe as a domestic servant, and then, when he was "between forty and fifty years of age, he accompanied a nobleman to England, in the capacity of a genteel dependent companion. . . ." The *Scots Magazine* claimed Heidegger came to

Harvard Theatre Collection

JOHN JAMES HEIDEGGER
engraving by J. Faber, Jr, after Van Loo

England as an ambassador from Switzerland, failed, and joined the guards as a private soldier. Just when and under what conditions he actually arrived in England is far from clear, but he may have come over as early as 1696 and seems certainly to have been in London by 1707.

Heidegger was involved with opera productions at the Queen's Theatre in the Haymarket as early as the 1707–8 season, for on 2 October 1707 he and the violinist and manager Charles Dieupart signed a contract (now among the Coke papers at Harvard) with the singer Littleton Ramondon. Another document in the same collection shows that on 31 December Heidegger was due £20—probably his monthly salary. The performers at the theatre begged of the Lord Chamberlain special consideration for Heidegger, saying he had spent a considerable sum of his own money on the opera project at the Queen's. Exactly what Heidegger did at the theatre is not clear; he seems at that early date not to have been the manager, though he was certainly involved in the business affairs of the house. He may also have busied himself as a musical arranger or selector; when the librettist Motteux published *Thomyris* in 1707, he said in his preface that since "the choice of the Songs was not my Province, I may better do justice to the Gentleman who provided that Part of the Entertainment. Tho' Musick is only his Diversion, the best Masters allow him to be so good a Judge that I have no Reason to doubt but his Collection [of music by Scarlatti and Bononcini] will be generally approv'd. . . ." The reference seems not to have been to Pepusch, who supplied the recitatives and added some bits of music, for Pepusch was a professional musician and not a dabbler.

A Critical Discourse upon Opera's in England (1709) attributed *Thomyris* and the opera *Clotilda* to Heidegger, calling him facetiously the "Swiss Count whose Earldom lies in the Land of the Moon." On 7 April 1708 he was, in fact, paid £120 for *Thomyris* (it had recently been revived), but we should probably understand that he served only as the arranger of the music and airs and as the opera's promoter. He may have been the translator of *Clotilda* in 1709; the original Italian libretto was by Neri, and the music was by Conti and others.

The *Tatler* took notice of Heidegger on 5 May 1709 in a piece devoted to theatrical af-

fairs. Calling the Queen's Theatre "the palace," the *Tatler* said it had been "put into the hands of a surgeon, who cuts any foreign fellow into an eunuch, and passes him upon us for a singer of Italy." On 14 January 1710 the same journal said, "You must needs know that such a Creature as Count Hideacre has been able to get 2 or 3000 guineas an Opera subscrib'd"—an exaggeration for effect, perhaps, but indicative of Heidegger's success in London. Through what Caulfield called his "sprightly, engaging conversation, and insinuating address," Heidegger had established himself firmly in London's musical and social circles.

The impresario's name was attached to a number of dedications in published opera librettos: *Almahide* (first performed at the Queen's Theatre on 10 January 1710 and published that year), *Antioco* (Queen's 12 December 1711; published in 1712), *Ercole* (Queen's 3 May 1712; published in 1712, according to Grove, but *The London Stage* says it was apparently not published), *Ernelinda* (a *pasticcio*; Queen's 26 February 1713; published that year), *Arminio* (Queen's 4 March 1714; published that year), *Lucio Vero* (*pasticcio*; King's [previously Queen's] 26 February 1715; published that year), and Handel's *Amadigi* (King's 25 May 1715; published that year; libretto attributed to Heidegger by several sources but questioned by Grove). It is likely that Heidegger signed the published opera librettos as opera impresario rather than as librettist, though in the case of *Antioco* he seems also to have served as translator.

The opera accounts show payments to Heidegger which are not always explained. Between March and May 1711, for example, he was paid £53 15s.; on 13 February 1713 he was to share with Handel and six of the singers the sum of £162 19s. It is not clear what Heidegger earned each year; instead of a regular salary he may have worked for a share of the profits. Colman's "Opera Register" at the British Library stated, in connection with the production of *Ernelinda*, that "Monr John James Heidegger managed both this & ye former Opera for ye Singers & ye Subscription was for Six Nights paying 10 Guin for 3 Tickets each Night, they not to give out above 400 Tickets a Night." The "former Opera" may have been Handel's *Teseo* (10 January 1713), though Owen Swiney was the opera manager when that work opened. Swiney fled London after two performances of *Teseo*, leaving his singers unpaid. The "Register" would seem to indicate that Heidegger took over the management for the third and subsequent performances. He remained London's chief opera impresario into the 1740s.

By early 1711 Heidegger had begun holding masquerades at the Queen's Theatre. Thomas Warton in "A Fragment of a Satire" alluded to Heidegger and explained in a note that he was "the introducer and manager of masquerades in this kingdom, to the great and irreparable depravation of English morals." The affairs became notorious, making from £400 to £500 each for Heidegger and giving him an annual income from masquerades alone of about £5000. They gained the approval of George I, who presented the impresario with a gift of £1000.

The "strange bird from Switzerland," as Pope called Heidegger in *The Dunciad*, correctly judged the taste of the English nobility. A London paper of 15 February 1718 (quoted by Michael Kelly in his *Reminiscences* as from *Mist's Weekly Journal*, which it is not) described one of Heidegger's subscription masquerades at the King's Theatre:

The Room is exceedingly large, beautifully adorned, and illuminated with five hundred Wax Lights; on the Sides are divers Beaufets, over which is written the several Wines therein contained, as Canary, Burgundy, Champagne, Rhenish, &c. Each most excellent in its Kind; of which all are at Liberty to drink what they please; with large Services of all Sorts of Sweetmeats. There are also two Sets of Music, at due Distance from each other, performed by very good Hands. By the vast Variety of Dresses (many of them very rich) you would fancy it a Congress of the principal Persons of all Nations in the World, as Turks, Italians, Indians, Polanders, Spaniards, Venetians, &c. There is an absolute Freedom of Speech, without the least Offence given thereby; while all appear better bred than to offer at any Thing profane, rude, or immodest, but Wit incessantly flashes about in Repartees, Honour, and good Humour, and all Kinds of Pleasantry. There was also the Groom Porter's Office, where all play that please; while Heaps of Guineas pass about, with so little Concern in the Losers, that they are not to be distinguished from the Winners. Nor does it add a little to the Beauty of the Entertainment, to see the Generality of the Masqueraders behave themselves agreeable to their several Habits. The Number, when I was there on

Tuesday, last week, was computed at 700, with some files of Musquetiers at Hand, for the preventing any Disturbance which might happen by Quarrels, &c. so frequent in Venice, Italy, and other Countries, on such Entertainments. At eleven o'Clock a person gives Notice that Supper is ready, when the Company pass into another large Room, where a noble cold Entertainment is prepared, suitable to all the Rest; the whole Diversion continuing from nine o'Clock till seven next Morning. In short, the whole Ball was sufficiently illustrious, in every Article of it, for the greatest Prince to give on the most extraordinary Occasion.

Italian operas had been suspended in 1717–18, so Heidegger's extravagant masquerades did not have to share the theatre with stage productions that season, as they did in others.

His events encountered considerable resistance from the clergy, as one might expect. On 16 November 1721 Vanbrugh wrote to Lord Carlisle that "Heydegger is much in fear the Bishops won't let his masquerades appear, till the Plague's over. I am told however, the King thinks that no very Stanch reason." When the King was once prevailed upon to sign a proclamation against the masquerades, Heidegger simply changed their name to *ridotti* and invited His Majesty to the next one. The *Weekly Journal* on 29 December 1722 carried an advertisement of one of Heidegger's affairs:

We hear that Count Heydreiggar has taken in a Subscription for three Redoltos, in which, besides the Musick and Entertainment of Sweet-meats and Wine, &c., every Lady is to have a Ticket for a Lottery, which will be drawn in the Presence of the Company; in which every Prize will be intitled to some curious Toy.

The Grand Jury for Middlesex petitioned the House of Commons on 12 February 1723:

Whereas there has been lately publish'd a Proposal for Six Ridotto's, or Balls, to be managed by Subscription at the King's Theatre in the Hay-Market, &c. We the Grand Jury of the County of Middlesex, sworn to enquire for our Sovereign Lord the King, and the Body of this County, conceiving the same to be a Wicked and unlawfull Design, for carrying on Gaming, Chances by Way of Lottery, and other Impious and Illegal Practices, and which (if not timely suppressed) may promote Debauchery, Lewdness, and ill Conversation: From a just Abhorrence, therefore, of such Sort of Assemblies, which we apprehend are contrary to Law and good Manners, and give great Offence to his Majesty's

HEIDEGGER at the harpsichord, musical gathering at Montagu House
by Laroon

good and virtuous Subjects, We do present the same and recommend them to be prosecuted and suppressed as common Nuisances to the Publick, as Nurseries of Lewdness, Extravagance, and Immorality, and also a Reproach and Scandal to Civil Government.

The petition brought about the cancelation of the last three *ridotti* scheduled, but in 1724 Heidegger held his masquerades again under the name of balls.

On 6 January 1724 the Lord Bishop of London preached against Heidegger's entertainments. His sermon provoked a letter from Vanbrugh to Lord Carlisle on 18 February:

The Masquerade flourishes more than ever—Some of the Bishops (from the true Spirit of the Clergy, to meddle in everything) had aimed to attack the King about them, which I believe, he did not like, for he took occasion to declare aloud in the Drawing room that whilst there were Masquerades, he wou'd go to them. This with what the Bishops understood from some Ministers they apply'd to, made them think it be as well to be quiet.

The Bishop of London however during this, preach'd one very Spiritless Sermon on the Subject which I believe has not lost Heydegger one Single Ticket.

The sermon also brought forth a verse letter in reply, dated Easter Monday and signed as though by Heidegger but actually written by Macey, Cox, and Povey, who were quickly arrested.

In June 1724 *A Seasonable Apology for Mr. H[eidegger]* tried to prove "the Usefulness and Antiquity of Masquerading from Scripture, and prophane History." The facetious work included a report by a committee headed by "The Countess of Clingfast" which listed a number of positive effects of masquerades. Typical was this item: "It having been made appear . . . to this Committee, that near four hundred Females doom'd to the Arms of old, or otherwise, impotent Husbands, have from the frequent Use of these Entertainments, receiv'd in good Part, relief and Supply." The committee concluded that masquerades should be

farther extended, in Order to extend their great Usefulness, that is, that in the good Cities of *London* and *Westminster*, there be two every Week, and one

likewise weekly in every City and County Town in England at least, Lent excepted, when 'tis (if ever) convenient to abstain from all Kinds of Flesh; and that for the Sake of Regularity, they be all under the Licence and Direction of Mr. H————r.

Hogarth, as might be expected, got in on the fun with a satirical print, *Masquerades and Operas* (1724), which was accompanied by a poem:

> Could new dumb Faustus, *to reform the Age,*
> Conjure up Shakespear's *or* Ben Johnson's
>   Ghost,
> They'd blush for shame, to see the English Stage
> Debauch'd by fool'ries, at so great a cost.
> What would their Manes *say?* should they be-
>   hold
> Monsters *and* Masquerades, *where usefull Plays*
> Adorn'd the fruitfull Theatre *of old,*
> And Rival Wits contended for the Bays.

The midnight masquerades of Heidegger were pictured by Hogarth as being on a level with the entertainments of the conjurer Fawkes and the pantomimes of John Rich. He showed a crowd of masqueraders led by a satyr and a fool, with the satyr holding £1000—the amount the Prince of Wales is said to have given Heidegger to support the masquerades. Shown in a window is Heidegger himself.

Montague Bacon in a letter to Lady Mary Montagu described how Heidegger converted his theatre into a ballroom for these occasions:

There was a masquerade on Thursday last at the Haymarket Playhouse. By laying planks over the Pit, they made a continued floor as far as the Boxes, which were blocked up with pieces of fine painting, and two or three of the side Boxes left open for wine and other things. 'Twas of Heidegger's projecting; the price of tickets a guinea and a half, and not only so but they that took them were obliged to subscribe too for the next.

Hogarth satirized John James again in his *Masquerade Ticket* in 1727. Heidegger's face appears on a clock face at a masquerade; the pendulum is called "nonsense," the minute hand "impertinence," and the hour hand "wit." The artist shows at the masquerade a niche dedicated to Priapus, decorated with signs of cuckoldry, and another dedicated to Venus. Two "Lecherometers" are shown, one on each side, with the following calibrations:

Ticket for HEIDEGGER's Masquerade, 1727
by unknown engraver, after Hogarth

Expectation	Cool
Hope	Warm
Hot desire	Dry
Extreem Hot	Changable
Moist	Hot
Sudden Cold	Moist
	Fixt

Another satirist, Henry Fielding, wrote Heidegger into his *Author's Farce* in 1729 as
"Count Ugly" and had him call himself "sur-
intendant des plaisirs d'Angleterre." Appropriately, George II made Heidegger his Master
of the Revels.

James Bramston's *The Man of Taste* in 1733
quipped about Heidegger's entertainments:

Thou, Heideggre! *the English taste has found,*
And rul'st the mob of quality with sound.
In Lent, if Masquerades displease the town,
Call 'em Ridotto's, *and they still go down:*

Go on, Prince Phyz! *to please the British nation,*
Call thy next Masquerade *a* Convocation.

If the Abbé Prevost was correct when he said
that one of Heidegger's masquerades brought
the impresario 2000 guineas, it is little wonder that he contrived to keep them going despite all opposition.

Perhaps it was for some of his masquerades
that he developed (or caused to be developed)
a remarkable lighting device. It was used in
October 1727 at Westminster Hall at the celebration of the coronation of George II. Mrs
Delany described its effect: "The room was
finely illuminated, and though there was 1800
candles, besides what were on the tables, they
were all lighted in less than three minutes by
an invention of Mr. Heidegger's, which succeeded to the admiration of all spectators. . . ."
Lysons claimed that Heidegger also used his
quick-lighting device at his house in Barn

Elms, where he entertained the King, but no description of its operation has survived.

Though Heidegger's masquerades must have consumed much of his time and energy over the years, his chief activity was in opera production. After Owen Swiney left the managership of the Queen's Theatre in Heidegger's hands in mid-January 1713, John James and the company struggled on to the end of May with fair success. With the advantages of music by Handel and singing by the castrato Nicolino, the opera troupe continued through 1716–17, presumably under Heidegger's management, though his name was not frequently mentioned in the scanty records that have survived. The bills, of course, rarely cited him, for the focus was on the singers and composers. But a manuscript account book at Winchester, studied by Sybil Rosenfeld, shows that Heidegger was given a benefit on 30 March 1717 and netted a handsome £141 14s. 9d.; the performance is not listed in *The London Stage*.

There was no Italian opera in London in 1717–18 and 1718–19; what with the high cost of talented singers the troupe had not been able to prosper, despite the support of the nobility. In 1719 the Royal Academy of Music was formed, with Heidegger as one of the directors and Handel as a principal composer. On 27 November of that year a list of proposals was drawn up (it is now among the Lord Chamberlain's papers); included was a directive that "Mr. Heidegger be desir'd to lay before the Directors on Monday next, an Estimate of the Charges of the Opera house, and of the Officers that are necessary to manage the Same." Unfortunately, his response has not survived, but on the following 2 April 1720 the new Academy began its first opera season.

The opera flourished through the 1726–27 season, with opera patrons gradually becoming more interested in the feuds between singers than in the operas themselves. When both Signora Faustina and Signora Cuzzoni were singing in London the factions supporting each grew so vehement that on 6 June 1727 at the King's Theatre there was a near riot. The disturbance inspired a satirical playlet called *The Contretemps; or, Rival Queans*, in which Heidegger appeared as "High-Priest to the Academy of Discord." Despite his pleading, his leading

ladies engaged in a stage brawl, supported by their cat-calling factions. The opera season was cut short, and though the Academy offered operas again in 1727–28, dissension within the company and within the board of directors brought the venture to an end, and London had no Italian opera in 1728–29.

Early in 1729 Handel and Heidegger were granted permission by the defunct Academy to use the scenes and machines and other opera paraphernalia at the King's Theatre for a period of five years. Both men went to the Continent on recruiting jaunts, and on 2 December 1729 they opened their new opera venture with Handel's *Lotario*. They had a modest success, but even with the King contributing £1000 annually to the undertaking they had difficulty. By 1733 the "Opera of the Nobility" had formed to compete with the Handel-Heidegger group. The partners lost most of their best singers to the rival organization. In 1733–34 the two groups performed in opposition, but on 6 July 1734 when Handel's agreement

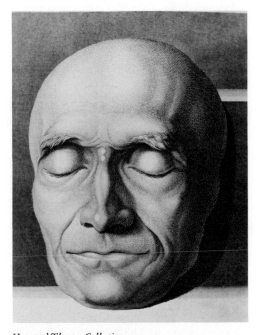

Harvard Theatre Collection

JOHN JAMES HEIDEGGER, death mask
engraving by Sharp

with Heidegger expired, the pair gave up their venture, each having lost £10,000. Heidegger rented the King's Theatre to the Opera of the Nobility for the 1734–35 season.

Lord Hervey wrote to Henry Fox on 2 November 1734:

By way of public spectacles this winter, there are no less than two Italian Operas, one French play house, and three English ones. Heidegger has computed the expense of these shows, and proves in black & white that the undertakers must receive seventy-six thousand odd hundred pounds to bear their charges, before they begin to become gainers.

The Opera of the Nobility came to an end in June 1737, and Heidegger and Handel came to a new agreement. They planned a season of operas at the King's Theatre, with Handel serving as music director. Their 1737–38 season was not successful enough to attract a full subscription for the following season. Heidegger needed 200 subscriptions at 20 guineas each; when they were not forthcoming he was forced to direct his banker to return the money to those who had subscribed. In the fall of 1738 he rented the King's Theatre to Handel and dropped out of operatic affairs for a time.

In 1741 Heidegger was granted a license good for four years at the King's Theatre. Grove quotes an agreement signed by eight fashionable young men who put up a total of at least £1000

to cause to be exhibited and performed in the Opera House of John James Heiddegger situated in the Hay Market . . . or in another Opera house . . . fifty publick Representations of such new or old operas . . . as they shall think fitt, between the dates of 1 Nov. 1741 and 1 July 1742.

The season was a financial disaster for the venturers but probably not for Heidegger. In 1742–43 Gluck offered a season of operas at the King's, and in 1743–44 Lampugnani replaced him as resident composer. Then London was without Italian opera.

In October 1745 Mrs Cibber wrote to Garrick that no operas were planned for 1745–46 (a season eventually materialized); she urged Garrick to join with Quin and her to act at the "Haymarket" (the King's Theatre, presumably). "Mr. Heidegger," she said, "shall pay scenes & c. and pay those that receive wages." Nothing came of her suggestion. Heidegger,

now well along in years, seems not to have renewed his license at the King's Theatre. His masquerades had lost their popularity (the last notice of one was in February 1743, when few people attended) and his direct concern in opera productions seems to have waned in the 1740s.

John James Heidegger died at his house in Richmond on the morning of 5 September 1749, according to the *General Advertiser* (Grove gives 4 September). He left a natural daughter, Elizabeth Pappet, who married Captain (later Vice-Admiral) Sir Peter Denis on 2 September 1750. Heidegger's house in Maid of Honour Row in Richmond was richly decorated with views of Italy and Switzerland, executed by Heidegger's scene painters at the theatre. The house still stands, and the paintings are in good condition.

Heidegger's ugliness was frequently alluded to. Pope in the first book of *The Dunciad* said "And lo! her bird (a monster of a fowl, / Something betwixt a Heideggre and owl)." Mary Granville called him "the most ugly man that was ever formed," and Caulfield said Heidegger was tall and well-made but, "owing to an ugly face, scarcely human." Heidegger joked about his ugliness and is said to have wagered with Chesterfield that his lordship would not be able to find an uglier face in London. Chesterfield lost the bet. Dr Burney noted that Dr. Arbuthnot "inscribed to [Heidegger] a poem called *The Masquerade*, in which he seems more severe upon the count's *ugliness*, which he could not help, than on his voluntary vices."

Portraits of Heidegger include:

1. By Marco Ricci, c. 1720, showing Heidegger listening to opera singers rehearse. Very little detail. Versions are owned by Sir Watkin Williams-Wynn, Bart., Major Christopher Turnor, and Mr George Howard.

2. Drawing by Marcellus Laroon, 1736, showing Heidegger at the harpsichord, for a gathering at Montagu House. In the British Museum.

3. Etching by Worlidge reported by *The Dictionary of National Biography*. Present location unknown.

4. Death mask, engraving by W. Sharp.

5. Engraving by John Faber, after John Baptist Van Loo, 1749 (but Deutsch in *Handel* dates it 1742). Published in Caulfield's *Remarkable Persons*, 1820.

6. Engraving by Joseph Goupy, after sketch by Marco Ricci, 1728–29, showing Signora Cuzzoni and the *castrato* Farinelli standing in front of a seated Heidegger. Heidegger's figure in the sketch may have been supplied by Cuzzoni's patron, the Countess of Burlington.

7. Engraving by Hogarth, "Masquerades and Operas," 1724, shows Heidegger at a window looking down on the street.

8. Engraving by Hogarth, "Masquerade Ticket," 1727. Heidegger's face appears on the clock face at the top of the print.

9. Engraving by W. Sharp, showing Heidegger in a nightcap, lying on his back. The same picture was engraved by Barlow with the legend, "From Lavater."

10. Anonymous engraving, "Heidegger in a rage," c. 1740.

11. Anonymous engraving, "Hei! Degeror, o!," 1724.

"Heifer, The Surprising." *See* "SURPRISING HEIFER, THE."

Heinel, Anne Frédérique, later Mme. Fierville, then Mme. Gaëtan Apolline Balthazar Vestris *1753–1808, dancer.*

Anne Frédérique Heinel (sometimes Heynel or Ingle) was born on 4 October 1753. As a child she studied dance in the studio of Lepy and then continued her training under Noverre. At the age of about 14 she made her debut at the Académie Royale de Musique (the Opéra), probably in *Ernelinde* on 24 November 1767, and was a very great success. In 1768 she danced there in *Dardanus*, *Daphnis et Alcimadure*, *Sylvie*, and *Tithon et l'Aurore* and in 1769 in *Erigone et Psyché*, *Enée et Lavinie*, *Hippomène et Atalante*, *Omphale*, *Sandomir*, and *Zaïs*, among other pieces.

Soon after her debut at Paris she was seen by Grimm, who in his *Correspondance littéraire* wrote of her precision, sureness, and aplomb; taken by her beautiful eyes and legs and her very pretty figure, Grimm echoed the prediction of connoisseurs that within several years Mlle Heinel would become "la première danseuse de l'Europe." Later Grimm wrote that she was a creature of heavenly grace.

Mlle Heinel's youthful charms attracted many admirers, among them the Comte de Lauraguais, who, it is said, in return for her attentions offered her 30,000 livres for herself

By permission of the Trustees of the British Museum

ANNE FRÉDÉRIQUE HEINEL as a sultana

engraving by Proud, after Brandoin

and 20,000 livres for her brother. Among the favors she bestowed on the Comte was a very disagreeable skin disease.

Finding Mlle Heinel's name listed as a principal dancer in the 1770 edition of Badini's comic opera *Il Disertore* (with music by Guglielmi), *The London Stage* assumes that cast list to be for a production at the King's Theatre on 19 May 1770, for which no cast was listed in the bills or in the advertisements. We question, however, the presence of Mlle Heinel in London on that night, since she had danced in *Persée* at Versailles only two nights before. The spectacle there was "magnificent," according to the Duchess of Northumberland, who was present and who acclaimed Mlle Heinel as "the finest woman I ever saw, & an excellent Dancer." Indeed Mlle Heinel was not engaged for London until over a year later. On 25 August 1771 Horace Walpole wrote to Lord Strafford:

There is a finer dancer [than Mlle Guimard] whom Mr. Hobart is to transport to London; a Mademoiselle Heinel, or Ingle, a Fleming. She is tall, perfectly made, very handsome, and has a set of attitudes copied from the Classics; she moves as gracefully slow as Pygmalion's statue when it was coming to life, and moves her leg round as imperceptibly as if she was dancing in the Zodiac. But she is not Virgo.

Announced as then making her first appearance, Mlle Heinel danced in a *New Grand Ballet* at the King's Theatre on 17 December 1771. Throughout the season she was featured on almost every bill. Probably she appeared in *Il Disertore* on 21 December and its subsequent performances and perhaps in other operas, but most of the time the billing was for her *New Grand Ballet* or solo dancing. For her benefit on 12 March 1772 she danced a *Half-Comic Ballet* and in *Admete and Alceste* (previously danced on 10 March). In May 1772 her appearances included a *Grand Turkish Dance*, *Admete and Alceste*, *Le Triomphe du Magie*, and *Le Jaloux sans un rival*. The bills for 3 June announced the "Last time of Mlle Heinel's dancing before she leaves England," but she reappeared, by desire of several of the nobility, on 5 June.

Her first season in London had been a sensational success. In addition to a salary reported to have been £600, her income was increased by the tribute of £600 from the Macaroni Club. Burney wrote that her "grace and execution were so perfect as to eclipse all other excellence." In letters to his friend the Abbé Morellet in France, Garrick called her "most amiable" and "a delicious young woman!"

Mlle Heinel returned to the King's Theatre in January 1773, making her first appearance of the season on the fifth in several serious ballets. She continued to perform regularly throughout the opera season, frequently dancing a pas de deux or chaconne with Fierville. For her benefit on 1 April 1773 she and Fierville danced a minuet in *La Fête du Village*, two new entrées, and a new grand ballet in the characters of Savages. She danced a Sultana in a *Turkish Ballet* on 23 April. On 8 June, probably her last night of the season, she and Fierville danced *Les Tartares* at the end of the opera *Orfeo*. In that year the minuet she had danced with Fierville and her "celebrated Dances" as performed at the King's Theatre, arranged for the harpsichord, violin, and flute, were published in London. In his epilogue to *She Stoops to Conquer*, Goldsmith acknowledged her popularity by referring to his heroine as one who "Dotes upon dancing, and in all her pride, / Swims round the room, the Heinel of Cheapside."

Although regularly engaged at the Opéra in Paris, Mlle Heinel returned to London for several special appearances at the King's Theatre in connection with the benefits of Fierville, whom she had married in London in 1773. On 24 March 1774 she danced a chaconne and a *Polish Ballet* with him, and on 30 May 1776 she performed in several pieces including *Le Triomphe du Magie*, evidently her last London appearance.

Mlle Heinel retired from the Opéra after 1782 with pensions of 2000 livres from that theatre and 4100 livres from the King. About that time she became the mistress of the great dancer Gaëtan Apolline Balthazar Vestris (1729–1808), called sometimes "le dieu de la danse." Previously Vestris had lived with the dancer Marie Allard (1742–1802), who had borne him a son, Auguste Vestris (1760–1842), also a dancer. In earlier years a feud between Mlle Heinel and Gaëtan Vestris at the Opéra, occasioned by his insults prompted by jealousy, had been a *cause célèbre* and had resulted in a public apology by Vestris. After Mlle Heinel had with some difficulty had her previous marriage to Fierville annulled, she finally married Vestris on 16 June 1792, eleven months after the birth of their son Adolphe on 9 May 1791. A clipping in the Burney papers at the British Library (manifestly misdated by hand 6 November 1783) asserts:

Mlle. Heinel, the famous dancer, who some time ago appeared with so much eclat at the Opera-house in the Haymarket, and who was since married in the Church of England to one Monsieur Fierville, a ballet-master, very much pitted with the small-pox, not finding herself satisfied with her match, has thought proper to avail herself of the authority of the Popish laws, which pronounce every Marriage void that has not the rites performed by a priest of the Church of Rome: She has therefore broke her matrimonial ties with Fierville, and given her hand to Signor Vestris the father. The ceremony took place about twelve days ago in Paris.

In October 1797 the *Monthly Mirror* reported that "Madame Vestris, wife of the famous dancer, lately stabbed herself in a fit of jealousy. The wounds are thought to be mortal." Anne, however, did not die until 17 March 1808, at Paris, some six months before the death of her husband on 23 or 27 September.

Information on Mlle Heinel's career in Paris may be found in Campardon's *Académie royale* and in the *Enciclopedia dello spettacolo*.

An engraving by Proud, after C. Brandoin, of Mlle Heinel in the role of a Sultana was published by Sayer & Smith, 1772. Two bust portraits by an unknown engraver depicting her and Charles Fox accompanied an account of Fox's amorous and gambling character that was published in the *Town and Country Magazine* in September 1773. So infatuated had Fox become with Heinel that he was reported to have bought and distributed 200 tickets for her benefit. Verses "To the Young Cub on his keeping Madam H–n–l" were published in the *Westminster Magazine* in September 1773. Mlle Heinel is represented as a nymph in a statuette "en talc" done in 1780 by the sculptor Merci.

Heinnitz, John   *d. 1803, oboist.*

John Heinnitz played second oboe at the Handel Memorial Concerts at Westminster Abbey and the Pantheon in May and June 1784. Writing from No 5, Princess Street, Soho, on 6 February 1785 Heinnitz sought aid from the Royal Society of Musicians:

I am very sorry my necessity obliges me to lay my case before you, and sue for relief. I am at this time under trouble, having been arrested for ten pounds, and am only indulged to do my duty in the Guards, and I have not had any employment since the closing of Vauxhall [Gardens], and am discharged with several others from the Opera House [i.e. the King's Theatre], I have four in family to maintain which case I hope Gentlemen you will take into consideration.

The Society granted Heinnitz 10 guineas.

John played oboe at the St Paul's concerts on 10 and 12 May 1785, and he was paid £5 10*s*. for playing for the Academy of Ancient Music in 1787–88. But he was in trouble again in 1789 and turned once more to the Royal So-

ciety of Musicians. On 7 June he attended a meeting of the Board of Governors and informed them that he had been discharged from the guards and had no employment whatever. He had apparently been receiving two and a half guineas monthly from the Society, and he was raised to three guineas. In 1789 the Society was also asked by Mrs Heinnitz for aid; she needed money to provide the necessaries for her daughter preparatory to her going into service. The Board agreed to investigate the matter and provide assistance up to £5. Then, on 6 December 1789, Mrs Heinnitz reported that her husband and her daughter had retired to the country and left her totally unprovided for. The Society decided not to interfere, since it was a family matter.

On 6 February 1791 Heinnitz informed the Society that he was employed teaching a band (in the country? in London?) at a salary of 50 guineas annually; the Society thereupon cancelled the allowance they had been giving him. A month later, on 7 March, the Society reconsidered and, as an encouragement to Heinnitz for his industry, granted him an allowance of one guinea monthly. On 6 May 1792 the Society agreed to continue that allowance.

Though Heinnitz claimed to have been discharged from the guards in 1789, he was evidently reinstated, for on 1 June 1794 he wrote to the Society that "by age and infirmity" he was rendered incapable of doing regimental duty and had therefore been dismissed again. The Society granted him four guineas monthly as relief. Four years later, on 7 October 1798, John complained to the Society that his family had been afflicted with a putrid fever, and he had been put to great expense; the Society responded with a grant of four guineas for medicine. On 6 July 1800 the Society felt that it could not help Heinnitz further when he begged for relief to compensate for illness, for they were already giving him a full allowance.

Hapless Heinnitz fractured his arm in a fall and asked for help in 1802; on 2 May the Board of Governors of the Society gave him three guineas for medical assistance. The amount was evidently not sufficient, for John asked for more relief, and on 4 July 1802 an additional five guineas was authorized. His miseries ended in 1803. On 7 August Mrs Heinnitz informed the Royal Society of Musicians that her husband had died. The Board ordered that she be given an allowance of £2 12s. 6d. monthly, £8 for funeral expenses, and £1 1s. for medical assistance.

On 6 March 1814 Mrs Heinnitz requested a loan from the Society, but lending was not one of their practices, so she was refused. However, she was granted five guineas for medical relief on 7 January 1816, another five guineas on the following 5 May, £5 on 4 May 1817, £5 on 4 January 1818, and £5 on 5 July 1818. Mrs Heinnitz followed her husband to the grave in late 1819.

Heiterkeit. *See* DE HIGHTREHIGHT.

Hele. *See* HEALE.

Helena and Judith   *1701–1723, curiosities.*

Twins named Helena and Judith, "Born with their Backs fastn'd to each other, and the Passages of their Bodies . . . both one way," were placed on exhibition at the Angel, Cornhill, in the middle of 1708. They were described as seven-year-old Hungarian sisters who were "very Handsome, and Lusty, and Talk three different Languages. . . . Those who see them, may very well say, they have seen a Miracle, which may pass for the 8th Wonder of the World." Prior to their public display, an account of the twins had been given in a letter read before the Royal Society on 12 May 1708. Swift viewed them and thought they raised an "abundance of questions in divinity, law, and physic." An advertisement in the *Daily Courant* on 28 October 1808 advised that the twins could be viewed privately at a fee double the general admission.

In his *The Shows of London* (1978), Richard Altick cites their deaths at Presburg in 1723. Descriptions of the twins may be found in the Royal Society's *Philosophical Transactions* published in 1757.

Hellendaal, Petrus   *1721–1799, violinist, organist, composer.*

Eighteenth-century printers wrestled in vain with the name of the Dutch musician Petrus Hellendaal. His Christian name was sometimes spelled Pieter or Peter, and his surname was turned into Hallandall, Helendaal, Hellendael, Hellendahl, Holdandael, Hollan-

dall, Hollendale, and Hollandula. Grove settles for Petrus Hellendaal and states that he was christened in Rotterdam on 1 April 1721. He journeyed to Italy when he was 15 and studied in Padua under Tartini. Though he is usually said to have come to England in 1752, we believe he was the "Hellend Zall" who played the violin at Hickford's Music Room, for his benefit, on 17 March 1741. He was married in Amsterdam by 1744 and matriculated at the University of Leyden on 8 January 1749, according to van der Straeten's *History of the Violin.*

Hellendaal came again to London to present concerts in 1752. He played a violin solo at the Haymarket Theatre on 13 February 1754. About 3 November 1759 he played the violin at the Oxford Music Room, and perhaps it was then that he applied for (but did he win?) the post of leader of the band there. On 15 February 1760 in London he played a solo on the violin at the Haymarket. On 5 November 1760 Hellendaal accepted an appointment in King's Lynn as organist of St Margaret's Church. He gave up that post on 21 September 1761 to become organist of Pembroke College, Cambridge.

In addition to being accomplished on the violin and organ, Hellendaal was a composer (Grove lists a number of his sonatas, lessons, and glees), and in 1769 he won the Catch Club's medal. He was appointed organist of St Peter's College in April 1777 and established a fine reputation as a teacher as well as a performer at concerts in Cambridge, Oxford, Norwich, and other provincial towns. The Pieter Hellendaal listed as a musician and music seller in Humphries and Smith's *Music Publishing in the British Isles* was probably our subject, though Grove speaks of Hellendaal's son, Peter, as a publisher (he was also a clarinet virtuoso, but he seems not to have performed in London in the eighteenth century). The Hellendaal shop in Cambridge was at his house in Trompington Street, opposite St Peter's College. There about 1770 was offered *Eight Solos for the Violoncello with a Thorough Bass, composed . . . by . . . Peter Hellendaal*. Grove lists that opus as by the elder Hellendaal. About 1785 the elder and younger Hellendaals printed and sold *Two Glees for four Voices* at their shop opposite Peterhouse College, where they still were about 1790 when *A Collection of Psalms*

Courtesy of the Royal College of Music

A Concert in Cambridge, 1770 Back Row: JOHN NOEL, FREDERICK RANISH, John Wynne, DAVID WOOD Front Row: PETRUS HELLENDAAL, Mr West, GEORGE NOEL

artist unknown

was published. The last work was advertised as "compos'd & harmoniz'd by Peter Hellendaal Junr."

The elder Hellendaal played first violin in the Handel Memorial Concerts at Westminster Abbey and the Pantheon in May and June 1784, but he seems to have confined most of his performing to the provinces. Petrus Hellendaal died at Cambridge on 26 April 1799. He is today considered perhaps the only Dutch composer of consequence in the eighteenth century. The lack of interest in his work in Holland drove him to England. A revival of interest has taken place in the twentieth century.

At the Fitzwilliam Museum in Cambridge is an etching showing Hellendaal playing the violin at a concert at Christ's College on 8 June 1767. With him are Ranish, West, Wynne, Wood, and the elder and younger Noel, all Cambridge musicians.

Hellnor, Mr $_{[fl.~1789]}$, *bassoonist.*
The bassoonist Hellnor was listed in the Minute Books of the Royal Society of Musicians as playing at the St Paul's concert on 12 and 14 May 1789.

Helme, Mrs $_{[fl.~1781]}$, *actress.*
A Mrs Helme acted at Richmond in the summer of 1781. Perhaps she was the mother

of the actor (Jack?) Helme, who also acted at Richmond about that time.

Helme, [Jack?] [fl. 1774–1805], *dancer, singer, actor.*

Mr Helme made his first appearance in England at Covent Garden Theatre on 7 October 1774 in a new ballet *The Vintage Festival*, dancing with D'Egville and Sga Vidini. Probably he previously had been a dancer in France, for later London account-book entries often listed him as Mons Helme. He made a second appearance in *The Vintage Festival* on 14 October and danced in the banquet scene in *Henry VIII* the next evening. During the remainder of the season he appeared in numerous performances of *The Druids* and in a *New Dance of Forresters* that had been interpolated into Act V of *As You Like It*.

The next season found Helme as a member of the ballet ensemble for the opera at the King's Theatre, where he first danced on 31 October 1775 as L'Ombre in the ballet *Le Triomphe d'Euthime sur le génie de Liba* with Fierville and Mlle Baccelli. He also appeared in the dancing for *Didone* and in a number of ballets such as *Il filisofo amoroso*, *Les Evénements*

Harvard Theatre Collection

JACK HELME as Black Beard

engraving by Tomkins, after Roberts

imprévues, *Les Deux soeurs rivales*, and *La Générosité de Scipion*.

Engaged in 1776–77 at Drury Lane, Helme made his first appearance there in *The Savage Hunters* on 24 October and then performed regularly in *The Double Festival* and *The Triumph of Love*. On 22 April 1777 he danced with Signora Crespi, Miss Armstrong, and Sga Ricci in *The Garden of Love*, a new pastoral ballet of his own choreography. A draft of £70 to him "to pay Sundry dancers" on 5 October 1776 suggests that he functioned in some supervisory capacity. During the summer of 1777 he was employed at Liverpool at £2 per week, where perhaps he remained for several seasons.

In the winter of 1779 a Mr Helme acted twice at the Haymarket, as Carbuncle in the farce *The Prejudice of Fashion* on 22 February and as Monsieur in the interlude *A Mirror for the Ladies* on 15 March. Presumably neither assignment was in the dancing line. Indeed, the Mr Helme who was to appear regularly in the London theatres over the next decade played an enormous variety of modest roles, which embraced straight acting, dancing in pantomime, and singing in musical pieces. It is possible, therefore, that a second Mr Helme began a London career at that time, but this notice continues on the assumption that only one performer of the name was concerned.

In any event, Helme was at Drury Lane in 1780–81 and 1781–82, playing principal characters in *Fortunatus* (pantomime), *Deaf Indeed* (farce), a vocal part in the funeral procession of *Romeo and Juliet*, a Spouter in *The Apprentice* (farce), Putty in *The Flitch of Bacon* (comic opera), a Servant in *The Divorce* (musical farce), Beau Trippit in *The Lying Valet* (comedy), and a Servant in *The Fair American* (comic opera); he shared benefits with minor performers on 18 May 1781 and on 16 May 1782.

After playing at Richmond in the summer, Helme engaged for the season of 1782–83 at the other patent house again, where he remained for seven consecutive seasons at a constant salary of £1 5s. per week. At Covent Garden he performed regularly and variously: Francisco in *Hamlet*, Seyward in *Macbeth*, the Second Officer in *The Count of Narbonne*, Burgundy in *King Lear*, a Reaper in *Rosina*, Sylvius in *As You Like It*, Jeffrey in *Barnaby Brittle*, Pistol and Bardolph in *The Merry Wives of*

Windsor, Darby Tattoo in *The Funeral*, the Lord Mayor in *Richard III*, Jack Stanmore in *Oroonoko*, a Planter in *Inkle and Yarico*, and numerous other roles, including a host of servants and officers.

After 1788–89, Helme's name was no longer to be found on the Covent Garden bills until February 1798, ten years later, when he performed a Herald in 14 performances of the ballet pantomime, *Joan of Arc*. But he may have been anonymously in the dancing chorus during that period. On 31 August 1795 he was at Sadler's Wells playing in *England's Glory* a character named Jack Helme, a possible indication of his own first name. That summer at the Wells he also performed Vulcan in *Pandora's Box* and a Naval Officer in *Momus's Gift*. By 1796 he was performing at the Royal Circus, St George's Fields, for about that time was published the song *Little Kilty* from *the Jew and the Gentile* as sung by him there. At the Royal Circus, at least through 1805, he appeared in such burletta and pantomime roles as Sawney Beane (with songs) in *Harlequin Highland* (the *Monthly Mirror*, April 1799, complimented his "ferocity" in the part), Corydon Careful, the elder, in *Haste to the Wedding* (1801), Tichée in *The Eclipse, or, Harlequin in China* (1801), and Deputy Bull in *The Knights of the Garter* (1805).

In 1800 Helme married Harriot Cabanel (fl. 1791–1806), a dancer at the Royal Circus and the sister of Rudolphe Cabanel (1763–1839), the architect and machinist. After 1805, we have no record of him.

A portrait of Helme as Black Beard was engraved by C. Tomkins, after I. F. Roberts.

Helme, Mrs [Jack?]. *See* CABANEL, HARRIOT.

Helme, Susanna *d. 1788, actress, dancer, singer.*

Susanna Helme was acting at Bath perhaps as early as 1750 and is known to have performed Charlotte in *The Gamester* at Simpson's Theatre in that city on 27 February 1753. Her first performance known to us, however, was as Miss Sealand in *The Conscious Lovers* at Richmond, Surrey, on 13 June 1752. In that summer at Richmond she acted a number of attractive and spirited young women, including Mrs Prim in *A Bold Stroke for a Wife*, Mrs

Gadabout in *The Lying Valet*, Lucy in *The Recruiting Officer*, Tag in *Miss in Her Teens*, Isabinda in *The Busy Body*, Beatrice in *The Anatomist*, Dorinda in *The Beaux' Stratagem*, Mrs Fainall in *The Way of the World*, Lady Grace in *The Provok'd Husband*, Centaur in *The Silent Woman*, Margaret in *A New Way to Pay Old Debts*, the Duchess in *Duke and No Duke*, and Favourite in *The Gamester*. She also performed the more serious roles Leonora in *The Mourning Bride*, Lady Percy in *Henry IV*, and Goneril in *King Lear*.

After playing at Bath in the winter of 1752–53, Miss Helme returned to the Richmond summer theatre, adding to her repertoire Lady Loverule in *Love's Last Stake*, Mrs Lovejoy in *The Fine Lady's Airs*, Lady Graveairs in *The Careless Husband*, a Witch in *Macbeth*, the Fairy Queen in *The Oracle*, Sylvia in *The Double Gallant*, Bisarre in *The Inconstant* and Peggy in *The King and the Miller of Mansfield* for her benefit on 20 August 1753, and Colombine in *Harlequin Skeleton*.

In the autumn of 1753 Miss Helme was engaged at Covent Garden Theatre, where she made her first appearance on 8 October as the maid Mincing in *The Way of the World*. Over the season she also played Lucy in *The Country Wife*, Engine in *The London Cuckolds*, Molly Brazen in *The Beggar's Opera*, Charlotte in *The Mock Doctor*, and Mademoiselle in *The Provok'd Wife*.

Miss Helme continued to be regularly engaged at Covent Garden for the next 20 years, specializing in the supporting roles of pert and pretty ladies and appearing in the pantomimes as a singer and dancer. Her salary from 1760–61 through 1767–68 was £1 5s. per week. In 1769, her costume allowance was a modest £11. Her annual benefits shared with other performers brought her little: £2 19s. 6d. on 22 April 1758, £3 12s. 6d. on 12 April 1760, £3 15s 6d. on 17 April 1761, and £4 16s. 6d. on 9 May 1767. In a letter to the *Theatrical Monitor* on 5 November 1768 from Covent Garden performers, she signed as Susanna Helme, the form in which her name was listed as a subscriber to the edition of Thomas Hull's *Original Letters* in 1772. Most of the time, however, her name was printed in the bills simply as Miss Helme, though several times in April 1774 as Mrs Helme.

A selection of her roles at Covent Garden

includes: Situp in *The Double Gallant*, Prudentia in *A Duke and No Duke*, the Milliner in *The Suspicious Husband*, Cherry in *The Stratagem*, Emira in *Alzira*, Betty in *A Bold Stroke for a Wife*, the Player Queen in *Hamlet*, Flareit's Maid in *Love's Last Shift*, and Isabella in *The Merry Counterfeit*. She had also numerous dancing and singing assignments in such pieces as *Harlequin Doctor Faustus*, *The Rape of Proserpine*, *Apollo and Daphne*, *Harlequin's Jubilee*, and *Mother Shipton*. Her last performances were as Dolly in *The Commissary* on 25 May and Molly Brazen in *The Beggar's Opera* on 26 May 1774.

According to Wewitzer, Miss Helme died in 1788, leaving a bequest to the Covent Garden Theatrical Fund.

Hemet, Miss [*fl.* 1780–1785], *singer, actress.*

Announced in the bills as a Young Lady "who never appeared on any stage," Miss Hemet made her debut at the Haymarket Theatre on 24 June 1780 in the roles of Euphrosyne and a principal Bacchante in *Comus*. In July 1780 the *Westminster Magazine* identified her as Miss Hemet, after the *Morning Chronicle* earlier on 26 June had incorrectly called her Miss Hargrave. The latter paper described her as "a blooming girl about twenty, with a tolerable figure, a fine face, and an agreeable, though . . . not a very powerful voice." She had sung several airs "with some taste & very pleasingly," despite her inexperience. The *Morning Post* of 26 June reported that "Her figure, except when she stoops, is much in her favour, and her voice, in its present state, is a pleasing one, but evidently capable of considerable improvement." After five more appearances, she was replaced in the *Comus* roles by Mrs Cargill on 1 August. Miss Hemet returned to the Haymarket on 13 November to act Miss Fanny Lovewell in *The City Association*, and on 22 January 1781 she played there as Amadea in *A Wife to be Lett*.

Over the next four seasons Miss Hemet appeared infrequently at the Haymarket. In the spring of 1782 she acted Peggy in *The Gentle Shepherd* on 18 March and 9 April, singing "The Huntsman's Sweet Halloo" on the former date and "The Merry Roundelay" on the latter. On 6 May she sang the roundelay again as well as "The Soldier tir'd of War's Alarms." Subsequent performances were as one of the Taylors'

Ladies in *The Taylors* on 25 November 1782, principal characters in *Cheapside* on 17 September 1783 and in *The Patriot* and *The Reprisal* on 23 February 1784, and Polly in *The Beggar's Opera* (the last act only) on 31 January 1785.

Possibly Miss Hemet was related to Jane Hemet, who as Mrs Lessingham (1739–1783) was a featured actress at Drury Lane.

Hemet, Jane. *See* LESSINGHAM, JANE.

Hemings. *See* HEMMINGS.

Hemingway, David [*fl.* 1775], *exhibitor.*

Though the London papers seem not to contain mention of the machinist and exhibitor David Hemingway, the following notices from Bristol newspapers of 28 October 1775 indicate that he had shown his works in London. An advance puff for Cox's Museum stated:

Lest any one should be misled by a Person who in a certain Bill, handed about Town, *pretends* to have finished the grand Pieces of Mechanism, which compose the Museum in London, Mr. COX respectfully acquaints the Public, that the said Person has *no Pretensions* to merit thereon, as not a single Piece in that Museum was executed by him.

The proprietor of the mechanism, David Hemingway, put an advertisement in the paper saying he had been invited to exhibit in Oxford, Bath, and Gloucester but that he intended to remain in Bristol until after 4 November and then proceed to Bath for the season. Then he responded to Cox's notice:

N.B. Mr. HEMINGWAY, the proprietor and contriver of these curious and astonishing pieces of mechanism, humbly begs leave to inform the public in general, and the lovers of real merit in particular, that he was principally employed in finishing several of those grand pieces of mechanism which compose the Museum in London notwithstanding the insinuating false assertions of an advertisement in this paper to the contrary; and moreover is ready to prove on oath, that he was not only employ'd in compleating the Museum in London, but contrived and wholly executed and finished, several pieces of mechanism now going to be exhibited and imposed on the inhabitants of this city as the invention of another person.
DAVID HEMINGWAY.

A newspaper notice dated 21 October had described the display:

THE LONDON MUSEUM,
Or, POLITE ARTS DISPLAYED.

Just arrived in this City, and to be seen, for a few Days, at No. 12, near the Center of Bridge-street, from Ten in the Morning, till Eight at Night, at 1s. each, Servants and Children 6d. Automata performing on the German Flute &c. The Figures are as large as life, being near six feet high, and most magnificently habited in the Characters of a Sultan and Sultana and a Musical Young Lady richly dressed in the English fashion.

Hemley, Mrs [fl. 1788–1789], actress.

On 22 December 1788 Mrs Hemley acted Selima in *Tamerlane* and Charlotte in *Who's the Dupe* at the Haymarket Theatre. She was seen at the same house on 23 February 1789 as Athenais in *Theodosius* and Miss Tittup in *Bon Ton*. Perhaps the Mr Hemley who acted at Norwich in 1793 was related.

Hemmings, Mr [fl. 1740–1741], dancer, singer.

Mr Hemmings danced the role of a Priest in *The Imprisonment, Release, Adventures, and Marriage of Harlequin* at Goodman's Fields Theatre on 15 December 1740. The following 19 February he sang in the chorus in *King Arthur*.

Hemmings, Mr [fl. 1790s], actor.

According to Lillywhite's *London Coffee Houses*, "Mr. Hemmings, an esteemed actor," was at one time (about the 1790s, apparently) the landlord of the Wrekin Coffee House and Tavern in Broad Court, Bow Street. It is possible that he was the Mr "Hemings" who acted Don Whiskerendoes in *The Spaniard Well Drub'd* at the old Yates and Shuter booth at Bartholomew Fair in 1790.

Hemmings, Elizabeth [fl. 1710], singer, harpsichordist.

At York Buildings on 1 May 1710 a benefit was held for Elizabeth Hemmings. The advertisement stated that "Mrs Hemmings and others will sing in English and Italian several new Cantatas, and other Pieces of Musick. She also accompanies to her own Voice on the Harpsichord, being the first Time of her Appearance in Publick."

Hempson, Celeste, née Gismonde d. 1735, singer.

Celeste Gismonde, a native of Italy, was engaged by Handel for the 1732–33 opera season in London at the King's Theatre. On 4 November 1732 she sang Emilia in *Catone*; two days later the *Daily Advertiser* noted that she was "lately arriv'd here" and "perform'd a principal Part in it with universal applause." The following 20 November, according to the Earl of Egmont's *Diary*, she sang in a concert at the Crown Tavern. Then at the King's Theatre from November on she was Lisaura in *Alessandro*, Elisa in *Tolomeo*, Dorinda in *Orlando*, and probably Jael in the oratorio *Deborah*.

In 1733–34, as Signora "Celestina" Hempson, she deserted Handel and sang with Porpora's opera troupe at the Lincoln's Inn Fields playhouse. During the season she sang Antiope in *Arianna in Nasso*, Elisa in *Astarto*, a role in *Ferrando*, in the oratorio *David*, and Camilla in *Enea nel Lazio*. But Mrs Hempson was the second woman in the troupe, and with the return of Signora Durastanti to London in the fall of 1733, Mrs Hempson's services were no longer essential. She had, in any case, not been well. On 15 March 1735 the *Bee* reported:

Signora Celeste Gismundi, a famous Singer, Wife to Mr. Hempson an English Gentleman, died on Tuesday [11 March], after a lingering illness. She performed in Mr. Handel's Operas for several Winters [*recte*, one winter] with great Applause, but did not sing this Season on any Stage, on Account of her indisposition.

Her death in March 1735 was also noted by the *London Daily Post* on 12 March, in Reed's "Notitia Dramatica," and in Dr Burney's biographical notes at the British Museum, though Grove gives her death date as 28 October of that year and cites the *Daily Post* of 3 November.

Hempstead. *See* HEMSTED.

Hemskirk, J. [fl. 1745], singer.

J. Hemskirk played Peachum in a performance of *The Beggar's Opera* on 30 December 1745 at the New Wells, Clerkenwell.

Hemsted, Mr [fl. 1784], actor.

Advertised as "A Young Gentleman" making his first appearance on any stage, Mr

Hemsted (or Hempstead, Hampstead) played Young Norval in *Douglas* at the Haymarket Theatre on 13 August 1784. The *European Magazine* that month identified the actor and said he had a tolerable voice and figure, some defect in his pronunciation, and was generally not above mediocrity.

Hendel. *See* HANDEL.

Henderson, Mr [*fl.* 1789–1798], *singer.*

A Mr Henderson was a chorus singer at Drury Lane Theatre between 1789–90 and 1797–98. He shared in benefit tickets with minor performers and house servants on 29 May 1790, 31 May 1791, and 15 May 1792 (when the company was at the King's Theatre). His name appeared in the bills as one of the Chorus of Guards in *The Mountaineers*, performed eight times in 1794–95 and six times in 1795–96. At the end of 1797–98 his name was still found on the list of Drury Lane personnel.

Henderson, John *1747–1785, actor.*

John Henderson was born in Goldsmith Street, Cheapside, in February 1747 and was baptized, according to his contemporary biographical notices, on 8 March. His family was Irish, but they claimed descent from the Scots Hendersons of Fordel, related to Dr Alexander Henderson, a leading Covenanter, who is remembered for his conference with Charles I on the Isle of Wight. About a year after John Henderson's birth, his father, an Irish factor in London, died. His widow took John and his brother to Newport Pagnell, Buckinghamshire, where they lived on the interest of a £2000 legacy. John's older brother eventually was apprenticed to Mr Clee, an engraver in Oxendon Street, London; he "fell into a decline," moved to Paddington, and in a coughing fit died in the arms of a fellow lodger, Kitty Fisher, later a celebrated courtesan.

According to an early memoir in the *Morning Herald* of 3 January 1786, young John lived some ten years in Buckinghamshire under the "watchful care and assiduity" of his mother, whom he recompensed in his later, successful, years by rendering "her life happy by every means in his power." It was she, as the story goes, who put Shakespeare into his hands and

National Portrait Gallery

JOHN HENDERSON

by Gainsborough

trained him to recite select passages from the English classics. At the age of 11, Henderson was sent to school at Hemel Hempstead, Hertfordshire, where he was taught English, French, and arithmetic by Dr Sterling. A year later he returned to London to study drawing with David Fournier; at the age of 14, it is said, Henderson made a drawing of a fisherman, in the style of Teniers, that was exhibited at the Society of Arts and Sciences and won a prize. He then went to live with Mr Cripps, a silversmith in St James's Street and a near relative, evidently with the intention of entering that craft, but when Cripps died, Henderson found himself, at about the age of 20, with no prospects.

About 1768 Henderson determined to take up the stage. He auditioned for George Garrick, David's assistant at Drury Lane, and was told that his voice was too weak for the theatre, a deficiency owing to incipient consumption. Henderson was at that time a member of a convivial club of 14 men, called the Shandean Society, which met weekly at a house in

Maiden Lane. According to John Ireland in *Letters and Poems by the Late Mr. John Henderson* (1786), the club was organized "to unite to the festivity of Anacreon, the humour of Prior, the harmony of Pope; and above all the sensibility and pleasantry of Sterne." The affable Henderson was called "Shandy" by his fellows, because of his particular admiration of Sterne. Ireland printed Henderson's "Ode. Intended to Have Been Spoken at the Tomb of the Late Laurence Sterne on his Birth Day," a sentimental effusion of 140 lines which reveals some competency in versification.

The various memoirs differ slightly in the chronology of subsequent events in Henderson's quest for a theatrical engagement, but essentially it seems that he solicited Paul Hiffernan, a dramatist, to introduce him to David Garrick, but Hiffernan declined with the judgment that Henderson was too short, a curious excuse, inasmuch as Garrick himself was below average height. Henderson began in 1770 to deliver recitations in a large room on the upper floor of the Old Parr's Head, located in the Terrace, Upper Street, Islington. Among his selections was an imitation of Garrick's ode for the recent Stratford Jubilee, which Garrick may or may not have heard him recite. Presumably it was the bookseller Becket who prevailed upon Garrick to give Henderson a hearing. The manager rejected him because of a weak voice and bad articulation—"he had in his mouth too much wool or worsted," Garrick was supposed to have said, "which he must absolutely get rid of before he would be fit for Drury-Lane stage."

But evidently Garrick believed that the novice had promise, for he recommended Henderson to Palmer at Bath, who engaged him for three years at one guinea per week, rising to two. Adopting the stage-name of Courtney, Henderson made his debut at Bath on 6 October 1772 as Hamlet. In his *Genuine Narrative of the Life and Theatrical Transactions of Mr. John Henderson* (1778), Thomas Davies claimed that:

When it was buzzed about in the Rooms, in the walks, and all over the city of Bath, that a new actor was arrived from London under the patronage of the great Roscius, all people of whatever rank were eager to see the phenomenon. The house was soon filled, and he had the satisfaction to act Hamlet to a very brilliant audience.

Henderson won immediate favor. A letter in the *Bath Chronicle* of 15 October 1772 stated that Henderson performed Hamlet so "inimitably well" that he drew "such showers of deserved applause as hath not been heard these thirty years in the absence of Mr. Garrick." Despite a clumsy figure, he played the character with excellent understanding, though somewhat in imitation of Garrick. Henry Giffard, the manager with whom Garrick had made his debut, saw Henderson's Hamlet and supposedly assured him he would have a great career. Giffard spent a morning instructing him, and Keasberry offered him guidance throughout the season.

After repeating Hamlet on 13 October, Henderson appeared as Richard III on the twentieth. In November he played Benedick in *Much Ado about Nothing* on the fifth, Macbeth on the twelfth, Bobadil in *Every Man in His Humour* on the twenty-first, and Bayes in *The Rehearsal* on the twenty-eighth. In a letter he wrote on 24 October 1772, Henderson stated:

The continual practice I am in here is of great advantage to me—I once thought it a hardship to be forced upon so many characters. I think so now no longer, being convinced that every part I play, however unsuited to me, does me good. In London it would do me harm for this reason: there are computed to be thirty different audiences in London, here there are but two; and those who see me to a disadvantage one night, see me to an advantage the next.

He played Don Felix in *The Wonder* on 12 December and the title role in *The Earl of Essex* on the fifteenth. On 26 December 1772, playing Hotspur in *1 Henry IV*, he appeared for the first time under his own name, a billing he retained for the rest of his career. By the end of his first season Henderson had acted about 20 major roles, including King Lear, and earned for himself the name of the Bath Roscius. He became friends with John Beard, Paul Whitehead, and also Thomas Gainsborough, who cautioned Henderson against over-indulgence at the table and later painted at least two portraits of him.

On 5 January 1773 Garrick wrote to congratulate Henderson on his Bath success and proceeded to point out the "rocks" upon which former young men of merit had split, warning him against drink, telling him to study hard, to enter polite conversation, read much and wisely, and to be honest and responsible in keeping engagements and promises. In his reply on 21 January Henderson assured Garrick that "idling and drinking" were not his vices. Soon afterward, Richard Cumberland recommended that Garrick engage Henderson for Drury Lane. But the manager remained aloof from the new sensation, evidently believing negative reports from others, particularly from his brother George who had gone to Bath to recuperate and had seen Henderson act, through what Cumberland called his "distempered eyes."

After passing the summer of 1773 in London, where he failed to persuade any of the managers to engage him, Henderson returned for his second Bath season, in which he added to his repertoire Pierre in *Venice Preserv'd*, Don John in *The Chances*, Comus, Othello, Archer in *The Beaux' Stratagem*, Ranger in *The Suspicious Husband*, Sir John Brute in *The Provok'd Wife*, Belville in *The School for Wives*, and Beverly in *The Man of Business*. Despite his enormous success he still could not obtain an engagement when he again came up to London in the summer of 1774, so he returned to Bath for a third season.

During 1774–75 Cumberland and others pressed upon Garrick their case for Henderson. In a letter written sometime in 1774, Cumberland told Garrick that though "Nature has not been beneficent to him in figure or in face; a prominent forehead, corpulent habit, inactive features, and not a quick eye," nevertheless the Bath actor had "great sensibility, just elocution, a perfect ear, good sense, and the most marking pauses (next to your own) I ever heard; in the latter respect he stands next to you, very near you. His memory is ready to a surprising degree." Discouraged by Garrick's cool responses, Cumberland told Henderson he would get him an engagement at Covent Garden "on whatever terms" he desired, but whether or not Harris, that theatre's manager, was approached is not known. Garrick's aloofness may have stemmed from his concern for the competition he might face in the twilight of his career from Henderson, but more likely it had to do with the somewhat presumptuous conditions being demanded by Henderson.

Both Henderson and John Taylor, another

of his negotiator-friends, proposed terms to the effect that he would play only two characters for his trial at Drury Lane. Sometime in December 1774 Garrick replied to Taylor that the proposal would be a very injurious one to Henderson, for "could Mr. H. have an opportunity of performing ten or twelve different characters, his genius would have fair play, otherwise, as his well-wisher, I protest against the other scheme." Garrick remained interested, for on 28 December 1774 he asked Colman at Bath, "pray tell me truly w^t you think of *Henderson?*" From Garrick's letter of 13 January 1775 to Taylor, it is evident that Henderson was being intractable. Through Taylor, Henderson had demanded to be absolute manager of himself in choosing and rejecting all parts, terms to which Garrick could not agree under any circumstances, calling them "not only both *uncivil, & improper*, but *unpracticable*."

On 20 January Garrick wrote to Cumberland that he could not alter his opinion of Henderson's proposals. The Bath actor—"as I have not seen him Act, & cannot guess at his Merit, which is so variously Spoken of"— could be engaged only on Garrick's terms: Henderson could perform any two roles of his own choice at the beginning of the next season, and then Garrick would determine the subsequent characters; after some dozen performances, when they would know something of Henderson's talents and public reception, his salary would be fixed by the arbitration of two persons knowledgeable of the theatre, one representing Garrick, the other Henderson, with a third party available upon disagreement; Henderson's salary would not be less than £5 per week, nor more than £10, with a benefit, and after the salary was fixed he must become like all other performers "subject to my management *wholly*."

Despite Cumberland's advice to accept Garrick's offer, Henderson declined, and after some fruitless overtures to Covent Garden, reengaged with Palmer at Bath for another three years. In April of 1775 Garrick visited Bath, finally saw Henderson act, and wrote to Colman on the fifteenth:

. . . I have seen y^e great Henderson, who has Something, & is Nothing—he might be made to figure among the puppets of these times—his Don John is a Comic Cato, & his Hamlet a mixture of Tragedy Comedy pastoral farce & nonsense—however, tho'

Harvard Theatre Collection

JOHN HENDERSON as Hamlet

artist unknown

imitation of Garrick in his presence, including the great one's faults, had greatly incensed the Drury Lane manager.

Henderson continued at Bath through 1776–77, playing many more of the leading roles of the eighteenth-century repertory, both tragic and comic, including Posthumus in *Cymbeline*, Shylock, King John, Oakly in *The Jealous Wife*, and Valentine in *Love for Love*. In the summer of 1775 he also acted at Bristol in Samuel Reddish's company. On 15 July 1775 *Felix Farley's Bristol Journal* offered guarded praise:

> This prince of country performers, though avowedly inferior to the deceased tragedian [Powell], in expressing the finer sensations of humanity, is very happy in the expression of other passions, and though a little awkward in his manner, and disagreeable in his voice, may be considered as a very valuable acquisition to the Bristol theatre.

According to Ireland, "from the accidental indisposition of a performer," Henderson acted Falstaff in *The Merry Wives of Windsor* for the first time on 17 August 1775, but as Kathleen Barker points out in *The Theatre Royal Bristol, 1766–1966*, that date was not a playing day at Bristol, so the debut in that character probably occurred on 11 September, for his benefit. In the summer of 1776 he played under Yates's management at Birmingham, where he first met Mrs Siddons, who had recently acted at Drury Lane without great stir. She so impressed Henderson, however, that he wrote to Palmer advising her immediate engagement at Bath, but the manager paid no attention.

By 12 February 1777, while still acting at Bath, Henderson was engaged by Colman for the following summer at the Haymarket. On that date Henderson wrote to the London playwright-manager of his apprehension about making his debut in Shylock, because Macklin was so firmly entrenched in the character. In a subsequent letter on 16 March he admitted he was frightened by what he had heard of the severity of London critics. Moreover, William Woodfall, the publisher, who had seen him act at Bath, had advised him not to attempt London but to take up a private life and give up hopes of fame and fortune "to those who are better qualified by nature to contend for them." In that letter to Colman, now in the Harvard Theatre Collection, Henderson related that Woodfall did not think much of his

my Wife is outrageous, I am in yᵉ Secret, & see sparks of fire which might be blown to warm even a London Audience at Xmas—he is a dramatic Phenomenon, & his Friends, but more particularly Cumberland has ruin'd him—he has a manner of [r]aving, when he wᵈ be Emphatical that is ridiculous, & must be chang'd, or he would not be suffer'd at yᵉ Bedford Coffeehouse.

Several days later, on 20 April, Garrick again wrote Colman after having seen Henderson in Hannah More's *The Inflexible Captive*: "Henderson play'd Regulus—& you would have wish'd him bung'd up with his nails before yᵉ End of yᵉ 3ᵈ act"—a reference to the killing of Regulus by placing him in a nail-studded barrel and rolling it down a hill. Perhaps there is some truth in the story, told by Henderson, that his figure, voice, or manner; the nervous actor thanked Palmer for the promise of correcting his faults when he should arrive in London. (A letter now in the Westminster Public Library, written by Woodfall to the actor John Quick, after he had seen Henderson act in London, repeats the publisher's opinion: "his figure is bad, his voice dissonant (though melodious in the lower tones) his acting too uniform and sometimes ungracefull, his face too rotund and his features not so perfectly at his command as is requisite in a first rate player.")

Henderson's long-awaited London debut, as Shylock, occurred at the Haymarket on 11 June 1777. He had prepared well. His performance, according to the *Morning Chronicle* of 12 June, revealed "a dramatic mind, & from every sentence he uttered, it became more and more evident that he had studied the part till he had made himself perfect master of the poet's meaning." The *Gazetteer* of that day offered a mixed, but encouraging notice:

Mr. Henderson has some time past engaged the conversation of the frequenters of theatrical amusements. His friends, with more zeal than discretion, magnified his abilities to the utmost, & raised expectation too high. The choice he made of a character to give an impression of his merit . . . was as injudicious as the zeal of his friends. Nothing decisive can be said of his abilities from the specimen seen; though it is acknowledged he played the Jew inferior to none of the gentlemen who played the part in our winter theatres, Mr. Macklin excepted, who conceived the part, beyond the power of censure. In Shylock, then, Mr. Henderson stands a second to our favourite veteran, which is paying him no small compliment; but he really deserves it. His face & figure were so disguised by the necessary dress of the character, that nothing can be said of them. His voice, whether from nature or imitation, is exceedingly like Mr. Garrick's in many of his tones, but without his power.

The London Magazine of June 1777 thought that he promised more "to attain the character of a player of consummate judgment than a great player, properly so called." The *Public Advertiser* of 13 June reported that for all his faults Henderson received "loud & Unanimous Plaudits . . . richly merited." Macklin, himself, encouraged Henderson. Garrick, who had retired the previous year, saw the performance, but said nothing.

After three more performances of Shylock,

Henderson's next character was Hamlet on 26 June 1777. In his *Essay on the Character of Hamlet, as performed by Mr. Henderson* (1777), Frederic Pilon made some petty criticism but provided specific information:

Mr. Henderson's person is far from striking; it is rather under the middle size, and moulded with no extraordinary elegance, or symmetry. His eye is good, and all his other features, bold and marking; but his countenance seemed incapable of assuming the pathetic engaging look, which should particularly distinguish the character; his deportment was easy, but not graceful; and was considerably injured by his appearing over solicitous about the disposal of his hands; it is particular, and ungraceful, to confine them too much to the bosom. . . . But . . . he was not deficient in judgment and feeling.

In acting Hamlet's madness, Henderson "diminished the fine effect his disordered appearance would have had, by inattention to attitude and grace." He was not wild or desperate enough in his struggle with Horatio and Marcellus while attempting to follow the ghost, and he failed to drop his sword when the spirit told him he was his father. He was "too tame" with Ophelia, "too boisterous and irreverent" with Gertrude, "languid and unimpassioned" in the speech on Yorick's skull, and ignorant of fencing. The soliloquies, though not excellent, were "far from reprehensible." In all, despite his youth and inexperience, Henderson was proclaimed by Pilon as "the best performer now left to support the drooping trophies of the stage."

Henderson strengthened his reputation with five other characters that first summer at the Haymarket. On 15 July 1777 he acted Leon in *Rule a Wife and Have a Wife*, a role he had first played at Bath on 4 February 1777. On 24 July he acted Falstaff in *1 Henry IV*, a character in which he became famed. "In the frolicksome, gay, and humorous situations of Falstaff Henderson is superior to every man," wrote Davies; "His soliloquy in describing his ragamuffin regiment, and his enjoying the misuse of the king's press-money are so truly excellent that they are not inferior to any comic representation of the stage." On 7 August his Richard III (first seen at Bath on 20 October 1772) was so enthusiastically received that, according to Walpole, Garrick was "dying of the yellow jaundice." That role was followed by Don John in *The Chances* on 19 August (first

Harvard Theatre Collection

JOHN HENDERSON as Iago
engraving by Bartolozzi, after Stuart

played at Bath on 23 October 1773) and Bayes in *The Rehearsal* on 25 August, for his clear benefit when tickets were available of him at No 21, Maiden Lane, Covent Garden. According to Oxberry in his *Dramatic Biography*, the benefit brought Henderson £200. On 3 September 1777 he acted Falstaff in *The Merry Wives of Windsor*. It is said that Henderson's powerful charm allowed Colman to take in some £4500 that summer, though the manager became offended when Henderson imitated him to his face.

Sheridan engaged him at Drury Lane for the 1777–78 season at £10 per week, but first Henderson, who was under articles with Palmer which called for a penalty of £300 if broken, had to agree to play eight characters in succession at Bath before gaining his release. Henderson made his first appearance at Drury Lane, as Hamlet, on 30 September 1777. A notation by Sheridan in a memorandum book now in the Folger Shakespeare Library indicates that Henderson was paid £29 of the £228 4s. taken in that night (*The London Stage* lists receipts of £225 8s.). In his *Memoirs of Mrs*

Siddons (1827), Boaden stated that "The *style* of Henderson did not assimilate with the tone" of the Drury Lane company—among whom were Farren as Horatio, Baddeley as Polonius, Mrs Hopkins as the Queen, and Mrs Robinson as Ophelia—"They declaimed in a higher key, and more upon the level. The frequent undertones of the former hardly struck the ear at any considerable distance." Henderson followed with Richard III, Shylock, Falstaff in *1 Henry IV*, Horatius in *The Roman Father*, King John, Bayes, Brutus in the premiere of Shirley's *The Roman Sacrifice* on 18 December 1777, and Bobadil in *Every Man in His Humour*. His playing of Falstaff on 17 October 1777 caused an innovation in stage business resulting from his inability to lift the corpse of Hotspur, acted by Smith, upon his back. In previous performances of the play, especially when the characters had been acted by Quin and Barry, the business had always provided an opportunity for an extended joke. But Henderson encountered so much difficulty in getting Smith on his shoulders that the spectators tired of the *lazzo*. So it was decided in subsequent performances in which Henderson appeared to have several of Falstaff's ragamuffins carry off the body. The change was praised by the press as for the better because there had been "too much buffoonery" in the matter.

On 24 January 1778 Henderson played Edgar Atheling in the first performance of Cumberland's *The Battle of Hastings*. In the opinion of the author he was miscast and failed to have "the happiest effect, for he did not possess the graces of person or deportment, and as that character demanded both, an actor might have been found, who with inferior abilities would have been a fitter representative of it." Henderson's other roles in his first Drury Lane season were Benedick in *Much Ado about Nothing*, Valentine in *Love for Love*, and Macbeth, the last on 31 March 1778 for his benefit, when the receipts were £278 18s. (less £105 house charges) and Henderson was still lodging at No 21, Maiden Lane.

In the early summer of 1778 Henderson went to Dublin to play at Crow Street. In mid-August he acted at Liverpool and then played several nights at Bath, where he was bothered by rheumatism. He returned for a second season at Drury Lane, playing his repertoire of the previous year, to which he added Don

John, Falstaff in *2 Henry IV* and *The Merry Wives of Windsor*, the title role in *Aesop*, Father Dominick in *The Spanish Fryar*, and Bireno in the premiere of Jephson's *The Law of Lombardy* on 8 February 1779. For his benefit on 22 March he acted King Lear for his first time in London; receipts were £259 9*s*. (less £105 charges). Tickets could be had of him at new lodgings in Buckingham Street, York Buildings. On 10 April 1779 he played the title role in *The Gamester*. That season he also appeared several times at Covent Garden Theatre, playing Richard III on 5 October 1778, the Prologue and Chorus in *Henry V* on 1 January 1779, Falstaff in *1 Henry IV* on 24 April, and Hamlet on 26 April. (The Henderson who acted Bauldy in *The Gentle Shepherd* at the Haymarket on 11 January 1779 was no doubt another, but obscure, actor.)

After another visit, in the summer of 1779, to Ireland, where he played again at Crow Street and at Cork and Limerick in August, Henderson returned to London to act in the 1779–80 season, not at Drury Lane but at Covent Garden, at a salary increased to £12 12*s*. per week. He made his first appearance as a regular member of the Covent Garden company on 18 October 1779, as Macbeth. Next day the *Morning Chronicle* complained about his costume: "Last night the modern custom of making the principal actor fine was followed without any regard to propriety, or any care about the other personages of the drama." When he acted Sforza in the premiere of *The Duke of Milan* on 10 November, the same paper hoped that he "might surely break himself of the awkward custom of clapping his hands together almost perpetually, and running on and off the stage with so ungraceful a levity." To his regular characters he added Jaques in *As You Like It* on 17 December 1779 (which he also played at Drury Lane on 7 April 1780 for Mrs Robinson's benefit), Alwin in *The Countess of Salisbury* on 12 January 1780, and Tamerlane on 1 May. For his benefit on 14 March 1780 his role was Sir John Brute in *The Provok'd Wife*, his net receipts were about £129, and he still lived in Buckingham Street, his London home for the remainder of his life.

Returning from the summer of 1780 at Liverpool, Henderson acted the Duke in *Measure for Measure* at Covent Garden on 11 October 1780 and Cardinal Wolsey in *Henry VIII* on 30 October. His acting of Iago on 10 November 1780 was called by Boaden "perhaps the crown of all his serious achievements."

It was profoundly intellectual like the character. Any thing near this, I have never seen. . . . You must hear his insinuations with curses, and yet confess that you also would have been deceived. Other Iagos were to be seen through at once. . . . Though a studious man, there was no discipline apparent in the art of Henderson; he moved and looked as the humour or passion required . . . and he cared little about the measure of the line; he would not consider the fame of the versifier while the heart was to be struck.

His other new characters in 1780–81 were Pharnaces in *The Siege of Sinope*, Sir Charles Easy in *The Careless Husband*, Hastings in *Jane Shore*, and Sir Giles Overreach in *A New Way to Pay Old Debts*.

Except for a performance as Falstaff in *The Merry Wives of Windsor* at the Haymarket on 24 August 1781 to accommodate Edwin's benefit, he passed the summer of 1781 at leisure. Perhaps he had been ill. On 17 September

Harvard Theatre Collection

JOHN HENDERSON as Falstaff, with Charteris as Bardolph

by Kay

1781 he returned to Covent Garden to act Sir Giles Overreach. He acted Don John on 2 October and on 13 October "created" the character of Mr Osborne in Holcroft's new comedy *Duplicity*. Because of his "sudden Indisposition" his performance of Richard III scheduled for 22 October was postponed, as were performances of *Duplicity* on 23 and 26 October. He was sufficiently recovered to play in the latter on 30 October and in the strenuous role of Lear the next night. *Duplicity* was played again on 1 November, but the next night *King Lear* was canceled on account of Henderson's "infirm state of health." *Duplicity* was postponed on 3 November for the same reason; and when it was finally played for the author's benefit on 6 November, Wroughton played Henderson's role of Mr Osborne.

Whatever the extent of his illness, Henderson during those weeks was supervising the rehearsals of Jephson's *The Court of Narbonne*, in which he also acted Austin at its opening on 17 November 1781. On 1 November the *Public Advertiser* announced that Henderson in the forthcoming tragedy was "to wear a Dress which is lent him from the Antiquities at Strawberry Hill," provided by Horace Walpole, who was very solicitous of the event to the extent that he supervised the scenes and dresses. In a letter to Jephson the day after the opening, Walpole wrote that "Henderson was far better than I expected from his weakness, and from his rehearsal yesterday, with which he was much discontented himself." Henderson played the remainder of the season at Covent Garden in evident good health, acting, along with his regular roles, Lusignan in *Zara* for the first time on 10 January 1782, Maskwell in *The Double Dealer* for his benefit on 19 March, Essex in *The Earl of Essex* on 17 April, and Father Sullivan in *The Walloons* on 19 April. On 15 May 1782 he played Macbeth at Drury Lane, the last time he ever performed at that theatre.

Henderson continued to be engaged at Covent Garden for the rest of his career. His salary in 1782–83 was £14 14s. per week; it was raised to £15 15s. in 1783–84 and to £17 17s. at the beginning of 1785–86. Among his roles in 1782–83 were Evander in *The Grecian Daughter*, Sir Anthony Branville in *The Discovery*, the title role in the premiere of Bentley's *Philodamus* on 14 December 1782, Lord Da-

venant in the premiere of Cumberland's *The Mysterious Husband* on 28 January 1783 ("a fine bold-faced villain" character suggested to the author by Henderson), Chamont in *The Orphan*, Malvolio in *Twelfth Night*, and Leontes in *The Winter's Tale*. In 1783–84 he added Old Norval in *Douglas*, Sciolto in *The Fair Penitent*, Biron in *Isabella*, and Comus for his benefit on 23 March 1784. Roles added to his repertoire in 1784–85 included Posthumus in *Cymbeline*, Pierre in *Venice Preserv'd*, Caled in *The Siege of Damascus*, Theseus in *Phaedra and Hippolitus*, Alcanor in the premiere of Cumberland's *The Arab* on 8 March 1785, and Mr Ordeal in the premiere of MacNally's *Fashionable Levities* on 2 April.

Henderson had been at Liverpool in the summer of 1782 and 1783, and in 1784 he was seen for the first time at Edinburgh, where he offered a round of his most popular roles, including Hamlet, Richard III, Shylock, and Sir Giles Overreach. In the summer of 1785 he returned to Dublin to perform for a few nights and was invited to the Castle, where he entertained the Duke and Duchess of Rutland and their company with readings from *Tristram Shandy*. During the Lenten season of 1785 he and Thomas Sheridan commenced a series of readings at Freemason's Hall, London, which were highly successful and stimuated sales in the book shops. It was said that one bookseller sold 6000 copies of Cowper's *John Gilpin's Ride* after they offered selections from it, though it had scarcely been noticed at the time of its publication, several years before.

On 21 September 1785 Henderson began his seventh season at Covent Garden with Richard III. He then played Falstaff, Bayes, Sir Giles, Horatius, Leon, Evander, and Benedick. When he became suddenly ill on 4 November, he was replaced as Evander by Bensley of Drury Lane. On 8 November he again acted Horatius in *The Roman Father*, the performance which was to prove his last. After being seized with a fever, Henderson seemed to be responding to treatment, when he died in his sleep on 25 November 1785.

In his *Reminiscences*, T. J. Dibdin wrote that he had been told by the Covent Garden actor John Ledger that Henderson had fallen victim to an opiate administered by mistake. In the *Catalogue Raisonné of the Mathews Gallery of Pictures* (1823), it was said that he was "poisoned accidentally by his wife, who never knew the cause of his death." Other reports claimed that he had been seized unexpectedly with "a spasm in the brain." It was also reported that when his body was opened his liver was discovered to be "almost totally gone."

But the truth seems to be that Henderson had suffered a heart attack, though he was only 38. The autopsy report given by Mr Cruikshank, the anatomist, in the *Morning Herald* on 5 December 1785 stated that his liver was undiseased, his lungs in perfect health, his brain "had no extravasation whatever," and his stomach was strong. "His heart was the only part of the system which failed—his heart was literally broken—that is, it had lost its accustomed firmness of tone . . . and the leading vessels were all ossified, or ossifying." It was, Cruikshank claimed, the heart one would have expected to find in a person of 90.

On Saturday, 3 December 1785, Henderson was buried in the South Cross ("Poet's Corner") of Westminster Abbey, near the monument of

JOHN HENDERSON
artist unknown

Shakespeare and a few steps from the grave of Garrick. Over his crypt were placed the following words: "Underneath this stone are interred the remains of John Henderson, who died the 25th day of November, 1785, aged 38 years." A large congress of mourners in some 34 coaches formed the funeral procession. Dignum and Brett sang, assisted by voices from the Chapel Royal. Among the principal mourners were his friends Steevens, Malone, Byng, Murphy, and Whiteford, as well as Kemble, Macklin, Quick, Pope, Hull, Holman, and others from the theatres.

A long manuscript epitaph to Henderson, now in the Folger Shakespeare Library, proves to be the one published by J. H. Storer and J. Norris Brewer in *Histrionic Topography* in 1818. It had appeared during Henderson's lifetime in a collection of anticipated tributes to living characters by George Parker called *Humorous Sketches, Satirical Strokes, and Attick Observations*.

Though we have found no will for Henderson, administration of his estate was granted on 20 December 1785 to his widow Jane Henderson, of St Martin-in-the-Fields. She was the former Jane Figgins of the parish of St Clement Danes, whom Henderson had married at St Paul, Covent Garden, on 13 January 1779. They had, it was said, lived "in great domestic felicity." It is assumed that Henderson left her and an infant daughter well-provided for from his substantial earnings in salaries and benefits. Cumberland stated that in laying up a provision for his wife and daughter, "he was at least sufficiently careful and economical." Ireland believed that had Henderson lived longer he might have become at least as rich as Garrick. At Covent Garden Theatre on 25 February 1786 a benefit was held for Mrs Henderson, at which Mrs Siddons acted Belvidera in *Venice Preserv'd* and delivered a very dull and long address in praise of the deceased, written for the occasion by Arthur Murphy; the lines were printed by Wewitzer in his *Dramatic Chronology* (1817). Mrs Henderson died on 24 February 1819, at the age of 67, and was buried on 3 March beside her husband in Poet's Corner. The burial register gave her last address as No 56, Warren Street, Fitzroy Square, and stated that originally she was from Chippenham in Wiltshire. There is no evidence that Mrs Henderson ever performed or that she or her husband were related to the Mr (John?) Henderson who acted at the Haymarket in 1779–80 or the Mr Henderson who was a chorus singer at Drury Lane between 1789 and 1798.

Henderson had many natural disadvantages as an actor. He was short, ill proportioned, tending to corpulence, with a face not particularly flexible. His voice was neither mellifluous nor strong and handicapped him in roles requiring the softness of a lover or the rage of a tyrant. Yet he was regarded by his contemporaries as second only to Garrick. His greatest strengths lay in his intellect, uncommon powers of concentration and judgment, and a prodigious memory. It was said that in the delivery of soliloquies he was unequaled.

Cumberland, among others, praised his "strong colourings":

In broken and abrupt speakings, where the workings of the mind break forth into soliloquy, and more is to be conveyed to the spectator than the tongue utters, he was an unrival'd master; he could give its full weight to every incident of terror; and whether in the meditation or execution of the deepest catastrophe, he was the very soul of the scene.

In a review of Henderson's playing of Richard III, the *Public Advertiser* on 12 October 1784 claimed that he "is the soul, the animating particle of the person he represents—and never takes *punctuation* for *passion*." The "critical knowledge" which he displayed in his Shakespearean portrayals, according to the *Morning Herald* of 31 March 1783, was "no-

Harvard Theatre Collection

JOHN HENDERSON as Macbeth
engraving by J. Jones, after Romney

where better shown" than in his acting of King John. His chasteness and keenness of judgment are revealed in Boaden's description of his Falstaff: Henderson "stands before me with the muster of his recruits legible in his eye, and I hear the fat and chuffy tones by which he added humour to the ludicrous terms of the poet's description. . . . The bursts of laughter he excited by this, which he did not hurry, but seemed mentally to enjoy, as the images rose in succession, were beyond measure delightful. He made his audience for the time as intelligent as himself."

As Shylock, "Henderson exceeded Macklin in comprehension, but was inferior to him in execution," according to a press account about

Harvard Theatre Collection

Monument to JOHN HENDERSON

artist unknown

1787. "In the prominent display of Iago's jealousy, a material question of the play—slightly handled by the poet, and almost untouched by every preceding player," wrote a critic in the *Public Advertiser* of 25 April 1785, "in this, Henderson's claim to praise is quite unrivalled." His portrayals of Posthumus, Horatius, and Sir Giles Overreach were "perfection," thought William Dunlap, the American manager, and his Falstaff the only one "worth remembering, Cooke's being professedly a copy of it." He was, according to John Taylor, "a truly great actor." Mrs Siddons pronounced him "a fine actor, with no great personal advantages indeed, but he was the soul of intelligence." Boaden, Mrs Siddons's biographer, declared him "a man of great genius, and possessing the most versatile powers that I ever witnessed," no faint praise from the early editor of Garrick's correspondence.

In his eulogy on Henderson written for the *Public Advertiser* of 28 November 1785, Cumberland stated that his loss was to be lamented not only as a fine actor, but "as a most valuable man," who was benevolent and affectionate. Other memoirs published at the time of Henderson's death praised his humanity, candor, domestic tranquillity, hospitality, and devotion to his aged mother.

Though lacking in formal education, Henderson was well acquainted with arts and letters. He spoke French fluently. Some of his own verses, published by Ireland, are not particularly meritorious, but bespeak his literacy. With Thomas Sheridan he wrote *Sheridan's and Henderson's Practical Method of Reading and Writing English Poetry*, published, after his death, in 1796. In Fournier's *Theory and Practice of Perspective* (1764) are to be found some etchings by Henderson. He possessed a very large and fine library, including a Shakespeare first folio and many scarce old plays. His books were auctioned off by T. & J. Egerton, Scotland Yard, beginning 20 February 1786. The *Catalogue of the Library of John Henderson, late of Covent Garden Theatre*, published in 1786 for the sale, consists of 71 pages listing 1059 books (many sets) and 103 lots of prints, many of which were portraits of theatrical people.

While Henderson was still alive, Thomas Davies published *A Genuine Narrative of the Life and Theatrical Transactions of Mr. John Henderson, commonly called the Bath Roscius* (1777).

Soon after his death, *Letters and Poems, with Anecdotes of his Life* (1786) was published by John Ireland. An account of his life was printed in the *European Magazine* for December 1785. G. D. Harley's *Monody on the Death of Mr. John Henderson* appeared in 1787. A discussion of Henderson's acting is in Stephen Joseph's *The Tragic Actor* (1959).

Portraits of John Henderson include:

1. By Thomas Beach, 1773. Painting in the Garrick Club (catalogue No 452). Presented to the Garrick Club by Sir Squire Bancroft, 1897.

2. By Thomas Gainsborough, c. 1773. Exhibited at the Grosvenor Galleries in 1885, when it was owned by Andrew McKay; present location unknown. Engraving by J. Jones, published as a plate to *European Magazine*, 1786. A copy, after Gainsborough, is in the Garrick Club (catalogue No 24), and a similar picture, not by Gainsborough, was offered for sale at Christie's on 8 July 1938.

3. By Thomas Gainsborough, 1777. Exhibited at the Royal Academy in 1780 (No 194). Presented by Miss Julia Carrick Moore, Henderson's granddaughter, to the National Portrait Gallery (No 980) in 1895. Engravings by J. Jones, 1783; R. Josey, published by H. Graves & Co; Annon & Swan, plate to Doran's *Annals of the English Stage*, 1888; and unknown engraver, undated.

4. By W. Palmer, 1787? In *Notes and Queries*, 21 March 1857, H. T. Ellacombe reported that he owned "a large oval print" of John Henderson "published by Hogg, 1792, from a picture at Hanham painted by W. Palmer, 1787. Mr Strong, late Brooks, Bristol, had the copper-plate of it." Since we have found no other record of such a portrait, perhaps Ellacombe actually owned an engraved portrait of some other John Henderson, maybe the Oxford linguist and astrologist (1757–1788).

5. By Thomas Rowlandson. A watercolor caricature showing Henderson rehearsing in the Green Room with Sarah Siddons and her father Roger Kemble. With the National Trust, Ellen Terry Museum, Smallhythe; another copy in the Victoria and Albert Museum.

6. By unknown artist. Painting of Henderson in powdered wig and Van Dyck costume. In the Garrick Club (catalogue No 427c).

7. By unknown artist. Painting of Henderson in powdered wig, dark coat, and striped waistcoat. In the Garrick Club (catalogue No 236).

8. By S. Percy. Contemporary wax portrait. Sold at Christie's, 1800. Present location unknown.

9. Engraving by J. Coyte, based on Gainsborough's portrait in the National Portrait Gallery (above, No 3). Published 1787.

10. By unknown engraver. Published by J. Wingrave, 1786.

11. A design for a monument to Henderson's memory, with a medallion portrait. By unknown engraver. Published by J. Robinson as a plate to *Lady's Magazine*, 1786.

12. As Bayes in *The Rehearsal*. Engraving by Pollard, after J. Roberts. Published as a plate to *Bell's British Theatre*, 1777.

13. As Bireno, with William Smith as Paladore and Elizabeth Younge as the Princess, in *The Law of Lombardy*. By unknown engraver, undated, but no doubt 1779, since the engraving is marked "Scene in the New Tragedy of the Law of Lombardy," which opened on 8 February 1779 at Drury Lane. Rare copy in the Huntington Library.

14. As Count Biron in *Isabella*, with actress playing Isabella. Engraving by Walker, after D. Dodd. Published as a plate to *New English Drama*, 1777. We have found no record of Henderson's playing of this role by 1777.

15. As Dominick in *The Spanish Fryar*. Pencil and wash drawing by unknown artist. In the Folger Shakespeare Library.

16. As Dominick. By unknown engraver, undated.

17. As Don John in *The Chances*. Engraving by Terry. Published as a plate to an edition of the play, published by J. Harrison, 1780.

18. As Don John. Engraving by Thornthwaite, after J. Roberts. Published as a plate to *Bell's British Theatre*, 1777.

19. As Falstaff. Pencil drawing by Thomas Rowlandson. In the Yale Center for British Art.

20. As Falstaff. Sepia drawing by unknown artist. In the Harvard Theatre Collection.

21. As Falstaff. By unknown engraver. Published by Harrison & Co, 1781.

22. As Falstaff in *Falstaff's Wedding*. Red chalk drawing by J. Roberts. In the British Museum. Engraving by R. H. Cromek published as a plate to *British Library*, 1795, and *Bell's British Theatre*, 1795.

23. As Falstaff in *1 Henry IV*. Engraving by J. Coyte, undated.

24. As Falstaff in *1 Henry IV*. Pencil, pen and ink drawing by George Romney. In the Yale Center for British Art, on loan from the Yale Art Gallery.

25. As Falstaff in *1 Henry IV*, with Mr Charteris as Bardolf. Engraving by J. Kay, 1784. Probably of a provincial performance, as Mr Charteris seems not to have appeared in London.

26. As Falstaff in *The Merry Wives of Windsor*. Colored drawing by H. Ramberg. In the British Museum. Engraving by C. Grignion, published as a plate to Bell's *Shakespeare*, 1784.

27. As Falstaff in *The Merry Wives of Windsor*. By unknown engraver. Published by J. Wenman as a plate to an edition of the play, 1778.

28. As Hamlet. Chalk drawing by Robert Dunkarton, 1776. Exhibited at the Royal Academy that year (No 91). Presented by E. E. Leggatt to the National Portrait Gallery (No 1919) in 1921.

29. As Hamlet. Engraving by J. Goldar, after D. Dodd. Published as a plate to *Hibernian Magazine*, August 1778.

30. As Hamlet (?) with Mrs Elizabeth Hopkins (?) as Gertrude. By James Roberts. In the Garrick Club (catalogue No 439). This painting usually has been referred to as representing Mr and Mrs Spranger Barry, but Raymond Mander and Joe Mitchenson in *Theatre Notebook*, 16, suggest the possibility that it may depict Henderson and Mrs Hopkins.

31. As Hamlet, meeting the Ghost. Engraving by S. F. Ravenet, after J. Gwin. In the Harvard Theatre Collection, but not listed in Hall catalogue. Perhaps the vignette of Hamlet alone, published as a plate to an edition of the play by Harrison & Co, 1779 (and listed in Hall as No 22) is taken from this Ravenet engraving.

32. As Hamlet, with Richard Wilson as Polonius, as performed at Covent Garden on 26 April 1779. Painting by unknown artist, perhaps Benjamin Wilson. In the National Theatre. Another version, three-quarter length, in the Garrick Club (catalogue No 22) seems incorrectly attributed to Romney. When the National Theatre painting was exhibited at the Victoria and Albert Museum in 1951 it was incorrectly identified as a painting by William Beechey of J. P. Kemble and John Quick. See Mander and Mitchenson, *The Artist and the Theatre*, pp. 231–33.

33. As Hamlet ("To a Nunnery go"). By unknown engraver, undated.

34. As Horatius in *The Roman Father*. Engraving by J. Goldar, after D. Dodd. Published as a plate to *New English Theatre*, 1777.

35. As Iago. Painting by Gilbert Stuart, unfinished. In the Victoria and Albert Museum. Perhaps this is the portrait by Stuart of Henderson as Iago which was originally included in the *Mathews Collection Catalogue* (No 144) but is not located at the Garrick Club. An engraving by F. Bartolozzi was published by J. Bell, 1786; another state was published by Baldwyn; in the Harvard Theatre Collection is a third state, without line of publication. Another engraving by W. Read, after Stuart, was published as a plate to *Dramatic Table Talk*.

36. As Iago. Engraving by Thornthwaite, after H. Ramberg. Published as a plate to *Bell's Shakespeare*, 1785. Another engraving by E. Scriven, after Ramberg, also appeared.

37. As Iago. Drawing by A. Wivell. In the Players Club; gift of C. W. Couldock.

38. As Julius Caesar. By unknown engraver, undated.

39. As Macbeth, with the Witches. Painting (54½ × 64½) by George Romney, 1780. After Henderson's death the painting was won in a raffle at the Unincreasable Club by W. J. Long. It brought 250 guineas in the Long sale at Christie's on 28 June 1890 (lot 116). Present location unknown. Two of the Witches are said to be Charles Macklin and John Williams (who wrote as "Anthony Pasquin"). The original was engraved and published by J. Jones in 1787, three-quarter length. Other engravings were by J. Hopwood as a plate to *The Cabinet*, 1807, and by Kennerley as a plate to Oxberry's *Dramatic Biography*, 1826. A smaller version of the painting (35 × 28) is in the Garrick Club (No 435), acquired from the Mathews Collection. A third version (20 × 16) is in the Folger Shakespeare Library, acquired from the Montmartre Gallery on 1 October 1927; perhaps this is the version that was offered at the Grafton Gallery in 1897 (No 106).

40. As Macbeth. By George Romney. The single figure of Henderson was done by Romney in several studies and versions. A study in the Romney sale in April 1807 (lot 84)

brought £3 3s; perhaps that was the study, owned by J. P. Knight, exhibited at the Society of British Artists in 1832 (No 207). A watercolor and pencil drawing, after Romney, was sold for $50 in the sale of the property of the American Shakespeare Theatre (lot 168) at Sotheby Parke Bernet, in New York on 15 January 1976. An oil painting of the single figure of Henderson (30 x 25) was exhibited at the Grafton Gallery in the autumn of 1900 (No 94), as owned by Miss M. A. Nicholson. It was sold at Christie's on 23 June 1901. Perhaps this is the painting owned by R. R. Inglis-Jones, a photograph of which is in the Enthoven Collection at the Victoria and Albert Museum. A version is reported to be at the Museo Teatrale alla Scala, Milan.

Henderson, [John?] [fl. 1779–1796?], actor, singer.

At the Haymarket Theatre a Mr Henderson acted Bauldy in *The Gentle Shepherd* on 11 January 1779 and Byron (with songs) in *The Students* on 17 January 1780, performances given by actors from Scotland. He was no doubt the Henderson who acted at Edinburgh from 1781 to 1789, playing in the latter years such roles as Archer in *Robin Hood*, the Cook in *Love in a Village*, Midas in *The Countryman*, Westmoreland in *1 Henry IV*, and Trap in *The Prisoner at Large*. He was at Liverpool in 1786, Chester in December 1787, Newcastle in February 1788, and Coventry in June 1790. His wife, who did not appear in London, performed with him in most of those towns. Possibly he was the John Henderson who as a member of Fox's company at Brighton in July 1790 resided at No 11, King Street. A Henderson played at Salisbury in 1790–91. Actors called Mr and Mrs Henderson were with a company at Charleston, South Carolina, from January 1794 to March 1796.

There was no evident relationship between this Henderson and the famous actor John Henderson (d. 1785).

Hendrick. *See* KERMAN, HENDRICK.

Henery. *See* HENRY.

Hengler. *See also* HANGLER.

Hengler, Signor [fl. 1798–1822], pyrotechnist.

At Ranelagh Gardens on 9 July 1798 was discharged a fireworks display which included "an imitative Wheel of Boreas in angelic white, royal blue, green, yellow, rayonant and brilliant fires" and "A Superb Piece of Mechanism solely invented and executed by Signior Hengler, representing two Rattle Snakes in pursuit of a Butterfly (whose beautiful colours will be represented by blue, yellow, green, and other diversified fire-works). . . ." In July 1798 and again in 1800 and 1801 Hengler provided fireworks at Vauxhall after the sailing races. He was also at Vauxhall in June 1802, in August 1815, and in 1822.

Hengler was probably related to Hengler the tight-rope performer and pantomime actor who appeared at the Royal Circus from 1803 to 1808 and to the Miss Hengler who exhibited her tightrope ability there in 1803. A Mrs(?) Hangler was at Astley's Amphitheatre in 1786 and may also have been related to the pyrotechnist.

Henley, Mr [fl. 1785–c. 1798], singer, prompter.

Mr Henley sang principal characters in *The Fair Refugee* and *A Musical Interlude* at the Haymarket Theatre on 10 February 1785. He sang at the Royal Circus that year. Between that time and about 1798 he was associated with Astley's Amphitheatre as a prompter and occasional singer. There he is known to have played a Pilot in *The Royal Naval Review at Plymouth* in September 1789. At Astley's in Peter Street, Dublin, in January 1793 he sang a character in *The Natural Son*.

He was the husband of Elizabeth Henley, who sang at various London theatres between 1784 and 1817. Henley's name was entered on the Covent Garden pay list on 7 December 1793 for £1 per week, but we have found no mention of him in that theatre's bills. Mrs Henley's name was entered on the same day for £3 per week, and she performed frequently in that season.

Henley, Elizabeth [fl. 1784–1817], singer, actress.

Elizabeth Henley perhaps had been singing at Astley's Amphitheatre prior to her appearance at the Haymarket Theatre on 13 December 1784 as Lucy in *The Beggar's Opera*, a role she repeated there on 31 January 1785. Several weeks later at the same theatre she performed principal vocal characters in *The Fair Refugee* and *A Musical Interlude* on 10 February. In the same productions that night was her husband, Mr Henley (fl. 1785–1798), a singer and sometime prompter at Astley's. At the Haymarket on 15 March 1785, Mrs Henley played Miss Bridget Pumpkin in *All the World's a Stage* and Mrs Peachum in *The Beggar's Opera*.

Between 1785 and 1793 she was associated with Astley's musical performances. Her name was in Astley's advertisements as Nanny in *Love from the Heart* in September 1786, Joan in *The King and the Cobbler* in May 1791, and Old Mary in *The Tythe Sheaf* in July 1791. In Astley's Royal Amphitheatre in Peter Street, Dublin, she performed a Female Rower in *The Royal Naval Review at Plymouth* in September 1789 and was also there in 1785, 1788, 1791, and in January 1793 when she played Mrs Saveall in the musical farce, *The Miser*.

Announced as from Astley's, Mrs Henley made her debut at Covent Garden Theatre as Miss Di Clackit in *The Woodman* on 7 December 1793. The *European Magazine* that month reported that she had acquitted herself to the satisfaction of the audience. The following day her name was put on the Covent Garden salary list at £3 for a six-day week. Her husband, also engaged, was paid only £1 per week. Next she performed Mrs Peachum in *The Beggar's Opera* on 11 December, Lady Tereza Pancha in *Barataria* on 18 December, and the Landlady in *Harlequin and Faustus* on 19 December, playing the last role a total of 52 times before the end of the season. She also acted Mrs Fulmer in *The West Indian*, Margery in *The Travellers in Switzerland*, Miss Spinster in *Every One Has His Fault*, Mrs Maggs in *The London Hermit*, and Johayma in *Don Sebastian*. For her benefit on 11 June 1794, when she performed Mrs Bundle in *The Waterman*, she shared receipts of £295 13s. 6d. (less house charges) with Powel, Thompson, and Rock.

In 1794–95, when she lived at No 14, Broad Court, Drury Lane, Mrs Henley was again at Covent Garden with a salary of £3 per week, playing Huncamunca in *Tom Thumb*, Marcelina in *The Follies of a Day*, Mrs Ferret in *Arrived at Portsmouth*, Mysis in *Midas*, and a Country Girl in the chorus of *The Mysteries of the Castle*.

Absent in 1795–96, she returned to Covent Garden in 1796–97 at a reduced salary of £2 per week. That season and the next, still at £2 per week, she continued to swell the choruses of the pantomimes and musical spectaculars such as *Bantry Bay*, *Harlequin and Oberon*, *Crotchet Lodge*, *Harlequin and Quixotte*, *Joan of Arc*, and *Harlequin's Return*. The song *If a Body meet a Body*, as sung by her in *Harlequin Mariner*, was published in 1796.

The author of the *Authentic Memoirs of the Green Room* (1799) suggested that Mrs Henley "should forego Covent Garden entirely and attend Jones's company, (to whom her husband is prompter), for certainly she meets with more applause at the Circus than on the regular boards." Evidently she did just that, for her name was not in the Covent Garden bills after 1797–98.

Mrs Henley played at Norwich in 1798, at Richmond, Surrey, in 1804, and with the English Opera at the Lyceum in the Strand in 1810, 1816, and 1817. On 15 July 1815 she signed her full name to a Drury Lane salary receipt and was a member of that company in 1812–13, 1813–14, and 1814–15 with a constant salary of £2 per week. A Drury Lane casting book from that period, now in the Folger Library, gives her roles about 1815 as Mrs Casey in *Fontainebleau*, Landladies in *The Farmer*, *The Turnpike Gate*, and *Crotchet Lodge*, Mrs Neighborly in *Beggar on Horseback*, a Witch in *Macbeth*, Mabel Flourish in *Love in a Camp*, a Fishwoman in *The London Hermit*, Cicely in *The Quaker*, and Glumdalca in *Tom Thumb*.

Henman, Richard ₁*fl.* 1685–1697₎, singer.

On 23 April 1685 Richard Henman marched in the coronation procession of James II as one of the Children of the Chapel Royal. By 15 June 1692 his voice had broken, but he was granted livery on that date and as late as 1697 was still receiving material for clothes—a traditional grant to former Chapel boys.

Henney. *See* DE HENNEY.

Henning, Joseph [fl. 1760–1795], pit office keeper, doorkeeper.

On 22 September 1760 Joseph Henning was earning 2s. nightly at Covent Garden as a pit office keeper. He was mentioned occasionally in the account books, and by 1794–95 he had moved up to a weekly salary of 15s. and was serving as a doorkeeper.

Henniz, Mr [fl. 1766], musician.

In Carse's The Orchestra in the 18th Century is quoted a newspaper announcement of 1766 which indicates that Messrs Frickler, Henniz, Seipts, and Rathyen played on "the Clarinets and French horns" at Marylebone Gardens.

Henrey. See HENRY.

Henrie, Mrs [fl. 1752], dancer.

A Mrs Henrie was one of the Followers of Daphne in the pantomime Apollo and Daphne; or, The Burgomaster Trick'd at Covent Garden Theatre on 26 October 1752.

Henry, Mr [fl. 1704–1705?], equilibrist, musician.

A Drury Lane bill, not cited by The London Stage or seen by us, is quoted by Robert Gore-Brown in Gay Was the Pit (1957): "'Next a gentleman will perform several mimic entertainments on the ladder. First he stands on the top rung with a bottle in one hand and a glass in the other and drinks a health, then plays several tunes on the violin.'" Gore-Brown supplies the name "Henry" for the gentleman. He does not date the bill, but the context and the presence of Clinch of Barnet in the company point to 1704 or 1705.

Henry, Mr [fl. 1769], actor.

A Mr Henry played Iago in Othello and Flash in Miss in Her Teens in a pickup company at the Haymarket Theatre (usually dark in winter) on 28 February 1769. He is not otherwise known.

Henry, Mons [fl. 1788], pyrotechnist.

Astley's Amphitheatre at Westminster Bridge in 1788 advertised the addition to its attractions of a "Double Display of Fire-Works" with "Numerous Devices prepared in the usual way from Powder, etc." which were "alternatively played off with the newly invented Philosophical Fire-Works, under the direction of Mons. Henry [Henri?], the inventor and Professor of Natural Philosophy from Paris." A. St. H. Brock, in A History of Fireworks, thought that "The 'philosophical fireworks' were evidently an imitation of those exhibited at the Lyceum by Diller, which he described as 'Philosophical Fireworks from Inflammable Air, without smell, smoke or Detonation.'" There gas jets, both stationary and revolving, were arranged in patterns. Air from a bladder was forced through an ether-saturated sponge.

Extant Astley's programs of 16 May, 8 June, 22 and 31 August, and 4 September 1789, and 6 April 1790 included Henry's fireworks, "inflammable arrangements of exquisite colours."

Henry, Mrs [fl. 1788–1798?], actress, singer.

"A Young Lady" made her "first appearance on any stage" as Beatrice in Much Ado about Nothing at Covent Garden Theatre on 25 January 1788. She was identified as "Mrs Henry" in the European Magazine of February 1788. The reviewer felt that she had nothing but "personal beauty" to recommend her for the part. The World of 26 January 1788 called her a sister to Mrs Lawrence, a provincial actress.

On 24 July 1788 Mrs Henry was at the Haymarket to play Mrs Sullen in The Beaux' Stratagem. On that occasion the bill emphasized that she was appearing for the second time only. Thomas Lee Shippen, in his manuscript "Journey to Ireland 1789," in the Library of Congress, records that on 30 March 1789 he saw a play, presumably at Dublin, in which acted "a Mrs. Henry who played at the Haymarket Theatre last summer."

Mrs Henry returned to London and made her Drury Lane debut on 21 November 1789, again as Mrs Sullen. "She is a fine woman and a bad actress," wrote John Philip Kemble in a note now at the Folger Library. Her name appears in the manuscript pay book of Drury Lane (also at the Folger) each week all that season. It is not known what she did to justify her salary of £2 per week, unless she was singing in the choruses, not all of the members of which were always carried in the bills. She repeated Mrs Sullen on 29 May 1790, but except for that, and one appearance as Miss Hardcastle in *She Stoops to Conquer* on 26 May, her name did not appear in any playbill in London. At the time of her benefit she lived in Bruton Street, Berkeley Square. She was on the company roster at Drury Lane in 1790–91 at £2 per week.

She may have been the Mrs Henry cited by the *Thespian Magazine* as a member of Duckworth's company at the New Theatre, Parson's Green, Fulham, in 1792; and perhaps she was the Mrs Henry performing at Birmingham in the summer season of 1798.

Our Mrs Henry appears not to have been the Mrs Sarah Henry who was in the Drury Lane accounts at £3 per week in the 1801–2, 1804–5, and 1805–6 seasons. Nor is it likely that she was the Mrs Henry who played two characters—Miss Ogle in *The Belle's Stratagem* and Claudine in *The Hunter of the Alps*—and performed in "A New Ballet Dance" at Lancaster on 22 May 1805.

Henry, Master [*fl.* 1793], *acrobat.*
A Master Henry, advertised as "from London," performed various acrobatic feats at Bryant's Hall in Boston in the summer of 1793. He is otherwise unknown.

Henry, John 1746–1794, *actor, manager, musician.*
John Henry was born in Dublin in 1746. William Dunlap in his *History of the American Theatre* (1832) said that Henry had been "liberally educated, and [had] made his *debut* in London, under the patronage of the elder Sheridan," but had not been successful there. The London playbills do not, however, speak of anyone named Henry in 1762, a date put forward by Seilhamer in his own *History* (1889) and adopted by W. S. Clark in *The Irish Stage in the County Towns*—no doubt because 1762 was the year Thomas Sheridan was starring with Garrick at Drury Lane. In an index roster, Clark identifies him as the Henry who acted at the Vaults in Belfast on 7 August 1761. The part played by the 15-year-old boy is not known. But he had evidently acted at Dublin as well, for it was there that he must have begun his strange relationship with the Storer family of actors and singers.

Charles Storer, a journeyman Irish actor who had a brief London career, and his wife Eliza-

Harvard Theatre Collection

JOHN HENRY as Ephraim
engraving by "C. B.," after Tiebout

beth Clark Storer, an excellent singing actress, were parents of seven daughters of beauty and talent. In 1762 the family departed Ireland for Jamaica. Young John Henry seems to have gone with them. Charles Storer died in Jamaica. Henry married Jane Storer there. The next certain news we have of any of them is tragic. The story is told in dreadful detail in the *Newport* [Rhode Island] *Mercury* of 24–31 August 1767:

The following is a particular and authentic Account of the melancholy Accident which happened on board the Brig Dolphin, commanded by Capt. John Malbone, of this town, viz. Last Wednesday night she arrived off Point Judith, from Jamaica and when within about five Miles from Land, at half after ten o'clock the same Night, a Negro Boy went down between Decks, amongst the Rum where there stood several Puncheons of Water, and (as he says) with an Intention to draw some Water, but mistook and broached a Case of Rum; at the same Time the Door of the Lantern, in which he carried the Candle, being open, and the Candle falling into the Rum, set it on Fire; This so affrighted the Boy, that he neglected to stop the Running of the Rum, and in less than half a Minute the Head of the Cask flew out, and the Flames were immediately communicated to fifteen Casks more, all between Decks, so that all possible means used to extinguish it proved entirely ineffectual; the Vessel was all in Flames in a very few Minutes, and consequently reduced twenty-six Persons, being the Number of People, including Passengers, on board, to a Distress and Horror that must be left to the Reader's Imagination;— . . . There were eleven Passengers, viz.—Mr. John Henry, Mr. William Brooks Simson, Mr. Nathaniel Green, Mrs. Storer, Mrs. Henry, Miss Ann Storer, Mrs. Frances Storer, Miss Maria Storer, Miss Sarah Storer, and Mr. Henry's two Children, one sixteen months and the other four months old; five of whom perished in the following Manner, viz. Mrs. Storer, Miss Sarah Storer, and Mr. Henry's two Children being in the Cabbin, were suffocated with the Smoke before the two small Boats could be got out, they being thrown over with the utmost Difficulty, not having any Thing ready to hoist them: Mrs. [Jane Storer] Henry was upon the Deck, with her Sisters, and might have been saved with them, but overcome with maternal Love and Affection on hearing her Mother cry out, *The Children, oh the Children*, she ran and threw herself headlong down the Companion, into the Flames, and was there instantly consumed. The Remainder of the People, to the number of twenty-one, got ashore with Difficulty, in the two small Boats, not without being wet in landing; some of them, the same Night, with Trouble and Fatigue, got up to the House of Mr. Silas Niles, who received them with great Humanity, and afforded them all the Assistance in his Power, as did also the Rest of the Neighbours.— The Vessel burnt till eight o'clock the next Day, when she sunk. The above Brig belonged to Messrs. Evan and Francis Malbone, of this Town, was upwards of 200 Tons Burthen, was allowed to be the best Vessel belonging to the Colony, and was returning from the first Voyage, with a rich and valuable Cargo, and had got within three or four Hours Sail of this Harbour when the above Misfortune happened.

The unfortunate Storers and Henrys had been on their way north to join the American Company of Comedians, whose New York theatre was then being erected in John Street. Despite the tragedy and shock, the survivors had their livings to make and went almost at once to the Southwark Theatre in Philadelphia, where Douglass and Hallam had booked

the company to play a short season which opened on 7 September. Henry made his first American continental appearance in Philadelphia on 5 October 1767 as Publius Horatius in *The Roman Father*, and Ann Storer played Biddy Bellair in the farce *Miss in Her Teens*. Thereafter that season, Henry played Charles in *The Jealous Wife*, Jaffeir in *Venice Preserv'd*, Lovewell in *The Clandestine Marriage*, and probably Aimwell in *The Beaux' Stratagem*, Horatio in *Hamlet*, and other parts.

Henry's New York debut was on 7 December 1767 at the John Street Theatre, the season's opening night, when he played Aimwell in *The Beaux' Stratagem*, with Lewis Hallam playing Archer. It was a relationship—Hallam in first leads, Henry in either second leads (or minor parts)—which was to continue throughout most of their early association, since Hallam's mother, Mrs David Douglass, and her husband were running the company. During the remainder of that first season Henry demonstrated versatility with (in addition to parts played in Philadelphia), Heeltap in *The Mayor of Garratt*, Richmond in *Richard III*, Belarius in *Cymbeline*, Tybalt in *Romeo and Juliet*, the Tailor in *The Taming of the Shrew*, Eustace in *Love in a Village*, Edmund in *King Lear*, Tubal in *The Merchant of Venice*, Freeman and Lord Harry in *High Life below Stairs*, Castalio in *The Orphan*, Captain Brazen in *The Recruiting Officer*, Young Wilding in *The Citizen*, Blunt in *1 Henry IV*, Malcolm in *Macbeth*, Gargle in *The Apprentice*, List in *The Miser*, Portius in *Cato*, Sir Harry Harlow in *Neck or Nothing*, Sciolto in *The Fair Penitent*, Cassio in *Othello*, Carbuncle in *The Country Lasses*, Sir John Bevil in *The Conscious Lovers*, Lady Pentweazle in *Taste*, Timurkan in *The Orphan of China*, and Sir Callaghan O'Brallaghan in *Love à-la-Mode*. Neither Henry nor the Storers were in the bills during the last fortnight of the season.

The American Company returned to Philadelphia from 4 October 1768 to 6 January 1769, and with it returned John Henry, to add to his known repertoire only Lysimachus in *Alexander the Great*, so far as the surviving bills show. By 9 January 1769 the company was again in New York, and Henry was playing Hubert in *King John*. In the next six months, to 19 June, he remained with the company, but his roles are not known. But on 29 June

Henry delivered at the theatre "a moral, satirical and entertaining *Lecture* on HEARTS (Being the first Time of its Exhibition in America)," and rendered the monologue "Hippisley's Drunken Man." Between the parts of his performance Maria Storer sang several selections.

The American Company played for a month in Albany from 10 July 1769. From 8 November 1769 through 24 May 1770 they were in Philadelphia again, where Henry's only new parts preserved for history were Clerimont in *The Tender Husband* and Harlequin in *Harlequin Collector* ("in which character he will run up a perpendicular scene 20 Feet high"). On 30 March 1770 the bills were advertising that "*Mrs Henry*" (who was Ann Storer; there seems to have been no marriage ceremony) would play Tag in *Miss in Her Teens*. Her sister Maria Storer was still in the company. The troupe moved on to Annapolis and Williamsburg.

In 1772–73 Mr and Mrs Henry played again at Philadelphia, and in April 1773 they began, with the rest of the Douglass-Hallam company, the last season in which New York was to enjoy professional theatricals until after the war of the Revolution. In April and May 1774 Henry was recorded in a few roles at Charleston, on his way to Jamaica, where the American Company went early in 1775. John Henry managed and played in the company which served three theatres in Jamaica—Kingston, Spanish Town, and a new one at Montego Bay—from 17 March through 10 May 1777. Lewis Hallam had left for England in 1775 to attempt to scale the battlements of Drury Lane. Apparently the instant the 1777 season was over in Jamaica, or perhaps before it was over, John Henry also set sail for England, for he was almost certainly the Henry who acted a series of a dozen or so roles at the little China Hall Theatre in Rotherhithe from 18 June through 21 August 1777. Some of them, like Sciolto in *The Fair Penitent*, Iago in *Othello*, and Blunt in *George Barnwell*, were in John Henry's repertoire, and others were in his "line": Sir Jealous Traffic in *The Busy Body*, Ledger in *Polly Honeycombe*, Gloster in *Jane Shore*, Lissardo in *A Woman Keeps a Secret*, Frank Bevil in *Cross Purposes*, Marlow in *She Stoops to Conquer*, and the Conjuror in *The Devil to Pay*.

How Henry occupied himself for the next two years and more is not known. Perhaps he was strolling in the provinces. He may have gone back to Jamaica. John Durang in his *Memoir* assures us that "He was at one time an officer in the British Army, and you would always discover the deport of the soldier in him, erect and firm." Could he have been on British service in Jamaica during this period? (It would be tempting to think that he was the dancer named Henry who had been employed at Drury Lane in October and November 1776 and who returned to that theatre in 1777–78 and alternated between Drury Lane and the corps de ballet at the King's Theatre in 1778–79 and 1779–80, except that individual demonstrably was Luigi Henry [Henri].)

John Henry's (probably common-law) wife Ann Storer had not gone with him to Jamaica in 1775. She turned up at Smock Alley that year, and so did her sister Maria. By the summer of 1779 Maria had come to London, perhaps intending to join John Henry. At any rate they made debuts at the two chief London patent houses—he at Drury Lane as Othello (billed only as "A Gentleman") and she at Covent Garden as Patty in *The Maid of the Mill* (billed only as "A Young Lady")—on the same night, 16 October 1779. The news of their dual coup, with a criticism, was reprinted from some London daily in the Kingston, Jamaica, *Mercury* for 22–29 January. The London reporter had evidently badly garbled some of the details:

Oct. 19th. Saturday night last the play of Othello was performed at Drury-Lane Theatre for the purpose of bringing forward a young gentleman in the character of the Moor: we heard that his name is Henry, brother [-in-law?] to the young lady who made her appearance on the same evening at Covent-Garden, and son to an unfortunate pair of the Thespian tribe, who were drowned in their passage to the Indies.

Several passages in the part of Othello proved that he was more capable of giving dignity and ease to the temperate, than to the violent style of declamation. He has a good deal of that weakness which affects most spouters and country-players, tearing passion to fritters: There is, however, no part which is more difficult, nor more ineligible for a first appearance, than Othello; and he must indeed possess very capital ability who comes off with success. We shall therefore wish to see Mr. Henry again, before we ultimately decide on his merits.

The comic opera of the Maid of the Mill was, on Saturday night last, represented at Covent-Garden Theatre, in order to introduce a young lady in the character of Patty, being her first appearance on any stage. . . .

This young lady's name is said to be Storer, the daughter of an actress some twenty years ago equally celebrated for her vocal abilities, as for the propriety of her private character, but who had the misfortune, along with her husband, and others of her family, to be burnt on shipboard, going from one of the West India Islands to another.

An unidentified clipping in the Enthoven collection provides a more detailed criticism of Henry's London debut:

he wanted almost all the well-remembered dignity of a BARRY to support him, nor was he by a great deal sufficiently declamatory, besides that when he *did* exert himself, his voice grew harsh and coarse, and lost that melody he was able to preserve where its natural strength could compass his purpose. When his jealousy, however, first took fire from the insinuations against the honor of his wife, he began to *feel himself*, and to discover those abilities, which, we are inclined to think, were in a great measure suppressed in the more early scenes from a too studied desire of pleasing. From this period, he won more and more upon us; the dreadful workings of his mind, and the raging tempests of his soul, were executed in a masterly manner, and the symptoms of distraction [upon] his learning, that he had killed DESDEMONA without a cause, finely discovered and pursued till the fatal stab he receives from his own desperate hand.

The step of this gentleman, whose name we understand is HENRY, is easy and natural; his person somewhat about the middle size; his action exceedingly graceful, indeed in some parts of it . . . exuberantly so; and his speech clear, distinct, and forcible. With respect though to his *pronunciation*, we must, however he may have *decided* upon it in his own mind, submit it to him, whether handkerchief would not be better English than handker*cher*.

He'll be better when he has a better acquaintance "with *our* stage (for we are told he has performed elsewhere)".

On Saturday evening a woman fainted away in the two shilling gallery of Drury lane theatre when Othello strangled Desdemona—A better proof of the power of the poet than a whole volume of criticism!

But another anonymous critic wrote that "his gait was vulgar, and more resembled stalking than walking. . . . His voice had great extent but no variety. . . . in level speaking it was flat and inharmonious."

Henry's success was considerable enough to enable the managers to advertise him as "(The Gentleman who perform'd Othello)" when on 15 November he essayed the title role in *The Gamester*. According to the bills he acted sparingly in principal characters for the rest of the season: he repeated Othello on 8 January, was Cassius in *Julius Caesar* on 24 January 1780, Adam (for the first time) in *As You Like It* on 28 January, and for his benefit on 18 April he was both Posthumus in *Cymbeline* (for the first time) and Mungo in *The Padlock* (first appearance "in that character in Europe"). The benefit night produced for him £80 after house charges of £105. On 21 April he finished his season playing for Bannister's benefit (and for the first time) the Ghost in *Hamlet*. He had not been seen in the bills for over two and a half months after the announcement on 2 February that *Julius Caesar* had been deferred "on account of Henry's illness," and perhaps he had been held back by illness during all that time.

Henry had probably formed a permanent alliance with a third Storer sister. Very likely the unidentified "Young Lady" who made her first appearance on the Drury Lane stage playing Leonora in *The Padlock* on the night of Henry's one and only London benefit was Maria. Ann had disappeared from his life long since but was acting as Mrs Henry at Smock Alley, Dublin, from 29 January until at least midsummer 1775. She married the actor John Hogg (1770–1813) many years later. The date of the marriage of John Henry and Maria Storer—if they were, indeed, formally united—is not known. By about 1788 she was known to the public as Mrs Henry. Their life together was said to have been unusually happy.

We do not know when Henry left England to return to the Western Hemisphere. There is a story that on his passage he was captured by the Spanish and imprisoned at Cadiz but that he convinced his captors that he was a West Indian planter neutral about the war and indifferent whether Spanish or British were in control of Jamaica. On 30 June 1781 the Kingston, Jamaica, *Gazette* carried an announcement: "Mr. Henry respectfully acquaints the Public that he has jointly with Mr. [Lewis] Hallam [the younger] undertaken the superintendence of the American Company of Comedians and flatters himself, by attention and perseverance, to merit (the summit of his wishes) their Approbation."

David Douglass had retired and had sold his rights in the Jamaican enterprise and the American company to Hallam and Henry. Henry seems to have done the managing while the company remained in Jamaica. He signed an advertisement for a wardrobe keeper on 18 August, and while Hallam got the best parts, heading every surviving Jamaican bill from 18 July 1781 through 21 September 1782, Henry acted only a few roles early in the period.

On 25 August 1781 Henry brought out his own new comedy *School for Soldiers; or, the Deserters* in which he took the principal part. (It was published in Kingston in 1783. The editor of the *Royal Gazette* gave it a puff. He had "been informed by some friends of the author . . . that it possesses a very considerable share of dramatic merit and that it is written with an elegance of diction and purity of sentiment which would do credit to a more experienced son of Apollo. . . ." The piece was played at John Street in New York on 24 April 1788. The company continued to perform through the destructive Kingston fire and the threat of invasion from French and Spanish fleets in 1782.

With the drawing to a close of the Revolutionary War John Henry left Jamaica and went to Maryland, securing the passage of an act by the Assembly to confirm title of the American Company to the theatre the company had built at Annapolis in 1771. He then went to Philadelphia, seeking by a letter of 1 July 1782 to William Moore, President of the Executive Council of Pennsylvania, to secure property rights to theatres Douglass had erected there, a move which failed.

In New York, which was still occupied by the British, Henry gave monologues at the John Street Theatre on 1, 8, and 16 August 1782. He apparently went back to Jamaica and then on to London to collect performers. He returned to Jamaica in the summer of 1783, as a clipping in the British Library, taken from a current periodical, shows:

Extract of a letter from Jamaica, Sept 14, 1783: "Mr. Henry, who formerly belonged to Drury-lane Theatre, and who is the proprietor of the play-house, in the town of Kingston, upon this Island, arrived here the latter end of June, with some new performers, the want of whom occasioned his voyage to England last spring. Bad news awaited his return. The wardrobe of the Kingston theatre had

. . . been plundered to the amount of 500 1. and an account had the day before been received, that a very fine theatre, which belonged to him at Charlestown [S. C.], was entirely burnt to the ground. However, he turned his thoughts towards the entertaining [of] his Jamaica friends with great spirit, had the Play-house new painted, and opened it about a fortnight after his arrival, with *Venice Preserved*, and *Miss in her Teens*; since which they have gone very well, tho' they play only once a week. (Saturdays.) Mr. Henry's benefit . . . on the 6th of September, produced 291 1. In about a month's time they move off for Philadelphia, where Mr. Henry has a good theatre also. The company at present consists of Messrs. Henry, Hallam, Wignell, Giffard, More, Morris; Mrs. Giffard, Miss Fanny Storer, Miss Wainwright, Miss Kirk, Miss Quin, Mrs. Hamilton, and Miss Storer from Bath, who is Mr Henry's sister."

The Montego Bay *Cornwall Chronicle*, according to Richardson Wright's *Revels in Jamaica*, reported on 10 January 1784 the arrival of "the schooner Polly, Capt. Ogle, from Kingston, having on board the scenery etc. belonging to the American Company of Comedians," and on 28 January Henry announced that the new theatre at that town would open on 4 February. During the absence of Hallam in the States, Henry acted more frequently and seems to have been assisted in management by Thomas Wignell throughout the seasons of 1783 and 1784. The *Chronicle* of 5 November 1785 stated that the American Company had left Montego Bay "in July last" and "have arrived in Maryland; and were to open the theatre at Annapolis this [*sic*] first of this month."

Henry and Hallam's forces now rejoined, and on 21 November 1785 they reopened the John Street Theatre in New York. Henry and his wife moved into a house in Fair Street (now Fulton Street). Henry resumed a full schedule of acting and directed as well.

Hallam and Henry remained in partnership over the next seven years, dominating American theatricals from New York to Washington. On 5 June 1790 they even petitioned the Massachusetts legislature to open a theatre in Boston, but the petition failed. They were often in competition for parts and quarreled frequently. When in 1791 Wignell, an important member, resigned from the company and formed his own troupe, Henry grew alarmed. In 1792, he sailed once more for England to recruit players, one of whom was John Hodgkinson, whose character was both ruthless and devious. Hodgkinson set about at once to dominate Henry and to despoil him of his characters, which he did with the aid of Hallam. In addition to these troubles, the illnesses, both real and imagined, of Maria Storer Henry drove Henry deeper into despair and illness of his own. On 5 May 1794 John and Maria Henry took their farewell benefit, she in the title role of *Jane Shore* and he as Dumont, he as Obadiah Prim in *A Bold Stroke for a Wife* and she as Ann Lovely. At the end of the season Henry sold out his share (for $10,000) to Hallam, who at once transferred the property to Hodgkinson. (The original indenture of transferral to Hallam from Henry is in the Huntington Library.)

Henry died at sea near Fisher's Island, on a voyage from New York to Newport, Rhode Island, on 16 October 1794. ("He expired very suddenly of gout of the stomach," according to the *Columbian Centinel* of 1 November 1794.) Seilhamer says that he was buried at Bristol, Rhode Island. Dunlap says that he was "buried without ceremony under the sand of an island in the sound. His wife, who was with him [on the voyage], is supposed never to have recovered from the shock, and died, deprived of reason, at Philadelphia, 25th April, 1795, after having had the dead body of her husband brought to her, from its first place of unceremonious interment."

Henry was over six feet in height and uncommonly handsome, according to Dunlap. Durang said he was "a sterling actor, the American Sir Peter Teazle, great in Irishman [*sic*] and good in operas, the best gentleman Irishman I ever saw on any stage." While admiring his professional abilities and military bearing, Durang criticized him several times for parsimony: "Mr. Henry gave very low salaries to his performers, which kept most of them very poor."

Henry was a musician of "more than respectable acquirements," according to W. B. Wood in his *Personal Recollections:* "I can well remember that it was a common circumstance to see Henry in the orchestra, seated next the leader, giving his aid to the band, himself a good musical performer, when not otherwise engaged in the business of the evening." Several anecdotists among Henry's associates, including Durang, mention his carriage, the only one owned by an actor in New York in the nineties. Wood describes it: "The carriage was a curious and rather crazy looking affair, and lest the gout, which rendered it indispensable to him, might not be generally known as an excuse for such a luxury, he decorated the pannels with two crutches, crossed; the motto— 'This or These.'"

Besides the two young children by Jane, his first wife, who perished with their mother in the conflagration aboard the *Dolphin*, Henry is said to have been the father of a son by Ann Storer.

In addition to his comedy *A School for Soldiers*, John Henry staged *The Convention; or, The Columbian Father*, "A Serious Dramatic Pastoral," at John Street on 7 April 1787. It was revised and published as *Orvidus*. In addition, he left in autograph manuscript "The American Soldier, a Comedy" and "True Blue; or, The Sailor's Festival. A Farce," both now in the library of the Players Club, New York.

John Henry was shown as Ephraim Smooth in *Wild Oats* in an engraving by C. Tiebout, after "C. B." It was published by John Reid as a plate to an edition of the play in 1793.

Henry, Mrs John the second. *See* STORER, ANN.

Henry, Mrs John the third, Maria, née Storer *d. 1795, actress, singer.*

The third Mrs John Henry was a daughter of Charles and Elizabeth (née Clark) Storer, Irish performers. Maria had at least six sisters, Ann (Nancy, who became the *second* Mrs John Henry), Elizabeth, Frances (Fanny), Hannah, Jane (Jenny, who became the *first* Mrs John Henry), and Sarah. There may have been other siblings. Some or all of them are concealed in the bills of the Smock Alley Theatre, Dublin, in the season of 1757–58 under such descriptions as that in the advertisement for *The Oracle* on 25 April 1758: "All the Characters to be performed by Mrs. Storer's Children. With the original Epilogue to be spoke by Miss Storer in the Character of Cynthia." Only "Miss A.," "Miss E.," and "Miss M." were specified in the bills that season.

The entire Storer family emigrated to Jamaica in 1762. Their story is largely tragic after that year. Jane Storer and the young actor John Henry were married. Two children were born. At some time before Mrs Elizabeth Storer and John Henry gathered up their amalgamated families and fled toward the mainland colonies in 1767, the island's notoriously malign climate killed both Charles Storer and Maria's sister Hannah. Worse was over the horizon. On the night of 26 August 1767, as the brig *Dolphin* neared Newport, a cabin boy, sent to fetch water from a row of casks on a lower deck, dropped his candle and ignited a cask of rum, starting a fire which consumed the ship and, with it, Mrs Storer, Maria's sisters Sarah and Jane Henry, and Jane's two babies. Maria, her sisters Ann and Fanny, and John Henry were among the vessel's few survivors.

Ann Storer, John Henry (who soon took Ann into keeping; after 1768 she acted as "Mrs Henry"), and Frances Storer began to perform in Philadelphia and New York in 1767. In New York on 8 January 1768, "Miss M. Storer," "being her first Appearance on this Stage," sang a song at the end of *The Taming of the Shrew*. She sang once more, on 11 February, and mimed Agrippina, one of the "Children of Antony," in *Antony and Cleopatra* on 28 April 1768. The next season she stepped tentatively into speaking dramatic roles as young Prince Arthur in *King John*, a traditional debut part for youngsters. On 1 May 1769 Ann and Maria Storer had their benefit and invited ticket seekers to come to "the Miss Storers of Cart and Horse Street, facing the Church." Maria also sang that spring in a concert at Burns's Room for the benefit of Mr Tuckey.

Maria accompanied the American Company to Albany for a month of playing in July 1769, and from 8 November 1769 through 24 May 1770 the troupe was in Philadelphia, afterwards traveling to Annapolis and on to Williamsburg in 1771. In Philadelphia again from 28 October 1772 to 31 March 1773, they returned to New York and John Street on 14 April 1773 to begin the last theatrical season New Yorkers would enjoy until after the war of the Revolution. During this period Maria Storer was maturing early and rapidly and amassing a formidable list of characters, almost all in comedy, farce, and ballad opera: Clarissa in *Lionel and Clarissa*, Lady Bob in *High Life below Stairs*, Milliner in *The Suspicious Husband*, Cinthia (with a song in character) in *The Oracle*, Miss Willoughby in *A Word to the Wise*, Lucinda in *Love in a Village*, Louisa Dudly

in *The West Indian*, Miss Biddy in *Miss in Her Teens*, Leonora in *The Mourning Bride*, Kate in *The Miller of Mansfield*, Lucy Waters in *The Shipwreck*, Mrs Riot in *Lethe*, Lady Constant in *The Way to Keep Him*, Fanny in *The Maid of the Mill*, Betty in *The Fashionable Lover*, Maria in *George Barnwell*, Nell in *The Devil to Pay*, Lady Scrape in *The Musical Lady*, Miss Marchmont in *False Delicacy*, Ariel in *The Tempest*, Lucy in *The Beggar's Opera*, Marissa in *Theodosius*, First Aerial Spirit in *Edgar and Emmeline*, the Second Nun in *The Conquest of Canada*, the First Shepherdess in *Cymon*, Flora in *Hob in the Well*, Gypsy in *The Beaux' Stratagem*, Donna Isabella in *The Wonder*, Maria in *The Register Office*, Fanny in *The Clandestine Marriage*, Muslin in *The Way to Keep Him*, Lucinda in *The Englishman in Paris*, Miss Neville in *She Stoops to Conquer*, Nysa in *Midas* and Miss Nancy in *Neck or Nothing*.

On 25 November 1773, Maria arrived at Charleston with the manager David Douglass and his wife, the Henrys, and other elements of the American Company, on the brigantine *Sea Nymph*. The rest of the company followed later, and the actors opened performances at the New Theatre on Church Street on 22 December 1773. Maria's first recorded performance at Charleston was as Dorcas in the afterpiece *Thomas and Sally* on 31 January 1774. She repeated a number of her New York and Philadelphia parts that winter and spring in Charleston.

The next few years of Maria Storer's life must be carefully pieced together from fragmentary evidence. Douglass's American Company assembled in Jamaica in the late winter or early spring of 1775. Richardson Wright prints the only bill extant for the early part of the year, that for 1 July 1775, and in it a Miss Storer has one of the "vocal parts" in the "Solemn Dirge" traditional in *Romeo and Juliet*. But that lady was probably Fanny Storer. Apparently Maria had joined Ann, who was in the summer of 1775 appearing in Dublin, advertised as Mrs Henry, though she was never to rejoin her "husband."

But Maria was in Jamaica with the American Company—and John Henry—in the season which began at the New Theatre in Montego Bay on 17 March 1777. On that date she was Alicia and he was Dumont in *Jane Shore*. They played through 10 June 1777, and then the theatres in Jamaica seem to have been shut for a long period. Henry left for England and played at the China Hall Theatre in Rother-hithe in the summer of 1777. Nothing is known of him or of Maria until they made their London patent theatre debuts, on the same night but at different theatres, he at Drury Lane, she at Covent Garden, and both anonymously, on 16 October 1779.

The Kingston, Jamaica, *Mercury* for 22–29 January 1780 reprinted a criticism from some London newspaper of Maria's debut. The London reporter obviously made some errors:

The comic opera of the Maid of the Mill was, on Saturday night last, represented at Covent-Garden Theatre, in order to introduce a young lady in the character of Patty, being her first appearance on any stage. . . .

This young lady's name is said to be Storer, the daughter of an actress some twenty years ago equally celebrated for her vocal abilities, as for the propriety of her private character, but who had the misfortune, along with her husband, and others of her family, to be burnt on shipboard, going from one of the West India Islands to another.

In point of person she is rather below the middle size, neatly made, but not handsome. She seems to possess a good ear, some taste, and a knowledge of music; but her voice is thin, and without much compass, which seems to arise from the delicacy of her constitution. She spoke the part of Patty with propriety, but the thinness of her voice was equally conspicuous in speaking as in singing.

After the performances of 16 October 1777 John Henry disappeared for some time. Maria evidently went to the Bath-Bristol circuit where a Miss Storer is found by Kathleen Barker, playing singing heroines in the 1780–81 season. She was again at Bristol on 28 March 1782, singing in an oratorio with Rauzzini. She evidently also was much in request at "harmony" meetings in the cathedrals of the South and West.

On 7 February 1784 John Henry again opened the theatre at Montego Bay, and Maria Storer appeared as Rosetta in *Love in a Village.* She played all season, until 8 May, alongside Henry and her sister Fanny. Maria accompanied the troupe to Kingston for a short winter season and gave her last Jamaican performance on 24 February 1784. When Henry took the company back to Montego Bay in April, her place had been taken by an amateur, a Miss H. Haughton.

The *South Carolina Gazette* of 11 March 1785 informed its readers of the imminent arrival in Charleston of Maria: "We are assured that Miss Maria Storer, that celebrated Disciple of Calliope, intends taking her departure for Charleston the latter end of this month and from thence will sail for Great Britain in order to be in time to get a winter engagement at one of the theatres in London." The *Gazette* of 26–30 March announced her arrival in Charleston. She did not go to England at the time, however, but rejoined her comrades of the American Company in New York. That company was now under the joint management of Lewis Hallam and John Henry.

On 29 May 1786 (her previous New York service apparently forgotten) she was introduced by Henry simply as a "Gentlewoman," to sing Patty in *The Maid of the Mill* and Daphne in *Daphne and Amintor*. On 31 May the *Independent Journal* gave her praise and advice:

The Performance at the Theatre last night, was honored with one of the most numerous and brilliant Audiences ever known in this City: The powers of Miss Maria Storer, in particular, afforded the highest satisfaction to every individual; and, it is wished, that her much admired vocal abilities may be called forth for the entertainment of her kind patrons, in the line of Sacred Music, in which branch of composition we are informed she established an exalted reputation at Bath, Salisbury, Gloucester, Winchester, &c. Cathedrals, and other elegant harmony meetings, where the first company in England were collected to partake the divine songs in the Oratorios of the unrivaled Handel.

It is not known at what point Maria became the third Storer sister to come to John Henry's bed and board. Though all early historians agree that she married him, none say when. It was, however (if at all), by 1788, when complete bills become available again for New York and Philadelphia. Maria was the acknowledged tragedy queen of the American Company, and not merely by virtue of the fact that her husband was for so long co-manager.

Dunlap called her a small, fair woman whose figure gave no aid in tragedy. Her judgment, however, made her effective in everything. She had made a "lasting impression" on W. B. Wood. He recollected her as "a perfect fairy in person."

She usually came full dressed to the theatre, in the old family coach; and the fashion of monstrous hoops worn at that day, made it necessary for Mr. Henry to slide her out sideways, take her in his arms, and carry her like an infant to the stage entrance.

She possessed also all of the most desirable singing roles and was, indeed, the finest singer in America in ballad opera, oratorio, and concert, until the advent of Mrs Pownall in 1793. But by that time Maria's career was near its close. That it was so was partly the fault of her virago temperament which certainly qualified her for the title of America's first prima donna. Her husband's quarrels with Hallam and with Hodgkinson, who took Henry's best parts and ultimately forced him out of the theatre, were exacerbated by her imperious arrogance and her rages. John Durang wrote: "I have seen Mrs. Henry set in a chair in front of the stage crying thro' passion while the orchestra play'd her music through of a song in an opera. The performers at the same time concealing themselves behind the wings."

Henry sold his share of the theatre and his rights in the company in 1793. He died on 16 October 1794 during a voyage from New York to Newport, accompanied by his wife. She died on 25 April 1795, reputedly from grief over his death.

Henry, John Anthony [*fl.* 1784–1805], *instrumentalist.*

John Anthony Henry, a violist and subscriber to the New Musical Fund, was listed as resident at No 1, Sherrard Street, Golden Square, in Doane's *Musical Directory* in 1794. Was he the Mr Henry whom Burney listed as among the first violins at the Handel Memorial Concerts at Westminster Abbey and the Pantheon in May and June 1784? He was on the books of the New Musical Fund as late as 1805.

Henry, Luigi [*fl.* 1774–1808], *dancer.*

Luigi Henry was first noticed ("Henery") in a bill of the King's Theatre for 13 December 1774, when he was announced to dance on that date a pas de deux with Mlle Sophie at the end of the opera *La buona figliuola*. But that performance seems to have been canceled because of the illness of one of the principals. His first confirmed appearance was on 17 January 1775, when he ("Henry") and Mlle Sophie danced a pas de deux and an allemande, which they repeated on 18 April. On 6 June he and four companions figured in a *champêtre comique* after Act II of *La donna spirito*, a dance repeated on 24 June. On each of those occasions his name was spelled "Henery."

Henry was prominent in the ballet at Drury Lane Theatre every subsequent season through 1782–83. He danced also in the corps at the King's Theatre during the opera seasons from 1778–79 through 1782–83 and continued there (after leaving Drury Lane) until the date of the last London bill which carries his name, that of 28 June 1787. A document in the Lord Chamberlain's accounts in the Public Record Office shows him to have been on an annual salary of £80 at the opera house in 1784–85. C. B. Hogan identifies him as Luigi Henry, who was said by Giovanni Chiappari, in *Serie cronologica . . . dei principali teatri di Milano* (1818) to have been dancing in the opera house at Milan in 1808.

Between 1787 and 1808 there is a 21-year blank in Luigi Henry's record. Did he join strollers in the British provinces? There was a Henry on the York Theatre Royal company list in 1788, and a Henry "from Norwich" appeared at Derby on 14 March 1793. One night at the theatre at Buxton, near Sheffield, according to the author of *The Wonderful Theatrical Progress of W. H. West Betty* (c. 1805):

One of the Performers, a Mr. Henry, happened to step upon a trap, near the back part of the stage, which had been incautiously left unsecured, and he instantly fell through a space of more than twelve feet. A large hook caught the sleeve of his dress, which in some measure broke his fall, but lacerated his arm. He was taken up with very little symptoms of life. Medical assistance being on the spot, he was immediately bled, and carried home to his apartments. He was dreadfully bruised, and a considerable time elapsed before he was completely recovered.

The dancer Henry had a daughter, Victoire, born 24 June 1785, who was a piano virtuoso and married the composer Giacomo Gotifredo Ferrari.

Henry, Victoire. *See* FERRARI, SIG-NORA GIACOMO.

Henshaw, Thomas [fl. 1784–1794], singer.

Thomas Henshaw sang bass in the Handel Memorial Concerts at Westminster Abbey and the Pantheon in May and June 1784. Doane's *Musical Directory* of 1794 listed Henshaw as a member of the Concert of Ancient Music, the Academy of Ancient Music, and the choir of the Chapel Royal. He lived at No 24, James Street, Westminster. He was perhaps related to Joseph Henshaw of Edgeware Road, who was cited by Doane as an organist and music teacher but who seems not to have been a public performer.

Henslowe, Cecilia. *See* BARTHÉLEMON, CECILIA MARIA.

Henwood, Mr [fl. 1800], carpenter.

The Drury Lane account books show wages of £2 8s. paid on 4 January 1800 to one of the theatre carpenters, Mr Henwood.

Hepden. *See* HEBDEN.

Heptinstall, Thomas [fl. 1794–1841], singer.

Doane's *Musical Directory* of 1794 listed Thomas Heptinstall of No 3, Wood Street, Spa Fields, as a bass who sang for the Choral Fund and in the Handelian performances at Westminster Abbey. When the musician Joseph Mazzinghi made his will on 16 January 1841 he left £5 for a mourning ring to Thomas "Heptonstall" of Dorvuside College, but he revoked the bequest the following 1 November.

Herauld, George [fl. 1714], drummer.

In the Lord Chamberlain's accounts, George Herauld was listed as a drummer in the King's Musick in 1714.

Herbage. *See* D'HERBAGE.

Herbert, Mr [fl. 1769–1798?], actor, singer?, dancer?

Mr Herbert played a Recruit in *The Recruiting Officer* at Covent Garden Theatre on 30 September 1769. Between then and 17 October he appeared also as Faustus's Man in *Harlequin Doctor Faustus*, Sir Jasper in *The Mock*

Doctor, a Passenger in *Man and Wife*, and Charino in *Love Makes a Man*. He was probably the Mr Herbert who performed at the Capel Street Theatre in Dublin in 1770 and 1771 and was given a benefit at Sadler's Wells in London on 3 October 1772. On the latter occasion tickets were available from him at his lodgings in Bowling Green Lane near the Pantheon. Herbert shared a benefit with Crown at Sadler's Wells on 23 September 1774, and he was probably the entr'acte dancer Herbert who appeared at China Hall, Rotherhithe, on 27 June 1777.

Herbert was one of the performers at Sadler's Wells in the summer of 1780, and we take him to have been the Herbert who played a Wool Stapler ("with songs") in *Momus's Gift* at the Wells in April 1795. A Mr Herbert played Heli in *The Mourning Bride* at the Haymarket Theatre on 22 February 1796 (for that night only), and he was probably the Herbert cited in the *Catalogue of Printed Music in the British Museum* as singing, with Helme and Pilbrow, *An enemy appears in view* in *Black Beard*, published in 1798. Another song from the same work, *No longer heave the heart-felt sigh*, published in 1798, was sung by Herbert and Mrs Herbert. *Black Beard* was a music and dance spectacle performed at the Royal Circus.

Herbert, Mrs [fl. c. 1796–1807], singer, actress.

About 1796, according to the *Catalogue of Printed Music in the British Museum*, two songs were published "as sung by" Mrs Herbert at the Spa Gardens, Bermondsey: *I'll wait a little longer* and *'Tis Pity to die an Old Maid*. The following year was published another song, *Cottage on the Moor*, which Mrs Herbert had sung in *Niobe*, probably at the Royal Circus. The bills for the circus mention Mrs Herbert regularly from 1798 through 13 April 1807, singing hunting songs between the acts and playing Theresa in *The Nuptials*, Cheerfulness in *The Eclipse*, the Nymph of Spring "(with Songs)" in *The Golden Farmer*, Edith in *The Mysterious Freebooter*, the title role in *The Sorceress of Strozzi*, and Zada in *Solima*. The *Catalogue of Printed Music* shows that she also sang in *Black Beard*, *The Algerine Corsair*, and *The Jubilee of 1802* at the Royal Circus. Her husband sang with her in *Black Beard* in 1798 but seems to have had a much less extensive career. The

Miss Herbert who performed in London in the 1790s may have been their daughter.

Herbert, Miss [*fl. 1794–1798*], *actress.*
At the Haymarket Theatre Miss Herbert, possibly the daughter of the Mr and Mrs Herbert active in London in the 1790s, played Laura in *Tancred and Sigismunda* on 22 May 1794, Marcia in *Cato* on 4 December 1797, and Eliza Ratcliff in *The Jew* on 26 March 1798.

Herbert, John [*fl. 1710*], *musician.*
The Court of Burgesses of Westminster heard a complaint in January 1710 against John Herbert and "other Musitians living in the Parish of St. James, [Westminster]" who had "not only this last but Christmas was twelve months taken & received severall Sumes of money."

"Hercule, Mr." *See* DUCROW, PETER.

"Hercule Du Roi." *See* PORTE, LOUIS.

"Hercules, The Flemish." *See* DUCROW, PETER.

"Hercules, The Infant." *See* "INFANT HERCULES, THE."

"Hercules, The Modern." *See* "MODERN HERCULES, THE."

"Hercules From Paris, The." *See* PORTE, LOUIS.

Hergess. *See* STERGESS.

Heriot, John, stage name Herrington 1760–1833, *actor, author, editor, naval officer.*
John Heriot was born at Haddington, Scotland, on 22 April 1760, the son of a sheriff-clerk of East Lothian. After early schooling at Edinburgh High School he entered the University of Edinburgh, but a series of misfortunes broke up his family and he soon went to London. On 13 November 1778 Heriot was appointed a second lieutenant in the Royal Marines; he became a first lieutenant in 1780. He served in the *Vengeance*, the *Preston*, the *Elizabeth*, and the *Brune* and was put on half-pay in 1783.

Using the stage name of Herrington (given as Harrington in the *Thespian Dictionary*), Heriot waged a brief campaign in the theatre. He appeared as Orlando in *As You Like It* on the opening night of John Palmer's short-lived Royalty Theatre on 20 June 1787. Afterward, announced on the bills as a Gentleman but identified by name in the *Public Advertiser*, he played Lord Hastings in *Jane Shore* at the Haymarket Theatre on 29 August 1787, the second and evidently the last time of his appearance on the stage.

Heriot wrote two novels, *The Sorrows of the Heart* in 1787 and *The Half-pay Officer* in 1789. He also edited an account of the battle of the Nile and wrote for the *Oracle* and the *World*. On 1 January 1793 he started the *True Briton* and for a time edited the *Sun*, a newspaper in support of Pitt's policy which first appeared on 1 October 1793. He then published both papers until 1806. Afterward, he served as a clerk in the lottery office and from 1810 to 1816 as the deputy paymaster-general of troops in Barbados. His last years were passed as comptroller to the Chelsea Hospital, where he died on 29 July 1833, at the age of 73, about a week after the death of his wife. Information on his naval career may be found in *The Dictionary of National Biography*.

Herle, Mrs [*fl. 1733–1738*], *actress.*
Mrs Herle made her first appearance on the Drury Lane stage on 5 May 1733 playing Dorcas in *The Livery Rake*. During the 1733–34 season she was seen in *Harlequin Doctor Faustus* and as Mrs Wisely in *The Miser*, Altea in *Rule a Wife and Have a Wife*, Lucetta in *The Cornish Squire*, Ceres in *Cupid and Psyche*, and Mrs Cloggit in *The Confederacy*. On 15 April 1734 she played Mrs Wisely again at Lincoln's Inn Fields, and she repeated that part once more at the James Street playhouse on 31 May. Mrs Herle acted Mrs Mixum in *The Imposter* at Bartholomew Fair on 24 August.

She was not a member of any regular company in 1734–35. She acted Mrs Foresight in *Love for Love* at the Haymarket on 7 October 1734 and Arpasia in *Tamerlane* in the Great Room at the Ship Tavern on 4 November. After an absence she returned to Lincoln's Inn Fields on 31 March 1736 to play Mrs Day in

The Committee, and on 23 August of that year she was seen at Bartholomew Fair as Mrs Grey Goose in *The Modern Pimp*. Joan in *The Country Wedding*, at Pinkethman's booth at Bartholomew Fair on 23 August 1738, was the last recorded role for her.

Herold. *See* HAROLD.

Heron, Claudius [*fl.* 1739–*c.* 1760], *violoncellist.*

Claudius Heron was one of the original subscribers to the Royal Society of Musicians when it was founded on 28 August 1739. In May 1754 he was paid 10s. 6d. for playing the violoncello at the Foundling Hospital when the *Messiah* was performed, and he was a participant again, on the same instrument and at the same fee, when the work was given on 27 April 1758. About 1760 Claudius Heron's name appeared in the imprint of Salvador Lancetti's *Six Solos . . . for the Violoncello* ("Printed for Claudius Heron, at Mr. Burchell's Toy Shop, the upper end of Long Acre, near Drury Lane and sold at the music shops."). About the same time Heron had printed for him *Six Trios for two German Flutes, or two Violins with a Violoncello obligato* by "D'Hotel" (Dothel?).

Heron, [Henry?] [*fl.* 1760–1790?], *musician.*

A Covent Garden paylist dated 22 September 1760 cites a Mr Heron as a musician receiving 4s. 2d. daily. On 14 September 1767 he was still on the payroll at the same salary. The Mr Heron cited in the theatre's accounts on 28 December 1767 and 14 January 1774 ("The King's Footmen Xmas Box by Heron £2/2") was probably a royal servant and not the musician. The Covent Garden Heron may well have been the composer Henry Heron, who wrote a number of light songs, some of them sung by popular entertainers at London's pleasure gardens, and ten voluntaries for organ or harpsichord. Henry Heron's compositions, according to the *Catalogue of Printed Music in the British Museum*, were published between 1760 and 1790.

Heron, Mary d. 1736, actress, dancer?

Mrs Mary Heron was first mentioned in London playbills on 25 April 1721, when she took over the role of Emilia in *The Man of Mode* at Drury Lane from Mrs Younger, who had been graduated to Belinda. On the following 16 May Mrs Heron acted Valeria in *The Rover*, and on 26 May she and Mrs Seale shared a benefit. *The Funeral* was performed at the benefit, but neither of the women was listed in the cast; perhaps they were the unnamed dancers who performed between the acts. On 28 July Mrs Heron played Frisk in *The Country Wit* to conclude the season. She continued acting at Drury Lane through 1734–35, growing in public esteem, handling serious parts well, and becoming one of the leading comediennes in the company.

Among her roles over the years were Anna Bullen in *Henry VIII*, Julia in *The Fatal Marriage*, Lady Centaur in *The Silent Woman*, Hillaria in *Love's Last Shift*, Lucinda and Indiana in *The Conscious Lovers*, Araminta and Laetitia in *The Old Bachelor*, Mlle D'Epingle in *The Funeral*, Dorinda and Mrs Sullen in *The Stratagem*, Goneril in *King Lear*, Teresia in *The Squire of Alsatia*, Night in *Apollo and Daphne*, Clara and Estifania in *Rule a Wife and Have a Wife*, Emilia in *Othello*, Alithea in *The Country Wife*, Eliza in *The Plain Dealer*, Mrs Fainall in *The Way of the World*, Mrs Foresight and Mrs Frail in *Love for Love*, Cephisa in *The Distrest Mother*, Colombine in *The Comical Distresses of Pierrot*, Loveit in *The Man of Mode*, Lady Brute in *The Provok'd Wife*, Rachel in *The Jovial Crew*, Lady Sadlife in *The Double Gallant*, Lady Betty in *The Careless Husband*, Ruth in *The Committee*, Berinthia and Amanda in *The Relapse*, Biddy in *The Tender Husband*, the title role in *The Scornful Lady*, Queen Mary in *The Albion Queens*, Lady Townly in *The Provok'd Husband*, Lady Anne in *Richard III*, Lady Lurewell in *The Constant Couple*, Mrs Ford in *The Merry Wives of Windsor*, and Cleopatra in *All for Love*.

Mary Heron joined Theophilus Cibber in his protest against the management of John Highmore at Drury Lane in 1733. The malcontents complained of low salaries, among other things, and in retaliation the manager published in the *Daily Post* on 4 June 1733 a paylist that showed Mrs Heron to have been receiving £5 weekly—the highest scale among the actresses named and equal to what Cibber himself received. Highmore noted bitterly that he had raised Mrs Heron from £2 to £5 weekly, and that then she had refused to play several parts assigned her and had acted but seldom.

Cibber led his dissenters to the Haymarket Theatre, where they acted from September 1733 to March 1734. There, in addition to several of her standard parts, Mrs Heron added to her list Angelica in *Love for Love*, Arpasia in *Tamerlane*, Mariana in *The Miser*, and (since Mrs Horton stayed at Drury Lane) Millimant in *The Way of the World*. The rebels finally won their case, and Cibber dictated his own terms to the Drury Lane management when he and his group returned in March 1734. He demanded that each of his players should be paid £200 annually, that Mrs Heron should have benefits free of house charges, and that she should be given £100 yearly for clothes.

In her new and stronger position after she returned to Drury Lane Mrs Heron was able to join nine others in the troupe in a plan to lease the theatre for 15 years for £900 annually, but perhaps the plan did not materialize. Just when Mary was at the peak of her career she had an accident which forced her to retire and left her in financial straits. On 5 June 1735 she acted Indiana in *The Conscious Lovers* and then left the stage. On the evening of 5 March 1736 she died at her lodgings in Knightsbridge after a long and expensive illness which the *Daily Post* explained the following day. She was, the paper said,

justly esteemed of late the most celebrated actress on Drury Lane stage; but by the misfortune of breaking or putting out both her kneepans by a fall down stairs at her late dwelling house in Brownlow St. the Town has been deprived of her agreeable performances all this season, and the consequence has prov'd fatal to her, by throwing her frequently into convulsive fits, in one of which she died.

On 9 April 1736 the *Daily Advertiser* reported:

We hear, the late Mrs. Heron, on Account of her long and expensive Illness, having contracted some Debts more than she apprehended her Effects would discharge, in order to do justice to her Creditors, in almost her last Moments made her Entreaty, that the Profits arising from a Benefit Play . . . might be distributed amongst them. . . .

The benefit was held at Drury Lane on 16 April 1736. *Julius Caesar* was performed, and Kitty Clive spoke a special epilogue on Mary Heron's death.

A manuscript at the British Library contains a note calling Mrs Heron "a feeble actress, but correct," and most comments on her acting talent were tepid. Victor, in his *General History of the Stage* in 1761, said that Colley Cibber picked Mrs Heron to succeed Anne Oldfield in the roles of Lady Betty Modish and Lady Townly, two of his favorite characters. "On that Account he took extraordinary Pains, which was of singular Happiness to her; because with that Advantage, she made but a decent Actress. She was naturally well formed, with an easy, elegant Air and Mein; and though her Voice was bad, she had a sensible Pronunciation." *The Comedian* (1732) said she never appeared on the stage without giving audiences pleasure, but it gave no details.

Of Mary Heron's personal life almost nothing is known beyond the story of her accident. She was called Mrs Heron, though that did not necessarily mean that she was married. The following entry in the parish registers of St Paul, Covent Garden, may well have concerned the actress: on 23 September 1727 William, the illegitimate son of Sir William Yonge and Mary Heron, was baptized. The actress Mary Heron, interestingly, did not begin the fall season at Drury Lane that year until 13 October, and other actresses had taken her roles beginning the previous May.

Mary Heron was one of the players pictured by Laguerre in his satirical print, *The Stage Mutiny*, published in April 1733. She is the only actress shown, and she is at the center of the picture, at Theophilus Cibber's elbow.

Herpst, Mr ₍fl. 1768₎, *house servant?*

Mr Herpst was probably one of the house servants at Covent Garden. On 2 January 1768, according to the account book, he delivered a Christmas box worth £2 2*s.* to the Duke of Cumberland's footmen.

Herriette, Mons ₍fl. 1675₎, *dancer.*

Monsieur Herriette danced in the court masque *Calisto* on 15 February 1675.

Herriman, Mr ₍fl. 1775₎, *actor.*

Mr Herriman was one of the characters in *The Snuff Box*, an afterpiece, when it was given a single performance at the Haymarket Theatre on 23 March 1775.

Herring, John Frederick [*fl.* *1794*], *organist, violist.*

In 1794 John Frederick Herring of No 68, Leman Street, was listed in Doane's *Musical Directory* as a violist and as the organist at the Sion Chapel, Whitechapel.

He was probably related, perhaps as uncle, to John Frederick Herring (1795–1865), the animal painter, who was born in Surrey in 1795. According to the latter's notice in *The Dictionary of National Biography*, his father was an American of Dutch extraction who had settled in London as a fringe maker in Newgate Street.

Herring, [**Samuel?**] [*d.* *1760?*], *painter.*

A Mr Herring was paid 6s. 8d. on 29 September 1749 for two days' work at Covent Garden Theatre. He received various small sums, ranging from 11s. 6d. to £6 0s. 6d., between 18 January and 7 July 1750 and was referred to as "Herring[,] Painter." Perhaps he was the Samuel Herring who was buried at St Paul, Covent Garden, on 13 October 1760.

Herringman. *See* HERRYMAN.

Herrington. *See* HERIOT, JOHN.

Herron, Master [*fl.* *1796*], *actor.*

Master Herron played a Postboy in *Harlequin Captive* at Drury Lane on 9 and 11 November 1796, but his part was omitted in subsequent performances.

Herryman, Mr [*fl.* *1767–1788*], *singer, actor.*

Mr Herryman was a singer at Sadler's Wells Theatre for at least 21 years between 1767 and 1788. As a youngster, billed as Master Herryman, he sang there with Mrs Lampe and Miss Brown on 20 April 1767 and in *Merlin* on 13 May and 13 June 1767. Still as Master Herryman he sang at Marylebone Gardens on 17 August 1769. By 1776 his name was appearing in the Sadler's Wells bills as Mr Herryman. He was at Manchester in 1775–76, and in the winters of 1776 and 1777 he was engaged at the Theatre Royal, Liverpool. When Herryman received a benefit at Sadler's Wells on 2 October 1786, at which he per-

formed the title role in *The Old Woman of Eighty*, he lived at No 63, Leather Lane, Holborn. In 1788 he sang in *The Clown Turn'd Beau* and *Saint Monday*.

Songs published as sung by him at Sadler's Wells included: *As bringing home the other Day* (n.d.), *How d'ye do* (n.d.), *Fickle Chloe* (n.d.), *Ye French Hairdresser* (1770?), and *There's Beef and Mutton Roast and Boil'd*, in the interlude *A Trip to Cox Heath* (1778).

Herschel, Alexander [*fl.* *1760–1815*], *violist, violoncellist, optical technician.*

On 15 February 1760 at the Haymarket Theatre when the oratorio *The Universal Prayer* was sung, a "Mr Herschell" played the viola. We believe that person to have been Alexander Herschel, who was the son of Isaac Herschel (d. 1767), an oboist in the band of the Hanoverian Guard, by his wife Anna Ilse Moritzen. Alexander was one of ten children, including Jacob Herschel (c. 1740–c. 1792), a violinist, and Sir William Herschel (1738–1822), the famous astronomer and amateur musician at Bath and Slough. One of the Herschel sisters, Sophia Elizabeth, married Johann Heinrich Griesbach, also a musician in the band of the Hanoverian Guard and the patriarch of a large musical family, including five sons who are entered in this dictionary. In a letter to his daughter Fanny on 23 July 1799, Dr Burney reported attending a concert in the Music Room at Windsor Castle on the previous evening with Sir William Herschel, whose five nephews formed a principal part of the band.

Alexander left Hanover for England about 1757 to join his brother William at Bath, where he became a violoncellist in the Bath orchestra and at the Three Choirs' festivals. When his brother William, an organist and promoter of musical life at Bath, turned to astronomy by 1773, Alexander served as his expert mechanical assistant in the construction of telescopes. Their sister Caroline Lucretia Herschel (1750–1848) also abandoned music for astronomy.

Living many years at Bath and Slough, primarily employed by his brother, Alexander also appeared in concerts from time to time. Unfortunately the record of his musical career has become almost inextricably mixed with those of his brothers William and Jacob, neither of whom performed in London, although

Jacob had at least two of his compositions printed there. Possibly Alexander was the Herschel who played in concerts at Bristol on 5 November 1768, 13 June 1772, and 30 March 1784. His full name was advertised for playing the violoncello at a concert given for Kingsbury in the Assembly Rooms, Bristol, on 23 November 1776. He also played in the subscription concerts given in the Long Room, Bristol Hotwells, in June 1788 and in the Assembly Rooms in that city in November 1791.

In 1794 Alexander was listed in Doane's *Musical Directory* as a violoncellist, resident at Bath, and a subscriber to the New Musical Fund. His name was on the list of that fund's subscribers in 1805 and in 1815.

Hertford, Mr [*fl.* 1778₁], *actor.*

Mr Hertford wrote the prologue for a performance of *The Clandestine Marriage* and played Lord Ogleby, at the Haymarket Theatre on 30 May 1778. That would appear to have been his first and last stage appearance.

Hervey. *See also* HARVEY.

Hervey, Mrs [*fl.* 1736₁], *actress.*

A Mrs Hervey played Mrs Clearaccount in *The Twin Rivals* and spoke the epilogue at the Haymarket Theatre on 14 January 1736, for a benefit she shared with Miss Pattison.

Hervey, Miss [*fl.* 1800–1816?₁], *oddity.*

Miss Hervey, "The Beautiful Nyctalops"— an albiness who had normal vision in the daytime but was blind at night—was exhibited in Brookes's Original Menagerie, No 242, Piccadilly, in May 1800. A portrait of her, by an unknown engraver, was published as a plate to *La Belle Assemblée* in November 1816. Two other portraits by anonymous engravers—one titled "The Beautiful Albiness" and the other in color—were published without dates.

Hervigni. *See* D'HERVIGNI.

Hescot. *See* ESTCOURT.

Hesse. *See* DESHAYES, FAUSTINA, HASSE.

Heuette. *See* HUETTE.

By permission of the British Library Board

MISS HERVEY

artist unknown

Heurin, Mr [*fl.* 1776–1777₁], *performer?, house servant?*

The Drury Lane accounts for the 1776–77 season list a Mr Heurin, otherwise unknown, at a season salary of £70. He may have been one of the minor performers whose name was never cited in the bills, but his salary suggests that he held a position of some importance— among the house servants, perhaps.

Heutte. *See* HUETTE.

Hewerdine, William 1763–1799, *actor, composer.*

William Hewerdine made his first stage appearance as Young Philpot in *The Citizen* at Covent Garden on 14 May 1787; the playbill called him only a gentleman, but the *European Magazine* identified Hewerdine and said, "The confidence with which he exhibited himself before the public could only be excelled by the imperfection of his performance. We do not remember to have seen so complete a failure, so little modesty and so little merit." Hewerdine played the part again, but not until 16 April 1792 at the Haymarket Theatre.

WILLIAM HEWERDINE
artist unknown

In 1790 was published *A Collection of Odes, Songs, and Epigrams, against the Whigs . . . In which are included Mr. Hewerdine's Political songs.* The *European Magazine* in June 1799 reported that he died at Port Witham, Lincolnshire, on 5 June at the age of 36.

A portrait was made of Hewerdine by an unknown engraver, undated; it probably dates from the 1790s.

Hewes. *See* HUGHES.

Hewetson, Mr [*fl.* 1729], *proprietor.*
Mr Hewetson operated a "Great Room, the Upper End of Bow-Street, Covent Garden" where Richardson's Lilliputian Theatre held forth in January 1729. Hewetson advertised on 25 January that "This Theatre is proportioned to the Actors, and contains a great Variety of correct and beautiful Scenes, Machines, and all the regular Decorations and Changes incident to a Theatre, and will be varied to the Subject. The Musick is set and performed by some of the best Hands."

Hewitt, Mr [*fl.* 1784–1794], *singer.*
Mr Hewitt (or Hewit) sang tenor in the Handel Memorial Concerts at Westminster Abbey and the Pantheon in May and June 1784. Doane's *Musical Directory* of 1794 cited the Handel performances and gave Hewitt's address as West Smithfield.

Hewitt, Elias *d.* 1751?, *musician.*
The manuscript registers of the Worshipfull Company of Musicians at London Guildhall show that on 7 August 1751 Elias Hewitt, a musician from Spitalfields, became a freeman. Two added notes indicate that Hewitt was excused as poor (excused from some of his duties?) and that he died, apparently before the year was out.

Hewitt, James 1770–1827, *violinist, violoncellist, composer.*
According to Grove, James Hewitt was born in Dartmoor on 4 June 1770. He was the son of Captain John Hewitt of the Navy and entered the naval service himself but left it soon after because he objected to the cruel treatment of the sailors on his ship. He displayed a remarkable talent for music, and by the early 1790s he had become the leader of the orchestra at the court of George III. The J. Hewitt listed as a composer in the *Catalogue of Printed Music in the British Museum* was probably James; he was, in 1791, living at Preston and had published some songs and marches. On 7 November 1791 he was recommended for membership in the Royal Society of Musicians, but the following 5 February 1792 Hewitt told the Board of Governors that he had married (a Miss Lamb) since he was proposed to the Society, and his recommendation was declared void. Doane's *Musical Directory* of 1794, published after Hewitt left England, described him as a composer, violinist, and violoncellist who had performed in the Handel concerts at Westminster Abbey and who had played at Drury Lane.

Lowens in *Music and Musicians in Early America* states that Hewitt's wife and infant child died in 1791, but that must be an error for 1792. It was, perhaps, the loss of his wife and child that made James Hewitt decide to move to America, where he spent the rest of his career. In New York on 20 September 1792 he announced a subscription concert for the following day at Corre's Hotel to be presented by Hewitt, Gehot, Bergman, Young, and Phillips, "from the Opera House, Hanover Square, and professional concerts under the direction of Haydn, Pleyel, &c., London." Grove, however, states that Hewitt first appeared in concert in New York on 25 January 1793.

Hewitt established himself quickly as an impresario, composer, performer, teacher, and operator of a music publishing and selling shop. He conducted the band at the John Street Theatre (and, later, the Park Theatre), played the organ at Trinity Church, directed military bands, organized concerts, and wrote one of America's first operas, *Tammanny, or The Indian Chief* (1794). As a concert manager Hewitt was in direct competition with Peter Van Hagen, though they joined forces for a short while beginning in 1795. Hewitt traveled up and down the coast, performing, and in 1810 (or, according to some sources, 1812) settled in Boston. There he ran concerts in opposition to the Graupners and took charge of the music at the Federal Street Theatre.

Hewitt had married Eliza King in December 1795. They had at least two sons, James Hewitt and John Hill Hewitt (who had a musical career). About 1825 or 1826 husband and wife separated. He returned to New York, according to Lowens, and she remained in Boston. But they may have been reconciled, for James Hewitt died in Boston on 1 August 1827.

In addition to *Tammanny*, the music for which has been lost, Hewitt composed a number of piano and violin pieces, overtures, marches, songs, incidental music for plays, and music to accompany Collins's ode at the Anacreontic Society in New York on 11 June 1795 (that music has not survived).

A formal portrait of James Hewitt, in oil, artist unknown, was once in the possession of the Hewitt family. It was reproduced in Oscar Sonneck's *Early Opera in America*, but the original has evidently been lost. The portrait is not at the Library of Congress, as was once believed, and its location is not known by the Bicentennial Inventory of American Paintings, National Portrait Gallery.

Harvard Theatre Collection

JAMES HEWITT

artist unknown

Hewitt, John [*fl.* 1733–1737], *actor, playwright.*

At Lee and Harper's booth at Bartholomew Fair on 23 August 1733 John Hewitt (or Hewet) played Jethro in *Jeptha's Rash Vow* and Jupiter in *The Fall of Phaeton*. He performed at Drury Lane in 1733–34 and 1734–35, appearing as Alonzo in *The Tempest*, Atticus in *Theodosius*, Castro and Juan in *Rule a Wife and Have a Wife*, Worthy in *The Recruiting Officer*, Socrates in *Timon in Love*, the Governor in *Love Makes a Man*, Buckingham and Ratcliff in *Richard III*, Mortimer and Worcester in *1 Henry IV*, Albinus in *Junius Brutus*, the Governor in *Oroonoko*, Kister Aga in *The Christian Hero*, Raymond in *The Spanish Fryar*, Southampton in *The Unhappy Favourite*, Norfolk in *Henry VIII*, Morton in *The Albion Queens*, Morelove in *The Careless Husband*, Cassio in *Othello*, Decius in *Cato*, Decoy in *The Miser*, Heartly in *The Mother-in-Law*, and Decius Brutus in *Julius Caesar*.

During those seasons Hewitt also appeared at Lincoln's Inn Fields in April and May of 1734 to play Morelove in *The Careless Husband* and Castro in *Rule a Wife and Have a Wife*. At the Haymarket in May and June of the same year he played the King in *1 Henry IV*. He was not named in the Drury Lane bills in 1735–36, though his benefit tickets were accepted on 28 May 1736 (according to Latreille), so his connection with that theatre had not been severed.

In 1736–37 Hewitt worked for Henry Giffard at Lincoln's Inn Fields, but the season was not successful, and Giffard closed his theatre early. For Giffard, Hewitt played Merlin in *King Arthur* on 28 September 1736 on his first appearance and then such new parts as Lucius in *Cato*, a Player in *The Beggar's Opera*, Dulman in *Ignoramus*, the Beggar in *The Beggar's Pantomime*, Pizarro in *The Indian Emperor*, and the Constable in *The Recruiting Officer*. His last appearance may have been as Pizarro on 7 May 1737, though he shared benefit tickets on 27 May. During the season he signed an affidavit with his full name; it appeared in the *Daily Post* on 31 December 1736.

John Hewitt had a modest career as a playwright. *The Fair Rivals*, a tragedy, was published at Bath in 1729 and, according to the title page, was acted there by the Duke of Grafton's troupe. *The Fatal Falsehood* was published in 1734 and performed on 11 February that year at Covent Garden Theatre; it lasted four performances. A comedy, *A Tutor for the Beaus; or, Love in a Labyrinth*, was published in 1737 and presented in February of that year at Lincoln's Inn Fields Theatre.

Hewitt, Thomas [*fl.* 1754], *musician.*
Thomas Hare was bound apprentice on 6 May 1754 to Thomas Hewitt of the Worshipfull Company of Musicians.

Hewlet. *See* HULETT.

Hews. *See also* HUGHES.

Hews, James [*fl.* 1794], *singer.*
According to Doane's *Musical Directory* of 1794 James Hews of Poplar sang bass in the Handel performances at Westminster Abbey.

Hewson, Mr [*fl.* 1675], *violinist.*
Though he is not otherwise known, Mr Hewson appears to have been one of the regular band of 24 violinists in the King's Musick. He played in the court masque *Calisto* on 15 February 1675. Since one would expect to find other references in the Lord Chamberlain's accounts to anyone in the King's band of violins, perhaps "Hewson" is an error for another name.

Hewson, Mr [*fl.* 1730–1734], *actor.*
Mr Hewson evidently began his acting career as an amateur and eventually turned professional. He acted Archer in *The Stratagem* for his benefit on 18 September 1730 at the Haymarket Theatre and then, "for his Diversion," was King Arthur in *Tom Thumb* at Goodman's Fields on 15 and 18 March 1731. He held another benefit for himself at the Haymarket on 4 May and played Polydore in *The Orphan*. Perhaps when he was seen as Shift in *A Cure for Covetousness* on 23 August 1733 at the Fielding-Hippisley booth at Bartholomew Fair, he had turned professional. He certainly had done so for the 1733–34 season, during which he acted regularly at Drury Lane.

At the patent house from 1 October 1733 through 2 March 1734 he appeared as Sanchio in *Rule a Wife and Have a Wife*, a Countryman in *Harlequin Dr Faustus*, Poudre and Pierrot in *The Harlot's Progress*, a Noble Venetian in *Cephalus and Procris*, Nicias in *Timon of Athens*, Stephano in *The Tempest*, the Fencing Master in *Timon in Love*, Jack in *Oroonoko*, Lord Pride in *The Intriguing Chambermaid*, Dash in *The Author's Farce*, and Mars and Quadrille in *Cupid and Psyche*. The company at Drury Lane was a weak one, Theophilus Cibber having attracted some of the theatre's stronger performers to the Haymarket. When Cibber and his seceders returned to Drury Lane, Hewson left.

Hewson made a few appearances at the Haymarket in the spring of 1734. On 5 April he played John in *Don Quixote in England* and subsequently was see as Bilkum in *The Covent Garden Tragedy* and, for his benefit on 27 May, as Hotspur in *1 Henry IV*. He and Warwell had planned a performance of *The Stratagem* at Lincoln's Inn Fields on 17 May for their benefit, but, according to the *Daily Advertiser*, "a Disturbance . . . entirely hinder'd the Performance of the Play."

Hey. *See* HAY.

Heyborn, Mrs [*fl. 1782*], *actress.*
Mrs Heyborn played Mrs Joyner in *An Adventure in St James's Park* at the Haymarket Theatre on 21 January 1782.

Heyborn, Miss [*fl. 1782*], *actress.*
Miss Heyborn, very likely the daughter of the actress Mrs Heyborn, played the Duke of York in *Richard III* at the Haymarket Theatre on 4 March 1782 for that night only.

Heydon, Miss, later Mrs George Parker
[*fl. 1771–c. 1775*], *actress.*
In his *View of Society* George Parker tells us that he married a Miss Heydon in Edinburgh during his first engagement there under Digges. The Edinburgh *Evening Courant* of 16 November 1771 reported that Miss "Hayden" and Parker had been married a few days before. She was, Parker said, "no devotee to cleanliness," and her drinking, promiscuity, and spendthrift ways drove Parker into debt. He finally left her and set off for London. Miss Heydon got to London, too, for about 1775 she was seen at Bartholomew Fair as Mrs Bundle in the ballad opera *The Waterman* as a member of Sarah Baker's Sadler's Wells troupe.

Heyman. *See* HAYMAN.

Heynel, Mlle. *See* HEINEL, ANNE FRÉDÉRIQUE.

Heynes. *See* HAINES and HAYNES.

Heyward. *See also* HAYWARD and HAYWOOD.

Heyward, Mr [*fl. 1767*], *dancer.*
A dancer named Heyward was on the Drury Lane paylist on 24 January 1767 at 2*s*. 6*d*. daily, or 15 *s*. weekly.

Heywood. *See also* HAYWOOD.

Heywood, Thomas [*fl. 1672–1688*], *singer, lutenist.*
Thomas Heywood, who was perhaps related to the famous dramatist of that name, was one of the Children of the Chapel Royal as of 25 December 1672. By 12 April 1673 his voice had broken, and he received the usual grant of clothing and maintenance. On 23 April 1674 he was admitted as a musician in ordinary for the French lute, but without fee. On 23 October 1676, after John Rogers's death, Heywood was awarded a yearly salary of £100. He replaced Charles Husbands as a Gentleman of the Chapel Royal on 29 March 1678.

From 14 August to 26 September 1678 Heywood was one of the tenors singing for the King's entertainment at Windsor, for which service Heywood received an extra 6*s*. daily. James II renewed Thomas's appointment in the King's Musick, and Heywood was listed among the countertenors. He resigned his post on 24 October 1688.

Hicken, Mr [*fl. 1790*], *actor.*
The Bartholomew Fair puppeteer Flockton put on a performance of *Miss in Her Teens* in 1790; in the cast was a Mr Hicken.

Hickes, F. [*fl. 1706*], *impresario.*
The *Daily Courant* of 4 March 1706 cited a series of musical concerts usually presented monthly at Mr F. Hickes's lodgings in Finch Lane, near the Royal Exchange, Cornhill.

Hickey, Mr [*fl. 1753*], *house servant?*
Tickets for a Mr Hickey, possibly one of the house servants, were accepted at Covent Garden on 21 May 1753.

Hickey, Edward. *See* SEYMOUR, EDWARD HICKEY.

Hickford, Thomas [*fl. 1697–1739?*], *impresario, dancing master.*
Though the concert room named after Thomas Hickford was one of the most important ones in London in the first half of the eighteenth century, remarkably little is known about Hickford himself. Elkin, in his *Old Concert Rooms*, gives Hickford's first name as John and says a son took over the management of the concert room at some point. The earliest

mention of Hickford's Room was in 1697 and the last in 1779, though there is no certainty that during that long period there was always someone named Hickford concerned in the management.

Hickford's chief source of income at first was evidently as a dancing master, as an advertisement in the *Post Boy* of 20 November 1697 suggests:

These are to give Notice to all Lovers of Musick, and the Art of Singing, that Mr. *James Kremberg* is lately come out of Italy, and shall keep a new Consort of Musick by very great Masters, of all sorts of Instruments; with fine singing in Italian, French, English, Spanish, German, Dutch and Latin, after the newest Italian and French Manner, at Mr. *Hickford's* Dancing School in *Panton-street*, near the *Hay-Market*, or in *James-street*, over against the Tennis-Court, just by the *Blew-Posts*, there being a Door out of each street to the Room. This Consort will begin on *Wednesday*, the 24th of this instant at Eight a Clock at Night and will continue Weekly the same day; always with New Compositions. Price Half a Crown.

That may have been the first use of Hickford's Room as a concert hall.

The following 9 December a similar advertisement appeared for a performance of Jeremiah Clarke's St Cecilia's Day music, but after December 1697 Hickford seems not to have used his establishment for concerts until January 1706, when he was again calling it a Dancing School. Perhaps during the interim, unless we are simply missing evidence of regular concerts, Hickford found it more profitable to work as a dancing master.

From 1706 to 1738 Hickford's Room was in regular use, usually for musical offerings but also for dance performances. Most of the continental musicians of eminence who performed in London during that period appeared at Hickford's: "the Baroness," Dubourg, Valentini, Castrucci, Nicolini, Francesco Scarlatti, Geminiani, and many others who were sometimes not cited by name in the bills. The best of the native performers were also featured at Hickford's. Hickford seems to have leased his Room on occasion to musicians who organized their own series of concerts, and, indeed, that may have been his normal practice. The advertisements seldom make clear whether Hickford managed the concerts or simply rented his hall.

In 1738 Hickford's Room was apparently not used, probably because Hickford (or his son, perhaps, by that time) was preparing a new concert room. On 9 February 1739 was advertised a benefit concert for Valentine Snow at "Mr. Hickford's *new* Great Room in Brewer Street near Golden Square." The new hall was built at the rear of Hickford's house. It measured, Grove tells us, 50' × 30', had a coved ceiling, and was lit by a large window at the southern end "in front of which was the platform, small and rather low, and there was a gallery opposite, over the door." From 1739 to 1779 the new hall was regularly used for concerts, and again the foremost musicians of the period appeared there, among them Mrs Arne, John Beard, Mozart and his sister (on 13 May 1765), Johann Christian Bach, and Abel. After 1775 the Room was used less frequently, and Hickford's name was not mentioned in connection with concerts after 1779. By April 1789 the concert hall had become Rice's Great Rooms. The place was still in existence and in good condition in the 1930s.

Hickman, Mr. [*fl.* 1799], *bill deliverer and stage doorkeeper.*

Among the papers at the Richmond, Surrey, Reference Library relating to the Richmond Theatre are accounts concerning the house servants in 1799. Mr Hickman is listed as a bill deliverer and stage doorkeeper, and his wife is cited as the fruit seller.

Hickman Mrs [*fl.* 1799], *fruit seller. See* HICKMAN, MR.

Hickman, John d. 1751, *porter, stage doorkeeper.*

John Hickman was paid 18s. weekly for a season total in 1749–50 at Drury Lane of £28 16s. for his work as a porter. He held a different position before the prompter Cross noted in his diary on 28 December 1751: "Jack Hickman dy'd, Stage Door-keeper."

Hicks, Mr [*fl.* 1729–1734], *actor, singer.*

Mr Hicks was first noticed in London bills on 31 January 1729, when he played Appletree in *The Recruiting Officer* at the Haymarket Theatre. From that date through the end of the 1732–33 season Hicks performed at that playhouse in the winters and made occasional excursions to the fairs in the late summers. His roles at the Haymarket included Puny in *Hurlothrumbo*, Hearsay in *The Smugglers*, a Countryman in *The Humours of Harlequin*, the second Felon in *Love and Revenge*, Joan in *The Author's Farce*, a Forester in *The Amorous Adventure*, Secret in *The Fall of Mortimer*, Maiden in *Tunbridge Walks*, Cymon in *Damon and Phillida*, Father Pedro in *The Miseries of Love*, Lockit in *The Beggar's Opera*, Scrub in *The Beaux' Stratagem*, the Welshman in *The Mock Doctor*, and Truman in *The London Merchant*.

In August and September of 1730 he was a Forester in *Harlequin's Contrivance* at both Bartholomew and Southwark fairs; in September 1731 he played a Demon in *Merlin* at Southwark Fair; in August 1732 at Tottenham Court he was seen as Davy in *The Mock Doctor* and Dr Faustus in *The Metamorphosis of Harlequin*; and in August 1733 he played Diddimo in *Jeptha's Rash Vow* at Bartholomew Fair.

On 19 January 1734 Hicks turned up at Drury Lane in *Cupid and Psyche*, playing a Cobbler and a Satyr. Drury Lane apparently had no other use for him, or the company did not put him in any other parts that were mentioned in the bills. He kept playing in *Cupid and Psyche* into early March, and he was probably discharged from the troupe when Cibber and his rebel players returned to Drury Lane on 10 March 1734. Hicks went back to the Haymarket and appeared as Mr Sneak in *Don Quixote in England*, beginning on 5 April. At Southwark Fair on the following 7 September he was Taylor in *The Siege of Troy*, after which his named disappeared from London bills. There was a Mr Hicks acting at Norwich from 1746 to 1756, but judging by that performer's roles he was probably not the Hicks we have been following.

Hicks, Mr *d. 1796*, boxkeeper.

Mr Hicks, one of the boxkeepers at Drury Lane, shared a benefit with three others on 20 May 1780, the first mention of him in the bills. He shared similar benefits annually through 14 June 1796. His weekly salary as of 19 September 1789 was 9s. The newspapers reported on 8 June 1796 that Hicks had died recently, but his name still appeared on the benefit bill a week later. Perhaps he was the

father of Mr Hicks (fl. 1799–1804) and the Hicks girls who performed at Drury Lane around the turn of the century.

Hicks, Mr [*fl. 1799–1804*], *performer?*

A note in the Drury Lane accounts on 16 October 1799 shows that a Mr Hicks was paid on account "10—" (pounds, apparently). Hicks "and sister" were down for £2 per week in the 1800–1801 and 1801–2 seasons. Hicks was cited again on 22 September 1804 at £2 10s. The sister referred to was probably Charlotte; if so, Hicks also had two other sisters at Drury Lane around the turn of the century, Amelia and Louisa.

Hicks, Mrs [*fl. 1798*], *actress?*

Sybil Rosenfeld in *Theatre of the London Fairs* reports that Mrs Hicks was a member of Richardson's troupe when it performed at Bartholomew Fair in 1798.

Hicks, Amelia [*fl. 1799?–1806?*], *performer. See* HICKS, CHARLOTTE.

Hicks, Charlotte [*fl. 1797–1805*], *singer.*

Richard Brinsley Sheridan agreed to engage Miss Charlotte Hicks in 1797 at 10s. weekly, "the Theatre to find her instruction 'till a further arrangement shall be made." As far as can be determined from the Drury Lane account books, Charlotte was a singer who by the end of the 1804–5 season was earning £2 weekly, apparently for serving in the chorus. Perhaps the Mr Lanza who was paid £10 on 8 October 1799 to teach a Miss Hicks music was the instructor Sheridan found for Charlotte. What makes it difficult to be certain of Charlotte's work at Drury Lane is the fact that two other Hicks girls, Louisa and Amelia—Charlotte's sisters it seems—were also at Drury Lane, and the accountant did not always distinguish them carefully.

Louisa and Amelia apparently joined the company later than Charlotte, perhaps in 1799–1800 but possibly not until the following season. Louisa and Amelia seem to have earned £1 weekly in the 1800–1801 season, but one of them was being paid £5 weekly by 1804–5 and continued with the troupe at least through 1805–6.

Hicks, George ₍*fl.* 1794₎, *violist, violinist, flutist.*

Doane's *Musical Directory* of 1794 listed George Hicks as a tenor (violist), violinist, and flutist who performed in the Handel Concerts at Westminster Abbey. Doane gave Hicks's address as the Polygraphic Manufactory, Woolwich Common.

Hicks, Louisa ₍*fl.* 1799?–1806?₎, *performer. See* HICKS, CHARLOTTE.

Hickson, Mrs ₍*fl.* 1740–1748₎, *actress.*

Mrs Hickson acted Rhodope in *Orpheus and the Death of Eurydice* at Yeates's Bartholomew Fair booth on 23 August 1740. At the same fair on 24 August 1748 at the booth of Lee and the elder Yeates she appeared as Lady Betty in *The Unnatural Parents.* On 5 September at the Haymarket Theatre she was Miris in *Busiris,* and on 31 October at the James Street playhouse she donned breeches to play George Barnwell in *The London Merchant.*

Hide. *See* HYDE.

Hidoux, Margaret Catherine ₍*fl.* 1774–1775₎, *dancer.*

On 29 August 1774 David Garrick mentioned in a letter to the dramatist Richard Cumberland that he had engaged the Parisian dancer Mlle Margaret Catherine Hidoux to dance with Slingsby in the coming season. She had been recommended to Garrick by Antonio Carara, his former valet and sometime talent scout on the Continent. Mlle Hidoux made her debut at Drury Lane Theatre on 5 November 1774 dancing with Slingsby in *The Maid of the Oaks;* their performance was praised as "uncommonly fine" by the *London Chronicle* (5–8 November), and the prompter Hopkins noted in his "Diary" that they "were Amazingly well rec'd." Her low-cut costume put "modesty to the blush," according to a critic who recalled his embarrassment over a year later in the *Middlesex Journal* (7–9 October 1775).

In addition to her appearances during the season in *The Maid of the Oaks,* Mlle Hidoux danced frequently with Slingsby in specialty numbers. On 8 December 1774 they offered a *New Grand Provencalle,* with new dresses and a new scene of the port of Marseilles, and on 6 April 1775 they presented a *Grand Garland Dance.* For her benefit on 3 April, at which she made a net profit of £103 9*s.* 6*d.,* she and La Ravière performed a new ballet called *The Force of Love.*

For her season's work at Drury Lane Mlle Hidoux was paid 500 guineas, in several installments; the last payment of £27 5*s.*—"in full"—was made on 27 May 1775. On 18 January 1775 she had been reimbursed £31 18*s.* for the cost of lace for her costumes.

Mlle Hidoux returned to Paris to dance at l'Opéra in the last years of the 1770s.

Hiem, R. ₍*fl. c.* 1780–1797?₎, *proprietor.*

Wroth in *The London Pleasure Gardens* tells us of the proprietor Hiem:

In 1781 (or 1780) [Cromwell's Gardens] were in the hands of Mr. R. Hiem, a German florist, who grew his cherries, strawberries, and flowers there. About that time he changed the name to Florida Gardens, erected a great room for dining in the centre of the gardens, and opened the place to the public at a charge of sixpence. A bowling-green was formed and a band (said to be subscribed for by the nobility and gentry) played twice a week during the summer. An air-balloon and fireworks were announced for 10 September 1784. It was a pleasant place where visitors could gather flowers, and fruit "fresh every hour in the day," and take the light refreshment of tea, coffee, and ice creams, or wine and cyder if they preferred it. Hiem specially recommended his Bern Veckley as "an elegant succedaneum for bread and butter, and eat by the Noblesse of Switzerland." However, like many proprietors of pleasure-gardens, he subsequently became bankrupt, between 1787 and 1797(?).

The gardens adjoined Hale House in Brompton.

Higgins, Mr *d. c.* 1710, *posture maker.*

On 7 December 1709 the *Daily Courant* advertised that the Dutch posture maker Mr Higgins was to perform that night at the Queen's Theatre in the Haymarket. He "turns himself into such variety of Amazing Shapes and Figures that the particulars wou'd be incredible to all Persons who have not seen him." Addison saw a performance by Higgins and wrote about it in the *Tatler:*

I found the audience hushed in a very deep attention and did not question but some noble tragedy was just then in its crisis, or that an incident was to be unraveled which would determine the fate of a hero. While I was in suspense, expecting every moment to see my old friend Mr Betterton appear in all the majesty of distress, to my unspeakable amazement there came up a monster with a face between his feet; and as I was looking on, he raised himself on one leg in such a perpendicular posture that the other grew in a direct line above his head. It afterwards twisted itself into the motions and wreathings of several different animals, and after great variety of shapes and transformations, went off the stage in the figure of a human creature. The admiration, the applause, the satisfaction of the audience during this strange entertainment is not to be expressed.

Higgins performed at the Rummer in Bow Lane on 10 February 1710. In 1711 another posture maker was performing in London and was said to be better than the late Higgins. We would guess, then, that Higgins died about 1710.

Higgins, Mr [fl. 1782], actor.

A Mr Higgins played two roles at the Haymarket Theatre on 21 January 1782: Dapperwit in *An Adventure in St James's Park* and Colonel Manly in *The Beaux' Duel*.

Higgins, Miss [fl. 1776–1777], performer?

Miss Higgins received £5 from the Drury Lane management on 31 May 1777 for services rendered during the 1776–77 season. She may have been a minor performer.

Higgins, Parmenas [fl. 1794], singer.

Doane's *Musical Directory* of 1794 listed Parmenas Higgins, of No 14, Hemlock Court, Carey Street, as a bass who sang for the Choral Fund and the Handelian Society and in the Handel performances at Westminster Abbey.

Higgins, William d. 1806, violinist.

The violinist William Higgins was listed in the Drury Lane accounts on 20 August 1775 as a member of the theatre band. It is not clear how long he was employed at Drury Lane. Higgins played second violin in the Handel Memorial Concerts at Westminster Abbey and the Pantheon in May and June 1784, and as a member of the Royal Society of Musicians he played in the annual spring concerts at St Paul's in 1790 and from 1793 through 1797. The Minute Books of the Royal Society of Musicians reveal that William Higgins died in 1806. On 7 December of that year Ann Higgins, his widow, was granted £8 for funeral expenses and given a stipend of £2 12s. 6d. monthly. On 1 July 1810 the Society provided £5 to pay for Mrs Higgins's funeral expenses.

Higginson, Mr [fl. 1715–1718], actor.

At Drury Lane on 6 December 1715 *Richard III* was performed, and the 1718 edition of the play listed Mr Higginson as Dighton. At the same theatre on 6 August 1717 Higginson acted Burndorp in *The Old Troop*, and on 28 May 1718 he shared a benefit with three others.

Higginson, Mrs. *See* CUSSANS, MRS.

Higginson, [Miss?] [fl. 1776–1777], dancer.

The Drury Lane accounts in 1776–77 refer on 31 May 1777 to a Miss Higginson, who was paid "in full of this season" the sum of 5s. Another entry that season, not dated specifically, cited her as Mrs Higginson and described her as a dancer at a salary of £1 10s. weekly.

Highat, Mr [fl. 1735], performer?

Mr Highat's benefit tickets were accepted at Lincoln's Inn Fields Theatre on 2 September 1735. His function at the playhouse is not known.

"Highlander, The Prince's." *See* MACDONALD, SAMUEL.

Highman Palatine. *See* PALATINE, HIGHMAN.

Highmore, John 1694–1759, patentee, manager, actor.

The manager and actor John Highmore was baptized at St James, Westminster, on 7 February 1694, the son of Thomas and Joan Doggett Highmore. His father, noticed in *The Dictionary of National Biography*, was appointed Sergeant Painter on 25 April 1702 and died in 1720. Thomas Highmore was the son of Abra-

Harvard Theatre Collection

JOHN HIGHMORE
by Hogarth

and had then succeeded his master as Sergeant Painter.

Nothing is known of John Highmore's early life and education, but he evidently enjoyed a circle of influential and wealthy acquaintances as a consequence of his father's positions at court. John Nichols in his *Biographical Anecdotes of William Hogarth* mentions Highmore's poem "Dettingen," which "would have disgraced a Bell-man." In his *Apology for the Life of T[heophilus] C[ibber]* in 1740, Fielding described Highmore as "A Gentleman who had a great likening for theatrical Affairs, and who played some Parts on the Stage, meerly . . . to Shew what a Judge he was of acting, and consequently of Actors." Evidently to win a wager made in a coffee house, Highmore ventured onto the Drury Lane stage in the role of Lothario in *The Fair Penitent* on 19 February 1730. The bills listed the actor only as "A Gentleman," but Thomas Davies, Theophilus Cibber, and John Genest all confirm him as Highmore. He repeated Lothario on 21 February and then acted Polydore in *The Orphan* on 21 March and Torrismond in *The Spanish Fryar* on 2 April, playing the latter role, according to Davies, "very much to his disreputation."

At the end of the season, on 3 June 1730, he acted Othello at Goodman's Fields Theatre, where he was announced as the "gentleman who never appeared on any stage since he perform'd the Part of Castalio at the Theatre Royal in Drury Lane." The announcement erred in respect to Highmore's role in his previous performance in *The Orphan*, unless he had been the player of Castalio at Drury Lane on 16 April 1730 (when, according to *The London Stage*, Wilks acted that role). Highmore returned to Drury Lane for one performance as Hotspur in *1 Henry IV* on 31 December 1730, when he was announced as "the Gentleman who oblig'd the House by his Performance last Year."

The wealthy Highmore evidently had not seriously intended a career as an actor. His eye was on management. On 13 July 1732 the presumptuous Highmore ventured into the lion's den, purchasing the ailing Barton Booth's share of the patent for a sum reputed to be £2500. Anticipating a severe financial loss, Colley Cibber then sold his share of the

ham Highmore, a lieutenant colonel in the service of Charles I, and Mary Highmore, daughter of Thomas Bettesworth of Chidden, Hampshire. One of Thomas's brothers was Edward Highmore, a coal merchant in Thames Street, London, who was the father of three sons: Samuel Highmore (1682–1752), a schoolmaster and pastor of a dissenting congregation; Nathaniel Highmore (1689–1749), woodmonger and member of the London Common Council; and Joseph Highmore (1692–1780), the well-known painter and author. Our subject John Highmore's sister Margaret (1691–1717) married William Burroughs (d. 1727) of Chiswick and the Inner Temple in February 1718. John also was related to the artist Sir James Thornhill, who had been apprenticed to John's father Thomas Highmore

"Cloaths, Scenes, and Patent" to Highmore on 24 March 1733, thereby alienating his son Theophilus and provoking a rebellion, a lockout, and the secession of the actors to the Haymarket. Although an intrepid intruder into that intricate world, Highmore seems to have done his best to keep the theatre operating under the management which he now shared with Mary Wilks and Hester Booth, widows of the actors, and the painter John Ellis.

The details of Highmore's quarrel with the actors and their defection are given in Theophilus Cibber's notice in this dictionary (III, 244–47) and by Arthur Scouten in *The London Stage* (pt. 3, vol. 1). The events spawned considerable controversy and some pamphlets, including *A Letter from Theophilus Cibber, Comedian, To John Highmore, Esq.* (1733), which was a windy but explicit answer to the case the patentees had made in their statement in the *Daily Post* on 4 June 1733. In *The Theatrical Squabble* (1733), Highmore was characterized as "A Dancing Warrior, whom Mankind might say, / Frighten'd, not beat, his Enemies away," and in a reference to his brief acting career he was denigrated as "a Spindle-Lord," who "gay in Spangles" would first spout a tragic speech and then cut a caper. If Hotspur himself had seen Highmore's playing of that character, sneered the pamphleteer, he would have driven "the Mongrel Mimick from the Stage."

When Highmore's case against Harper, one of Cibber's actors whom they caused to be arrested as a vagrant, would not stand up in court, the position of the managers was severely weakened. By 2 February 1734 Highmore had sold his shares in the patent at about half their value to Charles Fleetwood (d. 1747), another wealthy dabbler whose tribulations at Drury Lane were eventually greater than Highmore's.

Little more is known about Highmore's private and public life after the squabble of 1733–34. His will suggests that he remained occupied profitably in real estate. But he may also have found a career at law. *The Register of Admissions to Gray's Inn, 1521–1889* (1889) lists, on 12 May 1736, "John Highmore, of St. James, Westminster, Esq." He did, however, make two other appearances on the stage: on 8 March 1743 he acted Lothario at Lincoln's Inn Fields Theatre for the benefit of Giffard,

and on 29 March 1744 he performed the same role at Covent Garden for the benefit of Mrs Horton.

Highmore made his will on 2 August 1756 and added a codicil on 30 January 1757. He died on 14 April 1759, at the age of 65, according to information provided by a descendant, N. J. Highmore, in *Somerset & Dorset Notes & Queries* (1917). The will was proved at London by his nephew and executor Thomas Burroughs on 4 April 1759. In the will he described himself as of the parish of St Paul, Covent Garden, but expressed his wish to be buried at St James, Westminster, with a funeral not to exceed £60 in costs. He further particularly enjoined his executor that his body be tenderly and carefully treated "and not unnecessarily exposed to the view of any Body and that it be put in a substantial Leaden Coffin within one of the most durable kinds of Wood and that my said Coffin be kept open and not fixed or screwed down until immediately before my Interment and which I desire may not be made with the Space of Ten Days after my decease unless my Corpse shall become offensive and will not admit of being so long kept."

Highmore made bequests of £10 to the poor in the parishes of St James and Hampton; £20 to his cousin May Sheafe; and £20 to the spinster daughter of his late cousin Thomas Burnel. A substantial amount of plate, china, gold rings, silver watches, books, linen, and other properties were left to his nephew William Burroughs. All else, including notes, bonds, lands near Ipswich, a freehold house in Old Bond Street, a freehold house in Albemarle Street, stables and other tenements in Ormond Mews near St James's Square, and lands near Islington, was bequeathed to his nephew Thomas Burroughs, a trustee of the estate. Highmore also invited to his funeral his cousin Joseph Highmore of Lincoln's Inn Fields and the sons and daughters of his late cousins, the Reverend Samuel Highmore and Nathaniel Highmore. No mention was made in the will of a wife or children.

Highmore was depicted among the figures in John Laguerre's satirical etching called "The Stage Mutiny," which was published in June 1733. He stands to the right in this print, holding a paper which reads, "*It costs £6,000*". He also is represented in the background as an

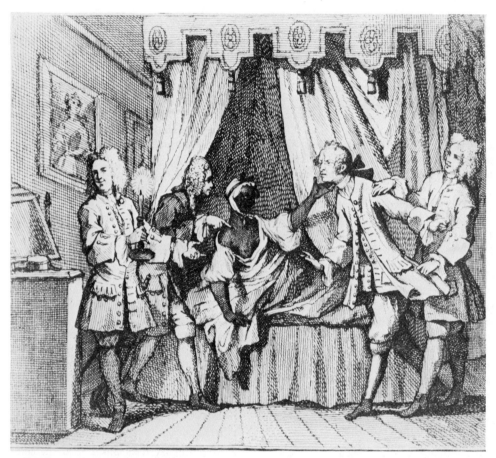

From the collection of Edward A. Langhans
JOHN HIGHMORE, "The Discovery"
by Hogarth

ape on a tightrope, carrying a sign which reads "*I am a Gentleman.*" The same design was represented on the show-cloth in Hogarth's engraving of "Southwark Fair," published the same year (with copies also engraved by Dent, T. Cook, T. Clerk, T. E. Nicholson, and T. Phillibroun). Hogarth also depicted Highmore in his print of "The Discovery," published about 1743, in which Highmore finds a black woman in his bed. It is intended as an allusion to his reputation as a real-life Lothario. Only about ten prints were taken before the plate was destroyed at the request of Highmore's friends. The original print is in the collection of Her Majesty, Queen Elizabeth II; a proof

before lettering is in the British Museum. An engraving by S. Ireland was published in May 1788 and in Ireland's *Graphic Illustrations of Hogarth* in 1794. An engraving of the single figure of Highmore from "The Discovery," after Hogarth, a rare copy of which is in the Harvard Theatre Collection, was published later in the century.

Hightrehight. *See* DE HIGHTREHIGHT.

Hilbourn, Abell [*fl.* 1724–1727], *house servant?*

The Lincoln's Inn Fields Theatre accounts in the 1720s make occasional references to Abell

Hilbourn, who may have been one of the house servants. He was paid £1 7s. on 5 October 1724 for 18 days' arrears, £2 2s. on 25 March 1727 on account, and 10s. on 5 June. He was also cited on occasion on the company's free list.

Hilbourn, Ann ₍fl. 1724–1729₎, sweeper.

Ann Hilbourn (or Hilborne) was very likely related to Abell Hilbourn, the Lincoln's Inn Fields employee. She was a sweeper, and the account books show occasional payments to her in the 1720s. Her weekly salary was 9s. She was first cited in the accounts on 5 October 1724, and she was on the company's free list from 1726–27 through 1728–29.

Hilisberg. See HILLIGSBERG.

Hill, Mr ₍fl. 1695–1696₎, actor.

Mr Hill played with Christopher Rich's troupe at Drury Lane during the 1695–96 season, appearing first as Junius in *Bonduca* in September 1695 and then as Diego in *Agnes de Castro*, Lysander in *Neglected Virtue*, and Petruchio in *The Unhappy Kindness*.

Hill, Mr. ₍fl. 1705–1721₎, impresario, dancing master.

On 2 January 1705 a benefit concert for Henry Eccles the younger was held at Hill's Dancing Room in Bishopsgate Street. He was most likely the Hill whose dances were included in *A Collection of Minuets, Rigadoons, & French Dances* in 1721.

Hill, Mr ₍fl. 1728–1729₎, actor.

A Mr Hill was a member of the company at the Haymarket Theatre in 1728–29. His roles included: Nickum in *The Metamorphosis* and Lookout in *The Craftsman* on 15 October 1728, then Pedro in *The Spanish Fryar*, Truelove in *The Lottery*, the Marquis of Posa in *Don Carlos*, Polydore in *The Orphan*, Brazen in *The Recruiting Officer*, a role in *The Royal Captives*, Genius in *Hurlothrumbo*, and Couch in *The Smugglers*.

In January 1729, Hill married Mrs. Anderson, a dancer at the Haymarket, and with the new Mrs Hill he took a benefit on 27 January 1729 as Polydore. Although Mrs Hill continued to perform in London for some years, we lose track of Mr Hill after this season.

Hill, Mr ₍fl. 1729₎, performer?

The London Stage lists a benefit at the Lincoln's Inn Fields Theatre for a Mr Hill on 12 April 1729, with no indication of Hill's participation in the performance. The gross receipts came to a very respectable £138 4s. 6d. No Hill is known to have been in the company at that time, yet "Hill" could hardly be an error for John Hall, since he received his benefit, shared as usual, the following 24 April.

Hill, Mr ₍fl. 1731?₎, actor.

In the Harvard Theatre Collection is an engraving by B. Cole of "The Humrous Farce of Jobson and Nell from an original painting in Vauxhall Gardens." Penciled under the three characters depicted are the names of "Hill," "Harper," and "Clive." Presumably the scene is from *The Devil to Pay*, at Drury Lane, on 6 August 1731, in which Harper acted Jobson and Kitty Clive acted Nell. But the name Hill appeared in no cast lists for the new ballad opera and we are unable to identify such a person with other Hills active about that time. We have reproduced the engraving with the notice of John Harper in this volume, where the third performer is tentatively identified as Richard Charke playing Ananias.

Hill, Mr ₍fl. 1736–1740₎, actor.

A Mr Hill played an unspecified character in performances of *The Cheats of Scapin* given at Southwark Fair between 23 and 26 August 1736 at Fielding and Hippisley's booth. Probably he was the same Mr Hill who acted Bravo in *Harlequin Grand Volgi* at Tottenham Court Fair on 4 August 1740. Possibly those appearances were the earliest ones of John Hill (c. 1716–1775).

Hill, Mr ₍fl. 1739–1754₎, puppeteer.

At Punch's Theatre, adjoining the Tennis Court in James Street near the Haymarket, beginning on 29 March and ending on 5 May 1739, Mr Hill, a puppeteer, gave 17 performances of *The Covent Garden Tragedy*. For his benefit on 1 May, when Hill was described as "Maker and Performer of Mr. Punch and his Company," tickets were to be had of him at the Lancashire Witch opposite the theatre.

Fifteen years later, on 19 September 1754, "at Hill's Large Theatrical Booth on the Bowling Green," Southwark, the "not'd Hill" presented *Harlequin Conjurer, or Pantaloon Dissected* and a *Grand Assembly of Lilliputians*.

Hill, Mr *[fl. 1774]*, *numberer.*

On 6 July 1774 the *Morning Chronicle* reported that Mr Hill, a numberer at Covent Garden Theatre, had a few days previously married a Miss Heaviside.

Hill, Mr *[fl. 1783?–1806?]*, *actor.*

A Mr Hill was a member of a company which acted on Mondays, Wednesdays, and Fridays at the Windsor Castle Inn, King Street, Hammersmith, during the summer of 1786. The variety of roles he played suggests provincial experience: Gayless in *The Lying Valet* on 5 June, one of the Mob in *The Mayor of Garratt* and Young Norval in *Douglas* on 7 June, Belville in *The Country Girl* on 28 June, Carmine in *Taste*, Laertes in *Hamlet*, and Hortensio in *Catherine and Petruchio* on 30 June, Bedamer in *Venice Preserv'd* and Eugene in *The Agreeable Surprise* on 5 July, Mervin in the *Maid of the Mill* on 7 July, Romeo on 12 July, Don Garcia in *A Bold Stroke for a Wife* on 19 July, Courtall in *The Belle's Stratagem* and Beaufort in *The Fool* on 26 July, and Blushingly in *The Natural Son* and Carlos in *The Wrangling Lovers* on 5 August.

A person or persons named Hill acted at Chester in 1785 and 1788, at Manchester in 1783, 1788, 1794, and 1799, at Newcastle in 1788 and 1789, and at Edinburgh in 1791–92 and 1805–6.

Hill, Mr *[fl. 1784?–1794]*, *singer.*

A Mr Hill from Winchester sang in the Covent Garden oratorios in the spring of 1794. Perhaps he was the Mr Hill, a tenor of Salisbury, who was listed by Dr Burney as one of the vocalists in the Handel Memorial Concerts at Westminster Abbey and the Pantheon in May and June 1784.

Hill, Mr *[fl. 1785–1803]*, *doorkeeper.*

A Mr Hill was a doorkeeper at Covent Garden Theatre between 1785–86 and 1802–3. He shared annually in benefit tickets with other minor personnel. His salary from 1794–95 through 1802–3 was 12*s.* per week (though some versions of the account manuscripts show a salary of £1). From 1800–1801 through 1802–3, two Mr Hills were being paid £1 and 12*s.* per week respectively, so there may have been two house servants by this name working at Covent Garden in the 1790s.

Hill, Mr *[fl. 1793?–1797]*, *dancer.*

A Mr Hill danced one of the Notaries in seven performances of *The Governor*, a new ballet pantomime, at Covent Garden Theatre between 11 March and 23 April 1793. He was probably the Mr Hill who performed in the historical ballet *Alfred the Great* at Sadler's Wells in 1797.

Hill, Mr *[fl. 1794]*, *bassoonist.*

A Mr Hill, of Hemlingdon, was listed in Doane's *Musical Directory* of 1794 as a bassoonist and a performer in the Handelian concerts at Westminster Abbey.

Hill, Mrs *[fl. 1723–1744]*, *singer, actress.*

Mrs Hill, announced as making her first appearance on any stage, sang in Italian and English at Lincoln's Inn Fields Theatre on 3 May 1723. She also sang on 10, 20, and 22 May. The following season she was noticed in the bills as singing at the Haymarket Theatre on 12, 13, 17, and 23 December 1723, and 3, 13, and 16 January. For her benefit on 6 May 1724 she sang in a concert at Lincoln's Inn Fields, and several weeks later she sang at Drury Lane. Her other appearances included 30 April 1725 at Stationers' Hall, 9 August 1728 at the Haymarket, 13 May 1731 (singing "Si Caro") and 19 May 1732 at Goodman's Fields Theatre.

Evidently this person was the same Mrs Hill who acted in musical and comic plays during the 1730s and early 1740s. Her first such performance seems to have been as Jenny in *The Lottery* at the Haymarket on 19 November 1728. On 20 May 1737 she played Lady Henpeck in *The Man of Taste* at Drury Lane. Playing Horatio in the same cast was Charles Hill, a nephew of Aaron Hill, but of no evident relationship to Mrs Hill. She played Dolly in *The Beggar's Opera* at Drury Lane on 25 October 1737. At Bartholomew Fair she acted Mother Catterwawl in *The Rumbling Lovers* in August 1740, Lady Grey Goose in *The Modern Pimp* in August 1741, and Doublescore in *The Glorious Queen of Hungary* in August 1743.

At the Haymarket in the autumn of 1744 she acted the Nurse in *Romeo and Juliet*, Dorcas in *The Mock Doctor*, Mrs Sealand in *The Conscious Lovers*, Peggy in *Love in Low Life*, Serjeant in *The Prodigal*, and Margery's Mother in *The Gardner's Wedding*. She also sang "the Noon Tide Air" from *Comus* on 20 October, and offered other vocal selections on 1 and 5 November. At Goodman's Fields on 3 December 1744, she played Lucy in *The Beggar's Opera*. Her last known performance was singing at James Street Theatre on 10 December 1744.

On 18 October 1744 at the Haymarket she sang the song "Was ever Nymph like Rosamond," suggesting that perhaps she was also the "Miss" Hill who had sung that favorite number at Goodman's Fields and York Buildings in 1734.

About 1740 was published *Tho' Baucis and I*, as sung by Mr Johnson and Mrs Hill in *Baucis and Philemon*.

Hill, Mrs, formerly Mrs Anderson   [*fl.* 1724–1740?], *dancer, actress.*

Mrs Anderson, a student of the dancer John Essex, made her first appearance on any stage in the dances at Drury Lane on 26 September 1724. (Probably she had been born Anderson; several times in subsequent bills she was listed as Miss Anderson.) On 2 November 1724 she danced again, and on 20 February 1725 she played Daphne's Follower in *Apollo and Daphne*.

The following season Mrs Anderson was at Lincoln's Inn Fields Theatre, where her roles included a Scaramouch Woman in *The Necromancer* on 3 November 1725, Atropos in *Harlequin a Sorcerer* on 13 November, and a Nymph and a Bacchante in *Apollo and Daphne* on 14 January. For her benefit shared with Salway on 9 May 1726 she danced a chaconne and, with Burney, a *Pastoral Dance* and a *Venetian Dance*; gross receipts for the night were £158 4s.

She began the season of 1726–27 at Lincoln's Inn Fields at a salary of 10s. per week, but by the end of September she had joined an Italian *commedia dell'arte* company which played at the King's Theatre until 10 May 1727. The following season, 1727–28, she returned to Lincoln's Inn Fields, playing a Mezzetin Woman in *The Necromancer* on 6 October and similar roles until 25 June 1728, when she acted the Niece in *The Successful Strangers*.

In January 1729 she married the actor Hill (fl. 1728–1729) and shared a benefit with him at the Haymarket Theatre on 27 January, at which time she was billed as Mrs Hill, "the late Miss Anderson." At the Haymarket during the remainder of the season she danced Diana in *The Humours of Harlequin* and Cuzzonida in *Hurlothrumbo*. Back at Lincoln's Inn Fields in 1729–30 she appeared in *The Triumphs of Love*, *The Dutch and Scotch Contention*, *Harlequin a Sorcerer*, and *The Rape of Proserpine*; she also played in *Hurlothrumbo* again at the Haymarket on 27 December 1729.

In September 1730 she danced at Lee and Harper's booth at Southwark Fair. She was probably the Mrs Hill who played the Nymph in *Orpheus and the Death of Eurydice* at Tottenham Court Fair between 23 and 27 August 1740.

Hill, Mrs   [*fl.* 1786]. *See* BURTON, PHILIPPINA.

Hill, Miss   [*fl.* 1729–1731], *dancer.*

At the Haymarket Theatre on 25 February 1729 a Miss Hill performed Venus and Ceres in *The Humours of Harlequin*; playing Diana in the same piece was Mrs Hill, late Mrs Anderson, but there seems to have been no relationship between them. Miss Hill danced a Nymph in *Apollo and Daphne* at Lincoln's Inn Fields Theatre in 1729–30 and 1730–31.

Hill, Miss   [*fl.* 1734], *singer.*

A Miss Hill sang at Goodman's Fields Theatre on 18 April and 8 May 1734; on the latter day her song was "Was ever Nymph like Rosamond." At a benefit that she shared with Pearce, Sandham, and Boucher several weeks later on 22 May 1734, Miss Hill sang the title role (by desire) in *Flora*. At the York Buildings on 28 August 1734, she gave the epilogue—in boy's clothes—to *The Orphan* and sang again "Was ever Nymph like Rosamond." Possibly this person was the singer and actress Mrs Hill (fl. 1723–1744).

Hill, Miss   *b.* 1777, *actress.*

Miss Hill made her debut at Covent Garden Theatre on 24 September 1794 as Miss Hardcastle in *She Stoops to Conquer*. She had been billed then as a Young Lady making her first appearance on any stage; the *European Magazine* in October 1794, however, identified her as Miss Hill from the Plymouth theatre. According to a notation in a manuscript at the Folger Library, she was 17 years old at the time of her London debut. On 28 March 1795 she acted Flavia in *The Absent Man*, and she replaced Mrs Mountain as Clara Sedley in *The Rage!* on 6 April. Her salary for the season was £2 per week, according to the account books. Though she was named in the bills for only the three performances noted, perhaps she also served in other minor parts.

Hill, Miss [*fl.* 1796], *dancer.*

Miss Hill, probably a child, danced the role of Petit Amour in a new ballet *Flore et Zéphire* at the King's Theatre on 7 July 1796 and four other times that month.

Hill, Aaron *1685–1750, playwright, manager, critic, poet.*

Aaron Hill was born in Beaufort Buildings in the Strand on 10 February 1685. He was the eldest surviving son of George Hill, an attorney of Malmsbury Abbey, Wiltshire, who died during Aaron's childhood. George Hill, it is said, had illegally sold an estate of about £2000, which had been entailed upon Aaron. Left without an inheritance, Aaron and his brother Gilbert were reared by their mother, née Gregory, and their grandmother, Ann Gregory. Aaron was sent at the age of nine to the free grammar school at Barnstaple in Devon, where John Gay was his schoolfellow. Then he received a classical education at Westminster; there he began his friendship with another Westminster boy, Barton Booth, who was destined to become a great tragic actor.

Rather than proceeding to one of the universities, the normal route for a lad of his background, Hill determined at the age of 14 to visit a distant relative, the sixth Lord Paget, who was at that time ambassador to Constantinople. Aaron's grandmother, being a woman of "uncommon understanding and great good-nature," financed the voyage, and Hill embarked on 2 March 1700, traveling by way of Portugal and Italy. At Constantinople, Lord Paget provided a learned ecclesiastic under whose tutelage Hill visited Greece, Egypt, and Palestine. Hill later wrote about these adven-

From the collection of Kalman A. Burnim

AARON HILL

engraving by Hulsbergh

tures in his *Full Account of the Present State of the Ottoman Empire*, published at London in 1709. In Constantinople in 1702, seventeen-year-old Hill killed a Turkish fanatic in self-defense. Another time he was rescued by Turkish soldiers from Arab bandits who had shut up his party in a cave with the intention of killing and robbing them.

Hill started home with Lord Paget's suite in the early summer of 1702; after passing through Bulgaria, Roumania, Austria, Germany, and Holland, and surviving a sea battle with the French, they arrived in England in April 1703. Probably Hill remained in Paget's household for several years. Then for a time he was tutor to young William Wentworth, who succeeded to his baronetcy in March 1706.

In 1707 Hill published his poem *Camillus*, dedicated to the colorful Lord Peterborough, whom he served as secretary until 1710. In 1708 Hill published *The Invasion: A Poem to the Queen* and *The Celebrated Speeches of Ajax and Ulysses*; the latter was a translation from Homer into English verse in collaboration with

Nahum Tate. Some dozen of Hill's short poems appeared in the *British Apollo* the same year.

In 1709 Hill, a theatrical novice, surprisingly came into the management of a major London playhouse at the age of 24. After complaints from the actors against Christopher Rich's oppressive management, Drury Lane Theatre was closed by order of the Lord Chamberlain in June 1709. One of the shareholders in the patent, William Collier, M.P., used his influence at court to negotiate a license which would allow him to operate Drury Lane. He obtained a new lease from the landlord—despite the fact that Rich already held a lease—and on 22 November 1709, as the *Tatler* related, drove Rich ("Divito") and his supporters from the theatre. The next night Collier reopened it with his license, with Aaron Hill as his manager. It is unclear how Hill could have persuaded Collier of his fitness for such a post, but perhaps the influence of Lord Peterborough had been exerted in his behalf. That Hill would accept the helm in such a maelstrom is testimony to his naïveté or nerve, probably both.

On 3 January 1710 Hill brought out his tragedy *Elfrid; or, The Fair Inconstant* and on 9 January added his farce afterpiece *The Walking Statue; or, The Devil in the Wine Cellar* to the bill. Hill confessed to having written *Elfrid* in less than a fortnight. Full of bombast, it was acted about five other times. Both pieces were published together that year with a dedication to the Marquis of Kent. (Twenty years later Hill revised *Elfrid* and saw it produced at Drury Lane on 10 December 1731 under the title *Athelwold*.) On 27 April 1710 Hill's comedy *Squire Brainless, or, Trick upon Trick* was given and damned; it was repeated on 28 and 30 April but was never published.

Hill's management was highly flattered in the friendly *British Apollo* of 3 April 1710, where verses extolled his abilities for reforming the stage. But his efforts at controlling his actors brought him only grief. During most of the season, Hill shared the managerial duties with seven of the leading actors, Barton Booth being the foremost among them. When Hill balked at giving the actors what they regarded as sufficient say in the casting, a bloody rebellion ensued, some of the facts of which may be gleaned from a letter Hill wrote to Vice Chamberlain Coke on 10 June 1710. After Hill had

withdrawn "the useless power of the seven Managers," an act which was "a great surprise to em, resented warmly by all," he appointed Pack director of rehearsals. But Pack gave up the post after two days, whereupon Hill offered it to Booth, who refused to accept unless all seven were restored. Hill delegated his brother Gilbert Hill to the job. Soon after, when Aaron left town to visit in Essex, Gilbert found it necessary to exact a fine from several players for neglect of duty, thereby causing Booth, Powell, Keene, Bickerstaff, and Leigh to refuse to act and to threaten to run off with the costumes. Bickerstaff had also pushed Gilbert Hill off the stage. Aaron rushed back to London, suspended Keene and Bickerstaff, and had harsh words with Booth. Fearful that the rebels would make good their threat to abscond with the costumes, Hill ordered the theatre closed.

On the afternoon of 2 June 1710 Hill, his brother, and the treasurer Zachary Baggs were attacked in the theatre office by Booth and his followers. Gilbert was struck on the head from behind by Leigh, and Aaron, almost stabbed by Powell, escaped; when he came back after an unsuccessful search for the Vice Chamberlain Aaron found himself locked out of Drury Lane. By an order dated 14 June 1710, the Lord Chamberlain dismissed Powell and suspended Booth, Keene, Bickerstaff, and Leigh from acting. It was a shallow victory for Hill, for the season was over anyway.

The following season the rebellious actors were reinstated at Drury Lane, though Hill was not. He had not been dismissed, however, but had simply changed his venue. While Hill had been struggling at Drury Lane in 1709–10, Swiney, in partnership with Cibber, Wilks, and Betterton, had prospered with plays and operas at the Queen's Theatre in the Haymarket. Again Collier used his influence, this time to force Swiney and his colleagues to take Drury Lane while he got control of the operas at the Queen's. The arrangements were completed on 6 November 1710, and on 22 November Hill took over the management of the Queen's, having persuaded Collier to farm it out to him at a rent of £600 per year, a figure Hill could then afford, inasmuch as his recent marriage to Margaret Morris, the only daughter of Edmund Morris of Stratford, Essex, had brought him a comfortable fortune.

The first three operas produced by Hill, *Idaspe*, *Pirro e Demetrio*, and *Etearco*, were neither critical nor popular successes. But the next was noteworthy. Hill solicited an opera from George Frideric Handel, who had recently arrived in London. The result was *Rinaldo*, composed by Handel in a fortnight to a text written in Italian by Giacomo Rossi and based upon a plan provided by Hill from Tasso's *Jerusalem Liberata*.

Rinaldo was first produced at the Queen's Theatre on 24 February 1711. An immediate and great success, it ran a total of 15 performances before the end of the season. The text was hardly distinguished. It possessed the typical imbecilities found in opera libretti of the period, but as Hill explained in the preface to his translation of Rossi's verses, published that year and dedicated to Queen Anne, his aim had been to fill the eye as well as the ear. Addison ridiculed the orange grove and the caged sparrows which, when let loose for dramatic effect, wreaked havoc with the ladies' dresses. He described the opera as an entertainment filled "with thunder and lightning, illuminations and fireworks; which the audience may look upon without catching cold, and without much danger of being burnt; for there are several engines filled with water, and ready to play at a moment's warning." The scenic effects described in the libretto were impressive nevertheless—including chariots drawn by fire-belching dragons, black clouds filled with monsters, and a crystal gate of a palace on a mountain which was transformed into a rock in mid-ocean. Despite the sarcasms heaped upon the production by Addison in the *Spectator* and Steele in the *Tatler*, *Rinaldo* was a landmark event in the history of English dramatic music, "superior in composition," in the opinion of Dr Burney, to any opera "which had ever been performed in England."

Hill's triumph as opera impresario was short-lived, for Collier took the Queen's Theatre back into his own hands before the end of the season, while Hill, according to Charles Dibdin's *History of the Stage*, "too wise or too powerless to contend with him, relinquished his right without murmuring." In his *Apology*, Colley Cibber, who lived closer to the events, was vague about the circumstances. On 3 May 1711 Collier was ordered by the Vice Chamberlain to pay back to Hill whatever Collier had received from subscription money in excess of the amount due him.

Throughout his life Hill was an optimistic promoter of money-making schemes involving all manner of projects. In 1712 he took up the first of his speculations, the development of a process for extracting oil from the beech mast, which occupied him for the following four years. Hill's studies convinced him that the demand for beech oil would be enormous and that his process promised to be one of the greatest benefactions to trade ever conceived. Through imaginative promotion he capitalized the project with securities to the amount of £120,000, but bad crop years burst the bubble, and in November 1716 the scheme failed. He had made little profit in four years, and only skillful stock manipulation had prevented his ruin. His poem *Dedication of the Beech-Tree* was published in 1714. In that and the subsequent years he issued various prospectuses and pamphlets on his scheme.

After his beech-mast failure, Hill turned once more to tragedy. *The Fatal Vision; or, The Fall of Siam* was produced by John Rich at Lincoln's Inn Fields Theatre on 7 February 1716. It ran seven nights with moderate success. No notice of a benefit night for the author can be found in the bills. *The Fatal Vision*, moreover, was produced at Hill's own expense with new costumes, decorations, and scenery. In this production—and in the preface to the published text—Hill pressed his doctrine of realistic but artistic scenic propriety: "The Decoration, which, however slighted, or ill-understood, among us, is a fifth Essential: And without it, 'tis impossible but that the finest Tragedy must be maim'd, and strain on Probability: to this I paid a very great Regard, in the Contrivance of the Play: And all the Dresses and Scenes were new: And such, who saw 'em, in the Representation, will confess them not unpleasing, and extremely differing from anything which has been lately seen upon the English Stages." Scenic descriptions for *The Fatal Vision* are strikingly operatic in their flavor, and it is possible that in that production Hill introduced to the English stage the *scena per angolo*, or angular perspective, a scenic technique which, having been perfected by Ferdinando Galli-Bibiena, was by 1716 commonplace in continental productions. With *The Fatal Vision*, Hill also claimed that his objective had been to combine the "necessary strictness" of French form with the liveliness of the Elizabethans.

For several more years Hill became absorbed in commercial ventures, including a proposal to colonize Georgia. In 1718 he engaged with a "society of gentlemen" in a plan to publish each month an essay account of some new invention. In December of that year the group issued *Four Essays*, specifically: *On making China Ware in England*; *On a method for furnishing Coals at a Third Part of the Price they are usually sold at*; *On the Repairing of Dagenham, or other Breaches*; and *On our English Grapes, proving that they will make the best of Wines*. A manuscript note on the title-page of a copy of the *Four Essays* in the British Library credits Hill with writing the first; no doubt he also had a hand in the other three. Also in 1718 he wrote a complimentary poem to Peter the Great called *The Northern-Star*, of which there were subsequent editions in 1724, 1725, and 1739. Before he died in 1725 Peter had ordered a gold medal to be forwarded to Hill, but it never arrived. Though the Czarina promised Hill materials for a life of Peter, only a few sheets were sent, and Hill never wrote the biography.

Hill's next play resulted from a philanthropic impulse. In order to assist his friend, the poet Joseph Mitchell, he wrote a tragedy called *The Fatal Extravagance*, which he allowed to be brought out under Mitchell's name at Lincoln's Inn Fields. The first recorded performance occurred on 21 April 1721, when Mitchell had a benefit supported by Hill, but there probably were two prior performances. The piece was repeated on 22 April and 22 November 1721 and on 11 January and 7 May 1722. On 2 May 1724, though *The Fatal Extravagance* was not played, its "author" received a benefit. The tragedy had been printed in 1720 with Mitchell's name on the title-page; in the preface he confessed his debt to Hill for "much in the scheme, in the sentiments, and language." Authorship of *The Fatal Extravagance* was credited to Hill by Theophilus Cibber, and in 1760 the play was printed in Hill's *Dramatic Works*. Hill had also obliged Mitchell with a prologue and an epilogue. A month earlier, he had provided an epilogue to Eliza Haywood's *The Fair Captive* at Lincoln's Inn Fields on 4 March 1721.

Soon Hill made an attempt to return to theatrical management. In that aspiration he was destined to constant frustration. In the autumn of 1721 he began negotiations to take over the new little theatre in the Haymarket, which had been built on speculation by the carpenter John Potter in 1720. The Haymarket had first been occupied by a group of French players under the patronage of the Duke of Montague. Their run ended in May 1721, and on 18 November next the *Weekly Journal* announced: "We hear that the Theatre in the Hay-Market . . . will be opened in a little time. . . . The Actors, as well as the Plays, they say, will be entirely new, and the whole to be under the Management and Direction of that noted Projector, Aaron Hill, Esq." First Hill had tried to persuade Rich to rent Lincoln's Inn Fields Theatre for two nights a week, but that manager, secure in his patent, had refused. Hill then had made "an absolute agreement" with Potter, as he wrote the Duke of Montague, "to pay him 540 pounds for two seasons." His plans were thwarted when the French players returned in November 1721 and Potter allowed them to act more than the ten nights that his agreement with Hill had stipulated. Hill complained to the Duke about Potter's double-dealing, but the Duke was not very accommodating. When Montague suggested that Hill try the larger King's Theatre, Hill pointed out that his scenery, already built—"after a model perfectly out of the general road of scenery"—would fit only the little Haymarket stage. Hill thus was obliged to abandon hopes for a theatre.

It was probably for his *King Henry V*, intended for production at the Haymarket, that Hill had prepared the scenery. This play, which well illustrates the methods of most of the uninspired Shakespearean adapters of the period, was produced at Drury Lane on 5 December 1723 with Booth, Wilks, and Mrs Oldfield in the leading roles. It had five additional performances that month and then was promptly and properly forgotten, despite an opinion in the satirical periodical *Pasquin* that Shakespeare's soul had "transmigrated" to Hill. But its importance rests in the announcement that the scenery was "to be disposed in a new Manner and Method." Like *The Fatal Vision*, this production was subsidized by Hill, at a cost of £200. The *Daily Journal* of 6 November 1723 reported that the scenes were "to be designed by Signior Angelo, an Italian." Possibly the reporter confused *scena per angolo*, the perspective technique which seems to have been employed in painting the scenes, with the name of the scene painter, who perhaps was John De Voto, then resident at Drury Lane.

Except for an occasional prologue or epilogue, such as those he wrote for Savage's *Sir Thomas Overbury* at Drury Lane on 12 June 1723, Hill occupied himself for the remainder of the 1720s outside the theatre. Much of his time was busied with yet another great "projection," the development of his idea for floating Scottish timber down the Spey to supply the navy. But again the result was financial disaster when it was discovered that there were really no trees in the Highlands tall enough for masts for a "first-rate" vessel. Otherwise, however, Hill's private affairs prospered and his prestige in literary circles rose.

Between 23 March 1724 and 7 May 1725, in collaboration with William Bond, Hill published a periodical called *The Plain Dealer*, which consisted primarily of essays on friendship, marriage, morality, business, history, and literature, which essays were later collected and published in two volumes in 1730. Of the 117 numbers only four were concerned with the theatre. In No 59, on 12 October 1724, Hill wrote, "It is the Duty of a Patriot to mourn for those growing Evils, which seem to threaten, either the Safety, or the Honour of his Country: And, for this Reason, I have often been irresistably chagrin'd, at the Corruption of our Public Theatres." In a similar vein in No 80, on 12 December 1724, he observed, "Either the Taste of our Audiences must be depraved, to a Degree of Horror; or the Judgement of the Master-Players corrupted, to a Degree of Pity!"

As a man of some wit and influence, Hill served the interests of such struggling writers as Mitchell and Mallet (for whose *Eurydice* he provided a prologue at Drury Lane on 22 February 1731) and enjoyed the friendship of James Thomson and a group of minor poets. He contributed many poems to Savage's *Miscellany*. His circle of platonic literary acquaintances called him "Hillarius" (a name evidently given him by Eliza Haywood) and his wife "Miranda." Hillarius wrote some letters and love-poems to "Clio" (Martha Fowke), about

whom Miranda seems to have been complacent.

Over the years Hill also suffered an uneasy relationship with Pope. Their contentions were complex and evidently had started when Hill, incited by a misreported remark, attacked Pope in the preface to *The Northern-Star* (1718). Despite Hill's apology in the preface to *The Creation* (1720), Pope in *Bathos* (in the third volume of his *Miscellanies*, 1727–28) provided a list of bad authors in which "A. H." was characterized as a flying fish. Hill retaliated with an epigram on Pope, Swift, and Arbuthnot in the *Daily Journal* of 16 April 1728. The following month in *The Dunciad*, Pope described Hill at the diving-match in the games sacred to dullness and dirt:

> H—— tried the next, but hardly snatched from sight,
> Instant buoys up, and rises into light;
> He bears no token of the sable streams,
> And mounts far off among the swans of Thames.

In his note to the next edition (1729), Pope explained that he had softened his satire into compliment, because Hill had once apologized and perhaps was "capable of a second repentance."

Still feeling affronted, Hill satirized Pope as "tuneful Alexis" in his poem *The Progress of Wit: a Caveat. For the use of an eminent writer*, "By a fellow of All-Souls" (1730). Eventually they formed a truce, but Hill continued to bombard Pope with letters and manuscripts to be critically scrutinized. Though his patience must have been severely tried, Pope usually responded. In a letter to Hill on 22 December 1731 Pope claimed to have read *Athelwold*, Hill's new tragedy, six times. It would seem that Hill had extracted punishment enough.

Athelwold, a revision of *Elfrid*, was produced at Drury Lane on 10 December 1731, preceded by Hill's extensive campaign to assure its success with entreaties to Wilks (who refused to play the leading role) to mount the play in antique costumes. He sent drawings "in the old Saxon dresses," based on Verstegan's *Antiquities*, accompanied by a letter on 28 October 1731 in which he argued that "as to impropriety in the custom of dressing characters so far back in time after the common fashions of our days, it weakens probability." A trial for any audience, *Athelwold* was repeated only twice, on 11 and 13 December. Hill wrote to

Pope "how it dragged itself along for two lean nights after the first; as lame and wounded as the snake in your poem, but not half so delightfully. It would be affectation, not modesty, to deny that I am nettled at the monstrous reception which the Town has given this tragedy."

Hill's next writing for the stage was a prologue for *The Tuscan Treaty*, a tragedy written by his friend William Bond, which was produced at Covent Garden on 20 and 21 August 1733. (The prologue was delivered by a "young gentleman," a student. In a letter to Benjamin Victor, Hill identified him as a young man named Harvey, about 18 or 19 years old.) Hill also supplied a prologue and epilogue to *The Lady's Revenge*, a new comedy by his friend and sometime associate William Popple, which was given at Covent Garden on 9 January 1734, and an epilogue to John Hewitt's *The Fatal Falsehood* at Drury Lane on 11 February 1734.

In 1733 Hill's urge to venture into management was revived. By April of that year he was considering an arrangement with John Highmore, a fashionable enthusiast who had recently acquired the Drury Lane patent. When Highmore's actors, led by Theophilus Cibber, defected to establish a rival operation, Hill wrote to the deserted manager on 5 July 1733:

If to have surfeited the town with a choking succession of absurdities; if to have dressed . . . Mr Cibber and his string of comedies; if to consider the new pieces which are offered them in no other light than whether their authors will make interest to support them; if to revive so few old ones that . . . our audiences are able to bear part with the actors; and, finally, if not to have found, made, or left one promising genius for the stage to succeed to the fame of such notable instructors:—if these are the marks of a capacity for directing a theatre, then the players have a title that can never be questioned.

Hill then offered to give up his own plans for "attempting a new theatre" if Highmore should care to accept his advice and assistance at Drury Lane that fall. In a letter to an unidentified recipient on 31 August 1733, Hill forwarded his design to establish "an academical theatre for improving the taste of the stage, and training up young actors and actresses for the supply of the patent theatres." He claimed that his company was formed and

could begin in November to perform "a race of plays and entertainments so new in themselves and the manner in which they will be acted that the success will, I think, be insured by the novelty." Though he had been offered a patent at £400 a year, Hill preferred that his correspondent should secure him a license.

His appeal came to nothing; for in the autumn of 1733 Hill was marking parts for Highmore at Drury Lane, providing such services as advice to Bridgewater as Tamerlane to "speak like an angel and move like a god," and a detailed analysis of Imoinda in *Oroonoko* for Mrs Porter's edification. When in February 1734 Highmore sold his patent to Charles Fleetwood, Hill was bitterly disappointed.

At that point Hill turned once more to journalism. With William Popple, who was a civil servant and another disappointed dramatist, Hill began to publish on 12 November 1734 a periodical called *The Prompter*, a two-penny half sheet which appeared twice weekly on Tuesdays and Fridays and continued until 2 July 1736. The 173 numbers ranged over a wide spectrum—ethics, sociology, economics, prison reform, slavery, and the Georgia colony—but 68 of them dealt with the theatre. These offer a lively account of the London stage in the mid-1730s and thus possess a particular importance.

In *The Prompter*, Hill and Popple were critical of managers, actors, operas, spectators, and playwrights. Those papers dealing with the opera are most entertaining, sounding the clarion call to repel the "foreign plague." Especially important are the essays, mostly by Hill, devoted to the actor and his art, which in some ways foreshadow the triumph of the naturalistic school of Macklin and Garrick. In his poem on "The Actor's Epitome" (No 113, on 9 December 1735) Hill began to formulate a system of acting which subsequently developed into his 416-line poem *The Art of Acting* (1746) and his prose *Essay on the Art of Acting*, published posthumously in his 1753 *Works*.

The theory was based on the belief, as summarized by William Appleton and Kalman A. Burnim in the preface to their modern edition of *The Prompter* (1966), "that the actor must first develop his imaginative powers in order to experience the emotions he is portraying and then transfer the expression of those emotions, in physical terms, to the stage." Hill perfect, with an Intention to keep them from going wrong. I have often observed the most expert and couragious Generals tremble thro' Fear of missing his Instructions, and the wisest of Monarchs lend him an attentive Ear. I have seen the merriest of Mortals not dare to crack a Joke, till he gave them the *Cue*, and the most despairing of Lovers refrain from Sighs and Tears, till they had his Permission to be miserable. I have seen a discontented Statesman hush Sedition, at his Nod ; and a very habile Prime Minister, not able to pay Pensions without his Advice and Concurrence. In short, I have seen so much, that I shall not hesitate to pronounce him, A Director of the Ignorant, a Comforter of the Afflicted, a Terror to the Evil Actor, and a *Counsellor to the Counsellors of Kings*.

I HAVE already taken notice of the Scouts, and Messengers, which attend him ; by dispatching one of these, he can, at a Minute's Warning, bring the greatest Characters of Antiquity, or the pleasantest of the present times, upon the Stage, for the Improvement or Diversion of the Audience. I mention this here again, because 'tis a Part of his Conduct, which I intend strictly to imitate.

AMONG his *Instrumenta Regni*, his Implements of Government, I have taken particular Notice of a little Bell, which hangs over his Arm : By the Tinkling of this Bell, if a Lady in Tragedy be in the Spleen for the Absence of her Lover, or a Hero in the Dumps for the Loss of a Battle, he can conjure up soft Musick to sooth their Distress ; nay, if a Wedding happens in a Comedy, he can summon up the Fidlers to dispel *Care* by a Country Dance. I must inform my Readers, that I have procured an emblematical Bell for these Purposes, and that whenever any of these Misfortunes shall befal them, I can call up a musical Spirit of Chearfulness, and make them as *merry*, as is consistent with the old *Proverb*.

ANOTHER Tool of his Authority, is a Whistle, which hangs about his Neck : This is an Instrument of great Use and Significance : I won't say but the Sound of a Boatswain's Whistle may be sometimes more terrible ; but I am sure, it cannot be more punctually obeyed. Dr. *Faustus's* celebrated Wand has not a more arbitrary and extensive Power, than this musical Machine : At the least Blast of it, I have seen Houses move, as it were, upon Wings, Cities turned into Forests, and dreary Desarts converted into superb Palaces : I have seen an Audience removed, in a Moment, from *Britain* to *Japan*, and the frozen Mountains of *Zembla* resembling the sunny Vales of *Arabia Fœlix* : I have seen Heaven and Earth pass away, and Chaos ensue, and from thence a new Creation arise, fair and blooming, as the Poet's Fancy ; and all by the powerful magic Influence of this Wonderworking Whistle. No body will be surprized, after this, to hear, that I have made use of all my Interest, to procure from the ingenious Mr. *Cheetwood*, an attested Copy of this marvellous Instrument, by virtue of which, and some Directions from that eminent *Adept*, I shall be able to present my Readers with a never-failing Variety of Objects.

THUS qualified, and fired by such Examples, I enter, boldly, upon my Province. The Comparison between the World and the Stage will hold in all Points : I could go thro' with it, if it were not too old to be repeated, as well as too certain to be doubted : Therefore, when we daily see so many Men *act* amiss, can we entertain any Doubt, that a good PROMPTER is wanting ? I will do my best to make up for that Defect, by closely imitating that worthy Officer at the Play-house. I shall give the *Word* impartially to every *Performer*, from the Peasant to the Prince, from the Milk-maid to her Majesty ; every Part, whether Male or Female, serious or humorous, high or low, shall be carefully and equally *prompted*.

NOR can I think it any Dishonour, since the Stage has so long been transcribing the World, that the World should now make Reprisals, and look as freely into the *Theatres*. —— Let their *Managers* therefore be upon their Guard ; and their *Dependents*, Tragic or Comic, take good heed to their Parts, since there is, from this Day forward, arisen a PROMPTER, *without Doors*, who hath a *Cat-call*, as well as a *Whistle* ; and, whenever the Players grow *flat*, will himself make bold to be *musical*.

NOW if, after what I have said, any of my Readers should be still of Opinion, that I have chosen too humble a Character, let them remember, that Travellers who go *incog.* may take what Appellation they please, and are never the worse Company. Let me also inform them from History, that a Prince of a Royal House undertook a Pilgrimage to *Jerusalem*, under the humble Name of *Planta Genistæ* (which his illustrious Successors afterwards assum'd for their Surname, and were proud to be called *Plantagenets*) that is, in plain *English*, neither better nor worse than Mr. *Broomstick*. I mention this, not without some Tincture of secret Pride : As I have the Honour to be a *Broomstick* my self, by Paternal Descent, from a *Stock* of immemorial Antiquity, transplanted from a *Mountain* in *Scotland*, at least as ancient as *Ararat*. —— I wou'd have the *Great*, whom I may see Cause to *prompt* in their *Parts*, take due Notice of this, that they may know, I am *Gentleman* enough to be *wise* in Right of my *Ancestors*, and not neglect my Instructions, as the good Sense of an *Upstart*, too obscure to deserve Notice.

catalogued these passions as those of joy, sorrow, fear, scorn, anger, amazement, pity, hatred, jealousy, love, and shame. "To act a passion well," he wrote later in his *Essay on Acting*, "the actor must attempt its imitation, till his fancy has conceived so strong an idea or image of it, as to move the same springs within his mind, which form that passion when 'tis undesigned and natural." Davies praised Hill as "almost the only gentleman who laboured assiduously to understand the art of acting, and who took incessant pains to communicate his knowledge of it to others."

The essays in *The Prompter* on theatrical management must be seen against the background of the events which led to the Licensing Act of 1737 and Hill's own attempts to undertake the direction of a theatre. Condemning the theatres as schools of "public effeminacy and corruption," Hill implied in No 38 that he could convert them to "academies of courage, good taste, and humanity." He pressed his campaign in No 53, and in No 136 he called for a patron, perhaps in the royal family. Within a year, however, parliament determined the need to regulate theatres by passing the Licensing Act. Hill was not satisfied with that outcome, for the restrictions were placed mainly on players and playwrights when he believed the managers were the culprits who most desperately needed to be reformed.

On 25 April 1735 at Covent Garden a prologue by Hill introduced *The Double Deceit*, a new comedy by his collaborator William Popple. According to next day's *Grub Street Journal*, the house was sparse, amounting to only about £30, and consisted mainly of the author's friends, "notwithstanding which, little or no applause was given." Though the play was announced again for 28 April, the house was so empty (about £5) the audience was dismissed and the performance canceled. (In *The Prompter* of 6 May 1735, Popple blamed the cancellation on Walker's not knowing his part.)

For several years Hill had been trying to bring his adaptation of Voltaire's *Zaïre* upon the stage. One scene was printed in the *Gentleman's Magazine* of May 1733, and in the previous issue it had been reported that Rich had refused to produce the play. Evidently Highmore had accepted it for a showing at Drury Lane in the autumn of 1733 but had delayed until the theatre was no longer his. In November 1733 Hill sent copies of the play to Pope, James Thomson, and Lord Bolingbroke, telling each that he would bring it out in a month or two.

Finally *Zara* was produced in late spring of 1735 in the Music Room at York Buildings, Villiers Street, by a group of amateurs for the benefit of William Bond, who, as the *Daily Post* of 29 May 1735 announced, "brings it out at a great Expence (tho' all that act in it, are so good to appear Gratis for him) who has lain ill of the Gout, and Rheumatism, upwards of Four Years." Bond acted Lusignan, and Hill's nephew, also named Aaron, appeared as Osman. The title role was played by a young actress, probably Miss Ferguson. On 28 May 1735 *Zara* was rehearsed "before a great Appearance of Nobility and other Persons of Distinction." It opened the next night and was announced again for Saturday 31 May; that performance, however, was deferred until Monday 2 June "At the Desire of several Persons of Quality" who wished to support Bond's benefit but had commitments at the opera on Saturday. At the 2 June performance the sick and feeble Bond fainted away while playing the death scene of the aged monarch Lusignan and died within a few days. For the third performance, Friday 6 June, the bill announced, "Lusignan—by particular Desire, by the same Gentleman who plays Osman."

In his *Prompter* essay of that date Hill praised his nephew, young Hill, without naming him, for playing both roles in the same performance: "The part of Osman a gay, violent, imperial, amorous conqueror, and the part of Lusignan an old, dejected, miserable captive . . . " The tragedy was presented at York Buildings again on 13 and 18 June and at the Haymarket, by the same cast, on 9 July. Hill's epilogue, which had been spoken by Miss Ferguson in boy's clothes, was printed in *The Prompter* of 4 July 1735. (On 17 July "little Miss Ferguson" spoke Hill's original prologue and a new epilogue for a revival of *The Fatal Extravagance* at York Buildings.)

The history of the production of *Zara* continued in a bizarre manner. Hill finally succeeded in getting Fleetwood to offer the tragedy at Drury Lane in 1735–36. Under the author's direction *Zara* had its first professional production there on 12 January 1736, with Milward as Lusignan, Theophilus Cibber as Nerestan, Mrs Pritchard as Selima; Susanna Cibber, Theophilus's young wife, made her debut as a dramatic actress playing Zara. Mrs Cibber's father-in-law, Colley Cibber, provided and spoke a prologue begging the audience's indulgence for the novice. Mrs Cibber played "to the Admiration of every Spectator that had their auricular Faculties," according to the prompter Chetwood, and proved herself "the Daughter of Nature in Perfection." Hill had underlined her speeches with "a kind of commentary," marking, as Davies said, "every accent and emphasis; every look, action, and department proper to the character, in all its different situations, he critically pointed out."

Hill's success with Mrs Cibber was dampened, however, by the failure of his nephew as Osman on the first night. Young Hill was severely criticized by all critics except his uncle, who defended him in *Prompter* No 129 on 3 February 1736. The nephew did not play on the second night, 13 January, and next morning the *Daily Advertiser* announced: "The Gentleman who perform'd the Character of Osman . . . the first Night, having since declin'd it, that Part was read last Night; and it being submitted to the Determination of the Audience, whether the Play should be continu'd, or the Repetition of it deferr'd 'till somebody was study'd in the Part, they unanimously declar'd for the Continuation of the Play; and 'twas desir'd the Part might be read till one of the Players could be studied in it." Osman continued to be read until the seventh performance on 19 January, when Mills assumed the role. The play ran 14 consecutive nights. As the best of Hill's dramas, it continued to be acted in the repertory throughout the rest of the century and was frequently printed in separate or collected editions. Hill's nephew remained the focus of a controversy waged in the periodicals over the next six months; he later acted for several seasons at Drury Lane and Covent Garden, but he died on 15 April 1739 from wounds received in a street fight.

A prologue by Hill was spoken by Quin at the premiere of Connolly's *The Connoisseur; or, Every Man in his Folly* at Drury Lane on 20 February 1736. No doubt encouraged by the success of *Zara* that season, Hill adapted Vol-

taire's *Alzire* soon after its introduction at Paris in January 1736. As *Alzira* it was quickly brought on by Giffard at Lincoln's Inn Fields on 18 June 1736. Though it ran for nine nights and was given "warm and weighty applause" by the Prince of Wales on the fourth night, 1 July, *Alzira* did not enjoy the artistic or critical success accorded to *Zara*. In adapting both plays, in the judgment of Davies, Hill forgot the distinguishing character of the two nations by failing to "have interrupted, by an easy interposition, those long speeches which are equally tiresome to the speaker and the hearer" in the English theatre.

Hill's letters indicate that he occupied himself during the remainder of 1736 with the printing arrangements for *Alzira*. By the spring of 1737 he found himself "under an unexpected obligation" to retire from London, as he wrote to Richardson, with whom he developed a firm friendship and a steady correspondence. No doubt Hill was suffering some temporary financial difficulties. He was at Southampton in April 1737 (where he penned some verses), in Guernsey and Jersey in May, and in Edinburgh in June. The following spring he completed a "solitary ramble" along the various seacoasts. By July 1738 he had returned to settle some of his financial affairs in London, where for some time he had kept a house in Petty France, Westminster, overlooking St James's Park. At the end of that year he settled at Plaistow, Essex, with several of his daughters. Hill's wife had died on 25 June 1731, at the age of 37, and had been buried in the West Cloister of Westminster Abbey on 30 June.

Except for his letters to Richardson, Hill's literary output diminished in the late 1730s. In 1737 he published a poem, *The Tears of the Muses*, and in 1738 *An Enquiry into the Merit of Assassination*. He had intended to be a contributor to the new periodical *The Citizen, or the Weekly Conversation of a Society of London Merchants on Trade and other Public Affairs* when it began in February 1739, but it is doubtful that he ever was. At Plaistow he revived his scheme for making wine, planted some vineyards and sent bottles of the vintage to Richardson.

Hill lived about a dozen years at Plaistow, in constant hope of moving closer to London, but an interminable litigation, evidently involving money left by his wife's family in trust for his daughters, kept his finances precarious. During the 1740s he published *The Fanciad: an heroic Poem in Six Cantos* (1743), dedicated to the Duke of Marlborough; *The Impartial. An address without flattery* (1744); *The Art of Acting* (1746); *Free Thoughts on Faith; or, the Religion of Reason, a poem* (1746); and *Gideon, or the Patriot*, an epic poem in twelve books (1749).

By 1745 Hill had finished a translation of Voltaire's *Mérope*, but not until after many delays and letters from him to Garrick did the Drury Lane manager bring it out on 15 April 1749. There were difficulties in casting since no one seemed anxious to appear in it. Garrick took on Eumenes. After promising to accept the title role, Mrs Cibber decided against it, and Mrs Pritchard was prevailed upon to play it. Barry turned down Polyphontes, obliging the author to settle for Havard in the role, although Barry agreed to the smaller part of Norbas. As was his custom, Hill provided Garrick with all sorts of advice, especially in respect to the setting, which called for wings set obliquely, an uncommon technique at the time:

As to the last act of *Merope*, I rather chuse to *break* the scene, than *lose* an added beauty, of such striking force, as that will carry. . . . The chief difficulty will be found your *painter's*: For, considering, how crowded a confusion, has, before, been represented to the *audience*, in the speech of *Euricles*, 'twill call for all the *pencil's* art, to fill the temple (through side opening, seen twixt columns, standing separate from the slanted scenes, which are to be set back as far as possible) with such significantly busied groupes of interested people, as were spoken of in the description, and to lessen off their view, in gradual depth of *keeping*, so as to extend the prospect with scarce a sensible distinction, from the real life, before, and near the altar: such as the kneeling *queen* and *prostrate* guards, together with the *priests*, and *virgins*. . . .

On its opening night, *Merope* was received with "great applause," according to the prompter Cross, and ran for nine nights. At his author's benefits on the third, sixth, and ninth nights, Hill received net amounts of £77, £31, and £77, respectively. Davies considered *Merope* to have been Hill's masterpiece: "The scene between Merope and Eumenes is a beautiful ex-

ertion of genius, in describing the workings of natural affection in a son and mother unknown to each other." Hill, in a sense, had written the play as a retaliation against Voltaire's beliefs about the incapacity of the English for tragedy. "I undertook this piece," Hill wrote Mallet, "upon a motive more malignant than it should have been; for I but sought to mend with the bad view to mortify him." In the "Advertisement" to the printed edition that year, Hill turned Voltaire's comments back upon the French:

he must pardon me, if I am sensible that our unpolished London stage . . . has entertained a nobler taste of dignified simplicity than to deprive dramatic poetry of all that animates its passions; which, from an affectation to shun figure, sinks to flatness; an elaborate escape from energy into a grovelling, wearisome, bald, barren, unalarming, chillness of expression, that emasculates the mind instead of moving it.

Hill's version served as a vehicle for actresses in the grand pathetic style through the 1780s. He received £100 from Miller the publisher for printing *Merope* in 1749, having given the copyright reluctantly to him instead of Richardson, who had printed most of his works since 1736. The play was reprinted in separate London editions in 1753, 1758, 1777, 1786, and 1803, at Edinburgh in 1755, and in *Bell's British Theatre* in 1776 and 1797 and the *English Theatre* in 1776.

During a run of the revival of *Merope* at Drury Lane in 1749–50, Hill was confined to his bed with kidney disease on 3 February 1750. A benefit for him was commanded by the Prince of Wales for 9 February, but Hill died the night before, on the eighth, "at the instant of the earthquake," reported the *London Magazine* that month. (The prompter Cross wrote in his diary that Hill died on "Wed last," 7 February, and Davies claimed 5 February.) The posthumous benefit brought in £170, less house charges of £63. On 18 February he was buried in the West Cloister of Westminster Abbey in the same grave as his wife, Margaret, who had died in 1731.

By his wife, Hill had nine children, four of whom were still alive in 1760: a son Julius Caesar and three daughters, Minerva, Urania, and Astraeia—names which perhaps testify to a certain eccentricity on Hill's part. The registers of St Giles in the Fields reveal the names of several other children. Margaret, daughter of Aaron and Margaret Hill, was born on 19 July 1712 and baptized the following 16 August; Harley Hill, the son of Aaron and Margaret, was born on 22 March 1714 and baptized the following 15 April. Aaron Hill, of the parish of Aldingham in Hertfordshire, who married Elizabeth Rowe of the same parish at St Giles on 25 July 1741, was perhaps a son.

Hill's son Julius was a disappointment to him; according to letters written to Richardson in the 1740s, Julius tended to take "the shortest and dirtiest way to a Waste and Infamy." Administration of his father's estate, however, was granted to Julius on 10 March 1750.

Urania, the daughter who managed the Hill household after the death of Mrs Hill, kept up a correspondence with Richardson in the 1750s and tried her hand at writing a novel, which he criticized. In 1739 she married a London actor named Johnson. On 12 April 1746 the press announced: "Last week died at Wandsworth, in Surry, *Mr. Johnson* late a comedian belonging to the Theatre Royal in Covent Garden. He married the daughter of Aaron Hill Esq. and was a man well respected by all that had the pleasure of knowing him." Latreille's identification of this person as Benjamin Johnson is incorrect, for that actor died in 1742 and was never associated with Covent Garden. Urania's husband was more likely "Tall" Johnson, who had been acting at Lincoln's Inn Fields and Covent Garden in the late 1730s and up to March 1740. Johnson had acted Zamor in Hill's *Alzira* at Lincoln's Inn Fields on 18 June 1736, and Hill had written a special prologue for an unrecorded performance by Johnson of Cato. The marriage offended Aaron Hill, but after Johnson's death in 1746, Hill described him in a letter on 10 July of that year as a modest, honest man, despite the fact that he had run through his own substantial fortune and a good part of his wife's.

Aaron Hill's pomposity and long-windedness no doubt often made him seem tedious, but he does not deserve Thomas Lounsbury's sweeping condemnation as "the most persis-

tent and colossal bore of the century." Highly respected by his contemporaries, Hill was a vigorous and inquisitive man, evidently kind and liberal, if perhaps overly zealous on occasion. Today his plays are insignificant, but his ideas about acting and staging had impact in their time and remain of interest to students of the art. His criticism, sometimes garrulous and eccentric, but often vigorous and entertaining, reflects a period of vitality and experimentation in the English theatre. He had, as Davies said, "an uncommon grandeur of thinking, and a nervous manner of expressing his sentiments." His style was often bombastic, but his ideas often made good common sense. Moreover, though it was erratic, Hill's career in the theatre was founded on more practical experience than that of any critic of his century. In person Hill was tall and genteel; in later life his figure, air, and manner were gracefully "venerable."

After Hill's death *A Collection of Letters never before printed: written by Alexander Pope, Esq; and other ingenious Gentlemen, to the late Aaron Hill, Esq.* was published in 1751. *The Works of the Late Aaron Hill, Esq; in four volumes. Consisting of Letters on Various Subjects, and of Original Poems, Moral and Facetious* was printed in 1753 "for the Benefit of the Family." Hill's tragedy *The Roman Revenge*, an adaptation of Voltaire's *Le Mort de César*, which he had unsuccessfully solicited with incessant letters for performance in London, was published in 1754. Another tragedy, *The Insolvent, or Filial Piety* (based on works by Davenant and Massinger), was produced posthumously, with an epilogue by him, at the Haymarket on 6 and 16 March 1758, and was published the same year. In 1760 *The Dramatic Works of Aaron Hill, Esq.* with a life of the author by "J. K.," appeared in two volumes. Included were some dramatic pieces which had never been produced: *The Muses in Mourning*, a short opera; *Merlin in Love*, a pantomime opera; *Saul*, a tragedy; *Daraxes*, a two-act pastoral opera; and *Snake in the Grass*, a burlesque of pantomimes.

Dorothy Brewster's *Aaron Hill, Poet, Dramatist, Projector* (1913, reprinted 1966) is an important modern study, especially of his literary and commercial ventures, and contains a checklist of his publications. An annotated collection of *The Prompter*, edited by William

Appleton and Kalman A. Burnim, was published in 1966.

A portrait of Aaron Hill at the age of 24 was engraved by H. Hulsberg in 1709. A copy, engraved by R. Newton (and marked "G. Clint del."), was published by W. Walker in 1822. Another copy, by an unknown engraver, was published by E. Evans, without date.

Hill, Aaron *c. 1715–1739*, actor.

Aaron Hill, the namesake of his uncle the playwright and manager, was born about 1715 and perhaps was the son of Gilbert Hill, a brother of the elder Aaron Hill. The younger Aaron figured prominently in the controversy surrounding the productions of his uncle's *Zara* in 1735 and in 1736. When the tragedy was first performed by a group of amateurs in the Music Room at York Buildings, Villiers Street, in the spring of 1735, he acted Osman in the open rehearsal presented on 28 May "before a great Appearance of Nobility and other Persons of Distinction," as well as at the opening the next night. *Zara* was announced again for Saturday 31 May but was deferred until Monday 2 June. After that performance, the ailing William Bond, who acted Lusignan and for whose benefit the production had been arranged, died. For the next performance on Friday 6 June the bill announced "Lusignan— by particular Desire, by the same Gentleman who plays Osman."

In his *Prompter* essay on 6 June 1735, the elder Hill praised him, without mentioning that he was a nephew:

. . . I saw the parts of Osman and of Lusignan performed by one and the same actor—The part of Osman a gay, violent, imperial, amorous conqueror, and the part of Lusignan an old, dejected, miserable captive—Both performed full up to the elevated grace of nature, attitude, force, glitter, and perfection, by a youth quite new upon the stage, and who has scarce seen twenty years of life yet!

The *Gentleman's Magazine* of May 1735 identified the young actor in *Zara* as Hill's nephew and claimed that he was the "young Gentleman, a Student," who had spoken Hill's prologue to William Bond's *The Tuscan Treaty* at Covent Garden several years earlier, on 20 and 21 August 1733. That prologue speaker, however, was identified by Hill in a letter to Benjamin Victor on 18 August 1733 as a young man of 18 or 19 named Harvey.

Additional performances of *Zara*, with young Hill presumably playing both roles, were given at the York Buildings on 13 and 18 June 1735 and at the Haymarket by the same cast the following 9 July.

Still not named in the bills but announced as "the Gentleman who performed Ozman in *Zara*," our subject acted Marcus in *Cato* at Drury Lane on 20 September 1735. When *Zara* was given its first professional production at Drury Lane on 12 January 1736 (the night that Susanna Cibber made her dramatic debut in the title role), the bills announced that Osman was to be played by a gentleman, "by particular Desire, during the first Run only." The gentleman, of course, was young Aaron Hill, and he was hissed off the stage. Either he judiciously withdrew from the role or it was taken away from him, for at the second performance on 13 January the lines of Osman were read by one of the other players. Next day the *Daily Advertiser* reported: "The Gentleman who perform'd the Character of Osman . . . the first Night, having since declin'd it, that Part was read last Night; and it being submitted to the Determination of the Audience, whether the Play should be continued, or the Repetition of it deferr'd 'till somebody was study'd in the Part, they unanimously declar'd for the Continuation of the Play: and 'twas desir'd the Part might be read till one of the Players could be studied in it." Osman continued to be read until the seventh performance on 19 January, when Mills assumed the role.

In his *Prompter* of 3 February 1736 the elder Hill printed some bitter verses, which purported to have been written by his unfortunate nephew, and then defended the novice's performance:

. . . I saw him, too . . . when he appeared in the same character the first night the play was acted at the theatre in Drury Lane, to which house, I am assured by those who will maintain it to be fact, it had been given, *gratis*, merely at his request. . . . There may be household fools (for aught I know) of dullness thick enough to feel no differences. But, I am sure (among the audience) there could not be a judgment so depraved as not to know, and own, in spite of prejudice, that hardly ever a part was looked, or spoke, or acted, with more beautiful propriety and less affectation!—To what, then are we fallen! And when, or whence must we expect to see improvement on our theatres!

In the next issue of *The Prompter* on 6 February 1736, a correspondent reported that the young actor seemed to have been the victim of a party against him. The controversy over the actor was taken up by the *Grub Street Journal*, which on 25 March 1736 was highly critical of both Hills, affirming that the appearance of an amateur gentleman on a public stage, especially at a major patent theatre, was a sign of vanity and ostentation: "the Hero takes the Stage, and with much gesticulation, flies over a cracked instrument, in many artless and unnatural divisions. All the Audience laugh, and some hiss;—he bursts away indignant; and is very positive that the other Performer [Mrs Cibber?], apprehensive of being eclipsed, hired a party to mortify him." On 1 April the *Grub Street Journal* printed a letter from J. English, who claimed that the young actor overemphasized single words, stretched his voice unnaturally, and kept his profile to the audience; yet he had shown a variety of manner and gave "a just idea of the Character." In his *History of the Theatres*, Benjamin Victor wrote that young Hill had done "Injury both to the Play and himself."

Despite the bad notices, Hill was allowed to act at Drury Lane Theatre in the 1736–37 season, making his next appearance as Abergavenny in *Henry VIII* on 30 December 1736. He also played Phoebus in *Phaeton* on 12 April 1737, Horatio in *The Man of Taste* on 20 May, when he shared a benefit with Winstone and Miss Cole, and Worthy in *The Recruiting Officer* on 26 May. He was a regular member of the Drury Lane company in 1737–38, when he acted Marcus in *Cato*, Blunt in *1 Henry IV*, Shamwell in *The Squire of Alsatia*, Bedamar in *Venice Preserv'd*, Octavius in *Julius Caesar*, Lurewell and the King in *The King and the Miller of Mansfield*, Greenwood in *Sir John Cockle at Court*, Hotman in *Oroonoko*, a Spirit in *Comus*, Artamon in *The Siege of Damascus*, Fenton in *The Merry Wives of Windsor*, Abergavenny in *Henry VIII*, and Lysimachus in *The Rival Queens*. On 26 May 1738 he shared a benefit with Boman and Martin. According to John Williams's footnote to *A Pin Basket to the Children of Thespis* much later (in 1797), Aaron

Hill's nephew prompted a performance of *The Orphan* given by Eton scholars at York Buildings in 1738 in which the young David Garrick played Chamont. There is, however, no record or other authority for such an event. Moreover, Williams cited the first name of the younger Hill as "Colley."

Hill began the 1738–39 season at Drury Lane by playing Blunt, Octavius, and Catesby in *Richard III* on 14, 21, and 30 September, respectively. But on 21 October 1738 he acted Cornwall in *King Lear* at Covent Garden, where he continued to play through most of the season in such roles as Stratocles in *Tamerlane*, Aquilius in *Mithridates*, Leander in *The Cheats of Scapin*, Westmoreland in *1 Henry IV*, Hastings in *2 Henry IV*, Gloucester in *Henry V*, Oswald in *The Royal Convert*, a Servant in *The Parracide*, Alcander in *Oedipus*, Cabinet in *The Funeral*, Perdiccas in *The Rival Queens*, and Ernesto in *The Orphan*.

His last performance seems to have been as Narbal in *Mariamne* on 9 April 1739, a Monday. The next day while walking along Hart Street, he accidentally ran his elbow against one of two persons passing by, whereupon one of them struck him with a cane. Hill retaliated by collaring his assailant, according to an account given by Isaac Reed in his "Notitia Dramatica." "When immediately the other who was disengaged stabbed Mr. Hill twice with a knife once in his Side & the other near his navel." The *Daily Post* of 17 April 1739 reported that Mr Hill of Covent Garden Theatre had died on Sunday, 15 April, about seven o'clock, "of the Wounds he received by Villains unknown." He was buried on 19 April at St Paul, Covent Garden, in whose burial register his full name is recorded.

Hill, Benjamin   *b. 1755, instrumentalist.*

When Benjamin Hill was recommended by Charles Linton for membership in the Royal Society of Musicians on 7 March 1784 he was described as 29 years of age, single, with engagements at Covent Garden and Haymarket theatres. The variety of instruments on which he played included violin, violoncello, double bass, and harpsichord. Hill was admitted to the Society on 6 June 1784. His name appeared on the Society's lists to play the double bass, his primary instrument, at the annual May concerts at St Paul's in 1785 and 1789. Probably he was the musician named Hill who was employed at the King's Theatre in 1783 and in 1791 (when the company was at the Pantheon). In May and June 1784 he had played the double bass in the Handel Memorial Concerts at Westminster Abbey and the Pantheon. Perhaps he was the Benjamin Hill who married Ursula Treis at St Marylebone on 8 July 1787.

Hill, Colley. *See* HILL, AARON *c.* 1715–1739.

Hill, Eliza, née Warrell. *See* ATKINS, MRS WILLIAM.

Hill, Frederick [*fl.* mid-eighteenth century], *flutist. See* HILL, JOSEPH [*fl* 1715–1766].

Hill, George *d.* 1706, *musician.*

George Hill was sworn a musician in ordinary in the King's Musick upon the surrender of Frederick Steffkins, according to a Lord Chamberlain's warrant dated 29 November 1705. He was listed as deceased on 12 April 1706 and probably died shortly before that date.

Hill, Gilbert [*fl.* 1694–1750], *assistant manager, translator.*

Gilbert Hill was the son of George Hill, an attorney of Malmsbury Abbey, Wiltshire, and his wife, née Gregory. By the time his elder brother, Aaron Hill (1685–1750), the future playwright and manager, entered the grammar school at Barnstaple in 1694, Gilbert was being cared for by his mother and grandmother, Mrs Ann Gregory, for George Hill had died.

Little is known of Gilbert's life. On 17 September 1709 his brother Aaron wrote to Archdeacon Warley that Gilbert was "sure of a considerable curacy and promise of a presentation from the Earl of Peterboro', on the death of an old and sickly incumbent." Evidently Gilbert had not been living a saintly life and wished to make atonement by taking orders; though "unqualified by the Formality of a Degree," it

was hoped that Gilbert would be recommended by the Archdeacon to the Bishop of London for ordination.

Gilbert was appointed by his brother in the spring of 1710 to assist him in the management of Drury Lane Theatre. Gilbert, in his brother's absence, fined several players for neglect of duty. On the afternoon of 2 June 1710 a group of actors broke into the treasurer's office; in the melee, Aaron was almost stabbed and Gilbert was struck on the head by Leigh. (Details of that incident are related in the notice of Aaron Hill.)

Gilbert does not surface again in accounts of Aaron Hill's life until 1724, when a second edition of Aaron's poem *The Northern-Star* was published, accompanied by a Latin translation by Gilbert. On 5 July 1738 Gilbert wrote to Sir Hans Sloane, in Latin, that the absence of his brother from London had increased his own troubles, a suggestion that he relied on Aaron for financial support. After his brother's death in February 1750, Gilbert sent Samuel Richardson his expression of gratitude for services to the family. That is the latest evidence we have of him.

Possibly Gilbert Hill was the father of the young actor Aaron Hill (c. 1715–1739), who performed in London between 1735 and 1739.

Hill, James *d.* 1817, *singer, actor.*

According to the unreliable *Authentic Memoirs of the Green Room* (1801), James Hill was born in Kidderminster, Worcestershire. His father dying when James was four, the lad was adopted and educated by his maternal uncle, the Reverend Mr Hale, Rector of Allbrighton, Shropshire. When that uncle died James was cared for by another uncle at Wolverhampton who apprenticed him at the age of 16 to a painter.

At the completion of his indentures, young Hill decided "to take a tour of the world before settling to business." Presumably his travels brought him to London in 1796 for a fortnight, but then he went to Bristol where he was introduced to Dimond, the manager of the theatres there and at Bath. Dimond's company was full, but he was persuaded to allow Hill to play one night free "as an amusement." Thus Hill made his debut as Belville in the comic opera *Rosina*. That first appearance oc-

Harvard Theatre Collection

JAMES HILL as Leander

engraving by Schiavonetti, after De Wilde

curred in June 1796 at Bristol, according to the *Authentic Memoirs*, but on 1 October 1796 at Bath, according to *The Dictionary of National Biography*.

So impressive was Hill's debut that he was articled by Dimond for five years. After preparatory lessons under Richards, leader of the band at the Bath theatre, and from Xamenes and others, Hill was taken on as a pupil by Rauzzini upon the recommendation of Signora Storace. After two years as a principal tenor at Bath and Bristol—where it was said he was the "possessor of one of the finest voices on the stage"—Hill was released from his articles by Dimond in order to accept an engagement at Covent Garden in 1798–99 at a salary of £5 per week.

Hill made his debut at Covent Garden on 8

October 1798 as Edwin in *Robin Hood*. That season he also performed characters in *Ramah Droog* and *The Magic Oak*, Belville in *Rosina*, a Male Bard in *Oscar and Malvina*, Campley in *Inkle and Yarico*, Nicolo in *False and True*, Bouquet in *The Son-in-Law*, Joe in *Poor Vulcan*, Frederick in *No Song No Supper*, Lorenzo in *The Merchant of Venice*, and a principal Baccanal in *Comus*. On 7 June 1799, when tickets could be had of him at No 24, Bow Street, opposite the pit door, Hill took in gross benefit receipts of £287 7s.

In 1799–1800 at Covent Garden, still earning £5 per week, Hill added to his repertoire Lord Aimworth in *The Maid of the Mill*, Dermot in *The Poor Soldier*, Michael in *The Mouth of the Nile*, Montauben in *The Mysteries of the Castle*, Captain Greville in *The Flitch of Bacon*, Harold in *Peeping Tom*, Count Murville in *The Social Songsters* and Medley in *The Woodman*. On 14 November 1799 he was the original Sir Edward in *The Turnpike Gate*, Thomas Knight's successful comic opera, which enjoyed a total of 27 performances that season. He also was the original Don Antonio in James Cobb's *Paul and Virginia* on 1 May 1800.

Although he created no great stir, Hill evidently acquitted himself well as a singer of inconsequential roles. In 1801 he was described by the author of the *Authentic Memoirs* as still young and attractive, "with a pleasing figure," and a possessor of a nose of "as fair and goodly proportion, as though he had accompanied Sterne's traveller to the Promontory of Noses, and there culled for himself, as the fairest among ten thousand, his promising and prominent member!" He wanted ease, humor, and sprightliness as an actor, but nevertheless he was a great favorite among the ladies and devoted himself to pleasurable pursuits at the expense of improving his craft.

He continued to be engaged at Covent Garden through 1805–6, playing such roles as Abdalla in *Il Bondocani*, Young Inca in *The Blind Girl*, Lorenzo in *Who's the Rogue?*, and De Montefort in *The English Fleet in 1342*. His salary was about £8 per week in 1801–2; it was raised gradually until it was £12 in 1805–6. He also performed at the Haymarket in 1800 and at Liverpool in 1799 and 1801. At Preston on 7 September 1802 for the benefit of Mr and Mrs Siddons, he played Lord Alford in *The Children in the Wood* and sang "Black Ey'd Susan," a hunting song, and a duet with Atkins. At the end of 1805–6 Hill left Covent Garden over some presumed injury to his pride and became lost in the provinces. Possibly he was the Hill who performed at the Royal Circus, Surrey, in 1810 and at Edinburgh with a Mrs Hill in 1810–11.

In 1816 Hill and his wife joined a company headed by W. Adamson in Jamaica. He gave concerts at Montego Bay and Falmouth in July and August of that year and in 1816–17 played at Spanish Town. This company had evidently also performed on St Thomas, St Croix, and other islands. According to Monk Lewis, who saw some of the Jamaican performances, that Hill was the former Covent Garden singer. Hill died at Mount Bay, Jamaica, on 27 June 1817. Administration of his estate was eventually granted to his brother Charles Hiss, a bachelor and medical practitioner in northern Britain.

A pencil and red-chalk drawing by Samuel De Wilde of James Hill as Leander in *The Padlock* is in the British Museum; an engraving by Schiavonetti was published as a plate to Cawthorn's *Minor British Theatre*, 1806.

Hill, John   *d. 1667, cornettist.*

One of the manuscripts in the Harleian collection listed John Hill as "one of the waites of the citie of Westminster" in 1663. He was probably the John Hill who played cornet in Westminster Abbey in 1664; Dr Busby's account book cited Hill as receiving £4 for his services that year. John Hill was buried in the cloisters of the Abbey on 12 February 1667. He was very likely related to the court musician Roger Hill.

Hill, John   *c. 1716–1775, critic, playwright, actor, author.*

John Hill was born at Peterborough about 1716, the second son of the Reverend Theophilus Hill. After an apprenticeship to an apothecary, Hill operated a small shop in St Martin's Lane. His studies in botany brought him employment from the Duke of Richmond and Lord Petre as caretaker of their gardens and plant collections. In his travels throughout the country Hill collected specimens of rare plants which he later described in books on vegetable and herb life, especially as related to

Harvard Theatre Collection

JOHN HILL
engraving by Houston, after Cotes

his various patent medicines. By 1738 his apothecary's shop was in James Street, Covent Garden.

It is not surprising that a person of such varied enterprise, living in the heart of the theatrical district, would make early attempts at a stage career. In 1738 Hill sent John Rich a manuscript libretto of an opera about Orpheus, which the Covent Garden manager rejected. When Rich was readying a production of Lewis Theobald's pantomime opera *Orpheus and Eurydice*, with music by Lampe, for February 1740, Hill accused the manager of stealing his work and published *Orpheus: an English opera. By Mr. John Hill. With a preface, appealing to the publick for justice, and laying before them a fair and impartial account of the quarrel between the author and Mr. Rich, who intends in a few weeks to perform such an entertainment without his concurrence* (dated 1740, but actually 1739).

Rich countered with *Mr. Rich's answer to the many falsities and calumnies advanced by Mr. John Hill, apothecary, and contained in the preface to Orpheus, an English opera, as he calls it, published on Wednesday the 26th of December last* (1739). Whereupon in his *An answer to the many plain* and notorious lyes advanc'd by Mr. John Rich. Harlequin (1740), Hill claimed that the title page of Rich's answer was by Theophilus Cibber, the beginning, end, and "certain dark passages in the middle" were by Theobald, the impertinence was by Captain Egan, and "the folly, Mr. Rich's own." On 6 February 1740 the *Daily Post and General Advertiser* contained a letter "To Mr John Hill, on his Answer to Mr Rich's Defence," and further letters were published on 11 and 12 February, the latter date being the night on which Rich brought out his production.

Announced as a "Gentleman" who never appeared on the stage before, Hill acted Constant in *The Provok'd Wife* at Drury Lane on 13 March 1742. (The "Gentleman" was identified as Hill in Rylands MS 1111.) In his *Letter from Henry Woodward to John Hill* (1752), Woodward recalled Hill's "rape" of Mrs Woffington as Lady Brute on that occasion, "when, in a certain Passage, where, at least, a *seeming* Manliness was necessary, you handled her so awkwardly, that she join'd the Audience in laughing at you. . . ." When *Love Makes a Man* was performed on 25 March before the royal family, the role of Carlos was played by Hill, now announced as "a Gentleman (who never appear'd on any stage but once before)." Hill reappeared to act Charles in *The Stratagem* on 8 May 1742 and Hotman in *Oroonoko* on 12 May. No salary or benefit for Hill at Drury Lane that season is known.

According to Genest, Hill acted Roderigo when Samuel Foote made his stage debut as Othello at the Haymarket Theatre on 6 February 1744. Additional performances of *Othello* occurred on 13, 20, and 23 February, 2 March, and 26 April. Possibly Hill also appeared in other plays presented under Macklin's guidance at the Haymarket that season. From Woodward's *Letter* to Hill we also learn that the apothecary acted the "Character of the Reverend *Botanist*" (Friar Lawrence) in the production of *Romeo and Juliet* with which Theophilus Cibber opened his short-lived season under a shaky license at the Haymarket on 11 September 1744.

Before Cibber was required to abandon that venture he presented *Romeo and Juliet* seven other times in September and October. Indeed the bill for 29 September 1744 listed Friar Lawrence by Mr Hill. *The London Stage*, how-

ever, states that in this instance Hill was the stage name for a Mr Johnson. Such an ascription seems doubtful, inasmuch as Johnson's name appeared in other Haymarket bills that season, for instance for Balance in *The Recruiting Officer* on 27 September and for Sealand in *The Conscious Lovers* on 4 October. Also in Cibber's company was a Mrs Hill who acted the Nurse in *Romeo and Juliet* and several other roles, but we can establish no relationship for her with John Hill. His first wife, whom he married early in life, was a Miss Travers, the daughter of Lord Burlington's household steward; she seems not to have been a performer.

It is highly possible, however, that before those performances at the Haymarket between 1742 and 1744, Hill had actually appeared as a pantomime player. So asserts Woodward in his *Letter*: "It has been mentioned in a late Weekly Paper, and with Truth too, that the first Efforts of your universal Genius were to excel in Pantomime." Woodward claimed that Hill was as much a failure in that genre as Woodward himself had been a success. Indeed, we find that a Mr Hill had played an unspecified character in performances of *The Cheats of Scapin* given at Southwark Fair between 23 and 26 August 1736 in Fielding and Hippisley's booth and Bravo in *Harlequin Grand Volgi* at Tottenham Court Fair on 4 August 1740.

Hill's performances as Friar Lawrence at the Haymarket in 1744 seem to have been his last. In a pamphlet published in 1752 during Hill's squabbles with Woodward, the pseudonymous Simon Partridge claimed that Hill had taken to the stage because he needed money but had made a bad figure at the Haymarket—"Damn this Apothecary, he can give nothing but Vomits, for his acting is enough to turn ones Stomach."

His acting career behind him, Hill's fortunes turned upward. While holding a modest appointment as apothecary to several regiments in the Savoy, he published in 1746 Greek and English versions of *Theophrastus's History of Stones. . . . To which are added two Letters . . . on the Colours of the Sapphire and Turquoise, and . . . upon the effects of different Menstruums on Copper &c.* (second edition enlarged, 1774). Having been introduced into the company of men of letters by Martin Folkes and Henry Baker, Hill submitted a paper to the Royal Society entitled *Lucina sine concubitu,* "in which it is proved . . . that a woman may conceive . . . without any commerce with men"; signed as by "Abraham Johnson," it was published in 1750 and translated into French in the same year. About that time, surprisingly enough, he received a diploma in medicine from St Andrew's. In 1750 Dr Hill wrote *A Dissertation on Royal Societies. In Three Letters from a Nobleman on his Travels to a Person of Distinction in Sclavonia*, and in 1751 he issued *A Review of the Works of the Royal Society of London, containing animadversions on such of the papers as deserve particular observation*, which had been motivated by his failure to receive the requisite number of votes for nomination to membership in the Society.

In March of 1746 Hill had begun publication of his monthly *British Magazine* (later he issued supplements for January and February to complete the year), which he continued until December 1750. He offered therein a number of moral essays but did not devote many to the theatre. He criticized audiences in one number in 1746 and in 1748 wrote a paper on "Theatrical Performances and their Influence on the Minds of Audiences." In January 1749 he offered "Some Remarks on the New Entertainment Lethe" (on the occasion of the revival of Garrick's farce at Drury Lane on 2 January 1749), in which he attacked the actor-manager for self-puffing and political scheming. An "Essay on the Art of Puffing" appeared in June 1749, some more criticism of theatrical management in October, and an account of French players in November. Letters from occasional correspondents, both those in favor of and those opposed to Garrick, were printed throughout 1750.

For over two years from 4 March 1751, Hill was responsible for a daily letter called "The Inspector," which appeared in the new *Advertiser and Literary Gazette* (after 17 April 1751 the *Daily Advertiser and Literary Gazette*). Of those, 19 papers were devoted to theatre, particularly to performers, and contained excellent critiques. His attitude toward Garrick had softened, and in several numbers he praised his acting and managing. On 8 March 1751 Hill offered a most appreciative review of a revival of Mallet and Thomson's masque *Alfred* at Drury Lane on 23 February. In her *Apology* George Anne Bellamy told a colorful story about Hill's absentee reviewing which prob-

ably is much exaggerated for humorous effect. Hill had recently praised her in a review of *Romeo and Juliet* when

he one evening swept into the Green-Room during the representation of that play, and when I was called to go to the balcony, the scene on which he had been most exhuberant in his eulogiums, he greatly astonished me by saying, 'I must go and see it, for I hear it is the finest piece of acting in the whole performance.' I could not resist turning back to ask him if he had not wrote a critique upon it? To which he replied, with a becoming *non chalence*, that he had written it from what he had heard at the Bedford, and never till that evening had an opportunity of seeing it.

It is clear, however, as Charles Gray concludes in *Theatrical Criticism in London to 1795* (1931), that Hill "had some excellent powers as a critic of acting," but his private quarrels and scurrilous reputation prevented a full appreciation of his ideas.

These "Inspector" essays drew Fielding into a paper war in the *Covent-Garden Journal*, causing Hill to attack the sometime magistrate in *The Story of Elizabeth Canning considered. With remarks on what has been called a clear state of her case by Mr. Fielding* (1753). In the solitary number of *The Impertinent* on 13 August 1752, and subsequently in "The Inspector" for 6 and 7 December 1752, Hill attacked Christopher Smart, who retorted in *The Hilliad; an epic poem*, "Pimp! Poet! Puffer! 'Pothecary! Player!" Hill's character assassination of Mountefort Brown in "The Inspector" of 30 April 1752 provoked Brown to assault him at the entrance to the Ranelagh Rotunda on the evening of 6 May 1752. A satirical print captured the event for posterity (British Museum No 3183). Fielding reported in the *Covent-Garden Journal* for 12 May 1752: "On Saturday last Mountefort Brown, Esq., surrendered himself before the Justice, to answer the Complaint of Dr. Hill, for a supposed Assault at Ranelagh, on Wednesday last; when upon the Affidavit of an eminent Physician, that Dr. Hill was not in any Danger of his Life, Mr. Brown was admitted to Bail, two Housekeepers of great Credit and Substance becoming his Sureties."

The most notable squabble provoked by "The Inspector" was with Henry Woodward. In the autumn of 1752 Woodward inserted into his afterpiece *Harlequin Ranger* a new scene that ridiculed the town's flocking to Cov-

JOHN HILL, "A Night Scene at Ranelagh"
engraving by "Telltruth," after "Clody"

ent Garden to see the rope-dancer Maddox. On Friday evening, 10 November 1752, a party led by Thaddeus Fitzpatrick attended Drury Lane for the purpose of damning Woodward's afterpiece. When Woodward announced *Harlequin Ranger* again for the next night, Fitzpatrick threw an apple at him from a stage box. The actor's remark, "Sir, I thank you," was judged insolent by some of the audience and was received by Fitzpatrick as a challenge. The next night there was hissing throughout the mainpiece, *The Silent Woman* (in which Woodward acted Sir John Daw), especially at the passages which Hill had pointed out in "The Inspector" as being indecent. Noise and fighting about the afterpiece then ensued in the pit.

On Monday night Garrick told the house that the new scene in *Harlequin Ranger* would be withdrawn after that performance. But now others insisted on the scene being kept in, and after more noise Lacy announced that it would be. The next morning, 14 November, in "The Inspector" Hill attacked Woodward's supposed insolence toward Fitzpatrick. Contention and contradiction followed. Woodward published an affidavit in the *General Advertiser* denying ay intention of insolence or challenge, and Fitzpatrick used "The Inspector" column to claim that Woodward had said more to him than the simple "Sir, I thank you." Fitzpatrick waited on the Lord Chamberlain to complain of Woodward's behavior, as Cross the Drury Lane prompter related in his diary: "my Lord sent for Garrick who told ye whole Story; & upon Mr Fitz owing [*sic*] he threw an apple at him, my Lord said, that act put [him] upon a Footing with ye lowest, & judg'd him the Agressor;— —upon wch Fitz; desir'd all affidavids &c shoul'd cease & he wou'd drop his resentment. which was done." (Eleven years later Fitzpatrick would not be so accommodating; in protest at the elimination of a half-price policy at both theatres, mobs harangued by him broke the chandeliers and vandalized the house at Drury Lane on 25 January 1763 and caused even more severe destruction at Covent Garden in February.)

The affair spawned humorous and vituperative pamphlets from all sides. On 2 December 1752, in response to "The Inspector" No 524, Woodward issued his *Letter from Henry Woodward, comedian, the meanest of all characters; to*

Dr. John Hill, Inspector-General of Great-Britain, the greatest of all characters. Anonymous publications included *An Essay on the Rationality of Brutes* [1752], a reply to Hill's "Inspector" pieces of 30 November and 1 December 1752; *The Theatrical Contention. A fable* [1752]; *Whipping rods for trifling, scurrhill, scriblers; as Mr F———t . . . Spectorhill his late pamphlets* (1752); *The Geese Stript of their Quills* (1753); *A letter to Mr. Woodward, on his triumph over the Inspector. By Sampson Edwards, the merry cobler of Haymarket* [1752]; and *A Letter to Henry Woodward, comedian, occasion'd by his letter to the Inspector. By Simon Partridge, the facetious cobler of Pall Mall* [1752?]—in which it was stated that Woodward had sought Hill at George's Coffee House with the intention of beating him with a stick, but Hill escaped.

Hill's best known and most important works related to the theatre were his two treatises on acting. In 1750 he published anonymously *The Actor: a Treatise on the Art of Playing*. Essentially it was a paraphrased translation of Pierre Rémond de Sainte-Albine's *Le Comédien*, which had been published at Paris in 1747. In 1755 Hill published a more expanded version, again anonymously, with the title *The Actor; or, a Treatise on the Art of Playing. A new Work, written by the author of the former, and adapted to the present state of the theatres*. The second was a decided improvement over the first, being really a new work in his own style and containing many fine observations on the performances of such leading actors as Garrick, Barry, Woodward, Foote, Havard, Ryan, Mrs Cibber, Mrs Clive, Mrs Bellamy, Mrs Pritchard, and Mrs Woffington. The result was one of the major works of the century on acting theories, in which Hill claimed that "Playing is a science, and is to be studied as a science," and "A perfection in the player is the hiding himself in his character." A useful discussion of *The Actor* is in Edwin Duerr's *The Length and Depth of Acting* (1962).

Generally, opinions of Hill by his contemporaries were not high. Frequently he got the worst in the controversies which he provoked. In 1756 Arthur Murphy satirized him, Theophilus Cibber, and Samuel Foote in *The Spouter; or, The Triple Revenge*, an unproduced but published comedy. On 24 April 1756, *The Maiden Whim; or, The Critical Minute*, a farce credited to Hill by Nicoll and *The London*

Stage, was produced for a single disastrous performance at Drury Lane. But *The Maiden Whim* seems to have been the work of Dr Paul Hiffernan. Cross wrote in his diary: "A new farce by Doctor Heffinal for his benefit. O Sad!" On the day of the performance a letter was sent to the editor of the *Public Advertiser*, in which the characters in the farce were specified; their names were the same as those in the piece when it was brought on at Covent Garden under its alternate title *The Lady's Choice* on 20 April 1759. It was published as *The Maiden Whim* in 1759.

Hill's great quarrel with Garrick came late in 1758 over the production of Hill's farce *The Rout*. Letters received from Hill that autumn should have been warning enough for Garrick. In reply to one, Garrick wrote Hill, "The[re] is a certain Air of incivility in y^r last Letter which I think is y^e *Idlest* thing of all—I Use Every Gentleman with Justice & Good Manners, & Expect from Dr Hill a return in Kind." That month Garrick sent his recommendations for changes, which Hill incorporated, and *The Rout* was settled for production on 20 December 1758 for the benefit of the General Lying-in Hospital. Early in December Arthur Murphy claimed that the farce had been pirated from him, an accusation of which Garrick denied knowledge, stating that he had not solicited the piece:

The Managers can receive no advantage from the Farce, it was sent to 'Em from the Hospital, We have promis'd to perform it for the Benefit of the Charity and must do it, unless it is recall'd by the Governors, To them therefore you should apply; for our Word has been given & cannot on any Account be retracted.

The Rout was hissed on its opening night and the next. The third performance, normally the author's benefit, was deferred from 23 December "on account of the indisposition of a principal performer" and was again deferred for the same reason on the twenty-eighth. (It was, no doubt, a most troublesome period for the manager, as he was being badgered by Murphy about the forthcoming production of *The Orphan of China*, his scene designer Oram died on 29 December, just a few days before a revival of *Antony and Cleopatra* was to appear, and Taswell, a good utility actor, died on 8 January 1759.) Hill hissed venom upon Gar-

rick in the press, although he had not announced himself as the author, giving it out that the farce had been written by a "Person of Honour." In his review of *The Rout* in the *Gentleman's Magazine* for December 1758, Garrick's friend Hawkesworth disclosed Hill's duplicity in connection with the production and publication of the piece:

Who now, after all this, would imagine, that the *veritable* author of the Rout is no other than Dr *Hill*; that it was written and offered for representation *before* the public charity was in view; that the representation of it was *not* interrupted by the indisposition of a performer, but by the distaste of the public; that the primary view of it was *profit to the author*; that the managers, who, in the advertisement [to the printed play], are said to be *welcome* to any advantage that may result from it, have been solicited for a gratification, even after the performance was set aside.

Hill was also vigorously attacked in an anonymous pamphlet *A Letter to the hon. author of the new farce, called "The Rout." To which is subjoined, An epistle to Mr. G———k, upon that, and other theatrical subjects* (1759), in which it was stated that the dispute had reached such proportions that "the *Inspector* was no longer hawked at the Bow-Lamp in Southampton-Street, and Dr. H——was struck off the list of freemen of the theatre." Garrick neatly demolished Hill with his well-known epigram: "For Physick & Farces, his Equal there scarce is, / His Farces are Physick, his Physick a Farce is." In a letter to Hawkesworth about January 1759, Garrick related how the epigram was born:

. . . I was in Company the other day with some Gentlemen, & His Print [probably the engraving by Houston, after Cotes] was produc'd (which by ye bye is a very good one) & it was propos'd that Each of us sh^d try to make a Motto for it Extempore—We did so, & Mine was fix'd upon as ye best for ye purpose . . .

On 1 March 1759 Garrick declined to reply to Hill's letters: "You must Excuse Me, if I drop all farther Correspondence." The answer he had penned but did not send was "there are some People so void of honour, Gratitude or Ev'n Common honesty, that it is both vain & injurious to hold any Correspondence wth them." On 3 March Garrick wrote Hawkesworth, "could you have imagin'd that there could Exist such a Being as Hill?—Matters are very low with him & he wants to make a printed Quarrel of it—but I'll write no more Except with my Crabstick upon his back & Shoulders—it grieves me that so wretched a fellow should be capable of writing his Name." Hill persisted, trying to get a financial settlement or a benefit night without a performance of *The Rout*, but Garrick refused. In a pamphlet entitled *To David Garrick, Esq: the petition of I. in behalf of herself and her sisters* (1759), Hill criticized Garrick for pronouncing in such words as "virtue" the "i" as if it were "u"—to which Garrick retorted with another happy epigram:

> *If it's true, as you say, I have injur'd a letter.*
> *I'll change my note soon, and hope for the better.*
> *May the just rights of letters as well as of men*
> *Hereafter be fix'd by the tongue and the pen;*
> *Most devoutly I wish, they may both have their*
> *   due,*
> *And that I may be never mistaken for* YOU.

According to Garrick's letter to Hawkesworth on 20 March 1759, Hill petitioned the Duke of Devonshire against him; but, as Garrick had assumed, the petition came to nothing. The matter seems to have ended with Hill's publication in May 1759 of the anonymous pamphlet *Observations on the importance and use of theatres; their present regulation, and possible improvements*—reviewed in the *Gentleman's Magazine* that month—which proposed that

the conduct of theatrical entertainments be for the future taken under the care of the government, and a person of judgment and integrity appointed by the name of comptroller, or conductor of the stage, who *alone* shall determine what old plays shall be acted, and what new ones received; and who shall take charge of the money received, and defray the necessary expenses, accounting for the remainder to the public. . . .

Hill then turned his attention to the publication of *The Vegetable System*, undertaken in 1759 with the patronage of Lord Bute. He finally completed it in 1775, a total of 26 folio volumes, with 1600 copper-plate engravings illustrating 26,000 different plants. The effort ruined him financially but won him a deserved and lasting reputation as a botanist as well as the order of Vasa from the King of Sweden in 1774. Thenceforth he styled himself as Sir

John. He applied himself to the study and preparation of various herbal medicines, such as "the essence of waterdock," "tincture of valerian," and "pectoral balsam of honey," which brought him great income but also the epithet of quack. His gardens at Bayswater, where he cultivated his plants and concocted his medicines, covered the area about Lancaster Gate. Bute helped him obtain an appointment as superintendent of Kew Gardens but the grant seems not to have been confirmed. According to Walpole's *Letters*, Hill once earned 15 guineas a week "by working for wholesale dealers" and on the accession of George III made £2000 as gardener of Kensington Palace. It is said that he was "forbid Chelsea garden for making too free with it." Hill lived in extravagant style when his fortunes were high but, according to Nichols's *Literary Anecdotes*, could one month be in a chariot, and the next in debtor's prison. He arranged plants native to the British Isles in a catalogue on Linnaean principles, even though he was critical of Linnaeus's work on classification.

Over 80 publications by Hill are listed in his notice in *The Dictionary of National Biography*. In addition to the comparatively few on theatrical matters and his plays cited above, they range over an amazing variety of subjects, including studies of herbs and gardening, essays on natural history and philosophy, astronomy and theology, patent medicines and cures, and insects and fossils. Hill was also a justice of the peace for Westminster, a member of "the Imperial Academy," and a fellow of the Royal Academy of Sciences at Bordeaux. He contributed numerous articles to the *Supplement to Mr Chambers Cyclopaedia, or, Universal Dictionary of Arts and Sciences* (1753).

Hill died in Golden Square on 21 November 1775 of gout, despite his having written *The Management of the Gout. By a Physician, from his own case. With the virtues of an English plant, Bardona, not regarded in the present practice, but safe and effectual in alleviating that disease* in 1758 and another book on the same subject in 1771. He was buried at Denham. His second wife, the Hon Henrietta Jones, sister of Charles, fourth viscount Ranelagh, survived him. In 1788 she published *An Address to the Public . . . setting forth the consequences of the late Sir John Hill's acquaintance with the Earl of Bute*, in which she blamed Bute for her husband's

168   *The* A C T O R.

taught it; by means of which we are able to converse with people of all nations; and nature has
been fo determinate in the fenfe of every particle of
it, that art would attempt in vain to make it either
more intelligible or more expreffive.   The ut-
moft that can be done by the niceft hand, is to
polifh and ornament it; and all that the player
needs, or indeed is able to do, is only to avoid
improprieties in it, and to be careful to ufe it only
in fuch parts as nature fhews it to be neceffary
and ufeful in.

The judgment of the player muft inform
him, that when he acts the part of a man of
high rank and quality, he is to ufe fewer geftures, and thofe lefs violent than when he acts
a clown; nor is it difficult to guefs from whence
this neceffary diftinction arifes. Nature left to
herfelf, is under lefs reftraint, and runs into
more irregular emotions, than when curb'd and
regulated by a proper education.

People in high life have the fame affections
with the vulgar; but they have more hypocrify.
Their very paffions put on the air of diffimulation,
which has been inculcated into them in all their
other actions, and appear moderate and rea-
fonable even when they are the moft inordinate and ungovern'd. A man of high rank
is in a manner fedate and tranquil even in his
refentment, while a cobler under the fame cir-
cumftances wou'd be outrageous, kick the tables
and chairs about the houfe, and half murder his
wife and children, tho' they did not even know
what it was that put him in this fury.

If the frequent ufe of paffionate geftures is on
this account not allowable in genteel comedy,
                                                      much

The A C T O R.   169

much lefs is it fo in tragedy: As much as the
gentleman is above the vulgar, fo much is the
king or heroe above the private gentleman:
If the former is expected to maintain a certain
dignity and refpect adequate to his rank above
the commonalty; the latter is under infinitely
greater neceffity of fupporting his character by a
majeftic deportment, and keeping up, by a grave
and fedate carriage, the high idea we have formed
of his virtues and accomplifhments.

No lefs eminent a player than Mr. *Garrick* has
been accus'd of not keeping up this dignity in
fome of his tragedy characters. We can by no
means agree with thofe who are for making the
charge general againft him, but are apt to believe
that the people who do fo, are influenced merely
by his want of figure; and give no little proof
of their own incapacity of being ftruck by things
of much greater confequence.

His *Macbeth* and *Richard*, we take to be
mafter-pieces in this kind; and many of his
other characters are kept up at leaft with fo
much dignity, that a candid fpectator will not
think him cenfurable in this refpect; but there
are fome in which he is evidently wanting.
In *Pierre*, perhaps, we fhou'd not fee this defect
in him, if we had not an unlucky comparifon at
hand, with that player in the fame part, who certainly excells all the world in this peculiar article. When *Jaffeir* mentions honefty as a virtue that is not fit for this world, Mr. *Garrick*
forgets the dignity of his character to give into
a fhrewdnefs and feverity very natural to him,
and in general very becoming, when he an-
fwers him,

Opening from *The Actor*,

by JOHN HILL

decline of fortune and health. The anonymous
*Short Account of the Life, Writings, and Character
of the late Sir John Hill, M.D.* was published in
1779.

The characterization of Hill in *The Dictionary of National Biography* as "a versatile man
of unscrupulous character, with considerable
abilities, great perserverance, and unlimited
impudence" is appropriate. Johnson told the
King that Hill "was an ingenious man, but
had no veracity," and if he would have "been
content to tell the world no more than he knew
he might have been a very considerable man,
and needed not to have recourse to such mean
expedients to raise his reputation."

Garrick's poem *The Sick Monkey* and Kenrick's *Pasquinade* are only two of many publications in which he was ridiculed. In a verse

among the manuscripts of William Havard
now at the Folger Library, that actor wrote:

Upon the Inspector's fixing up the Lyon at the
Bedford-Coffeehouse, formerly us'd by ye Wits at
Button's

*An ass once found Apollo's Lyre
And with his Hoof began to play;
Full masterly he touch'd the Wire—
'Twas heavn'ly Music we may say.
Th' Inspector next a Lyon found,
That erst cou'd sweetly roar—
John H——l, I'll lay you fifty Pound
The ass is at your Door.*

In *The Rosciad*, Churchill wrote of him:

*With sleek appearance, and with ambling pace,
And, type of vacant head, with vacant face,
The* PROTEUS H[I]LL *put in his modest plea—*

Let favour speak for others, worth for me.
For who like him his various pow'rs could call
Into so many shapes, and shine in all?
Who could so nobly grace the motley list,
Actor, Inspector, Doctor, Botanist?
Knows any one so well sure no one knows,
At once to play, prescribe, compound, compose?

A drawing of John Hill by Francis Cotes is in the British Museum print room; it was engraved by R. Houston. Copies were engraved by T. Priscott, published by C. Dyer; and by J. Vendramini, published as a plate to Thornton's *Sexual System of Linnaeus*, 1799. A version of the Cotes portrait, reversed by an unknown engraver, was published with the subscription: "Sir John Hill, M.D., Knight of the Polar Star, First Superintendent of the Royal Gardens at Kew." Hill was also pictured in several satirical prints described in the *Catalogue of Prints and Drawings in the British Museum*. No 3183, "A Night-Scene at Ranelagh on Wednesday 6th of May 1752," is referred to in our text above. In No 3187, "Lusus Natural, *or* Carracaturas *of the present age*," a scene of recognizable eccentrics published on 5 March 1752, he is shown on the extreme left; at his feet is a paper inscribed, "*not to know me argues thyself unknown*." In No 3279, "JUMPEDO *and* CANNING in Newgate," published in 1754, Hill appears at the door of the cell.

Hill, Jonathan [*fl. 1702*], *mountebank*.
The *Post Man* on 8 September 1702 advised strolling mountebanks to pay 2s. daily to town constables whenever they performed. Among those cited was Jonathan Hill.

Hill, Joseph [*b.c. 1715–1766*], *musical instrument maker, music seller and publisher, instrumentalist?*
The musical instrument maker Joseph Hill was born about 1715, according to *Grove's Dictionary*. He may have been the son of the Joseph Hill who was a music seller in the Minories, near Aldgate, between 1731 and 1734.
Hill had his shop first at "Ye Harp and Hautboy" in Piccadilly, subsequently in High Holborn at "The Violin" in Angel Court, Westminster, and from about 1762 at "The Harp and Flute" in the Haymarket. From the last location Hill published *Six Easy Lessons for the Harpsichord*, "Compos'd by Sigr: Binder-Mazzinghi-Ritschel Sigr: Legne-Galuppi-

Zamperelli, Book I" (c. 1765); and *A Set of Easy Lessons for the Harpsichord . . . Opera Trentesima Prima*, with a preface signed "J. M." (1766).
Hill was one of the founders of the Philharmonick Society in the 1730s and the patriarch of a line of violin makers who descend to the present firm of W. E. Hill and Sons in New Bond Street.
His son Frederick Hill was a flutist, "a celebrated player closely associated" with the Philharmonick Society, according to *Grove's Dictionary*. Frederick's son Henry Hill (d. 1839) was an instrument maker and publisher in partnership with Tebaldo Monzani (d. 1839) at No 3, Old Bond Street until 1813, at No 24, Dover Street until about 1819, and then at No 28, Regent Street until 1829 when the partnership dissolved and the firm became known as Hill & Co, then Hill & Sons.
Not much is known about the Philharmonick Society in which Joseph and Frederick Hill were active, but the Society supplied the orchestra for Handel's *Esther* in 1732 and was led by the professional violinist Michael Festing from 1735 to 1737. The Hills presumably played in the orchestra.

Hill, Joseph [*fl. 1784–1805*], *double-bass player*.
Joseph Hill was one of the double-bass players in the Handel Memorial Concerts at Westminster Abbey and the Pantheon in May and June 1784. In 1794 he was listed in Doane's *Musical Directory* as a member of the New Musical Fund and a player in the Concerts of Ancient Music, the Professional Concerts, the opera, the Covent Garden oratorios, the Oxford Meeting of 1793, and the Handelian concerts in the Abbey. He lived in Stangate Street, Lambeth. Joseph Hill was a subscriber and a member of the Court of Assistants of the New Musical Fund in 1794 and 1805.

Hill, Roger d. 1674, *singer*.
Roger Hill and Edward Coleman were double cast as Alphonso in Davenant's "opera" *The Siege of Rhodes* when it was first presented in 1656. By May 1661 Hill was one of the singers in the Chapel Royal, and on 25 November of that year he officially replaced the deceased Roger Nightingale. Hill attended the King at Windsor in May, June, and July

1671, but his activity in the Chapel Royal was otherwise rarely mentioned. He died on 2 March 1674 and was buried in the cloisters of Westminster Abbey two days later. It is possible that Roger was related to John Hill, one of the Waits of the City of Westminster in 1663.

Hill, Thomas   *c. 1747–1800, trumpeter, horn player.*

Thomas Hill was probably the musician named Hill who was a member of the theatre band at York in 1781–82 and played a horn concerto at his shared benefit there on 2 May 1782. When he was recommended by John Coyne for membership in the Royal Society of Musicians on 7 November 1784 he was described as a performer on the trumpet and French horn, about 37 years old, a married man with a daughter age 13 and a son age 12. Hill was admitted to the Society on 2 January 1785. Hill was on the Society's lists to play the trumpet in the annual May concerts at St Paul's in 1789, 1794, and 1795. In 1797 and 1798 he served as a Governor of the Society. On 2 March 1800, his widow, Laetitia Hill, was granted £8 for his funeral costs and an allowance of £2 12s. 6d. per month.

Hill, William   [*fl.* 1672–1710?], *musician, composer?*

On 2 October 1672 the Lord Chamberlain ordered William Hill and several other London musicians apprehended for playing without a license from the Corporation of Music. A William Hill witnessed a power of attorney made by the court musician William Gregory on 13 February 1675 and may have been our subject. In January 1710 a William Hills published *Fifty two Minuets and Rigadoons* and *A Collection of New Minuets;* and he, too, may have been our man.

Hill, William   [*fl.* 1769–1811?], *instrumentalist, music publisher?*

William Hill, of St James's Street, Haymarket, became a freeman of the Worshipfull Company of Musicians on 31 October 1769 and was admitted to its livery on 17 January 1775. When he was recommended by William Duncombe for membership in the Royal Society of Musicians on 7 November 1779, Hill was identified as a violinist and violoncellist

and as the organist of Trinity Chapel, Conduit Street. At that time he was married, with two children, ages four and seven. After his admission on 2 January 1780, Hill's name appeared on the Society's lists as playing the violoncello in its annual May concerts at St Paul's in 1785 and 1790. He had also been one of the violoncellists in the Handel Memorial Concerts at Westminster Abbey and the Pantheon in May and June 1784.

Perhaps he was the W. Hill, publisher of No 4, Bridge Road, Lambeth, near the Westminster Hospital, who advertised in October 1811: "Flute and Flageolet—Just published, complete in 9 numbers, Hill's Magazine of Music, for the Flute and Flageolet."

Hillard, Mr   [*fl.* 1784], *acrobat.*

The summer season of 1784 at Brighton featured "Hillard's acrobatic entertainment from Sadler's Wells. . . ." but his presence at the Wells cannot be established from any known bills.

"Hillarius." *See* HILL, AARON 1685–1750.

Hillerberg. *See* HILLIGSBERG.

Hilliar, Ann. *See* DIBDIN, MRS THOMAS JOHN.

Hilliard. *See* HILLYARD.

Hillier, Mr   [*fl.* 1734], *actor.*

At a special benefit for Mr Ward at York Buildings on 8 July 1734 a Mr Hillier played Dervise in *Tamerlane.*

Hillier, Mr   [*fl.* 1768–1775], *actor.*

The Mr. "Hilliard" reported by a W. J. Lawrence manuscript notation at the University of Cincinnati Library as acting somewhere in Dublin in 1768 may have been the "Hillier" who was at Dublin in 1773 and, according to the *Morning Chronicle* of 2 August 1775, was acting at Richmond, Surrey, that summer, announced as "from Dublin." No roles are known.

Hilligsberg, Mlle E. *See* HILLIGSBERG, JANET.

Hilligsberg, Janet [*fl.* *1793–1801*], dancer.

On 1 June 1793, the young dancer Janet Hilligsberg made her first appearance at the King's Theatre in *La Jaloux puni*, a new ballet composed by D'Egville, which had a total of eight performances that month. The bills for her debut advertised her as "Mlle Hilligsberg, Jun" to distinguish her from her elder sister, the more famous Mme Hilligsberg. A year later, on 2 July 1794, when the afterpiece *The Glorious First of June* was presented at Drury Lane, listed in the bills among the dancers were Mme Hilligsberg and a Mlle E. Hilligsberg, but the latter billing, we believe, was a printing error for Janet, our subject.

Miss J. Hilligsberg performed the role of Statira in *Alexander the Great*, D'Egville's lavish three-act pantomime ballet which had its premiere at Drury Lane on 12 February 1795 and continued for a total of 36 performances that season. On 26 March 1795, for her sister's benefit at the King's Theatre, Janet performed with her in a Russian dance and in *Paul et Virginie*. When Mme Del Caro became ill on 16 May of that year, Janet again danced the role of Virginie to her sister's Paul.

In 1797–98 Janet began a regular engagement at the King's Theatre, where her sister was a leading dancer. Janet's performance in *L'Offrande à Terpsichore*, a new ballet by Gallet on 28 November 1797, was a success, though, according to the *Morning Chronicle* of 30 November, she was "overcome by her terrors." She danced the role of Africa in *Le Triomphe de Thémis* on 20 December 1797 and performed in *Énée et Didon* on 19 April 1798 and *Elise; ou, Le Triomphe de la nature* on 10 May 1798. On 9 May, the evening previous to her appearance in *Elise*, she danced at Drury Lane Theatre in the ballet *Bacchus et Ariadne*.

At the King's Theatre in 1798–99 she danced in *Peggy's Love*, *Bacchus et Ariadne*, *Télémaque*, and *Tarare et Irza* and in 1799–1800 in *Les Jeux d'eglié*, *Témire*, *Le Mariage Mexican*, and *Hyppomène et Atalante*. During that period she appeared as Clytre in *Télémaque* and in other dances for Michael Kelly's benefit at Drury Lane on 8 May 1799; and on 14 May 1800 she again appeared at that theatre in several dances, again for Kelly's benefit.

The *Morning Chronicle* of 18 June 1800 announced that Janet Hilligsberg had married and retired from the stage. Her role of Elise in *Télémaque* on 17 June had been performed by Mlle Parisot. On 27 February 1801, the *Morning Herald* reported that "Little Hilligsberg," having wed a French émigré count, was about to lie in; the birth of a daughter in the last week of May was announced in the same paper on 2 June 1801.

Hilligsberg, Mme [*M. L.?*], later Mme **Beaumont** *d. 1804,* dancer.

Mme (sometimes Mlle) Hilligsberg, a pupil of Gaëtan Vestris in Paris, joined the King's Theatre dancing chorus in 1787–88, making her first appearance on 8 December 1787 in Noverre's ballet *Les Offrandes à l'amour*. On 12 January 1788 she appeared in the same ballet and also performed a *Military Dance* with Didelot, Chevalier, Vestris, and others.

Her other dancing that season included a pas de deux with Vestris on 15 January, Psiché in *L'Amour et Psiché* on 29 January (her success in which, according to the *Public Advertiser* of 7 February 1788, gave her "an opportunity of

Harvard Theatre Collection

MME HILLIGSBERG in *La Jaloux Puni*

engraving by Condé, after de Janvry

making herself perfect in her profession"), a pas de Russe with Vestris on 21 February, a pas de quatre with Gardel, Mlle Coulon, and Vestris on 3 April, a role in the ballet *Adela de Ponthieu* on 19 April, Louisa in D'Auberval's ballet *The Deserter* on 29 May, and *La Bonté du seigneur* on 31 May. At her benefit on 28 February 1788, when tickets were available from her at No 1, Suffolk Street, Charing Cross, she danced Psiché and appeared in Noverre's new ballet, *Les Fêtes de tempe*.

After a year's absence, Mme Hilligsberg returned to London in 1789–90 to dance with the opera company then playing at the Haymarket Theatre because of the late fire which had destroyed the King's Theatre. Her first appearance at the Haymarket was on 7 January 1790 in *La Bergère des Alpes*. Other ballets in which she performed that season were *Les Mariages Flamands*, *Les Caprices* and *La Jalousie sans raison* (for her benefit on 25 March 1790, when she lived at No 7, Great Suffolk Street), *Lauretta*, and *The Generous Slave*. In July 1790 she danced at Covent Garden. That year she also participated in the private theatricals at Wargrave.

During the 1790s Mme Hilligsberg enjoyed popularity at the new King's Theatre, where she appeared in numerous ballets and specialty dances. She also performed at the Haymarket and the Pantheon in 1791–92. Her address in the spring of 1791 was No 11, Haymarket; by March 1795 she lived at No 115, Jermyn Street; in April 1796 at No 10, St Alban's Street; in May 1797 at No 36, Great Pulteney Street, Golden Square; and in May 1798 at No 43, Gerrard Street, Soho, where she still was to be found in May 1800.

Her popularity was enhanced by her custom of dancing in men's trousers. At her benefit on 26 March 1795 she and her younger sister Janet Hilligsberg performed a Russian dance in men's clothes and also appeared together in *Paul et Virginie*. Several days later the audience interrupted the proceedings at the King's Theatre with their demands that Mme Hilligsberg perform the ballet she had danced at her recent benefit. When a spokesman announced that despite the fact that the manager would have to pay her £300, Mme Hilligsberg would perform again as Paul the following week, the audience calmed down and allowed the scheduled dance, *L'Espiègle Soubrette*, to go on. Per-

haps the claim that Mme Hilligsberg commanded so high a sum was exaggerated, but in 1795–96 her salary for the seven-month season at the King's was £1000. When she performed at Covent Garden Theatre for a while in 1797–98 she was paid £16 per night.

Reviewing Mme Hilligsberg's performance in *Paul et Virginie*, the *Morning Chronicle* of 13 January 1796 noticed that her "graceful figure, and the naivety of her attitudes gives this little ballet irresistible interest." When Mme Hilligsberg danced with Mme Laborie as the Twin Sisters in the ballet *Les Deux Jumelles* at the King's on 29 January 1799, the critic in the *Morning Chronicle* the next day wrote that she owned "the first rank among the dancers of London" and described her as a "woman of distinguished merit," who "succeeds with peculiar happiness in sportive and jocose expressions, and . . . is bewitchingly graceful as a Welch or Scotch country girl. Her figure is very handsome, but her arms are somewhat long and thin."

Mme Hilligsberg remained a featured dancer at the King's through 1802–3, receiving her last benefit there on 5 May 1803. She also danced at Drury Lane in 1800–1801. According to the *Gentleman's Magazine*, she died in France in January 1804. (In his *Reminiscences*, Michael Kelly stated incorrectly that she had died at Calais in August 1803.) A few months before her death she had married a M. Beaumont, "a French gentleman of good birth." She left a daughter by a former marriage.

In 1793–94, the King's Theatre bills had listed Mme Hilligsberg as "Mme M. L. Hilligsberg Sen," to distinguish her from her sister Mlle Janet Hilligsberg, who was also in the company. A Mlle E. Hilligsberg was also listed in Drury Lane bills of 2 July 1794 as dancing with Mme Hilligsberg in *The Glorious First of June*, but we believe that billing to have been a printing error for J. Hilligsberg. Instead of four female Hilligsbergs listed in *The London Stage* as dancers in the 1790s, we believe there were only two—Mme [M.L.?] and her sister Janet.

Engravings by Condé, after H. de Janvry, depict Mme Hilligsberg dancing in *Le Jaloux puni* (published 12 May 1794) and in *Ken-si and Tao*, for her benefit on 14 May 1801 (published 1801). A sketch by Alexandre Moitte of her as a Fairy in *Alcindor* is in the Beard Collection, Victoria and Albert Museum. Mme Hilligsberg also appears in an engraved caricature by Thomas Rowlandson that shows King's Theatre performers begging in the streets; this engraving is one of two by Rowlandson entitled "The Prospect Before Us." In *John Hoppner R. A.* (1914), William McKay and W. Roberts reported a large canvas (90 × 60) of a dancer, full-length, in a white low dress, sometimes called Mme Hilligsberg. The painting was owned by Mrs Howard Smith when it was reproduced in William Sharp's "Fair Women" issue of *The Portfolio* in July 1894. McKay and Roberts were "doubtful as to the authenticity of this picture," presumably in respect to its attribution to Hoppner.

Hillingham. *See* ALLINGHAM.

Hillingsworth, Mrs. *See* ILLINGSWORTH, MRS.

Hillisberg. *See* HILLIGSBERG.

Hills, Mr [*fl.* 1741], *singer.*
Mr Hills sang "The Life of a Beau" at the James Street playhouse on 27 October 1741 at Mrs Careless's benefit.

Hills, William. *See* HILL, WILLIAM.

Hillyard, Mrs [*fl.* 1782], *singer.*
At Cooper's Hall, King Street, Bristol, on 2 March 1782 a company from Sadler's Wells led by a Mr Andrews gave performances of rope-walking and tumbling. Between the turns there were "several select SONGS by Mrs. Hillyard."

Hillyard, Miss [Mrs?] *d.* 1744, *dancer, actress, singer.*
The first notice in the London theatrical bills of a Miss Hillyard (sometimes Hilliard or Hillier) was on 16 March 1734, when she appeared at Covent Garden as the Bridal Virgin in *The Nuptial Masque*, a spectacle seen several times that season. She rejoined the ballet corps at Covent Garden in the fall of 1734 to dance 172 nights for 3*s*. 4*d*. per night, sustaining a few named parts in pantomime— Proserpine in *The Rape of Proserpine*, Andromeda in *Perseus and Andromeda*, Diana in *Apollo*

and Daphne, Diana in *The Royal Chace*, Lettice in *Sylvia*, and the like—through the season of 1737–38.

On 9 November 1737 Miss "Hillyard" appeared in a straight dramatic part, Advocate in Charles Shadwell's comedy *The Fair Quaker of Deal*. In 1737–38 there were parts in which Miss Hillyard employed her talents both acting and singing: Arethusa in *The Contrivances* and Arabella in *The Honest Yorkshireman*. The Covent Garden playbill for 15 May 1741 announced that "At the End of the Second and Fourth Act" of *Double Falsehood* would "be performed an Interlude in two Comic Scenes in Musick, betwixt Signor Capoccio, a Director from the Canary Islands, and Signora Dorinna a Virtuosa." Capoccio was sung by Gustavus Waltz and Dorinna by "Miss Hillier."

When Miss Hillyard returned to Covent Garden in 1741–42 she resumed several of her old parts dancing and singing, but moved further into dramatic roles with Audrey in *As You Like It*, Mrs Squeamish in *The Country Wife*, Clara in *Rule a Wife and Have a Wife*, and Mrs Farthingale in *The Funeral*. In 1742–43 she added Lettice in *The Plain Dealer* and Betty in *The Old Bachelor*. In 1743–44 her new parts were Myrtilla in *The Provok'd Husband*, Jenny Diver in *The Beggar's Opera*, Juletta (Juliet) in *Measure for Measure*, and Lucia in *The Squire of Alsatia*.

The *Daily Advertiser* of 8 December 1744 reported the death of "Miss Hilliard" of Covent Garden Theatre on 6 December 1744. The relationship of Miss Hillyard to the Miss P. Hillyard (Hilliard) of 1746 and twenty years following is not understood. Perhaps they were sisters; in view of the time-spread, it does not seem likely. It may be that they were mother and daughter (see next entry).

Hillyard, Miss P. [née Cavendish?] [*fl.* 1746?–1768], *dancer.*
The actress George Anne Bellamy recalled in her *Apology* (the time of which she speaks would have been around mid-eighteenth century) that her

little house in the Vineyard [Lisle Street, Leicester Fields] was always crowded. I had with me, besides my own family [nieces and nephews of her lover, George Metham], the widow of Mr. Delany, and Miss Hilyard, a daughter of Lord Frederick Cavendish, who had made such a proficiency in dancing, that she afterwards appeared with great eclat, upon the stage, and though she was far from handsome, she might have made her fortune, had she been inclined to enter the lists of gallantry.

Lord Frederick Cavendish (1729–1803) was the third Duke of Devonshire. He died unmarried. No one can vouch for the accuracy of Miss Bellamy's gossip. There is a good chance that the girl of which Miss Bellamy spoke was the Miss "Hilliard" who was dancing with Muilment, Desse, Picq, and Miss Scott at Drury Lane theatre on 6 February 1746. She may have been there earlier or later that season, but the bills do not reveal it.

Not until 20 April 1748, apparently, was Miss Hillyard again in a London bill. She danced on that night with Lalauze and Madame Delagarde in a ballet called *The Amorous Swain; or, Rival Nymphs* at Covent Garden and then disappeared again until the season of 1749–50. She was on the Covent Garden books by 16 December 1749 at £3 per week but was not recorded dancing until 31 January 1750, when she and Cooke did a *Grand Scotch Ballet*. She was then advertised in the bills as appearing on that stage for the first time, and on the face of it that should mean a different Miss Hillyard. But printers or managers often accidentally or deliberately made the "first appearance" claim, especially after a lapse of some time since the last previous appearance. A British Library manuscript records that on 8 January 1750 Mr Broadas the Covent Garden tailor made a dancing dress for Miss Hillyard. She danced on 7 February in a new pantomime *The Fair*, used to introduce Mons Jossett to the London stage. It was repeated many times, and she was otherwise much employed. On 23 April she took her benefit. Cooke, her frequent partner that season, joined her in a *Dutch Dance*, a *Grand Scots Dance*, a minuet, and a louvre. She gained £27 1s. The fact that she was given her own separate benefit might suggest that she was a principal dancer and no novice.

Miss Hillyard's dancing (under that spelling) was frequent at Covent Garden in 1750–51 and 1751–52. She was not seen until 7 December in the 1752–53 season. The *General Advertiser* of 17 November had reported that she had suffered a painful sprain. On 30 April she shared a benefit with Signor Maranesi. She

returned to Covent Garden only once in the fall of 1753, on 3 November, when she and Cooke danced a minuet in *Romeo and Juliet*.

A year later Miss Hillyard was in Ireland with the Smock Alley company, where on 29 November 1754 she joined McNeil and others dancing *The Hibernian Meggot*. A letter to *Faulkner's Dublin Journal* on 26 April 1755 was signed "P. Hilliard." When she returned to Covent Garden to dance with Granier on 14 November 1755, she was said to be appearing there for the first time "these two years." Her name was then spelled "Hilliard" in the bills. (Whether that spelling in the newspaper letter and the bills reflected her preference or not is not known.)

Miss Hillyard's winter service to the theatre was unbroken for the next five years, through 1759–60. (As "Hillerd" she was apparently dancing at Liverpool in the summer of 1758.) Then she again disappeared into the provinces for two years. She danced at Drury Lane at least three times in the fall of 1763 and at Covent Garden at least once in the spring and once in the fall of 1766. Arthur Murphy's list of salaries at Covent Garden as of 14 September 1767 shows her in the dance company at 4s. 2d. per night. There is no other evidence that she danced that season, but the bills were not very informative. After the 1767–68 season nothing more was heard of a Miss Hillyard (or Hilliard) in London.

What relation Miss P. Hilliard may have been to the earlier dancer Miss Hillyard is not known. Both may have been related to the provincial strollers, the family Hillyard reported by Richard Ryan in *Dramatic Table Talk* (1825) as "well known in Lancashire and Yorkshire" toward the end of the eighteenth century. "At a large room, in the New Street, Ashton, Friday Evening, June 30th, 1797" they presented *The School for Scandal* and *Barnaby Brittle* and took all of the parts in both the mainpiece and the afterpiece. Involved were Mr Hillyard, Mr Hillyard, Jun, Mrs Hillyard, Miss Hillyard, Miss P. Hillyard, Master Hillyard, and Master T. Hillyard.

Hilsberg. *See* HILLIGSBERG.

Hilton, Mr [*fl.* 1718–1719], *actor*.
The 1718 edition of *The Stage Coach* lists a Mr Hilton as the Hostler. He probably acted

that part when the play was given at Drury Lane on 13 May 1718. Hilton shared benefits at that house on 28 May 1718 and again on 19 May 1719.

Hilton, Mr [*fl.* 1755], *proprietor.*

The *Gentlemen's Magazine* contained the following report:

Tuesday 9 [September 1755]. A Warrant, granted by my lord Mayor, to search the house of Mr and Mrs Hilton, at the *Rose* in *Cursitor-Street*, where public dancing and musick were carried on twice a week, without the license which the late act requires, was executed by eight or nine constables, who brought away about 30 young men and women, and lodged them in the two Compters.

The following morning the group was examined by the Lord Mayor and a magistrate and released with "a severe reprimand for resorting to such houses, for the suppressing of which this statute was so wisely made." The report did not indicate what punishment, if any, Mr and Mrs Hilton received.

Hilton, Mrs [*fl.* 1755], *proprietress. See* HILTON, MR [*fl.* 1755].

Hilton, Mrs [*fl.* 1792], *actress.*

Mrs Hilton played Tag in *Miss in Her Teens* at the Crown Inn, Islington, on 16 January 1792.

Hilyard. *See* HILLYARD.

Hime, Humphrey [*fl.* 1784?–1840], *violinist, violist.*

The Mr Hime who played first violin in the Handel Memorial Concerts at Westminster Abbey and the Pantheon in May and June 1784 was probably Humphrey Hime of Liverpool. Doane's *Musical Directory* of 1794 gave Hime's address as Lord Street, Liverpool, and noted that he played the violin and viola. In addition to performing at the Abbey in London, Hime also played for the New Musical Fund.

In the late 1780s Humphrey was in the music-selling and publishing business with his brother Maurice. After Maurice left Liverpool for Dublin, Humphrey set up shop at No 14, Castle Street, Liverpool, from about 1790 to 1805. He continued business as Hime and Son

at various premises in Castle Street and in Church Street from about 1805 to 1840. His son apparently carried on the business after the latter year.

Himet, Miss. *See* HEMET, MISS.

Hinchly, Hildibrand [*fl.* 1725], *singer.*

A Lord Chamberlain's warrant dated 24 June 1725 ordered an allowance for Hildibrand Hinchly, a former child of the Chapel Royal whose voice had broken.

Hind. *See* HEARD AND HINDE.

Hinde, Samuel [*fl.* 1730?–1747], *actor, dancer, singer, manager.*

There were a number of performers named Hinde (or Hind) in the British Isles in the eighteenth century, and distinguishing them is difficult. A dancer named "Hind" appeared at the Lee-Harper booth at Southwark Fair on 24 September 1730, at the Miller-Mills-Oates booth at Bartholomew Fair on 23 August 1732, and at Goodman's Fields Theatre on 5 October 1732. A Mr Hind acted Archer in *The Beaux' Stratagem* at the Haymarket Theatre on 19 March 1733, and it is possible that he was the same person.

Beginning with the 1733–34 season at the Smock Alley playhouse in Dublin, a Mr S. Hinde (almost certainly Samuel Hinde) appeared on the Irish stage. We know none of Hinde's roles that season. A "Hind" acted Simon in *The Siege of Troy* at Southwark Fair in London on 7 September 1734. S. Hinde was in the Aungier Street company in Dublin in 1734–35, but we do not know in what months he acted there; if he performed only in the spring and summer of 1735, then the Mr Hind who essayed pantomime roles at the Goodman's Fields Theatre in London in 1734–35 could easily have been the same person. At Goodman's Fields from 25 September 1734 through 15 April 1735 Hind was seen as a Londoner in *Britannia*, a Londoner in *Harlequin in the City*, Pierrot in *The Chymical Counterfeits*, and Argus in *Jupiter and Io*. Hind's London record is blank between mid-April and 23 August 1735 (when, if he was, in fact, S. Hinde, he may have been in Dublin). On 23 August 1735, "Hind," Yeates, and Warner ran a booth at "Welch" Fair at which they presented *The Author's Farce* with six-foot-high wax figures and *The Mistake* with live actors.

S. Hinde was at the Aungier Street playhouse in Dublin in 1735–36; "Hind" was at Covent Garden the same season. But the Covent Garden player appeared only once, on 22 November 1735 as the Soothsayer in *Julius Caesar*. S. Hinde's only known role at Aungier Street that season (though he may have acted more frequently than the scanty records show) was Gaylove in *The Honest Yorkshireman* on 15 January 1736.

A Mr Hind, a dancer, appeared with Mme Violante's company at Carubber's Close playhouse in Edinburgh in a pantomime on 9 February 1736, according to Dibdin's *Annals of the Edinburgh Stage*.

On 24 March 1737 a Mr Hinde sang and danced at Smock Alley in Dublin, advertised as making his first appearance on that stage—not a true statement if that was S. Hinde. "Hind" and Miss Barnes danced the popular *Dutch Skipper and His Frow*, and "Hinde" sang "The Song of New Mad Tom." S. Hinde was at Smock Alley again during the 1737–38 season, after which we find no further references to a Hind or a Hinde for three years. At Goodman's Fields on 10 and 11 December 1741 a Mr Hinde played Macheath in *The Beggar's Opera*. Again there is a gap in the records until 12 June 1745, when a Mr Hind began an engagement at the Jacob's Wells Theatre in Bristol for a fee of 2s. each performance; he was occasionally paid extra if he played two or three roles—which suggests a bit-part player. At Southwark Fair on 16 October 1746 a Mr Hind was seen as Foigard in *The Stratagem*. Finally, Samuel Hinde, an actor with the Smock Alley troupe in 1746–47, signed a petition at the end of February 1747 urging that the theatres be reopened.

Samuel Hinde, who, we think, is the performer cited throughout these years, had a wife who appeared with him in Dublin. As will be seen in her entry, there was a Mrs "Hind" who danced and acted in London in the early 1730s and whose career partly parallels that of our subject.

There were several other Hindes active about the same time or somewhat later, and it is probable that they were related. J. Hinde acted at the Rainsford Street playhouse in Dublin from 1732 to 1736. William Hinde and his wife and children appeared at Norwich, and it is probable that they were the Hindes who were at Edinburgh in mid-century. Also at Norwich and later at Belfast were Edward Hinde and his wife.

Hinde, Mrs Samuel [*fl.* 1732?–1748?], dancer, actress, singer.

A Mrs "Hind" played Lucy in *The London Merchant* at the Haymarket Theatre on 1 June 1732, and at the Miller-Mills-Oates booth at Bartholomew Fair she danced on 23 August. *The London Stage* lists Mrs Hind as a dancer in the Goodman's Fields troupe in 1732–33, but her only known appearance was as Lady Bountiful in *The Beaux' Stratagem* on 19 March 1733. Appearing with Mrs Hind at most of these performances was a Mr Hind, presumably her husband.

Mrs S(amuel) Hinde made what was advertised as her first appearance on the (that?) stage on 21 March 1737 at Smock Alley in Dublin when she played Lucy in *The Beggar's Opera*. Three days later Mr Hinde made his first Smock Alley appearance, according to the bills. The scanty Dublin records show Mrs S. Hinde in the Smock Alley troupe again in 1737–38, her only known role being Betty in *The Squire of Alsatia* on 14 November 1737. After that Mrs Hinde's name disappeared from the bills. A Mrs Hind played Mrs Cheatwell in *The Rival Lovers* at the Phillips booth at Southwark Fair on 24 August 1748, and perhaps she was the woman whom we have been following.

Hindle, John 1761–1796, singer, harpsichordist, organist, composer.

When John Hindle was recommended to the Royal Society of Musicians for membership on 1 June 1783 he was described as a single man 22 years old, a harpsichordist and teacher, and a student of Dr Benjamin Cooke. His father was Bartholomew Hindle of Westminster. In addition to playing the harpsichord, John was a countertenor and sang in the Handel Memorial Concerts at Westminster Abbey and the Pantheon in May and June of 1784. In August 1780 he had sung at the Worcester festival. In March and April 1786 Hindle sang in the Tottenham Street concerts. He matriculated on 16 November 1791 at Magdalen College, Oxford, and evidently received a bachelor's degree in music (his published songs so indicate). Hindle sang in the oratorios at Covent Garden in March 1792 and, according to Doane's *Musical Directory* of 1794, he was a member of St Peter's choir and an organist. In 1794 he was living at No 4, Tufton Street, Westminster.

Hindle was a lay vicar of Westminster Abbey, and on 3 June 1792 the Royal Society of Musicians, of which he was a member, ordered that he should be summoned to a general meeting to explain why he should not be expelled for nonattendance at St Margaret's the previous year.

John Hindle died in London in 1796. His mother, Mary Hindle, a widow, was granted administration of his estate. Hindle was described as of Tufton Street in the parish of St John the Evangelist. Hindle composed a number of glees and other light songs during his lifetime, his most popular work being the glee "Queen of the silver bow."

Hindmarsh, George [*fl.* 1740–1759], *musician.*

The musician George Hindmarsh, according to the records of the Worshipfull Company of Musicians, had three apprentices bound to him between 3 July 1740 and 21 May 1759. Hindmarsh was probably related to the violinist John Hindmarsh, who was born about 1759.

Hindmarsh, John *c.* 1759–1796, *instrumentalist.*

John Hindmarsh was born about 1759, the son of James Hindmarsh, a shoemaker of the parish of St Botolph, Bishopsgate, and his wife Mary. By 16 January 1773, when John was apprenticed, his father had died. Young Hindmarsh was bound first to the musician Edward Boxley, according to the records of the Worshipfull Company of Musicians, but on the same day it was agreed by all parties to turn the boy over to George Buckland, a plaisterer but a musician by profession, of No 1, New Street, Bishopsgate Street. John became a freeman on 28 November 1782, by which time he was living in Spitalfields. At some point he studied under Salomon.

On 4 May 1783 Hindmarsh was recommended for membership in the Royal Society of Musicians, his sponsor reporting that he was a single man of 24 and proficient on the violin, viola, and clarinet. He was admitted in 1784. He was one of the first violinists in the Handel Memorial Concerts at Westminster Abbey and the Pantheon in May and June 1784, and in May 1785 and several subsequent years he played in the Society's annual St Paul's concert. Among his students was John George Henry Jay, who had a career as a violinist and composer.

In 1787 Hindmarsh became leader of the band at the Royalty Theatre, but that playhouse had a very short life. He also served as leader of the band at Astley's Amphitheatre. On 16 February 1790 at the Paul's Head Tavern in Cateaton Street a benefit concert was held for Miss Newman, with Hindmarsh serving as violoncello soloist and director, and the following 29 September at the Haymarket Theatre Hindmarsh played a concerto on the violin. Doane's *Musical Directory* in 1794 listed Hindmarsh as a member of the Royal Society of Musicians, the Concert of Ancient Music, and the Amicable Society. Doane said that the musician had played at the Oxford Meeting in 1793 and had participated in the Handel concerts at Westminster Abbey. Hindmarsh's address was given as Vauxhall House, Hampstead Common. The *Oracle* reported on 5 November 1796 that John Hindmarsh had lately died. The Royal Society of Musicians on 6 November entertained a request from Mary Ann Hindmarsh, John's widow, for an allowance. They granted her a present, "but as the Governors are informed she possesses talents that will enable her to support herself, they trust that she as soon as decency permits, will exert herself to obtain an engagement." Mrs Hindmarsh was a singer and actress.

On 4 February 1797 administration of the estate of John Hindmarsh, late of Ealing, was granted to his creditor John Druce—Mary Ann Hindmarsh and Mary Brownell, formerly Hindmarsh (John's mother), having renounced their rights. The estate was valued at £300.

Hindmarsh, Mrs John, Mary Ann, née Williams [*fl.* 1792–1815], *singer, actress.*

On 29 May 1792 Mrs (John) Hindmarsh sang at the Crown and Anchor Tavern. Doane's *Musical Directory* of 1794 listed Mrs John

Hindmarsh ("late Miss Williams") as a soprano. She and her husband lived at Vauxhall House, Hampstead Common. On 11 March 1795 Mrs Hindmarsh made what the *Morning Herald* called a successful first appearance singing in the *Messiah* at Covent Garden Theatre. She participated in the oratorios at the theatre through 27 March. John Hindmarsh died in late 1796, and on 6 November of that year his widow requested a widow's allowance from the Royal Society of Musicians. The Governors granted her request but noted that since Mrs Hindmarsh was capable of earning her own living through singing, they felt they could not continue the pension once she returned to her career. On 7 January 1798 she wrote to the Society that she had accepted an engagement at the Theatre Royal in Edinburgh but needed money to defray her travel expenses. She was granted 15 guineas, provided she relinquish her allowance for a year.

On 20 January 1798 she sang the title role in *Rosina* in Edinburgh, after which, through March, she appeared as Caroline in *The Prize*, Gillian in *The Quaker*, Laura in *Lock and Key*, Leonora in *The Padlock*, Margaretta in *No Song No Supper*, and Wilhelmina in *The Waterman*. She also sang at the Oxford Music Room in 1798, and on 23 August she sang at the Haymarket Theatre in London. But she evidently had a difficult time supporting herself. She appealed for relief to the Royal Society of Musicians in October 1798 but was denied help. When she applied again in January 1799 she was granted £2 12s. 6d. per month. In mid-1799 she again had an engagement at Oxford, for which she received (the Royal Society of Musicians learned) £76 15s. When she requested her regular allowance from the Society, they summoned her to a meeting to explain her actions. On 1 September she came before the Governors and confessed that she had received more salary within a year than the Society allowed if she was to be granted a pension, so her allowance was stopped.

By June 1800 she was in York, writing again to the Society for financial assistance, but she seems to have earned 55 guineas during the first half of the year and was once again denied aid. In February 1802 she was apparently in London; she told the Society she was afflicted with a severe indisposition and once more needed financial aid; a committee investigated, found her representation true, and granted her five guineas. In April 1805 she was again put on a monthly allowance of £2 12s. 6d. Over the years that followed there was much correspondence concerning Mrs Hindmarsh, but the evidence in the Minute Books reveals little. She seems, however, to have been energetic in her attempts to get aid from the organization. On 1 March 1812 she was told that she had no further claim on the Society, but that did not stop her from appearing a month later to plead for her widow's allowance. When the Society discovered that she had refused an offer to sing in the oratorios for six guineas, her allowance was reduced to two guineas monthly.

In 1813, though she had told the Society that she had no property, they had found that she owned a house in High Street, Brighton. Once again they cut off her allowance. Mrs Hindmarsh replied that she had, indeed, purchased the house, but that she derived no financial advantage from it. That claim turned out to be true, and the Society granted her all her arrears and a renewal of her monthly allowance. The Governors must have been relieved to hear on 5 March 1815 that Mrs Hindmarsh had married Dr Henry Harington of Bristol, a composer who had been active from the 1770s to the 1790s. She requested and was granted a widow's dowry.

Hinds, Ann. *See* HATTON, MRS WILLIAM THOMAS P. THE SECOND *1775–1841.*

Hingeston, John *d. 1683, singer, organist, violist, composer.*
John Hingeston (or Hingston) of York was the student of the musician Orlando Gibbons (d. 1625). John served as a court musician under Charles I, and by 1651 John Playford listed "Hinkston" as a teacher of organ or virginal in his *Musicall Banquet*. Hingeston was in the service of Oliver Cromwell, taught the Protector's daughters, and about 1654 was appointed as the ruler's organist at Hampton Court at £100 yearly. Roger L'Estrange in *Truth and Loyalty Vindicated* in 1662 told of playing the viola with Hingeston in "a little low room of Mr. . . . Hinkson's" in St James's Park; Cromwell himself dropped by, unexpected, to listen for a while. On 19 February 1657 Hingeston joined other London musi-

Faculty of Music, Oxford

JOHN HINGESTON

artist unknown

cians in an unsuccessful effort to establish a College of Music.

On 23 June 1660 Hingeston was appointed "for a Viol, in the place of Alphonso Ferrobosco" in the King's Musick. His livery fee was the usual £16 2*s*. 6*d*. annually, though the King rarely paid it on time; the musician's regular salary at that early date is not known. On 2 July 1660 he was given the added post of "tuner and repairer of organs, virginalls, and wind instruments," replacing Arthur Norgate. A warrant in the Lord Chamberlain's accounts dated 15 March 1661 directed that Hingeston should be paid £121 13*s*. 6*d*. for a new cabinet organ, four violins, and several other instruments and for the stringing and repairing of yet more instruments. Similar warrants in later years show him busy caring for the instruments required by the King and Queen at the Hampton Court Chapel. By 1662 his annual salary as tuner and repairer of the wind instruments was £60, but he also earned at least £50 more each year as one of the court instrumentalists. Warrants show that his duties also involved furnishing the organ loft at Hampton Court, enlarging and furnishing

the loft at Whitehall and setting up an organ there, moving organs from one royal building to another, accompanying their majesties on trips to Windsor, and performing. Warrants also list Hingeston among the lutenists and singers at court. By 1663 he had a room at Whitehall, near the organ loft.

Hingeston was a friend of Samuel Pepys', and on 19 December 1666, Pepys was just leaving Whitehall after a conference with the Duke of York when he

met Mr. Hingston the Organist (my old acquaintance) in the Court, and I took him to the Dogg tavern and got him to set me a bass to my *It is decreed*, which I think will go well; but he commends the song, not knowing the words, but says the ayre is good, and believes the words are plainly expressed. He is of my mind, against having of eighths unnecessarily in composition. This did all please me mightily. Then to talk of the King's family: he says many of the Musique are ready to starve, they being five years behindhand for their wages. Nay, Evens, the famous man upon the Harp, having not his equal in the world, did the other day die for mere want, and was fain to be buried at the almes of the parish—and carried to his grave in the dark at night, without one Linke, but that Mr Hingston met it by chance and did give 12*d* to buy two or three links. He says all must come to ruin at this rate, and I believe him.

The following year, on 10 December 1667, Pepys met Hingeston by chance, "and I walked with him; and, asking him many questions, I do find that he can no more give an intelligible answer to a man that is not a great master in his art, than another man. And this confirms me that it is only want of an ingenious man that is master in musique, to bring musique to a certainty, and ease in composition."

By 1668 the accounts cited Hingeston not only as an organ repairer but also as organ maker to the King at £60 annually, plus £50 each year as a member of the King's private music. Hingeston seems to have managed his finances well. On 20 November 1668 his fellow musician Theodore Steffkin assigned £8 of his next salary payment to Hingeston, presumably in return for a loan. In October 1671 eight court musicians directed that one Thomas Townsend, esquire, "will be pleased to deliver our talleys, and order on the fee farmes for one year's liverie due at St. Andrew, 1669, unto our fellow John Hingeston, and his acquittance in the behalf of us shall be a sufficient discharge." He had evidently been lending all of them money. John was also high in the membership of the Corporation of Music; he was, as of 24 June 1672, the deputy marshal.

On 10 June 1673, when Hingeston must have been getting on in years, Henry Purcell was appointed his assistant as keeper of the organs; Purcell was unsalaried but was to receive Hingeston's post and income upon his retirement or death. Purcell had some time to wait. The Lord Chamberlain's accounts contain scattered references to Hingeston during the following few years. A vaguely dated entry indicates that sometime between 1673 and 1675 Hingeston was paid for "Repairing and amending two harpsichords and carrying them to the playhouse"—a reference, probably, to the court theatre at Whitehall, though perhaps the Theatre Royal in Bridges Street was intended. And on 15 June 1676 Hingeston was to appear in court for a debt owed to the organ maker Bernard Smith.

John accompanied the King to Windsor in the spring of 1682, for which he was paid £15, but the records show little more musical activity for him in the early 1680s. On 12 December 1683 Hingeston, describing himself as "infirme in body," had his will prepared. Within a few days he died. His burial was at St Margaret, Westminster, on 17 December, on which date Henry Purcell succeeded to John's post as organ maker and keeper. On 22 December Robert Carr replaced Hingeston among the violists at court.

John Hingeston's will was a lengthy one, full of bequests large and small to his many friends and relatives. He must have built up a considerable fortune during his life. To his brother Arthur Hingeston of Bickerton, Ainsty, York, he left his two houses in Chelsea, then occupied by Mr Robbins and Mr King. Those houses, after the death of Arthur Hingeston, were to go to the children of Hingeston's two sisters, Elizabeth Petty of Bickerton and Isabella Calfe, late of Benningbrooke, Yorkshire. To the children of Elizabeth Petty also went £5 and one of Hingeston's houses in Berry Street, lately occupied by John Webley. To the children of Hingeston's sister's

son Henry Petty, deceased, went £5 each. To John Calfe, the son of Hingeston's sister Isabella by her second husband, and to Isabella's daughter Mary Thorpe went £5 each.

Hingeston also owned a house called the Crowne and Scepter, in Piccadilly, which he gave to his nephew John Trayne and to the daughters of Isabella Calfe in trust. Trayne was to give one Mary Nelson upon her marriage £40 from the income of the Crowne and Scepter. Trayne and the Calfe girls were also to pay out of that income the following: £5 to Edward Goodgson of Skipton (Shipton?); £3 to Frances Grange, Hingeston's half-brother's daughter, lately living in St Dennis Churchyard, York; £5 to the poor of the parish of Londesburgh, York; £3 to the poor of the parish of St Lawrence, York, where John Hingeston was born; £5 to the poor of the parish of Skipton (Shipton?); and £3 to the poor of the parish in which Hingeston happened to die (possibly St Margaret, Westminster, but we do not know precisely where he died).

Hingeston left £50 and half of the arrears in salary, due him from the King, to his godson Richard Graham. The other half of his arrears he left to various relatives mentioned above. To George Wyatte of Westin (Westm?—that is, Westminster?) Hingeston left £5; to his godson Henry Purcell went £5; and to John Andrews of Hartshorne Lane went £6. To Elizabeth, Countess of Burlington and Cork, he bequeathed pictures of her and of Francis, Earl of Cumberland; Henry, Earl of Cumberland, his son; Edward, Earl of Sandwich; and Richard, Earl of Burlington and Cork. Hingeston left his friend Richard Bell £5 for a ring and his godson Richard Graham (his executor and residuary legatee) some property in Church Lane, alias Hogg Lane, Chelsea. Hingeston directed Graham to give 40s. to each of Hingeston's servants. Hingeston's friend Thomas Whitfield was to receive £3 for a ring.

Hingeston remembered many of his fellow court musicians with bequests. He left gold rings worth 8s. each to those "ffellow servants of his Maj^ties private Musique and gentlemen of his Chappell as shall be present at my funerall." To the court musician Thomas Blagrave he gave £10 and his best chest of viols; to his apprentice Peter Hingeston (probably John's nephew) he left £40; to the musician William

Gregory he left his "great" double bass; and to Raphael Courteville of the Chapel Royal he left an organ (the one with two sets of keys, the will specified) and a number of music books. Hingeston gave a picture of "my ever Hono^rd Master Orlando Gibbons" to the music school at Oxford. Morgan Harris, one of the Gentlemen of the Chapel Royal, was given one of Hingeston's bass viols (the one in a leather case, the will stated); Hingeston's student John Blagrave (the son of Anthony Blagrave of Norwich) was left one of Hingeston's violins; another violin was left to the son of the musician Humphrey Madge (another godson of Hingeston's) and yet another was bequeathed to Frederick Steffkin. Thomas Blagrave was named assistant executor of the will. Probably too weak to sign his will, John Hingeston made what the scribe certified was "his marke."

The British Library has a small collection of Hingeston's music in manuscript. Oxford owns six volumes of the musician's compositions and his portrait, by an unknown artist.

Hingeston, "Thomas." *See* HINGESTON, JOHN.

Hinner, Philipp Joseph *b. 1754, harpist, composer.*
According to Grove, Philipp Joseph Hinner was born in Wetzlar, Germany, in 1754. He lived as a boy in French Guiana, visited Paris and Naples, and came to London in 1781. He was much admired in London, according to Fétis's *Biographie des musiciens*, for his performances of adagios on the harp. Hinner returned to Paris, became Marie-Antoinette's harp teacher and chamber musician, and composed a number of works, including some songs for *Le Fausse délicatesse* (1776) and *Les Trois inconnues* (1783).

Hiorne, Miss [*fl. 1778*], *actress.*
Miss Hiorne and a number of other performers made their first stage appearances in *The Macaroni Adventurer* at the Haymarket Theatre on 28 December 1778. That night Miss Hiorne also acted Industrious Jenny in *The Covent Garden Tragedy*.

Hippersley, Tom [*fl. 1738*], *singer.*
William John Pinks in *The History of Clerkenwell* (1881) stated that in Bickham's *The*

Curious Entertainer (1738) was an engraving of Tom Hippersley, mounted in the singing rostrum of Bagnigge Wells, Clerkenwell, regaling the company with a song. We have not been able to identify *The Curious Entertainer*, though Bickham did publish *The Musical Entertainer*. The British Library copy of the latter does not, however, contain a print that shows Hippersley.

Hippisley, Mrs. *See* HIPPISLEY, ELIZABETH.

Hippisley, Elizabeth [*fl. 1742–1769*], *actress, singer.*
Elizabeth Hippisley, the second daughter of the actor John Hippisley, made her first appearance on any stage as Angelina in *Love Makes a Man* at Henry Giffard's playhouse in Goodman's Fields on 25 January 1742. Two days later she acted Mincing in *The Way of the World*, and on 3 February she appeared as Parthenope in *The Rehearsal*. During the remainder of the season she played Columbine in *Harlequin Englishman*, Rose in *The Recruiting Officer* (a role she was to play for many years), Kitty in *The Lying Valet*, Arante in *King Lear*, Prue in *Love for Love*, and Sylvia in *The Old Bachelor*. Throughout the season she was carefully identified in the bills as Miss E. Hippisley, to distinguish her from her sister Jane, who also acted in the Goodman's Fields troupe.

Reed in his "Notitia Dramatica" stated that on 24 September 1742 "Miss Hippisley removed to Cov. Gar^n" where her father, John, acted. On 4 October she was advertised as making her first appearance on that stage playing Lucy in *The Virgin Unmask'd*. Her sister Jane remained with Giffard's company and acted in 1742–43 at Lincoln's Inn Fields. At Covent Garden during the rest of the season Elizabeth acted Prince Edward in *Richard III*, Lappet in *The Miser*, Miss Hoyden in *The Relapse*, and Juletta in *The Pilgrim*. On 11 April 1743 "Miss Hippisley, from the Theatre Royal in Covent Garden," played Prue in *Love for Love* and Lucy in *The Virgin Unmask'd* at Lincoln's Inn Fields.

Through 1750–51 Elizabeth Hippisley performed at Covent Garden under the aegis of John Rich, playing such parts as Mademoiselle in *The Provok'd Wife*, Kitty in *The Lying Valet*, Peggy in *The London Cuckolds*, Corinna in *The*

ELIZABETH HIPPISLEY as Biddy Bellair, DAVID GARRICK as Fribble, HANNAH PRITCHARD as Mrs Tag, and HENRY WOODWARD as Captain Flash in a scene from *Miss in Her Teens*

engraving by C. Mosley

City Wives Confederacy, Lucy in *An Old Man Taught Wisdom*, Ascanio in *The Assignation*, Phoebe in *As You Like It*, Lucia in *The Squire of Alsatia*, the title role in *The Lying Valet* (at her father's benefit in March 1744), Betty in *Flora*, Flareit and Mrs Anne in *Love's Last Shift*, Mrs Slammekin and Jenny Diver in *The Beggar's Opera*, Mrs Hartshorn and Miss Notable in *The Lady's Last Stake*, Doll Mavis in *The Silent Woman*, Chloe in *Timon of Athens*, Cherry in *The Stratagem*, Jenny in *The Provok'd Husband*, Edging in *The Careless Husband*, Patch in *The Busy Body*, Farthingale in *The Funeral*, Harriet in *The Miser*, Lady Sadlife in *The Double Gallant*, Silvia in *The Old Bachelor*, Amarillis in *The Rehearsal*, Arabella in *The Fair Quaker of Deal*, Pert in *The Man of Mode*, Lady Blanche in *Papal Tyranny*, Damaris in *The Amorous Widow*, Tippet in *Phebe*, Nerissa in *The Merchant of Venice*, Margaret in *Much Ado about Nothing*, Diana in *All's Well that Ends Well*, Phyllis in *The Conscious Lovers*, Miss Biddy in *Miss in Her Teens*, Flora in *She Wou'd and She Wou'd Not*, Lucetta in *The Suspicious Husband*, Prince John in 1 *Henry IV*, Dorothy Slut in *The Consequences of Industry and Idleness* (at Bartholomew Fair, one of her few appearances

there), Lucetta in *The Rover*, Clarence in 2 *Henry IV*, the Wanton Chambermaid in *The Descent of the Heathen Gods* (at the Fair in August 1749), Francisca in *Measure for Measure*, an Amazon in *Perseus and Andromeda*, and Cynthia in *The Wife's Relief* (at the Haymarket in July 1750).

The accounts for Covent Garden show that Miss Hippisley's salary—in October 1746, at any rate—was 8s. 4d. daily. A *Mrs* Hippisley was paid £1 5s. on 29 May 1747 and 6s. 8d. for two days on 29 September 1749, but it is likely that those entries are errors for Miss Hippisley (or possibly Mr Hippisley); the only Mrs Hippisley active in the theatre during the 1740s seems to have confined her performing to Bristol.

Indeed, the Hippisleys were very active at the Jacob's Wells Theatre in Bristol, which Elizabeth's father managed. Scattered playbills from 20 August 1744 through 31 March 1755 show that Miss Hippisley spent many of her summers performing there. She usually received benefits each August. Only a few of her roles at Bristol were specified: in 1746, Rose in *The Recruiting Officer* (unless that should be assigned to Elizabeth's sister Jane) on 2 June,

Edging in *The Careless Husband* on 16 June, Emilia in *Othello* on 21 July, Mrs Fardingale in *The Funeral* on 4 August, Parley in *The Constant Couple* and Kitty in *The Harlot's Progress* on 20 August, Lavinia in *The Fair Penitent* on 25 August, Nerissa in *The Merchant of Venice* on 29 August, and Lady Troth in *The Double Dealer* on 1 September; in 1755 Charlot in *The Gamester* and Columbine in *The Spell* on 31 March. All references in Bristol bills match free periods in Miss Hippisley's schedule in London.

On 19 December 1752 Elizabeth appeared as Mrs Trusty in *The Provok'd Husband* at Drury Lane. Then she was seen there as Isabel in *The Double Disappointment*, an Attendant in *The Brothers*, Miss Crochet in *Bayes in Petticoats*, and Mrs Tatoo in *Lethe*. In 1753–54 she acted Betty in *The Non-Juror*, Clara in *Scapin*, and Myrtilla in *The Provok'd Husband*—advertised in the bills as Mrs Hippisley; when she appeared as Victoria in *The Grumbler* in late April 1754, she was cited as Miss Hippisley. Possibly the variant ascriptions could mean that there were two Hippisley women at Drury Lane that season, but well into the 1760s the bills carried what we take to have been the same actress sometimes as Miss and sometimes as Mrs. She seems to have settled for Mrs most of the time in the 1760s. A study of the roles in *The London Stage* suggests that the references to Miss and to Mrs Hippisley all concern Elizabeth.

During the 1750s at Drury Lane Elizabeth played such parts as the Kinswoman in *The Chances*, Cleora in *The Tragedy of Tragedies*, Advocate in *The Fair Quaker of Deal*, a part in *The Chinese Festival*, Dona Martona in *Marplot in Lisbon*, Fadladinida in *Chrononhotonthologos*, Betty in *The Gamester*, a Lady in *The Toyshop*, Ismene in *Merope*, Charmion in *Antony and Cleopatra*, Peggy in *The King and the Miller of Mansfield*, Serina in *The Orphan*, Lady Bab's Maid in *High Life below Stairs*, Jessica in *The Merchant of Venice*, Betty in *Woman Is a Riddle*, unnamed roles in *Fortunatus* and *The Ambitious Stepmother*, Charlotte in *The Apprentice*, Miss Pewit in *The Male Coquette*, Laetitia in *The Heiress*, Lucilla in *The Fair Penitent*, Anne Page in *The Merry Wives of Windsor*, Lucinda in *The Conscious Lovers*, Night in *Amphitryon*, and Harriet in *The Upholsterer*.

In the 1760s Elizabeth Hippisley, still occasionally cited as Miss, added such parts as Furnish in *The Way to Keep Him*, Betty in *A Bold Stroke for a Wife*, Miss Charlotte in *Love à-la-Mode*, Helen in *Cymbeline*, Sigea in *Hecuba*, Toilet in *The Jealous Wife*, Tippet in *All in the Wrong*, Trifle in *The Old Maid*, a Slave in *Barbarossa*, Ursula in *Much Ado about Nothing*, a Lady in *Philaster*, Corinna in *The Citizen*, Parisatis in *The Rival Queens*, Penelope in *Tunbridge Walks*, Isabella in *The Stage Coach*, Milliner in *The Suspicious Husband*, the Player Queen in *Hamlet*, Cleone in *The Distrest Mother*, Lucy in *The Platonic Wife*, Florella in *The Orphan*, Lettice in *The Plain Dealer*, Iras in *All for Love*, Delia in *Theodosius*, the Chambermaid in *The Clandestine Marriage*, and an Attendant in *Zenobia*. After 27 January 1764 she seems to have been advertised regularly as Mrs Hippisley.

Hopkins wrote in his diary after the performance of *Zenobia* on 3 December 1768 that "Mrs. Hippisley [was] d———k, and could not speak." She was replaced in that play on the sixth and performed infrequently the rest of the 1768–69 season. Her last known appearance was on 8 April 1769, when she played her familiar role of Myrtilla in *The Provok'd Husband*.

The Dictionary of National Biography claims that Elizabeth Hippisley became Mrs Fitzmaurice and, late in her career, was working as a dresser at Bath. That woman, however, would seem to have been a different person— a Miss Hippisley (doubtless related) who acted at Bath in the early 1750s and then, as Mrs Fitzmaurice, performed in Edinburgh in the late 1750s and in York in the 1760s and 1770s. She seems not to have appeared in London.

Thomas Dibdin said that a Mrs Hippisley died in 1792 at the age of 90, but that woman could hardly have been our Elizabeth, who was surely of a younger generation. Dibdin was probably referring to Mrs John Hippisley, who seems to have worked at Bristol from as early as 2 September 1741 and was asscciated with the Bristol theatre as late as 1763. John Hippisley's wife was also named Elizabeth and was separated from him from as early as 1748. She seems not to have acted in London (the listing in *The London Stage* of a Mrs Hippisley playing Lucy in *Lethe* at Goodman's Fields on 27 November 1741 would appear to be an error; that role was normally performed by John Hippisley's daughter Jane, who was a regular member of the Goodman's Fields troupe). Could Hippisley's wife have been the woman who became Mrs Fitzmaurice?

Elizabeth Hippisley was pictured as Biddy Bellair, with Garrick as Fribble, Mrs Pritchard as Tag, and Woodward as Captain Flash, in a satirical print by Charles Mosley of the duel scene in *Miss in Her Teens*, published in 1747. Supposedly this print is the earliest known picture of a performance at Covent Garden Theatre that shows players and audience.

Hippisley, Jane. *See* GREEN, MRS HENRY.

Hippisley, John   1696–1748,   *actor, dancer, singer, manager.*

According to L. G. Turner (cited in Leo Hughes's *A Century of English Farce*), John Hippisley was born on 14 January 1696 in Wookey Hole, near Bristol. He was trained by John Rich as a harlequin, and on 7 November 1722 he made his first appearance at Lincoln's Inn Fields playing Fondlewife in *The Old Bachelor*— but judging by Hippisley's roles the rest of the season it is probable that that appearance was not his first as an actor.

He went on to play a Citizen in *Oedipus*, a Parishioner in *The Spanish Curate*, Scrub in *The Stratagem*, Sir Davy in *The Soldier's Fortune*, Marplot in *The Busy Body*, Sir Hugh in *The Merry Wives of Windsor*, Gomez in *The Spanish Fryar*, Tipple in *Injur'd Love*, Sir Clement in *The Compromise*, Lolpoop in *The Squire of Alsatia*, Daniel in *Oroonoko*, Worm in *Cutter of Coleman Street*, a comic role in *Julius Caesar*, a Boor in *Beggar's Bush*, Francis in *1 Henry IV*, Hecate in *Macbeth*, Alphonso in *The Pilgrim*, Vellum in *The Drummer*, the title role in *Hob*, the Clown in *Jupiter and Europa*, Sir Paul in *The Double Dealer*, Day in *The Committee*, Polonius in *Hamlet*, and Pandarus in *Troilus and Cressida*, for his benefit on 3 May 1723. At his benefit he also danced a new *Drunken Miller*; receipts were £84 7s. before house charges.

Hippisley continued performing for Rich at Lincoln's Inn Fields and, beginning in 1732, at Covent Garden, through the 1746–47 season, and the number of his roles over the years was phenomenal. Among them, in addition to

Harvard Theatre Collection

JOHN HIPPISLEY as Scapin

by J. H. Green

those he played during his first season with Rich, were Charino, Cholerick, and Lewis in *Love Makes a Man*, Scruple in *The Fair Quaker of Deal*, Scapin in *The Cheats of Scapin*, Ginks and Higgin in *The Royal Merchant*, Barnaby in *The Amorous Widow*, Lyrick in *Love and a Bottle*, Kitely in *Every Man in His Humour*, Sir William in *Love's Last Shift*, Sancho in *The Rover*, Sir Jasper in *The Country Wife*, the Welsh Collier, Pearmain, and Appletree in *The Recruiting Officer*, Gripe in *The Confederacy*, Sir Oliver in *She Wou'd If She Cou'd*, the Mad Welshman in *The Pilgrim* (his Welsh parts earned him the nicknames Ap-Leek and David Ap-Shinkin), Fumble in *The Fond Husband*, Learchus in *Aesop*, Dorante in *The Gamester*, ancient Corbaccio in *Volpone* (in November 1727 when John was 31; aged characters were another specialty of his), Peachum in *The Beggar's Opera* (when it opened in 1728; John could sing, too), Obadiah Prim in *A Bold Stroke for a Wife*, Pyefleet, the Cobler, and Ap-Leek in *The Cobler's Opera*,

Antonio in *Venice Preserv'd*, Clodpole in *The Rape of Proserpine*, and Sir Thomas Testy in his own afterpiece *Hob's Opera* (later called *Flora*) on 17 April 1729.

Also Moneytrap in *The Confederacy*, Mother Griffin in *A Woman's Revenge* (he took skirts parts on occasion), Calianax in *The Maid's Tragedy*, the Spanish Servant and the Hussar's Servant in *Perseus and Andromeda*, the First Murderer in *Macbeth*, Cimberton in *The Conscious Lovers*, Smugler and Alderman in *The Constant Couple*, Dashwell and Wiseacre in *The London Cuckolds*, Scaramouch in *The Emperor of the Moon*, Manuel in *She Wou'd and She Wou'd Not*, the Old Woman in *Rule a Wife and Have a Wife*, Obadiah in *The Committee*, Sir Wilful in *The Way of the World* at the opening of Covent Garden on 7 December 1732, Plausible in *The Plain Dealer*, Phaeax in *Timon of Athens*, Sir Solomon in *The Double Gallant*, Sir Francis in *The Provok'd Husband*, Shorthose in *Wit Without Money*, Shallow in *2 Henry IV*, Muckworm in *The Honest Yorkshireman*, Tipkin in *The Tender Husband*, Fluellen in *Henry V*, Foresight in *Love for Love*, Dogberry in *Much Ado about Nothing*, Old Bellair in *The Man of Mode*, Sable in *The Funeral*, Scapin in *Harlequin Scapin*, the Clown in *Measure for Measure*, Coupler in *The Relapse*, Drudge in *Orpheus and Eurydice*, Mufti in *Don Sebastian*, the title role in *The Miser*, Alderman in *The Twin Rivals*, and Testimony in *Sir Courtly Nice*. Season in and season out he delighted London audiences with his skirts parts, dialect roles, and portrayals of fools, bumpkins, clowns, rascals, and eccentric old gentlemen.

Hippisley's financial situation would seem to have been good over the years. His benefit brought in £102 2s. 6d. in 1724 when his daily salary was £1; in 1726 the receipts came to £84 11s. 6d.; in 1727 they were £103 19s. 6d.; in 1728 they came to a handsome £176 11s.; in 1731 they were a whopping £212 4s.; in 1735–36 John was being paid £180 per season—which probably meant the same £1 daily salary; and in 1741 his benefit brought in £202 14s.

Hippisley augmented his patent house income with appearances elsewhere and had a separate career as a manager at Bristol and at the late summer fairs in London. Hippisley's theatrical career at Bristol began in the summer of 1728. *Farley's Bristol Newspaper* said on

13 July, "We hear, that the famous Mr. Hippisley (from the Theatre-Royal in London) is come to town; and designs in a short Time to Entertain his Friends and Countrymen with a Diverting FARCE, of his own composing, call'd *The English Thief: or, The Welsh Lawyer*." The work (unpublished?) was presented on 14 August for the author's benefit, and near the end of August John joined the Bath Company (which was, to a considerable extent, the Bristol troupe) to play Peachum in *The Beggar's Opera*.

According to Latimer's *Annals of Bristol*, toward the end of 1728 Hippisley, with the support of a number of Bristolians who lent him £300, leased some land adjoining the Horse and Groom in Jacob's Wells. He erected a theatre—Bristol's first permanent playhouse—which was opened with *Love for Love* on 23 June 1729. He seems not to have acted there much at first, though in 1730 his two-act farce *A Journey to Bristol* was probably given at his Bristol playhouse before being presented to London audiences on 23 April 1731 at Lincoln's Inn Fields, with Hippisley as the Faithful Welshman. In June 1736 the actor-manager obtained a lease of the Horse and Groom and subsequently used it as a dwelling. A newspaper notice dated 7 August of that year stated that "Mr. Hippisley's Play-House is now compleatly finished, and on Monday next, the 9th Instant, the Comedians are desir'd to play the Provok'd Husband . . . for Mr. Hippisley's Benefit." Having expanded his leasehold, John apparently made some improvements to his little playhouse. He eventually came into full possession of the property.

But his Bristol venture was in financial trouble by the fall of 1737. John advertised a benefit in London for 25 November, but the death of the Queen closed the theatres, and the benefit was not held until 17 January 1738 at Covent Garden. Hippisley then told the public that because of his Bristol speculation he had fallen into debt and had been forced to mortgage his salary as an actor at Covent Garden during the previous two years. In time his situation improved. He spent the summers of 1741 through 1747 at Bristol, and some of his roles are known from advertisements: the title role in *The Cheats of Scapin*, Pearmain in *The Recruiting Officer*, Day in *The Committee*, Testimony in *Sir Courtly Nice*, Sable in *The Funeral*,

Dogberry in *Much Ado about Nothing*, Sir Paul
Pliant in *The Double Dealer*, and Trincalo in
Albumazar. In June 1746 he was granted the
ground on which the Jacob's Wells playhouse
stood during the lifetime of his two children
(John the younger and Jane, later Mrs Green)
on payment of two rents of 5s. each.

Hippisley's theatre in Jacob's Wells was far
from lavish. Latimer says that

The accommodation for the players was so contracted that an actor who left the stage on one side
and re-entered on the other had to walk round the
outside of the house. Adjoining it was another alehouse, the Malt Shovel, and a hole was made in the
party wall, through which liquors could be handed
in to the players, as well as to the upper class
spectators who in those days crowded the stage.
Instead of footlights, the stage was illuminated by
tallow candles, stuck in four hoops, and suspended
over the actors' heads. And it is recorded that on
one occasion a personator of Richard III wielded his
sword so recklessly that he cut the rope of one of
the primitive chandeliers, and had to be rescued
from the hoop by the laughing spectators.

Undeterred by the fact that that humble playhouse had driven him into debt, in November
1747 Hippisley joined with a Mr Watts in a
proposal to build a new and larger theatre in
Bath, costing £1000. Though John died before the project was carried out, construction
of the Orchard Street Theatre in Bath seems to
have begun before his death.

Hippisley's summers, then, were often committed to Bristol and Bath over the years; yet
he was also often found in London at the late
summer fairs or at the theatre in Richmond.
On 22 August 1730, for example, he acted
Puzzle in *Scipio's Triumph* at Reynolds's booth
at Bartholomew Fair. On 1 July 1731 he joined
the Richmond troupe to play Smuggler in *The
Constant Couple* and then acted Sir Hugh Evans
in *The Merry Wives of Windsor* on 8 July, Sir
William in *Love's Last Shift* on 15 July, and
Cimberton in *The Conscious Lovers* on 22 July.
On 24 August he joined Fielding and Hall in
the management of a booth at Bartholomew
Fair where, incorrectly puffed as making his
first appearance, he acted Shallow in *The Emperor of China*. In September the trio offered
the same production at Southwark Fair. Hippisley and Fielding ran a booth at Bartholomew Fair in August 1732 at which John
played the Physician in *The Envious Statesman*,

Courtesy of the Garrick Club

JOHN HIPPISLEY

artist unknown

and the following year at their booth he acted
Scapin in *A Cure for Covetousness*. John sometimes danced his popular *Drunken Man* as an
added attraction.

In 1734 Hippisley joined Bullock and Hallam to run a Bartholomew Fair booth at which
he played Vizard in *The Imposter*. Then, on 2
September, he managed to act Sir Thomas in
Flora at Covent Garden after playing Scrub in
The Beaux' Stratagem at Hampstead. On 9 September at Richmond he appeared as Sir Francis
in *The Busy Body*, and he repeated the role on
16 September (though it is not recorded in *The
London Stage*). Two days later he began his
Covent Garden season playing Polonius and
then on 26 September, when Covent Garden
was conveniently dark, he turned up at Richmond again for his benefit to appear in *The
Drummer* and *Flora*.

John stayed away from Bartholomew Fair for a year but with Fielding ran a booth there in August 1736; they put on *Don Carlos* and *The Cheats of Scapin*, with Hippisley in the title role of the latter. Not until August 1739 did he work at the fair again; that year with Chapman and Legar he produced *The Top of the Tree*, in which he played a Clown, and *The Royal Chace*. He and Chapman ran a fair booth in 1740 with John appearing in the title role in *Harlequin Scapin*, and the following year the same pair produced *The Devil of a Duke*, with Hippisley as the Drunken Captain, and *The Matrimonial Squabble*. In 1742 they offered *Scaramouch Scapin*, featuring Hippisley, and in 1743 they put on *The French Doctor Outwitted*, with John as Old Fumble. That turned out to be Hippisley's last August at Bartholomew Fair.

John's career as a playwright was not extensive, but in addition to *The English Thief* of 1728, which seems not to have been published, he wrote the ballad opera *Flora* (also called *Hob's Opera*), first presented on 17 April 1729 and published that year; that reworking of Thomas Doggett's *Hob, or, The Country Wake* went through seven editions by 1768. Hippisley's next ballad opera, *A Journey to Bristol*, was published in 1731, and his last, *A Sequel to the Opera of Flora*, was given at Lincoln's Inn Fields on 20 March 1732 and published that year.

Only *Flora* achieved popularity, but *A Journey to Bristol* was extravagantly puffed in the *Grub Street Journal* in April 1732:

As Novelty meets with the greatest encouragement, and bids fairest to afford one at least of those two agreeables Profit and Delight, Mr. HIPPISLEY, we are inform'd, to shew that he can speak some Wit of his own, as well as that of others, has written a merry Farce, which he purposes to exhibit for his own Benefit on the 23d inst. This Piece has rais'd uncommon expectation from the character every where given of it: and what is most extraordinary, his Brethren the Poets, who are but too apt to discourage a beginner, affirm it to be written in so moving a strain, that 'tis impossible to be a spectator, and not have the passions touch'd. This is no artful Paragraph, as is too common in these cases, written with a view of enhancing the merit of the piece, which has not been read before the Society, and to which we shall therefore give no testimony. Our Author assures us, that he shall content himself with a full House, and submit the merit of his labours to the candour and good nature of his aud-

itors. Thus much we thought proper to communicate, as an instance of our impartial delight in the prospect of so rising a Genius, who may one day come to be famous, either as an Enemy, or as a Member of our Society.

One cannot be certain where Hippisley lodged in London over the years, but his benefit tickets on 23 April 1731 were available at a coffee house in Newcastle Court, Temple Bar; two years later his tickets could be had at Will's Coffee House; and the playbill for 22 March 1736 said that one could buy "Tickets at Hippisley's, at Will's Coffee House, Bow Street." His bill for 1740 placed his lodgings in Playhouse Passage, Bow Street, where he may have lived through 1747, though he had secondary lodgings in Bristol.

When Hippisley played Scrub in *The Stratagem* for his benefit on 2 April 1747 at the end of his career, the newspapers carried the following notice: "We hear Mr. Hippisley is so far recover'd from his late illness, that, tho' considerably altered in his physiognomy, and lower'd in spirits, he persuades himself a crowded House . . . will create a smile on his countenance, raise his spirits, and make him appear as much a Scrub as ever." The veteran actor was on the company list at his Jacob's Wells Theatre in Bristol from 10 June to 31 August 1747. Then, on 26 September, he acted Cimberton in *The Conscious Lovers* at Richmond. It was erroneously reported that he had died, and on 9 October Hippisley published a humorous denial. As though to prove that he was still among the quick, he appeared in Bristol in *Albumazar* on 3 November 1747, playing Trincalo for his benefit. That is the last role recorded for him, according to advertisements we have seen.

John Hippisley died at Bristol on 12 February 1748. The *Public Advertiser* on 14 February 1755 remembered him:

Epitaph on the late Mr. *John Hippisley*,
of facetious Memory; buried at *Clifton*
in *Gloucestershire*:
When the Stage heard that Death had struck her John,
Gay Comedy her Sables first put on;
Laughter lamented that her Fav'rite dy'd;
And Mirth herself ('tis strange) laid down and cry'd;
Wit droop'd his Head, e'en Humour seem'd to mourn,
And solemnly sat Pensive o'er his Urn.

Harvard Theatre Collection

THOMAS WALKER as Macheath, LAVINIA FENTON as Polly, and JOHN HIPPISLEY as Peachum
detail from a scene in *The Beggar's Opera* by Hogarth

Hippisley had drawn up his will on 1 February 1748, describing himself as of the city of Bristol. To "my beloved consort Mrs Mary Charley with whom I cohabit and dwell and whom I acknowledge and Esteem as my Wife" Hippisley left his house near Jacob's Wells in the parish of Clifton, Gloucestershire; to her also he left the nearby playhouse and related buildings and all his ready money and plate. The residuary legatees were her son John, "whom I had by her and called John Hippisley," and the actor's daughter Jane Hippisley Green. Hippisley also remembered his legal wife: the younger John Hippisley, Jane Green, and Mary Charley, during their successive lives, were to provide £5 annually to Hippisley's wife Elizabeth, then living in King Street, Holborn, London, if Hippisley's house and playhouse in Jacob's Wells should rent for £20 annually. The sum paid to Elizabeth was to be proportionately less if the rent was less.

To Elizabeth he also left the furniture in her lodgings. Mary Charley proved the will on 30 July 1748.

John Hippisley had a daughter Elizabeth who, like Jane and young John, was a performer, but he did not mention her in his will. Another Miss Hippisley, who became Mrs Fitzmaurice and acted in Bath, Edinburgh, and York, was perhaps another daughter, but she was not mentioned in the will either. Nor was Hippisley's niece Mrs Simpson cited; she acted in the 1740s, 1750s, and 1760s and died in 1769.

The *British Oracle* of 15 October 1748 carried an announcement of the disposal of Hippisley's property:

To be sold by auction, or otherwise, on Tuesday the 18th of this Inst. October 1748, The household goods, linen, and plate of the late Mr Hippisley, deceas'd, at his dwelling House near the Playhouse at Jacob's Wells. . . . There is a very good large spinnet almost as good as new, and many other curious things.

Davies called Hippisley a "comedian of lively humour and droll pleasantry" who was fine at depicting the excesses of avarice and amorous dotage. Davies was especially fond of Hippisley's Corbaccio, Fumble, and Fluellen. In *The Actor* (1750) John Hill said, "We all remember the late Mr. Hippisley's merit in comedy, yet perhaps no body ever wish'd to see him in the buskin." That opinion was shared by the anonymous author of a *Letter to a Certain Pantentee* (1748), who criticized John Rich for overpaying Hippisley and for casting him as Polonius, a role he felt was beyond John's abilities. The writer found Hippisley's Sir Francis Wronghead wanting (not a good Yorkshire accent), and his Miser he did not like, but he commended his Bishop of Winchester in *Henry VIII*. He disliked Hippisley's drunken characters: they were too brutish, he thought, as though the actor had "never observ'd a Man drunk in his Life. . . ." Rich apparently played up Hippisley's name in cast lists unnecessarily, but, the critic admitted, John certainly was a favorite with audiences, who would "clap him heartily, and fall a laughing at him as soon as he appeared upon the Stage, before he had opened his Mouth to speak one Word."

Hippisley had a "fine Chuckle and Crow" and a deformed but funny face. Samuel Foote in *Roman and English Comedy* (1747) said

This great Comedian was so fortunate, as in his Infancy to fall in the Fire, by which Means the left Corner of his Mouth, and the Extremity of his Chin, became very near Neighbours: how often that lucky Circumstance has recommended him to the Approbation of the Sky-parlour Gentry, I submit to the Critics on the Ground Floor.

Chetwood in *The British Theatre* agreed that the accident that "new formed his Countenance to a Risible Grimace . . . seemed greatly to aid the Comic parts he performed." Latimer has it that Hippisley's accident came "when he fulfilled the humble functions of a stage candle-snuffer," but the earlier sources probably had the correct story.

Hippisley's monologue on the *Drunken Man* was immensely popular and continued to be performed by other comedians, Shuter and Quick especially, long after Hippisley's death. The text, which was published in 1776, consists of five pages of nonsense interspersed with comic songs.

Portraits of John Hippisley include:

1. By G. P. Harding. A pencil drawing listed in the *Catalogue of the Effects of the Property of the Sublime Society of Beefsteaks*, sold for £1 18s. at Christie, Manson, and Woods on 7 April 1869. Present location unknown.

2. By unknown artist. Canvas in the Garrick Club (No 300).

3. As Sir Francis Gripe in *The Busy Body*. Engraving by Sykes, after Hogarth. There is a drawing in India ink in the Harvard Theatre Collection, but it is unlikely that it is the Hogarth original.

4. As Peachum in Hogarth's painting of the prison scene in *The Beggar's Opera*. There are a number of versions, including those in the Tate Gallery and the Yale Center for British Art.

5. As Scapin in *The Cheats of Scapin*. Drawn and engraved by his grandson John Hippisley Green, published 1801.

6. As Scapin. Same picture as above, but another plate.

Hippisley, John *d. 1767, actor.*

John Hippisley the younger, the son of the famous comedian of the same name, made his first appearance on any stage as Tom Thumb in *The Tragedy of Tragedies* on 26 April 1740 at Covent Garden. The following year Master Hippisley, as he was still called, played the role again on 10 March 1741 at his father's benefit. He may not have pursued a stage career further, though he shared a benefit with his father at the Jacob's Wells Theatre in Bristol on 3 September 1741.

On 1 January 1750 *A Dissertation on Comedy* by John Hippisley, Junior, identified as an Oxford student, was published. The work contained much praise for Garrick's reformation of the stage into a moral institution. No Hippisley is recorded in the *Alumni Oxoniensis* at that time, however. Hippisley, presumably the same person, published essays on Africa in 1764, and that author was Governor of Cape Coast Castle. He died, according to the *Gentleman's Magazine*, on 1 January 1767.

Hird. *See* HEARD.

Hirvey. *See* HARVEY.

Hitchcock, Mr [*fl. 1798–1799*], *singer.*

A Mr Hitchcock sang in the chorus of *Ramah Droog*, a comic opera which premiered at Covent Garden on 12 November 1798 and had a total of 35 performances that season.

Hitchcock, Mrs [*fl. 1746–1776*], *house servant?*

A Mrs Hitchcock was regularly employed at Covent Garden Theatre, probably as a house servant, from 1746–47 through 1775–76. In most seasons, she shared benefit tickets in the spring with various house servants and chorus dancers. Often she received full value for her tickets, while others received only half value, as on 11 May 1747 when her share was £20 6*s*., which she had in full, but eight others were given only half shares. Similarly she received £19 4*s*. on 27 April 1750 and £22 9*s*. on 11 April 1761. Her last benefit noted in the account bills was on 22 May 1776. Sometimes her name was given in the account books only as "Hitchcock," but in each instance it seems clear from the bills that Mrs Hitchcock was intended.

Hitchcock, Miss [*fl. 1769–1770*], *singer, dancer.*

A Miss Hitchcock was a singer at Sadler's Wells in 1769 and 1770. In September of the latter year she danced a minuet there with Master Mathews. She played Leonora in *The Padlock* at the Haymarket Theatre on 29 October 1770. She may have been one of the children of the performers Robert and Sarah Hitchcock, but she would have been too old to be their child Mary Anne, who was born in 1766.

Hitchcock, Mary Anne, later Mrs Jonas Greene *1766–1854, actress, singer.*

Mary Anne Hitchcock was born, according to the *Dublin Castle Pedigrees*, on 3 May 1766. Perhaps her birthplace was Norwich, where at that time her parents Robert and Sarah Hitchcock may have been performers in the theatre. Mary Anne performed at York as early as 1772, as Toadel in *Lilliput* on 22 February. She played children's roles at Bristol in 1776.

On 15 May 1777 she made her debut at the Haymarket Theatre with her brother Robert in *Lilliput*. In 1778 she was again in the York company, where she played Columbine to her brother's Harlequin in *Pigmy Revels* on 21 February. She returned to the Haymarket that summer to appear on 1 June 1778 as Sally in Colman's *Man and Wife*, a role she acted a total of six times by the end of the season. In that comedy her mother played Lettice. Mary Anne acted Sally several times at the Haymarket in the summer of 1780.

At the Haymarket in the summer of 1781 she played Nancy in *The Silver Tankard*, a musical farce that had its first appearance on 18 July and was repeated five times. On 22 August she appeared as Nancy in the interlude *Ripe Fruit*. When Miss Harper became ill on 4 September 1781, Miss Hitchcock read her role of Laura in *The Agreeable Surprise*. Two nights later, 6 September, she played the role, but Miss Harper recovered to claim it again on 10 September.

In the autumn of 1781 Miss Hitchcock accompanied her parents to the Smock Alley Theatre, Dublin, where her father became prompter and her mother acted. Miss Hitchcock made her Irish debut at Smock Alley on 3 January 1782 and became a popular favorite, acting there until 1787. She also played at Cork in 1782 and 1786, at Waterford and Limerick in 1786, and at Kilkenny in 1787. On 30 January 1786 she signed her full name to a letter sent by the Smock Alley performers to the *Hibernian Journal*.

In the autumn of 1787 she joined Wilkinson's company at Wakefield and Doncaster for several weeks, playing the title role in *Rosina*. By then, according to Wilkinson's description in his *Wandering Patentee*:

She was grown a handsome young woman, an improved actress, and could put her hand to anything, such as ladies, chambermaids, girls, singing, first and second characters, and like Mrs. Phillis, "All became her;" nay, sometimes she ventured on the gentle Desdemona and Ophelia; was attentive to her private conduct; was a strict oeconomist, and was well received by several respectable families.

She acted at York from 1788 to 1790. The critic in the *Theatrical Register* of 1788 found her figure engaging and her voice above the mediocre but advised her to abolish her "Sistine style for English" and to be more deliberate in pronunciation. She left Wilkinson's company in early spring, bound for Dublin, where at St Anne's on 11 April 1790 she married Jonas Greene, a barrister, and retired from the stage. Greene, who became recorder of Dublin, was knighted in 1821 and Mary Anne became Lady Greene. She died in Dublin on 23 November 1854.

Hitchcock, Robert *d. 1809, actor, prompter, deputy manager, playwright, theatre historian.*

Robert Hitchcock and his wife were members of the company of the Theatre Royal, Norwich, in 1769. On 22 May of that year their articles were renewed for the ensuing season, with Hitchcock to receive 15*s.* per week and his wife the larger sum of one guinea. On 19 April 1770 their salaries were advanced to a total of two guineas per week, and a month later on 12 May their articles were renewed at that combined salary for 1771. After completing their third season at Norwich in July 1771, the Hitchcocks joined Tate Wilkinson's company on the York circuit.

The Hitchcocks remained with Wilkinson at York until the summer of 1777. Hitchcock played small parts, his wife those of lively ingenues. On 4 March 1773 Hitchcock's five-act comedy *The Macaroni* was produced at York and met, according to Wilkinson in *The Wandering Patentee,* "with deserved success." It was played at the Haymarket Theatre on 16 September 1773, but Hitchcock seems not to have been in London at the time. The play was published at York that year and at Dublin the following year. Among the subscribers to the York edition were a number of actors from the York and London theatres.

The Coquette; or The Mistakes of the Heart, another comedy by Hitchcock, was first played at Hull on 14 November 1775. The subject, based on the novel *The History of Betsy Thoughtless,* had been suggested to Hitchcock by Wilkinson. Less successful than his first play, *The Coquette* was published at Bath in 1777. It was produced at the Haymarket Theatre on 9 October 1777. Another comedy by Hitchcock called *The Ladies' Stratagem* was published at York in 1775 but does not seem to have been produced.

In the summer of 1776 Hitchcock, his wife, and their young child Robert performed at Bristol and Bath. The following summer they were members of Foote's company at the Haymarket Theatre, where Hitchcock made his first appearance, on 6 June, as Broadbrim in *The Devil upon Two Sticks.* Though his wife played regularly that summer, Hitchcock's only other notice in the bills was for an unspecified role in *The Rehearsal* on 25 August 1777. They returned to the Haymarket in the summer of 1778, when Hitchcock assumed duties as the prompter, a position he held there for four summers.

Hitchcock served the elder Colman, the Haymarket manager, as a model for the character of the prompter in his prelude *The Manager in Distress,* which was first performed on 30 May 1780, but the role was played by Davis. That night, however, because Robert Baddeley had suffered a stroke earlier that day, Hitchcock read the role of Catchpenny in *The Suicide.* Hitchcock also appeared as himself in *The Hodge Podge,* an anonymous interlude about theatrical people that was performed on 28 and 31 August 1781.

Hitchcock continued to be engaged as an actor in Wilkinson's company on the York circuit in the winter seasons through the first half of 1781. In 1779 he and his family acted with Glassington's troupe at Stourbridge Fair, near Cambridge. He had also served as Wilkinson's deputy at Edinburgh in 1779–80.

After the summer of 1781 Hitchcock went to Dublin to become Richard Daly's prompter and assistant at Smock Alley, a position he held for many years. He was instrumental in persuading many English performers to join Daly's company. He moved to Crow Street when Daly remodeled and reopened that house in the summer of 1788. After Daly sold his interest in Crow Street to Jones in 1797, Hitchcock continued to work for the new management up to the year of his death, which occurred at No 5, Clarendon Street, Dublin, at the end of 1809.

In 1788 Hitchcock had published at Dublin his first volume of *An Historical View of the Irish Stage; from the earliest period down to 1788. Interspersed with Theatrical Anecdotes.* In the second volume, published in 1794, he explained that he had decided to end his history at 1774.

Hitchcock's wife, Sarah, who remained remarkably youthful in appearance over the years, was a favorite actress in Dublin until

January 1810. The date of her death is unknown to us. They had a large family. Their seventh and perhaps last child, Sarah, was baptized at St Michael le Belfry, York, on 14 March 1781. (In the baptismal register, Robert Hitchcock was identified as the son of John and Elizabeth Hitchcock.)

Hitchcock's son Robert, born in 1768, performed as a child in the provinces and at the Haymarket between 1777 and 1780. He entered Trinity College, Dublin, in 1783, received his LL.B. degree, and became a member of the Irish bar.

The Miss Hitchcock who played Leonora in *The Padlock* at the Haymarket on 29 October 1770 may have been a daughter of Robert and Sarah Hitchcock, but that role indicates she would have been too old to have been Mary Anne Hitchcock, their daughter who was born in 1766. Mary Anne performed at the Haymarket in 1781 and had a successful stage career in Dublin in the 1780s before her marriage in April 1790 to Jonas Greene; upon his knighthood in 1821 she became Lady Greene. She died at Dublin in 1854.

Of Robert Hitchcock's character, Tate Wilkinson wrote in his *Wandering Patentee*: "In few words, Mr. Hitchcock is valuable as a friend, and is *truly* an honest man, and that is saying a great deal, and to the purpose; but as he himself is not a man of many words, I am sure he will think I have said enough."

Hitchcock, Mrs Robert, Sarah [fl. 1766–1810], actress, singer.

Sarah Hitchcock and her husband Robert Hitchcock were acting at the Theatre Royal, Norwich, from 1769 to 1771. In 1770 she earned one guinea per week, a salary larger than the 15s. received by her husband. Their combined salary for the 1771 season was two guineas per week. In July 1771 the Hitchcocks joined Tate Wilkinson's Company on the York circuit. She made her debut at Leeds on the thirteenth of that month as Rosetta in *Love in a Village*. Wilkinson did not find her "proficient in singing," but she had "a neat figure, was easy in carriage, and very lively," attributes that qualified her for many ingenue roles.

The Hitchcocks remained engaged with Wilkinson in the winter seasons through 1776. In the summer of 1776 the family performed at Bristol and Bath. Announced as

from the latter city, Mrs Hitchcock made her first appearance as a member of Foote's company at the Haymarket Theatre on 9 June 1777 as Miss Neville in *She Stoops to Conquer* and Daphne in *Midas*. Throughout that summer she was seen almost every night in such parts as Jessica in *The Merchant of Venice*, the title role in *Polly Honeycombe*, Jenny Diver in *Polly*, Bell in *The Deuce is in Him*, the Mother in *The Recruiting Serjeant*, Ophelia in *Hamlet*, Mopsa in *The Sheep Shearing*, Columbine in *The Portrait*, Lady Miniken in *Bon Ton*, Matilda in *April Day*, and Belinda in *The Provok'd Wife*. In early September of 1777 she performed Polly in *The Beggar's Opera* with Glassington's company at Stourbridge Fair near Cambridge (where she returned with her husband in 1779).

Over the next four summers at the Haymarket she added many similar roles to her repertoire, among them: Miss Biddy in *Miss in Her Teens*, Lettice in *Man and Wife*, Lucy in *The Beggar's Opera*, Laura in *The Gipsies*, and Fanny in *The Maid of the Mill* in 1778; Molly in *The English Merchant*, Cherry in *The Stratagem*, and Miss English in *The Separate Maintenance* in 1779; a Bacchante in *Comus* and Susan in *The Wedding Night* in 1780; and the Goddess of Health and the Genius of Nonsense in *The Genius of Nonsense*, Mrs Page in *The Merry Wives of Windsor*, and Lucinda in *Love in a Village* in 1781. On 18 August 1779 the *Morning Chronicle* criticized her for overdressing her part of Cherry—"Boniface, we presume, would never have suffered a French frizeur to have approached his daughter." Again on 12 June 1780 that paper inquired, "Would the barmaid of an inn at Litchfield dress with the same regard to taste, which governs the toilet of a woman of fashion?"

Mrs Hitchcock had returned to Wilkinson's company for the winter season in 1779. When Wilkinson took his troupe to play at Edinburgh for several months in 1779–80, Mrs Hitchcock appeared there in some of the roles she had performed at the Haymarket and was also seen in a number of new ones, among which were Celia in *As You Like It*, Donna Clara in *The Duenna*, Miranda in *The Busy Body*, Miss Sterling in *The Clandestine Marriage*, Mrs Candour in *The School for Scandal*, and Phillis in *The Conscious Lovers*.

In the autumn of 1781, the Hitchcocks left

Wilkinson's employ to engage with Daly at Smock Alley, Dublin. Her husband served as prompter there, and later at Crow Street for many years, and she and her daughter Mary Anne became favorite actresses. Mrs Hitchcock performed regularly at Smock Alley from 1781–82 through 1786–87 and then at Crow Street for several decades more. She also played at Cork, Limerick, and other Irish towns.

In his *Wandering Patentee*, published in 1795, Wilkinson wrote that the "lively spirited Mrs Hitchcock retains the powers of youth in every respect. . . . To see her on the stage, a stranger would hardly suppose it creditable, that the little woman should have laboured so well in her vocation, and yet appear so youthful."

Sarah Hitchcock's husband died in late 1809 in their house at No 5, Clarendon Street, Dublin. She made her last appearance on the stage at Crow Street on 26 January 1810. The date of her death is not known to us. Information about her seven children, one of whom was born as early as 1766, is given in her husband's notice.

Hitchcock, Robert *b. 1768, actor.*

Robert Hitchcock, the son of the performers Robert and Sarah Hitchcock, was born in 1768, probably at Norwich. During his childhood, he appeared occasionally at theatres where his parents were playing. He performed at York in 1775 and 1776 and at Bath and Bristol in 1776–77. At the Haymarket Theatre in the summer of 1777 he appeared with his sister in *Lilliput*, a pantomime performed by children on 15 May, as the Printer's Devil in *The Author* on 7 July, and as Robin in *The Merry Wives of Windsor* on 3 September. At York on 21 February 1778 he played Harlequin to his sister's Columbine in *Pigmy Revels*. At the Haymarket in the summer of 1779 he delivered the monologue "Bucks have at ye all" on 10 August and played the Printer's Devil in *The Devil upon Two Sticks* on 13 August. The following summer at the Haymarket he played the latter role on 11 September 1780.

Young Hitchcock performed at York in 1781 and probably in Dublin after 1781, when his father joined the Smock Alley Theatre as prompter. In July 1783 at the age of 15, he entered Trinity College, Dublin, re-

ceived his LL.B. degree, and became a member of the Irish bar.

Hoard. *See* HEARD.

Hoare, Miss. *See* SAGE, MRS L. A.

Hoare, Katherine. *See* POWELL, MRS SPARKS.

Hoare, Sarah. *See* WARD, MRS THOMAS ACHURCH.

Hobart, George *1732–1804, manager.*

George Hobart, third Earl of Buckinghamshire, was born in 1732, the son of the first earl, John, and his second wife, Elizabeth, née Bristow. George was educated at Westminster as a king's scholar, beginning in 1746. He was elected a member of parliament for St Ives in 1754 and for Beeralston in 1761, 1768, and 1774. He was appointed secretary to the embassy at St Petersburg in 1762.

Hobart became the manager of the King's Theatre at the commencement of the 1769–70 opera season. His career was beset with problems, as one of Walpole's letters, quoted by Nalbach in *The King's Theatre*, reveals:

In the meantime our most serious war is between two operas. Mr Hobart, Lord Buckingham's brother, is manager of the Haymarket [i. e. the King's]. Last year he affronted Guadagni, by preferring the Zamperina, his own mistress, to the singing hero's sister. The Duchess of Northumberland, Lady Harrington, and some other great ladies, espoused the brother, and without a license erected an Opera for him at Madame Cornelys's. This is a singular dame, and you must be acquainted with her. . . . Her Opera, which she called HARMONIC MEETINGS, was splendid and charming. Mr Hobart began to starve, and the managers of the theatres were alarmed. To void the Act, she pretended to take no money, and had the assurance to advertise that the subscription was to provide coals for the poor, for she has vehemently courted the mob, and succeeded in gaining their princely favour. She then declared her masquerades were for the benefit of commerce. I concluded she would open a bawdy house next for the interests of the Foundling Hospital, and I was not quite mistaken for they say one of her maids, gained by Mr Hobart, affirms that she could not undergo the fatigue of making the beds so often. At last Mr Hobart informed against her, and the bench of justices, less soothable by music than Orpheus's beasts have pronounced against her. The Opera is quashed, and Guadagni, who governed so haughtily at Vienna, that, to pique some man of quality there, he named a minister to Viencie, is not only fined, but was threatened to be sent to Bridewell. . . .

One of Hobart's successes was Mlle Heinel, the Flemish dancer. She was paid £600 for the 1771–72 season and helped pack some of the houses. But in November 1773 the opera house changed hands; Hobart gave up the management to Mrs Brooke and Mrs Yates.

On 3 August 1793 Hobart succeeded as third earl of Buckinghamshire. Four years later he was made a colonel in the Lincolnshire militia, and in 1799 he became a colonel in the army. He died on 14 November 1804 at Nocton, Lincolnshire. He had married Albinia, daughter and coheir of Lord Vere Bertie, on 22 May 1757. They had eight children: George (who died young), Robert, Henry Lewis, George Vere, Albinia, Henrietta Anne Barbara, Charlotte, and Maria Anne.

Hobbes, Thomas Raphael   1777–1836, singer, organist.

The register book of the parish of Ealing, Middlesex, shows that Thomas Raphael Hobbes was born on 9 April 1777 and christened on 2 May; he was the son of Thomas and Lydia Hobbes. By 1794, when Doane's *Musical Directory* was published, Hobbes had been a member of the Chapel Royal, was then a member of the Academy of Ancient Music and the Concert of Ancient Music, and participated in the oratorios at Drury Lane and Westminster Abbey and the 1793 Oxford Meeting. He was cited as a bass singer and organist living at No 27, James Street, Westminster.

Hobbes was admitted to the Royal Society of Musicians in 1799 and was cited at the time as being a single man and a teacher of singing and pianoforte. The Society minutes on 6 August 1836 indicate that Hobbes had died, still single, on the previous 29 June; he had not had to become a claimant on the Society, thanks to the assistance of his friends.

Hobbs, Mr   [fl. 1800–1806?], oboist, bassoonist?

A Mr Hobbs played oboe in the St Paul's concert in May 1800. A "Hobbes" was on the list again (instrument not specified) in 1802,

and in 1803 "Hobber" was down as a bassoonist. The name Hobbes was on the list in 1804 and 1806, but there is no certainty that the same person was referred to.

Hobbs, John   c. 1760–1788, violinist.

When John Hobbs (or Hobbes) was admitted to the Royal Society of Musicians on 6 June 1784, he was said by his recommender John Ashley to have been about 24 years old, a sober, diligent, unmarried man, and a violinist. Ashley stated that Hobbs played in the Ancient Music Concerts and was annually employed by Sir Watkin Williams Wynn, probably at his private theatre at Wynnstay. Dr Burney's list of performers at the Handel Memorial Concerts at Westminster Abbey and the Pantheon in May and June 1784 included Hobbs as one of the first violinists.

John Hobbs was to have been employed by the Academy of Ancient Music during the 1787–88 season for £4 4s. but was replaced by John Fentum. Hobbs died in 1788. On 7 September of that year the Royal Society of Musicians received a plea from Mary Hobbs, John's widow. "Your petitioner has been at a very great expense with medicines for her late husband," she wrote, and "also for the burial therefore hopes the Governors will take it into their consideration, your Petitioner's Husband has been very ill upwards of six months." Hobbs's subscription to the Society had been paid through 24 June 1788. The Society minutes do not indicate whether or not Mrs Hobbs's plea was answered.

Hobgood. *See* HABGOOD.

Hobler, John Paul   [fl. 1783?–1794], singer.

John Paul Hobler was probably the P. Hobler who was an original professional member of The Glee Club, which was organized in 1783 and had its first public meeting on 22 December 1787 at the Newcastle Coffee House. He was undoubtedly the Hobler who sang tenor in the Handel concerts at Westminster Abbey in May and June of 1784. Listed as J. Paul Hobler he was paid £9 for performing for the Academy of Ancient Music in 1787–88. Hobler had an odd career as a chorus singer at the theatres; he was named in very few casts, and he had a record of being dropped, usually after one performance—if, indeed, he managed to show up at all. On 5 August 1788 he sang at the Haymarket in *The Gnome*; on the eighth he was omitted from the cast. Similarly on 11 August 1789 at the same house he had a vocal part in *The Battle of Hexham*, but two days later he was omitted.

In 1790–91 Hobler was not named in any casts, but the account books show that he was an extra alto chorus singer at Drury Lane (in 1791–92 he was cited as a countertenor). On 15 October 1791 with the Drury Lane troupe at the King's Theatre he was one of many Priests in *The Cave of Trophonius*, and he seems to have remained in that cast. The following 23 May 1792, however, he sang in the chorus of *Dido Queen of Carthage*, but two days later he was omitted. He ran true to form again in the summer of 1793 at the Haymarket: he sang in the performance of *The Mountaineers* on 3 August and was omitted on the fifteenth. Hobler was a Soldier in *Royal Clemency* at the Haymarket on 10 October 1793 and stayed with the production, but at Drury Lane in June 1794 he missed rehearsals for *Lodoiska* on the ninth and twelfth and on 23 and 25 June he absented himself from performances.

Doane's *Musical Directory* of 1794 provided us with Hobler's full name, gave his address as No 26, Berwick Street, Soho, and noted that the singer performed in the concerto sponsored by the Academy of Ancient Music and the Anacreontic Society, in St Paul's choir, at Drury Lane and the Haymarket, and in the Handel concerts at Westminster Abbey. He was also a member of the Court of Assistants of the New Musical Fund.

Hobson, Mr ₍*fl. 1735?–1751*₎, *house servant.*

A Mr Hobson, vintner, was named in a benefit bill at the Lincoln's Inn Fields Theatre on 21 May 1735. There is no certainty that he was the Hobson who for many years was an important house servant at Drury Lane, but he may have been. On 25 May 1737 Hobson the house servant shared a benefit at Drury Lane with two others. And so it continued each spring at benefit time, through Hobson's last benefit on 10 May 1751.

Not until 25 May 1739 was his function in the theatre mentioned in the bills; on that date he and the stage manager shared a benefit, and Hobson was described as the housekeeper, a post of considerable importance, and stage doorkeeper. From 1742 on, the bills frequently noted that places for the boxes could "be taken of Mr. Hobson, at the Stage-Door of the Theatre." In 1742–43 Hobson became the box bookkeeper as well as housekeeper and doorkeeper. He may have retired after his last benefit in 1751.

In 1749–50 a Mrs Hobson was paid various small sums (once, 5s. for a tub); she seems not to have been a theatre employee, but she may well have been related to Mr Hobson.

Hobson, Charles ₍*fl. 1690*₎, *drummer.*

Charles Hobson was appointed a drummer in the King's Musick on 19 January 1690, but his position carried no salary. He was not mentioned again in the Lord Chamberlain's accounts, so it is likely that a salaried post for him never materialized.

Hochbrucker, Christian *b. 1733, harpist, composer.*

Grove states that Christian Hochbrucker was born in Tagmersheim, Bavaria, on 17 May 1733. He was a harp virtuoso, as was his uncle Simon Hochbrucker and his elder brother Celestin (1727–1803). Yet another Hochbrucker, Johann Baptist, published some works for harp and may also have been a performer. Christian Hochbrucker, we believe, was the "Hochbrucher" who performed at the King's Theatre in London from 23 February to 27 April 1779 in the ballet in Act II of *Zemire e Azore*. He was advertised: "Hochbrucher, like a Genius of Instrumental Music, will play upon the Pedal Harp." Johann Hochbrucker was also in London about 1779 and published *Six Divertimentos* about 1780; there is no certain evidence that he performed professionally during his stay.

Christian Hochbrucker played at the Oxford Music Room about 6 May 1780. Much of his career, however, was spent in Paris, where he was largely responsible for popularizing the pedal harp. The French Revolution, according to Fétis's *Biographie des musiciens*, forced Hochbrucker to return to England, where, in 1792, he published some of his compositions.

Hochbrucker, Simon   *b. 1699, harpist.*

Simon Hochbrucker, who was born in Donawerth in 1699, was the reputed inventor, in 1720, of the pedal harp. He is known to have performed at the Imperial court in Vienna. He was probably the "Hockbrucker" who played a Handel concerto on the Welsh harp at the Lincoln's Inn Fields Theatre in London on 15 March 1743. He may have been "The Italian harper" named "Hochbroker" who performed at the Lord Cobham's Head, Cold Bath Fields, on 19 August 1762. That performance was recorded by George Daniel in a copy of *Merrie England*, now at the Huntington Library.

Simon's nephew Christian was probably the harpist in London in 1779.

Hockins. *See* HOSKIN.

"Hodge." *See* DUNSTALL, JOHN.

Hodges, Mr   [*fl. 1696*],   *trumpeter.*

The *Post Boy* of 26–28 May 1696 reported that "Hodges, the Trumpeter" and others "who were in the Custody of *Messengers* are Discharged." Nothing else is known of Hodges, nor have we knowledge of any Restoration musician of a similar name with whom Hodges may have been confused.

Hodges, Mr   *d. 1779, office keeper.*

Mr Hodges was an office keeper at Drury Lane Theatre from as early as 1761–62 through 1778–79, at a constant salary of 2s. per day, or 12s. per week. Usually he shared in benefit tickets annually with other house servants, the last such time being on 1 June 1779. He died at Kentish Town on 29 June 1779. His obituary line in the *Public Advertiser* of 1 July described him as "many years Keeper of the Cheque" at Drury Lane.

Hodges, Miss   [*fl. 1780*]. *See* HEDGES, MRS.

Hodges, William   *1744–1797,*   *scene painter, landscape artist.*

Born in London in 1744 the only child of a blacksmith in Clare Market, William Hodges had some early tuition in painting at Shipley's drawing school, where he had originally been employed as an errand boy. He was then taken on as assistant and pupil to Richard Wilson, under whom it is said he made such swift progress that he soon quit London and his master to engage as a scene painter in the Derby Theatre.

Hodges exhibited landscapes and views at the Society of Artists in 1766, 1768, 1770, and 1771. In 1772 some of his views of the Rhine and Switzerland were shown there. He also exhibited at the Spring Gardens Rooms in 1770 and 1772. In the latter year he departed England in the post of draftsman to Captain Cook's second expedition to the South Seas, whence he returned in 1775 to take up employment with the Admiralty, in which service he finished his drawings and supervised their

By permission of the Trustees of the British Museum

WILLIAM HODGES
engraving by Daniell, after G. Dance

engravings (by Woollett and others) for the published account of the voyage.

At the Royal Academy he exhibited a view of Otaheite in 1776 and views of New Zealand and England in 1777 and 1778. He also painted views of the scenery in India, where he resided under the patronage of Warren Hastings for six years between 1778 and 1784. Upon his return from India those views, to some of which animals were added by Gilpin, appeared in large engravings by J. Browne and Morris. Hodges himself engraved a set published in 1786; smaller versions also appeared in the *European Magazine*. In 1793 he wrote an account of his *Travels in India*, which was published with engravings and was translated into French. Hodges was elected an associate of the Royal Academy in 1786 and a full member the following year. He continued to exhibit there until 1794. He traveled on the Continent and visited St Petersburg in 1790.

From 1784, however, he spent most of his time at his studio in Queen Street, Mayfair. On 25 February 1788 at Drury Lane Theatre a production of *Love in the East* was presented with a variety of new scenery that included "A View of Calcutta, from a painting done on the spot by Hodges." When O'Reilly opened the Pantheon for operas after the fire at the King's Theatre, Hodges was employed there as a scene painter and "inventor of decorations." His work for the Pantheon in 1791 included scenes for *La bella pescatrice*, *Armida*, *Idalide*, and a ballet, *The Deserter*. But it is said that Hodges did not demonstrate much ability as a scenographer because of his slender knowledge of architecture and perspective.

A collection of 25 of his pictures, including two large allegories of "the Effects of Peace and War," were exhibited by him in Bond Street, but the venture failed, persuading Hodges to give up his profession. In 1795 he established a bank at Dartmouth but was ruined because of the unsettled economy.

Hodges was married three times. His first wife, Martha Nesbit, whom he wed at St George, Hanover Square, on 11 May 1776, died in childbirth within a year. Her loss induced him to take his India voyage. On 16 October 1784 he married Lydia Wright, who also soon died. Soon after, he wed Ann Mary Carr, a woman much praised by Romney and other friends of Hodges.

Hodges died from gout in the stomach at Brixham, Devonshire, on 6 March 1797 at the age of 53. Administration of his estate was granted on 20 May 1797 to Thomas Gritton, a creditor, his widow Ann Mary Hodges having first renounced the letters of administration. She died very soon after at Tunbridge, in May 1797. Her five children, left in poverty by Hodges, were also named in the administration: Catherine Hodges, spinster; Henry William and Caroline, minors; and Mary and Hernana, infants. The Ann Hodges, spinster, who married Thomas Jones, widower, at St Marylebone on 13 July 1791 in a ceremony witnessed by William Hodges, was probably his child by one of his earlier marriages.

Three contributions were made by Hodges to the Boydell Picture Gallery. "The Forest of Arden with the Wounded Stag," a scene from *As You Like It*, was acquired by the Folger Shakespeare Library in 1926; thence it went to Lincoln Kirstein in 1962, then to the American Shakespeare Theatre, from which it was acquired in 1976 by the Yale Center for British Art. The figure of Jaques was painted by Romney. An engraving of the scene was made by S. Middiman, 1791. The other two paintings by Hodges for Boydell, scenes from *The Merchant of Venice* and *A Winter's Tale*, are lost, though an engraving exists of the former by J. Browne. Hodge's landscape scene of *Cymbeline* (not for Boydell) was exhibited at the Royal Academy in 1788. His painting of a ruined castle is in the Victoria and Albert Museum.

Some of Hodges's pictures from the South Seas are preserved at the Admiralty and at the British Museum. A number of them are reproduced in color by Jane Roundell, "William Hodges Paintings of the South Pacific," *The Connoisseur*, February 1979. When a young man, Hodges engraved a portrait, after R. Wilson, of Torre del Greco at Naples.

A profile portrait sketch of Hodges by George Dance, signed and dated 10 March 1793, is at the Royal Academy of Arts; an engraving by W. Daniell was published in 1792. An engraved portrait by Thornthwaite, after R. Westall, was published as a plate to the *Literary Magazine*, 1792. Hodges was also pictured by H. Singleton in a large painting of "The Royal Academicians assembled in their Council Chambers to adjudge the Medals to the successful Students in Painting, Sculpture,

"Portia's Garden"

By WILLIAM HODGES, engraving by J. Browne

Architecture, and Drawing in 1793" which is in the Royal Academy; an engraving by C. Bestland, with key-plate, was published by the engraver in 1802.

Hodgins, Mr [*fl.* 1792–1827], *scene painter, actor.*

The scene painter commonly called Hodgins the Younger, whose mature career did not begin until the nineteenth century, was probably the son of the Covent Garden scene painter Henry Hodgins (d. 1796), although no definite relationship has been established. He was probably the Master Hodgins who appeared as the Pudding Boy in the pantomime *Harlequin's Museum* at Covent Garden on 26 December 1792. Some of the scenery for this piece, which had a total of 48 performances in 1792–93, was painted by Henry Hodgins, one of the resident painters at that theatre.

The younger Hodgins did not begin to paint at Covent Garden until after the death of Henry Hodgins on 20 September 1796. In 1796–97 he was paid only 15*s.* per week. His salary was still at that figure in 1799–1800, and by then his name had not yet appeared on a playbill for painting. The name of Hodgins on the bills for revivals of *Harlequin and Faustus* on 28 May 1798 and *Harlequin's Chaplet* on 13 May 1799 is that of Henry, who had contributed scenes to those productions several years earlier. The first production for which the younger Hodgins received credit in the bills for his scenic contributions was, as far as we can determine, the premiere of *Paul and Virginia* on 1 May 1800. Also painting for this production were Phillips, Lupino, and Hollogan.

Hodgins's career at Covent Garden as an artist of minor importance lasted at least through 1826–27. In 1800–1801 his salary was raised to £1 per week; it was £1 5*s.* per

Scene design, probably for *The Death of Captain Cook*, May 1804

by HODGINS, the younger

week in 1801–2, £2 by 1811–12, and £2 10*s*. by 1817–18.

Nine drawings for scenery by Hodgins survive in the British Museum. They are described and reproduced in *Theatre Notebook*, 27, by Sybil Rosenfeld, who also provides a list of over 100 productions to which Hodgins contributed in the nineteenth century.

Hodgins, Henry *d. 1796, scene painter, landscape artist, actor.*

Henry Hodgins was the son of Joseph Vernon's Dublin landlady. Hodgins became a pupil of the scene painter Robert Carver (d. 1791), with whom he worked at the Crow Street Theatre, Dublin. After receiving a farewell benefit there on 30 April 1762, young Hodgins accompanied Vernon to England to seek his fortune, but his activities for some 15 years are unknown until he was employed by

Younger as a scene painter for the theatre at Liverpool commencing the week of 13 July 1776 at a salary of £2 10*s*. per week. In the winter season of 1776–77 Hodgins was retained at Liverpool on a salary of £2 per week, and he also received payments for "Potts Lime, Chalk & Charcoal."

From the account books of the Liverpool Theatre (at the Folger Library) it appears that Hodgins also doubled as an actor in Younger's company from time to time. He worked at Liverpool through the summer and winter of 1777, receiving in addition to his regular £2 per week occasional sums to reimburse his expenses: on 10 June 1777, "By Ballance of Mr Jodgin's [*sic*] Bill, of Sallaries pd himself, Banks, Bowman, Singleton, Houghton, & Sundrys laid out while Painting the Theatre scenes—11/5/7"; on 16 August 1777, "By Mr Hodgins for Venetian Lake, Bread, & for

Cleaning Scenes o/6/o"; and in the winter of 1777, "By Mr Hodgins for Canvas o/3/9."

In January 1777 Hodgins traveled with Younger's company to Manchester, where he provided scenery for a performance of *Semiramis*, with Mrs Siddons in the title role. The *Mercury* reported that "the two scenes painted purposely for this play by Mr. Hodgings are truly Elegant and Picturesque; the outside of the Palace of Semiramis, with the Hanging Gardens on one hand and the Mausoleums on the other, are allowed to be very near representations of the descriptions given by Historians." No doubt that month Hodgins also painted the scenes for *Cymon* which promised "a view of the Burning Lake, the Flying Chariot drawn by Eagles, Inchanted black Tower, Transparent Cave of Merlin, etc." For *King Arthur* in February 1777 at Manchester, his scenes included "a very fine wintry view of Frost and Snow, which changes to an extensive Summer Prospect of a Garden, etc., the Bleeding Tree, the Golden Bridge at which two Syrens or Mermaids appear and sing their deluding strains."

At Stourbridge Fair, Cambridge, in 1779 Hodgins provided scenes for Glassington's productions of *The School for Scandal* and *The Camp*. He also worked at York, at Norwich, and probably for Mrs Baker's company in Kent. In 1778–79 he had been engaged as a resident scene painter at Covent Garden Theatre. Although his name did not appear on the pay list until 13 November 1779 when he received £36 15s. to cover 14 weeks of salary (or £2 12s. 6d. per week), he had, however, with Richards, Carver, and Garvey, painted scenes for the premiere of *The Touchstone* the previous season on 4 January 1779. With Richards, Carver and Cipriani he prepared scenes for *The Mirror; or Harlequin Everywhere*, which played first on 30 November 1779.

Hodgins continued to be employed at Covent Garden regularly through 1795–96. In 1781–82 his salary was £3 13s. 6d. per week; it rose to £4 4s. in 1788–89, to £5 5s. in 1793–94 (with an apprentice at 30s.), and to £6 10s. in 1795–96. He was also paid £54 12s. for work during the dark period at Covent Garden between 24 June and 16 September 1786.

With other painters Hodgins contributed scenes to *Harlequin Free-Mason* in 1780–81 (on

28 May 1781 he was paid £141 15s.); *The Choice of Harlequin* in 1781–82; *Lord Mayor's Day* in 1782–83; *Friar Bacon* and *Harlequin Rambler* in 1783–84; *All the World's a Stage* and *The Magic Cavern* in 1784–85; *Omai* (designed by De Loutherbourg) in 1785–86; *The Enchanted Castle* in 1786–87; *The Dumb Cake* in 1787–88; *Alladin* in 1788–89; *Harlequin's Chaplet* in 1789–90; *The Picture of Paris* in 1790–91; *Oscar and Malvina* and *Blue-Beard* in 1791–92; *Columbus, Harlequin's Museum*, and *The Governor* in 1792–93; *Harlequin and Faustus* (his scenes were the study of Faustus, a view of a country inn, Smithfield on market day, and a street with two Irish sedan chairs), *The Travellers in Switzerland*, and *Hercules and Omphale* in 1793–94; *Mago and Dago* and *Windsor Castle* in 1794–95; and *Merry Sherwood* and *Harlequin's Treasure* in 1795–96.

During his career at Covent Garden, Hodgins also provided his earlier manager Younger with a model of De Loutherbourg's scenery for *The Critic*, for use in a production at Manchester in 1780. He also painted most of the scenery for the new theatre at Margate, built by Charles Mate and Thomas Robson on the east side of Hawley Square in 1787, and models (evidently his specialty) of scenes for Daly at Dublin, including some for *The Castle of Andalusia*. These models, according to the Irish dramatist O'Keeffe, were "done and painted most accurately on card paper by little Harry Hodgins. . . . His celerity in painting was wonderful." Charles Lee Lewes praised him as "an excellent scene-painter, an art of more difficulty and real skill than public estimation."

Hodgins, also a landscape painter, became a Fellow and Director of the Society of Artists. The *Gentleman's Magazine* for September 1796 reported his death at Maidstone on the twentieth of that month. The scene painter known as Hodgins the Younger, who also worked at Covent Garden in the 1790s and flourished into the 1820s, was probably his son, although no definite relationship can be established.

Hodgkinson, Mrs John the second, Frances, née Brett 1771–1803, *actress, singer.*

Frances Brett was born in 1771, somewhere in rural England, while her father William and mother Hannah were on tour as performers.

She and her (at least) four siblings: her brother William and sisters Arabella Hannah, Elizabeth, and "W." grew up in the world of actors, dancers, and musicians, as their parents shuttled back and forth between the Bath-Bristol company and Foote's Haymarket. The father finally settled down to a steady engagement at Covent Garden Theatre. In due course Elizabeth, William, "W.," and possibly Arabella, became performers also (but William was only nine when he died in 1782).

Frances played juvenile parts at Bath and Bristol in 1781–82 and 1782–83. She first appeared in London at the Haymarket Theatre as a Dwarf in 10 performances, from 2 August through September 1784, of Thomas Holcroft's new comic opera *The Noble Peasant*. On 10 May 1786, for the benefit of her father, she played Nancy in the afterpiece *True Blue; or, The Parting Lovers* at Covent Garden, her only recorded appearance at either of London's winter patent houses. In the summer of 1786 both

Harvard Theatre Collection

FRANCES HODGKINSON as Cora

engraving by Tiebout, after Dunlap

her father and mother were at the Haymarket, and Frances was Maria in *Hunt the Slipper* and a Bacchante in *Comus*, each several times repeated.

On 18 September 1786, just as the fall season at Covent Garden was about to begin, William Brett was for some reason notified he would not be rehired there. He played at Brighton and then went to Smock Alley, Dublin, in the 1786–87 season. He continued at Smock Alley in 1787–88 and switched to Crow Street in 1788–89.

Frances had evidently accompanied her father to Ireland, though the first known references to her there were performances at Smock Alley in the summer of 1788. She was in the Crow Street company that fall and the entire season of 1788–89, along with her father and her sister "W." (who came back as a Crow Street regular from 1791–92 until about 1796, when she married Chapman, the boxkeeper and treasurer at the theatre). On 2 April 1789, William Brett died at Dublin.

On 23 September 1789 Frances was advertised in a Bristol bill as "from Dublin." She acted and sang with the Bath-Bristol company that season and in February and March gave a series of subscription concerts with Incledon and others at the Assembly Rooms, Prince's Street, Bristol.

On 4 October 1790 the rising young actor John Hodgkinson came from Exeter to join the Bath-Bristol troupe, accompanied by his somewhat older wife Mary Ann (née Jones), formerly common-law wife of Joseph Shepherd Munden, and four of her children by Munden. Hodgkinson became a star of the company almost immediately. One of his successes was in the sprightly afterpiece *No Song, No Supper*, in which Frances Brett played the ingenue Louisa (and Mrs Hodgkinson the Grandmother!).

Frances Brett and John Hodgkinson played opposite each other in a number of productions in 1790–91 and in 1791–92. They discovered not only a dramatic affinity but also, before long, a mutual attraction. Hodgkinson—never, then or afterward, notable for ethical behavior—began to seek ways of deserting his wife (as, indeed, she had deserted Munden). Refusing several offers of a London debut, he wrote in December 1791 to Lewis Hallam and John Henry, managers at New York, inquiring for positions for himself and a first-line female singer—by whom he meant Frances Brett. In June 1792 Henry, on a recruiting mission, saw Frances and Hodgkinson act at Bath and concluded an agreement which included Hodgkinson, Frances, her mother Hannah, and at least one of the other Brett girls. (Mrs Brett and a daughter seem to have remained in England for some time after Frances and Hodgkinson left. The daughter remaining behind must have been the youngest, Arabella, who was then just nine years old. It is not certain that she ever acted. The Miss Brett who played ingenue roles with Mr and Mrs Hodgkinson in Philadelphia in 1792–93 was the one who married the actor William King by September 1794.)

The four Munden children were sent to their father in London, and their mother Mrs Hodgkinson was abandoned at Bath. She died at Tiverton on 6 October following. In August 1792 Hodgkinson, Frances Brett, and eight other provincial actors (including King, the future brother-in-law) had set sail for America. Frances married Hodgkinson soon after their arrival. The couple made their American debut at the Southwark Theatre in Philadelphia on 26 September with "An Introductory Address by Mr. Hodgkinson, written by himself." He played Don Felix in *The Wonder* and she was Leonora in *The Padlock*. During the remainder of the season she offered the title role in *Rosina*, Priscilla Tomboy in *The Romp*, Molly in *The Farmer*, Margaretta in *No Song, No Supper*, Kathleen in *The Poor Soldier*, Cowslip in *The Agreeable Surprize*, Amanthis in *The Child of Nature*, Kitty in *Ways and Means*, and probably other roles.

William Dunlap left a description of Frances Hodgkinson at that period and an analysis of her powers:

As an actress in girls and romps she was truly excellent. In high comedy she was much above mediocrity, and even in tragedy she possessed much merit. In Ophelia she was touching in a powerful degree, as her singing gave her advantages in this character which tragic actresses do not usually possess. Her forte was opera. From her father she had derived instructions; and her husband's practice on the violin continued to improve her in knowledge of this branch of her profession. Her voice, both in speaking and singing, was powerful and sweet.

Mrs. Hodgkinson was very fair, with blue eyes, and yellow hair approaching to the flaxen. Her nose was prominent or Roman; her visage oval, and rather long for her stature, which was below the middling. Her general carriage on the stage was suited to the character she performed; and in romps, full of archness, playfulness, and girlish simplicity. As a general actress, she was as valuable in female as her husband in male characters.

Dunlap's last statement was a considerable compliment and perhaps an exaggeration, for John Hodgkinson was certainly the finest actor who had appeared in America up to his day. He was not, however, an agreeable theatrical colleague or business partner, as Dunlap and others began soon to discover. He began to use his undoubted abilities to gather all the first roles for himself and his wife. The particular victim of his machinations was Mrs Lewis Hallam, wife of John Henry's co-manager. In 1794 Hallam, disgusted, sold his half of the company to Hodgkinson—as had been foreseen by Hodgkinson. In 1796 William Dunlap bought half of Hodgkinson's part of the concern. He, too, found himself overmatched by the greed of Hodgkinson for more money and better parts. In 1797 Hallam gave up.

Meanwhile Hodgkinson, trying to maintain simultaneous summer companies, one at Hartford and Boston and one at New York, lost large sums. In 1798 Hodgkinson left New York to manage at Boston—decamping, it seems, with some properties he had sold to Dunlap. But when, after failure and debts at Boston, he offered to return to New York to act, Dunlap generously engaged both him and Mrs Hodgkinson. The greed and consequent rancor, predictably, continued. Frances Brett Hodgkinson did not have to witness the denouement. Frances died of tuberculosis, at Philadelphia, on 27 September 1803 at 32. She was buried in St John's cemetery in New York City, beside her sister Arabella, who had died, also of tuberculosis, on 12 September. In its obituary the *Columbian Centinel* said accurately that "The various characters which her versatile talents enabled her to sustain" in tragedy, comedy, and opera "will rarely be found united in any one actress." John acted two seasons at Charleston and then obtained the lease of the Park Theatre, which Dunlap, now bankrupt (in part because of Hodgkinson's actions) had lost. Traveling South in quest of actors, Hodgkinson died of yellow

Harvard Theatre Collection

Tombstone of FRANCES HODGKINSON

fever at a tavern near Bladensburg, Maryland, on 12 September 1805.

The Hodgkinsons had two daughters and a son Thomas. Both daughters, Frances and Rosina, were briefly on the American stage. Aaron Sargent in *The Sargent Genealogy* (1895) says that Mrs Rosina Hodgkinson Lewis, who married Nathan Sargent (1794–1875) on 14 February 1821, had been born 15 October 1798 and had died on 15 February 1878. Sargent was judge of the Washington, D.C., Court of Common Pleas and of the Probate Court and at various times was Sergeant at Arms of the House of Representatives, commissioner of customs, and a well-known political writer under the nom de plume Oliver Oldschool.

A portrait by William Dunlap of Frances Hodgkinson as Cora in *Pizarro* was engraved by C. Tiebout and published by Dunlap as

frontispiece to an edition of the play, 1800. The same picture was also engraved by S. Hollyer. She is pictured as Moggy McGilpin, with John Martin as Charley, in *The Highland Reel* in an engraving by J. Scoles, after Martin. A drawing of her tombstone, with inscription, is in the Harvard Theatre Collection. A portrait in oil by an unknown artist, inscribed on the back, "Mrs John Hodgkinson in the character of Queen Elizabeth in John Street Theatre, N. York," was sold for $17.50 in the Evert Jansen Wendell sale at the American Art Association, 15–20 October 1918.

Hodgson. *See also* HUDSON.

Hodgson, John [*fl.* 1689–1741?], *actor.*

A warrant in the Lord Chamberlain's accounts dated 23 August 1689 listed John

Hodgson (spelled Hudson in some sources) as a member of the United Company. His first recorded role was Orgillus, one of the title characters, in *The Treacherous Brothers* by George Powell at Drury Lane in January 1690. Hodgson also provided Powell's play with a Latin poem, "Ad amicum in hujusce Tragoediae Authorem," which Powell prefaced with this comment: "My Friend, against my will, puts this Complement upon me, had he not been a particular Acquaintance, and a Brother-Actor, I shou'd have took it as an Affront; yet though he writ it, I dare swear neither you nor I think it; and so take it among ye." Both the size of the role Hodgson played and Powell's consideration of him would suggest that by 1690 Hodgson was no stripling and may well have had previous acting experience.

Several manuscript casts which seem to belong to the very early 1690s name some other roles Hodgson played: Harry Clare in *The Merry Devil of Edmonton*, Harry in *Madam Fickle*, Brabantio in *Othello*, Rivers in *Richard III*, Ford in *The Merry Wives of Windsor*, and Medley in *The Man of Mode*. He is also found in several printed cast lists for the 1690–91 season: Count Canaile in *Sir Anthony Love*, Audas in *Distressed Innocence*, Sir Robert Holland in *Edward III*, Tachmas in *Alphonso*, Don Juan de Mendoza in *The Mistakes*, Will Merriton in *Love for Money*, Monsieur in D'Urfey's *Bussy D'Ambois*, Lord Worthy in *Greenwich Park*, and Conon in *King Arthur*. A warrant dated 12 June 1691 indicates that Hodgson was sued by one Tobias Langdon for a debt.

Before the United Company divided in 1695 Hodgson acted, usually at Drury Lane, Captain Darewell in *The Marriage-Hater Matched*, Briomer in *The Rape*, the Duke of Florence in *The Traytor*, Coenus in *Cleomenes*, Sussex in *Henry II*, Welford in *The Volunteers*, Hotspur in *The Richmond Heiress*, Wellborn in *A Very Good Wife*, and Meanwell in *The Female Vertuosos*—and, we should assume, other roles for which no records have been found. During the early 1690s Hodgson (cited as Hudson) testified at the trial of Lord Mohun following the killing of the actor William Mountfort on 9 December 1692. In the course of his testimony Hodgson spoke of having been invited to supper with Lord Mohun at the Rose Tavern in Covent Garden. Captain Hill, Mohun's friend, was there and spoke of his passion for

the actress Anne Bracegirdle and how he was "obstructed by *Mountford*, whom I design to be the Death of. . . ." Hodgson was at the theatre the evening Mountfort was murdered, for he testified that Captain Hill "came into the Scene-Room of the Play House, and my Lord *Mohun* had Captain *Hills* Coat on, and Captain *Hill* had my Lord *Mohuns* Coat on, and they changed their Cloaths in the Play House. I saw them change their Cloaths; but what their Design was, I cannot tell." Later that evening, though Hodgson was not a witness to it, Hill and Mohun sought out Mountfort near Anne Bracegirdle's house and killed him.

During 1693 Hodgson was again in financial difficulties. On 2 November a Mr Lawrence sued him for the rent of a house; a hearing was called for 22 November, but the outcome is not known.

When Thomas Betterton and the older players in the United Company broke away to form their own troupe, Hodgson joined them, and for the rest of his career he acted at Lincoln's Inn Fields Theatre. There he is known to have appeared as Lovewell in *She Ventures and He Wins* in September 1695 (the earliest notice of him there), the prologue to *Lover's Luck*, Abradatas in *Cyrus*, Philabel in *The She-Gallants*, Ismael in *The Royal Mischief*, Lord Lovewel in *Love's a Jest*, Young Mr Gerald in *The Anatomist*, Lovebright (and the prologue) in *The City Lady*, Heartfree in *The Provok'd Wife*, Count de Fiesque in *The Intrigues at Versailles*, Beaumont in *The Innocent Mistress*, Decius in *Boadicea*, Alfonso in *The Italian Husband* (*The London Stage* shows Hodgson playing that role; the 1698 edition actually has Mrs Hodgson listed, in error), the prologue to *Europe's Revels* (at court, in conjunction with the Drury Lane company), Count Andrea in *The Deceiver Deceived*, Fabiano in *Beauty in Distress* (later called *The French Beau*), Mardonius in *Xerxes*, Bucarius (and the prologue) in *The False Friend*, Glendower in *Henry IV*, Pacuvius Clarius in *The Fate of Capua*, Demetrius in *The Czar of Muscovy*, and Dumnacus in *Love's Victim*. The last-named role he acted about April 1701, after which he seems to have retired from acting.

During Hodgson's years with Betterton's troupe he figured in a few adventures. The *Post Man* of 13–15 July 1697 reported that a Mr

H., an actor at Lincoln's Inn Fields, fought and won a duel with a Mr D. on 13 July. The actor in question was probably Hodgson, though he may have been one of the Harrises or Benjamin Husband. Hodgson was, it should be noted, sometimes called Captain and may well have had a military background. Indeed, he was called that when, on 17 June 1699, according to Narcissus Luttrell, "one Brown, a baylif, with 13 more, beset the playhouse, in order to arrest Capt. Hodgson; but the players comeing out in a body, beat and wounded them, and in the scuffle Captain Hodgson's man was cowardly run through the back by a baylif, and immediately dyed, having nothing but a stick in his hand."

On 24 June 1700, according to the Coram Rege Roll for Michaelmas Term 1701, Hodgson and others were cited for having performed the "obscene" play *Love for Love* (*The London Stage* does not list a performance on or before that date, though the play was given on 28 June). Hodgson was one of several players on trial the following November for using profanity on the stage during a performance of *The Anatomist*. On 29 November he was indicted and fined £10. John and the others were listed as from the parish of St Clement Danes.

On 2 June 1721 there was held at Drury Lane a benefit for "Mr Hodgson, formerly a Comedian in the King's Company." *The Fair Penitent* was performed. If Hodgson had been a King's Company player before 1682 when the United Company was formed, this is the only evidence of it, unless the Drury Lane managers in 1721 were using the term "King's Company" loosely. Still, Hodgson was obviously still alive in 1721 and should have provided them with accurate information about his background in the theatre. A John Hodgson was elected a member of the Sublime Society of Beefsteaks on 16 May 1741, but that date is too long after the previous reference to the actor to permit safe identification. If Hodgson was still living in 1741 he was doubtless well along in years.

The parish registers of St Paul, Covent Garden, show a John Hudson of St Clement Danes marrying a Sarah Bawden of the same parish on 27 July 1701. A Mrs Hodgson, possibly the wife of John the actor, was working in the theatre in the 1690s; John could have married a second time in 1701.

Hodgson, Mrs [John?] [*fl.* 1690?–1719], *singer, oboist.*

The Prophetess was performed about 3 June 1690 at the Dorset Garden Theatre, and perhaps Mrs Hodgson (or Hudson) sang in it. She may have been related to the actor John Hodgson, who was active in the United Company at the same time. According to the printed edition of *The Maid's Last Prayer*, which was given at Drury Lane at the end of February 1693, Mrs Hodgson sang Purcell's "Tho you make no return to my passion" and other songs. During the two years that followed, before the United Company broke up, she was listed in printed plays as singing in *The Villain*, *Rule a Wife and Have a Wife*, *The Prophetess*, *Love Triumphant*, *The Lancashire Witches*, *The Fatal Marriage*, *The Ambitious Slave*, *2 Don Quixote*, and possibly *Macbeth* (in the British Library manuscript of that work, as performed in late 1694, her name was entered on some songs and then crossed out). The only name role known for Mrs Hodgson was Herse in *The Rape of Europa* at Drury Lane in 1693–94; she sang specialty pieces but did not portray characters in straight plays.

When Betterton and the older actors in the United Company complained of the management of Christopher Rich and Sir Thomas Skipwith, Mrs Hodgson did not sign the bill of particulars and evidently remained at Drury Lane as late as 22 February 1695. As of the following 20 July, however, she was in Betterton's company at Lincoln's Inn Fields. In August she sang in their production of *Pyrrhus*. By September John Hodgson was working with Betterton's company; indeed, except for a gap in John's record from June 1693 to September 1695, the careers of the two Hodgsons run parallel. Possibly they were man and wife; they seem not to have performed as a team.

For the rest of the 1695–96 season Mrs Hodgson appeared as a specialty singer in the Lincoln's Inn Fields productions of *Generous Enemies*, *She Ventures and He Wins*, *Lover's Luck*, *The Country Wake*, *The Royal Mischief*, and *Love's a Jest*, and in December 1695 she sang in *Pausanius* at the rival Drury Lane Theatre. In *The Loves of Mars and Venus* at Lincoln's Inn Fields on 14 November 1696 she sang "Erato, the Muse that presides to Love Songs, &c." in the prologue, and in the play proper she was Aglaia, one of the Graces, and Jealousy. In late

June 1697 she sang in *The Innocent Mistress*. Her name appeared less frequently in printed plays during the last years of the century, but she is known to have sung the Messenger of Peace in the combined Drury Lane-Lincoln's Inn Fields production at court of *Europe's Revels*. The Lord Chamberlain's accounts show her as a member of Betterton's troupe as of 14 November 1698 (and presumably for the full 1698–99 season), but no appearances are known for Mrs Hodgson either during that season or the one following. On 25 April 1698 a concert was presented at York Buildings, according to the *Post Man* of 21–23 April (as reported in *The London Stage*), for the benefit of "Mr" Hodgson—very likely a misprint for Mrs Hodgson, inasmuch as no Mr Hodgson is known to have been connected with London concerts.

When *The Charms of bright Beauty* from "*Orensebe*" (*Aureng-Zebe*) was published about 1698, Mrs Hodgson was named as the singer; Dryden's play was reprinted in 1699 and probably was revived during the 1698–99 season. On 5 March 1700, when *The Way of the World* was performed, Mrs Hodgson probably sang Eccles's "Love's but the frailty of the Mind." Mrs "Hudson" and Mr Williams shared a benefit concert at York Buildings on 20 March 1700 at which the famous comedian Joe Haines spoke a prologue. Mrs Hodgson sang "Ah! Cruel Damon" at Lincoln's Inn Fields about 1700; according to the *Mercurius Musicus*, she was a singer in *The Fate of Capua* when it was given in mid-April 1700; and in some play she sang Eccles's "Fy Amarillis." *The Mad Lover* must have been revived in 1700–1701, for the *Mercurius Musicus* of January-February 1701 contained songs from it as performed at Lincoln's Inn Fields by Mrs "Hudson" and others. She also sang Barrett's "Melinda cou'd I constant prove" at Lincoln's Inn Fields, according to the same periodical. In a lost play, *The Morose Reformer* (c. 1700), she sang "You Ladyes who are young and gay."

Mrs Hodgson was Juno in *The Judgment of Paris* at Dorset Garden on 21 March 1701 and was praised by the author, Congreve, in a letter to his friend Keally. During the first six years of the new century Mrs Hodgson sang at Lincoln's Inn Fields and then the new Queen's Theatre, and occasionally the records show her to have appeared in concerts at York Buildings.

A document among the Lord Chamberlain's papers that dates about 1703 indicates that as a potential singer in a proposed new company Mrs Hodgson would have received an annual salary of £30—the second highest fee among the singers.

At a York Buildings concert on 11 December 1703 Mrs Hodgson revealed another talent: she played the oboe and Mrs Cook played the violin in a duet. She was not otherwise advertised as an instrumentalist. But she was clearly one of the more popular singers of her day, for the printed songs of the time often mentioned her as the soloist. Eric White has suggested that she may have sung Dido in the revival of Purcell's masterpiece at Lincoln's Inn Fields on 29 January 1704, but the cast was not listed in the papers. Mrs Hodgson is known to have sung between 1700 and 1706 in such works as *Tamerlane*, *Love Betray'd*, *The Fair Penitent*, *The Country Wife*, *Timon of Athens*, and *Love at First Sight*. When Finger's *Shee that wou'd gain a faithfull Lover* was published about 1715 (error for 1705?), Mrs Hodgson was listed as having sung the song at York Buildings; if 1715 is correct, she is not otherwise known to have been active at that late date.

D'Urfey's *Wit and Mirth* contained in 1719 several lyrics to songs with Mrs Hodgson listed as the soloist, but they were all songs from the early years of the century. The last mention of Mrs Hodgson was on 18 May 1719, when she shared a benefit with Mrs Cook at a performance of *Circe* at Lincoln's Inn Fields.

Hodson, Miss ₍*fl.* 1782–1804?₎, *equestrienne, dancer.*

A Miss Hodson performed feats of horsemanship with Griffin and Jones at Astley's Amphitheatre in April and June 1782. She was probably the "Miss Hudson" who danced an Attendant in the music spectacle *Love from the Heart* at Astley's on 4 September 1786. Perhaps she was the Miss Hodson who danced in an allemande at the Royal Circus on 8 October 1804.

Hodson, ₍**R.?**₎ ₍*fl.* 1798–1807₎, *manager, costume designer?*

In June 1798 a Mr Hodson became joint manager and proprietor of the Royal Circus in St George's Fields with George Jones and John Cartwright Cross. Perhaps he was the R. Hod-

son who also designed costumes for that theatre between 1801 and 1807. Some of the
productions the latter dressed were *Rinaldo
Rinaldini* and *The Fire King* in 1801; *The
Golden Farmer, Gonsalvo de Cordova*, and *The
Jubilee of 1802* in 1802; and *The Rival Statues*
in 1803. On 22 September 1807 an advertisement announced that tickets could be had of
Mr Hodson at No 6, Fore Street, Lambeth.

Hodson, William *b. 1748, kettle drummer.*
See HODSON, WILLIAM *d. 1789.*

Hodson, William *d. 1789, organist,
violinist.*
William Hodson was one of the second violinists who performed in the Handel Memorial
Concerts at Westminster Abbey and the Pantheon in May and June 1784. He was a member of the Royal Society of Musicians by 1785,
and probably much earlier, for that year he
served on the Society's Court of Assistants and
played the violin in the annual May concerts
at St Paul's.

Sometime in April of 1789 William Hodson
died. His will, drawn on 31 May 1776, in
which he described himself as a gentleman of
the parish of East Greenwich in Kent, was
proved on 2 May 1789 by his widow and sole
executrix Elizabeth Hodson. On 3 May 1789
the Royal Society of Musicians awarded Mrs
Hodson the widow's allowance of two and a
half guineas per month.

On 28 May 1747, William Hodson, organist, of Princess Square, and his wife Elizabeth
had baptized their daughter Elizabeth (25 days
old) at St George-in-the-East, Stepney. At the
same church on 23 August 1748 their son
William (born on the previous day) was baptized. This son was probably the Mr Hodson
who played the kettle drum at St Paul's in May
1785 in the same concerts in which the father
played the violin.

Hoffman, Mr *[fl. 1798–1804?], bassoon-
ist?*
A Mr Hoffman played in a performance of
the *Messiah* at the Haymarket Theatre on 15
January 1798. Perhaps he was the musician
named Hoffman who played at the Park Street
Theatre in New York in 1798. Dunlap in his
Diary cited a Mr Hoffman, a bassoonist, in his

preliminary list of orchestra members. On 14
April 1803 Hoffman participated in a concert
at the City Assembly Room, and he was in one
of the series of professional concerts presented
at Mechanics' Hall in February and March
1804.

Hoffman, John *[fl. 1794], pianist,
drummer.*
Doane's *Musical Directory* of 1794 listed
Master John Hoffman, evidently the son of
John Andrew Hoffman, as a performer on the
pianoforte and drums. His address was given
as No 214, Oxford Street (possibly an error for
124; see the entry of John Andrew Hoffman).

Hoffman, John Andrew *[fl. 1794–
1822], musician, music seller.*
Doane's *Musical Directory* of 1794 listed John
Andrew Hoffman, of No 214 (124?) Oxford
Street, as a trumpeter, violinist, violist, and
organist who performed for the Choral Fund
and in the Handel performances at Westminster Abbey. Doane may have been mistaken in
Hoffman's address; Kidson's *British Music Publishers* and Humphries and Smith's *Music Publishing in the British Isles* give his address as No
124, Oxford Street. There from about 1795 to
1799 Hoffman ran a music-selling and -pub-
lishing business. From about 1799 to 1808 his
premises were at No 9, Princes Street, Cavendish Square, and from about 1808 to 1822
they were at No 21, Manchester Street,
Manchester Square. John Andrew was surely
the father of young John and Sophia Hoffman,
both musical prodigies and both listed in
Doane as living at the same address.

Hoffman, Sophia *b. 1785?, pianist,
organist, harpist, singer.*
Sophia Hoffman was almost certainly the
daughter of John Andrew Hoffman. According
to the *Gentleman's Magazine* of January 1788,
Sophia was two years and four months old in
November 1787 and had already developed a
piano repertoire of 60 pieces. Doane's *Musical
Directory* of 1794, giving her address as No
214 (124?), Oxford Street, claimed that Sophia was not only a pianist but an organist,
harpist, and singer. When she appeared at
Drury Lane Theatre on 18 May 1797 to play
a piano piece, she was (incorrectly?) advertised
as being nine years old.

Hogarth, William *1697–1764, artist.*

We believe that William Hogarth should not be included in this dictionary, and normally we silently omit such persons. But some readers may be aware that in *Theatre Notebook* in 1964–65 Hogarth was included in a census of scene painters. The evidence for his having painted scenery for the professional theatre derives from a source that we feel cannot be relied upon: J. T. Smith's *Antient Topography of London* (1810). In that work Smith tells the story he heard from Edward Oram to the effect that Oram's father and Hogarth had painted scenery at Drury Lane Theatre and for a booth at Bartholomew Fair. Sybil Rosenfeld in the eighth volume of *Theatre Notebook* conjectured that if Hogarth did paint scenery for a fair booth, it may have been for *The Siege of Troy* in 1724.

But there seems to be no concrete evidence, and had so important an artist as Hogarth actually painted scenery for professional productions, some proof of it should have survived. It is worth noting that in his definitive works on Hogarth, Ronald Paulson does not mention any theatrical activity by the painter.

Hogg, Mr ₁*fl. 1778?–1794*₁, *trumpeter, singer?*

The Drury Lane accounts contain several references to a trumpeter named Hogg, and he may also have been the Mr Hogg who, in the 1778–79 season, sang occasionally in the chorus. Most of the notes, however, cite Hogg as an extra trumpeter, and it may be that he was not on the regular paylist but was hired occasionally. The earliest reference to him as a trumpeter was on 19 January 1782 and the last on 3 June 1793. A singer named Hogg performed in Derby in the summer of 1794.

Hogg, Mr ₁*fl. 1784–1785*₁, *bassoonist.*

Mr Hogg played bassoon in the Handel Memorial Concerts at Westminster Abbey and the Pantheon in May and June 1784. He was probably the Mr Hogg who served on the Court of Assistants of the Royal Society of Musicians in 1785.

Holberg, Ludwig von *1684–1754, violinist.*

Born in Bergen, Norway, on 6 November 1684, Baron Ludwig von Holberg, the father of modern Danish literature, was also a violin virtuoso. He studied theology and through teaching earned money to visit Holland, France, Germany, and England before settling in 1718 in Copenhagen. In England, according to the violin historian van der Straeten, Holberg appeared with success as a violinist. After establishing his home in Copenhagen he devoted most of his time to writing. He was created a baron in 1747 and died in Copenhagen on 27 January 1754.

Holcomb, Henry *c. 1693–c. 1750?, singer, composer.*

According to Grove, Henry Holcomb was born about 1693, probably in Salisbury, where he was a chorister as a boy—though *The Dictionary of National Biography* says he was born in Shrewsbury, about 1690. Henry came to London in the early years of the eighteenth century and sang at Drury Lane as early as 26 February 1705, when he was cited merely as "the New Boy." He may have been the "new Italian Boy" who sang at the Queen's Theatre on 14 April 1705, for we know from later references that he was fluent in Italian. In the fall of 1705 the Drury Lane bills called him "the Boy"; on 30 March 1706, when he sang Prenesto in the first performance of *Camilla*, he was cited as Holcomb. The bill for 1 June, when he sang a new English cantata, called him Henry Holcomb. On 13 October and 1 November 1706, with the Drury Lane troupe at the Dorset Garden playhouse, Holcomb sang between the acts at performances of *The Recruiting Officer* and was called "Holcomb, the late Boy" (the earlier of the two dates is from a presentation copy at the London Guildhall and is not listed in *The London Stage*). On 4 March 1707 Holcomb sang the Page in the opera *Rosamond* at Drury Lane.

The Dictionary of National Biography claims that Henry sang in revivals of *Camilla* in 1708, but there is no confirmation of that fact elsewhere. He sang on 8 August 1709 at a concert in York, according to notes given us by the late Emmett Avery (Professor Avery may have meant York Buildings). Henry sang at the Queen's Theatre in 1709–10, though he did not make his first appearance there until 29 June 1710, when he offered three "select Entertainments" in Italian. He seems not to have appeared there again, and his name has not yet been found in another London bill until 26 February 1729, when he sang six songs at a concert at Drury Lane held for his benefit. On 28 August 1739—ten years later—he became one of the original subscribers to the Royal Society of Musicians. By that time, and perhaps much earlier, Henry Holcomb earned his living by teaching singing and harpsichord.

In 1748 Holcomb was living in Russell Street, Covent Garden. He died about two years later, according to Grove and *The Dictionary of National Biography*, but it is worth noting the following entry in the parish registers of St Paul, Covent Garden, which seems to imply that Holcomb was still alive in 1752: Martha, the wife of Henry Holcomb, was buried on 16 August of that year. There could, of course, have been a second Henry Holcomb in the parish.

Holcomb composed a number of songs. The "Holdecombe" who set to music Pope's *Duke upon Duke*, "An Excellent New Play-house Ballad" (1720), was our subject. The piece was reprinted frequently in the years that followed. Other songs that were published separately were *Arno's Vale* (1740?), *The Forsaken Nymph* (1740?), *The Garland*, a collection of songs and cantatas (1750?), *Go, happy Paper* (1742?), *The Happy Man* (1720?), *The Musical Medley*, a collection of songs and cantatas (1740?), *Six Solos for Violin and Thorough Bass, with some Pieces for the German Flute and Harpsichord* (1745?), and *The Syren of the Stage* (1728?). Another song of his which proved very popular was "Happy Hour all Hours Excelling," which was included in *Musical Miscellany*.

Holcroft, Thomas   1745–1809, *actor, singer, violinist, dramatist, novelist.*

Thomas Holcroft was born in Orange Court, Leicester Fields, London, on 11 December 1745 and baptized at St Martin-in-the-Field's on Christmas Day, the son of Thomas and Sarah Holcroft. In a narrative of his life (which he brought down through his fifteenth year and which was completed after his death by William Hazlitt) Holcroft said that until he was six years old his father kept a shoemaker's shop in Orange Court. He added, "I have a faint recollection that my mother dealt in greens and oysters." The father also dabbled in horse trading until he suffered financial reverses which sent him away "into

National Portrait Gallery

THOMAS HOLCROFT
by Opie

Berkshire, somewhere beyond Ascot Heath, about thirty miles from London," where the parents and several children stayed a year.

When Thomas was seven, his father, who was both stern (and occasionally violent) and sentimentally affectionate, took the boy with him on a wandering tour of the country. Then for a period Thomas accompanied his mother and father "*tramping* the villages, to hawk our pedlary," and on at least one occasion the boy was set to begging from house to house. From Cambridge to the Isle of Ely, to Coventry, Macclesfield, Lichfield, Nottingham, Buxton, Chesterfield, Mansfield, and other localities, the family wandered. Sometimes Thomas went peddling, sometimes he drove asses loaded with coals through the knee-deep mud of country traces. Often he was put in the care of strangers. Often, too, he went hungry. Sleeping under a damp hedge for want of money for a lodging, Holcroft contracted a fever and an "asthma," the effects of which he felt all his life. But his father taught him to read, and he developed an early and astonishing proficiency with language and, somehow, a devotion to honesty and a sensitivity to human suffering.

Holcroft was, successively, cobbler's helper, apprentice to a stocking weaver, and Newmarket stableboy. He remained at Newmarket for nearly three years and, despite a riding accident which nearly cost him his life, was happy, being well-fed and well-treated by his master, the trainer John Watson, and enjoying the bustle and routine of stable and racecourse. While at Newmarket he joined a small singing-society under the direction of a musical breeches-tailor and discovered that he had a fine singing voice. At 16 he moved back to London to work with his father in a cobbler's stall in South Audley Street. In 1764 he went with his father to Liverpool, taught school for a few months, and in 1765, at 19, married the first of his four wives, a girl whose name is not now known.

Holcroft's career continued varied. He returned to London, wrote a few political articles for the *Whitehall Evening Post*, and secured a position, probably secretarial, in the family of the churchman and abolitionist Granville Sharpe. He was dismissed from that post because of his insistence on attending a "spouting-club," a tavern-meeting of young apprentices giving dramatic readings, probably at the Red Lion, Cripplegate.

Without a situation, in the spring of 1770 he was despondently on his way to enlist in the army of the East India Company when he was accosted by a companion from his dramatic society who took him for an interview with Charles Macklin. Macklin heard him, corrected him with his usual rough abuse, and gave him a letter of introduction to William Dawson, the manager at the Capel Street Theatre, Dublin. Hazlitt's narrative makes it seem that Holcroft then went directly to Ireland. But Holcroft had also interviewed Samuel Foote, who signed him to the company at the Haymarket for the summer of 1770. The tyro walked on as one of a four-man mob in *The Mayor of Garratt* on 28 May 1770 and two nights following. From then until mid-September he gave scattered performances as the Butler in *The Devil to Pay*, the Tapster in *The Stratagem*, Mercury in *Midas*, a Footman in *The Old Bachelor*, and Philpot's Servant in *The Citizen*.

Holcroft borrowed six guineas from Macklin, redeemed his pawned clothes, and set off for Dublin in late September 1770. The Capel Street season did not commence until November. He had been hired for 30s. per week, but Dawson peremptorily reduced his pay to a guinea. When Macklin arrived he refused either to intercede or to stand by a bargain he had made to instruct Holcroft. Hazlitt wrote: "Unable to extricate himself, [Holcroft] endured the insults of malice and ignorance for five months, till the money which he had borrowed had been deducted from his stipend, and then *Dawson* immediately discharged him."

Left in a strange country without funds, Holcroft joined the perennially insolvent Henry Mossop's company at Smock Alley. "It soon appeared that there was no probability of his being paid for his performance at Mossop's theatre: he was therefore forced to quit Dublin, and went on board the Packet for Parkgate, in March, 1771." After a violent storm and a passage of eight days in which the ship ran out of provisions and Holcroft was almost thrown overboard as a "Jonah" by some superstitious Irishmen, the vessel finally made port.

Holcroft now received several offers from country managers because of his talents as a singer and his new reputation as "from the Theatre Royal, Dublin." He joined a strolling company at Leeds, Yorkshire, which collapsed from internal dissension, after which he walked, nearly penniless (and arrived near starvation), 160 miles to Hereford to join Roger Kemble's company. With the Kembles he strolled, probably through Ludlow, Worcester, Leaminster, Bewdly, Bromsgrove, Droitwich, Gloucester, Wolverhampton, Monmouth, and Swansea.

Evidently while Holcroft was in the Kemble company he married Matilda Tipler of Nottingham. About 1773 their son William was born while Holcroft was acting in Samuel Stanton's company at Kendal. The comedian William T. P. Hatton recommended him to the country manager and sometime London performer C. J. Booth. To plead his case Holcroft wrote Booth a letter offering himself in multiple capacities. Hazlitt summarized the letter:

He engaged to perform all the old men, and principal low-comedy characters; he was to be the music, that is, literally the sole accompaniment to all songs, &c., on his fiddle in the orchestra; he undertook to instruct the younger performers in singing and music, and to write out the different . . . parts in every new comedy; and, lastly, he was to furnish the theatre with several new pieces, never published, but which he brought with him in manuscript, among the rest Dr. Last in his Chariot [by

Samuel Foote and Isaac Bickerstaff] which character he himself performed.

He proposed a share and a half of the profits (which could amount to only about 17*s*. weekly) as his salary. He joined Booth at Carlisle in the autumn of 1774, and on this circuit Matilda Holcroft began also to act. From their lodgings at the house of George Bowes, hatter, on 1 June 1775, Holcroft addressed a letter to David Garrick, in which he pleaded for an engagement for a "trifling salary":

I have played in the country with applause, and my friends, I am afraid, have flattered me: some of them have ranked me among the sons of genius, and I have, at times, been silly enough to believe them. I have succeeded best in low comedy and old men. I understand music very well, something of French and fencing, and have a very quick memory, as I can repeat any part under four lengths at six hours' notice. I have studied character, situation, dress, diliberation, enunciation, but above all, the eye and the manner; and have so far succeeded, as to be entirely at the head of my profession here in all those characters which nature has any way qualified me for.

He informed Garrick that his wife was then lying in and enclosed 10 quatrains of his own composition entitled "Hope; or, The Delusion." Garrick's reply, if there was one, never reached him. Mrs Holcroft died during or after the birth of their daughter Sophy.

After a year and a half with Booth, Holcroft joined John Bates in a circuit which included Durham, Sunderland, Darlington, Scarborough, and Stockton-upon-Tees. On one occasion Holcroft walked from Durham to Stockton-upon-Tees with the composer William Shield "studying Lowth's Grammar, and reading Pope's Homer." During this period of his country service he "practised a good deal on the fiddle, which he continued ever after to do occasionally, but he never became a good performer." He also became friendly with Joseph Ritson the antiquarian and John Cunningham the actor-poet and continued to interest himself in social questions.

Holcroft arrived in London for his second assault on the patent theatres in 1777, shortly after the assumption of the managership of Drury Lane by R. B. Sheridan. According to Hazlitt he tried to secure an engagement at Drury Lane and then at Covent Garden but had no success at either:

As a last desperate resource when his money was nearly exhausted, he sat down and wrote a farce [actually a comic opera], called The Crisis, or Love and Fear, which Mrs. Sheridan was prevailed on to read; and this, with his musical knowledge (as he was able to sing in all choruses), procured him an engagement at twenty shillings a week. On his being engaged, Mr. Holcroft was desired by Mr. Sheridan to give in his cast of parts to Mr Hopkins, the prompter.

The parts were: Don Manuel in *The Kind Impostor*, Hardcastle in *She Stoops to Conquer*, both Hodge and Justice Woodcock in *Love in a Village*, Giles, Ralph, and Sir Harry Sycamore in *The Maid of the Mill*, Scrub in *The Beaux' Stratagem*, Sir Anthony Absolute in *The Rivals*, General Savage in *The School for Wives*, Colin Macleod and Mortimer in *The Fashionable Lover*, Sir Benjamin Dove in *The Brothers*, Major O'Flaherty, Fulmer, and Varland in *The West Indian*, and Colonel Oldboy in *Lionel and Clarissa*. They were parts of considerable range as to age and importance—in farce, sentimental comedy, and comic opera—and reflected the usual requirements for actors in small traveling repertory companies. But in the large pond of Drury Lane where, for instance, Holcroft's three characters in *The West Indian* were played, respectively, by the first-rate comedians Moody, Baddeley, and Parsons, Holcroft was a rather small fish. Moreover, according to his recollection, Hopkins the prompter "who had the regulation of the inferior parts in the theatre, entertained a very low opinion" of his "powers as an actor." Thus, when his name first appeared in a Drury Lane bill, on 4 January 1777, it was as one of some two dozen in a "Chorus of Spirits" in *The Tempest*. For the rest of the 1777–78 season, chorus-singing was his usual lot. He was, however, allowed a few named characters: Taffy in *Harlequin's Invasion*, Tom in *The Jealous Wife*, Rovewell in *The Fair Quaker*, an unspecified "principal Character" in *St Helena*, Simon Pure in *A Bold Stroke for a Wife*, and the interesting Mungo in *The Padlock*. When Sheridan saw him in Mungo, said Hazlitt, "he was so much pleased as to order his weekly salary to be raised to five and twenty shillings." Holcroft in 1777 subscribed his 10*s*. 6*d*. to the Drury Lane Theatrical Fund, apparently confident of a London career.

After the close of the London season, in the summer of 1777 Holcroft went to Canterbury, where he played, often opposite Mrs Inchbald, in W. W. Dimond's company. He acted some 30 times and added 25 new characters to his repertoire: Cimberton in *The Conscious Lovers*, Salisbury in *Henry II or the Fall of Rosamund*, Fag in *The Rivals*, Canton in *The Clandestine Marriage*, the Duke of Richmond in *King Charles I*, Don Alvarez in *The Revenge*, Shylock in *The Merchant of Venice*, Don Lewis in *Love Makes a Man*, a Citizen in *The Roman Fathers*, Sharp in *The Lying Valet*, Peachum in *The Beggar's Opera*, Lord Minikin in *Bon Ton*, Justice Woodcock in *Love in a Village*, Polonius in *Hamlet*, Grub in *Cross Purposes*, the Miller in *The Miller of Mansfield*, the Poet in *The Author*, Doctor Cantwell in *The Methodist Preacher*, the Squire in *Thomas and Sally*, Charles Stanley in *All the World's a Stage*, Coupler in *The Man of Quality*, Arcas in *The Grecian Daughter*, Mr Druggit in *Three Weeks After Marriage*, Byron in *The Rival Candidates*, and Linco in *Linco's Travels*. On the night of his benefit performance, 12 September (shared with Miss Lings), when he made his unaccustomed venture into the first-line serious part of Shylock, he also brought out his own new comedy, *Rosamond; or, the Dutiful Daughter*, in which he played Young Handfield and composed and delivered a prologue and address "to the Ladies and Gentlemen of Canterbury and its environs."

Holcroft returned to, and chafed under, the same anonymous and trifling parts at Drury Lane in the winter of 1777–78 and added only a Watchman in the oft-repeated *Queen Mab*, Issachar in *The Note of Hand*, and another Watchman in *Much Ado about Nothing*. He also repeated some old roles and sang in choruses. But his obvious eagerness and abilities gained him the position of Secretary to the Theatrical Fund in April 1778. On 1 May 1778 he perhaps curried favor with the prompter Hopkins by furnishing *The Crisis; or, Love and Fear* for the afterpiece on the night the Misses Elizabeth and Priscilla Hopkins took their benefit. He played Orak in the feeble farce, which was seen only once.

Holcroft's personality commended him to a widening circle of Londoners, some of whom, like Richard Fulke Greville and his wife Mrs Frances Macartney Greville, were influential for him with his manager. After another summer in the country, at Nottingham and elsewhere, and another season (1778–79) at Drury

Lane, in which he added only Pistol in *The Merry Wives of Windsor*, Joe in *The Miller of Mansfield*, and Jerry Sneak in *The Mayor of Garratt*, he began to lose hope in lasting theatrical success. He had lobbied Mrs Sheridan again, and unsuccessfully, in favor of his "Shepherdess of the Alps" and "The Maid of the Vale," a translation of the Goldoni-Piccini comic opera *La buona figliuola*. After a third season of obscure activity, he took his plight directly to Sheridan in a letter (undated) remarkable for its combination of imaginative expressions of despair and crafty appeals to Sheridan's ego.

Depressed, dejected, chained by Misfortune to the rock of Despair, while the vultures Poverty and Disappointment are feasting with increase of appetite upon me, I have no chance of deliverance but from you. You, Sir, I hope, will be my Alcides! Mr. Evans says, he must increase the deductions he already makes from my salary (9s. per week), unless I can obtain your order to the contrary. It is scarcely possible I should maintain my family, which will shortly be increased, upon my present income. [He had now married for a third time; and in a letter to his father of about 1779 he speaks of "three little ones." Hazlitt says that in 1783 there were Ann by his first wife, Sophy, and William by his second, and Frances by his third.] Were I not under deductions at the office, my receipts would very little exceed sixty pounds a year; and this I enjoy more through your favour than any consequence I am of to the theatre, though continually employed. But then it is either to sit in a senate or at a card-table, or to walk in a procession, or to sing in a chorus, which is all that the prompter, who has the direction of this kind of business, thinks me capable of. Nay, in so little esteem am I held by Mr. Hopkins, that he took the part of a dumb steward in Love for Love from another person, and made me do it; and when by your permission I played Mawworm, he said, had he been well and up, it should not have been so. I do not mention this as a subject of accusation against Mr. Hopkins, but merely to shew that if I am consigned to his penetration, I am doomed to everlasting oblivion.

Unhappily for me, when I performed Mawworm, you were not at the theatre. Interest rather than vanity makes me say, I was more successful than I had any reason to expect. The audience were in a continual laugh. I played Jerry Sneak for my own benefit last year, and with the same success; and if I could only be introduced to the town in old men and burletta singing, I know from former experience how soon I should be held in a very different estimation from what I am at present. You do not know, Sir, how useful I could be upon a thousand emergencies in the theatre, if I were but thought of; but this I shall never be till your express mandate is issued for that purpose.

You have frequently been pleased to express a partiality towards me, as well as a favourable opinion of my abilities. But, Sir, if you do not immediately interest yourself in my behalf, I may grow grey, while I enjoy your favour without a possibility of confirming or increasing it. "Who's the Dupe" prevented the Crisis from being played [again] last year: now you tell me you will talk to me after Christmas; in the mean time "the Flitch of Bacon" and a new pantomime are preparing. I told those to whom I am indebted, I should have a chance of paying them soon, for that the Crisis would come out before the holidays. When I said so, I believed that it would; but they will think I meant to deceive them.

In short, I am arrived at the labyrinth of delays, where suspense and all his busy imps are tormenting me—*You alone, Sir, hold the clue that can guide me out of it.*

Like most such appeals to the inefficient and procrastinating Sheridan the letter went unheeded; and for the rest of Holcroft's associa-

tion with Drury Lane—1779–80, 1780–81, 1781–82—he fared no better, continuing to walk on in Soldiers, Plebeians, Gardeners, Spirits, and Watchmen, some of whom were melodious, others dumb, with an occasional sop in the form of a named character: Dapper in *The Citizen*, Hecate in *A Fête*.

With the 1781–82 season Holcroft's acting career was virtually concluded, but his connection with the stage was far from over. On 13 October 1781 his comedy *Duplicity* was put on at Covent Garden but survived only so far as the third, or author's, night despite the efforts of John Henderson and Elizabeth Inchbald in the leads. But the failures of his plays on the stage seemed only to fire his determination to succeed in letters. He had in 1777 published in a single pamphlet his *Elegies: I. On the Death of Samuel Foote, Esq.* and *II. On Age.* In 1780 he published his first novel, *Alwyn, or the Gentleman Comedian*, in which the adventures of the character Hilkirk parallel his own adventures as a stroller. He also wrote a number of songs for Vauxhall, set by his friend Shield. By 1780 he had begun with a spate of articles for the *Town and Country Magazine* that prolific production for periodicals, which was to continue for the rest of his life. After 1783 his commitments become increasingly political and philosophical, but his interest in the stage continued strong. Frequently his social philosophy appeared under the surface of his plays, which were often produced anonymously because of violent objections to his radical politics.

In 1783 he went to Paris as correspondent of the *Morning Herald*. He was also commissioned by the publisher John Rivington to furnish notices of new continental works for translation. After preparing his comic opera *The Noble Peasant* for its debut at the Haymarket on 2 January 1784 and singing at the Handel memorial concerts at Westminster Abbey and the Pantheon in May and June, he went again to Paris. During the second trip, he pirated *Le Mariage de Figaro* of Beaumarchais soon after its first appearance. The translation was produced at Covent Garden on 14 December 1784 under the title *The Follies of a Day*, with Holcroft taking the part of Figaro. It was a great and lasting success, playing 27 times the first season and entering the permanent repertory. Holcroft was supposed to have

Harvard Theatre Collection

THOMAS HOLCROFT
by Condé

received £600 for his author's nights and a large sum for the copyright.

After the performances of Figaro in 1784–85, Holcroft seems to have acted no more. As an actor, he could never have risen above the third-rate, despite his higher estimate of his abilities. His early style, according to several testimonies, was modeled on the action of Thomas Weston, and he never achieved an original approach.

Holcroft was an ardent apologist for the French Revolution in its earlier phases, a friend of many of the radical and republican theorists of the day, including William Blake and William Godwin (who numbered him among his "four principal oral instructors"). Charles Lamb called him "one of the most candid, most upright, and single-meaning men" he had known. That candor—and his indifference to consequences—made much trouble for him. In November 1792 he became a member of the radical "Society for Constitutional Information." In 1793 he reviewed Godwin's *Political Justice* with warm approval in *The Monthly Review*. In 1794, along with Horne Tooke, Thomas Hardy, and nine others, he was indicted for high treason. On 6 October 1794 the Middlesex grand jury returned a true bill against him and he was committed to Newgate until 1 December. In consequence of Hardy's acquittal, Holcroft was not tried and was released.

Holcroft's financial position, always precarious, grew critical in 1799; he sold his books and a considerable collection of pictures and moved to Hamburg in May. Before he left he married his fourth wife, young Louisa Mercier. At Hamburg he published, for two numbers only, a journal, *The European Repository*. He then moved to Paris. He returned to England in 1803, setting up a printing firm with his brother-in-law, Mercier. That, too, failed utterly.

Holcroft died after a long illness in Clipstone Street, Marylebone, on 23 March 1809. He was buried in Marylebone Cemetery. His very curious and unorthodox will was signed on 18 January 1809. As transcribed in the records of the Prerogative Court of Canterbury it reads:

William Nicholson and I understand from Mrs. Holcroft that it is your wish & will in the event of that termination of life which we must all expect she and ffanny should jointly possess all that you are worth in order to enable them to the best of their judgment to support the ffamily and bring up the children Thomas Holcroft answered I mean that that is right I can speak no more now it hurts me exceedingly good bwye The above written interrogatories and answer were made and given in the Chamber of Mr. Thomas Holcroft at a ¼ of an hour past 4 of the clock in the afternoon of the 19th Day of Dec! 1788 [*recte* 1808; a mistake acknowledged in an addendum statement] Louisa Holcroft his Wife being present. . . .

William Godwin attested that the signature was Holcroft's. No value was assigned to the property, of which administration was granted Louisa Holcroft on 8 January 1810.

Holcroft's rise from the humblest of beginnings was marked by gallant and stoical behavior in the face of repeated reversals. He acquired a good knowledge of French, German, and Italian and a sophisticated understanding of music, philosophy, and letters. He was an intimate of Muzio Clementi and belonged to a musical club, the membership of which included Shield, Villeneux, Crompton, Clementi, and Salomon. Hazlitt said that Holcroft

once gave a considerable sum of money for a couple of Cremona fiddles at a sale; one of which he afterwards presented to his friend Shield. . . . The only extravagance with which he could reproach himself was an occasional gratification of that inordinate love which he had for everything connected with learning, or the fine arts. A fine-toned instrument, a curious book, or a masterly picture, were the baits which luxury always held out to him. . . . Sales of books and prints belonging to him were held on 13 January 1807 and on 17 October 1809.

An admirably complete list of his writings is Elbridge Colby's "A Bibliography of Thomas Holcroft," *Bulletin of New York Public Library*, 1922. For the plays alone, see the "Hand-List of Plays" and "Supplements" in Allardyce Nicoll, *A History of English Drama: 1660–1900*, second edition, 1955.

The Life of Thomas Holcroft Written by Himself Continued to the Time of His Death from His Diary Notes & Other Papers by William Hazlitt was edited by Elbridge Colby in 1925.

Portraits of Thomas Holcroft include:

1. By George Dance, 1795. Pencil drawing in the British Museum. Sold at Christie's on 1

July 1898, as property of the Reverend George Dance, grandson of the artist.

2. By Thomas Lawrence. Black and red chalk drawing of Holcroft seated with William Godwin; sketched at the Old Bailey during the trial of John Thelwall 1–5 December 1794. Bought by Cox in Francis Broderip sale at Christie's on 6 February 1872; with Peter Murray Hill, Ltd, London, after 1945; and with Stonehouse, Inc, New Haven, Connecticut, 1960.

3. By John Opie, about 1782. Canvas painted for Mrs Holcroft. Eventually the painting passed to Dr Henry A. Miers, who owned it in 1911.

4. By John Opie, about 1798. Exhibited at the Royal Academy, 1798(?). Probably the picture sold at Christie's 18 July 1891 for five guineas, bought by Graves. Present location unknown.

5. By John Opie, 1804. Exhibited at the Royal Academy, 1804. Purchased by the National Portrait Gallery in 1878 from Kenney. Engravings by T. Blood published as frontispiece to Holcroft's *Memoirs* by Longman & Co, 1816; by T. Blood for Hazlitt's edition of *Holcroft's Diary*, 1816; and by T. Hodgetts (two states).

6. By George Romney. Bought at Christie's on 18 July 1891 (lot 83) for 30 guineas by Irving. Present location unknown.

7. Engraving by J. Condé. Published as a plate to *European Magazine*, 1792.

8. Engraving by S. Freeman, after E. Smith. Published by Longman & Co, 1806.

9. Engraving by W. Ridley, after S. Drummond. Published as a plate to the *Monthly Mirror*, 1799.

10. By unknown engraver. Published by B. Crosby, 1794.

Holden, Mr [fl. 1784], singer.

Mr Holden, from Birmingham, sang bass at the Handel Memorial Concerts at Westminster Abbey and the Pantheon in May and June 1784.

Holden, Miss [fl. 1660?–1662], actress.

Miss Holden was probably the daughter of the printer John Holden, who published Davenant's *Works* and to whom Thomas Betterton was once apprenticed. If so, that might explain her presence among the first actresses in Davenant's troupe at Lincoln's Inn Fields. Downes the prompter numbered her among the original actresses, at any rate, so we may guess she was in the company in 1660–61. The only role known to have been hers was "Count Paris's Wife" (Lady Montague?) in *Romeo and Juliet*, of which Downes wrote:

> Note, There being a Fight and Scuffle in the Play, between the House of *Capulet*, and House of *Paris*; Mrs. *Holden* Acting his Wife, enter'd in a *Hurry*, Crying O my Dear *Count*! She Inadvertently left out, O, in the pronuntiation of the Word *Count*! giving it a Vehement Accent, put the House into such a Laughter, that *London* Bridge at low-water was silence to it.

The play was performed on 1 March 1662 at Lincoln's Inn Fields, and perhaps that was the performance to which Downes referred.

Miss Holden (or Mrs Holden, as contemporary sources refer to her) probably left the stage after 1662, for we find no other notice of her. (But see Mrs Holten.)

Holdendael. *See* HELLENDAAL.

Holder, Joseph William 1765–1832, *organist, composer.*

Joseph William Holder was born in 1765 in the parish of St John, Clerkenwell. At the age of seven he became one of the children of the Chapel Royal under James Nares. During his years with Nares he assisted his master with the younger boys and played the organ. After seven years in the Chapel Royal, Holder returned to his father for two or three years, during which time he served as assistant organist to Reinhold at St George the Martyr, Queen Square.

Holder was then appointed organist of St Mary's Church, Bungay, Suffolk, where he lived for 17 or 18 years. While there he married the daughter of a local surgeon. After his stay in Suffolk he moved near Chelmsford, Essex, where he was living in 1823, when he supplied Sainsbury with the details of his musical career.

In 1792 Holder had received his bachelor's degree in music at Oxford and had been elected an honorary member of the Royal Society of Musicians. He became one of the examiners of potential members for that organization. He

By permission of the Trustees of the British Museum

JOSEPH WILLIAM HOLDER

engraving by Jones, after Woodin

was also elected an honorary associate of the Concentores Sodales. Holder forgot to mention that he had been a subscriber to the New Musical Fund; his name appears in the lists for 1794 and 1805, and he doubtless subscribed in other years and performed with the group in London. He wrote a number of anthems, glees, canons, songs, and piano pieces. According to Grove, Holder died in 1832.

The will of a Joseph William Holder has survived; the name and date seem right, but it is difficult to determine whether or not it is actually the will of our subject. The will was written on 16 February 1831; a codicil was added on 8 May 1832; and the will was proved on 8 December 1832. Holder gave his address as Burton Street, Burton Crescent, in the parish of St Pancras. He made no mention of a wife, who may have died before the will was written. To his nephew Joseph William Love he left £4000 in trust, the income from which Love was to use to provide an annuity for

Holder's sister, Sarah Lydia Love, widow. After his death the annuity was to go to Joseph William Love and his sister Charlotte Roberts Elizabeth Love. Joseph William Love was bequeathed the rest of the estate and appointed executor. In the codicil Holder directed that £500 should be given to Mary Ann Hough, the wife of Captain Henry Hough of the Artillery. (Holder the musician in his autobiographical letter to Sainsbury referred to a musical amateur friend, Major John Lemon of the Royal Horse Guards, so we know that he had military connections.)

A portrait of Holder was engraved by Jones, after Woodin; private plate, no date. It was published by G. E. Madeley.

Holder, William [fl. 1674–1677], singer.

William Holder was one of the Children of the Chapel Royal under John Blow in 1674. From 18 May to 3 September of that year Master Holder earned 3s. daily for attending the King at Windsor. By 1 April 1675 his voice had changed, and the Lord Chamberlain's accounts began referring to him as a former Chapel boy. As late as September 1677 he was still receiving the traditional grant of clothing for boys who had left the Chapel. Holder may have been the son of Dr William Holder, subdean of the Chapel Royal in 1674, but the elder Holder was born in 1616, married in 1643, and made no mention of a son William in his will written on 26 June 1694.

Holicourt. See BALICOURT.

Holiday, Mr [fl. 1791], actor.

At the Haymarket Theatre on 24 October 1791 Mr Holiday played Lord Dupe in *Taste*.

Holiday, Miss. See MILLS, MRS WILLIAM THE SECOND.

Holinds, Mr [fl. 1799], puppeteer.

According to the Pie Powder Court Book at the Guildhall Library, Mr Holinds exhibited puppets at Bartholomew Fair in 1799.

Holladay, Miss. See MILLS, MRS WILLIAM THE SECOND.

Holland, Mr [fl. 1740], performer?

The London Stage indicates that a Mr Holland shared in benefit tickets at Covent Garden Theatre on 29 May 1740.

Holland, Mr [fl. 1782–1785], actor.

A Mr Holland acted Richmond in *Richard III* and Squire Badger in *Don Quixote in England* at the Haymarket Theatre on 4 March 1782 for the benefit of Mrs Lefevre. He played a principal character in *The Fair Refugee* at the same theatre on 10 February 1785.

This performer may have been one of several performers of that name who were often seen in the provinces—perhaps William Holland, who made his debut at Smock Alley Theatre, Dublin, on 10 January 1772. A Holland was with Roger Kemble's company at Worcester in 1772. Hugh Holland (1732–1792) and his wife Margaret (1732–1820) were principal performers at the Norwich Theatre between 1765 and 1786. An actor named Holland performed Oroonoko for his debut at Ipswich on 31 December 1789, then played at Norwich in 1790, at Edinburgh in 1792, and at Smock Alley, Dublin, in 1794.

Holland, Mr [fl. 1796], actor.

A Mr Holland acted the role of Watchall (for the first time) in *A New Way to Pay Old Debts* at Covent Garden Theatre on 19 April 1796.

Holland, Mrs [fl. 1728], singer.

A Mrs Holland's name was given in the 1728 edition of *Penelope* as playing Doll in that new dramatic opera when it was produced at the Haymarket Theatre on 8 and 9 May 1728.

Holland, Master [fl. 1785], dancer.

A Master Holland appeared in a new dance *The Sailor's Return* at the Royal Circus on 21 October 1785. On the same night Jack Holland, no doubt his father, performed in *A New Jockey Race*.

Holland, Miss [fl. 1764?–1777], actress.

A Miss Holland acted Mrs Strictland in a performance of *The Suspicious Husband* at the China Hall Theatre, Rotherhithe, on 23 June 1777. Perhaps she was the Miss Holland who, billed as a "Young Gentlewoman," had made her debut at Crow Street Theatre, Dublin, on 29 December 1764 as Hero in *Much Ado about Nothing*; her name was printed as Miss Holland in the bills for her third appearance in that role on 24 January 1765.

Holland, Miss [*fl. 1800*], *singer.*

A Miss Holland, announced as making her first appearance, sang in the new oratorio *Britannia* at Covent Garden Theatre on 16 June 1800. She had been recruited at short notice as a substitute for Miss Tennant, who evidently was ill.

Holland, Charles *1733–1769, actor, manager.*

Charles Holland was born on 12 March 1733 and was baptized at Chiswick Church the following 3 April, the son of a baker of that parish, John Holland (1697–1764), and his wife Sarah (d. 1778). After completing an apprenticeship with a turpentine merchant in Old Street (Ealing?), to whom he had been bound at the age of 14, and having enjoyed

Harvard Theatre Collection

CHARLES HOLLAND

engraving by J. S. Müller

some success in private theatricals, Holland applied to David Garrick, who it is said gave him "good encouragement and good advice." Announced as "A Young Gentleman," Holland made his debut at Drury Lane on 13 October 1755 as Oroonoko with a cast that included Mrs Cibber as Imoinda, Palmer as Blanford, Yates as Daniel, and Edmund Burton as the Governor. The novice "perform'd very well & had great applause," reported the prompter Richard Cross in his diary, until the last scene, when in attempting to stab the Governor he struck Burton on the cheek and "upon hearing him cry, O God! was so shocked that he did not die so well as was expected—Burton was taken off, & dress'd by Mr Bromfield, who was accidentally behind the Scenes."

After two more performances of *Oroonoko* on 14 and 16 October, Holland acted Dorilas in *Merope* on the twenty-eighth "to great applause." He repeated both roles several times in November and December, and then on 1 January 1756 he played his third character, George Barnwell in *The London Merchant*. His other roles in his first season at Drury Lane included Florizel in Garrick's alteration of *The Winter's Tale* for the first time on 21 January and Hamlet for the first time at his benefit on 20 April, when tickets could be had of him at his lodgings with a peruke maker opposite Cecil Street in the Strand. On the latter night, when the benefit brought him £270 (less house charges of £65), he had another accident but this time displayed more control. While Holland was speaking his first lines to the Ghost, his hat fell off at the sight of the spectre, as was traditional in the scene. An "Ignorant Man" seated on the stage (as was also the custom at benefits at that time) "took up his hat & clapt it upon [Holland's] head," wrote Cross in his diary; "Holland unconcern'd play'ed with it so, & went off with it, (great Prudence)." (In his *Memoirs*, Tate Wilkinson embellished this event, claiming that the helpful spectator was a woman friend of Holland, who placed the hat on his head when Hamlet complained of the cold biting air.) He also acted Chamont in *The Orphan* for Burton's benefit on 29 April. In the character of the Genius of England he had spoken the prologue at the premiere of *Athelstan* on 27 February 1756, although he did not play a role in that tragedy.

Holland was attached to Drury Lane for the

remainder of his 15 years on the London stage. He continued to enjoy a warm friendship with Garrick upon whose acting he had modeled himself to the extent that he was called by one critic a "shadow" of the great actor. With a handsome, manly figure and a deep-toned voice, Holland's abilities improved with experience, although he could never be regarded as a truly superior performer. Among his numerous capital roles (with date of first performance) were Jaffeir in *Venice Preserv'd* on 26 April 1757, Romeo on 28 April 1757, Essex in *The Earl of Essex* on 1 June 1758, Tancred in *Tancred and Sigismunda* on 19 April 1759, Douglas on 11 January 1760, Richard III on 1 May 1760, Young Bevil in *The Conscious Lovers* on 30 December 1760, Pierre in *Venice Preserv'd* on 20 October 1762, Macbeth on 17 March 1763, Horatius in *The Roman Father* on 27 March 1764, and Iago in *Othello* on 19 March 1765.

His original parts included Rhesus in *Agis* on 21 February 1758, Hamet in *The Orphan of China* on 21 April 1759, Colonel Medway in *The Discovery* on 3 February 1763, Sir John Melvil in *The Clandestine Marriage* on 20 February 1766, Moody in Garrick's *The Country Girl* (an adaptation of *The Country Wife*) on 25 October 1766, the title role in *The Earl of Warwick* on 13 December 1766, General Melmoth in *The Widow'd Wife* on 5 December 1767, Colonel Rivers in *False Delicacy* on 23 January 1768, Teribazus in *Zenobia* on 27 February 1768, Timur in *Zingis* on 17 December 1768, and Sir William Evans in *The School for Rakes* on 4 February 1769.

Holland's repertoire consisted of dozens of additional leading and supporting roles, among which were Ferdinand in *The Tempest*, Charles in *The Busy Body*, Thyreus in *Antony and Cleopatra*, Young Knowell in *Every Man in His Humour*, Clerimont in *The Double Gallant*, Titus in *The Siege of Aquileia*, Altamont in *The Fair Penitent*, Jachimo in *Cymbeline*, Hotspur in *1 Henry IV*, Carlos in *Love Makes a Man*, Osmyn in *The Mourning Bride*, Osman in *Zara*, Achmet in *Barbarossa*, Don Pedro in *Elvira*, Oakly in *The Jealous Wife*, Hastings in *Jane Shore*, and Bajazet in *Tamerlane*. In 1768–69, his last full season at Drury Lane, Holland acted, in addition to some of the roles already mentioned, Dorilant in *The School for Lovers*, Zanga in *The Revenge*, Lovemore in *The Way to Keep Him*, the title role in *The Plain Dealer*,

Lothario in *The Fair Penitent*, and Prospero in *The Tempest* (for the first time on 16 March 1769).

According to Francis Gentleman in *The Theatres* (1772), Garrick had kept Holland at a "poor, penurious pittance" in the earlier years of his career. Davies in his biography of *John Henderson* (1778) claimed that Holland "acted all the principal characters in tragedy, five years successively, under £5 per week," but after Garrick was obliged to pay his new star William Powell from £10 to £12 per week in his second season (after paying him only 50 shillings per week in his first season, 1763–64), it was necessary to put Holland on the same footing. Holland's salary in 1766–67, the only season for which a Drury Lane paylist is available during those years, was £12 per week. His benefit receipts, though not spectacular, were consistently respectable: £150 on 26 April 1757, when his address was No 17, New Crown Court, Bow Street; £200 on 22 April 1758; and £170 on 19 April 1759, when he lodged next door to the Bedford Arms, in the Piazza, Covent Garden. All figures are presumably less about £65 for house charges; receipts for subsequent years are not known. In 1766, according to the Fund Book in the Folger Library, Holland had subscribed £2 2s. to the Drury Lane Fund, but he died before it was formally established.

Relatively few summer excursions to provincial theatres are known for Holland in his earlier years. In the spring of 1757 he went north to act at the New Concert Hall in Edinburgh, where he was seen that summer in such roles as Constant in *The Provok'd Wife*, Dolabella in *All for Love*, Gifford in *The Albion Queens*, Laertes in *Hamlet*, and Phoenix in *The Distrest Mother*. He returned to Edinburgh in the spring of 1758. He acted at Birmingham in 1762 along with Jane Pope and Thomas King; on 18 June 1762 he wrote to Garrick that the Birmingham summer was going "prodigiously well." He was at Bath for a while in 1762–63. For playing at Smock Alley, Dublin, in the summer of 1763 he received £100 for ten nights, plus a benefit, according to one press notice, and £150 for 12 nights, according to another.

About the winter of 1768, Holland became involved in a scheme with Thomas King and George Garrick to buy James Lacy's share of the Drury Lane patent. Holland raised £15,000 from his friends, but Lacy suddenly decided not to retire.

Several years earlier, however, in the autumn of 1766 Holland had begun to negotiate for a share in the lease of the new King Street Theatre in Bristol. Since its opening on 30 May 1766, the Bristol theatre had been managed by John Arthur, Matthew Clarke, and William Powell. But Arthur's "insolence and tyranny" caused him to be driven from the triumvirate, and Holland was nominated in his place. On 6 September 1766 Powell wrote to Garrick that the proprietors had permitted him to take Holland, his Drury Lane colleague and very dear friend, into the management. Although it was not until 28 August 1767 that Holland, Powell, and Clarke signed a retroactive seven-year lease at a rent of £450 for each of the first two years and £300 a year thereafter, Holland had begun his association with the Bristol theatre earlier that summer.

Holland and Powell were a powerful acting team at Bristol and their performances for two summers drew enthusiastic praise, with Holland being commended for a voice "the most manly, and at the same Time the most harmonious . . . that ever pleased the public ear," nor was he criticized for the rant and exagger-

Harvard Theatre Collection

CHARLES HOLLAND
engraving by J. R. Smith

ated effects which were reported to mar his London performances. They also enjoyed financial success their first two summers, 1767 and 1768, but early in their third season, on 3 July 1769, William Powell succumbed to pneumonia at the age of 34. He died at seven in the evening, just before the performance of *Richard III* was to begin; upon hearing of the death, Holland broke down and had to apologize to the audience for his inability to go on. Within six months, Bristol would suffer a second tragic loss by the death of Holland himself.

Holland began the 1769–70 season at Drury Lane by playing Hamlet on 19 September. On 20 November 1769, during his last performance as Prospero, it is said that Holland was greatly shocked by a large rat which ran across the stage. That trauma was compounded by his having discovered earlier in the evening that he had been talking with a person who had just left a small-pox patient. Holland, who had intended for several years to be inoculated but could never work up the resolution, had indeed caught the disease. Bills were printed for his appearance in *Zingis* on 27 November, but *Amphitryon* was substituted. The prompter Cross entered in his diary on that date: "Mr Holland Ill, Small Pox." Stricken blind and attended by eminent physicians provided by Garrick, he died ten days later in his house in Cecil Street, the Strand, about four in the morning of 7 December 1769, at the age of 36.

The burial of Holland in his family vault at St Nicholas, Chiswick, on 15 December 1769 was attended by a large representation of London actors, including Samuel Foote, who despite his warm friendship with the deceased could not forbear quipping that he had seen Holland "shoved into the family oven," a joke which alluded to the trade of Holland's father and to the fact that the family mausoleum looked like an oven. Garrick, however, was suffering from a severe attack of the stone, so he could not be one of the bearers; on the day before the funeral he wrote to the Reverend Evan Lloyd, "Poor Holland has dy'd much lamented, & is to be bury'd tomorrow—I am too bad to attend the doleful Ceremony." (Garrick did not perform until two weeks later, on 28 December, as Sir John Brute.) An inscription was placed on Holland's tombstone in the

church yard (where Hogarth and De Loutherbourg are also buried) reading:

In a Vault under this Stone
Lieth the Body of
Mr. Charles Holland
Late of Drury Lane Theatre
Of Whose Character and Abilities
David Garrick, Esqr. has given Testimony
On a Monument Erected to his Memory
In the Chancel of the Church by Permission
Of His Grace the Duke of Devonshire

The monument referred to originally occupied a place on the north wall of the chancel
but was later moved to a place high on the
north tower wall beneath the belfry. In the
form of a pyramid, with a bust in front, on a
medallion, the monument bears Garrick's inscription (of which manuscript versions in
Garrick's hand are in the Harvard Theatre Collection):

If Talents
to make entertainment instructive
to support the credit of the Stage
by just and manly Action
If to adorn Society
by Virtues
which would honour any Rank and
Profession
deserve remembrance
Let Him with whom these Talents were long
exerted
To whom these Virtues were well known
And by whom the loss of them will be long
lamented
bear Testimony to the Worth and Abilities
of his departed Friend
Charles Holland
who was born March 12, 1733
dy'd December 7, 1769
and was buried near this place.
                                        D. Garrick

Three elegies for Holland were published by
versifiers in the *St James's Chronicle* on 21 December 1769, one of which, signed "Bristo-
liensis," lamented that eyes scarce dry over the
latterly-wept Powell should now weep again
over Holland.

The specifications for Holland's interment
had been directed in his will drawn on 6 December 1769, the day before he died. He asked
his executors James Madden of "Craggs Court
the Strand" and George Garrick (David's

brother) of "Somerset Stableyard the Strand"
to purchase the "piece of Ground in the Chiswick Church Yard and that they do build a
vault wherein I may be interred and I do earnestly desire that my poor deceased ffather may
be removed from the place wherein he lies unto
the said vault and that the same do belong to
the ffamily." Further he beseeched his "good
ffriend David Garrick . . . to make an Inscription of a few decent lines upon my Tomb Stone
as the last token of his regard for me."

Holland made small bequests to his friends
"as a Mark of My affection and Great Regard"
including: his "gold headed cane" to Samuel
Foote, his "Best Diamond Ring" to David
Garrick, £30 to James Madden, and his "other
Diamond Ring and the Sum of Twenty
pounds" to George Garrick. The residue of his
estate, unspecified in the will but later reported to have been from £5000 to £6000, he
left to his mother Sarah and his brothers John
and Thomas Holland. Holland also directed
his executors to make "strict Inquiry whether
Harry fforand Son of [blank] fforand Spinster"
who was thought to be his son ("but of which
I am doubtfull") really was. Should they be
satisfied of the truth of the claim they were to
place £200 in trust for the boy until his majority and "pay the Interest thereof towards his
Maintenance."

Evidently Holland had never married, although at one time he was engaged to the
actress Jane Pope. She discovered him, however, in a boat on the river at Richmond with
another actress—that "seductive piece of mischief" Sophia Baddeley, and when Holland
would not apologize or explain, Miss Pope
never spoke another word to him except on the
stage.

The well-proportioned, athletic, and handsome Holland was indeed something of a gallant. Among the chief of his amours was a Mrs
K. Earle, who had "strongly excited" his curiosity by sending him numerous letters signed
"Leonora." After he met her under bizarre circumstances through the machinations of her
confidante, they "came to a perfect understanding and were so well pleased with each
other that the lady moved to a house in Arundel Street in order to be able to carry out her
affair with convenience. In 1765 her husband
William Earle brought charges of criminal

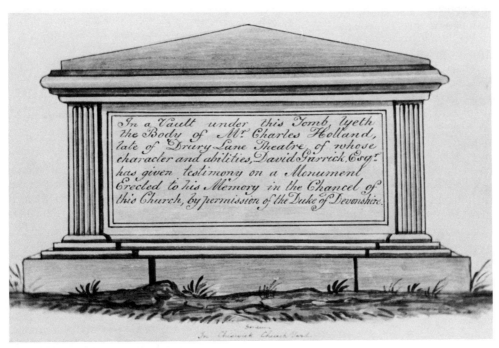

In a Vault under this Tomb, lyeth the Body of Mr Charles Holland, late of Drury Lane Theatre, of whose character and abilities, David Garrick, Esqr. has given testimony on a Monument Erected to his Memory in the Chancel of this Church, by permission of the Duke of Devonshire.

Harvard Theatre Collection

Monument to CHARLES HOLLAND
artist unknown

conversation against Holland, who was fortunate enough to escape with a judgment of only £50 against him. It was said that the whole event had been engineered by Earle himself, with the aid of the confidante Mrs Gilbert, in order to get rid of his wife without refunding her considerable fortune. (Details of the case may be found in *Trials for Adultery* [1779], Ryan's *Table Talk*, and the *Town and Country Magazine* of December 1769.) In 1768 Holland had begun his affair with Sophia Baddeley, and "under a pretence of being privately instructed by him" in acting, she used to call at his lodgings three or four times a week. Although it was said that she was deeply disturbed by Holland's death, one of his physicians, Dr. Hayes, quickly assumed his place in her affections.

A number of Charles's relatives are buried with him in the family vault at St Nicholas. His father had died in 1764, his mother in 1778. His brother John died in 1789, unmar-

ried. His other brother Thomas, born in 1725, died on 27 February 1793. Thomas Holland had three sons and a daughter by his wife Sarah (d. 1795): the first son Charles (1768–1849), like his namesake uncle, became an actor at Drury Lane and is entered separately in this dictionary; the second son, Thomas, became a wine merchant and died unmarried in 1841; the third, John Henry Holland, was born in 1775, followed a military career, and died unmarried in 1865 at the age of 90; the daughter Elizabeth, born in 1771, married the eminent surgeon Joseph Constantine Carpue and had six unmarried daughters. The scene painter John Joseph Holland, who worked in the London theatres in the 1790s and then in America, does not seem to have been related to Charles Holland's family.

In private life, despite his weakness for the flattery of women, Holland was neither conspicuous for his vices nor remarkable for his virtues. Garrick spoke of him warmly. Other contemporaries praised him as being "free, good, natural, cheerful, and generous," as well as sober, firm in his attachments, and punctual in paying his debts.

Holland was devoted to his profession. He was often accused of being an imitator of his master—Garrick "taught him," wrote Gentleman in *The Theatres*, "and by teaching spoil'd." But when the manager made his grand tour from 1763 to 1765, Holland took over such capital roles as Hamlet, Chamont, Hastings, and Tancred, in all of which he enjoyed success. *The Theatrical Review* of 1757–58 placed him immediately after Garrick, "as the shadow follows the body:"

. . . he has all the merit a copy can pretend to; his face and voice are not disagreeable; and he cannot fail of being an actor of note, when a little more experience shall have given him the command of both; he may then please in his own right; but at present his deportment is faulty, it wants freedom; but that may be easily remedied by observation, fencing, dancing, &c.

About the same time another critic wrote that despite the heavy stamp of Garrick upon him, in his own right

. . . this performer has genius . . . Holland, upon the whole, is always perfect; he knows what he is about; he can taste the essence of a part. . . . We have beheld him daily improve. He performed Hamlet in a manner that merited the approbation with which he was received. There is a great tenderness in his Dorilas; and I think he must cut a very good figure in a serious cast in Comedy. His figure is agreeable; his features well-proportioned, and pleasingly disposed. Some tones of his voice, which is not strong, remind us of that of Mr. Garrick, which it resembles. . . .

In his *Musical Tour*, Dibdin claimed that although Holland lacked a liberal education (Tom Davies wrote that he was illiterate), his intellect was of a "strong, clear, and decided kind" that served him well in artistic decisions. He was, according to Kirkman in his memoirs of Macklin, if not originally excellent, "one of the best copies of excellence."

In their *Thespis* (1767) and *Rosciad* (1761), Kelly and Churchill, respectively, were harshly critical of Holland, the former labeling him "sententious, dull, and heavy," the latter writing:

Next Holland came—with truly tragic stalk,
He creeps, he flies—a hero should not walk.
As if with Heaven he warr'd his eager eyes
Planted their batteries against the skies.
Attitude, action, air, pause, start, sigh, groan,
He borrowed, and made use of as his own.
The actor who would hold a solid fame,
Must imitation's servile arts disclaim:
Act from himself, on his own bottom stand;
I hate e'en Garrick thus at second-hand.

Against Gentleman's assertion in his *Dramatic Censor* that as Iago Holland was "hunting after a meaning he never found" must be measured Sylas Neville's opinion, entered in his *Diary* on 31 October 1767, that "Holland is the best Iago we have." According to Hopkins's notations in his prompter's diaries, Lovemore in *The Way to Keep Him* was "a character in no way proper to Mr Holland" (3 January 1764); Hopkins could not "say much" for him as Don Carlos in *The Mistake* (14 January 1764), and when Holland played Oakly in *The Jealous Wife* (12 October 1764) the prompter recorded that he was "coolly received." His Romeo, at least, was praised by an enthusiastic correspondent to the *Public Advertiser* on 6 January 1766; signing himself "G. F. Theatricus," he reported his delight at seeing Holland's performance as Romeo on 23 December 1765: "I never saw Garrick himself in that part with more pleasure. He was admirable throughout the whole play, but more so in that last act, where he receives the news of Juliet's death. The sudden surprise and strong passions of grief were worked up with the utmost propriety in his face."

Tate Wilkinson eulogized Holland as "a shining ornament, and an honest, truly agreeable man, [who] was universally beloved, but death snatched him in the bloom of life and improvement, and deprived the stage of an actor of merit and a worthy character."

A portrait of Holland, attributed as a copy after Hugh Barron, is in the Garrick Club and is similar to the engraved portrait of him by J. R. Smith, after "H. B.", which was published by the engraver in 1771. A watercolor drawing of Holland by an unknown artist is in the Harvard Theatre Collection, as is an engraved portrait by J. S. Müller. Engraved pictures of his tombstone and the monument at Chiswick are also in the Harvard Theatre Collection. A miniature of Holland by J. Hutchinson, 1760, is in the National Portrait Gallery.

Holland, Charles   *1768–1849,   actor, manager.*

Charles Holland was born in 1768, probably at Chiswick, and was the son of Thomas Holland (1725–1793) and his wife Sarah (d. 1795). He had two brothers: Thomas, a wine merchant who died unmarried in 1841, and John Henry (1775–1865), who followed a military career. His sister Elizabeth, born in 1771, married the eminent surgeon Joseph Constantine Carpue. Charles's uncle was the well-known actor Charles Holland (1733–1769), friend of Garrick and performer at Drury Lane between 1755 and 1769, but the nephew never saw him act.

Adopting the pseudonym of Harford, the younger Holland made his debut on the stage at Bath, as Pierre in *Venice Preserv'd*, on 4 January 1791. Possibly he was the Holland who acted at Edinburgh in 1791–92 and at Liverpool in June 1792. Using his own name, Holland made his second appearance at Bath on 19 June 1792 and played at Bristol in 1792–93. Probably he was the Holland who acted at the Theatre Royal, Edinburgh, in the first half of 1795, playing such roles as Antonio in *The Merchant of Venice*, Frederick in *The Jew*, Earl Osmond in *Tancred and Sigismunda*, Jemmy in *Auld Robin Gray*, and Sir Charles Freeman in *The Stratagem*.

On 31 October 1796 Charles Holland made his first appearance in London at Drury Lane Theatre in the modest role of Marcellus in *Hamlet*. The press reported that he had "a very genteel figure, with a voice of good tone and distinct articulation" and that he had performed on the provincial stages "with much credit." After playing Marcellus again on 7 November, he was the Duke of Norfolk in *Richard III* on the ninth, Marcellus again on the twenty-first, and then Trueman in *The London Merchant* on the twenty-eighth. One critic, who also provided the information that Holland was from the Margate Theatre, regretted that the young actor had not been allowed to play Barnwell (acted by C. Kemble) instead of Trueman. After being put on the paylist at 6s. 8d. per day on 5 November and being paid £10 10s. on account on 7 December 1796, Holland was seen during the remainder of that season as Heli in *The Mourning Bride*, Aranthes in *Theodosius*, the Prince of Tanais in *Tamerlane*, Aviragus in *Cymbeline*, a Greek Herald in *The Grecian Daughter*, Ross in *Macbeth*, Jaques de Boys in *As You Like It*, the Sea Captain in *Twelfth Night*, and Don Manuel in *Love Makes a Man*.

In the summer of 1797 Holland went to Richmond for seasoning. An undated letter from him, now in the Enthoven Collection, was written during Holland's summer at Richmond. No addressee is noted on the letter, but evidently it was written to a provincial manager in hopes of getting better roles for a subsequent summer engagement:

I have played Macbeth, Richard, Irwin and two or three more of the characters I mentioned to you in the *Richmond Theatre*, and as Mr Cory's engagement is not likely to take place I hoped no objection would be made to the cast of characters I have given you. My only motive for attempting characters of that importance is the hope of improvement in acting, my benefit would be equally goo[d] were

Harvard Theatre Collection

CHARLES HOLLAND (1768–1849) as Duke Alberti

artist unknown

you to give me the worst of parts. I should be glad to be with you for a month, will you then be kind enough to let me know what parts you wish me to play.

Earning a salary of £2 per week in his second season, 1797–98, at Drury Lane, Holland did not find his assignments much upgraded, for he played some of the roles of his previous season and added to his repertoire Sanchio in *Rule a Wife and Have A Wife*, Mr Blandish in *The Heiress*, the Nephew in *The Irish Widow*, Baron de Courcy in *The Haunted Tower*, Mr Harlow in *The Old Maid*, Montano in *Othello*, a Brother in *Comus*, Sir Walter Blunt in *1 Henry IV*, Salarino in *The Merchant of Venice*, Leroches in *The Countess of Salisbury*, Belmour in *Jane Shore*, Hewit in *Hannah Hewit*, Sir Henry Loveit in *Know Your Own Mind*, Don Pedro in *Much Ado about Nothing*, and Spondee in *The Ugly Club*. On 16 October 1797 he acted the important role of Horatio in *Hamlet*, a part he played several more times that season and then regularly when that play was given in subsequent years.

During his next two seasons at Drury Lane, when he earned £3 per week, Holland continued as a utility actor in his familiar line, to which he added Kenrick in *The Castle Spectre*, the Count in *The Outlaws*, Lord Randolph in *Douglas*, the Count of Montval in *The Castle of Montval*, Gayless in *The Lying Valet*, Captain Beverly in *The Embarkation*, Courtal in *The Belle's Stratagem*, Colonel Townley in *A Trip to Scarborough*, and Hastings in *She Stoops to Conquer*. He played Count Wintersen in *The Stranger* on 15 September 1798 and was the original Centinel in *Pizarro* on 24 May 1799. Upon Charles Kemble's illness Holland replaced him in the role of Alonzo in *Pizarro*. On 26 February 1800 he acted Cassio in *Othello* for the first time.

Holland reengaged with Drury Lane for five years beginning September 1800, at a salary of £4 per week the first year, £5 the second, and £6 the final three. In an undated letter now in the Enthoven Collection, probably sent sometime in 1800–1801 to the Drury Lane treasurer Peake, he revealed he was suffering financial difficulties:

Pray oblige me in what I am going to ask you. I shall ever esteem it a favor for I have had losses of late [gambling?] which have much embarassed me. There will be three weeks salary due to me next Saturday—besides the arrears of last season and the Fourteen Pounds the first season I came to the Theatre. I have (as you know) been obliged to borrow small sums of my friends. I have promised to pay part of what I owe immediately. *I only ask you for the three weeks which will be due next Saturday.* Such a sum as Twelve Pounds can be of little importance to the Theatre but it is to me of *the greatest consequence.* I hope I shall some time or other have an opportunity of repaying the obligation.

Holland's tenure at Drury Lane was uninterrupted until his retirement in 1821 (from 1796–97 he had subscribed to the Drury Lane Fund). Between 1809–10 and 1811–12 he acted with the Drury Lane company at the Lyceum while their new theatre was being built, and when it opened on 10 October 1812 he was Horatio to Elliston's Hamlet. His salary was £10 per week in 1812–13, £11 by 1814–15, £12 in 1815–17, £13 in 1818–19, and £14 in 1819–20.

At the Haymarket Theatre he made his first appearance as Steinfort in *The Stranger* on 6 June 1809, and there on 25 July 1810 he was the original Henry Mortimer in *High Life in the City*. In the summer of 1811 he became comanager of the Brighton Theatre, where he had acted in previous seasons.

A casting book for Drury Lane, dating from about 1815 and now in the Folger Library, lists 46 roles for Holland, showing continuing subordinate service, mostly in unimportant plays. Later he played York to Kean's Richard II, Buckingham to his Richard III, and Gloucester to his Lear. He was the original Infirmier in *Julian and Agnes*, Hassam in *The Bride of Abydos*, Mendizabel in *Manuel*, the Earl of Angus in *Flodden Field*, and Cedric in *The Hebrew* (Soane's adaptation of *Ivanhoe*). Sometime in 1819–20 he wrote to Russell, Elliston's assistant in the management of Drury Lane (letter in the Folger Library), that he wished "to be retired from the Walking Gentleman in Farces Dumb Lords and attendants in Tragedies" and requested "to act only such parts as Banquo—King Henry—Reinhold. . . ."

According to Gilliland, Holland had a refined education but suffered from a "delicacy of nerve" that hampered his success. In October 1807, he was described by the press as "a very respectable actor, and a gentleman." Although he had good looks and some elegance, Holland seems to have deserved Winston's opinion that he was "of very moderate talent."

After 1820–21, Holland retired from the stage to become a gentleman farmer. He died in 1849, probably at Chiswick. According to information about the Holland family found in *Notes and Queries*, 3 May 1890, Charles had been married but had no children.

Holland was depicted as Duke Alberti in *The Peasant Boy* in an anonymous engraving published by West in 1811 and as Buckingham in *Richard III* in an undated engraving by an unknown artist.

Holland, John [fl. 1769–1796], dancer, ballet master, equestrian, actor.

In 1769 the child John Holland was a pupil of the Drury Lane dancing master Peter D'Egville. On 19 October of that year Peter D'Egville signed an agreement with Thomas King, then manager and director of Sadler's Wells Theatre, "for and in behalf of himself and his five pupils namely John Holland, Richard Scriven, Mary Ross, Elizabeth Armstrong, & Harriet Medlicot," who were to receive jointly £175 for dancing "as often as required" and were not to dance anywhere else except the Theatres Royal in London without consent of King.

Master Holland's performances at Sadler's Wells are unknown to us, but he did dance at Drury Lane on 21 November 1772 with Elizabeth Armstrong in a minuet and allemande, at which time they were still scholars of D'Egville. On 25 March 1773 he appeared with D'Egville and Miss Holland in a comic dance, and on 1 April, that threesome and Mary Ross, along with other unnamed pupils, performed in a new dance called *The Surprize*.

In the following season Master Holland and Miss Armstrong danced at the King's Theatre on 28 April and 12 May 1774. In 1774–75 D'Egville took them to Covent Garden where Master Holland appeared in *The Provençale* on 28 September 1774, in the dances of *The Druids*, beginning on 19 November, and in a program of minuets, allemandes, and cotillions on 26 May 1775. At the same house the next season he danced a new comic dance on 18 November 1775, *La Soirée à-la-mode* on 7

December, and in the new dances *The Academy* and *The Humours of the Newmarket Races* on 3 May 1776, for the benefit of D'Egville.

After performing at Bristol in the summer of 1776, Master Holland returned to London where he danced at Drury Lane in a minuet and allemande with Miss Armstrong between 3 April and 2 May 1777. Except for a performance at Drury Lane in a *Minuet de la Cour* on 6 November 1777, Master Holland was engaged at Covent Garden for the next three seasons, through 1779–80, performing in similar dances. He was probably the Master Holland who danced a hornpipe at the Haymarket on 18 March 1782, at which time he was identified as a student of Mr Holloway, the ballet master of Covent Garden Theatre.

In 1779–80, his name appeared in the Covent Garden bills sometimes as Master Holland and sometimes as Mr Holland (judging from the titles of the dances, we believe that the same person was involved). As Mr Holland, he danced with D'Egville, Miss Vallois, Miss Matthews, and Langrish in *The Dockyard* on 22 September 1779 and throughout the season. On 18 May 1781 at Covent Garden he appeared in a *Minuet de la Cour en Quatre* with Holloway, Miss Francis, and Miss Matthews, and in *The Humours of New-Market, with the Pony Races*. We next find him on the bills on 21 October 1785 at the Royal Circus playing the Wildman in *A New Jockey Race*. On that evening, a Master Holland, probably his young son, danced in *The Sailor's Return*.

By 1785, Holland was established at the Royal Circus as the ballet master and a principal dancer on the stage and horse. That year, named often in the advertisements as Jack Holland, he appeared in *The Padlock*, *The Garland*, as Harlequin in *The Defeated Harlequin*, and in feats of horsemanship performed with Jones and the Little Devil. In the spring of 1786, he appeared in *The Cricketteers*, a new dance of his composition. He was most likely the Mr Holland who danced at Smock Alley Theatre, Dublin, in 1786–87.

At the Royalty Theatre, London, in 1787–88, Holland danced in *Don Juan; or, The Libertine Destroyed* on 31 October 1787, in *Harlequin Mungo* in November, and in *The Merry Sailors* and *The Deserter of Naples* in January and February 1788. Whn Holland danced with

Miss Bithmere in *The Cobler Outwitted* on 12 May 1788 at Sadler's Wells, they were both advertised as making their first appearances at that theatre; but in the case of Holland, at least, who had danced there when a child, the announcement was incorrect or was intended to indicate his adult debut there. At the Wells on 7 June 1788 he danced with Dubois, Miss Bithmere, and others in *Love and Opportunity*. Advertised as from Sadler's Wells, Holland performed at Norwich in the early months of 1789 and 1790.

Between 1789 and 1796 he was to be found regularly at the Royal Circus in the summers and between 1792–93 and 1795–96 regularly at Covent Garden in the winters. At the latter house he appeared in such pieces as *The Governor* and *The Sailor's Festival* in 1792–93, *Harlequin and Faustus* and *Oscar and Malvina* in 1793–94, *Windsor Castle* and *The Tythe Pig* in 1794–95, and *The Shipwreck* and *Harlequin's Treasure* in 1795–96. He may have been the Mr Holland who acted Watchal in *A New Way to Pay Old Debts* on 19 April 1796, but possibly that person was one of the several provincial actors of that name. Holland's salary at Covent Garden in 1793–94 was £2 per week. According to *The Oracle* of 21 April 1796 Holland was to be appointed ballet master at Covent Garden to succeed Byrn, who was bound for America, but we have not found his name in the bills for the rest of the century.

The actor Charles Holland (1768–1849), who began to play at Covent Garden in 1796 while John Holland was still employed there, does not seem to have been related to John. The *Oxford Companion to the Theatre* states that the American actor George Holland (1791–1870) was the son of a London dancing master, so possibly our subject was his father, but we find no evidence.

Holland, John [*fl.* 1770–1777], proprietor.

In 1770 Islington Spa was taken over by John Holland and became popular as an afternoon tea garden. Although the *Sunday Rambler* styled the Spa genteel during this period, it would seem, judging from Colman's farce *The Spleen; or, Islington Spa*, that its clientele consisted largely of publicans and tradesmen. Holland became bankrupt in 1777.

Holland, John Joseph *c.* 1776–1820, scene painter, landscape artist, architect, decorator, manager, actor.

John Joseph Holland was born in London about 1776, but nothing is known of his parentage. Possibly he was related to the "John Holland, Herald Painter, Deceased," whose will was proved under the authority of the Archbishop of Canterbury in 1760. According to William Dunlap, the American manager who later became his friend, young Holland was neglected by his father but at the age of nine taken in as a pupil by Gaetano Marinari, chief scene painter at the King's Theatre. Marinari trained him in architecture and scene painting; in his leisure time Holland taught himself landscape painting.

Presumably Holland assisted Marinari at the King's Theatre. After completing his apprenticeship he was employed by Covent Garden Theatre from 2 August 1794 to 23 February 1795 for 7*s*. 6*d*. a day. His name was on the bills there as one of the assistant painters for the pantomime *Mago and Dago*, which opened on 26 December 1794, and he must have worked on other productions.

Soon Holland returned to the King's Theatre, where Thomas Wignell discovered him in 1796 and engaged him for the Chestnut Street Theatre in Philadelphia. Holland was in America by the autumn of 1796 and served for nine years as assistant to C. Milbourne at Chestnut Street, during which time he also appeared on stage as a harlequin. In 1805–6 he replaced Milbourne as head scene painter, a position he then held until 1807.

In 1797 Holland was also employed to rebuild and decorate the Greenwich Street Theatre in New York as a summer playhouse. Thomas Abthorpe Cooper engaged him to direct the alterations and decorations of the Park Theatre in the summer of 1807, thereby offending that theatre's scene designer Charles Ciceri, who resigned. The refurbished Park was described by the *New York Evening Post* on 28 August 1807 as having "more of taste, grandeur, room, convenience and elegance tha any one in the United States." Holland stayed on at the Park as chief designer until 1813. Then he became co-manager of a company called the Theatrical Commonwealth at Broadway and White Street. In 1814 with William

Metropolitan Museum of Art

Design by JOHN JOSEPH HOLLAND

for *Adelmorn, the Outlaw*, Baltimore, 1802

Twaits he ran the Olympic Theatre; then he returned to work at the Park from 1816 through 1818–19.

During the War of 1812, Holland served in the American army. He also made drawings of the fortifications on Manhattan and Long Island. According to Dunlap:

Though short in stature, Mr. Holland was well formed, active and athletic. In his personal appearance, always extremely neat. When he entered the workshop, he uniformly changed his dress; and both by precept and example, forwarded the business of his employers with wonderful dispatch. Streets, chambers, temples or forests, grew under his hand as by magic.

After "a Lingering illness," Holland died in New York on 16 December 1820, in his forty-fifth year, according to the *Commercial Advertiser* of 18 December. His first wife was an Englishwoman who died in Philadelphia; his second wife was the daughter of a Mr Jackson of Staten Island. Evidently there were no children by either marriage.

Details of Holland's American career may be found in Richard Stoddard's "Notes on John Joseph Holland," *Theatre Survey* (May 1971) and in *The New-York Historical Society's Dictionary of Artists in America, 1564–1860* (1957).

A portrait of Holland painted by Dunlap in 1814 was in the possession of Holland's widow

Harvard Theatre Collection

JOHN JOSEPH HOLLAND
by Evers

in 1834. Dunlap thought it "the best head I had painted." It was reproduced in Dunlap's *Diary*. A miniature portrait of Holland by John Evers is in the collection of the New-York Historical Society. A bust portrait of Holland drawn in india ink by an unknown artist was bought by a Mr King in the Evert Jansen Wendell sale at the American Art Association, 15–20 October 1918.

Holland, William   [*fl.* 1762], *entrepreneur.*

In June 1762, at the Long Room, Richmond Wells, a "Will" Holland conducted assemblies and offered a "good band of Musick." Previously he had operated at St Alban's Tavern, according to a newsclipping in the British Library.

Hollandall, Hollendale, Hollendulla. *See* HELLENDAAL.

Holles, Mr   [*fl.* 1798], *musician.*

Charles Beecher Hogan in his introduction to Part 5 of *The London Stage* states that in October 1798 Mr Holles, a member of the

Drury Lane band, was hit by an apple thrown from the gallery by Andrew Fleming, against whom Holles began legal proceedings. Fleming made a public apology in the papers, and Holles seems to have withdrawn his action.

Hollicomb, William   [*fl.* 1794], *singer.*

William Hollicomb, according to Doane's *Musical Directory* of 1794, lived in Strutton Ground, Westminster, and was an alto tenor. He had been in the Wells choir and, in London, participated in oratorio performances at Westminster Abbey and Drury Lane.

Holliday or **Hollyday, Miss.** *See* MILLS, MRS WILLIAM THE SECOND.

Hollier, Richard   [*fl.* 1794], *singer.*

Doane's *Musical Directory* of 1794 listed Richard Hollier, of No 2, Cheapside, as an alto who sang with the Longacre Society and the Cecilian Society.

Hollingsworth, Mr   [*fl.* 1708], *boxkeeper.*

A paylist in the Coke papers at Harvard lists Mr Hollingsworth as a boxkeeper at the Queen's Theatre on 8 March 1708. His daily salary was 5s.

Hollingsworth, Miss   [*fl.* 1793], *actress.*

Miss Hollingsworth played the role of Hibernia in *The Hall of Augusta* at Sadler's Wells in 1793, according to the printed text of that piece.

Hollingsworth   [Thomas?]   [*d.* 1767?], *men's dresser.*

A Mr Hollingsworth's name was on the Covent Garden paylist in 1760–61 as a men's dresser at a salary of 1s. per day. The Mrs Hollingsworth who was a charwoman there at that time was probably his wife. Probably the dresser was the Thomas Hollingsworth, from St Giles in the Fields, who was buried at St Paul, Covent Garden, on 10 September 1767. He may have been the father of Thomas Hollingsworth, who as a child first appeared at Covent Garden in 1766–67.

Hollingsworth, Mrs [Thomas?] [fl. 1760–1761], charwoman.

Mrs Hollingsworth's name was on the Covent Garden paylist in 1760–61 as a charwoman at a salary of 1s. per day. Probably she was the wife of the (Thomas?) Hollingsworth, who was a men's dresser there at that time, and she may have been the mother of the actor Thomas Hollingsworth.

Hollingsworth, Thomas 1748–1814, actor, singer, dancer.

Born in 1748, Thomas Hollingsworth was perhaps the son of the Covent Garden house servants Mr (Thomas?) and Mrs Hollingsworth. Entered in the Covent Garden account books as Master Hollingsworth, he was paid £2 2s. on 10 March 1767 for appearing as one of the fairies, along with ten other young people, in eight performances of *The Fairy Favour*, a masque that was first produced on 31 January 1767. At the time of his debut he would have been 19, perhaps too old ordinarily to appear as a fairy, but several accounts of Hollingsworth in his maturity described him as having been very short.

His father dying in September 1767, Hollingsworth was taken under the protection of the actor Joseph Younger, who, according to *The Secret History of the Green Room* (1790), "taught him to play some trifling parts in Covent-Garden." Young Hollingsworth's name appeared on that theatre's paylist in 1771–72 as the lowest paid actor, at a salary of 7s. 6d. per week, though he was not assigned any roles in the playbills for that season. He was first noticed on a bill for Daniel in *The Conscious Lovers* on 22 May 1773, when he received the modest sum of £1 13s. 6d. in shared benefit tickets and was called Mr Hollingsworth. The following season his name appeared in the Covent Garden bills as Damaetas in *Midas* on 24 September 1773, a character in the new pantomime *The Sylphs* on 3 January 1774, and a character in *Mother Shipton* on 11 April 1774, for Younger's benefit. In 1774–75 he again appeared as Daniel in *The Conscious Lovers* and in *The Sylphs* and also played Tom in *The Jealous Wife*, a Gravedigger in *Hamlet*, List in *The Miser*, and characters in *The Rehearsal*, *The Druids* (a masque first performed in *The Winter's Tale* on 19 November 1774), and *St Patrick's*

Day. On 4 May 1775 he shared benefit tickets with Mrs Morris and Miss Cranfield.

In September 1775 Hollingsworth joined Younger's company at Birmingham. That October he was with Younger for the winter season at Manchester. For the following 12 years, through the spring of 1787, he played regularly at Liverpool and Manchester, becoming a popular favorite in low comedy roles and an excellent clown in pantomimes. At Liverpool he was paid £1 10s. per week in the summer seasons and £1 in the winters; for his benefit there on 25 August 1786 he received net proceeds of £71 5s. 6d. His known roles at Manchester included Rowley in the first Manchester performance of *The School for Scandal* on 9 June 1778, a Gravedigger in *Hamlet* in 1778–79 (a role in which he was often featured in the provinces), Dangle in *The Critic* on 17 April 1780, and Little John in the comic opera *Robin Hood* on 2 February 1785.

While playing at Liverpool, Hollingsworth suffered an accident that nearly ended his career. One night, according to *The Secret History of the Green Room*, "between the Play and Farce, while he was looking through the aperture made in the green curtain, there was an apple with a pen-knife stuck in it, thrown at him, the latter of which penetrated so deeply near his eye, that he was a long time confined, and it was generally thought he would lose his sight."

Between December 1781 and May 1782 Hollingsworth also was a member of Jackson's company at Edinburgh, where he played over three dozen roles, among which were Blunt in *The London Merchant*, Bullock in *The Recruiting Officer*, Cloten in *Cymbeline*, David in *The Rivals*, Jobson in *The Devil to Pay*, Justice Woodcock in *Love in a Village*, Mr Hardcastle in *She Stoops to Conquer*, Peachum and Mrs Peachum in *The Beggar's Opera*, Old Philpot in *The Citizen*, Peter in *Romeo and Juliet*, Sir Charles Clacket in *The Guardian*, Sir Francis Wronghead in *The Provok'd Husband*, Touchstone in *As You Like It*, Varland in *The West Indian*, and a Witch in *Macbeth*.

After his long stint in the northern provinces, Hollingsworth was engaged by Sheridan at Drury Lane, where he made his first appearance on 12 December 1787 as Hodge in *Love in a Village*. On 26 December he performed the Clown in *Harlequin Junior*, a type he then played in that and other pantomimes at Drury Lane over the next decade. His other roles in his debut season were Gobbo in *The Merchant of Venice*, Serjeant Flower in *The Clandestine Marriage*, a character in *'Tis an Ill Wind Blows Nobody Good*, a Peasant in *The Pilgrim*, Crow in *The School for Wives*, Lint in *The Mayor of Garratt*, Bunkle in *The Waterman*, and Sir Hugh Evans in *The Merry Wives of Windsor*.

Hollingsworth remained at Drury Lane through 1803–4, playing dozens of roles in his line. Toward the end of his career there he was confined to older characters. His salary in 1789–90 was £2 10*s*. per week; by his last season, 1803–4, it was £4 per week. Though he had promised to be an excellent performer, the few critical comments on his acting were not favorable. In *The Druriad* (1798), he was condemned.

Of acting I have seen enough,
Most vile, most execrable stuff;
But none so bad as thine, I vow to God!

When he replaced Aickin in several roles in 1799–1800, he was regarded by Thomas Dutton in the *Dramatic Censor* as poor compensation. *The Secret History of the Green Room* described Hollingsworth as "remarkably short in person, but rather lusty."

A selection of Hollingsworth's many roles at Drury Lane includes Tom Errand in *The Constant Couple*, Lucianus and a Gravedigger in *Hamlet*, Justice Guttle in *The Lying Valet*, the Governor in *Henry V*, the Farmer in *Harlequin's Frolicks*, Squire Sapscull in *The Fairy Favour*, Michael in *The Siege of Belgrade*, the Lord Mayor in *Richard III*, Robin in *First Love*, the Clown in *Robinson Crusoe*, Sir Epicure in *Harlequin Captive*, and Hassan in *Blue-Beard*. In 1799–1800, one of his last seasons at Drury Lane, he acted at least 36 different parts, many of which were bailiffs, coachmen, servants, and other minor characters.

His occasional performances at the Haymarket Theatre, usually for a colleague's benefit, included Cranky in *The Son-in-Law* on 13 October 1790, the Governor in *Henry V* on 24 September 1793, and Sir Felix Friendly in *The Agreeable Surprise* on 13 June 1797. He participated in the private theatricals at Wargrave in 1790, played at Liverpool again in the summers of 1792, 1797, 1798 (when his death

there was incorrectly reported on 27 August), and 1799, and at Manchester in 1801–2.

After leaving his engagement at Drury Lane at the end of 1803–4, Hollingsworth was employed at Manchester and Edinburgh for several years. He also performed in pantomimes at the Royal Circus, London, in the summers from 1805 to 1808 and at the Royalty Theatre in Wellclose Square in 1809–10; among the burlettas he appeared in at the latter place were *The Magic Picture* and *The Hero of Hungary* on 27 November 1809 and *The Wedding Portion* and *The Mystic Cup* on 25 January 1810. In an account of the 1813 summer season at Liverpool, the *Theatrical Inquisitor* of October 1813 reported that in the company "Last and least, in size, is our old veteran Hollingsworth, who is seldom now more than a senator, villager, &c. though when he assumes a more prominent part, has still some little humour left." He had just married, at age 65, and looked, according to the *Theatrical Inquisitor*, "quite spruce and gay."

In the spring of 1814 Hollingsworth performed at the Surrey Theatre, one of his roles being Harlequin in *The Hall of Mischief*. By the autumn he was back in Liverpool, where he died on 17 October 1814 and was buried at nearby Warton. According to a manuscript in the O. Smith Collection in the British Library, at the time of his death Hollingsworth was 66. In a manuscript book of "Theatrical Nicknames," Harper wrote that Thomas Hollingsworth was called "The Father of the Manchester and Liverpool Theatres."

Hollogan, [J.?] [*fl.* 1790?–1834?], *scene painter.*

Mr Hollogan, a scene painter at Covent Garden Theatre between 1794 and 1818, may have been the Master J. Hollogan who as "An Honorary Exhibitor" showed two heads, in chalk, at the Society of Artists in 1790. The first recorded payment to Hollogan at Covent Garden was on 12 April 1796 when he received £4 14*s*. 6*d*. for six days, but in 1794–95 with Hodgins, Walmsley, Phillips, and Lupino he had painted scenes for *Hercules and Omphale*, *Mago and Dago*, and *Windsor Castle*. In 1795–96 he worked on *Merry Sherwood*, *Wicklow Gold Mine*, and *The Lad of the Hills* and repaired scenery for *Harlequin's Treasure*. His other painting in the eighteenth century—

always in collaboration—was for *Olympus in an Uproar*, *Harlequin and Oberon*, and *Raymond and Agnes* in 1796–97; *The Round Tower*, *Harlequin and Quixote*, *Joan of Arc*, and *Harlequin's Return* in 1797–98; *Ramah Droog*, *Albert and Adelaide*, and *The Magic Oak* in 1798–99; and *The Volcano* and *Paul and Virginia* in 1799–1800.

Hollogan's salary was £2 per week in 1797–98, £2 10*s.* in 1799–1800, £3 in 1800–1801, and £3 10*s.* in 1801–2. He was listed as a member of the Covent Garden Theatre in 1812–13 and 1813–14. In 1820 he painted scenery at Drury Lane for Kean's *King Lear* and *Coriolanus*. He was probably the Hollogan who painted at the Brighton theatre in 1827 and who was an assistant painter at Drury Lane between 1831–32 and 1833–34, although that person may have been his son.

Holloway, [Richard?] *d. 1800? dancer, dancing master, violinist.*

The dancer named Holloway who was first noticed in the bills as performing a Soldier in the new pantomime dance *The Recruits* at Covent Garden Theatre on 1 May 1772 perhaps had been engaged as a chorus dancer all season at that theatre. Possibly he was the Richard Holloway, from St Martin-in-the-Fields, whose son Thomas, presumably an infant, was buried at St Paul, Covent Garden, on 12 February 1775.

Holloway remained engaged in the ensemble at Covent Garden through 1781–82 though his name seldom appeared in the bills. On 24 April 1773 he was listed as dancer in a new ballet called *The Festival of the Black Prince*. Also dancing in the chorus was his wife, who was at Covent Garden Theatre between 1772–73 and 1776–77. On 21 May 1773, when tickets were delivered by Mr Holloway, he and his wife danced a louvre and a minuet. They appeared together again in a double hornpipe on 11 May 1774. In 1774–75 Holloway danced in *The Sylphs* and shared in benefit tickets on 8 May 1775. On 4 May 1776 he danced a minuet with Miss Cranfield and shared tickets on 15 May.

Most of Holloway's benefits were taken with Harris and Dumay, also dancers, as on 16 May 1780 when they shared £277 18*s.*, less £105 and on 25 May 1782, £238 0*s.* 6*d.*, less £105. Holloway's salary from 1779–80 through 1781–82 was £1 10*s.* per week. His address

between May 1776 and May 1778 was in Great Maddox Street, Hanover Square, and in May 1779 it was Newington Butts. On 18 March 1782 Master Holland, described as a pupil of Holloway, danced a hornpipe at the Haymarket Theatre.

He was probably the Mr Holloway listed in Doane's *Musical Directory* of 1794 as a violinist and dancing master living in Kennington Lane. A Mr Holloway performed at Birmingham in the summers of 1798 and 1799. On 15 September 1800 a benefit was given at Birmingham for Mrs Holloway and her two infant children, "unfortunately now left to claim the patronage of the Public."

Perhaps Holloway was related to the J. Holloway who was listed in Doane as an instrument maker at No 31, Gerrard Street, Soho. A Thomas Holloway received from Drury Lane a total of £180 in nine payments of £20 each in February 1798, presumably for music supplied to the various musical productions of that season. The firm Holloway & Co, wholesale music sellers, instrument makers, and publishers, was located at No 40, Hart Street, Bloomsbury, London, from about 1805 to 1820. It was probably the establishment later run by a Thomas Holloway (d. 1867) at No 5, Hanway Street, from 1821 to 1859, and at No 41, Hanway Street, from 1859 to 1868.

A Miss M. Holloway, perhaps the daughter of the dancers, was a performer at Drury Lane from 1803–4 through 1807–8 at £4 per week.

Holloway, Mrs [Richard?] [*fl. 1772–1800*], *dancer.*

The wife of the dancer Holloway (d. 1800?) whose first name may have been Richard was a member of the chorus at Covent Garden Theatre by 1772–73. On 24 April 1773 she danced with her husband and others in the new ballet *The Festival of the Black Prince*, and on 21 May she performed a louvre and a minuet with him. On 11 May 1774 the Holloways offered a double hornpipe. On 15 May 1776 she danced in minuets and cotillions. Her last known performance at Covent Garden was in a minuet de la cour and allemande with her husband on 20 May 1777.

On 15 September 1800 at Birmingham a benefit was given for her and her two infant children, "unfortunately now left to claim the patronage of the Public." A Miss M. Holloway, perhaps their daughter, performed at Drury Lane from 1803–4 to 1807–8.

Holman, Master ₁*fl.* *1737–1739*₁, *dancer, actor.*

Master Holman danced as Harlequin in *The Burgomaster Trick'd*, a pantomime dance performed by "Lilliputians," scholars of Leviez, at Drury Lane on 19 November 1737 and several other times that season and the next. He also played Puck in *Robin Goodfellow*, another pantomime entertainment, which opened at Drury Lane on 30 October 1738 and was performed some 34 times by the end of February 1739.

Holman, Joseph George *1764–1817*, *actor, manager, playwright.*

Joseph George Holman was born in August 1764, the son of Major John Holman, of Denmark Street, St Giles, who was an officer in the British service and, it was said, was descended from the younger brother of Sir John Holman, of Warkworth Castle, Oxfordshire. Sir John, who had been created a baronet by Charles II, died without male issue. His

Harvard Theatre Collection

JOSEPH GEORGE HOLMAN

Engraving by Ridley, after Taylor

younger brother, who was killed fighting the northern rebels in the battle of Dunblain in Scotland in 1715, left a young male child (subsequently John George Holman's grandfather), who was deprived of his inheritance because the register of his father's birth was destroyed in a fire at the Sardinian ambassador's chapel. Had the claim held up in litigation, presumably the baronetcy eventually would have passed to Joseph George Holman through his father.

After the death of Major John Holman in 1766, the two-year-old Joseph George Holman was placed in the care of an uncle, who eventually sent him to the Soho Academy for schooling under Dr John Barwis and then under Dr Barrow. During the latter's mastership, especially, the school was noted for amateur theatricals, in which Holman performed with his classmate, the future dramatist Thomas Morton. Though Holman, intending to enter the clergy, matriculated at Queen's College, Oxford, on 7 February 1783, he soon gave up the pursuit of a degree and set his course for the stage.

Without any evident provincial training—announced as a young gentleman making his first appearance on any stage—Holman played Romeo to Miss Younge's Juliet at Covent Garden on 25 October 1784. For the occasion, Thomas Hull, who played Friar Lawrence, before the play delivered an address written by Barwis that was printed in the *European Magazine* that month:

> *From Isis banks, just wing'd his daring flight,*
> *A College Soph presents himself to-night;*
> *From heathen Greek, short commons, and long*
>   *pray'r,*
> *Begging admission, and protection here.*
> *From Logic's fetters, and pedantic schools,—*
> *From Aristole's* [sic] *cold and cumb'rous rules,*
> *To Shakespeare's gentler Muse, and sprightlier*
>   *scene,*
> *His active mind and youthful fancy lean.*

Holman repeated Romeo on 26 October and 1 and 5 November. His name appeared in the bills for the first time on the last date, but the *Public Advertiser* of 1 November had already identified him in an encouraging notice: "This easy and natural performance of Holman . . . will prove a fatal blow to the cause of the Attitudinarians and Face-makers; to those who think dramatic excellence consists in . . . finding out meanings that were never meant . . . in stretching out their fingers like monkies dying in convulsions . . . in uttering their words like minute-guns at royal funerals." The *Gazetteer* of 28 October 1784 had questioned Holman's wearing of black in the last act since at that point in the action Romeo has not heard of Juliet's death. (Over a year later, commenting on a performance of the play on 28 November 1785, the *Public Advertiser* complained that Holman's manner after the killing of Tybalt was "most censurable," for the "horror and concern for an action should not be expressed by appearing out of breath.") Despite his inexperience, Holman's debut was a success and drew considerable applause, though it would be an exaggeration to claim, as did one of his memoirs, that "his fame, like Garrick's, was thoroughly established."

His second character was Macbeth on 12 November 1784. The *Gazetteer* critic the next day reported that Holman "had not the weight, the slow action nor the dignity of Macbeth." His "too light and rapid" action and speech failed to convey the deep passions, a criticism often leveled at him early in his career. Next he acted Don Felix in *The Wonder* on 3 December, Achmet in *Barbarossa* on 13 December, and Richard III on 12 January 1785. When he played Chamont to Pope's Castalio in *The Orphan* on 4 February Holman received high praise; the critic in the *European Magazine* that month expressed the opinion that there was a rapport between the actor's style and the character: "the general spirit of Chamont seemed to accord with that of Holman." In the uttering of the gentler passages, however, his delivery, like that of Pope, was defective, "modulated by the ear, not produced by the heart."

For his first benefit on 15 February 1785 Holman acted Hamlet, at which time he was living at No 24, Bedford Street, not far from the theatre. His other roles that debut season were Hippolitus in *Phaedra and Hippolitus* on 3 March, Morcar in *Matilda* on 7 March, and Lothario in *The Fair Penitent* on 12 April 1785.

In the summer of 1785 Holman went to Ireland, where he acted at Smock Alley, Dublin, and at Limerick in August. Returning to Covent Garden for his second season, in which he was paid £11 per week, Holman played in

1785–86 some of his previous characters and added Hotspur in *1 Henry IV*, Leon in *Rule a Wife and Have a Wife*, Hastings in *Jane Shore*, Benedick in *Much Ado about Nothing*, Orestes in *The Distrest Mother*, Edgar in *King Lear*, Bevil in *The Conscious Lovers*, the title role in *Werter*, Zaphna in *Mahomet*, Young Belmont in *The Foundling*, and Timon in *Timon of Athens*. He also delivered occasional prologues to *The Roman Father*, *Appearance Is Against Them*, and *Small Talk*, pieces in which he did not act. For his benefit on 19 April 1786 he chose Osmyn in *The Mourning Bride*; his receipts were £219 4s., less house charges of £105, and he was still living at No 24, Bedford Street, an address he retained through the following season.

On December 1785 a critic in the *Public Advertiser*, writing of Holman's Richard III, praised him for not adopting the rants and mouthings of the "present rising theatrical generation" and was pleased to note that the actor "was not more violent than the character required him to be." After playing again in Ireland in the summer, Holman was back at Covent Garden in 1786–87, still earning £11 per week. His new roles were Philotas in *The Grecian Daughter*, Valentine in *Love for Love*, Villiers in *Eloisa* (a new tragedy by Frederic Reynolds on 20 December 1786), Carlos in *Love Makes a Man*, Dorilas in *Merope*, Elvirus in *Such Things Are* (a new drama by Mrs Inchbald on 10 February 1787), the title role in *Comus* (for his benefit on 14 April when his receipts were £241 8s., less charges of £105), Posthumus in *Cymbeline*, Flutter in *The Belle's Stratagem*, and Florizel in *The Winter's Tale*.

Quitting Covent Garden after his third season because of a dispute over salary, Holman returned to Ireland. He played at Smock Alley and Crow Street, Dublin, in 1787–88 and also at Cork on occasion. Early in 1789 he joined Jackson's company at the Theatre Royal, Edinburgh, for several months, playing such characters as Hamlet, Macbeth, Benedick, Posthumus, Romeo, Mahomet, and Petruchio. In May of that year he acted six nights in Manchester. About that time, perhaps in the autumn of 1788, Holman returned to Oxford for a term and, according to a memoir in the *Monthly Mirror* of March 1798, delivered a Latin oration "which evinced his grateful respect for the university, no less than his classical eloquence."

The Museum of London

JOSEPH GEORGE HOLMAN as Chamont
by De Wilde

In the autumn of 1789, after a two-year absence, Holman returned to Covent Garden on the same terms as those he had left, £11 per week, making his reappearance on 14 September as Romeo. The critic in the *European Magazine* that month thought Holman had acquired some bad habits in the provinces. Probably his faults were those alluded to in the anonymous *Modern Stage Exemplified*, published the previous year.

> HOLMAN *at first with partial eye is seen,*
> *His graceful figure and his noble mien.*
> *Thus be his silence prais'd: but who can bear*
> *To see the* GENTLEMAN *become the play'r;*
> *To hear him speak, and bellow, rant and rage.*
>
> . . . .
>
> *Then, when he starts, or stamps the harmless*
> *ground,*
> *To see him look with confidence around,*
> *And hint, 'tis now I justly claim your hands,*
> *While the bold look the ready clap commands.*

The wild extravagance which characterized his acting served Holman well in the feigned madness of Edgar but often marred his other roles. When he acted Young Bramin in the premiere of Mariana Starke's tragedy *The Widow of Malabar* on 5 May 1790, a critic in the *Biographical and Imperial Magazine* condemned him: "This young man will never be a player till he ceases to swim in the air, and display his fine proportions with such ostentatious vanity—in short, till he ceases to be a consummate coxcomb; which we fear is next to saying he will *never* be a player at all."

Though he never overcame to any great degree his mannerisms and a certain lack of judgment in interpretation, Holman remained a popular and serviceable actor at Covent Garden throughout the 1790s. His salary was raised to £12 per week in 1791–92, the level at which it remained through 1799–1800. In the Harvard Theatre Collection is a Covent Garden paysheet for 1795–96 with Holman's signature acknowledging the receipt of a total of £386 for 193 nights of playing. His benefit receipts were usually ample; for example, £278 11s. on 14 April 1790, £273 1s. 6d. on 11 April 1793, £263 3s. on 24 April 1795, £290 11s. 6d. on 29 April 1797, and £350 2s. on 9 April 1799 (all less house charges). In 1789–90 and 1790–91 he lived at No 2, Tavistock Row; by April 1792 he had chambers at No

12, John Street, the Adelphi, where he resided through 1797.

During his years at Covent Garden, Holman played dozens of leading roles in comedy and tragedy. In addition to those given above, among the original characters he "created" were Raymond in Hayley's *Eudora* on 29 January 1790, Dorville in Marshall's *The German Hotel* on 11 November 1790, the title role in Merry's *Lorenzo* on 5 April 1791, Harry in O'Keeffe's *Wild Oats* on 16 April 1791, Ibrahim in Mrs Coweley's *A Day in Turkey* on 3 December 1791, Harry Dornton in Holcroft's *The Road to Ruin* on 18 February 1792, Alonzo in Morton's *Columbus* on 1 December 1792, Charles in O'Keeffe's *The World in a Village* on 23 November 1793, Charles Seymour in Holcroft's *Love's Frailties* on 5 February 1794, Darnley in Reynolds's *The Rage!* on 23 October 1794, Conway in Mrs Cowley's *The Town Before You* on 6 December 1794, Surrey in Watson's *England Preserv'd* on 21 February 1795, Shatter in Benjamin Hoadly's *The Tatlers* on 29 April 1797 (the manuscript was given to Holman by Hoadly Ashe, the late Dr Hoadly's nephew), Algernon in Cumberland's *False Impressions* on 23 November 1797, Egerton in Morton's *Secrets Worth Knowing* on 11 January 1798, Mortimer in Reynolds's *Laugh When You Can* on 8 December 1798, and Lazarra in Cumberland's *Joanna* on 16 January 1800.

Among his numerous first appearances in plays of the established repertoire were Frankly in *The Suspicious Husband*, Marc Antony in *All for Love*, and Touchstone in *As You Like It* in 1789–90; Lord Townly in *The Provok'd Husband* in 1790–91; Tancred in *Tancred and Sigismunda*, Faulkland in *The Rivals*, and the title role in *Oroonoko* in 1791–92; Captain Plume in *The Recruiting Officer* and Henry VIII in 1792–93; Charles Oakly in *The Jealous Wife* in 1793–94; Horatio in *The Fair Penitent*, Welborne in *A New Way to Pay Old Debts*, and the title role in *The Earl of Warwick* in 1795–96; Juba in *Cato* in 1796–97; and Antonio in *The Merchant of Venice* in 1797–98.

Holman also acted twice at Drury Lane Theatre: Hamlet on 27 May 1796, for Sedgwick's benefit, and Leon in *Rule a Wife and Have a Wife* on 6 February 1800, before the King and Queen. On 29 June 1799 he made his first appearance on the Haymarket stage as Harry Dornton in *The Road to Ruin*, a role he repeated

there the following 3 July. In 1795 Holman,
Pope, Incledon, and Fawcett had been granted
a license to conduct readings and music at
Freemasons' Hall, Queen Street, for 10 nights
between 20 February and 27 March.

Reviews of his acting during the 1790s revealed no real abatement of his energetic style,
which one supporter claimed Holman had
adopted in order to avoid the monotonous,
steady Kemble school. The *Morning Herald* of
6 November 1792 believed that Hamlet
(which he had played the previous night) was
well within his powers but that Holman had
failed to provide any of the character's subtle-
ties: "He 'out Heroded Herod' throughout,
with more than his usual perseverance." By
1796 he was growing corpulent. That year in
A Pin Basket to The Children of Thespis, John
Williams complained that Holman carried his
shoulders high and ungracefully; because of his
continual rant and roar, stemming from his
want of judgment, the good impression and
promise of Holman's first appearances were,
for Williams, being gradually eroded. Though
described as possessing a fine intelligence,
Holman was unfavorably anatomized by F. G.
Waldron in *Candid and Impartial Strictures on
the Performers . . .* (1795):

His person is well formed, manly, and elegant;
would his gait and manners were conformable; but
in the first there is an unpardonable roll from one
side to the other; and in the last, a seeming studied-
stiffness, that is uniformly the same in every thing
he undertakes: there is also a continual haughty
erection and toss of the head, that he practices in
most of his characters;—this may do well in the
proud . . . *Hotspur*; but is absurd and ridiculous
in . . . *Romeo*, or . . . *Jaffier*.—This gentleman
possesses a very handsome countenance, animating
and expressive: which is considerably heightened
by brilliant sparkling eyes. There is a deficiency in
the length of his upper lip, that continually exposes
his teeth to the audience; which defect occasioned
the following whimsical observation, made one
night by a gentleman in the pit—"that Mr. Holman's head painted would make a most excellent
sign-post to a dentist." We think Mr. Lewis would
be a most powerful competitor with him for this
palm of distinction. . . .

His mind is powerful, and gifted with that divine quality called genius . . . yet Mr. Holman . . .
is always endeavouring to do what the situation
does not require should be attempted, or what Nature is shocked at when done. An ardent wish to
deliver passages in a manner different to what has

Harvard Theatre Collection

JOSEPH GEORGE HOLMAN as an Irish Cherokee

artist unknown

been ever offered to an audience before, frequently
hurries him into a singularity of expression that has
nothing but its oddity to attract attention. . . . An
intemperate violence is also frequently practised by
this gentleman, accompanied by an extravagance of
action that often inclines us to risibility. He has
likewise a method of hurrying over the latter part
of a sentence, as if to give it more effect, but in
reality destroys the intention and solemnity of the
scene.

After acting at Covent Garden during the
winter seasons in the 1790s, Holman regularly
traveled out to the provinces during the summers, playing at Liverpool each year between
1791 and 1798, at Cheltenham in 1793, at
Crow Street, Dublin, for six nights in 1794,

and at Chichester and Portsmouth in 1795. In May of 1797, he visited his friend Morton on the Isle of Wight.

In the autumn of 1792 Holman's quarrel with his common-law wife, Maria Hughes, an Irish actress, became public matter. He had met her when both were members of the Crow Street company in 1788. Maria had been born in 1761, the daughter of Jacob Hughes, a country squire of Thurles, Tipperary. When she was five, her father died, leaving all his property to Maria, save a jointure of £100 per year to his widow, the former Miss English, of Seskin. Her mother took Maria for her education to Dublin, where all their money was soon squandered and the high-spirited girl went upon the stage, making her first appearance at Crow Street as Euphrasia in *The Grecian Daughter* on 10 April 1788. Her dress at her debut caused a small sensation—it was such "as was never seen on the stage before," reported the *Hibernian Journal*; "Grecian taste and Asiatic magnificence united to surprise the beholder." Holman, too, was attracted. Together they acted *Romeo and Juliet* at Belfast in November 1788, and in early 1789 they went off together to act at Edinburgh. Her career took her back to Crow Street in February 1790, then to York and Manchester the same year. In a manuscript in the Folger Shakespeare Library is a notation for the week of 21 December 1790: "Miss Hughes the Dublin Actress & the bon ami of Holman is playing at Portsmouth. Holman went down last Week to play for her benefit."

On 17 October 1792 Maria advertised from an address at No 14, Tavistock Row, her proposals for publishing by subscription, "An Account of the unparalleled Conduct of JOSEPH HOLMAN . . . towards Mrs. Holman, late Miss Hughes . . . written by herself, with a view of exciting a generous public to alleviate her distress, and to obtain a support for herself and two infants left destitute, in consequence of his desertion, as also being a necessary apology due to the public previous to her professional appearance in London, which Mr. Holman has most artfully and illiberally exerted every means to prevent." In a letter to the papers dated that same day, Holman denied ever marrying Maria Hughes or promising he would do so. He had left her because of "her horrible temper," he asserted, and contrary to her claim, he had not deserted the two children, whom he admitted having sired, but had left them in the care of his mother with a guinea a week for their maintenance. Further, he claimed to have proposed a settlement of 100 guineas per year for Miss Hughes and the children or £50 per year solely for her own use if she would resign the children to him. Though she had rejected the offer with contempt, Holman stated that he continued to provide for the children.

Maria Hughes, though she never performed in London, eventually prospered, becoming the second wife of Major John Scott-Waring (1747–1819), former chief lieutenant in India to Warren Hastings and a descendant of William Wycherley. At Peterborough House in Parson's Green, Fulham, they offered lavish entertainments to the fashionable. One such event was a masked ball in honor of the Prince Regent on 3 February 1812, the morning after which Maria Scott-Waring was found dead at the bottom of the grand staircase with her neck broken. Within eight months the Major married another actress, Harriet Esten (1765?–1865).

Holman, meanwhile, married Jane Hamilton at St Martin-in-the-Fields on 12 February 1798. She was one of the daughters of the Reverend Frederick Hamilton of Lichfield House, Surrey, son of Lord Archibald Hamilton, who in turn was the seventh son of William, third Duke of Hamilton. Jane's sister was Lady Aldborough, the first wife of Edward Augustus Stratford, second Earl of Aldborough. Holman's marriage to Jane Hamilton, an accomplished amateur singer who often performed at Richmond House, was regarded by most of her friends as a misalliance and had been opposed by her father, but he finally consented. Soon after their marriage the Holmans moved into a house at No 73, New Street, Covent Garden. As predicted, the union proved unhappy. By 9 August 1799 Jane had suffered three miscarriages and subsequently she brought forth no live issue. By 1803, when she visited for two months with Mrs Thrale-Piozzi, who often mentioned her in her diary, the rift in the Holman marriage had begun. Soon after they separated, and she died in London on 11 June 1810. It was said that during her final illness, Holman by sheer accident had come to her door looking for a doctor to treat

Harvard Theatre Collection

JOSEPH GEORGE HOLMAN as Romeo and
ANNE BRUNTON as Juliet

engraving by Park, after M. Brown

an injured servant, so Mrs Holman died happy
in the belief that he had intended to see her.

During the 1790s Holman also turned author. He appeared in his adaptation of *Hamlet*
at Covent Garden on 9 October 1793 and at
Dublin on 29 July 1794. *Abroad and at Home*,
his comic opera, was produced with music by
Shield on 19 November 1796 and enjoyed a
successful run of 28 performances in its first
season; it was published at London in 1796
and at Dublin in 1797. His next effort, *The
Votary of Wealth*, a comedy, was first played at
Covent Garden on 12 January 1799 and was
performed 21 times before the end of the season. Its original title, *The King's Bench*, was
changed because of the Lord Chamberlain's objections. The comedy was published at London
and Dublin in 1799. Holman's melodrama,
The Red-Cross Knights, based on Schiller's *Die*

Räuber, with music by Attwood, was played
for the first time at the Haymarket Theatre on
21 August 1799; moderately successful for six
performances that summer, it was published
the same year.

In 1799–1800 Holman and seven other performers were involved in a dispute with the
Covent Garden proprietors over the management's reducing the amount of free tickets provided to actors and increasing the benefit
charges. In 1800 was published *A Statement of
the Differences subsisting between the Proprietors and
Performers of the Theatre Royal Covent Garden. . . .
By John Johnstone, Joseph George Holman, Alexander Pope, Charles Incledon, Jos. S. Munden,
John Fawcett, Thomas Knight, Henry Erskine
Johnston*, a pamphlet probably written by Holman.

In *The Dramatic Censor* (1800), Thomas
Dutton, sympathetic to the managers, asserted
that Holman's total income, including salary
and benefit, in 1799–1800 had been £517
14*s*. 2*d*. In earlier numbers the biased Dutton
had called Holman "a very indifferent Hotspur" and criticized him for ranting and strut-
ting as Lazarra in *Joanna* and for being so
"Sombre, saturnine, and soporific" in the
sprightly role of Comus. "Mr. HOLMAN's acting operates on the audience by *reverse* principles," ridiculed Dutton. "He makes us *laugh*
most, when most he endeavours to be serious:
he never discovers any portion of the *vis comica*,
except when he aims at *sentiment* and *pathos*."
Dutton also hinted that the pamphlet *Defence
of the Profession of an Actor*, published in 1800
and dedicated to Mrs Siddons, was also written
by Holman, notwithstanding the prefatory
disclaimer that the author was an actor.

When the Lord Chamberlain ruled against
the actors, Holman either decided to resign or
was discharged from Covent Garden. At his
last benefit he played Drooply in *The Votary of
Wealth* on 17 April 1800, when the gross receipts were a disappointing £195 7*s*., leaving
him little after house charges.

Holman's last performance at Covent Garden was on 11 June 1800, as Harry Dornton.
He never returned to a London winter theatre,
though in 1800 his career was only at mid-
point. That summer he played at the Haymarket Theatre as Count Alphonso d'Esparza in
his comic opera *What a Blunder*, with music
by Davy, which premiered on 14 August and

ran nine performances; it was published that year. After playing a few nights in Birmingham at the end of the summer, Holman made for Ireland.

For the first time in 12 years he showed up at Belfast, to play six nights, beginning on 23 February and taking a benefit on 3 March 1801. He then joined the Theatre Royal, Dublin, where for several seasons he shared the management with Jones. In May 1801 the *Monthly Mirror* reported that Holman had been offered £1000 per year at Dublin "for his exertions as actor and manager, besides the profits of a benefit." "His talents as a performer, and his character as a gentleman," the bulletin continued, "are in the highest possible estimation in this city; and it is a credit to any city to have such an actor and such a man in the character of its *arbiter elegantiarum*."

In the National Library of Ireland is a manuscript journal kept by a Dublin playgoer who often saw Holman perform between 1801 and 1803. The anonymous journalist thought highly of Holman's abilities but, as with previous critics, found his acting too overwrought. His passionate scenes as Alexander on 16 March 1801 "tho certainly good pieces of acting, were . . . too vehement . . . the delerium excited by the poison, the last, was highly natural. . . . It is the only representation of madness which I have seen without unpleasant sensation." Holman's *Votary of Love* was "villainously" performed to a "wretched house" on 26 May 1801. For his benefit on 17 June, Holman performed a pasticchio of scenes from *As You Like It*, *Much Ado about Nothing*, *Romeo and Juliet*, *King Lear*, and *Macbeth*. In the last, Holman was superior to Kemble, thought the playgoer, with "the voice of guilt, fearful of betraying itself by rising above a whisper, the rolling eye, the haggard countenance, the breathless anxiety."

In 1802 Holman exhibited "considerable merit" as Osmyn in *The Mourning Bride* (with Mrs Siddons as Zara) on 7 June, indulged in "sometimes disagreeable ranting" as Jaffeir in *Venice Preserv'd* on 10 June, was "tolerable" as Orestes in *The Distrest Mother* on 14 June, and was "excellent" as Varanes in *Theodosius* on 19 June. As Macbeth during that summer he provided "very excellent support to the Siddons." He spoke the dagger soliloquy down front, to the audience—"the effect was uncommonly fine, when his straining eye-ball began to express the removal of the vision." His headpiece in *Macbeth* caused a new fashion called "The Witch Bonnet," a hat of "straw with high crown, leaf cocked, and thrown as far on the territory of the cheek as could be reckoned consistent with the usual purposes of a hat;" it was "worn with taste" by elegant women but was "otherwise frightful."

About that time, it is said, Holman took up farming, but his name was in the Dublin bills in 1803, 1806, and 1808. On 31 July 1806 he received a benefit at which he acted Antony to the Ventidius of Cooke in *All for Love*. On 13 February 1804 Holman's comedy *Love Gives the Alarm* had been acted at Covent Garden, but Holman had not played in it. The piece

Harvard Theatre Collection

JOSEPH GEORGE HOLMAN as Alexander
by De Wilde

was damned and was never acted again nor printed. In November 1804 he was a guest actor for six nights at the Orchard Street Theatre, Bath.

Holman played at Edinburgh in 1808–9 and at Glasgow in April 1809. Acting with him in Scotland was Agnes Holman, his daughter by Maria Hughes. In the summer of 1811 Holman returned to London after an absence of 11 years to play at the Haymarket, reappearing on 22 August as Jaffeir to Miss Holman's Belvidera. He acted Lord Townly to her Lady Townly in *The Provok'd Husband*, Horatio to her Calista, Osmond to her Angela in *The Castle Spectre*, and, for his last appearance, on 12 September 1811, Faulkland to his daughter's Julia in *The Rivals*.

Encouraged by the reports of George Frederick Cooke's enormous success in America, Holman set off for New York in 1812, taking with him his daughter and a letter of introduction from James Wilson, in which it was stated that he had been "the first actor in Covent Garden theatre" and a fellow of Queen's College, both exaggerations. Holman was announced to make his debut as Hamlet at the Park Theatre on 21 September 1812, but he fell ill. He appeared as Lord Townly with his daughter as Lady Townly on 5 October, and on 6 November he acted Edgar and she Cordelia to Thomas A. Cooper's Lear. Later in 1812 the Holmans went to play at the Chestnut Street Theatre in Philadelphia, where Holman had an old friend, Mr Westray, the father of Juliana Westray Wood. According to William B. Wood's *Personal Recollections*, Holman was "frequently the object of dislike" at the Philadelphia theatre because "he had acquired a dictatorial manner in business. . . ." He made his first appearance in Boston as Hamlet at the

JOSEPH GEORGE HOLMAN, William Jackson, and John Taylor
"A Theatrical Chymist" by Rowlandson

Federal Street Theatre on 2 January 1813. For a while Holman managed the Walnut Street Theatre in Philadelphia, without success, and then in 1815–16 became manager of the theatre in Charleston, South Carolina.

At the end of his first year of management in Charleston, Holman returned to London for recruits, two of whom were James H. Caldwell (1793–1863) and a Miss Lattimore from Liverpool. Caldwell proved a favorite light comedian in Charleston, but Holman fired him in March 1817 for refusing a tragedy role. Caldwell consequently provoked a riot which resulted in damage to the theatre, and subsequently he wounded Holman in a duel on Sullivan's Island. At the end of 1816–17 Holman left Charleston with the intention of opening a new theatre in Richmond, Virginia. On or about 22 August 1817 he married Miss Lattimore. Two days later, on 24 August, at Rockaway, Long Island, Holman died at the age of 53, of a fever, according to one report, or of a stroke, according to another.

Holman's widow continued her stage career and in March 1819 married Isaac Star Clewson. In the summer of 1824 she again married, this time to C. W. Sanford, a lawyer and military officer, and retired from the stage. But when Sanford became proprietor of the Lafayette Theatre in New York, she appeared there in October 1826. She also acted at the Chestnut Street Theatre in January 1829 and at the Park Theatre in the summer of 1829. She died in New York on 1 September 1859.

In 1815 Holman's daughter Agnes had married Charles H. Gilfert, who had opened a theatre at Richmond, Virginia, after his father-in-law's death. Gilfert, the son of a German immigrant who had been president of the Musical Society of New York in 1789 and a member of Dunlap's theatre orchestras in that city, was the musical director of the Commonwealth Company at the New Theatre in New York in 1813 and became leader of Holman's orchestra at Charleston in 1815. Later he managed the new Pearl Street Theatre in Albany in 1825 and the new Bowery Theatre in New York from 1826. There his wife was his leading actress and the young Edwin Forrest his star actor. Financial reversals from his several theatrical enterprises left him impoverished before his death on 30 July 1829. We do not know when Agnes Holman Gilfert died. The

Mr Holman who acted in Philadelphia in 1791–92, some 20 years before Joseph George Holman went to America, possibly was related to him. *The True Briton* of 8 May 1797 announced that an uncle of our subject had died suddenly on 6 May, causing Holman to take that night off from his duties at Covent Garden.

In addition to the stage pieces cited above, Holman wrote *The Gazette Extraordinary*, a comedy that was produced at Covent Garden on 23 April 1811 and was printed that year. Probably he was also the author of *Frost and Thaw*, an operatic farce with music by Cooke that was first played at Covent Garden on 25 February 1812.

When Holman had first appeared on the London stage in October 1784 he possessed the attributes that promised a fine actor. As described by Boaden (in his memoirs of Kemble):

His person was genteel and his manner extremely prepossessing. His face originally was not only handsome, but expressive; and he had a manly sonorous voice, which, though it had more strength than sweetness, yet discovered no signs of being rebellious to the ear; and as the actor had the character of being a man of study, of judgment and good taste, as he showed high spirit and great ardour to excel, there were very sanguine hopes that he would leave a name in the art.

From a description of him in the *Monthly Mirror* of May 1809, written 24 years after his debut, it is clear that Holman had failed to realize his great potential, though he continued to demonstrate substantial talents:

Though his action and manner are uncommonly elegant, his face and figure are certainly not now in his favour; and his voice, though admirable in volume and extent, is deficient in pathetic feeling; indeed the want of pathetic expression is his greatest defect. In elegant declamation he is very superior, but it is in the delineation of the stronger passions that his genius shines forth with the most astonishing power.

It was perhaps his agitated manner that caused him while acting Macbeth on 28 October 1793 to be wounded in the mouth during the last fighting scene by Pope, who played Macduff. But, even accounting for his improprieties, Holman afforded great satisfaction to audiences, who perhaps mistook his *hauteur* for feeling. No other actor, for example, could "pretend to speak a prologue with him," according to *The Secret History of the Green Room*. Lamb described him as the "jolliest" Hamlet he had ever seen. In his *Reminiscences*, W. C. Macready recalled Holman as having lost his fire at the end of his career and as having become "as cold and artificial in his practised tones and movements as an automaton."

Holman enjoyed the warm friendship of Thomas Morton and the actor Thomas Hull. The latter left a portrait of himself to Holman and his two small medallions carved "on pieces of Shakespeare's Mulberry tree with the Heads of Shakespeare and Garrick" to Jane Holman in his will proved in 1808. Holman was also a second-wave member of the actors' club called "The School of Garrick," though he had never known the great master.

Portraits of Holman include:

1. By Daniel Dodd. Ink miniature, in the Victoria and Albert Museum.

2. By H. Bone, 1800. Present location unknown. Engraving by J. Heath. Published by J. P. Thompson, 1812.

3. By Taylor. Miniature. Present location unknown. Engraving by W. Ridley. Published as a plate to *Monthly Mirror*, March 1798.

4. By Gilbert Stuart. Painted in America. Noted by C. M. Mount, *The Works of Gilbert Stuart*; present location unknown.

5. Engraving by W. Angus, after D. Dodd. Published as a plate to *European Magazine*, 1784.

6. Engraving by J. Condé. Published as a plate to *Thespian Magazine*, 1794.

7. By unknown engraver. Published in *Ireland's Mirror*.

8. As Alexander in *The Rival Queens*. Painting by Samuel De Wilde. In the Garrick Club (catalogue No 243). Engraving by Chapman. Published as a plate to *Bell's British Library*, 1793.

9. As Alexander. Watercolor drawing by De Wilde, dated 1814. In the Harvard Theatre Collection. Similar to the painting in the Garrick Club.

10. As Arden in *Arden of Feversham*. Watercolor drawing "Taken from Life" by W. Loftis, 1787. In the Folger Shakespeare Library.

11. As young Belmont, with Mrs Warren as Rosetta, in *The Foundling*. Engraving by J. Scott, after T. Stothard. Published as a plate to *New English Theatre*, 1786.

12. As Chamont in *The Orphan*. Painting by De Wilde. In the Museum of London.

13. As Chamont. Painting by De Wilde. In the Garrick Club (catalogue No 266). Same costume as in De Wilde's painting of him in the Museum of London, but different pose, drawing sword. Engravings: by Audinet as a plate to *Bell's British Library*, 1791; by Godfrey, published by J. Bell, 1792; by Thornthwaite, as a plate to *Bell's British Theatre*, 1791; by unknown engraver, as a plate to *British Drama*, printed for C. Cooke, 1807; and a reversed copy of the preceding by unknown engraver.

14. As Cyrus in *Cynthia and Cyrus*. Painting by De Wilde. In the Garrick Club (catalogue No 257). Engravings by Audinet as a plate to *Bell's British Library*, 1795; and by Wilson as a plate to *Bell's British Theatre*, 1795.

15. As Douglas in *Douglas*. Painting by De Wilde. In the Garrick Club (catalogue No 221). Engraving by W. Bromley as a plate to *Bell's British Library*, 1791; and the same as a plate to *British Drama*, published by C. Cooke, 1807. Engraving by Ferguson was published by William Jones as a plate to *British Theatre*, 1792.

16. As Edgar (as Mad Tom) in *King Lear*. Painting by Gainsborough Dupont. In the Garrick Club (catalogue No 412).

17. As Edward in *Albina*. Engraving by J. Thomson, after J. Graham. Published as a plate to Cawthorn's *British Library*, 1797.

18. As Faulconbridge in *King John*. By J. Stewart. Listed in the *Mathews Collection Catalogue* (No 145), but not in the Garrick Club. Engraving by Thornthwaite as a plate to *Bell's British Library*, 1786 ("M. Brown del."), and the same (also "M. Brown del.") also published by J. Cawthorn, 1806.

19. As Hamlet. Watercolor by W. Loftis. In the Folger Shakespeare Library.

20. As Hamlet. Painting by unknown artist. In the Garrick Club (catalogue No 585), presented in 1915 by Sir Edward Marshall Hall.

21. As Hippolitus in *Phaedra and Hippolitus*. Engraving by W. Leney, after J. Graham. Published as a plate to Cawthorn's *British Library*, 1796.

22. As Hotspur in *1 Henry IV*. Watercolor by W. Loftis. In the Folger Shakespeare Library.

23. As Lazarra in *Joanna of Montfaucon*. By unknown engraver. Published by Harrison, Cluse & Co, 1800.

24. As Richard III. Engraving by N. C. Goodnight, line vignette, undated; the same was published as lithograph in color, undated.

25. As Romeo, with Miss Brunton as Juliet. Painting by M. Brown. In the Mander and Mitchenson Collection. Engraving by T. Park, after M. Brown. Published by the engraver, 1787.

26. As Romeo. By unknown engraver. Published by J. Walker, 1784. A reversed engraving published in *Hibernian Magazine*, June 1785.

27. As Romeo, looking up at Juliet in balcony. By unknown engraver, undated.

28. As Selim in *The Mourning Bride*. By unknown engraver, undated.

29. As Tancred in *Tancred and Sigismunda*. An engraving by Thornthwaite, after De Wilde, was published as a plate to *Bell's British Theatre*, 1791, and as plate to *British Theatre*, 1817. An engraving by Matthieu of the same picture by De Wilde was published as a plate to *Bell's British Library*, 1792.

30. As Zaphna, with Miss Brunton as Palmira, in *Mahomet*. Engraving by J. Heath, after Stothard. Published as a plate to *New English Theatre*, 1786.

31. Caricature: "A Theatrical Chymist." By Thomas Rowlandson, published 1786. Holman emerges from the mouth of a retort heated over a furnace tended by the "Theatrical Chymist," supposedly William Jackson, editor of the *Morning Post*. The man at the bellows probably is John Taylor, that paper's drama critic.

32. Caricature: "An Irish Cherokee," standing with club in hands. By unknown engraver. Published as a plate to *Hibernian Magazine*, 1792.

33. Caricature: "The Road to Ruin," similar to preceding except that Holman carries hat in hand instead of club. By unknown engraver. Published as a plate to *Attic Miscellany*, 1792. Another state was published with title, "A Jolly Toper."

34. In a caricature burlesque of F. Reynold's

Werter. Engraving by J. Sayers, published 1786.

Holmes, Mr [fl. 1708], *musician*.

Mr Holmes played in two benefit concerts at Stationers' Hall: one on 4 February 1708 for the younger Thomas Dean and one on 26 March 1708 for Leigh.

Holmes, Mr [fl. 1719?], *manager*.

In D'Urfey's *Wit and Mirth* in 1719, the song "War, War and Battle" by John Barrett was noted as "Sung at Holmes's Booth in Bartholomew Fair." Holmes is not otherwise known, and there is no assurance that he was active in booth management at the time D'Urfey's work was published.

Holmes, Mr [fl. 1747], *actor*.

A Mr Holmes played Duncan in *Macbeth* on 5 January 1747 at the Goodman's Fields theatre.

Holmes, Mr [fl. 1779–1802?], *actor*.

On 15 March 1779 at the Haymarket Theatre a Mr Holmes played Mr O'Carney in *A Mirror for the Ladies* and Don Carlos in *The Wrangling Lovers*. The following 10 May at the same house he acted the title role in *Douglas*. He had a principal part in *The Touchstone of Invention* at the Haymarket on 18 October of the same year; then his name disappeared from London bills. On 22 January 1781 he was back at the same house with a group of mostly provincial performers playing a major but unnamed role in *The Sharper's Last Shift*.

Holmes was not seen in London again until 21 September 1795, when he played a Peasant in *Love and Madness!* at the Haymarket. In January 1797 he was in the cast of *The Battle of Eddington* (though he was dropped when the work was repeated in May), and he played Scruple in *Ways and Means* and Sir Peter Pride in *Barnaby Brittle*—all at the Haymarket.

It seems likely that the Holmes we have been following was a provincial actor who turned up from time to time in London. There was a Holmes acting at Derby in the spring and at Nottingham in the summer of 1799; he appeared at the theatre in Chesterfield on 17 January 1800 as the title character in *Pizarro* and Charles in *The Village Lawyer* and was in Hoy's troupe at Halifax in 1801. The *Monthly Mirror*'s Halifax correspondent wrote that the theatre there opened on 11 November 1801 with *The West Indian*; "Mr. Holmes, a favourite, after two years absence is returned." When the same periodical reported on theatrical activity at Nottingham in 1802, the correspondent called Holmes "a very respectable performer, though too much addicted to rant. But in another issue, on 13 May 1802, the Nottingham correspondent said, "Mr Holmes maintains a very respectable distinction."

Holmes, Mr [*fl.* 1794], *performer?*

The Drury Lane accounts in 1794 show a payment to a Mr Holmes, possibly a performer, of £4 10*s.* for 12 nights.

Holmes, Agnes. *See* KENNEDY, MRS THOMAS.

Holmes, George [*fl.* 1656–1705], *painter.*

The Painter-Stainers Minutes mentioned George Holmes and his sons John and Thomas between 1656 and 1673. William Winde in 1683 called Holmes "certainly a great maister of his profession." He painted some works at Combe Abbey, Christ's Hospital, and Vintners' Hall, and from 1687 to 1702 he painted pageants for the Lord Mayors' Shows with the assistance of Richard Hayes and William Thompson. For his pageant painting he received as much as £212. His designs for *London's Triumph* in 1687 were etched by Isaac Beckett, but no copy is now known. His designs for Settle's *Glory's Resurrection* were etched by the second William Faithorne in 1698. On 7 May 1705 George Holmes applied for the position of drawing master at Christ's Hospital.

Holmes, James 1756–*c.* 1822, *bassoonist, violinist, clarinetist.*

James Holmes was recommended for membership in the Royal Society of Musicians on 3 August 1783, when he was 27 years old and had a wife and two children—one four years of age and the other two. He played the bassoon, violin, and clarinet and was engaged at Sadler's Wells. In May and June 1784 Holmes played bassoon in the Handel Memorial Concerts at Westminster Abbey and the Pantheon, and he also played that instrument at the spring concerts at St Paul's, beginning in 1785. In 1787–88 he was employed by the Academy of Ancient Music, for which he was paid, as a bassoonist, £6. He appeared at Covent Garden Theatre on 19 February 1790, was popular at Vauxhall, and engaged in a subscription concert series at the Assembly Rooms in Bristol on 18 November 1791. In March 1793 he played at the Haymarket Theatre.

Doane's *Musical Directory* of 1794 summed up Holmes's multiple activities, listing him only as a bassoonist, and noted that he had also played at the Professional Concerts, at Ranelagh, in the oratorios at Drury Lane, and, in 1793, at the Oxford Meeting—in addition to his participation in the Handel performances at the Abbey. Grove notes that Holmes also played in Salomon's concerts. His address was No 23, Berwick Street, Soho. Holmes was at the King's Theatre in February and June 1795, and Smith's *The Italian Opera* notes that the bassoonist was a regular player in the band at that theatre in 1795–96, 1796–97, 1800, 1817, and 1818—and Holmes may have played at the King's in other years. He performed in the *Messiah* at the Haymarket on 15 January 1798 and at the Oxford Music Room the following 16 June. Perhaps he was the Holmes who was in the band at the Haymarket Theatre during the summers from 1804 to 1810.

According to Sainsbury, the "celebrated Holmes" had been a pupil of the first bassoonist at the opera, a "German professor of the bassoon," and we take that teacher to have been Samuel Baumgarten.

On 5 May 1799 James Holmes proposed Thomas Holmes (not his son, but probably a relative) for membership in the Royal Society of Musicians. By 1805 James was one of the Governors of the Society, and from 1806 on he served on the Court of Assistants. The last mention of him in the Society minutes was in 1818. Grove says that James Holmes died about 1822.

Holmes, Thomas 1777–1812, *violinist, violist, violoncellist.*

The parish registers of St Sampson's in York show that Thomas Holmes, the son of Charles and Ellinor Holmes, was baptized on 12 June 1777. On 5 May 1799 Thomas was proposed for membership in the Royal Society of Musicians by the bassoonist James Holmes, doubtless a relative. On 4 August Thomas was elected unanimously, but when he attended his first meeting on 5 January 1800 the time had elapsed for him to sign the book, and his election was declared void. When he was recommended for membership a second time, on 2 March 1800, he was described as 22 years old, single, proficient on the violin, tenor (viola), and violoncello, and engaged at the King's Theatre in London and as leader of the band at Birmingham. Holmes was admitted to the Society the following June.

Thomas played violin in the annual spring concerts at St Paul's from 1802 through 1812. Perhaps the Holmes who played in the band at the Haymarket Theatre in the summers from 1804 to 1810 was Thomas, though that musician may have been James Holmes. In 1806 Thomas conducted the orchestra at Brighton.

On 25 September 1806 at St Paul, Covent Garden, Thomas and his wife, Hannah, had two of their children baptized: Charlotte Mason Holmes, who had been born on 24 August 1805, and Thomas Charles Holmes, who had been born on 12 August 1806. By 1811 our subject was in trouble. On 3 February he wrote from Fleet Prison to the Royal Society of Musicians saying that his two children were destitute; he made no mention of his wife, Hannah. Each child of Thomas Holmes was granted a temporary stipend of 7s. weekly, and Thomas Holmes was expected to indemnify the Society at some later date. He was out of prison in time to play in the St Paul's concert in May, but on 6 May 1811 he asked the Society to extend the allowances for his children for another month. That was done.

Holmes played in the May 1812 concert at St Paul's, but by 7 June he was dead. On that date the Royal Society of Musicians received an application for Holmes's funeral expenses, and the Secretary was ordered to ask Holmes's mother in York to take charge of Thomas Junior and Charlotte. On 5 July it was learned that Holmes's aunt was willing to care for Charlotte, and an allowance was granted to her; Holmes's son was to be sent to York. On 5 June 1814 the Board of Governors of the Society, evidently dissatisfied with the care Holmes's aunt was giving young Charlotte, ordered that the girl should be sent to her grandmother in York.

The last mention in the Minute Books of young Thomas Charles Holmes was on 7 May 1815, when his grandmother was noted as having had charge of the boy's schooling since August 1813. Charlotte, however, continued to attract the attention of the Society in London. On 5 January 1817 the minutes showed that Charlotte was then 14 but had a lame arm. An investigation into possible apprenticeships for her was ordered. On 2 March the Society learned that Mrs Holmes, a dressmaker (not Charlotte's grandmother; Holmes's widow Hannah, perhaps?), was willing to receive the daughter of the late Thomas Holmes as an apprentice. By 7 March 1819, when Charlotte wrote to the Society, her mistress had died; the Society sent Charlotte to her grandmother in York, who was granted an additional 2s. weekly as an allowance plus £2 for clothes for the girl. The last mention of the case in the Minute Books was on 2 February 1823. The Society in London received a letter from York acknowledging the receipt of £5 for our subject's father, Charles Holmes.

Holmes, Mrs Thomas, Mary [fl. c. 1759–1799?], *wardrobe mistress, performer?*

Charles Isaac Mungo Dibdin mentioned in his *Memoirs* that Mrs (Thomas, Mary) Holmes was the wardrobe mistress and mantuamaker at Sadler's Wells in 1787–88. She had brought up her granddaughter Miss Bates, who became Dibdin's wife. Mrs Holmes lived in a large house in Tunbridge Spa Gardens. She and her husband, Thomas, were the parents of Agnes Holmes, later Mrs Thomas Kennedy (c. 1759–1832), who had an acting career, and of another daughter, who married a Mr Bates. The Bateses had a daughter, Mary, who married Dibdin in 1797. Perhaps Mary Holmes was the Mrs Holmes who appeared at Sadler's Wells in the musical piece *The Oracle at Delphi* on 17 April 1799.

Holt, Mr [fl. 1706], *impresario.*

In the *Daily Courant* of 4 March 1706 was advertised a concert to be held on the sixth at

Holt's Dancing Room in Bartholomew Lane behind the Royal Exchange. Mr Holt was presumably the promoter of the event.

Holt, Mr ₁*fl. 1744*₁, *actor.*

Mr Holt played Marcellus in *Hamlet* at the Haymarket Theatre on 29 June 1744.

Holt, Mrs ₁*fl. 1721*₁, *actress.*

Mrs Holt played the Widow in *The Injur'd General* at Southwark Fair on 2 September 1721.

Holt, Henry ₁*fl. 1729–1739*₁, *dancer, actor, dancing master, impresario.*

Henry Holt's earliest notice in London bills seems to have been on 29 March 1729, when he played Darno in *Hurlothrumbo* at the Haymarket Theatre. At that theatre in 1728–29 was a Mrs Holt, possibly his wife. On 18 December 1729 Holt moved up to Genius in *Hurlothrumbo*; then, after an absence from the London stage, he played Aegon in *Damon and Phillida* on 27 May 1732 at the Great Booth on Windmill Hill. Holt was at Drury Lane in the summer of 1732, dancing in, among other pieces, *The Midsummer Whim* and a new *Scotch Dance*. The 1732–33 season found him at the Goodman's Fields playhouse, where he was seen first on 20 December 1732 as a Follower in *The Amorous Sportsman*. During the remainder of the season he danced a Peasant in a piece called *Masquerade*, participated in a number of untitled turns, and composed a new dance called *The North Country Maggot*, which he and Miss Wherrit danced at his benefit on 4 May 1733.

Holt joined Theophilus Cibber's rebel troupe at the Haymarket Theatre for the fall and winter of 1733–34. He was first mentioned in the bills on 6 October 1733 when he danced in *Les Bergeries*. After that, in addition to performing entr'acte dances, he was seen as a College Youth in *The Festival* and a Peasant in *The Burgomaster Trick'd*. When Cibber's group moved to Drury Lane in March 1734, Holt danced a Sylvan and Sailor in *Cupid and Psyche*. There he also played Pierrot in *The Harlot's Progress*, a Swain and a Peasant in *Britannia*, a Waterman and a Wind in *The Tempest*, and a Triton in *Cephalus and Procris*. His last appearance at Drury Lane was on 24 May 1734.

Henry Holt left England for America. Much information concerning Holt's American career has been found by Julia Curtis and incorporated in her dissertation "The Early Charleston Stage: 1703–1798." The "Charlestown" *Gazette* on 9 November 1734 carried the following announcement:

Mr. Henry Holt, lately arrived in this Province, takes leave to inform the public, that on Monday next he intends to open his Dancing Room at Mrs. Lory's in Church Street . . . where his constant attendance and utmost application on Mondays and Thursdays may be depended upon by those who shall be pleased to encourage him; the said Henry Holt is, he hopes sufficiently qualified to teach, having served his Time under Mr. Essex Jun the most celebrated Master in England, and danced a considerable Time at both the Play-Houses.

Holt's reference to "both the Play-Houses" implies that he danced at Covent Garden, for the Haymarket was not then a patent theatre, but Holt may have been merely embellishing his credentials.

Holt organized a ball in Shepherd's Court Room to help celebrate Christmas, 1734, and during the 1734–35 theatrical season he may have danced at the new playhouse in Queen Street. In May of 1735 he organized a ball at the theatre, but the playhouse was put up for auction soon after that. A poet denounced the sale in a published poem:

> *On the Sale of the Theatre*
> *How cruel Fortune, and how fickle too*
> *To crop the Method made for making you—*
> *Changes, tho' common, yet when great they prove,*
> *Make men distrust the care of mighty Jove.*
> *Half made in thought, (tho' not in fact) we find*
> *You bought and sold, but left poor H—— behind.*
> *P.S. Since so it is, ne're mind the silly trick,*
> *The Pair will please when Pierrot makes you sick.*

Holt may well be the person referred to, both as "H——" and as Pierrot.

Though the theatre reopened under new management by the fall of 1736, Holt announced in February 1737 that he intended to leave South Carolina. He wished to collect and discharge his debts by the beginning of May and to sell his carriage and horses. On 18 May he held his last ball at the theatre. By July 1737 he was in New York. Odell in his *Annals of The New York Stage* states that Henry Holt advertised in the New York *Journal* on 4 July 1737 that on the fourteenth he would conduct a ball "at the House of Mr. De Lancey, next door to Mr. Todd." The ball was later deferred until 21 July. At his new "Long Room" in February 1739 Holt announced a "New Pantomime Entertainment in Grotesque Characters, called the Adventures of Harlequin and Scaramouch, or the Spaniard Trick'd." The New York *Journal* advertisement promised a scenic display showing "the most noted Cities and remarkable Places both of Europe and America," and an epilogue was to be delivered by Master Holt.

Holt, Mrs ₁Henry?₁ ₁*fl. 1728–1737?*₁, *actress.*

A Mrs Holt acted Mrs Subtle in *The Lottery* at the Haymarket Theatre on 19 November 1728 and the second Countrywoman in *The Humours of Harlequin* at the same house on 25 February 1729. Since the actor-dancer Henry Holt performed at the Haymarket in March 1729, perhaps Mrs Holt was his wife. Henry Holt was in America by the end of 1734, and a Mrs Holt on 23 April 1737 was cited in the dancer Essex's benefit bill as running a lodging house (the dancer's lodgings were at "Mrs Holt's near the Playhouse Passage in Bow Street"). The landlady may have been the performer of 1728–29.

Holtam. *See* HOLTOM.

Holten, Mrs ₁*fl. 1682*₁, *actress.*

The 1682 edition of D'Urfey's *The Injured Princess* contains a trace of prompt copy which has preserved the name of an otherwise unknown actress: at the opening of Act III enter several characters plus "*a Viol, Mrs. Holten, Sue.*" The play was performed at Drury Lane by the King's Company in February or March 1682. There is a remote possibility that either Miss Holden or Amy Dalton, both King's Company actresses but from many years before, was intended. "Sue" was Susannah Verbruggen.

Holtham. *See also* HOLTOM.

Holtham, Mr ₁*fl. 1754*₁, *scene painter.*

Mr Holtham, a scene painter at Sadler's Wells Theatre, was included in a group called the Sadler's Wells Club painted by Francis Hayman in 1754. The painting hung for some time in the Sir Hugh Myddleton's Head Tavern, near the theatre, but has long been lost.

Holthom. *See* HOLTOM.

Holtom, Edward *d. 1780, actor.*

Little is known of the life of the actor Edward Holtom beyond the fact that he spent some 38 years on the stage, mostly in the humble roles of servants, messengers, ambassadors, foresters, sailors, and tertiary supporting characters. He was first noticed in London bills on 27 September 1744, when he acted Scruple in *The Recruiting Officer* with a company headed by Theophilus Cibber at the Haymarket Theatre. At that time his name was given as Holtham, a spelling which persisted in the bills through 1750–51 when it changed to Holtom (on occasion Holtam) for the remainder of his career. During Cibber's short-lived season at the Haymarket in 1744–45, Holtom also acted Benvolio in *Romeo and Juliet*, James in *The Mock Doctor*, Bluster in *The Prodigal*, and Lockit in *The Beggar's Opera*.

After the engagement with Cibber, four years passed before Holtom was again seen on the London stage, and it is quite possible that he spent that interval as an itinerant. On 17 October 1748 he made his debut at Covent Garden Theatre as Westmoreland in *1 Henry IV*. During 1748–49, his first season at Covent Garden, Holtom also played a Servant in *The Orphan*, Montano in *Othello*, Pistol in *The Merry Wives of Windsor*, Hotman in *Oroonoko*, a Merchant in *The Royal Merchant*, Ligarius in *Julius Caesar*, Kepler in *The Emperor of the Moon*, the Lawyer in *Love's Last Shift*, Jemmy Twitcher in *The Beggar's Opera*, and Sir T. Lovell in *Henry VIII*—a line of assignments which would vary little in status and type during an uninterrupted engagement at Covent Garden over the following 25 years. In 1749–50, for example, he played Cyclops in numerous performances of *Perseus and Andromeda*, Blunt in *Richard III*, a Beggar in *The Beggar's Opera*, Nym in *The Merry Wives of Windsor*, Peter in *A Cure for a Scold*, Steward in *The Recruiting Officer*, and Supple in *The Double Gallant*. Also, as a member of Cross and Bridge's company at Bartholomew Fair in August 1749, he performed Charles in *The Fair Lunatick*.

Holtom's salary in 1749–50 was 3*s*. 4*d*. per

day; by 1761–62 it was about 4s. 2d., and in 1767–68 it had risen to 6s. 8d. Usually Holtom shared in annual benefit tickets with other performers. On 5 November 1768 he signed his name as Edward Holtom in an open letter from the Covent Garden performers to George Colman; the letter was printed in the *Theatrical Monitor*.

His roles in 1763–64 will illustrate all of his career: a principal part in *Love in a Village*, Monsieur in *Love Makes a Man*, Lorenzo in *Rule a Wife and Have a Wife*, Caius in *The Merry Wives of Windsor*, Marquis in *The Englishman in Paris*, Jasper in *Miss in Her Teens*, Filch in *The Beggar's Opera*, a Frenchman in *Lethe*, Sneak in *The Country Lasses*, a principal character in *No One's Enemy but His Own*, the Valet de Chambre in *Perseus and Andromeda*, Humphrey in *Wit Without Money*, Varole in *The Relapse*, a Soldier in *The What D'Ye Call It*, the Apothecary in *Romeo and Juliet*, Paris in *The Jealous Wife*, and a Murderer in *Macbeth*.

In the summer of 1773 Holtom played an unspecified role in the premiere of Foote's comedy *The Bankrupt* at the Haymarket on 21 July. His last season at Covent Garden was 1773–74, but on 16 May 1775, according to a notation in a Kemble notebook, Holtom shared in benefit tickets. Holtom's last performance in London seems to have been as Canton in *The Clandestine Marriage*, given for the benefit of the Westminster New Lying-In Hospital on 30 April 1778 at the Haymarket Theatre.

In 1767 *The Rational Rosciad* claimed: "Holtom, in nothing able to excell, / Plays Filch or Frenchman tolerably well." Holtom died on 5 May 1780, according to manuscripts in the British Library and Fawcett's notebook in the Folger Library. The Miss Holton who acted at the Haymarket on 21 January 1782 may have been his daughter.

A portrait of "E. Holton" was listed in the *Mathews Collection Catalogue* (No 278), but is not in the Garrick Club.

Holton. *See* HOLTOM.

Holton, Miss [*fl.* 1782], *actress.*
A Miss Holton played Lydia in a specially-licensed performance of *An Adventure in St James's Park* at the Haymarket Theatre on 21 January 1782.

Holyday, Miss. *See* MILLS, MRS WILLIAM THE SECOND.

Homerston, Edward [*fl.* 1661–1677], *trumpeter.*
The elder Edward Homerston was appointed a trumpeter in ordinary in the King's Musick on 21 January 1661. He was active during the rest of the 1660s and into the 1670s but except for a trip to Tunbridge with the King from 10 June to 7 July 1663, which was noted in the Lord Chamberlain's accounts the following 17 October, he was rarely cited in contemporary records. On 29 December 1677 it was recorded that his son and namesake would replace him upon the elder Homerston's surrender of his position. After that the records made no mention of the elder Homerston, but the younger Edward Homerston (or Humerston) was listed as a trumpeter in the King's Musick at a salary of £60 annually on 13 December 1679. After that, his name, too, dropped from the records.

Homerston, Edward [*fl.* 1677–1679], *trumpeter. See* HOMERSTON, EDWARD [*fl.* 1661–1677].

Honour, John *d. 1792, carpenter.*
At Astley's Amphitheatre on 14 October 1785 John Honour (or Honor), Astley's head carpenter, shared a benefit with three others. He died on 3 June 1792 when the gunpowder he was using to make fireworks exploded. The *European Magazine* reported the accident. The machinist Mr Honour who worked at the Royal Circus in 1803 was probably a relative of John, perhaps his son.

Hoocfield, Elizabeth [*fl.* 1726?], *dresser.*
The Lincoln's Inn Fields accounts contain a note dated 2 March 1726 (1725/26 or 1726/27?) indicating that Mrs Elizabeth Hoocfield was paid 16s. for service as a dresser for Mrs Pelling.

Hood, Mr [*fl.* 1704–1705], *dresser.*
As early as 27 November 1704 the Lincoln's Inn Fields management, anticipating their move to the new Queen's Theatre in the Haymarket in 1705, tried to lure away from Drury

Lane Mr Hood, a dresser, and other servants and performers. The Drury Lane manager, Christopher Rich, complained to the Lord Chamberlain on 9 December 1705 about the matter. Hood apparently stayed at Drury Lane, though that theatre lost a number of other people to the Queen's in 1705.

Hook, James *1746–1827, organist, pianist, composer.*

James Hook, one of the most prolific English composers, was born on or about 3 June 1746 in the parish of St John, Maddermarket, in Norwich. Confusion exists over his parentage. According to *Grove's Dictionary* and Stacey's *Norfolk Tour*, his father was a cutler of Norwich, who died in 1757, when James was 11, thus leaving Mrs Hook to carry on the cutlery business. Information provided in *Notes and Queries* (15 September and 1 December 1883), however, argues that James's father was the Reverend John Hook, who succeeded Wesley at the Norwich Tabernacle and supposedly officiated there for 12 years until 1775, when the building was bought by the Countess of Huntingdon.

According to the Countess's memoirs, *The Life and Times of Selima* (1839), John Hook "was of a respectable family and left a son who was a musical composer and performer." In *The Life of George Whitefield*, the Reverend John Hook was said to have been "grandfather of the Rev. Dr. James Hook, Dean of Worcester, and of Theodore Hook, the celebrated novelist." Those two grandchildren were sons of our subject, James Hook, the composer. Testimony that the Reverend John Hook was James Hook's father would seem persuasive, except that, according to Grove, James Hook and his wife visited Norwich in October 1766, when he gave a benefit concert "for the widow Hook." But John Hook was very much alive, directing the Norwich Tabernacle between 1763 and 1775.

Early surgery on James Hook's legs, which had been crippled since his birth, left him with a limp. By the age of four he demonstrated musical gifts on the harpsichord, and by the age of six he played concerts. By seven his talent for composition was evident; at the age of eight he composed a ballad opera to a libretto written by a Miss Williams of Norwich.

Hook was placed under the instruction of Garland, organist of Norwich Cathedral. By the time he was a young lad he was teaching privately and at a local boarding school as well as playing in Norwich concerts.

About 1763, at the age of 19 or 20, Hook migrated to London. His first professional engagement, according to Busby's recollection in *Concert Room Anecdotes*, was as organist at White Conduit House, "where he daily entertained the visitors." In 1765 he was awarded the Catch Club medal for his "Parting Catch." He was also involved with productions at Richmond, Surrey. His music for the Richmond pantomime, *The Sacrifice of Iphigenia*, was published about 1765; he conducted the overture of that score at a Norwich concert in 1766. About 1767 he published a *Collection of New English Songs sung at the new Richmond Theatre.*

By the time Hook went back to Norwich in October 1766 to give the benefit concert for "the widow Hook," he was married to Harriet Horncastle Madden, daughter of a military officer. While at Norwich she advertised that "Mrs. Hook from London, Miniature Painter, intends during her stay in Norwich to take likenesses for Bracelets and Rings, at very Reasonable Rates."

In 1769 Hook became the organist at Marylebone Gardens. On 10 August he played an organ concerto and provided the music for the two-act pastoral serenata *Love and Innocence*, for which he received a benefit on 17 August. He continued as accompanist at Marylebone Gardens through 1773, also composing music for *Il dilettante* on 29 July 1773 and *Apollo and Daphne* and *The Divorce* on 27 August 1773.

Hook's compositions were also heard at other locations in London. At Drury Lane Theatre on 31 March 1770, Miss Radley sang one of his new songs in Act IV of *The Double Falsehood*. He played a concerto on the harpsichord at the Haymarket Theatre on 20 September 1770 and provided songs and accompaniments for the oratorio program there on 12 April 1771. At Covent Garden Theatre on 1 May 1771 he played a concerto on the harpsichord. His comic opera *Dido* was performed at the Haymarket on 24 July 1771; at the same place on 27 July 1772, Francis Gentleman's pastoral farce *Cupid's Revenge* was given, with music by Hook. He also wrote music for *The Country*

National Portrait Gallery

JAMES HOOK

by Abbott

Courtship and *Trick upon Trick*, both produced at Sadler's Wells in 1772.

For the first exhibition given by the Society of Artists in their new Exhibition Rooms, near the Exeter Exchange in the Strand, on 11 May 1772, Hook set to music an ode especially written for the occasion by E. Lloyd. The ode was sung at Marylebone Gardens on 28 August

1772, "by a number of Capital singers and young gentlemen of St Paul's Choir," with the principal vocal parts taken by Reinhold, Bannister, Mrs Cartwright, and Mrs Thompson.

Sometime about 1773 or 1774, Hook approached Garrick for a position at Drury Lane. In an undated letter addressed to Hook in Percy Street, Rathbone Place, Garrick advised him that it was his theatre's policy not to engage a permanent house composer. In 1774, Hook was appointed organist and composer at Vauxhall Gardens, positions he held for almost 50 years, during which he wrote hundreds of songs. Among the productions he composed there were *The Poll Booth* (c. 1785), *The Triumph of Beauty* (a musical entertainment perhaps written by his wife, 1786), and *The Queen of the May* (c. 1787). Many of his Vauxhall songs were published in numerous single and collected editions. His other musicals performed in London's theatres included *The Lord of the Manor* at Covent Garden on 23 November 1778, *Too Civil by Half* at Drury Lane on

JAMES HOOK

engraving by Blood, after Drummond

5 November 1782, *The Double Disguise* (written by his wife) at Drury Lane on 8 March 1784, *The Country Wake* at Sadler's Wells about 1785, *The Fair Peruvian* at Covent Garden on 18 March 1786, and *Wilmore Castle* at Drury Lane on 21 October 1800.

Most of Hook's music for the theatre after 1800 was composed for pieces written by his two sons, James Hook, born about 1772, and Theodore Edward Hook, born in Charlotte Street, Bedford Square, on 22 September 1788. The father provided the music for his son James's comic operas *Jack of Newbury* at Drury Lane on 6 May 1795 and *Diamond Cut Diamond* at Covent Garden on 23 May 1797. Thereafter he composed for the works of his younger son Thomas Edward Hook, including *The Invisible Girl, Tekeli; or, The Siege of Montgatz,* and *Catch Him Who Can* in 1806; *The Fortress* and *Music Mad* in 1807; and *The Siege of St Quintin* in 1808. Their musical farce *Killing No Murder,* intended for production at the Haymarket on 26 June 1809, was postponed because of the Lord Chamberlain's request for alterations; when it was given in revised form on 1 July 1809, it "was received throughout with shouts of Applause," according to a manuscript in the Folger Shakespeare Library. Their last productions together were *Safe and Sound* in 1809 and *Sharp and Flat* in 1811 (revived in 1813, 1815, and 1821), both at the Lyceum.

In 1776 Hook's oratorio *The Ascension* was sung at Covent Garden on 20 March but without success. The reviewer in the *Westminster Magazine* that month wrote that it would "make but a poor figure at the Day of Judgement" and that Hook had "mistaken dullness for dignity"—"if there were no other objection to the *Ascension* than its extreme length and tediousness, that circumstance alone would prevent it from ranking among the pleasing Oratorios now in performance." In March of 1778 he directed the Covent Garden oratorios. Hook was also a sometime organist of St John's, Horselydown, and of St George's Chapel, Windsor. He is known to have composed one full symphony; it was performed at Vauxhall on 11 August 1787, but the music is lost.

During the first two decades of the nineteenth century Hook performed at the organ almost every night that Vauxhall was open. In

1820 he abruptly and surprisingly resigned that position. According to Busby, the proprietor kept his station in the band open for him during the entire season.

Harriet Hook, his first wife and the mother of his children, died at South Lambeth on 19 October 1808. Of his second wife little is known except that she survived him for many years, dying on 5 April 1873. James Hook died at Bologna on a date unknown in 1827, evidently intestate. His widow was perhaps the Mrs Hook who sent a note of thanks on 7 February 1836 for a donation granted her by the Governors of the Royal Society of Musicians, though we find no record of James Hook's membership. Hook's music library was sold at Puttick and Simpson's on 30 January 1874.

His eldest son, James Hook, entered the clergy and advanced to Dean of Worcester in 1825, a position he held for three years, until his death on 5 February 1828. He was survived by his wife Anne, the daughter of the physician Sir Walter Farquhar. Their son Walter Farquhar Hook (1798–1875) became Dean of Winchester.

The elder James Hook's younger son, Theodore Edward Hook, was a novelist, playwright, journalist, and bon vivant of some consequence in the nineteenth century. Though judged by Coleridge to have possessed "as true a genius as Dante," T. E. Hook's enjoyment of drink prevented the full development of his gifts. He was the ghost-writer of Michael Kelly's *Reminiscences*, published in 1826. He died in 1841.

According to the *Thespian Dictionary* (1805), the Miss Hooke who sang in London between 1782 and 1787 was "supposed to be a near relation" of the composer James Hook. Possibly also related was Bridges Thomas Hooke, an obscure singer at the Haymarket in 1786–87.

James Hook composed, it is said, over 2000 songs and some 140 other pieces of music. Among his best and most popular songs were "Within a Mile" and "The Lass of Richmond Hill," both sung regularly with great success by Incledon. Extensive lists of his published pieces, including choral, instrumental, and miscellaneous music, may be found in *Grove's Dictionary* and the *Catalogue of Printed Music in the British Museum*. A list of his songs which were published in America is provided by Oscar Sonneck in *A Bibliography of Early Secular American Music*. Manuscripts of his music are in the University Library, Cambridge, the Minet Library, and the Royal College of Music. In the British Library is a collection of 225 folios (MS Add 28971), containing 46 songs set by Hook for Vauxhall Gardens.

In addition to his income from composing and playing, Hook earned some £600 per year by teaching. His *Guida di musica*, Part 1, was published about 1785; Part 2 appeared about 1794, and a *New Guida di Musica* about 1796.

An appreciation of Hook's music may be found in *Grove's Dictionary*, where it is stated that "Amid such an enormous amount . . . there was sure to be much of ephemeral interest, but there is also a good deal of delightful music." The *Thespian Dictionary* judged his compositions "very happy in ballad airs," but wanting variety and spirit sufficient for operas. Some of his detractors charged Hook with appropriating music and ideas from others, but there is originality in his numerous songs.

Good-natured and agreeable in personality, Hook enjoyed some reputation as a wit and punster. A painting of him by L. F. Abbott in the National Portrait Gallery shows a pleasant face, as does the engraving of him by T. Blood, after S. Drummond, which was published as a plate to the *European Magazine* in 1813.

Hook, Mary, later Mrs Harcourt [*fl.* 1698–1706], actress.

Mary Hook (or Hooke) acted at the Smock Alley Theatre in Dublin in 1698–99. Three of her roles were Mrs Rich in *The Comical Revenge*, Gatty in *She Wou'd If She Cou'd*, and Pert in *The Man of Mode*. She remained in Ireland through the season of 1701–2 and then went to London, where she entered into a five-year contract in October 1702 with Christopher Rich at Drury Lane. The only roles recorded for her during the 1702–3 season were Hoyden in *The Relapse* on 13 November 1702, Rosara in *She Wou'd and She Wou'd Not* on 26 November, and Aurelia in *The Twin Rivals* (and the epilogue) on 14 December.

On 9 December 1705 Rich complained to the Lord Chamberlain that Mrs Hook had been lured away by the management of the new Queen's Theatre; he called Mary "Mrs. Hooke, alias Harcourt." Her new name may have been that of a new husband, or perhaps Mary took a different name because of her breach of contract with Drury Lane. At the Queen's, as Mrs Harcourt, she played Camillo in *The Mistake* on 27 December 1705, Elvira in *The Spanish Fryar* on 8 January 1706, and Christina in *The Revolution of Sweden* on 11 February. She seems to have left the London stage after the 1705–6 season.

Hooke, Miss ₁*fl. 1782–1787*₁, singer, actress.

Announced as "A Young Gentlewoman" making her first appearance on any stage, Miss Hooke played the title role in *Polly* at the Haymarket Theatre on 11 June 1782. A week later, on 18 June, identified as the young lady who had performed Polly, her name was given in the bills for the roles of the Goddess of Health and the Genius of Nonsense in the pantomime farce *The Genius of Nonsense*. On 20 June she played Cecilia in *The Son-in-Law* and sang a song in *The Separate Maintenance*. That summer she was also seen as Maria in *The Fatal Curiosity*, Caroline in *None are so Blind as Those Who Won't See*, and Caroline in *The Dead Alive*.

Miss Hooke returned to the Haymarket in the summer of 1783 and added to her repertoire a Bacchante in *Comus* and Cecilia (with the "Cuckoo Song") in *As You Like It*. Though she was again at the Haymarket in 1784 and 1785, she played no new roles. She made no other summer appearances there, but on 8 January 1787, her last notice in the London bills, she played Margery in *Love in a Village*. Making his second-known and last appearance on the London stage that night as Hawthorn was Bridges Thomas Hooke, who may have been related. According to the *Thespian Dictionary* (1805), Miss Hooke was also "supposed to be a near relation" of James Hook (1746–1827), the composer and organist.

Hooke, Bridges Thomas ₁*fl. 1783?–1787*₁, singer.

Bridges Thomas Hooke was perhaps the Mr Hooke who sang at the Anacreontic Society meetings in 1783. He made his first and only appearance at Covent Garden Theatre on 14 November 1786 as Hawthorn in *Love in a Village* and several days later signed his full name in a letter to the *Morning Chronicle*. On 8 January 1787 he played the same role at the

Haymarket Theatre and then was not seen again on the London stage.

Two notations in the baptismal register of St Paul, Covent Garden, evidently relate to his family: on 24 January 1764, "Brydges David Son of Brydges David Hooke by Anne his Wife" was baptized; and on 26 February 1764, "Thomas Son of Thomas Hook by Sarah his Wife" was baptized.

Hooker, John ₁*fl. 1669–1670*₁, scenekeeper.

The London Stage lists John Hooker as a scenekeeper in the King's Company in 1669–70. The Lord Chamberlain's accounts cited him once, on 23 April 1670, as a member of the troupe.

Hool, Mr ₁*fl. 1741*₁, house servant?

The Covent Garden accounts in 1741 contain notations of small payments from time to time to a Mr Hool "for his men." He may have been the head of a crew of stage carpenters or stagehands. A Mr Hamersley was paid £1 1s. on 18 April "for makeing Mr. Hool's Artic^s." Hamersley was a tailor at the theatre.

Hoole, Samuel ₁*fl. 1739*₁, musician.

Samuel Hoole was one of the original members of the Royal Society of Musicians when it was founded on 28 August 1739.

Hooper, Mr ₁*fl. 1730–1731*₁, house servant.

Mr Hooper shared benefits with two others at Goodman's Fields Theatre on 17 June 1730 and 12 May 1731. Latreille identified Hooper as one of the house servants.

Hooper, Miss 1743–1769. See ELLIOT, ANN.

Hooper, Miss d. 1807. See LOVE, MRS JAMES.

Hooper, Rachael ₁*fl. 1742–c. 1760*₁, actress, singer.

Rachael Hooper made her first appearance on any stage on 13 December 1742 at Lincoln's Inn Fields Theatre attempting Sylvia in *The Recruiting Officer*. On 14 February 1743 she was

Polly in *The Beggar's Opera*, and for her benefit on 21 March she repeated Sylvia and played Nell in *The Devil to Pay*. Rachael gave her address as in Knightsbridge. On 5 February 1746, perhaps after gaining some provincial experience, Mrs Hooper played Polly for her first appearance at the Goodman's Fields playhouse. The only other role she is known to have acted there that season was Sylvia. Perhaps Rachael was the Mrs "Hoper" who wrote *Edward the Black Prince* (unpublished), which was performed as *The Battle of Poictiers* at Goodman's Fields on 5 March 1747. Mrs "Hoper" also wrote *The Cyclopedia*, a farce given at the Haymarket on 31 March 1748.

That same "Mrs Hoper" appeared in her own play, *Queen Tragedy Restored*, at the Haymarket on 9 and 11 November 1749. She took the principal part and for her benefit on 11 November pleaded in verse:

Left in distress what can a woman do?
By nature helpless and by want beset,
Is playing meaner than to run in debt?

Latreille noted that the *Biographia Dramatica* said "Mrs. Hoper was the widow of an Upholsterer and Cabinet Maker." That fact would not rule out the possibility that the playwright-actress Mrs Hoper was Rachael Hooper, but some of the evidence seems to argue that two different women were concerned.

On 9 April 1750 at the Haymarket Theatre for her benefit Rachael again sang and played Sylvia in *The Recruiting Officer*. The bill rather carefully stated that the actress-singer was "Mrs. Rachael Hooper who perform'd six years ago at the Theatre Royal in Lincoln's Inn Fields" and who had not performed at the Haymarket before. "Mrs. Hooper having been for a considerable time retir'd from the World, and being at a loss to know where to wait on her Friends" begged the audience's indulgence at her benefit.

Rachael Hooper sang at Sadler's Wells at its opening concert on 22 April 1751 and was at the New Wells in December 1751, according to the *General Advertiser*. She was at Sadler's Wells again in 1754, 1755, and 1756 as a singer. On 21 October 1757 she played in *A Medley Concert* at the Haymarket. Mrs Hooper was still performing about 1760, when the song *The Blooming Maid* was published, with her name given as the singer.

Hooton, Edward [*fl.* 1666–1702], *violinist, wind instrumentalist.*

On 7 December 1666 Edward Hooton (or Hooten) replaced Thomas Mell, deceased, in the King's Musick. Hooton was listed among the wind instrumentalists in 1668, but on 20 January 1669, when he was appointed to a second post, replacing the late Gregory Thorndell, he was named among the lutenists and singers at a salary of £40 yearly plus a livery allowance of £16 2s. 6d. The Lord Chamberlain's accounts contain other references to Hooton: he was ordered on 4 July 1674 to practice under Cambert at the court theatre; he attended the King at Windsor in the summers of 1674 and 1675; and on 10 September 1677 he was described as a violinist and appointed to the place of Thomas Fitz, who had recently died.

On 16 September 1677 Hooton resigned one of his positions, his place in the wind instruments, a few months after he had accompanied Charles II to Newmarket (from 16 to 30 April 1677). On 17 May 1682 a warrant directed that Hooton should be paid for having accompanied the King to Windsor; a warrant in 1683 indicated that the musician was still due livery payments from as early as 1678. On 31 August 1685 Hooton was reappointed to the private music under James II. He attended the King and Queen at Windsor and Hampton Court for 3s. daily in the summer of 1685, and he received on 21 September 1686 back livery fees totaling £112 17s. 6d. Hooton was with the King at Windsor again in the summers of 1686, 1687, and 1688.

Under King James the musician earned £50 annually (for one of his positions, at least), but under William and Mary his salary dropped to £30. He waited upon the King at Newmarket in 1689 and at the Hague from 1 January to 13 April 1691. By 1697 his salary had risen to £40 annually. Hooton was still serving at Court in 1702.

All that we know of Edward Hooton's private life is his marriage: the registers of St Andrew, Holborn, reveal that Edward Hooton, "one of the King's private Musicke," married Isabella Bower of the King's household, spinster, on 21 July 1674.

Hoper, Mrs. *See* HOOPER, RACHAEL.

"Hophye, Mme" ₍*fl. 1753*₎, *performer.*

When Christopher Smart ("Mrs Midnight") put on *The Old Woman's Concert* at the Haymarket Theatre on 13 March 1753, "Mme Hophye" was listed as one of the performers.

Hopkins, Miss, later Mrs Willoughby Lacy ₍*fl. 1790–1817*₎, *actress, singer.*

Miss Hopkins was probably born in Bath. She made her debut at the Orchard Street Theatre in that city on 16 April 1791, as Rosalind in *As You Like It*. She was a member of the Bath-Bristol company in 1791–92. Perhaps her father was the landlord of the Shakespeare Tavern who, as an amateur, had acted Boniface, the innkeeper, in *The Beaux' Stratagem* in 1786. On 7 November 1792 the Bristol press announced the death of "the wife of Mr. Hopkins of Bath, and mother of Miss Hopkins, late of our Theatre." Miss Hopkins acted at Brighthelmstone in the summer of 1792.

Subsequently Miss Hopkins joined the company at the Theatre Royal in Shakespeare Square, Edinburgh, on 23 January 1793 as Louisa Courtney in *The Dramatist*. Over the next six months at Edinburgh she was seen in at least 20 different roles, including Harriet in *The Reprisal*, Hero in *Much Ado about Nothing*, Isabinda in *The Busy Body*, Jessica in *The Merchant of Venice*, Laura in *The Agreeable Surprise*, Louisa Dudley in *The West Indian*, Ophelia in *Hamlet*, and a Singing Witch in *Macbeth*.

In the autumn of 1793 Miss Hopkins was engaged at Covent Garden Theatre at a salary of £3 per week, which, as the bills reveal, she earned by appearing almost every night, especially in the second half of the season. Announced as from Edinburgh, she made her Covent Garden debut on 20 September 1793 as Jacintha in *The Suspicious Husband*. That month the critic of the *European Magazine* suggested that "There is a mild cast of female character which this Lady may prove useful to the stage in filling." A manuscript notation on the playbill for her debut night, preserved in the British Library, reports that her "real name is said to have been Bennet," but we find no other evidence to substantiate that claim. Her next roles were Louisa in *The Irishman in London* on 25 September 1793, Lydia in *The School for Arrogance* on 8 October, Rachel in *The Prisoner at Large* on 16 October, and Lady Grace in *The Provok'd Husband* on 22 October.

Subsequently that season she acted Donna Clara in *Two Strings to Your Bow*, Lucilla in *The Fair Penitent*, Belinda in *Modern Antiques*, Lucy Oakland in *Netley Abbey*, Angelina in *Lovers' Quarrels*, Fatima in *The Widow of Malabar*, and Narcissa in *Inkle and Yarico*. She also played Philidel and sang a glee in 52 performances of *Harlequin and Faustus*, a pantomime which was first played on 19 December 1793, and a Shepherdess in 21 performances of *The Travellers in Switzerland*, a comic opera by Henry Bate which was premiered on 22 February 1794. At a benefit on 30 May 1794, when she acted Aspasia in *Cyrus*, she shared house receipts of £208 0s. 6d. (less house charges) with Hull. In the Harvard Theatre Collection is a pay sheet for 1793–94, signed by her, indicating she received a total of £104 for acting 208 nights that season.

In 1794–95 her salary was raised to £4 per week. She continued to be a busy performer, adding to her repertoire Fanny Pendant in *Arrived at Portsmouth* (a new musical farce by William Pearce on 30 October 1794), Lady Elizabeth in *The Town Before You*, Lady Charlotte in *Grief à-la-Mode*, Lady Blanche in *Windsor Castle* (a spectacular musical drama by Pearce on 6 April 1795), Emily in *The Telegraph*, Emmelina in *Bonduca, Queen of the Britons*, and Miss Emma Hale in *The Bank Note*.

The following season, however, Miss Hopkins was not to be found at Covent Garden, and the *Monthly Mirror* of December 1795 reported her at Exeter. She played next at Plymouth, where in late June 1796 she married the actor Willoughby Lacy (1775–1817), son of the elder Willoughby Lacy (1749–1831) by his first wife Maria Ann Lacy (1757–1788), née Orpen, and grandson of James Lacy (1696–1774), co-patentee of Drury Lane Theatre with David Garrick.

Mrs Lacy seems to have spent the rest of a modest career in the provinces with her husband. She was acting with him in a company circuiting Barnstaple, Taunton, Poole, and Guernsey in 1799–1800. The *Monthly Mirror* of February 1800 called her "a good scientific singer . . . though her voice is rather weak." Later, in November 1802, when she was performing at Bedford, the same journal praised her as "truly an excellent singer." Between 1802 and 1808 she played at St Neots, where her husband was manager.

Mrs Lacy was still alive when her husband died at Skibbereen, Ireland, on 12 November 1817 at the age of 42. The *Gentleman's Magazine* of that December reported that she and four young daughters had been left "totally destitute." One of the daughters, Maria Anne Lacy (1803–1877), acted at Covent Garden and married the dramatist George William Lovell.

Hopkins, Daniel [fl. 1714–1752?], trumpeter.

Daniel Hopkins was a trumpeter in the King's Musick by 1714. He was listed as one of the original subscribers, "being musicians," to the Royal Society of Musicians upon its establishment in 1739. By 1748 he held the post of deputy serjeant trumpeter; on 21 February of that year the serjeant trumpeter, John Shore, bequeathed £100 to his good friend and assistant, Daniel Hopkins, to be paid within six months of his decease. Shore's will was proved on 20 November 1752.

Hopkins, Edward [fl. 1663], trumpeter.

Edward Hopkins was appointed a trumpeter extraordinary (without fee) on 23 May 1663. He must have tired of waiting for a salaried position to become vacant, for the Lord Chamberlain's accounts made no further mention of him. He was very likely related to the Restoration trumpeter William Hopkins and to Christopher Hopkins, trumpeter under Charles I, and Peter Hopkins, a Gentleman of the Chapel Royal in 1625. The trumpeter Daniel Hopkins of the eighteenth century, and later musical Hopkinses, probably belong to the same line.

Hopkins, Edward 1757?–1790?, horn player.

Edward Hopkins, a horn player, according to *Grove's Dictionary* was born perhaps in 1757 and died perhaps in 1790. Edward Hopkins had at least two sons who became musicians. One, George Hopkins, a clarinetist, about whom little else is known, according to Grove died in 1869; he was the father of Edward John Hopkins (1818–1901) and John Hopkins (1822–1900), also musicians who are noticed in Grove. Edward Hopkins's other son, Edward Samuel George Hopkins (1779–1859), is noticed separately in this dictionary.

Our subject's wife, Frances Hopkins, of Dartmouth Street, Westminster, was still alive in November 1817, when she gave an affidavit to the Royal Society of Musicians attesting to the birth of her son Edward Samuel George Hopkins in 1779.

Hopkins, Edward Samuel George 1779–1859, clarinetist, violinist, bandmaster.

Edward Samuel George Hopkins, according to the records of the Royal Society of Musicians, was born on 25 February 1779 and was baptized at St Luke, Chelsea, on 4 April 1779, the son of the musician Edward Hopkins (1757?–1790?) and his wife Frances. On 1 November 1817, our subject's mother Frances Hopkins, of Dartmouth Street, Westminster, widow of the late Edward Hopkins, provided a record of her son's baptism to the Royal Society of Musicians.

In 1794 Hopkins was listed in Doane's *Musical Directory* as violinist and clarinetist and a member of the third regiment of guards. His address was in Brownlow Street, Longacre. On 3 May 1801 Charles Ashley proposed Hopkins for membership in the Royal Society of Musicians, but on 2 August of that year Hopkins withdrew himself from consideration. Seventeen years later, in 1818, Hopkins was again proposed for membership by C. F. Eley, at which time he was described as 39 years old, with engagements at Covent Garden Theatre and Vauxhall. By that year he was the father of four daughters: Isabella, born in July 1802; Mary Ann, born in April 1806; Elizabeth, born in November 1807; and Louisa, born in October 1817. Hopkins was elected to the Society on 5 July 1818.

Probably he was the Hopkins who was working in the Drury Lane band in 1821–22 for a salary of £3 per week. A "Hopkins Jr" was also receiving £1 5s. per week at the same time. On 1 January 1824, Hopkins, who was by then bandmaster of the Scots Guards, wrote to Sainsbury that he had little to contribute to that editor's biographical dictionary, "having been always in the quiet pursuit of his profession in a Military Band, under which circumstances he regrets he has nothing to communicate which could possibly interest the Public." In the letter, however, Hopkins gave his address as the "orchestra," Theatre Royal, Covent Garden.

Hopkins died at his home at No 10, Crosier Street, Stangate, Surrey, on 11 July 1859. His will with two codicils was proved on 10 October 1859 by his son John Larkin Hopkins, of Benet Street, Cambridge.

That son, born on 25 November 1820, was an organist and composer at Cambridge; he died on 25 April 1873. He is noticed in Grove, along with Edward Samuel George Hopkins's daughter Louisa Hopkins (1817–1880), who married Richard Lloyd and became the mother of the tenor Edward Lloyd, and his daughter Sophia Hopkins (born after 1818), who married the violist W. H. Hann.

Hopkins, Elizabeth. *See* HOPKINS, MRS WILLIAM and SHARP, MRS MICHAEL.

Hopkins, George [*fl.* 1739], *musician.*
George Hopkins was listed as one of the original subscribers, "being musicians," when the Royal Society of Musicians was established in 1739.

Hopkins, Hezekiah [*fl.* 1735–1749], *trumpeter.*
Hezekiah Hopkins was listed as one of the original subscribers, "being musicians," when the Royal Society of Musicians was established in 1739. According to the Lord Chamberlain's documents in the Public Record Office, he was a trumpeter in the King's Musick between 1735 and 1749.

Hopkins, Hopkins *1737–1754, dwarf.*
A facsimile advertisement in the London Guildhall Noble Collection, dated 7 March 1757 (*recte* 1754) announced the appearance of "Hopkin Hopkins / The Wonderful and Surprising Little Welchman," at Mr John Cafe's, carpenter, facing Salisbury Court, Fleet Street. Admission was 6*d.* to view Hopkins, who was "shortly to leave Town." He died several weeks later.

The *General Magazine* of April 1754 announced the death on 19 March, "In Glamorganshire in Wales, of mere old age and a gradual decay of nature, at seventeen years and two months," of Hopkins (or Hopkin) Hopkins, known as "the little Welchman," who had been lately exhibited in London. "He never weighed more than seventeen pounds, but for three

years past no more than twelve," reported the obituary, which also informed that "The parents have still six children left, all of whom no way differ from other children, except one girl of twelve years of age, and in all respects resembles her brother when at that age."

Hopkins, Priscilla. *See* KEMBLE, MRS JOHN PHILIP.

Hopkins, William [*fl.* 1641–1662], *trumpeter.*
William Hopkins was a trumpeter in the King's Musick in 1641, but at half pay. Subsequent warrants in the Lord Chamberlain's accounts on 17 March, 1 April, and 19 April 1642 indicate that he may have remained at half pay (8*d.* daily) for some time, though he was granted annual livery and called a trumpeter "in ordinary." He was very likely related to the trumpeter Christopher Hopkins, who served the King from 1625 to 1641, to Peter Hopkins, a Gentleman of the Chapel Royal in 1625, and to the trumpeter Edward Hopkins of 1663. On 11 June 1660 William Hopkins was reappointed to the King's Musick under Charles II at a salary of £60 annually, but the accounts made no mention of him after 1662.

Hopkins, William *d. 1780, prompter, actor, playwright.*
Though William Hopkins served in the very important post of prompter at Drury Lane for 20 years, 16 under Garrick's management and then four under Sheridan's, very little is known about his background or life. He began his theatrical career as a player. Announced as making his first appearance on any stage, Hopkins acted King Henry in *Richard III* at the New Concert Hall, Edinburgh, on 21 December 1750. At Edinburgh that season he was also seen as a Bacchanal in *Comus* on 14 January 1751, Escalus in *Romeo and Juliet* on 18 and 29 January, Lord Brumpton in *The Funeral* On 28 January, Solarino in *The Merchant of Venice* on 27 February, Doodle in *Tom Thumb the Great* on 13 March, and Priuli in *Venice Preserv'd* on 19 April.

In 1752 Hopkins was in the York company, one of his roles there being Albany in *King Lear* on 28 February 1752. While playing at York, Hopkins lodged in a public house operated by a Mr Barton, whose 22-year-old

April — Benefits Continued

144	Wed	10	Twelfth Night	1	The Man of Quality	2	Mr Palmer	
145	Thurs	11	Alchymist	3	Spleen	4	House	
146	Fry	12	As you like it	4	Waterman	1	Mr Bannister	

The Farce went off with great Applause the New Scene of the Regatta was properly introduced in the Farce

| 147 | Sat | 13 | Runaway | 15 | Spleen | 5 | House (Mr Parsons) Boughs by the managers |
| 148 | Mond | 15 | Matilda | 5 | Loves Metamorphosis | 1 | Mrs Wrighten |

This Farce was wrote by Mr Vaughan pretty well received

149	Tues	16	Much ado	7	Spleen	6	House {Mr Aicking night Boughs by managers
150	Wed	17	School for Wives	1	Bon Ton	14	Mr & Mrs Hopkins
151	Thurs	18	Runaway	16	Jubilee	34	House
152	Fry	19	Mahomet	1	Bon Ton	15	Mr Brereton
153	Sat	20	Maid of the Oaks	8	Waterman	2	Miss Abrams
154	Mond	22	Fair Quaker	1	Bon Ton	16	Mrs King
155	Tues	23	Jealous Wife	2	Elopement	6	Mrs Sutton
156	Wed	24	Recr. Officer	1	Man of Quality	3	Mr Jefferson
157	Thurs	25	Every man	4	Waterman	3	House
158	Fry	26	School for Rakes	1	Do	4	Mr Hurst & Mr Webb
159	Sat	27	Hamlet	4	May Day	16	House Mr Baddeley night Boughs by manages
160	Mon	29	Cymbeline	2	Rival Candidates	11	Mr Whitfield, Mrs Sharp
161	Tues	30	Provok'd Wife	4	Padlock	7	House Mr & Mrs Davies

When the Song was encored Mr Garrick said come let us give us that Song again for two very good Reasons, the first because your Friends desire it, and secondly because I believe I shall never be in such good company again.

	May							
162	Wed	1	Clandestine Marr	4	Irish Widow	3	Mr Bransby & Mr Burton
163	Thurs	2	Rule a Wife	4	Rival Candidates	12	House
164	Fry	3	Plain Dealer	3	Peep behind Curt	2	Signr Crespi
165	Sat	4	Committee	1	Genii	3	Mr Wright, Mr Carpenter & Mr Butler
166	Mond	6	Beggar's Opera	2	Bon Ton	17	Mrs Bradshaw, Mr Johnston
167	Tues	7	Stratagem	4	Man of Quality	4	Mrs Abington

Mrs Abington having wrote to Mr Garrick that she intended to quit the Stage at the End of the Season never to return to it again, he very kindly play'd for her Benefit

| 168 | Wed | 8 | Constant Couple | 1 | Deserter | 9 | Mr Waldron & Mr Greville |

Mr Greville St Harry Wildair very bad

169	Thurs	9	Much ado	8	Rival Candidates	13	House
170	Fry	10	As you like it	5	Waterman	5	Mr Fawcett, Mr Legg & Mr Kear
171	Sat	11	Rehearsal	1	Irish Widow	4	Mr Lamash, Mr Griffith, Mr Bluxton, Mr Cupett
172	Mond	13	King Lear	1	Spleen	7	House

The People flock'd about the doors by Two o'clock. There never was a greater Overflow — Mr G. was never happier in Lear — the Applause was beyond description 3 or 4 loud Claps succeeding one another at all his Exits & many cryd out Garrick for Ever &c &c

Folger Shakespeare Library

"Diary" of WILLIAM HOPKINS, April–May 1776

daughter Elizabeth he married at York Minster on 22 April 1753. She had acted in Yorkshire as Miss Barton. They performed at Edinburgh in 1757; one of his roles was Antonio in *Twelfth Night* on 18 August. They acted at Smock Alley, Dublin, in 1757–58 and at Belfast and Cork in the summer of 1758.

In the provinces his wife developed into a meritorious actress, but Hopkins had little success, and soon, as was reported in *The Secret History of the Green Room* (1790), he became "more remarkable for writing a neat expeditious hand, and being conversant in the regulation of the internal business of a Theatre, than for great abilities as an actor." When the Drury Lane prompter Richard Cross died on 20 February 1760, Hopkins was recommended to Garrick as one "who was perfectly qualified to superintend in getting up Plays" and was appointed to that position, which he held until his death.

Over the years Hopkins must have been one of the very busiest persons in the theatre, next in command to the managers James Lacy and David Garrick and the latter's brother George. In addition to the actual prompting of performances, he kept the promptbook library of the repertory, submitted plays for inspection by the Lord Chamberlain's Examiner of Plays, supervised rehearsals and the writing out of parts, and served as stage manager in the evenings. Hopkins also wrote out first and second drafts of Garrick's letters and negotiated as the managers' go-between with the actors. A letter written by Hopkins to the retired David Garrick on 6 January 1779—just a few weeks before the latter's death—illustrates the prompter's continuing devotion to his former manager and reveals the tribulations he often experienced in carrying out the responsibilities of his position:

We play'd last Night *Much Ado about Nothing* & had an Apology to make for the Change of three principal parts. About Twelve o' Clock Mr Henderson Sent word he was not able to play. We got Mr Lewis from Cov Gard supply'd the Part of Benedick. Soon after Mr Parsons sent word he could not play. Mr Moody supply'd the part of Dogberry and about Four in the afternoon Mr Vernon sent word he could not play—Mr Mattocks supply'd his part of Balthazar. I thought myself very happy in getting these wide Gaps so well stopt.—In the middle of the first Act a Message was brought me that M^r La

Mash (who was to play the part of Borachio) was not come to the House. I had no body there that could go on for it, so I was obliged to cut his Scenes in the first & Second Acts Entirely out & got Mr Wrighten to go on for the remainder of the part. . . . Mr Parsons is not able to play in the School for Scandal tomorrow Night dont yet know how we shall be able to settle that.

Hopkins's most important legacy to theatre historians was his continuation of the manuscript diary begun by Richard Cross, which in 13 volumes (now at the Folger Shakespeare Library) lists the evening's bill, the estimated house revenue, and many notices of unusual events during the performances throughout Garrick's management and for the first four-and-a-half years of Sheridan's. According to James Winston in "The Manager's Notebook," Garrick took a regular "morning peep" into the diary "which Hopkins took special care should always lie in his way accidentally." Additional information by Hopkins is provided in a manuscript memorandum book in the H. J. Smith Collection at the British Library and in manuscript notes transcribed by J. P. Kemble on playbills now in the Henry E. Huntington Library.

At the end of every season Hopkins was given a benefit which he sometimes shared with his wife, who acted regularly at Drury Lane from 1761–62 into the 1790s. Net benefit proceeds were £216 3*s*. on 27 April 1778, £162 15*s*. on 19 April 1779; and £145 5*s*. 6*d*. on 13 April 1780—his last benefit. His salary was £3 per week in 1776–77, less than that of his wife, who earned £4. From as early as April 1767 until his death, he lived at No 7, Little Russell Street, Covent Garden, opposite the stage door of Drury Lane Theatre.

The account books show many payments to him of fees for getting plays to the Licenser. In December 1768 Garrick sent a bill to the Calcutta Theatre for Hopkins's services—in the amount of 15 guineas in all—for cutting and preparing scripts to be shipped to India. When the new Liverpool Theatre was opened in the summer of 1765, Hopkins was prompter, a position he held still in 1775. There seems to be no record that Hopkins acted at Drury Lane, as we know his predecessor Cross did, but most likely he found himself on stage in some last-minute emergencies.

Hopkins played an important role in the

preparation of Bell's "acting" edition of Shake-speare (1773–74) by furnishing the Drury Lane prompt copies to the editor Francis Gentleman. In a letter to the *Morning Chronicle* on 4–6 January 1774, Tom Davies criticized Garrick for having allowed Hopkins "to deliver the Plays of Shakespeare in a State of Mutilation, as acted at his Theatre." In a letter to the *St James's Chronicle* on 29 December 1773 John Bell publicly thanked Hopkins and Younger, his counterpart at Covent Garden, for their cooperation. *Bell's British Theatre* (1776–78) was also published as regulated from the promptbooks.

Hopkins retired at the end of 1779–80 and was replaced by Harwood. On 22 December 1780 he died of "an inflammation in his bowels," probably induced by the gout from which he suffered. His wife survived until 1801. When young, their two daughters had acted as the Misses Hopkins. They enjoyed adult stage careers. Elizabeth Hopkins, born in 1756, married the musician Michael Sharp in 1778; she is noticed in this dictionary under her married name. The younger daughter, Priscilla Hopkins, born in 1758, is noticed as Mrs John Philip Kemble; she married the actor-manager in December 1787 after the death earlier that year of her first husband, the actor William Brereton.

Hopkins, Mrs William, Elizabeth, née Barton *1731–1801, actress.*

Born the daughter of a publican at York in 1731, at the age of 22 Elizabeth Barton married the provincial actor and future Drury Lane prompter William Hopkins at York Minster on 22 April 1753. According to *The Secret History of the Green Room*, her husband, who had been a lodger in her father's public house, introduced Elizabeth to the Yorkshire stage. An advertisement in the *York Courant* on 20 August 1782, some years later, when Mrs Hopkins was about to begin an engagement at York, reminded the public of that city that they had seen her act as Miss Barton.

Mrs Hopkins's professional activities for several years after her marriage, when she probably toured the provinces with her husband, are obscure until she engaged at the New Concert Hall, Edinburgh, in 1756–57. Her first known role at Edinburgh was Lady Brute in *The Provok'd Wife* on 7 July 1756, followed by

Harvard Theatre Collection

ELIZABETH HOPKINS as Volumnia
engraving by Grignion, after Roberts

Ophelia in *Hamlet* on 14 July and Mrs Marwood in *The Way of the World* on 21 July. Over the next year there she performed a repertoire of over 30 roles in comedy and tragedy, including Lucinda in *The Conscious Lovers*, Miranda in *The Tempest*, Mrs Strickland in *The Suspicious Husband*, Lady Touchwood in *The Double Dealer*, Olivia in *Twelfth Night*, Cleopatra in *All for Love*, Hermione in *The Distrest Mother*, Lavinia in *The Fair Penitent*, and Emilia in *Othello*. On 14 December 1756 she played Anna in the first performance of Home's *Douglas*.

The following season the Hopkinses were engaged at Smock Alley Theatre, Dublin, where she made her debut on 8 December 1757 as Juliet to Ryder's Romeo. The next day, however, if we are to believe the account of the aggrieved actress Mrs Beauclerk, Mrs Hopkins was discharged by Thomas Sheridan. In *Mrs Beauclerk's Letters* (27 February 1758), Sheridan is accused of a number of injustices toward his performers, including obliging Mrs Hopkins to play Juliet a few days after her arrival in Dublin after having "lain-in but a Fortnight before she set out on her journey." In mock quotation of Sheridan, Mrs Beauclerk wrote:

this very Season, I lured Mrs. Hopkins, from the North of *England*, where she had three Pounds a Week and tho' she played *Juliet* very prettily, yet I, the next Morning, sent my trusty *Victor* with *five Guineas* to her, and a Message, that I had no further Occasion for her on my Stage, *as it was full*; and tho' she and her Husband used all their Rhetorick, and pleaded their Distress, nay offered to stay, if I would keep them from starving, yet I had too much Honour and Humanity to regard their Complaints, and nobly told them, I would not employ them: and if you doubt me, Madam, go to *Drogheda*; there they worked their Way, and breathe Life in a strolling Company.

With the Drogheda company, Mrs Hopkins played at Belfast in February and March 1758; that summer she performed at Cork. In 1758–59 she returned to Smock Alley, which was no longer under Sheridan's management. In Ireland she grew into an "actress of some merit," according to *The Secret History of the Green Room*. When her husband was taken on as prompter at Drury Lane Theatre, Mrs Hopkins was also engaged by the management, making her first appearance in London on 14 November 1761 as Almeria in *The Mourning Bride*. She was announced in the bills only as "A Young Gentlewoman" but was identified by a notation by J. P. Kemble on a playbill. When she acted Irene in *Barbarossa* on 21 November, she was named in the bills as making her second appearance. After repeating Irene on 23 November and 13 January 1762, her next role was Sylvia in *The Double Gallant* on 22 January. Subsequently that season she was seen as Harriet in *The Jealous Wife*, Clarissa in *All in the Wrong*, Lucy in *The Minor*, and Elvira in *Love Makes a Man*. On 13 April 1762, when she performed Clarissa, she shared benefit tickets with her husband.

The following season, 1762–63, Mrs Hopkins added to her London repertoire Charlotte in *The Apprentice*, Mrs Marwood in *The Way of the World*, Lucinda in *The Conscious Lovers*, Arabella in *The Male Coquette*, Lady Macduff in *Macbeth*, Lady Candid in *The Elopement*, and the Countess of Nottingham in *The Earl of Essex*. Among her numerous other roles at Drury Lane in the 1760s were Lady Wronghead in *The Provok'd Husband*, Millwood in *The London Merchant*, Hermione in *The Winter's Tale*, Alithea in *The Country Wife*, the Queen in *Hamlet*, Roxana in *The Rival Queens*, the title role in *Jane Shore*, Regan in *King Lear*, Zara in *The Mourning Bride*, Mrs Heidelberg in *The Clandestine Marriage*, and the Queen in *Richard III*. In 1764–65 she and her husband were earning a combined salary of 16s. 8d. per night, or £5 per week.

For 34 years Mrs Hopkins had a regular and busy engagement at Drury Lane. She lived with her husband at No 7, Little Russell Street, opposite the stage door of Drury Lane, until his death in 1780; subsequently she resided at No 31, Bow Street, Covent Garden, in 1782. Her salary in 1776–77 was £4 per week; by 1789–90 it was £7, an amount she was still receiving in 1795–96, her last season. On 1 June 1775 she made an appearance at Covent Garden Theatre, playing the Queen in *Richard III*, for the benefit of Macklin, who

Harvard Theatre Collection

ELIZABETH HOPKINS as Lady Brumpton
engraving by Thornthwaite, after Roberts

acted the title role. In the summer of 1775 she performed at Richmond, in 1777 at Bristol, and in 1782 at York, where lived a sister who was married to a Mr Wilkinson (no apparent relation to the York manager, Tate Wilkinson). Probably Elizabeth was the Mrs Hopkins who joined the Liverpool company for the summer of 1786. In 1791 ten guineas were bequeathed to Mrs Hopkins in the will of the actress Elizabeth Bennet.

Among the many roles she "created" at Drury Lane in the 1770s and onward were, to list only a few, Lady Rusport in Cumberland's *The West Indian* on 19 January 1771, Mrs Bridgemore in Cumberland's *The Fashionable Lover* on 20 January 1772, Lady Rachel Mildew in Kelly's *The School for Wives* on 11 December 1773, Mrs Stapleton in Cumberland's *The Choleric Man* on 19 December 1774, and Dinah in Mrs Cowley's *The Runaway* on 15 February 1776. Seldom was she the object of unfavorable press comments like that of 4 October 1782, when the *Public Advertiser* criticized her and Mrs Ward for their costumes as Emilia and Desdemona, respectively, on 1 October: "Mrs Ward and Mrs Hopkins seemed to have forgot their Engagement on the Stage, and dressed themselves for a Card Party . . . frizzed, hooped and fly-capp'd." In *The Children of Thespis* (1786), John Williams (under the pseudonym of A. Pasquin) found "a sameness prevails in all the parts that she plays":

> *When she fails, 'tis apparent she did not intend it;*
> *The fault is in Nature, she cannot amend it;*
> *Who mix'd in her juices the Heidlebeurgh drop,*
> *Which, like oil in liquids, will swim at the top.*

J. H. Leigh's comments in *The New Rosciad* (1785), however, suggest Mrs Hopkins's usefulness to the theatre:

> *Tho not so great, a medium merit shines*
> *In* HOPKINS, *which judicious taste refines.*
> *View the old Maid, Coquette, or Mater staid,*
> *In each view Genius, Merit bright display'd!*

By the 1780s Mrs Hopkins's advancing maturity and girth required her to give up many of the parts in the line of tragic queen for those in the line of stage mother, old eccentric, or dowager. She acted Mrs Peachum in *The Beggar's Opera* for the first time on 5 October 1779 and Widow Lackit in *Oroonoko* on 17 May 1781. Her roles began to include Lady Wishfort in *The Way of the World*, Mrs Malaprop in *The Rivals*, Mrs Dangle in *The Critic*, Mrs Annaseed in *The Divorce*, the Duchess of York in *Richard III*, Lady Bountiful in *The Beaux' Stratagem*, the Nurse in *Romeo and Juliet*, and Mrs Ratcliffe in the premiere of Cumberland's *The Jew* on 8 May 1794. In the summer of 1793 she joined Colman's company at the Haymarket, where she played through 1796 a similar repertoire. In his *Candid and Impartial Strictures on the Performers* (1795), Francis Waldron commented that, though once a useful actress, Mrs Hopkins was on the decline. Though still a "good reader," she bloomed with all "the *full* imperfection of *nineteen stone*" (266 pounds).

Her last performance at Drury Lane was as Mrs Quickly in *The Merry Wives of Windsor* on 8 June 1796. That summer she played at the Haymarket. In reviewing her performance of Miss Hebe Wintertop in *The Dead Alive* at the Haymarket on 13 June, the *Monthly Mirror* commented that her "shrillness of voice, and the squabbishness of her figure are admirable accompaniments to the peevish expression of her features, and thus as far as natural requisites go, she is perfectly suited to old maids and crabbed aunts." Her last appearance on the stage was as Mrs Ratcliffe in *The Jew* at the Haymarket on 17 September 1796.

On 26 November 1796, Mrs Hopkins

Folger Shakespeare Library

ELIZABETH HOPKINS as Gertrude and DAVID GARRICK as Hamlet

by De Faesch

claimed the aid of the Drury Lane Theatrical Fund, to which she had subscribed since 1766. She died at Bath on 8 October 1801 in her seventieth year, according to her obituary in the *Gentleman's Magazine* that month, and was buried on 12 October at Walcot Church in that city.

Mrs Hopkins's two daughters acted under their maiden names and then married performers. The elder daughter, Elizabeth, born in 1756, married the oboist Michael Sharp in 1778 and acted and lived at Norwich; she was the mother of the painter Michael William Sharp. The younger daughter, Priscilla, born in 1758, married the actor William Brereton in 1777; after his death early in 1787, she married John Philip Kemble in December of that year.

In her will, made on 25 January 1797, Mrs Hopkins bequeathed her gold watch, £80 ("in the hands of my Nephew Mr William Wilkinson now living without Bootham Bar of the City of York"), and all her clothes and household goods to her daughter Mrs Sharp, with whom she was residing in Norwich at that time. To her daughter Priscilla Kemble she left £200 in Bank of England five-percent stock. Her son-in-law, John Philip Kemble, was to receive her diamond ring and serve as her executor; he proved the will at London on 31 October 1801.

Portraits of Mrs Hopkins include:

1. By Richard Crosse (?). Probably our subject was the Mrs Hopkins whose portrait was painted in miniature by this deaf and dumb artist of Henrietta Street, Covent Garden, on 10 December 1777.

2. As Gertrude, with David Garrick as Hamlet. Watercolor by Jean-Louis De Faesch. In the Folger Shakespeare Library.

3. As Gertrude (?), with John Henderson as Hamlet (?). By James Roberts. In the Garrick Club (catalogue No 439). This painting usually has been referred to as representing Mr and Mrs Spranger Barry, but Raymond Mander and Joe Mitchenson in *Theatre Notebook*, 16, suggest the possibility that it may represent Mrs Hopkins and Henderson.

4. As Lady Brumpton in *The Funeral*. Engraving by Thornthwaite, after J. Roberts. Published as a plate to *Bell's British Theatre*, 1776.

5. As Volumnia in *Coriolanus*. Pencil draw-ing by J. Roberts. In the Harvard Theatre Collection. This drawing, which shows only Mrs Hopkins's head, seems to have been Roberts's early version of his portrait of her in this character, which was engraved by Grignion (see below).

6. As Volumnia. Engraving by C. Grignion, after J. Roberts. Published as a plate to Bell's *Shakespeare*, 1776.

Hopper, Simon   *d. 1694, violinist.*

The violinist Simon Hopper was first cited in the Lord Chamberlain's accounts on 3 January 1642, when he was authorized £30 yearly as a replacement for Richard Dorney, deceased. The warrant implies that Hopper had just then been appointed to the royal service; of his earlier activities nothing is known.

On 12 September 1660 Simon was reappointed and described as "violin to his Majesty for his practise of dancing," a special post which he held in addition to his place in the band of violins. Hopper occasionally earned extra pay as well by playing on such occasions as the funeral of Princess Mary on 30 March 1661, for which service he received 7s. 4d. He attended the King on a trip to Portsmouth in April 1662 and served King Charles at Windsor at some point, for which he was paid on 10 July 1663. He went with the royal entourage to Oxford and Hampton Court from 30 June 1665 to 18 February 1666. Hopper's annual salary as of 1668 was £45 10s. 10d. plus livery—but his livery payments were frequently in arrears. On 9 January 1669, for example, he was owed £60.

Hopper made another trip with the King, to Dover, from 16 May to 4 June 1670. After 13 December 1679 the musician's name stopped appearing in the Lord Chamberlain's accounts. Simon Hopper was buried at Richmond, Surrey, on 25 September 1694; the Westminster Abby registers, recording the burial of his wife Ann on 29 August 1709, described Hopper as a sometime officer in the Exchequer and styled him "gentleman." The editor of the registers evidently misinterpreted the request in Hopper's will that any salary arrears from the Exchequer should go to Hopper's widow. Many musicians' wills of the period made such a request, and the statement should not be construed as indicating that a person worked in the Exchequer office.

Hopper's will was written on 12 October 1686, at which time he described himself as from Richmond. To his son Richard and his "now" wife he left £10; to his son Robert, provided he should live peaceably and not disturb his relatives, especially his mother, Hopper left £5. Should Robert misbehave, he was to be cut off with 5s. Simon left his sons-in-law Adam Swift and William Lownes and his friend Charles Francklin mourning rings. "Anne" Hopper was to be Hopper's residuary legatee and executrix. She proved the will on 2 October 1694.

Ann Hopper, widow, of Richmond, made her will on 20 September 1703, leaving the lease on her house in Richmond to Thomas Jeff the younger. To her granddaughter Ann Jeff, Thomas's wife, Ann left £200. To her grandson John Hopper, Richard Hopper's son, she granted forgiveness of his debts to her. Ann left everything else to her granddaughter Ann, she to give to granddaughters Ann Butterfield and Mary Hopper £20 each and some goods and to Ann Hopper's daughter-in-law Mary Hopper, £5. Ann Hopper made no mention of her son Robert. Ann was buried in Westminster Abbey on 29 August 1709, and her will was proved by Thomas Jeff on 11 September.

Hopton, Mr [fl. 1791], actor.

Dermot O'Whiskey in *The Humours of Sir John Brute* at the Haymarket Theatre on 26 December 1791 was played by a Mr Hopton.

Hopwood, William d. 1683, singer.

William Hopwood, a bass from Exeter Cathedral, was admitted to the Chapel Royal in London on 25 October 1664, replacing George Lowe, who had died. The Lord Chamberlain's accounts mentioned Hopwood only twice: he attended the King at Windsor from 1 July to 11 September 1675 and from 14 August to 26 September 1678, earning himself 6s. daily on each trip.

Hopwood's first wife, Blanch, was buried in the East Cloister of Westminster Abbey on 19 September 1671. She and William had had no children, so far as the registers show. William married a second time, to a woman named Elizabeth. The registers of St Margaret, Westminster, note the baptism of William Hopwood, son of William and Elizabeth, on 3 September 1674; a child named William Hop-

wood was buried in the cloisters of Westminster Abbey on 9 September 1680. We take these references to concern the musician, his wife, and his son. The Abbey registers contain several other entries which seem also to concern the musician's children, but the entries do not include the mother's name: John Hopwood, a child, son of William, was buried on 3 October 1676; Elizabeth Hopwood, daughter of William, was baptized in May 1677; Susanna Hopwood, a child, daughter of William, was buried on 12 August 1679; Frances Hopwood, daughter of William, was baptized on 22 July 1680; and Sarah Hopwood, a child, daughter of William, was buried on 5 August 1682.

William Hopwood died on 13 July 1683 and was buried on the seventeenth in Westminster Abbey. His widow, Elizabeth, married the court musician Richard Hart on the following 18 November.

Horden, Hildebrand d. 1696, actor.

Hildebrand Horden was the elder son of Dr John Horden (d. 1690) of Twickenham. John Horden took his B.A. at Trinity College, Cambridge, in 1661, his M.A. in 1665, and his B.D. in 1682. He was rector of St Michael Queenhithe, London, and vicar of Isleworth, Middlesex. His wife was Anne, the daughter of Thomas Morice, M.P. for Haslemere, Surrey.

Hildebrand received a liberal education and joined the United Company at Drury Lane Theatre in 1694, just before the troupe divided. He remained with Christopher Rich's players at that theatre after Thomas Betterton and his seceders moved to Lincoln's Inn Fields. The first roles known for Horden were Fairly in *The Mock Marriage* and Venutius in *Bonduca*, both of which he acted in September 1695. During the rest of the 1695–96 season he played Vilander in *The Rival Sisters*, Basilius in *3 Don Quixote*, Stanmore in *Oroonoko*, Thraselin in *Philaster*, Young Worthy in *Love's Last Shift*, Welborn in *The Younger Brother*, Artaban in *Neglected Virtue*, Wildman in *The Lost Lover*, and Lysander in *Pausanius*. He spoke the prologues to all but two of those plays and during the season contributed a preface to *Neglected Virtue*.

Jacob in his *Poetical Register* (1719) stated that when Horden died at the end of the 1695–

96 season he had been acting about seven years. Since we know of no roles for Horden before September 1695, perhaps he had been performing outside London. The *London News-Letter* No 10, dated 18–20 May 1696, reported that Horden was killed at the Rose Tavern, Covent Garden, on 18 May by Captain (Elizius) Burgess who was committed, escaped, and in 1697 was pardoned. The *Protestant Mercury* of 18–20 May 1696 gave details of the murder:

Some players drinking on Monday night, at the Barr, in the Rose Tavern, Covent Garden, made some noise, which offending some Gentlemen, that were in an adjacent Room, one of them lookt out, and spoke some words, which the Players retorting, a quarrel ensued, and several swords were drawn, and Mr. Horden the player was killed in the scuffle; on which the Gentlemen fled but Captain Burgis, who was lately tried for killing Mr. Fane, being of the company was taken and committed.

The coroner's inquest later brought in a verdict of murder against six gentlemen, though only Burgess was held.

The *Post Boy* manuscript letter of 21–23 May 1696 revealed that

On Sunday [17 May] Capt Burgis who killed Hordin the Player got Leave of his Keeper to go wth him [to] ye Cellar of the Prison which lay Crosse the way from his Lodgings and where he continued drinking sevll hours in Company of a Keeper and going over againe to his Lodgings about 6 sparks knockt down the Keeper rescued him and all made ye Escape.

Long after, in November 1697, the *Foreign Post* reported that Burgess had come over from Flanders, where he had fled, to stand trial and was pardoned by the King.

By the time Cibber retailed the murder story in his *Apology* in 1740, Burgess had become a colonel and resident of Venice; Cibber had it that Burgess and the other gentlemen involved in the tavern brawl stood trial and were acquitted. Cibber was active at the theatre when Horden was performing, so his description of Hildebrand is doubtless correct:

This young Man had almost every natural Gift that could promise an excellent Actor; he had besides a good deal of Table-wit and Humour, with a handsome Person, and was every Day rising into publick Favour. Before he was bury'd, it was observable that two or three Days together several of the Fair Sex, well dress'd, came in Masks (then frequently worn) and some in their own Coaches, to visit this Theatrical Heroe in his Shrowd.

Horden was buried at St Clement Danes.

Hordon, Mr [*fl.* 1701], *actor.*
Mr Hordon played Tancred in *The Generous Conqueror* at Drury Lane in December 1701.

Hornbolt, Mr [*fl.* 1705], *singer.*
At Drury Lane on 18 July 1705 Mr Hornbolt, "who never perform'd but once on the Stage before," offered an entr'acte song. The following 2 October at the same theatre "Mrs" Hornbolt sang. There may have been a misprint in the bill.

Hornbolt, Mrs? [*fl.* 1705], *singer. See* HORNBOLT, MR.

Horne, John [*fl.* 1782–1786], *actor.*
John Horne was cited in the Inner Temple records in 1782. On 20 August 1784 at Drury Lane, described as "(of the Temple)," Horne played the title role in Rev Thomas Stratford's fiasco, *Lord Russel.* The cast consisted of "Ladies and Gentlemen, who never performed on any Stage." Stratford had rented Drury Lane for the occasion. At that time, of course, Horne was an amateur. But, if we have identified him properly, he acted at Bristol after the 1784 affair; then, advertised only as "A Gentleman" making his first appearance, he played Lord Hastings in *Jane Shore* at the Haymarket Theatre on 20 June 1786.

Horne, Simon [*fl.* 1663–1670], *scenekeeper.*
The London Stage lists Simon Horne as a member of the King's Company at the Bridges Street Theatre in 1663–64, 1666–67, and 1669–70. A warrant in the Lord Chamberlain's accounts cited Horne as a scenekeeper on 3 March 1665.

Horner, Mr [*fl.* 1783–1785], *dresser.*
The opera house accounts show that Mr Horner was a dresser at the King's Theatre in 1783. He was also cited in the Lord Chamberlain's accounts as a men's dresser in 1784–85.

Horner, Mr [*fl. 1784*], *singer.*

The Reverend Mr Horner sang bass in the Handel Memorial Concerts at Westminster Abbey and the Pantheon in May and June 1784.

Horriban, Miss [*fl. 1732*], *actress.*

Miss Horriban played Lucy in *The Miseries of Love* at the Haymarket Theatre on 29 November 1732.

"Horse, The Little." *See* "LEARNED HORSE, THE LITTLE MILITARY."

"Horse of Knowledge, The" [*fl. c. 1772*], *performing animal.*

Charles Hughes exhibited "The Horse of Knowledge" about 1772, according to Disher's *The Greatest Show on Earth.* Hughes wished his animal to rival his competitor Philip Astley's "Little Military Learned Horse." "The Horse of Knowledge" fired a cannon and a pistol and was said by Hughes to be "the only Horse at present in this Kingdom that will fetch and carry."

Horsfall. *See also* HURSFALL.

Horsfall, James [*fl. 1784–1815*], *singer.*

James Horsfall sang countertenor in the Handel Memorial Concerts at Westminster Abbey and the Pantheon in May and June 1784. During the 1787–88 season he was paid £4 10s. for singing for the Academy of Ancient Music, and on 13 November 1789 he appeared, apparently for the first time, at Drury Lane, playing Carline in *The Island of St Marguerite.* If Horsfall sang in any other works at Drury Lane during the 1789–90 season, his participation did not warrant a listing in the bills. In 1791–92 he was with the Drury Lane troupe at the King's Theatre and sang a Priest in *The Cave of Trophonius* and was in the chorus in *Dido Queen of Carthage.*

On 22 June 1792 Horsfall witnessed the will of the eminent musician Benjamin Cooke, and in the late summer and fall of 1793 he appeared at the Haymarket Theatre in the chorus in *The Mountaineers* and as a Soldier in *Royal Clemency.* Horsfall was evidently in the Drury Lane company in 1793–94, but the only re-

cords of his work concern his participation, or, rather, lack of it, in May and June 1794. On 16 May he was at a rehearsal of *The Pirates*, but on 22 May he absented himself from a *Lodoiska* rehearsal. On 2 June he showed up to work on *Lodoiska*, but on the twelfth he was absent, and on 21 June he missed the first chorus when *Lodoiska* was performed. Two days later he was absent from an entire performance. Yet Drury Lane apparently kept him on for the following season. On 24 February 1795 he was up to his old tricks: he absented himself from the chorus in *Alexander the Great.* Still Drury Lane kept him on, as an extra chorus member, according to the account books, through at least 1795–96.

Doane's *Musical Directory* of 1794 had listed the musical activities in which James Horsfall was then engaged: the New Musical Fund (he was still a subscriber in 1815), the Academy of Ancient Music, the Concert of Ancient Music, Westminster Abbey choir, Drury Lane and Haymarket theatrical performances, and oratorios at Drury Lane and Westminster Abbey. His address was given as the Dean and Chapter Office, near the Abbey.

Horsington, Margaretta, later Mrs Denis Delane, [then Mrs Walker?] [*fl. 1732–1750*], *actress, dancer.*

Miss Margaretta Horsington may have been making her first stage appearance when she played Dainty Fidget in *The Country Wife* at Lincoln's Inn Fields on 29 February 1732. She was not named in the bills again until the following 2 May, when her benefit tickets were accepted. Her stage career lasted through 1747–48, traceable in the bills but sometimes confusing, for from 1739 to 1745 she was cited sometimes as Miss and sometimes as Mrs Horsington. From the roles, however, it is clear that the same woman was being referred to.

Miss Horsington performed for John Rich at Lincoln's Inn Fields and then at Covent Garden, acting and dancing, through 1740–41, building up a repertoire of a few serious characters, parts in pantomimes, and secondary comedy roles. Among them were Mrs Squeamish in *The Country Wife*, Ann Page in *The Merry Wives of Windsor*, Parly in *The Constant Couple*, Aglave in *Sophonisba*, Rose in *The*

Fancy'd Queen, Teresia in *The Squire of Alsatia*, a Lady in *The Lottery*, a Country Lass in *The Rape of Prosperpine*, Scentwell in *The Busy Body*, Betty in *The Gamester*, Lucy in *Oroonoko*, Honoria in *Love Makes a Man*, Gipsy in *The Stratagem*, the Maid in *Love's Last Shift*, a Peasant in *Apollo and Daphne*, Peg in *The Way of the World*, Parisatis in *The Rival Queens*, a Country Lass in *The Royal Chace*, Julia in *Theodosius*, Clara in *Rule a Wife and Have a Wife*, Teresa in *The Spanish Fryar*, Trusty in *The Provok'd Husband*, Philadelphia in *The Amorous Widow*, Belinda in *Tunbridge Walks*, Pindress in *Love and a Bottle*, Matilda in *The Paracide*, Mrs Anne in *Love's Last Shift*, Jenny in *Love for Love*, Cornet in *The Provok'd Wife*, Mrs Coaxer in *The Beggar's Opera*, Advocate in *The Fair Quaker of Deal*, a Country Lass in *Orpheus and Eurydice*, an Amazon and a Country Lass in *Perseus and Andromeda*, and Sylvia in *The Double Gallant*.

Under Rich's management in 1735–36 Miss Horsington's salary was 2s. 6d. nightly for 172 nights, for a total season salary of £21 10s. She did not receive a benefit that season, though occasionally the spring bills indicated that her tickets were accepted. By 1740–41 she had been raised to 3s. 4d. daily. On 28 January 1741 a note in the accounts for Covent Garden says, "Miss Horsington in part of a note of Hand Endors'd by her for 36 pounds & pd. to Mr. Evans 10–0–0."

Perhaps it was in hope of a better financial situation that Miss Horsington moved to Drury Lane in the fall of 1741. She remained there through 1747–48, now advertised usually as Mrs but sometimes as Miss. Her first appearance at that house was on 10 October 1741 as Clara in *Rule a Wife and Have a Wife*. Oddly, she did not perform again in a named role the rest of the season. On 14 September 1742 she acted Audrey in *As You Like It* at Drury Lane, and thereafter to the end of her career she was seen in such new roles as Arante in *King Lear*, Mrs Chat in *The Committee*, Jaquenet in *Women Pleased*, Myrtilla in *The Provok'd Husband*, Dame Pliant in *The Alchemist*, and Lettice in *The School Boy*. Most of her roles at Drury Lane were those she had tried before at Covent Garden.

Miss Horsington made a few appearances at other theatres. In February and April 1735 she appeared at Lincoln's Inn Fields, and she was there again in April, May, and October 1736 and June 1737. She appeared as Lady Anne in *Richard III* at Richmond on 8 September 1744.

On 19 November 1745 Margaretta Horsington married the actor Denis Delane at St Paul, Covent Garden. Both were from the parish of St Martin-in-the-Fields. She continued acting under the name of Horsington, and the bills no longer called her Miss. The Delanes buried a child at St Paul, Covent Garden, on 11 July 1746, from which evidence we can guess that either the baby was premature or the marriage had been forced. Delane died in the spring of 1750 and was buried at St Paul, Covent Garden, on 6 April of that year. His undated will left all of his estate to Margaretta, including inherited land in County Roscommon and land in County Galway. Margaretta proved the will on 16 April 1750.

Mrs Delane had left the stage before her husband's death, her last appearance being on 2 November 1747 at Drury Lane, when she played Audrey in *As You Like It*. Since Denis Delane's name was sometimes spelled Delany and may, indeed, have been so pronounced, perhaps Margaretta was the "Widow Delany" of whom George Anne Bellamy spoke in her *Apology*. If so, George Anne made no mention of the widow's having been married to an actor. George Anne said that Mrs Delany had accompanied her on a visit to Bristol (not dated), and that she had married one of John Calcraft's clerks, whose name was Walker. George Anne's story was that after her first husband's death Mrs Delany had refused assistance to his sister, who was in distressed circumstances. The sister sued Mrs Delany, and since the widow Delany's surviving child was now dead, Delany's sister won the estate.

Horsley, Mr ₍*fl. 1730*₎, *house servant.*

Mr Horsley shared a benefit with two others on 17 June 1730 at Goodman's Fields. Latreille identified him as one of the house servants.

Horsley, William *1774–1858, instrumentalist, singer, composer.*

William Horsley was born on 15 November 1774, the son of William and Frances Horsley of the parish of St George, Hanover Square.

National Portrait Gallery

WILLIAM HORSLEY

by Owen

He was christened on 11 December that year. His education was neglected, and when he was placed under the pianist Theodore Smith for musical instruction, he received much violent treatment and little useful training. He became acquainted with John Callcott, however, and also with Jacob, Joseph, and Isaac Pring, and his musical education was encouraged. He began writing vocal compositions, especially glees, canons, rounds, services, and anthems.

Horsley was appointed organist of Ely Chapel, Holborn, in 1794. That year Doane's *Musical Directory* listed Horsley as a bass singer, pianist, and teacher who had participated in the Oxford Meeting in 1793 and the oratorios at Covent Garden Theatre. Horsley lived at No 17, New Street, Fetter Lane. John Ashley recommended Horsley for membership in the Royal Society of Musicians on 5 March 1797. He noted that Horsley was married but at that time had no children. On 4 June Horsley was elected unanimously to the Society.

In 1798 Horsley suggested to Jacob Pring and John Callcott that England needed a society to cultivate English vocal music; out of that suggestion grew the Concentores Sodales. About the same time Horsley was appointed assistant organist to Callcott at the Asylum for Female Orphans; he relinquished his post at Ely Chapel. In May 1799 Horsley played viola at the annual St Paul's concert; in some later years he was listed as an oboist. On 18 June 1800 he received his bachelor's degree in music from Oxford.

Horsley composed a number of new works for the Vocal Concerts when they were revived in 1801, not only songs but full orchestral symphonies. In 1802 he served as a Governor of the Royal Society of Musicians, and in later years he was a member of the Court of Assistants. Also in 1802 he succeeded to Callcott's post as organist at the Asylum. Horsley took the post of organist at Belgrave Chapel, Halkin Street, Grosvenor Place, in 1812 and was allowed, by the help of an assistant at the Asylum, to continue at that post as well. In 1838 Horsley added a third organist's position to his chores: that at Charterhouse. He was one of the founders of the Philharmonic Society in 1813.

When Muzio Clementi drew up his will on 2 January 1832, he bequeathed to his friend William Horsley, of the Kensington Gravel Pits, £5 for a mourning ring and asked Horsley to assist Clementi's widow in arranging his musical manuscripts. In 1839 Horsley developed a close friendship with Mendelssohn. Horsley was elected in 1847 to the Royal Society of Music at Stockholm. During his career Horsley turned out a number of admirable glees and other compositions as well as an edition, with a biography and critical commentary, of a collection of glees by Callcott.

Horsley's first wife, who had been mentioned in his recommendation for membership in the Royal Society of Musicians, evidently died sometime between 1797 and 1813. In the latter year Horsley married Elizabeth Hutchins Callcott, John Callcott's eldest daughter. They had two sons, John Callcott Horsley (1817–1903), who became a painter and a member of the Royal Academy, and Charles Edward Horsley, who was born on 16 December 1822 and died in New York in 1876 after a career as a musician. William Horsley died on 12 June 1858 and was buried in Kensal Green Cemetery. Elizabeth Callcott Horsley died on 20 January 1875.

A portrait of William Horsley by W. Owen is in the National Portrait Gallery, a bequest of his son John. A portrait lithograph by R. J. Lane, after John Horsley, was published by J. Dickinson in 1832.

Horton, Mr [*fl.* 1727], *actor.*

Mr Horton acted Onomastus in *Philip of Macedon* at the Lincoln's Inn Fields Theatre on 2 May 1727.

Horton, Mrs [*fl.* 1798], *See* HEDGES, MRS.

Horton, Captain [*fl.* 1738], *actor.*

At "the Desire of several Ladies and Gentlemen" Captain Horton played More in *The Dragon of Wantley* at Covent Garden Theatre on 1 September 1738. Perhaps he was an amateur, but the bill did not carry the usual comment that he was acting for his own diversion.

Horton, Christiana *1699–1756, actress.*

Christiana Horton was born in 1699, according to reports of her age at her death. *The History of the Stage*, ascribed to Betterton, placed her birth in 1696 and claimed that she was from a good family in Wiltshire. That source said that she joined Booker's strolling company when she was a child, and Davies in his *Dramatic Miscellanies* said that when Christiana was very young she married a musician who was insensitive to her charms and treated her brutally. Davies claimed that Mrs Horton acted Marcia in *Cato* at Windsor in the summer of 1713 with a miserable troupe of players. Barton Booth, the *History* assures us, saw her act Cupid in the droll *Cupid and Psyche* at Southwark Fair in 1714 and introduced her to Drury Lane audiences the following year as Melinda in *The Recruiting Officer*. Though *The London Stage* does not record it, Christiana is listed in a British Library manuscript as making her first London appearance playing the role on 21 September 1714 at Drury Lane.

That she was given a fairly high position in the Drury Lane company is indicated by the fact that on 6 June 1715 she was granted a benefit with only one other performer when she played Amy in *The Jovial Crew*. She acted Dorinda in *Greenwich Park* on 1 July, but the scanty records for the 1714–15 season show no other parts for her. In 1715–16 at Drury Lane she appeared as Lady Anne in *Richard III*, Florinda in *The Rover*, Christina in *The Country Wit*, Juletta in *The Pilgrim*, and Marguerita in *The Duke of Guise*.

Mrs Horton remained at Drury Lane until 1734 playing, among other roles, Dainty Fidget and Lady Fidget in *The Country Wife*, Louisa in *Love Makes a Man*, Mrs Foresight in *Love for Love*, Lady Macduff in *Macbeth*, Margaretta in *Rule a Wife and Have a Wife*, Calpurnia in *Julius Ceasar*, Mrs Fainall and Millamant in *The Way of the World*, Arabella in *The Committee*, the Countess of Nottingham and the Countess of Rutland in *The Unhappy Favorite*, Lady Lurewell in *The Constant Couple*, Isabella in *The Squire of Alsatia*, Mrs Sullen in *The Stratagem*, Melissa in *Timon of Athens*, Lady Brumpton in *The Funeral*, Lady Graveairs in *The Careless Husband*, Olivia in *The Plain Dealer*, Araminta and Belinda in *The Old Bachelor*, Anna Bullen and Katherine in *Henry VIII*, Elizabeth in *Vertue Betray'd*, Phillis in *The Conscious Lovers*, Lady Wouldbe in *Volpone*, Lavinia in *The Fair Penitent*, Lady Fanciful in *The Provok'd Wife*, Harriet in *The Man of Mode*, Mrs Clerimont in *The Tender Husband*, An-

dromache in *The Distrest Mother*, Lady Dainty in *The Double Gallant*, Lady Macbeth, Zara in *The Mourning Bride*, Berinthia in *The Relapse*, Monimia in *The Orphan*, Belvidera in *Venice Preserv'd*, and Lady Townly in *The Provoked Husband*.

Once, on 5 April 1725, when Mrs Horton replaced Mrs Younger in *The Conscious Lovers*, she met, said Davies,

with very uncandid treatment from the audience; who so far forgot what was due to merit and the handsomest woman on the stage, that they endeavoured to discourage her by frequent hissing. She bore this treatment with patience for some time. At last, she advanced to the front of the stage, and boldly addressed the pit: "Gentlemen, what do you mean? What displeases you; my acting or my person?" This shew of spirit recovered the spectators into good humour, and they cried out, as with one voice, "No, no, Mrs Horton; we are not displeased; go on, go on."

She was praised by Steele for her Lady Brumpton and was considered by Booth and Wilks as the only possible successor to the roles of Ann Oldfield, especially Millamant.

During her years at Drury Lane Mrs Horton received annual solo benefits. She seldom acted in the summers. In the spring of 1733 she was with Theophilus Cibber when he complained to the Duke of Grafton about the management of Drury Lane, but, curiously, she remained at Drury Lane when Cibber and most of the other leading players defected. Near the end of the 1733–34 season she was appearing occasionally at the old Lincoln's Inn Fields Theatre with the Drury Lane troupe.

On 30 September 1734 Mrs Horton made her first appearance with John Rich's company at Covent Garden, playing Queen Mary in *The Albion Queens*. During the rest of the season she acted a number of her old roles—Millamant, Rutland, Monimia, Lady Townly, Mrs Sullen, Marcia, and others—and also played the title roles in *Jane Shore* and *Mariamne* and Cordelia in *King Lear*. She stayed at Covent Garden to the end of her career in the early 1750s, playing such new parts as Estifania in *Rule a Wife and Have a Wife*, Statira in *The Rival Queens*, Laetitia in *The Old Bachelor*, Cleopatra in *All for Love*, Mrs Ford in *The Merry Wives of Windsor*, Imoinda in *Oroonoko*, Caelia in *Volpone*, Blanche in *King John*, Indiana in *The Conscious Lovers*, the Queen in *Richard II*, Almeria in *The*

Mourning Bride, Biddy in *The Tender Husband*, Lady Froth in *The Double Dealer*, Lady Betty in *The Careless Husband*, Lady Brute in *The Provok'd Wife*, Portia in *Julius Caesar*, the Countess of Roussilon in *All's Well that Ends Well*, and Lady Capulet in *Romeo and Juliet*.

Aaron Hill in *The Prompter* in 1735 found Christiana Horton "undoubtedly the finest figure on any stage, at present." He could not see anyone else who could "go beyond her in personating a fine lady in genteel comedy." In 1739 Thomas Earl wrote that he knew of no one who could "look, or play, the Coquette like her." For her talents Mrs Horton received from the Covent Garden management £250 per season in 1735–36, during which year she took no benefit—though she received regular benefits in March in later years. In the spring of 1738 she was living in King Street, Covent Garden, but two years later she had lodgings at the Angel in Bedford Street, Covent Garden. Her daily salary in 1740–41 was £1 10*s*., and her benefit that season, free of house charges, brought her a total of £159 17*s*.

By 1740 Mrs Horton was, as Benjamin Victor put it, "in the meridian of life," but she still retained "her beauty without art, and even without the entire loss of her bloom, [she] is, by far, the handsomest woman on either stage." Her beauty and style were better suited to comedy than tragedy, and the few tragic roles she played were probably given her because of her eminence in the company. Henry Fielding in *An Apology for the Life of T.....C.....* in 1740 compared her favorably with Kitty Clive at the rival house, though their manner and parts were different. He found an "*inexpressible Somewhat*" in her Air, Face, and Mein [which] throws out such a Glow of Health and Chearfulness, that, on the Stage, few Spectators that are not past it, can behold her without Desire; and, in the Fullness of my Heart I may venture to confess, that the Desirable is so predominant in her that my Soul has a Taste or Tendre for Mrs. H..t...on." He found her good at "female foppery," said Millamant was "naturally her own," and called her a "giddy, lively, fantastick." Yet she could also "rise into the Decent Dignity of a fine Lady, and charm with the innocent Reserve of an Indiana. . . ."

Fielding also praised her work in tragedy. Since the death of Mrs Hallam, he said, Mrs Horton "stands without any equal Competitor; for she has that Grace in her Presence, that clear Melody in her Voice, with Strength enough to express the Violence of some Passions, and Softness to subside into the Harmony of others, that no Actress now performing on either Stage can, in this Light, be compared to her."

The *Daily Post and General Advertiser* on 15 September 1740 was at pains to point out that the "Report of Mr Cibber and Mrs Horton being engag'd to another Theatre, is entirely without Foundation"—but it appears that the Drury Lane Manager did engage Mrs Horton to get his 1743–44 season started. For in the spring of 1744 Fleetwood discharged a number of his players, and Mrs Horton was named among them. In *The Disputes* (1744) she was described as being cast out, buried alive by Fleetwood, despite the fact that she "makes so amiable a Figure and understands her Business so well." Mrs Horton, then, was briefly under contract to Drury Lane. She was not named in any of the bills.

By 1746–47 Christiana was acting less frequently and, in consequence, was being paid only £3 weekly. In her last full season, 1749–50, Covent Garden paid her £1 daily—probably only when she performed. Mrs Horton left the stage, but not permanently. On 20 April 1752 at Drury Lane she acted Queen Elizabeth in *The Earl of Essex* for her shared benefit with the subtreasurer. By that time she was living at Mr Havard's in Broad Court, Bow Street. She was also reported as acting Mrs Maggot in *Young Scarron* in 1752, probably in a summer touring group. On 25 May 1753, the last day of the season at Drury Lane, Mrs Horton was given a benefit which brought in £120, but she did not perform. She was similarly benefited on 30 May 1754. On 24 May 1756 the prompter Cross wrote in his diary that *Love for Love*, "A Gratis Play," was "put [on] for ye Benefit of Mrs Horton, an old Actress who left ye stage some years, but Mr Morgan (an old actor) is to have a third of it." The receipts were only £89.

Davies tells us that Mrs Horton grew corpulent as she aged and that she tried to preserve her once-fine shape by lacing herself "so tight that the upper part of her figure bore no proportion to the rest of her body." At 60 (he should have said 50) she still dressed like a girl of twenty and ogled and simpered to the last.

Her sole passion, Davies said, was to be admired, yet she rejected an offer from a nobleman who would have given her a large settlement to live with him.

On 20 October 1756 Christiana Horton drew up her will, leaving her entire estate to her daughter Penelope Wolseley, a spinster then living in Dublin. Had Mrs Horton married a second time? No evidence has been found. Mrs Horton died on 4 December 1756 at the age of 57 and was buried four days later at St Giles in the Fields.

The Elizabeth Horton listed in a British Library manuscript dated 1722 was certainly Christiana; either Elizabeth was her middle name or the name was put down in error.

Horton, Elizabeth. *See* HORTON, CHRISTIANA.

Horton, John [*fl.* 1767], *musician.*
John Horton, a musician living in the Strand, became a freeman of the Worshipfull Company of Musicians on 2 December 1767. He may have been related to James Horton, who was bound apprentice to Charles Seymour on 18 September 1760. There is no record of James's becoming a freeman.

Horwell, Mr [*fl.* 1779–1792], *actor.*
Mr Horwell had a role in *The Touchstone of Invention* at the Haymarket Theatre on 18 October 1779 and appeared in *The Spendthrift* at the same house on 12 November 1781. *The London Stage* lists him as at the Haymarket again on 25 November 1782 playing Hairbrain in *Wit Without Money* and on 16 April 1792 playing King Henry in *Richard III.*

Horwood. *See* HARWOOD.

Hosley. *See* HASELER.

Hosier, Mr [*fl.* 1783–1785], *carpenter.*
The opera house accounts show that in 1783 Mr Hosier was a carpenter's journeyman at the King's Theatre. He was similarly noted in 1784–85 in the Lord Chamberlain's accounts.

Hoskin, Ann [*fl.* 1770–1790], *actress.*
Ann Hoskin was, according to the will of Charles Hoskin, in 1770, his natural daughter. Mrs Charles Hoskin was an actress and probably coached young Ann. We believe that Ann, not Mrs Hoskin, was the "Mrs Hoskin" who made her first appearance in Ireland at Smock Alley in 1774–75, hailed as from the Covent Garden Theatre in London. The Covent Garden bills, unfortunately, contain no mention of any Hoskin, though Ann may well have been an unrecorded performer there. Clark in *The Irish Stage in the County Towns* placed Ann at the Crow Street Theatre in Dublin in 1778, and W. J. Lawrence's notes on the Dublin bills indicate that she was there through 1780. Clark traced Ann to Limerick in 1779, Belfast in 1783, 1786, 1787, 1788, and 1789, and Derry in 1790.

Hoskin, Mrs Charles J. [*fl.* 1770–1799], *actress, manageress.*
Faulkner's Dublin Journal reported on 24 February 1770 that Mrs (Charles) Hoskin from Drury Lane in London would make her first appearance at the Capel Street Theatre on 26 February playing Mrs Harley in *False Delicacy.* Mrs Hoskin may indeed have acted at Drury Lane before 1770, but her name has not been found in any of the bills there. She may have been a very minor member of the Drury Lane troupe.

Mrs Hoskin's husband, Charles, was the builder of the Capel Street playhouse. *Faulkner's Dublin Journal* on 26 May 1770 reported that Hoskin had died and that his widow's benefit was to be on 7 June. Hoskin's will was proved on 18 June and mentioned his natural children Ann and Frederick but made no mention of Mrs Hoskin.

During the 1770s Mrs Hoskin played fairly regularly in Dublin: at Capel Street through 1770–71 (and she evidently helped in the management), at Smock Alley through the summer of 1774, and at Crow Street from 1776 to 1781. Ann Hoskin, Charles's daughter, acted in Dublin and the provinces from 1774 on. Mrs Hoskin also appeared at provincial playhouses. She was in Limerick in 1771, Cork in 1776, Kilkenny in 1779, Belfast in 1783, 1788, 1789, 1791, and 1792, and Derry from 1790 through 1794 and in 1799.

William Smith Clark, in *The Irish Stage in the County Towns,* recorded a benefit bill of 24 November 1795, when Mrs Hoskin was acting in Derry: she begged the public to rescue "their poor old favourite from the greatest misery and distress, and enable her to support herself in her latter days without soliciting charity which her spirit had hitherto prevented her from."

Hotham. *See* HOLTOM.

Houbert, Marie. *See* MILLARD, MARIE ELIZABETH ANNE.

Illustrations

OFFICIAL DOCUMENTS AND LETTERS

31

The Deposition of Mrs Rebecca Marshall
against Sr Hugh Midleton. 8. Feb. 1666.

On Saturday last Sr Hugh entring into the Tyring house, or
behind the scenes of the Playhouse, Mrs Marshall taxed him
with some ill language he had cast out against the women actors
of that house, and added that shee wondred he would come amongst
them. Sr Hugh being disgusted at this after a short discourse
grew into heat, and told her shee lyed, and concluded the injurie
with calling her Jade, and threatning he would kick her and
that his footman should kick her.

Mrs Marshall on the munday following frightned with his
menaces complained of him to the King, and desired his Ma:ties
protection from farther injuries.

Vpon tuesday in the evening hauing acted in the Play that day
and returning to her lodging in the great Entrie going out of
the Playhouse into Drurie lane, shee saw Sr Hugh Midleton
standing there wch gaue her some apprehension that he lay in wait
to doe her some mischief or affront. wch shee declared to Mr Quin
who led her home. Some few doores from the Playhouse a
Ruffian pressed hard upon her, insomuch that shee complained
first of his rudenes, and after turned about and said I thinke the
fellow would rob mee, or pick my pockett. vpon wch he turned his
face and seemed to slink away. And when shee thought shee
was quite rid of him, neare the entrance of the Court where shee
lodgeth (the Street being there free of coaches) the same Ruffian
ran close up to her and clapd a Turd upon her face and haire and
fled away in a Trice.

That this was a formd designe, appeares by the

fellows pursuit of her from the Playhouse to her lodging and
that Sr Hugh suborned him, appeares

1. Because the said Mrs Marshall hath no difference at present
with any other man or woman in England.

2. Because it was the same day that the newes broke out that shee
had been at Court and received a gracious promise from his Ma.^{ty}
that shee should not bee injured.

3. Because Sr H. Midleton was seen by her in the Entrie of the
Playhouse a good while after the Play was done, a place where
no people of Qualitie do stop at any time longer then to take
coach or chaire, which he could not want, many coaches standing
emptie and all the Audience wholly retired.

Mrs Marshall is readie to take her Oath of this if required
and doth beleeve it may bee prooud, if need bee, that Sr Hugh
did the same day discour a malicious design of doing her a
mischief   And the premises duely considered
Shee humbly implores his Maties protection and Justice aswell
for her vindication from these barbarous injuries, as for her
securitie for the future.

Courtesy of the Public Record Office
Deposition of the actress Rebecca Marshall, 8 February 1666

Charles R.

Hereas Complaint hath often been made unto Us, That divers Perſons do rudely preſs, and with evil Language and Blows force their way into Our Theatres, (called the Theatre Royal in Bridges-ſtreet, and the Dukes Theatre in Dorſet-Garden) at the time of their Publick Repreſentations and Actings, without paying the Price eſtabliſhed at both the ſaid Theatres, to the great diſturbance of Our Servants, Licenced by Our Authority, as well as others, and to the danger of the Publick Peace: Our Will and Pleaſure therefore is, and We do hereby ſtraightly Charge and Command, That no Perſon of what Quality ſoever, do preſume to come into either of the ſaid Theatres before and during the time of Acting, and until the Plays are quite finiſhed, without paying the Price eſtabliſhed for the reſpective Places. And Our further Command is, That the Money which ſhall be ſo paid by any Perſons for their reſpective Places, ſhall not be return'd again, after it is once paid, notwithſtanding that ſuch Perſons ſhall go out at any time before or during the Play; And (to avoid future Fraud) That none hereafter ſhall enter the Pit, First, or Upper Gallery, without delivering to the reſpective Door-keeper the Ticket or Tickets which they received for their Money paid at the firſt Door.

And foraſmuch as 'tis impoſſible to command thoſe vaſt Engines (which move the Scenes and Machines) and to order ſuch a number of Perſons as muſt be employed in Works of that nature, if any but ſuch as belong thereunto, be ſuffer'd to preſs in amongſt them; Our Will and Command is, That no Perſon of what Quality ſoever, preſume to ſtand or ſit on the Stage, or to come within any part of the Scenes, before the Play begins, while 'tis Acting, or after 'tis ended; and We ſtrictly hereby Command Our Officers and Guard of Souldiers which attend the reſpective Theatres, to ſee this Order exactly obſerv'd. And if any Perſon whatſoever ſhall diſobey this Our known Pleaſure and Command, We ſhall proceed againſt them as Contemners of Our Royal Authority, and Diſturbers of the Publick Peace.

Given at Our Court at *Whitehall* the Second day of *February* in the Twenty ſixth Year of Our Reign.

LONDON,

Printed by the Aſſigns of *John Bill* and *Chriſtopher Barker*, Printers to the Kings moſt Excellent Majeſty. 1673.

Theatre Collection, The New York Public Library at Lincoln Center
Proclamation of Charles II relating to the theatres, 2 February 1673

African Compª

For the Com.rs of his Ma.ts Customes send direccon to the severall officers of the Customes at Barbados and all other his Ma.ts Plantacon in America that they doe not permitt any ship or ships to goe to sea on a tradeing voyage from any Ports or places under their respective care till the Master owners or other Proprietors of such shipp or vessell have given good security according to the direccon of the abovewritten Order of his Ma.ty in Councell And &c.ª
6. X.br 1676 ~ Danby

Mr Betterton

After &c I being informed by Mr Thomas Betterton one of his R.ll H.ss the D. of Yorks Comedians that y.e Particulars menconed in the annexed Schedule are consigned to him from Calais to be used in a new Pageon not yet acted called Circe These are to direct & require you to permitt & suffer the same to be imported & to cause y.e same (after the usuall fees) to be & so Custome free for which &c
7 x.br 76   Danby
To y.e Com.rs   The Schedule

In a Deale Chest weighing 81 li french weight ab.t 30 do.z of Italian Masques some Scarlet Colour some black
30 Plumes of ffeathers already used.
a Plume of ffeathers for a Woman Scarlet Colour
2 Tires for the head of embroydered Satin
A Bundle of Weaving Linnen for a man
A Steel Compass
3 Iron Tooles
2 Fire Pibles
Some pastboard Moles
in the little box 28 or 30 Italian Masques
                        Signed   Tho Betterton

Port of Sandwich

Lett a Comission for setting out of Ports Wharfes and Keyes in the Port of Sandwich, and the severall Members and Creets thereunto belonging be yssued out of his Ma.ts Court of Excheq.r according to this Draught the forme whereof is agreeable to a Precedent approved of by his Ma.ts Attorney Generall for w.ch &c.ª 7. X.br 1676.
To the Kings Remembrancer or Copy: Danby.

Com.rs names
        The Mayor of Sandwich Dover City of Rochester and
        Towne of Feversham now & for the time being, Charles
        Osborne and Giles Dastar Esq.rs Surveyors Gen.ll of y.e Customs
        Rich. Breton, & Tho. Beale Esq.rs Custom.r of Sandwich Walter
        Browne Esq.r Comptroll.r of Sandwich, John Watten, Tho. Tooke, James
        Crouseman, Hen. Shales, Rich. Brabant, Jn.o Kennett, Jn.o Johnson
        Hugh Atwoote, John England and W.m Potts. —— Gents

Courtesy of the Public Record Office
List of theatrical goods imported custom free by the actor Thomas Betterton, 1676

Articles of Agreem.t Indented made concluded
& agreed upon this fifteenth day off Aprill —
Anno Dni 1695 by & between William Bullock
of S.t Giles Cripplegate in County of Midd. gent
of the one part & S.r Thomas Skipwith of Inner=
=Temple in County aforesd. Bar.t of the other
part.

Jnp.s The said William Bullock doth hereby Covenant to & with the
said S.r Thomas Skipwith, his heires & Assignes that he the
said William Bullock shall & will from henceforth during
the Terme of three yeares next ensuing the date of these
presents with his best care & Skill Sing daunce, act, & represent
such persons & parts in any Play house within London
Westm.r or the Suburbs thereof under the said S.r Thomas
Skipwith his heires or assignes as shall bee by him or
them ordered or appoynted for him the said W.m Bullock
to act or represent And shall & will from time to time
observe and obey the Rules & orders of such house & of
the sd. S.r Thomas Skipwith his heires & assignes in &
about or concerning the same.

And further the s.d William Bullock shall not nor will
att any time hereafter act play or beare any part in any
other play house whatsoever then in such play house
appoynted or governed by the said S.r Thomas Skipwith
his heires or assignes without leave under the hand & seale
of the said S.r Thomas Skipwith his heires or assignes
first had or obtayned.

Item in Consideration hereof the said S.r Thomas
Skipwith doth hereby Covenant to and with —
the said William Bullock his Ex.rs & Adm.rs that
hee the said William Bullock or his Assignes shall
have and receive the Summe of Twenty shillings
weekly and every week for & during soe many weeks
as hee the said William Bullock shall from time forth
act or play his part in such Playhouse under the

Courtesy of the Public Record Office

The actor William Bullock's contract with the Drury Lane co-patentee Sir Thomas Skipworth, 15 April 1695

Folger Shakespeare Library

The actor James Aickin's contract with the Drury Lane patentees Richard Brinsley Sheridan and Thomas Linley, 31 March 1794

433

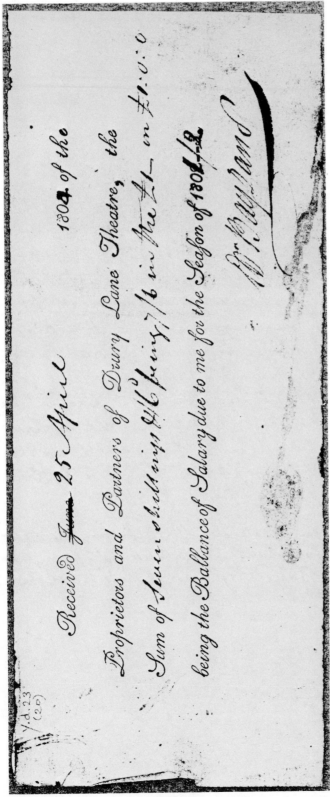

Folger Shakespeare Library
Salary receipt signed by William Bayzand, the Drury Lane dancer-actor, 25 April 1802

Nov. 9. 45

Sr

      I had a thousand pretty things to say to you, but you go to Ireland without seeing me, and to stop my mouth from complaining, you artfully tell me I am one of ye. Number you don't care to take leave of. And I tell you, I am not to be flamm'd in that manner.

      You assure me also you want sadly to make Love to me, and I assure you, very seriously, I will never engage upon the same Theatre again with you, without you make more Love to me than you did last year; I am asham'd that the audience should see me break the least rule of Decency (even upon the Stage) for the wretched Lovers I had last Winter; I desire you always to be my Lover upon the Stage, and my Friend off of it.

      I have given over all thoughts of playing this season; nor is it in the power of Mr Lacy with all his eloquence to inlist me in his Ragged Regiment; I should be very glad to

Command a Body of regular Troops, but I have no ambition to head the Drury Lane Militia.

What I wanted to speak to you about; was a letter sent me a fortnight ago; The purport of it was, Supposing the remainder of the Patent was to be Sold, wou'd you and Mr. Garrick buy it provided you cou'd get a promise of its being renew'd for ten or twenty years? As I was desired to keep this a strict Secret, I did not care to trust it in a letter, but your going to Ireland obliges me to it. After this it is needless to beg you not to Mention it, to any body, but let me know what you think of it, because I must return an answer.

I have no Theatrical News to tell you but that they have reviv'd the Trajedy of Lady Jane Gray at Drury Lane, and that Macklin has wrote a play which I hear is shortly to make its appearance. I accept the pleasure of your promise of writing to me when you are in Ireland, and am, Sr.

most Sincerely, yr friend,
and very humble Servt
S Cibber

P.S
I have no Commands but my best Compliments to every body that is so kind to enquire after me.

Novr 9 (1745)

Letter from the actress-singer Susanna Maria Cibber to David Garrick, 9 November 1745

Twickenham Feb 9th 1779

Dear Madam

    I can no longer resist enquiring after your Health; you have not been in a situation to admit of Letters – or visits of Ceremony; and even from your most sincere friends they must seem improper; I have fellt the greatest Concern for you in your great Calamity, but I won I not intrude upon you to tell you so, indeed what I fellt is not to be expressed. I hope by this time your spiritts are Reviving, I should suppose it must be so knowing the goodness of your understanding — these incurable Strokes must — Happen to all there is nobody Can give any Comfort to us upon these melancholy ocations but our Selves when we aske it – from a power above us.

    I shall be very happy to wait on you whenever you please If you think seeing Me will renew your Grief I will wait till your spirits are more settled and Composed; whenever it is it will give great pleasure to

        Dear Madam

My Brother and Sister beg their Respects .

        Your Most sincere and obliged
        C. Clive

Folger Shakespeare Library
Letter from the actress Catherine Clive to Eva Maria Garrick, 11 February 1779